JK   Lorch, Robert Stuart 27,089
2408
.L67 State and local politics
1989

DATE DUE

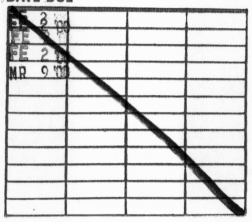

State
and
Local
Politics

State
and
Local
Politics

the great entanglement

third edition

ROBERT S. LORCH

*University of Colorado
at Colorado Springs*

Prentice Hall, Englewood Cliffs, New Jersey 07632

LIBRARY OF CONGRESS
Library of Congress Cataloging-in-Publication Data

Lorch, Robert Stuart
  State and local politics : the great entanglement / Robert S.
Lorch. — 3rd ed.
    p.   cm.
  Includes bibliographies and index.
  ISBN 0-13-844010-7
  1. State governments—United States.   2. Local government—United
States.   I. Title.
JK2408.L67   1989
320.473—dc19   88-11676
                                                                         CIP

Editorial/production supervision and
  interior design: Joy Moore/E. Rohne Rudder
Cover design: Photo Plus Art
Cover photo by Lou Odor, Photographer
Manufacturing buyer: Peter Havens

 © 1989, 1986, 1983 by Prentice-Hall, Inc.
A Division of Simon & Schuster
Englewood Cliffs, New Jersey 07632

Printed in the United States of America
10   9   8   7   6   5   4   3   2   1

ISBN 0-13-844010-7

Prentice-Hall International (UK) Limited, *London*
Prentice-Hall of Australia Pty. Limited, *Sydney*
Prentice-Hall Canada Inc., *Toronto*
Prentice Hall Hispanoamericana, S.A., *Mexico*
Prentice Hall of India Private Limited, *New Delhi*
Prentice Hall of Japan, Inc., *Tokyo*
Simon & Schuster Asia Pte. Ltd., *Singapore*
Editora Prentice-Hall do Brasil, Ltda., *Rio de Janeiro*

contents

preface   xi

1 introduction   1

Out of Sight, Out of Mind   2
Are the States Alike?   4
Why Study State and Local Governments?   7
Summary   9
Suggestions for Further Reading   10

2 state constitutions   11

Similarities among State Constitutions   12
The Amendment Process   13
Length of Constitutions   16
Revision of Constitutions   17
Summary   20
Suggestions for Further Reading   20

v

3 federalism   21

Dual Sovereignty   22
Constitutional Avenues for the Rise of Federal Power   26
Cooperative Federalism   28
Does Federalism Still Have a Useful Function?   34
Admission of States to the Union   35
Obligation of States to the Nation   37
Interstate Relations   38
Summary   41
Suggestions for Further Reading   42

4 election machinery   44

The System Dictates the Outcome   45
Control of Elections   45
Who May Vote?   48
Blacks and the Election System: A Case Study   51
Non-Racial Discriminations   54
Who Votes? Nonvoting in America   55
Does Democracy Work?   56
Other Forms of Political Participation   57
Nominations   58
The General Election   62
Nonpartisan Elections   67
Referendum and Initiative Elections   68
Recall Elections   69
Summary   71
Suggestions for Further Reading   72

5 parties, pressure groups, and elites   74

Party Functions   75
The Two-Party System   76
Party Organization   80
Campaigns   86
Campaign Finance   88
Two- and One-Party States   92
Elites   93
Pressure Groups   98
Ethnic Politics   99
Lobbying   100
Political Corruption   101

Summary   104
Suggestions for Further Reading   106

6 the governor   108

Governorship as an Institution   109
Some Advice for New Governors   110
Who Becomes Governor?   113
People Who Work in the Governor's Office   114
The War against Governors   119
The Governor's Appointment Power   119
The Governor as Legislator   123
The Governor's Ability to Influence Public Opinion   124
The Governor's Power to Call Special Sessions   126
The Governor as Party Leader   126
The Veto Power   127
The Governor's Term as a Power   129
The Governor's Budgetary Power   130
What Is a Power?   131
How Strong Should Governors Be?   133
The Lieutenant Governor   136
Summary   138
Suggestions for Further Reading   139

7 the legislature   140

The Triumph of Legislative Power   141
Decline   141
Democratization   141
Corruption   142
Reform   142
Sessions   143
Limitations on Legislative Power   146
Bicameralism   147
Size of the Legislature   150
Terms and Turnover   152
Compensation   154
Is the Legislature Representative?   155
Theories of Representation   156
Apportionment and Reapportionment   157
Staff Services to Legislators   160
Standing Committees   165
Speaker and President Pro Tem   168

Other Officers   169
How to Kill a Bill   169
Summary   176
Suggestions for Further Reading   177

8 courts and law   178

General Organization of the Court System   179
Local Courts   179
Trial and Appeals Courts of General Jurisdiction   181
Specialization of Courts and Judges   182
Some Specialized Courts   183
Administrative Tribunals   186
The Relationship of Federal and State Courts   187
Judges   189
Juries   193
Law   197
Criminal and Civil Procedure   204
Court Reform   209
The Ombudsman   210
Tort Liability of Governments   210
Barriers to Justice   212
Summary   213
Suggestions for Further Reading   215

9 counties, towns, townships, and special districts   216

Local Government in General   217
Counties   221
County Services   234
The New England Town   239
Townships   241
Special Districts   243
Summary   249
Suggestions for Further Reading   249

10 cities and metropolitan areas   250

Municipal Corporations   251
City Charters   252
Forms of City Government   255
Mayors   259

City Councils   264
Elections   267
Rural Government   271
Metropolitan Government   275
Two Cities   283
Summary   286
Suggestions for Further Reading   288

11 money

The Budget   290
The Fiscal Year   296
Appropriations   297
Auditing   297
Expenditures   300
Revenue and Taxation   304
Summary   315
Suggestions for Further Reading   317

12 civil servants

How Many and How Hired?   319
The Merit System   321
Public-Service Unionism   330
Privatization of Public Services   335
Our Ruling Servants: Bureaucrats as Judges and Legislators   337
Administrative Lawmaking   338
Administrative Adjudication   341
Summary   344
Suggestions for Further Reading   345

13 agencies and functions

The Bureaucracy   347
The Politics of Organization   347
What Does the Bureaucracy Do?   351
Summary   372
Suggestions for Further Reading   372

14 epilog

appendix   376

Journals   376
Other Reference Sources   377

glossary   378

index   389

preface

"Cover the subject, but don't give us an encyclopedia." "Don't make it too long; we plan to use some supplementary reading." "Give us about three-fourths state and one-fourth local." "Above all, write a book that will hold the interest of the students, especially students enrolled in their first political science course, who may never take another."

Those are some of the things I have been told by numerous teachers of state and local government. This book is an attempt to respond.

From my point of view, the nicest thing anyone could say about this book is that it is accurate, that it is lucid, that it broadly covers the subject, and that (in places at least) it is fun to read. In all sincerity I dedicate this book to those who are forced to read it at gunpoint, who are reading it because they have to— because it is assigned. You are with me in every paragraph. I understand you. I was a college student for eight years.

It is not easy to teach a course in state and local government or to study the subject. The 50 states vary so much that professors have difficulty saying anything definite that applies to them all. Yet the states do have many fundamentals in common. In a sense our states are like a pack of dogs (pardon the comparison). They all have four legs, two eyes, one tail, and a nose. Yet they have great differences. The bull terrier's tail is different from the foxhound's, and the doberman's legs aren't like the chow chow's.

The eighty some thousand local governments have lots in common, despite their differences.

In writing this book I often had to say "often"; frequently had to say "frequently"; commonly had to say "commonly." After hundreds of pages the sight of one of those fuzzy words was painful. I ached for something concrete and universal. But in the study of state and local government nothing is as lonesome as a concrete universal truth.

All purported conversations in this book, though entirely fictional, are based on actual conversations or on data acquired in other ways. They are simply intended to be a somewhat less formal way of presenting information. Any resemblance to persons living or dead is entirely coincidental.

The English language has no singular third-person pronoun that is both masculine and feminine. To correct this unfortunate circumstance we have used "he or she" rather than just "he," "his or hers" rather than just "his," and so on, except in passages where such double pronouns would impede the flow of language.

If any person reading this book is moved to write me a letter about it, please do so. I want to know what you like or don't like about the book. Future editions may reflect your observations. Your letter will be gratefully received, and answered if possible.

Certainly I would not want to lay responsibility on anyone but myself for these pages, but I must acknowledge with gratitude the numerous helpful criticisms made by W. Lee Johnston, University of North Carolina; Mavis Mann Reeves, University of Maryland; Donald Ranish, Antelope Valley College; and Ed Sidlow, Miami University of Ohio. I am also grateful to the reviewers: Karl Svenson, California State University; David Bingham, West Virginia University; Kenneth T. Palmer, University of Maine; Frank W. Essex, Middle Tennessee State University; and James Thomas, Illinois Central College.

ROBERT S. LORCH
Colorado Springs

State
and
Local
Politics

State
and
Local
Politics

1

introduction

PREVIEW

HOW ENTERTAINING IS A STATE?

The 56-year-old man with flowing white hair tried to hold his temper, tried to be polite. He tried to answer insinuations calmly. He tried to do what panelists at the American Political Science Convention usually try to do: avoid ruffling any feathers, avoid insulting anyone, avoid treating fools as if they were fools. But finally he exploded. His fist came down on the panel table. Water in drinking glasses splashed. An ashtray bounced to the floor. The great head of white hair flew in all directions as the editor of the *Capitol Crier* shouted at a frail and balding professor in the audience, "Don't you know what the newspaper business is all about, you bloody fool?"

Such language was unheard-of at meetings where learned scholars exchange ideas politely among themselves. But the editor was not a professional scholar. He owned and ran the most profitable newspaper in his state.

The target of his wrath, sitting near the back of the room, wasn't accustomed to being called a bloody fool by anyone except his wife. Color drained from his face.

The editor continued to erupt: "For the past ten minutes you've been trying to make me out as some kind of hideous ogre devoid of any shred of social consciousness. You act as though you think the job of a newspaper is to be an educational institution for the masses. Education is your job, not mine. I run a business. That business is to make money. My stock in trade is something called 'news.' It isn't really news all the time—quite often it's entertainment in the guise of

1

news. Whatever it's called and whatever it is, I'm not going to print it unless readers are going to read it. That's how I sell papers. I'm not going to print educational stuff that'll put me in the poorhouse."

The editor slowly sat down, eyes still glaring at his adversary. Stunned silence gripped the room. Finally the moderator, a young instructor from Nebraska who looked like Brooke Shields's twin brother, had the presence of mind to ask the professor whether he would care to respond to the editor's thoughtful remarks.

The professor paused and cleared his throat theatrically. This somehow produced a few giggles. Everyone turned around to see what he would say. "Now sir," began the professor, "I do not wish to paint you as any sort of ogre. I respect the important role played by the free press in America. I fully understand that a free press must be a private enterprise with a profit motive, and that you, unlike myself, have a payroll to meet and maybe some stockholders to satisfy. But your paper, which calls itself the *Capitol Crier,* gives almost no coverage of the state capitol— of state government. Why can't you entertain your readers with some state news?"

"I can't do that because the state government simply is not all that entertaining. I can't afford, and neither can anyone else, to hire a reporter to sit in the state capitol sending back dreary reports about a dreary government. People don't care about state government. They'd rather die than read about it. I'd go broke trying to get people interested in state government."

"But you do send a man to cover the legislature when it's in session, don't you?"

"Yes, because there's enough drama and idiocy there to amuse my readers. When the legislature adjourns, I pull my man back and put him to work writing up local murders."

"A good reporter," protested the professor, "can find drama, suspense, human interest, blood, and sex even in the state bureaucracy. A good reporter who is also a good writer can make the state department of agriculture as fascinating as a Shakespeare epic."

"If I had reporters who could write like that, they'd demand six times what I can pay."

OUT OF SIGHT, OUT OF MIND

States and the Mass Media

In America today the saying "out of sight, out of mind" can definitely be used to describe the governments of the states. They have a visibility problem. They are ignored, or at least overlooked, by the mass **media,** which probably give more coverage to foreign governments than to state governments. During the hostage crisis in Iran, for example, the U.S. media delved into every feature of Iranian politics; many Americans actually knew more about the government of Iran than about the government of their home state. The mass media are really not to blame for this. It's not their fault if people are more intrigued by hostages in Persia than by the sometimes dreary happenings in the statehouse.

State governments exist in the shadow of media coverage. Even local governments get more attention than states. One reason is that local newspapers and local television stations cover local events chiefly. There are very few state-oriented newspapers or television stations. True, some capital-city papers (the *Des Moines Register,* for example) have a strong statewide circulation, but they remain first and foremost local papers and are apt to regard happenings at the state capitol merely as local news.

Newspapers

Only the biggest newspapers are likely to have a full-time reporter stationed in the capital city to cover state government, except of course capital-city papers. Quite commonly that reporter will remain at the capitol only while the legislature is in session, which "implies a rather bizarre view of the governmental process—namely, that only the legislative branch makes decisions important enough to warrant sustained coverage."[1] An astonishing number of adult Americans do not read any newspaper at all and get no state news except for the rare items that happen to appear on television.

Some states are blessed with periodicals that address chiefly state politics—the *California Journal,* the *Empire State Report,* and *Illinois Issues,* to cite three examples—but they have a small readership, fewer than 10,000 per issue usually. Also, many states and cities have magazines that cover an assortment of topics from travel to cooking (*New York Magazine, Texas Monthly, Arizona, Philadelphia* magazine, for example) and that touch on state government, though not often.

Television

Few television stations are state-oriented. Television coverage is either local or national, not state—we get local news, or we get national news. There is Dallas TV but not Texas TV. And the network news—CBS, NBC, ABC—is not going to waste time on the Indiana legislature unless perchance the Indiana legislature does something silly like accidentally passing a bill abolishing Christmas, or unless it does something of national significance such as ratifying an amendment to the United States Constitution. Affairs of state in Lansing, Boston, St. Paul, and Jackson are usually left quietly to themselves.

What coverage of state government exists is likely to be more thorough in newspapers than in television. Because television requires some sort of movement suitable for camera and very expensive video cameras and crews, it is simply more difficult and more costly for television than for the print medium to cover state affairs.

Thus state governments don't get much publicity. If the public has a low opinion of state government, if the public doesn't think states do much of importance, how could it be otherwise when the doings of state officials occur in a gloom seldom pierced by media? When state government does make the front pages, the reason is all too often alleged corruption, as in Maryland, whose governor, Marvin Mandel, was accused in 1975 of mail fraud and racketeering,

[1]William T. Gormley, Jr., "Coverage of State Government in the Mass Media," *State Government* (Spring 1979), p. 47. Also, for a discussion of the question whether press coverage of legislatures is colored by a bias in the media against legislatures, see Robert W. O'Donnell, "What's Wrong with the Media's Coverage of the Legislature." *State Legislatures* (October 1985), pp. 29–30.

or in Tennessee, where former governor Ray Blanton was convicted of extortion, conspiracy, and mail fraud in 1981. Systematic analysis of states and their problems is found almost nowhere except in state government courses on college campuses.

ARE THE STATES ALIKE?

Physical Differences among States

It seems remarkable that the states, so diverse physically, can be so similar in the structure of their governments. In land area the states range from such giants as Alaska, Texas, and California to such microbes as Rhode Island. In mean elevation they vary from Colorado's dizzying average of 6800 feet (Ski Country USA) to Delaware's lowly mean of 60 feet. In total precipitation the states range from virtual deserts to virtual swamps—Phoenix, Arizona, is lucky if it gets 7 inches of rain in a whole year, whereas Mobile, Alabama, gets 67. Some states are a lot brighter and warmer than others—between sunrise and sunset in the Southwest the sun shines 80 percent of the time, whereas in the Midwest and East it generally shines only about 60 percent of the time. The states also vary greatly in forestation. New Hampshire is over three-fourths forest, whereas Iowa, which is almost totally cultivated, has only a few stands of timber.

These geographic and climatological differences among the states obviously produce striking differences in the way people live and striking differences in their economy. Climate and geography are what make oranges the number one crop in Florida, peanuts the most valuable crop in Georgia, wheat the salient crop in Kansas, corn the most important crop in Iowa, tobacco in North Carolina, soybeans in Louisiana, potatoes in Idaho, cotton in Texas, and hay in New York and Massachusetts.

Social and Economic Differences

The American states come in many sizes, shapes, and varieties, as we have seen, yet in most fundamentals their political institutions are the same. This is true despite their considerable social, cultural, and demographic differences. Economically the states are by no means equal or identical. For example, **per capita income** is about one-third higher in New Jersey, Delaware, and Maryland than in Mississippi and Arkansas. Family income in the Northeast and the West is significantly higher than family income in the South and the North Central states.

A significantly greater percentage of the population are high school graduates in Utah, Colorado, Washington, and Oregon than in Mississippi, Kentucky, Tennessee, and North Carolina. Likewise the per capita expenditure of states on education differs sharply: Delaware, Utah, Oregon, and Minnesota spend nearly 40 percent more than do Arkansas, Tennessee, Missouri, and Georgia.

In population the states range from mighty California, New York, and Texas on the one extreme to Wyoming, Alaska, and Vermont on the other (Box 1-1). Land area is no guarantee of population. True, California and Texas are among the largest states in both population and land area, but Alaska is both a

Box 1-1. *Population per State*

California	26.36 million
New York	17.78 million
Texas	16.37 million
Pennsylvania	11.85 million
Illinois	11.53 million
Florida	11.36 million
Ohio	10.74 million
Michigan	9.08 million
New Jersey	7.56 million
North Carolina	6.25 million
Georgia	5.97 million
Massachusetts	5.82 million
Virginia	5.70 million
Indiana	5.49 million
Missouri	5.02 million
Wisconsin	4.77 million
Tennessee	4.76 million
Louisiana	4.48 million
Washington	4.40 million
Maryland	4.39 million
Minnesota	4.19 million
Alabama	4.02 million
Kentucky	3.72 million
South Carolina	3.34 million
Oklahoma	3.30 million
Colorado	3.23 million
Arizona	3.18 million
Connecticut	3.17 million
Iowa	2.88 million
Oregon	2.68 million
Mississippi	2.61 million
Kansas	2.45 million
Arkansas	2.35 million
West Virginia	1.93 million
Utah	1.64 million
Nebraska	1.60 million
New Mexico	1.45 million
Maine	1.16 million
Hawaii	1.05 million
Idaho	1.00 million
New Hampshire	.99 million
Rhode Island	.96 million
Nevada	.93 million
Montana	.82 million
South Dakota	.70 million
North Dakota	.68 million
Delaware	.62 million
Vermont	.53 million
Alaska	.52 million
Wyoming	.50 million

Source: U.S. Bureau of the Census, *Current Population Reports, 1986.*

giant in land area and a dwarf in population, as are New Mexico and Montana. In density of population the states range from less than 6 persons per square mile in Alaska, Montana, Wyoming, and Nevada to a high of nearly 1000 persons per square mile in New Jersey (the Garden State).

The racial stock and therefore to some degree the cultural composition of states differ. Hundreds of thousands of persons of oriental ancestry, for example, live in California and Hawaii. Many American Indians live in California, Arizona, New Mexico, and Oklahoma. Large numbers of Spanish-surnamed persons live in Texas and the Southwest. States with the highest percentage of blacks are Mississippi, South Carolina, Louisiana, Georgia, and Alabama, but the largest populations of blacks are in New York, Illinois, Texas, and California.

States differ in a number of other intriguing ways. Most of the land in some states is owned by the federal government: Alaska is 90 percent federally owned, Nevada 88 percent, Utah 65 percent, Idaho 63 percent, Oregon 52 percent. States differ in their percentage of arable land. Iowa cultivates more acres than any state of the Union (more than two-thirds of Iowa is farmed), although 22 states are larger. On the other hand, Nevada, seventh largest state in the Union, cultivates less than one percent of its 109,889 square miles.

Uniformity of Political Culture

Despite the states' social and economic differences, they have an amazingly uniform **political culture.** One reason for this may be that the United States is probably the largest culturally homogenous nation in the world. A few other countries are larger in land area and population, but their populations are so culturally diverse that people in the various provinces can hardly understand one another. For example, the Soviet Union is much larger geographically than the United States and its population is slightly larger, but it is an empire composed of many nationalities, cultures, and languages, ruled primarily by Russians, the largest ethnic group, who constitute only about half the nation's population. The dominion of the English language nearly everywhere in the United States, the dominion of British political institutions in our early history, and the building on political traditions of the original 13 states by the other states as they entered the Union have all contributed to the uniformity of policial design among the 50 states. Nothing in the United States Constitution prevents states from having prime ministers, or presidents, or a master in chief instead of a governor. States are free to organize any way they want, as long as they retain a "republican form of government"[2] and do not grant titles of nobility.[3] This is by no means to say that the American states are political clones of one another; we speak only of similarities in broad design and general culture. States differ politically and culturally in many lesser ways, and this book will touch on some of those differences.

Governmental Similarities and Differences

Most state governments are essentially alike—the government of North Dakota is basically like the government of North Carolina, and so on. States differ more in their nongovernmental characteristics than in their basic frame of govern-

---

[2]*United States Constitution* [hereafter abbreviated *U.S. Const.*], Art. IV, Sec. 4.

[3]*U.S. Const.*, Art. I, Sec. 10.

ment. This sameness of structure is perhaps one of the reasons why many people do not find the contemplation of state government as mind-blowing as contemplation of Death Valley, the Grand Canyon, or Niagara Falls. If Colorado had a political feature as incredible as Pikes Peak—perhaps a parliament instead of a legislature—then that might make the study of its government a little more tangy. Think what attention we shower on Nebraska for having a one-house legislature. The same alikeness shows up in local government too; again we have literary overkill where there is some unique feature, such as the Louisiana parish or the New England town.

Size of Bureaucracy   Perhaps the greatest difference among state governments has to do with size rather than broad design. Some state governments are very big; some are rather minuscule. The size of a state government bears a close relationship to the size of a state's population. California, the most populous state in the Union, has more full-time employees than any other state; Wyoming, one of the least populous states, has the fewest state employees. The same general principle applies to local governments.

However, when one looks at the number of state employees per 10,000 population, it is apparent that states with a small population are likely to have a higher proportion of state employees than the large population states. Wyoming, for example, has 194 per 10,000; Ohio only 105; Alaska has 417; California only 102 at last report. Thus, the larger states do not always have a higher percentage of state employees than smaller states. Although Wyoming has the least number of full-time state employees, it has the second largest percentage of such employees in the nation (exceeded only by Alaska).

Elaborateness of Organization   The vast numbers of state employees in the populous states are arranged into state bureaucracies far more elaborate and complicated than one finds in less populated states. However, the basic institutions of government are the same: there is a legislature, a supreme court, and a governor in every state. The bureaucracy is roughly organized into the same types of departments nearly everywhere: most states have a treasury department, a law department, a state department, and so on. But these departments are more lavishly funded and staffed in the larger states.

WHY STUDY STATE AND LOCAL GOVERNMENT?

You would hardly expect the author of a book on state and local government to say the subject isn't worth studying. Still, one can easily understand why the federal government and its affairs seem more glamorous and important than "subnational" governments. Subnational governments don't fight wars, don't have international relations and Central Intelligence Agencies, and don't grapple with ultimate problems like inflation, depression, and national defense, at least not as visibly as the federal government does. The national government simply outshines and outranks the state governments. A United States senator in Washington. D.C., outshines a state senator at the state capitol. A justice of the United States Supreme Court outshines his or her counterpart on the state supreme court. The president is more radiant than a governor. Being attorney

Box 1-2. *What's in a Name? (Origin of the Names of U.S. States)*

Alabama: From an Indian word meaning "tribal town."
Alaska: From an Eskimo word (*alakshak*) meaning "peninsula" or "great lands."
Arizona: From an Aztec word (*arizuma*) meaning "silver bearing."
Arkansas: A French variant of Kansas, a Sioux word for "south wind people."
California: Bestowed by conquistadors. From the name of an earthly paradise depicted in a sixteenth-century Spanish romance.
Colorado: Spanish for "red."
Connecticut: From Algonquin words meaning "long river place."
Delaware: Named after an early governor of Virginia, Lord De La Warr.
Florida: From Spanish words meaning "flowery Easter."
Georgia: Named after King George II of England.
Hawaii: From a native word for "homeland" (*hawaiki*).
Idaho: A coined name supposedly meaning "gem of the mountains."
Illinois: French adaptation of an Algonquin word (*illini*) meaning "warriors."
Indiana: Land of the Indians.
Iowa: From an Indian word supposedly meaning "beautiful land."
Kansas: From a Sioux word meaning "south wind people."
Kentucky: From an Indian word supposedly meaning "meadowland."
Louisiana: Named after the French king Louis XIV.
Maine: From the name of an ancient French province.
Maryland: For Queen Henrietta Maria, wife of Charles I of England.
Massachusetts: From the name of an Indian tribe.
Michigan: From Chippewa words (*mici gama*) meaning "great water."
Minnesota: Indian word meaning "cloudy water."
Mississippi: From Chippewa words (*mici zibi*) meaning "great river."
Missouri: Missouri word meaning "muddy water."
Montana: Spanish for "mountainous."
Nebraska: From an Indian word meaning "flat river."
Nevada: Spanish for "snow-clad."
New Hampshire: Named after a county in England.
New Jersey: Named after England's Isle of Jersey.
New Mexico: Early Spanish term for "land northwest of the Rio Grande."
New York: Named for the Duke of York who sent an expedition to capture it.
North Carolina: Named after Charles I of England. (*Carolus* is Latin for "Charles.")
North Dakota: Sioux word for "friend."
Ohio: Iroquois word for "fine river."
Oklahoma: Indian word meaning "red man."
Oregon: origin unknown.
Pennsylvania: Named after William Penn, and after the word *sylvania* meaning "woodland."
Rhode Island: From the Dutch *roode eylandt,* "red island."
South Carolina: See North Carolina.
South Dakota: See North Dakota.
Tennessee: From an Indian word (*tanasi*) meaning "villages on the Tanasi River."
Texas: From an Indian word meaning "ally."
Utah: From a Navajo word meaning "higher up."
Vermont: From the French words *vert* ("green") and *mont* ("mountain").
Virginia: Named for Queen Elizabeth, the Virgin Queen of England.
Washington: Named after George Washington.
West Virginia: Named after the western counties of Virginia that refused to secede from the Union during the Civil War.
Wisconsin: From an Indian word (*ouisconsin*) meaning "grassy place."
Wyoming: From an Algonquin word meaning "large prairie place."

general of the United States is more lustrous than being attorney general of, say, Minnesota. Local government is also often associated with tasteless things like garbage collection, chuckholes, sewer systems, and water meters. Furthermore, because the mass media pay so little attention to states, people are left with the impression there isn't much going on at the capitol.

State and local governments actually do more than the federal government. In fact, they are doing more today than ever before—they are a growth industry, one might say. People who want a civilian job with government are more likely to find work with a state or local government than with the federal government. The state and local civil service of all subnational governments in the United States far exceeds the federal civilian bureaucracy in numbers. State bureaucracies alone almost equal the federal civil service: each is in the neighborhood of three million. Local bureaucracies, employing about eight million people, exceed state and federal bureaucracies combined.

State and local government touches our lives every day in all kinds of intimate ways. How? Thousands of schoolchildren and college students could answer this question easily. Their days are a constant entanglement with one of the greatest undertakings of state and local government: the public schools—grade schools, high schools, community colleges, state colleges, state universities, state institutes of technology. Automobile drivers are surrounded by a sea of state and local activities (road maintenance, for example) and by a sea of state and local laws governing who may drive, how they may drive, and where.

State and local governments touch the lives of each of us. When you turn on the tap for a drink of water you are probably getting service from a publicly owned water company, and you're probably going to rely on a publicly owned sewer system to carry away what you don't drink. When you turn on the lights you may well be using a publicly owned electric utility—in any event, a publicly regulated utility. The place you live in was in all probability built according to countless building standards and regulations enacted by local government. The sidewalk you pace along is very likely owned by government. The restaurant you eat in is closely regulated and watched by government health departments, as are hospitals, clinics, and all sorts of other establishments that could ruin your life if left entirely to a "buyer beware" system. If you ever have to go to court, chances are you will deal with state or local police, prosecutors, and codes. If you run for office, even for president, you deal almost exclusively with state and local political-party machinery and with state and local election machinery—in the United States there is almost no national election apparatus; nor can it be easily contended that we have national political parties.

The list of ways in which state and local government affect our daily lives is very long, as you will see throughout the remaining chapters.

SUMMARY

One reason why the public is so little informed about state government is that the mass-communication media pay little attention to that level of government. Although the states are characterized by great social and economic diversity, there remains an amazingly uniform political culture among them. The greatest difference among state governments has to do with size rather than broad design. Although state and local governments are not as glamorous as the national government, they offer an array of services that touch the daily lives of most citizens. State and local governments together employ many more civil servants than the federal government, they do more work, and the amount of work they do is increasing.

SUGGESTIONS FOR FURTHER READING

BEYLE, THAD L., ed., *State Government, CQ's Guide to Current Issues and Activities 1986–87.* Washington, D.C.: Congressional Quarterly Press, 1986. (A similar volume appears to be issued every two years by CQ.)

BOWMAN, ANN O., and RICHARD C. KEARNEY, *The Resurgence of the States.* Englewood Cliffs, N.J.: Prentice-Hall, 1986.

BURNS, JAMES M., J. W. PELTASON, and THOMAS E. CRONIN, *State and Local Politics: Government by the People* (4th ed.). Englewood Cliffs, N.J.: Prentice-Hall, 1984.

DYE, THOMAS R., *Politics in States and Communities* (5th ed.). Englewood Cliffs, N.J.: Prentice-Hall, 1985.

GLENDENING, PARRIS N., "The Public's Perception of State Government and Governors," *State Government* (Summer 1980), 115–20.

GRABER, DORIS A., *Mass Media and American Politics* (2nd ed.). Washington, D.C.: Congressional Quarterly Press, 1984.

HENRY, NICHOLAS, *Governing at the Grassroots: State and Local Politics* (2nd ed.). Englewood Cliffs, N.J.: Prentice-Hall, 1987.

HOUSEMAN, GERALD, *State and Local Governments: The Battleground.* Englewood Cliffs, N.J.: Prentice-Hall, 1986.

LITTLEWOOD, THOMAS, "What's Wrong with Statehouse Coverage," *Columbia Journalism Review* (March/April 1972), 39–45.

MOLLENHOFF, CLARK R., *Investigative Reporting.* New York: Macmillan, 1981.

2
state constitutions

PREVIEW

WHAT IS A CONSTITUTION?

The conference table in room 333 of the capitol was solid walnut. The three men could see their reflection in it. "Gentlemen," said the 57-year-old chief justice, "the constitutional convention which is now meeting to draft a new constitution for our state has named us to a Speech and Press Committee. Our job is to write up what we think the new constitution should say on those subjects. So let's get started."

The fat state senator and the skinny Baptist minister stopped playing ticktacktoe and settled down to business.

"Now here's what I think the constitution should say about freedom of speech and press." The chief justice unfolded a piece of paper and read, "No law limiting freedom of speech or press shall be made."

He stopped reading. There was a pause.

"Yes, go on. We're listening," said the minister.

"That's it," said the chief.

"You mean, that's all the constitution should say on the whole subject? Just those eleven words?" asked the senator.

The chief nodded.

"Surely," said the minister, "there's more to say than that."

"Why more?" asked the chief. "Doesn't that say it?"

"Well," protested the minister, "don't you think we should say in the constitution that publication of pornography is prohibited."

"And something about obscenities in public?" added the senator. "Your eleven words don't put any limits at all on speech, or on the press."

"Look," said the chief. "We can't include every conceivable limitation in a constitution. If we did, the thing would run longer than an encyclopedia."

"But a constitution should say something concrete," said the senator. "Your eleven words don't even tell us what 'speech' is or what 'the press' is. Are movies the press? Is burning a draft card speech?"

"Senator, those are things you legislators should spell out in the laws you pass. Then, if someone comes to court claiming your laws violate the constitution, we judges will decide whether they do or don't. Judges don't always take the constitution literally. We take it as a series of signposts. We follow its general direction. But in the process we divine its meaning in ways which we think the people want."

"But why not save the legislature and the courts all that trouble?" said the minister. "Why not get down to the nitty-gritty and say right here in the constitution just exactly what we mean by freedom of speech and freedom of the press?"

The chief justice stood up and looked at his colleagues. "Because we're not here to be a legislature, and we're not here to be a court. We're here to write a constitution—one that gives legislatures and courts some general guidance. That's what a constitution is supposed to do. A constitution points the way. A constitution does not spell out every detail."

SIMILARITIES AMONG STATE CONSTITUTIONS

The highest law made by a state is its constitution. A state constitution is written by a convention drawn from residents of the state (or proposed state) and is adopted by the people of the state (or proposed state). All other law made within the state is made under authority of the state constitution, and should conform to its commands. State constitutions may be thought of as higher in rank than other state law but lower in rank than the United States Constitution and federal law. Any provision of a state constitution that conflicts with anything in the United States Constitution or with a federal law may be declared invalid by the courts.

Basic Principles

Although all state constitutions differ in certain exotic ways, they are all nevertheless fundamentally alike. They all, for example, establish three separate branches of government—legislative, judicial, and executive—and grant to each of those branches a separate collection of powers, including powers with which to check the powers of the other two branches. We call that the principle of **separation of powers** and the principle of **checks and balances.** Each branch has the power not only to do its basic job but also to prevent other branches from exceeding their basic jobs. For example, legislatures are given power not only to legislate but also to remove members of the other two branches from office through impeachment. Separation of powers and checks and balances are found in every state constitution—either implied or directly stated.

Also found in every state constitution is the principle of **judicial review**—the power of courts to nullify laws that conflict with higher laws, most notably acts of the state legislature that conflict with the state constitution. Judicial review is also the power of courts to nullify the decisions and acts of lower courts, as well as the power to nullify the actions of executive officers that conflict with the law.

The idea of **popular sovereignty** is at the core of every state constitution. It is sometimes stated directly as a principle, sometimes merely implied by the fact that all public officials are either elected or receive their appointments from those who *are* elected and can exercise only such power as is given them by elected officials or by the people themselves.

State constitutions also set forth, often in great detail, the organization and power of *local governments,* especially of counties.

A **bill of rights** is another feature of state constitutions. Many of the civil rights set forth in these bills are identical to those found in the first eight articles of the federal Bill of Rights. They pertain chiefly to procedural rights of criminal defendants: the right to counsel, jury trial, bail, due process of law, freedom from compulsory self-incrimination and double jeopardy, and so on. State bills of rights also provide for freedom of speech, the press, religion, and assembly and other substantive rights identical to those in the federal bill. Most of these provisions have declined in significance now that the United States Supreme Court has applied almost every guarantee of the federal Bill of Rights to the states through expanded interpretation of the due process clause of the Fourteenth Amendment. However, most state constitutions were written long before this comparatively recent (post–World War II) application of the federal bill to states. Furthermore, some states have dreamed up a few incredible rights that might have surprised even Patrick Henry (of "Give me liberty or give me death" fame): the right to fish in public waters, for example.

THE AMENDMENT PROCESS

All constitutions have a provision describing how the constitution may be amended. The amendment process is harder in some states than in others, sometimes so hard that it is easier to abolish the whole constitution and adopt a new one than to repair the old one. The amendment process has two stages: initiation and ratification.

Initiation

Basically there are four ways to *initiate* (suggest) a state **constitutional amendment.** Of those four, two are used primarily for single-shot amendments. (The others are used mainly for broad constitutional revision, which will be discussed later in this chapter.) The most common way of initiating a single amendment is by vote of the legislature. Usually an extraordinary majority is required, such as two-thirds of each house, or three-fifths. The other is by petition—the so-called constitutional initiative. A proposal to amend the constitution may be put on the ballot if a certain number of signatures have been gathered on a petition supporting the proposal. The number of signatures required for a constitutional initiative varies from state to state but is usually about 10 percent of the total number of votes cast for governor in the last election—a staggering job for petition circulators. Initiation by the legislature is permitted in all states, and

---

Box 2-1.   *States in Which the People Can Initiate a Constitutional Amendment*

Arizona
Arkansas
California
Colorado
Florida
Illinois
Massachusetts
Michigan
Missouri

Montana
Nebraska
Nevada
North Dakota
Ohio
Oklahoma
Oregon
South Dakota

---

initiation by constitutional initiative is also available in 17 states (see Box 2-1). About 90 percent of all single-shot amendments are initiated by state legislatures. In one year recently, there were some 238 proposed state constitutional changes submitted to voters across the United States, of which about 211 were initiated by state legislatures. Also, the adoption rate for amendments submitted by state legislatures is much higher than for those initiated by petition.

Ratification

No matter how a constitutional amendment is initiated, all states except Delaware require that the proposed amendment be *ratified* (approved) by majority vote at a general election. Some of the most colorful and hard-fought elections in America revolve around the ratification of proposed state constitutional amendments. Vast sums and lots of effort and enthusiasm are poured into campaigns for and against provocative proposals to do such things as permit a state lottery, allow casino gambling, ban abortion, adopt an equal rights amendment, outlaw nuclear power plants, limit real estate taxes, or require a deposit on all bottles and cans sold in stores (bottle bills). A proposed amendment may threaten colossal financial interests; for example a proposal to tax the extraction of natural resources like coal or iron (severance taxes). Mining companies have spent fortunes fighting severance tax proposals. Yet it's cheaper for them to finance a $350,000 campaign to defeat the proposed tax, than to pay $10 million a year in taxes if it passes. Some critics of the amendment process, say it is too easy for "self-appointed reformers" to put "irresponsible" constitutional amendments on the ballot, which cost established interests huge amounts every two years to kill. Giant financial interests are by no means against using the amendment process themselves, although they generally find it easier to work their will through the legislature, and thus are not driven so often to the amendment process.

Should Constitutions Be Difficult to Amend?

Insofar as there is something to be said for stability and continuity of fundamental institutions and rules of the game, there is also something to be said for putting roadblocks in the path of those who would amend constitutions. Unfortunately, many state constitutions are stacked with provisions that have no business being in any constitution, but which should be in the form of ordinary legislation (exact dollar amounts, for example). Zealous to curb the power of officeholders (a lofty motive perhaps), constitution writers designed long and detailed constitutions. This cure may be worse than the disease.

A constitution, as some people view it, is a great listing of **civil rights,** rights that individuals and minorities—not only racial minorities but all minorities—have even against majorities. Civil rights include not only the right to freedom of speech, the press, religion, and assembly (protected by all American constitutions), but also the right to have a legislature popularly elected, a governor whose powers are limited, a court system with certain specific powers, and so on. The right to every fundamental institution is a civil right. We all have those rights, and they cannot be taken away in some wild moment by a mere majority; much more than a majority is needed to alter them. To combine basic rights of that sort in the same constitution with mere legislation is a corruption—a corruption of both the constitution and the legislature's right to legislate.

Frequency of Amendment

South Carolina's constitution has the prize for being the most amended state constitution in the United States—more than 450 times since its adoption in 1895. The California and Alabama constitutions have also been amended more than 400 times. New York and Texas have amended their constitutions 200 or more times (See Table 2-1.)

Table 2-1. State Constitutions: Oldest to Youngest, and Number of Amendments

Massachusetts	1780*
New Hampshire	1784*
Vermont	1793
Maine	1820**
Rhode Island	1843
Wisconsin	1848*
Indiana	1851
Ohio	1851*
Iowa	1857
Minnesota	1858*
Oregon	1859**
Kansas	1861*
Nebraska	1864**
Maryland	1867**
Tennessee	1870
West Virginia	1872*
Arkansas	1874*
Nevada	1875*
Colorado	1876*
Texas	1876***
California	1879****
South Dakota	1889*
North Dakota	1889*
Washington	1889*
Idaho	1890*

Continued.

Table 2-1   *(Continued)*

Mississippi	1890*
Wyoming	1890
Kentucky	1891
New York	1895**
South Carolina	1896****
Utah	1896*
Delaware	1897*
Alabama	1901****
Oklahoma	1907*
Arizona	1912*
New Mexico	1912*
Missouri	1945*
New Jersey	1948
Hawaii	1959*
Alaska	1959
Michigan	1964
Connecticut	1965
Pennsylvania	1968
Florida	1969
Virginia	1971
North Carolina	1971
Illinois	1971
Montana	1973
Louisiana	1975
Georgia	1983

*Amended more than 50 times.
**Amended more than 150 times.
***Amended more than 250 times.
****Amended more than 350 times.

The easiest constitutions to amend are probably those that require only a majority vote of the legislature to initiate and a majority vote of the electorate to ratify and that may also be amended by initiation of the voters without involvement of the legislature. About eight states fall into this category, and their constitutions have all been heavily amended. However, there is no ironclad correlation between ease of amending and the number of amendments adopted. Research might show that when a constitution is frequently amended, the frequency has a lot to do with how long and detailed the document is.

LENGTH OF CONSTITUTIONS

The typical length of state constitutions is about 26,000 words, four times the length of the United States Constitution. But there are some notable exceptions in both directions. Before 1983 Georgia had the longest constitution in the nation—600,000 words, about the length of *Gone With the Wind.* (Georgia's constitution is now much slimmer—25,000 words.) Alabama's constitution is nearly

130,000 (about the length of this book). The constitution of Vermont is the shortest. At 6600 words it is twenty times shorter than Alabama's, and about the same length as the United States Constitution.

REVISION OF CONSTITUTIONS

Constitutional Conventions

As we have seen, constitutions can be changed by formal amendment. But they can also be changed in other ways. They may be completely overhauled by **constitutional conventions** (and commissions)[1] or even thrown out and a new constitution proposed. Conventions tend to look at entire constitutions; amendments tend to zero in on single, isolated issues. (Although when faced by a large package proposed by a convention or commission, the electorate may adopt only a few isolated pieces of it.) We see constitution writing by convention when a new state is admitted to the Union. Congress generally will not admit a new state without first passing favorably on its proposed state constitution. In recent years Washington, D.C., has petitioned for admission to the Union. A constitutional convention drafted *A Constitution for the State of Columbia,* which was ultimately approved by the voters in 1982 and transmitted to Congress in 1983. This effort was discussed at length in Congress when hearings were held in 1983 on HR 3861, the New Columbia Admissions Act.[2]

Incidentally, some 14 states have written into their constitutions that every so many years the question shall automatically be put to the voters whether a constitutional convention shall be called. Usually the period of time is every 20 years, but one state has 16 years and 4 states have 10 years.

All but a handful of state constitutions provide a system for establishing constitutional conventions. Absence of such a provision doesn't prevent a state from holding a constitutional convention, however. The right of the people to change their state constitution is universally recognized. The Arkansas constitution of 1874, under which the state is presently operating, contains no such provision, yet this did not prevent the people of Arkansas from establishing a convention in 1976 by referendum. The system for calling a constitutional convention in those states where it is provided for in the state constitution is about the same everywhere. First, the legislature must decide whether it wants a convention, usually by majority vote, sometimes by two-thirds or three-fifths. Second, the proposal to have a convention must be submitted to the people. But even if the legislature and the people approve of having a convention, that does not necessarily mean they will approve what the convention does. The convention's proposals must be submitted to the people for ratification before they become the supreme law of the state. More than one convention has labored for years to design a wonderful new constitution only to have their work tossed in the trash on election day.

---

[1]State legislatures sometimes establish constitutional commissions and empower them to propose constitutional revisions to the legislature, which in turn may or may not refer such revisions to the electorate for ratification.

[2]*See also* Philip G. Schrag, *Behind the Scenes: The Politics of a Constitutional Convention* (Washington, D.C.: Georgetown University Press, 1985). An account of the D.C. Constitutional Convention.

Revision by Interpretation

Perhaps we spend too much energy trying to understand the tortuous process by which constitutions are formally amended or formally rewritten. After all, formal amendments are trivial in number compared with the great mass of constitutional change that occurs through **interpretation of constitutions** by public officials trying to apply supreme law to everyday affairs.

Judicial Interpretation   Courts are notorious interpreters of constitutions. Where there is dispute over the meaning of any provision of a constitution, courts have the last say. A constitution means what the judges say it means. If you want to find what any provision of a constitution means in practice, a good place to start looking is a law library where the decisions (reports) of state supreme courts are kept. Thousands and thousands of cases have spelled out the meaning of practically every word and punctuation mark. These court decisions vastly outnumber formal amendments, and are often at least as significant.

Legislative Interpretation   Courts are not the only ones who interpret constitutions. The legislature (usually through its bill-drafting service) looks at the state constitution to see whether a proposed new law would violate it. This obviously involves interpreting what the constitution means: how can you decide whether a proposed new law would violate the constitution unless you first decide what the words and provisions of relevant constitutional sections mean? Of course judges have the last say, but judges are often influenced by the legislature's view of what the constitution means. And of course the judges don't have a say unless they are asked to adjudicate the constitutionality of the law at some date after it is passed.

Executive Interpretation   Members of the executive branch—the bureaucrats—interpret constitutions in the process of determining the scope of their constitutional powers. In this they are helped by formal written advisory opinions given by the state attorney general. Again, in case of dispute, courts have the final say.

Constitutions are constantly being interpreted—and colored—by all who work with them, and under them.

How Many New Constitutions?

It is not altogether unusual for states to boot out their old constitution and adopt a new one. The 50 American states have had about 150 constitutions since 1776; Louisiana has had 11 and Georgia, 9, including their Civil War documents. The southern states, perhaps because of their tumultuous experiences in the Civil War, have had more constitutions than the typical northern or western state, but even Pennsylvania has had 5 and Michigan 4.

Some states, however, have clung to their original constitution. Massachusetts, one of the original 13 states, still has the constitution it adopted in 1780, though amended profusely. The Massachusetts document is older than the United States Constitution itself. Other durable constitutions are those of

Maine (1820), Wisconsin (1848), Ohio (1851), Minnesota (1858), and Kansas (1861). The first constitutions of Connecticut and Rhode Island evolved out of colonial charters dating back to the 1600s.

Constitution Writers Look to Precedent

Despite their differences in age and verbosity, the various state constitutions are substantially alike with regard to civil rights and fundamental institutions of government. One reason for these similarities is certainly the natural tendency of constitution writers in new states to use as models the constitutions of existing states as well as of the United States. Constitution writers plagiarize ideas, if not exact words, from existing constitutions. And why not?

Constitutional Revision Today

Constitution writing, amending, and interpreting is by no means a thing of the past. It is going on today at a steady pace as states try to modernize their somewhat archaic and ramshackle institutions and to solve current problems. Only about one-third of the states have constitutions written in this century; fewer yet are products of the last 25 years. On the other hand, since 1945 more than a dozen states have adopted brand-new constitutions and nearly all states have made important changes in their governmental machinery. Constitutional change reached a fever pitch in the 1960s, when at gun point (*Baker* v. *Carr*) every state was forced to bring its legislative apportionment into conformity with the one-person-one-vote rule. Annually a vast number of states amend their constitution: perhaps three-fourths of all state constitutions are changed in some way every year.

This annual nationwide collection of amendments usually touches all three branches of government. In recent years most states have reponded in one way or another to the checklist of reforms suggested by those who seek to modernize and strengthen state government. The most common subject of constitutional amendments has been the raising and spending of money; amendments including spending limitations, such as California's notable Proposition 13, have been ratified. Amendments affecting legislatures have included such provisions as increasing the frequency of their meetings and adjusting the terms of members. Amendments affecting courts have included attempts to establish a unified court system—that is, a system in which court and personnel procedures are more consistent throughout the state and more centrally controlled. In the area of civil rights, a number of states have attempted to write sex equality into their basic law. In the area of local government, some amendments have attempted to extend home rule. Miscellaneous amendments have aimed at protecting natural resources and the environment. Most of the more colorful proposals—such things as changing the state flower, calling the legislature a parliament, and moving the state capital—have failed to reach the ballot.

The Model State Constitution

Members of state constitutional conventions and other persons involved in revising a state constitution may want to look at the Model State Constitution published by the National Municipal League. Actually no state has adopted the

Model State Constitution in its entirety even though the document has been in circulation since 1928 and revised several times (most recently in 1968). Perhaps not even one of its provisions has ever been adopted word for word by any state. Nevertheless, the document does represent expert opinion about what ought to be in a state constitution. The main trouble with any so-called model constitution is that there is no model state: each state is unique in some way and therefore requires a tailor-made constitution.

SUMMARY

Although state constitutions differ in many ways, they all set forth roughly similar principles and basic structures of government. Constitutions may be revised or totally rewritten by constitutional conventions, or they may be changed by individual amendments adopted through the amendment process. State constitutions are generally amended by a two-stage process: initiation and ratification. Initiation is usually accomplished by an extraordinary majority vote in both houses, or by the people through a petition process. The amendment is then adopted or rejected by the voters (the ratification process). Insofar as there is something to be said for stability and continuity of the fundamental institutions and rules of government, there is also something to be said for making the process of amending constitutions difficult. Most state constitutions are too long and contain many provisions that could well have been written as ordinary legislation. The meaning of constitutions is determined by judicial, legislative, and executive interpretations.

SUGGESTIONS FOR FURTHER READING

BROWNE, CYNTHIA E., comp., *State Constitutional Conventions: From Independence to the Completion of the Present Union. A Bibliography.* Westport, Conn.: Greenwood, 1973.

CORNWELL, ELMER E., JR., *Constitutional Conventions: The Politics of Revision.* New York: National Municipal League, 1974.

ELAZAR, DANIEL J., ed., series of articles on American state constitutions and the constitutions of selected foreign states, *Publius* (Winter 1982), entire issue.

GRAVES, W. BROOKE, ed., *Major Problems in State Constitutional Revision.* Chicago: Public Administration Service, 1960.

MAY, JANICE C., "Constitutional Amendment and Revision Revisited," *Publius: The Journal of Federalism* (Spring 1987), 153–179.

McGRAW, BRADLEY D., ed., *Developments in State Constitutional Law, The Williamsburg Conference.* St. Paul: West Publishing Co., 1985.

Model State Constitution (6th ed. rev.). New York: National Municipal League, 1968.

SACHS, BARBARA FAITH, ed., *Index to Constitutions of the United States: National and State.* Dobbs Ferry, N.Y.: Oceana Publications, 1980.

SANFORD, TERRY, "Archaic State Constitution," *Judicature* (August/September 1968), 57–60.

STURM, ALBERT L., "State Constitutional Conventions during the 1970s," *State Government* (Winter 1979), 24–30.

———, *Thirty Years of State Constitution Making: 1938–1968.* New York: National Municipal League, 1970.

SWINDLER, WILLIAM F., ed., *Sources and Documents of United States Constitutions* (10 vols.). Dobbs Ferry, N.Y.: Oceana Publications, 1973–1979.

3
federalism

PREVIEW

WHY AN IOWA?

I almost didn't make it to college this quarter. They let me register late. And here I was—walking up the icy steps of Beardshear Hall on my way to class. Only 14 days ago my troopship arrived from Europe. We disembarked at Newport News on New Year's Day. What joy to be home again, alive, from Hitler's war! On the seventh of January we arrived at Camp Grant (in Illinois) and were discharged from the army. I took a train next day and didn't feel comfortable until we had crossed the Mississippi. Then I knew we were at last rolling home into Iowa.

I never cared much about the Corn State until this moment. I reached Ames, said hello again to my parents, and traded my five battle stars for five courses at Iowa State. Crossing the campus, I felt I should be saluting an officer somewhere. It was sunny and ten below zero. I climbed the granite stairs into Beardshear Hall and entered a classroom. It was a course on state and local government. I was late, and the hushed class was listening to a young professor with a bow tie explain states' rights. I took my seat and didn't even have my pen uncapped when this professor jumped me with a question. "Now, you in the khaki shirt, what shall we do with Iowa? Let's face that question. Why, really, do we need an Iowa? Why do we need *any* states any more?"

The sudden attention took my breath away. I stared at the bow tie, speechless. All I could think was, they sure didn't have bow ties in the Fourth Armored Division.

"Why Iowa, Mr. ahhh . . . I don't think I have your name on my class roll."

"Twomey, sir."

"Why Iowa, Mr. Twomey?"

He didn't let me answer but plunged on. "Why 48 divorce laws?" he demanded, looking out the window for the Atlantic Ocean. "Why 48 murder laws, why 48 court systems, why everything in 48s? Why not let Congress give us one national law? Do we need states anymore and their myriad laws?"

He paused and looked at me. I opened my mouth. But suddenly he resumed, now looking distantly through the wall to the Pacific Ocean. "Why 48 speed laws, why 48 assault-and-battery laws, why 48 income-tax laws?" He paused again. I wasn't sure he still wanted me to say anything. "Why, Mr. Twomey?" He glared at me fiercely, not with anger but with mounting concern for the question.

"Well," I began.

But he was off again, now searching for the North Pole, his gaze sweeping over the tops of our heads. "Why 48 systems for making a will? Why 48 systems of local government? Why 48 systems for making laws? Why 48 corporation acts? Why 48 partnership laws? Why 48 driver's-license laws?" The questions bore down like frenzied sharks. Now his eyes were piercing. "Why an Iowa, Mr. Twomey? Shall we do away with states, Mr. Twomey? Shall we do away with Iowa, Mr. Twomey? Why Iowa, Mr. Twomey?" shouted the professor, as the bell rang ending class.

I rose to leave, awash in self-consciousness. I floated out the door into the teeming hallway, and out the great east portal of Beardshear Hall, and picked my way carefully down the 25 massive steps. It was bitter cold. I walked alone, clawed by the cutting wind, clawed by the thought of Iowa. The sun shone brightly. The snow crunched under foot and glistened in blinding light. Again, the joy of being home embraced me. Iowa embraced me. Iowa was near to me. For the first time in my life, Iowa meant something. This rush of feeling slowed my stride. Freezing winds moistened my eyes. I stood still, cold yet warm, looking at the magnificent Memorial Union Building, looking at the skaters on Lake La Verne, looking at the towering Campanile, which just then struck 2 P.M. with chimes as crisp as ice flakes. Oh, how lovely, how sweet to be home in Iowa again. Yes, my God, we need an Iowa. Yes, God, we need an Iowa corporation act. Yes, we need an Iowa inheritance law, an Iowa speed law. Yes, we need all those things. Without them there wouldn't really be an Iowa.

Behind me a crunch in the snow. Behind me a pat on the back. Now beside me the bow tie. "Come on, Twomey, let's have a cup of chocolate."

DUAL SOVEREIGNTY

The United States Constitution might be described as a marriage contract drafted when a collection of sovereign states entered into wedlock with a central government (which they had created for the purpose). What is the status of that matrimonial relationship today? How is the federal government getting along with its 50 spouses, and how are the 50 getting along with their mighty bedmate, and finally, how are the 50 getting along with one another?

This gigantic union cannot always be called wedded bliss, for like so many marriages it is seasoned with occasional strife. In fact, the authors of the marriage contract did not intend the partnership to be entirely amiable—did not intend it to be all submissiveness on one side and mastery on the other. Competition among the partners, even feuding and brawling, was built into the system. This was not a union of vassals under a master, but a union of self-respecting sovereigns. It was a union in which each member surrendered a portion of its independent power to the other.

Roger B. Taney, chief justice from 1836 to 1864, viewed the Union as a system of **dual sovereignty.** A *sovereign* is a person or a government that has no legal superior. In Taney's view, the United States Constitution divided power into two heaps—one for the federal (central) government, the other for the states. When the federal government was doing the things it had power to do, it had no legal superior. Likewise with the states. Each side was sovereign and had no legal superior when it was acting within its exclusive sphere of authority— thus, dual sovereignty.

The Constitution lists the things the federal government has power to do, but it does not list things the states have power to do. States have power over almost everything the central government does not. Using the phraseology of the Tenth Amendment to the Constitution, we call the list of federal powers **delegated power** and the powers of the states **reserved power.** The **Tenth Amendment** says, "The powers not delegated to the United States by the Constitution, nor prohibited by it to the States, are reserved to the States respectively, or to the people."

The Division of Power

The authors of the United States Constitution, meeting that hot summer of 1787 in Philadelphia, certainly didn't want to set up a powerful central government that would overshadow the states. But they did want a central government that had enough power to handle several jobs that needed handling (such as defending the country). A confederacy would not do. They had tried confederacy, and it didn't really work to anybody's satisfaction. The Articles of Confederation had created a central government with no powers of its own. Each state under the confederacy was free to disregard anything the central government did, was free to disregard its laws and its requests for money. Each state was, in fact, entirely free to withdraw from the confederacy, because that is the nature of confederacies. A modern-day example of a confederacy is the United Nations: no member is bound to obey, no member is bound to pay, no member is stopped from quitting, no member surrenders any sovereignty. The central government under a **confederacy** has no power of its own—all its power is on loan, so to speak, from the member states, each of which is fully sovereign (in a legal sense) and therefore free to do as it pleases. The authors of the Constitution decided to put an end to the confederacy that had prevailed since the Declaration of Independence, to substitute **federalism,** to substitute dual sovereignty, and to ask the states to give up *some* of their sovereignty and transfer it to the central government. And that is exactly what was done. Yet 72 years later we had to fight a civil war to decide whether we really had substituted federalism for confederacy. The inefficiencies of the confederate system of government were again demonstrated in the southern Confederate States of America, which, because it had no power of its own, had to beg member states to send troops to General Robert E. Lee.

The general too often went into battle strong on promises but short on deliveries.

Surely no one at the Constitutional Convention in 1787 wanted to replace the weakness of a confederacy with any sort of centralized tyranny. After all, the Revolutionary War was a war against just such a central authority located in London. It was everybody's intention that the new central government not have power to do much. The states were to do most of the governing; the central government was limited to those items listed in Article I, Section 8, Clauses 1 through 18. To pay for these responsibilities, such as coining money, punishing counterfeiters, establishing post offices, building post roads, giving copyrights and patents, establishing federal courts, punishing pirates, raising and supporting an army and navy and making rules for them, and regulating interstate and foreign commerce, the Constitution gave the central government the power to lay and collect taxes and borrow money. The Constitution, in Article I, Section 8, Clause 18 (the **necessary and proper clause**), also allowed the federal government to make whatever laws were necessary and proper for carrying out its various powers, such as those mentioned.

Clearly the authors of the Constitution intended to cage almost all federal power within the fence of those delegated powers. To soothe the fears of those who questioned whether the central government would remain within that cage, the Tenth Amendment was added immediately after ratification of the Constitution. Patrick Henry and others who opposed the new Constitution and feared the power of the new central government wanted a bill of rights that would make it absolutely clear that there were a series of things the federal government could not do (interfere with freedom of speech, for example). Among the articles of the Bill of Rights is the aforementioned Tenth Amendment, which tries to make the boundary between state and federal power crystal clear.

If Patrick Henry were to rise from his grave and look at the vast government in Washington, D.C., today, he might feel that his misgivings about the new central government were absolutely justified. He worried that it would get out of hand and start doing all sorts of things the constitution writers of 1789 never intended. But if he could bring himself to sit down and ponder the changes that have occurred in this country since his death in 1799—changes in the size, complexity, and population of the country—he might be consoled that we have done a pretty good job of limiting federal power despite its great growth, and a pretty good job of preserving the states (they are doing more than ever before) despite the shrinkage of their independence. He might feel that the starring role played by the federal government today has become necessary because times have changed.

Why Has Federal Power Grown?

Let us look at the America of 1787 for a moment. The nation's population was only four million (including about a million slaves), scattered far and wide among the 13 states extending a thousand miles from New Hampshire to Georgia and inland an average of 200 miles. The largest city in America, Philadelphia, had only 42,000 people; the nation was distinctly rural, mostly farmers, frontier dwellers, tradespeople, and slaves. A New Yorker could not pick up the phone and talk to his or her agent in South Carolina, or drive down a freeway, or take a train to Charleston, much less a jet. In fact, it was next to impossible to move from state to state by land—much commerce was by sea, along the coast where the major cities were. The states were truly isolated: it took days or weeks to get from one to the other. News traveled no faster, for there were no national television hookups. Clearly if there was to be a central government at all, it needed to be designed to handle only the few common concerns of these 13 almost independent states—their common need for defense, their common need or wish for an economic union free of tariff barriers, and so forth. Most governing was still done by states—most of the lawmaking, most of the judging, most of the administering. No one looked upon the new central government as the star performer on the political stage, and no one thought of the president of the United States as more dazzling than a state governor.

The national government has grown in power not only because the nation has grown in size and population, but also because we have become less a collection of isolated states and more a single nation. The words of the Constitution remain the same, but the reality to which those words apply has changed. When the authors of the Constitution gave power to the central government to regulate commerce among the states, there really wasn't much interstate commerce—not by comparison with today's. If you analyze, say, the clothes you are wearing and ask "Where were these shoes made? Where were these socks made? Where was this shirt made? and How did they all get to me?" you will probably discover that nearly everything you wear was made in some other state. Of course, that applies not only to clothes but also to practically everything we use— the typewriter, the chair, the table, the plaster in the walls, the light fixture, the tile flooring, the briefcase, the file cabinet, the furnace, the toothpaste, the frozen peas, the canned corn. Nearly all of it comes from someplace far away and falls within the power of Congress to regulate. That would not have been true in 1787. When the Constitution writers gave the federal government control of interstate commerce, they did not give up control of the whole economic system. Today we have a **national economy,** and increasingly an international economy, rather than individual state economies, a fact that has given power to the national government. Furthermore, the problems of that national economy—unemployment, inflation and depression, the value of the dollar—cannot be doctored at the state level. They must be attacked nationally by national power.

Even crime has become national. Early in our history the job of drafting criminal laws was left largely to the states, but that too has changed. A kidnap victim can be moved a thousand miles in a matter of hours; negotiations for ransom may cross several states by phone. In fact, the federal kidnap law was enacted by Congress under its power to regulate interstate commerce (as have so many federal laws) because kidnapping is (or may easily be) interstate commerce. The existence of national police (the FBI, for example) reflects the increasingly national character of crime. Today great crime organizations operating out of such cities as New York, Chicago, Los Angeles, and Houston cover the nation with the efficiency of national corporations.

One would not want to say there is nothing for states to do anymore; states are finding a lot to do—state budgets and state employees have been increasing every year. All governments in America are doing more—federal, state, and local. What has declined is state independence, not state work; what has changed is the extent of national influence over the states. What remains basically unchanged is the overall legal relationship between the national government and the states. But that legal relationship masks a new reality. Increasingly the federal government is using states as field offices to carry out federal programs. More and more of what states do is done under federal supervision. States remain states, but the shadow of federal leadership falls across their independence. Local governments too are falling under federal leadership (as well as becoming more dependent on their state government).

CONSTITUTIONAL AVENUES FOR THE RISE OF FEDERAL POWER

Let us take a peek at the world of **constitutional law** to see how the rise of federal power and the decline of state independence has been legally possible under a Constitution that supposedly puts severe restrictions on federal power.

Style of the Constitution

One peculiarity of the United States Constitution is its unique style. The Constitution is only 10 or 12 pages long, hardly more than an outline. Whereas most state constitutions say too much, the United States Constitution says perhaps too little. Much is left unsaid, undefined, and unspecific. It establishes the fundamentals but leaves most of the details to be worked out by ordinary legislation. For example, the whole federal power over interstate and foreign commerce rests on a 16-word clause. This sketchiness of the Constitution allows a great deal to be read into the document that its authors may or may not have intended.

Spending Power

The very first item in the list of powers possessed by Congress allows Congress to spend money on anything it wants, the so-called **spending power.** Perhaps the authors of the Constitution assumed the government would spend money only for things the Constitution clearly authorized the federal government to do. But in fact, almost from the first hour of the Republic, Congress has spent money on things never imagined by the Framers in 1787. The Constitution does feebly try to say what Congress may spend for, but here we have an example of the monumental vagueness of the document: "The Congress shall have Power to lay and collect Taxes, Duties, Imports and Excises, to pay the Debts and provide for the common Defense and *general Welfare* of the United States" (italics added). This is the famous **welfare clause,** one of the most enigmatic of the entire Constitution. It defies definition; it ends up meaning nothing and everything. In the process of spending money for the general welfare, Congress has bought power—power to do many things the Framers did not envision, such as clearing slums in cities, "compelling" states to hire some of their civil servants through competitive examinations, preventing high blood pressure by underwriting medical research, and paying the states to do 500 other things.

Implied Powers

Another famous piece of vagueness in the United States Constitution is the fantastic language one sees at the bottom of the list of delegated powers in Article I, Section 8: the so-called necessary and proper clause. Here again it seems the central government was given power to do just about anything it wants, as long in this case, as it can somehow be related to the powers listed just before the necessary and proper clause. Such related powers are called **implied powers.** How necessary and how proper the related activity has to be is entirely up to Congress and ultimately the Supreme Court.

The Supreme Court confronted the question of how necessary and how proper a long time ago (1819) in the famous case of *McCulloch* v. *Maryland*.[1] The federal government had established the Bank of the United States and put a branch in Baltimore. Maryland bankers did not like competition from this "foreign corporation," nor did the state think the federal government had any delegated power to establish such a bank. To get rid of the bank, Maryland put a $15,000 tax on it (a staggering sum in those days). Mr. McCulloch, cashier of the federal bank in Baltimore, refused to pay the state tax, and that set the stage for a lawsuit. The Supreme Court conceded that nothing in the United States Constitution specifically authorizes the federal government to establish a bank. The Constitution, however, does authorize the government to collect money through taxes. It is obvious, said Chief Justice John Marshall, that the government has to keep that money somewhere, and the proper place to keep it is in a bank. It is also necessary for the government to have a bank so that the government can pay its bills in the East, West, North, and South by transferring funds among banks rather than moving money in great boxes around the country. Therefore, said Marshall (who was dedicated to making the central government strong and efficient), it is entirely proper for the federal government to do its banking through a bank chartered and controlled by the government itself, even though nothing in the Constitution specifically mentions a bank. As a result of this case, Congress has acquired wide powers from all its delegated authority.

Probably 95 percent of everything the federal government does today is done under the shield of the necessary and proper clause. That clause has been a major route for the expansion of federal power.

Commerce Power

The **commerce clause** is a short but crushingly important clause. It gives Congress the power "to regulate Commerce with foreign Nations, and among the several States, and with the Indian Tribes." The commerce clause has played a starring role in the collision of state and federal power and has proved to be one of the greatest constitutional limitations upon state power. Hundreds of cases concerning the commerce clause have reached the United States Supreme Court; every word of the clause has been litigated. Summing up all those cases, one senses that the Supreme Court has tried to favor federal power over commerce while trying to preserve as much state power as possible. The problem is that all commerce is related: it is hard to say exactly which commerce is between states and which is entirely within states. Almost all commerce today is directly or indirectly interstate. A hamburger stand in Elko, Nevada, might seem an example of commerce entirely within a state, yet the hamburger may come from Iowa or Argentina, and the customers may be from everywhere. A window washer in Trenton, New Jersey, may seem to have a strictly local business, but on closer examination we see that he earns money by washing windows on the 20-story headquarters of a firm doing business in 50 states and 63 foreign countries.

[1]4 *Wheat.* 316 (1819).

Practically any case concerning the commerce clause reveals the agony of the courts as they struggle to find the elusive boundary between state and federal power.

Supremacy Clause

If dual sovereignty exists (if the states are sovereign within their sphere of authority and the federal government is sovereign within its sphere of authority), what happens when the two sovereigns—each acting within its sphere of power—pass inconsistent laws? This has happened time and again. What if, for example, a state forbids banks to use the word *savings* in their business, and the Federal Reserve Act nevertheless authorizes banks to receive savings deposits? Or what if a state prohibits nonlawyers from representing clients in patent cases, and the United States Patent Office nevertheless licenses nonlawyers as patent agents? What if a state sets the minimum price of milk, and a milk dealer, acting under the Armed Services Procurement Act, sells milk below the minimum to a U.S. Army base in the state? What if state law prohibits use of oleomargarine, and the director of a federal soldiers' home nevertheless uses oleomargarine? What if a state law says that citizens of the state must have a state driver's license to drive in the state, and the U.S. Post Office nevertheless permits its employees to drive postal trucks without a state license? Such clashes of power are countless. They are dealt with in Article VI of the United States Constitution (the **supremacy clause**): "This Constitution, and the Laws of the United States which shall be made in Pursuance thereof; and all Treaties made, or which shall be made under the Authority of the United States, shall be the supreme Law of the Land. . . ."

The supremacy clause was carefully written into the Constitution because the Framers were clearheaded enough to see that if two sovereigns are to operate next to each other, they must agree on who is to be supreme in case of a conflict between them. The problem becomes especially sticky when Congress legislates in the foggy realm of its implied (necessary and proper) powers and when a state claims the federal law invades the state's reserved powers (an even foggier realm). One government must be superior to the other when they come into conflict, each exercising its supposed sovereign power. Federal power is so ill defined (yet supreme) that one must question whether any such thing as dual sovereignty is possible. No area of state power is safe from federal preemption under the supremacy clause.

Supreme Court as Umpire

It is significant that the United States Supreme Court is the ultimate umpire in all cases involving clashes of authority between the federal and state governments. The Supreme Court has not always decided in favor of the federal government in federal-state disputes, but it has commonly taken a broad view of federal power.

COOPERATIVE FEDERALISM

New, cooperative, creative, and the other adjectives that political scientists nowadays like to hang upon the word *federalism* are intended to tell us that governments today rarely work alone, but that usually all three levels of government—federal, state, and local—work together. **Cooperative federalism** is largely a matter of the national government paying subnational governments to do things in cooperation with it. There are some 500 tasks that the national government pays other governments to do, ranging from sewer construction to college education, and there are hundreds of other domestic assistance programs in which the federal government offers technical assistance but no money.

Federal aid is heavily, but not solely, financial. The federal government also studies in detail just what it wants other governments to do and how they should do it. Numerous federal bureaucrats are employed to develop standards and specifications for recipients of federal aid, and numerous others are employed to roam the nation making sure that state and local governments do what they are hired to do. If federal standards are disregarded—if highways financed partly by the federal government are not built the way the federal government wants them built—then federal money may be withheld.

Cooperative federalism is a matter not only of joint financing but also of joint planning and joint execution of projects. The actual work of, say, road building or sewer building or university building is done by state and local governments; the work shared by the federal government in these and other federal-aid projects is primarily in the areas of finance, planning, and inspection.

Federal payments to state governments for the purpose of enticing them into certain courses of action have been offered since the early years of the Republic. One of the greatest federal-aid programs of the last century was the Morrill Land-Grant College Act of 1862, under which the federal government gave public land to any state that would use it to establish a college for teaching agriculture and engineering. Some 69 colleges, including many famous ones, owe their existence to this enlightened piece of federal bribery.

We will not attempt to catalog every federal-aid program—there are hundreds. They touch almost everything state and local governments do in one way or another. Federal involvement with the work of state and local governments is so pervasive that today the latter are hardly distinct from the federal government.[2] Writers have begun referring to them as "subnational" governments. Not long ago a book was published with the fateful title *The Nationalization of State Government*.[3]

The Marble Cake

Federal payments to state and local government are earmarked primarily for such things as public housing, education, health, hospitals, agriculture, urban renewal, airports, libraries, welfare, and highways. Bureaucrats working within any one of those programs communicate closely with one another no matter what level of government they work for: there is a certain coziness among them and a certain mutuality of interest. This makes them the very symbol of cooper-

---

[2]For a discussion of the psychological effects of this upon voters see U.S. Advisory Commission on Intergovernmental Relations, "New Relationships in a Changing System of Federalism and American Politics," *National Civic Review* (November–December 1986), pp. 336–345. The foregoing article is based on Chapter 1 of ACIR's report *The Transformation in American Politics: Implications for Federalism* (Washington, D.C., 20575, August 1986, Report A-106) and excerpts from the Commission's Summary Findings and Recommendations.

[3]Jerome J. Hanus, *The Nationalization of State Government* (Lexington, Mass.: Heath, 1981).

ative federalism. Federalism today has been likened to a marble cake. At first glance the three levels of government appear to be a three-tier cake, each layer a different flavor. On closer examination, however, we find that it is a marble cake: all three flavors are mixed together in each layer, just as the three levels of government are separate but intertwined.

Today state governments receive about 20 percent of their revenue from the federal government. Local governments, taken as a whole, have lately received about 30 percent of their revenue from the state and federal government combined (These are lower percentages than in the early 1980s, when federal aid to state and local governments was greater).

Grants

Most federal aid to state and local governments is still in the form of grants-in-aid for specific programs (or categories), such as airports. This is called **categorical aid.** Although some more recent grants require no match, the federal government normally agrees to pay a certain generous portion of the cost of such a program if state or local governments will supply the remainder and do the work according to federal standards. The term *formula grant* is sometimes used to designate federal grants-in-aid offered under such a payment formula.

Obviously the purpose of a great many grants-in-aid is to establish at least minimum levels of health, highways, education, welfare, and so on. At first blush this seems entirely blameless and laudable. Actually, however, a good many of these grants-in-aid twist the arms of state or local government to spend money on certain programs they don't really need—or to spend more money on certain programs than they otherwise would if the "offer that can't be refused" were not constantly dangled before them. State and local budgets are distorted so that free money can be gotten: if the federal government is going to pay 40 percent of something, or 60 percent, or 90 percent, then what fool would not jump at the offer? In some cases, though, it is foolish for a state to spend, say, 10 million dollars on highways to get 90 million free dollars, when it really shouldn't be spending even the 10 million. However, very few state and local politicians are fearless enough to refuse the offer.

Another form of grant has risen to prominence in recent years: the *project grant,* which does not rely on a specific formula for payment. Project grants now number in the hundreds and are given one by one to governments that apply and that support their application with sufficient data and sufficient evidence of careful planning. These grants must be approved by experts in the bureaucracy (usually federal experts) who are given the discretion to accept or refuse such projects and to determine the scope of government aid for the ones accepted. This rise of project grants has given the professionals working within various programs (such as the airport program) a great deal of power and autonomy.

A grant somewhat related to the project grant is the **block grant.** Here the federal government makes funds available to support a collection (block) of activities and allows state governments to decide which activities within that block they wish to fund with the money. There is, for example, the community-development block grant administered by the Department of Housing and Urban Development. Regulations provide funds for a smorgasbord of activities aimed at eliminating slums, such as land acquisition, site clearance, parks and play-grounds, street and drainage improvements, removal of architectural barriers, historic preservation, and planning. Thus a block grant supposedly gives recipients freedom to reach a general goal by any of several routes.

Many state and local government officials like block grants better than categorical grants because of this freedom, and would like to see most categorical grants combined into block grants. For example, the 1981 block grant for Preventive Health and Social Services includes several former categoricals—rat control, emergency medical services, high-blood-pressure control, home health services, preventive health services. Some state and local officials are pleased to be able to decide for themselves which of these to emphasize, rather than be bound to a formula for each.

The advantages seen in block grants by state and local officials are accompanied by some worries. For one thing, although block grants supposedly allow states and municipalities greater freedom, federal bureaucrats who dole out the money do not always want to give greater freedom. To get block-grant money, a government has to apply for it. Federal bureaucrats then decide whether the application is worthy of being funded. In some cases those civil servants have their own ideas about what state and local governments should be funding with block-grant money. Thus the spirit of freedom can be snuffed out in practice.

State and local officials also worry that block-grant money can be cut by Congress more easily than categorical-grant money. It is politically easier to cut a fuzzy, ill-defined area like health care than to cut something specific like rat control.

Block grants also put the burden of deciding which programs to fund on state and local politicians. Such a burden may represent freedom, but it also represents having to say no to many applicants. Many state and local officials are not pleased with the prospect of having to make these hard decisions, or with the prospect of facing vocal pressure groups who want the money spent in some particular way. Under the categorical-grant system, funding is determined rather mechanically by formulas decided far away in Washington, D.C.

Grantsmanship

The proliferation of grants, both in dollar volume and in variety, causes state and local bureaucrats to spend tremendous energy applying for them. A whole new art has emerged called **grantsmanship.** It is so important that colleges even offer courses now in how to get grants. Professors in all disciplines spend an astounding number of hours dreaming up new ways to attract grant money and more hours putting together elaborate grant proposals. A new kind of hero has emerged: the person who gets a big grant, either personally or for the institution. State and local governments now hire people whose sole duty is to search for ways to get grants and sometimes even create whole bureaus for this purpose with high officials in charge. One can easily understand this sophisticated begging, because so much depends on it.

Recently an attempt has been made to reduce this endless pleading for federal grants without reducing the flow of federal money. General revenue sharing was thought to be the answer.

General Revenue Sharing

General revenue sharing is a somewhat new plan for distributing federal money to local governments. The plan helps liberate subnational governments from the compulsion to buy things they don't really want in order to get federal money. The federal government simply mails a check to subnational governments with a note attached saying "Do what you want with this." (There are, however, a number of crosscutting regulations touching such things as antidiscrimination, environmental protection, and citizen participation that apply to all federal grant programs.) Washington spends millions of dollars annually on such largess. The chief alleged virtue of general revenue sharing is also, according to some, its chief fault—the freedom it gives subnational governments to spend federal money according to their own priorities and preferences rather than the federal government's.

General revenue sharing is still in its experimental stage. It has not by any means replaced categorical aid, formula grants, project grants, or block grants, although some think it should. It has slightly lessened the dependence of subnational governments on the property tax (a tax already exploited to the limit), it has somewhat moderated the frenzy of grantsmanship and the systematic begging into which subnational governments are immersed, and it has given recipients more license in the use of federal funds.

Often this new freedom is used wisely and general-revenue-sharing money is spent sensibly. The reverse has happened just often enough, however, to call the whole system into serious question. Free money from Washington has occasionally been spent like Christmas money: on frippery that no one really needs—an airplane for the governor, new uniforms for the band. Although federal-aid money is supposed to help the downtrodden, very little of it gets to the downtrodden because governments are not run by the downtrodden. Revenue-sharing money is spent chiefly on things that delight the middle and upper classes, who do run governments, and only the smallest fraction gets to those in special need.

Have States Become "Middle Management"?

The rising volume of federal grants to state and local governments has changed the American system of government by virtually ending federalism. "The textbook distinctions between state and federal interests have been blurred by the evolution of the federal grant-in-aid system now consisting of almost 500 separate programs," said Governor Richard A. Snelling of Vermont. "States and local governments have lost much of their identity, becoming more like 'subnational units' than independent members of a federal system. The federal presence in state and local government does not even resemble the concept of federalism held by American political leaders a generation ago."[4]

Almost all of these grants-in-aid put the subnational units in a distinctly subordinate role—that of middle-management supplicants. If their supplications are granted, they must continually look up to a federal bureaucrat to see

---

[4]Richard A. Snelling, "American Federalism in the Eighties," *State Government* (Autumn 1980), p. 168.

whether they are behaving correctly in the administration of their grant. The relationship is not that of equals, but of superiors and subordinates. Commenting on the Environmental Protection Agency's management of the Clean Air Act, John Thorson observed that although the program is sometimes cited as a fine example of federal-state cooperation, the way in which EPA has administered it "reduces the states to the status of middle management under command of EPA."[5]

David B. Walker expressed a similar thought when he pointed out that "state and local governments have been 'used' to implement wholly national policies."[6] But Walker also noted that although Washington may "use" state and local governments, the reverse is also true—Washington has been "used" by state and local governments to further what not so long ago would have been a wholly local or state concern. Local governments have not resisted federal intrusion with any great vigor. In fact, they have seemingly relished it as a top-notch way to lighten their money problems. Complaints from state and local governments about federal mastery over them sounds a little like "It hurts so good."

Viewed from the federal government's standpoint, federal grants-in-aid allow the federal government to launch programs that are on or beyond the border of its constitutional powers and that allow it to use state and local bureaucracies as a convenient (and politically adroit) way of administering those programs without increasing the federal bureaucracy. It has been estimated that four out of every ten state and local employees are federal bureaucrats in disguise. One sometimes wonders why the federal bureaucracy has remained about the same size since the end of World War II while federal programs have multiplied. Is it that federal civil servants have increased their productivity spectacularly? No. The answer lies in the rapid growth of state and local bureaucracies supported in part by federal grants-in-aid.

The reduction of state and local governments to the status of middle managers for the federal government has alarmed some observers. Daniel J. Elazar notes that the American political system is not supposed to be a management hierarchy. "The federal system is not a power pyramid organized on the basis of the federal government on top, the states in the middle, and local governments on the bottom."[7] States, he observes, are supposed to be polities (political organizations) that govern and serve their people. Although their administrative responsibilities are important, this should not suggest that their primary function is managerial.

President Reagan established a Presidential Federalism Advisory Committee in 1981 and declared, "The federal government too often has treated elected state and local officials as if they were nothing more than administrative agents for federal authority."[8] In his inaugural address on January 20, 1981, he said, "All of us need to be reminded that the federal government did not create the states; the states created the federal government."

[5] John Thorson, "CSG Begins Clean Air Project," *State Government News* (March 1981), p. 13.

[6] David B. Walker, "Intergovernmental Relations and Dysfunctional Federalism," *National Civic Review* (February 1981), p. 69.

[7] Daniel J. Elazar, "States as Polities in the Federal System," *National Civic Review* (February 1981), p. 79.

[8] *State Government News* (May 1981), p. 9.

DOES FEDERALISM STILL HAVE A USEFUL FUNCTION?

Are States Closer to the People?

Federalism is said to bring government closer to the people. State governments are said to understand the people's needs better because they are closer to the people and know where the shoe pinches. The argument that state government is closer to the people than federal government may not be as true today as it once was. Admittedly people are closer to their state capital geographically (except for a few citizens in Maryland and Virginia who can practically see the Washington Monument from their front door), but geographic distance isn't as important perhaps as **psychological distance.** Actually most Americans may feel closer to the president than to the state governor, to Congress than to the state legislature, to the United States Supreme Court than to their own state supreme court. In fact, if the truth were known, a lot of people might feel closer to the president than to their mayor, their superintendent of schools, and so on. No doubt our enormous system of mass communication is more apt to feature news from Washington, D.C., than from Boise, Madison, Springfield, or Des Moines. People sitting in Durango, Colorado, are probably going to know a lot more about the habits and opinions of the president than of their governor. They may think of the president as their personal friend or enemy, whereas their governor remains distant and dim.

Therefore, the idea that state government is closer to the people is debatable. Logic may insist on it, but logic in this case is reversed by electronics. Through television and radio the federal government comes into our living rooms more frequently, more forcefully, and more intimately than state government.

Does Federalism Divide Power?

We are told that federalism is a defense against tyranny insofar as it splits power among the states and the national government. This supposedly deters a concentration of power in the national government. Certainly the authors of the United States Constitution were convinced that the best way to prevent tyranny was to scatter and divide power. Both federalism and separation of powers were intended to serve that purpose. As we have seen, however, it is not working as successfully today as the authors of the Constitution hoped. Legal divisions of power are overcome by powerful economic and political centralizing tendencies as well as by broad judicial interpretations of federal power.

But there are other divisions of power in our country—**pluralism,** for instance—and these may check the misuse of power better than federalism. Ours is a society with many centers of power, most of which are outside and beyond government: the great corporations, the giant labor unions, the huge pressure groups—dozens, hundreds, thousands of power centers. It can be argued that these conflicting interests—not federalism—are the best defense against tyranny we have. They curb one another, and they curb the government. The existence of powers outside and beyond government, most particularly the institution of private property, and the free press supported by private capital, may be our greatest check on tyranny. If federalism were totally abandoned in

America, the part it plays as a defender of liberty might not be seriously missed, as long as these other defenses existed.

Gymnasiums and Laboratories of Democracy

Federalism does give people opportunities to practice the arts of democracy. Like a muscle, democracy needs exercise. The process of electing state officers is an exercise in the process of self-government that keeps the system limber and educates thousands of citizens in the arts of politics and governance.

Furthermore, states serve as laboratories where solutions to various problems are tried and tested. In recent years states invented an ingenious variety of responses to the gasoline shortage. Although no states were able to end the shortage, they did create ways to distribute gasoline without rationing and without panic. Other pathfinding experiments by states have been immensely valuable: unemployment insurance was invented in Wisconsin, food stamps in Vermont. Thus federalism allows each state an opportunity to design its own answer to public problems—allows diversity in public policy.

ADMISSION OF STATES TO THE UNION

Original and Admitted States

The **original 13 state** were not really admitted. They became a union by ratifying the newly written Constitution. Other states were subsequently admitted. The United States Constitution was drafted in 1787 by an assembly of delegates convened for the purpose of suggesting amendments and repairs to the Articles of Confederation, under which the 13 original states had organized themselves in 1781 during the American Revolution. However, the delegates proceeded to draft an entirely new constitution, one article of which provided that as soon as 9 states ratified the document it would become a constitution among the states so ratifying. Delaware was the first to ratify and therefore nicknames itself the First State (technically an error because there were no states under the new Constitution until 9 of them ratified, and then these 9 together became the first states—an event that happened when New Hampshire ratified the Constitution, on June 21, 1788). The remaining 4 ratified shortly thereafter, Rhode Island being the last on May 29, 1790. From then on states were admitted individually by Congress, which is empowered to do so by Article IV, Section 3. The first admitted state was Vermont (1791), and the most recent Hawaii (1959).

Procedure for Admission

The usual procedure for admission to the Union is for a territory to draft a proposed state constitution and submit it to Congress together with a request for admission. A member of Congress then introduces a bill calling for admission. That bill goes through Congress just like any other bill and finally comes to the president for his signature. If he vetoes the bill, Congress may try to override the veto. President Andrew Jackson vetoed three attempts to admit Colorado. That state finally made it on the fourth try when President Ulysses S. Grant signed an enabling act (a law granting admission to the Union) and proclaimed Colorado the thirty-eighth state of the Union on August 1, 1876.

Legal Equality of Admitted States

Although delegates to the Constitutional Convention of 1787 couldn't make up their minds whether new states should be admitted on a basis of total equality of power with the other states, the issue was settled long ago by the United States Supreme Court in favor of equality. The most notable court case involving state equality resulted from an attempt by Congress to impose a curious restriction on Oklahoma as a condition for admission to the Union: Congress forbade Oklahoma to change the location of its state capital. The Court invalidated that restriction on the ground that Congress may not embrace in an enabling act conditions relating wholly to matters under state control.[9]

NATIONAL OBLIGATIONS TO THE STATES

Republican Form of Government

Not only does the Constitution mean what the Supreme Court says it means, it also appears to exist only when the Supreme Court says it exists. The following words seem to have been banished for all practical purposes from the Constitution by the Court: "The United States shall guarantee to every State in this Union a Republican Form of Government." No one seems to know what the authors of the Constitution had in mind when they adopted that "guarantee." The term **republican government** is somewhat mystical. Political scientists sometimes define republican government as a modified form of democracy—as rule by representatives of the people rather than by the people themselves. But if that is what the Framers had in mind, then all forms of direct democracy in the United States would be in jeopardy: the New England town meeting, the referendum, the initiative. Various forms of boss rule would also be in constitutional jeopardy, but for a different reason—they are not republican but dictatorial. The Supreme Court has shunned this provision of the Constitution and largely managed to escape deciding cases under it. The Court seems willing to assume that if Congress allows a state's representatives in Congress to keep their seats, this implies the state is republican. The Court uses other provisions of the Constitution to decide cases that might be decided under the republican-form-of-government clause. For example, the Court could perhaps find malapportioned legislative bodies unconstitutional as violations of the idea of republican government, but it has not done so. The term *republican* is so slippery and the whole business of deciding which governments are republican so political that the Supreme Court has chosen simply to pretend that the words guaranteeing a republican form of government were never written.

[9]Coyle v. Smith, 221 U.S. 559 (1911).

Territorial Integrity

The United States Constitution says, "New States may be admitted by the Congress into this Union; but no new State shall be formed or erected within the Jurisdiction of any other State; nor any State be formed by the Junction of two or more States, or Parts of States, without the Consent of the Legislatures of the States concerned as well as of the Congress." When West Virginia was torn out of the hide of Virginia, this provision of the Constitution seems to have been evaded (although one could argue that the "reconstructed" legislature of Virginia gave its consent). But that happened in 1863 during the Civil War, when western Virginia, now West Virginia, was sympathetic to the North and took steps to separate itself from the remainder of Virginia, which had joined the Confederacy. Vermont, Kentucky, Tennessee, and Maine were also once part of other states, but in their cases the procedure for separation was entirely constitutional.

Protection from Invasion and Domestic Violence

The United States is supposed to protect each state against invasion and, on application of the state legislature or state governor (when the legislature cannot be convened), against domestic violence.[10] This does not mean that the federal government must always wait for a state to "apply" for protection. If domestic violence threatens enforcement of federal law within a state, threatens execution of federal programs, or threatens the safety of federal property, the central government may move into any state with any force necessary to ensure that those threats are put down. The orders of federal courts may also be enforced within states by federal authorities without need of an invitation from the state government; the president has the discretion to send troops. However, if a state asks for help in repelling invasions and putting down domestic violence, the federal government is obligated under the Constitution to help.

OBLIGATION OF STATES TO THE NATION

Election of Federal Officials

One of the curiosities of American government is that the federal government does not conduct elections for its own officers. United States senators and representatives are elected by the electoral system of each state, and the president and vice president are chosen by electors who in turn are (now) elected through the state electoral system. "The Times, Places and Manner of holding Elections for Senators and Representatives, shall be prescribed in each State by the Legislature thereof; but Congress may at any time by Law make or alter such Regulations," says the United States Constitution. Nevertheless, as we shall see in Chapter 4, the election process is becoming increasingly nationalized.

---

[10]*U.S. Const.*, Art. IV, Sec. 4.

Consideration of Amendments

Perhaps it is stretching the point to say that states are fulfilling an obligation to the nation when they consider amendments to the United States Constitution, but since the states have so few clear-cut obligations to the Union other than to stay in it, we will use this space to discuss the amendment process. Usually the process of amending the United States Constitution is reserved for books on American national government and is more or less ignored in state government books. But if the Constitution is the marriage contract that binds the states and the federal government together and binds the states with one another, then the procedure by which the terms of that contract are changed should be examined.

The authors of the Constitution did not totally agree on the best way to amend the Constitution. One group thought all proposed constitutional amendments should originate with Congress and then go to the states for ratification. Another group thought Congress should be brought into the process only after two-thirds of the states had proposed a constitutional amendment. The complaint against the second system was that it would limit constitutional amendments to proposals that would increase state power, since Congress couldn't consider anything that hadn't first been approved by two-thirds of the states. However, the objection to the opposite system—limiting constitutional amendments to proposals first made by Congress—was that all amendments would tend to increase the power of the central government because the Congress is itself part of the central government. Article V of the Constitution is something of a compromise between those positions: it provides two systems for amending the Constitution. The first system allows Congress to propose amendments to the states for their ratification; the second allows the states to petition Congress to call a constitutional convention. The convention, without any involvement of Congress, may propose constitutional amendments to the states for ratification.

Proposal of constitutional amendments by Congress to the states has been used for all amendments; never has the convention system been used, although it has come close on several occasions. Congress has to call a constitutional convention if two-thirds of the states ask for one. Advocates of direct election of United States senators came within one state of achieving the necessary two-thirds, when Congress finally caved in and proposed the Seventeenth Amendment (requiring such direct election of senators). Advocates of an amendment to curb the effect of the Supreme Court's reapportionment decisions also came within one state of getting the two-thirds necessary for a convention.

INTERSTATE RELATIONS

Full Faith and Credit

No matter where you get married, chances are the marriage will be recognized (and, if necessary, enforced) in all other nations of the planet. It has long been the practice among sovereign nations to recognize and enforce many of the rights acquired by people under the laws or civil proceedings of other nations— not only marriages, but contracts of most sorts and various other legal rights.

Since this practice existed among sovereigns, perhaps it wouldn't have been necessary to put a **full faith and credit** clause in the United States Constitution. Apparently, however, the Framers thought it best to elevate those reciprocal recognitions and enforcements from the status of comity (voluntary courtesy) among sovereign states of the Union to the status of a constitutional command. The Constitution, therefore says, "Full Faith and Credit shall be given in each State to the Public Acts, Records, and judicial Proceedings of every other State."

The most common use of the full faith and credit clause has been in cases where a court has found that one party owes another money and orders it paid. If the person who owes the debt goes to another state, the creditor may take his "judgment" (the finding of the court) to that other state and have it enforced upon the debtor by courts there. It isn't necessary for a creditor to argue his case all over again; the matter is considered *res judicata* (adjudicated and decided), and the prior proceedings are entitled to the same faith and credit as in the state of origin.

Complaints about the full faith and credit clause have arisen mainly because of "quickie" divorces given by some states, such as Nevada. Several states, such as North Carolina, New York, and Massachusetts, have balked at recognizing these divorces. The legal argument against recognition is that states are not required under the full faith and credit clause to recognize the judgment of any "foreign" court that did not have legal authority to give that judgment. No state has authority to give a divorce to someone who is not a citizen of the state. To become a citizen, one must live in a state with the intent to reside there permanently. One may not acquire state citizenship by merely visiting a state. Therefore, it has been alleged that people who go to, say, Nevada for the sole purpose of getting a divorce and then return to their home state never really, except in some narrow technical sense, become citizens of Nevada and never really become subject to the divorce-granting powers of Nevada courts. However, that's only a theory. Since 1945 the United States Supreme Court has not been disposed to question the right of any state to determine what constitutes the requisite length of residence for divorce purposes.

Although the Constitution says full faith and credit shall be given by each state to the *judicial proceedings* of every other state, this does not apply to penal judgments.[11] However, the Constitution does say that states shall deliver up persons who have been charged with crimes, when properly asked to do so by the state from which such a person has fled.[12]

Extradition

Nations sometimes make **extradition** treaties with one another, but it is not necessary for the states of the Union to make such agreements with one another. It is already provided for in the United States Constitution: "A Person charged in any State with Treason, Felony, or other Crime, who shall flee from Justice, and be found in another State, shall on demand of the executive Authority of the State from which he fled, be delivered up, to be removed to the State having Jurisdiction of the Crime." If someone charged with a crime in, say, California

---

[11]Nelson v. George, 399 U.S. 224 (1970).
[12]*U.S. Const.*, Art. IV, Sec. 2.

flees to Illinois, the governor of California conveys his request for extradition to the governor of Illinois. But what if the governor of Illinois declines to extradite? In that case there really isn't anything the governor of California can do about it. The United States Supreme Court has held that the duty to comply with an extradition request is purely "moral"; that the federal government has no power to compel the governor (or any other state officer) to comply; and that the governor of one state may not go to federal court and ask for a *writ of mandamus* compelling the governor of another state to comply with an extradition request.[13] The main thing compelling a governor to comply with extradition requests is the knowledge that if he doesn't, then others won't comply with his own requests. Comity prevails in these matters, although a governor will occasionally decline to extradite someone he feels should not be returned to face criminal charges—perhaps a mother who "kidnaps" her child from its legal guardian (a situation that recently motivated a Colorado governor to refuse extradition) or an old man who committed a crime 30 years ago in another state but who during the intervening 30 years has dwelled in a community as a flawless citizen. These rare refusals to extradite do not normally upset relations between governors.

Another reason governors usually comply with extradition requests is that they are reluctant to have their states regarded as havens for criminals. Most states receive 500 to 1000 extradition requests every year. Naturally, a governor hasn't time to personally investigate them all and will assign someone on his staff to handle them. The state attorney general may assign one or more full-time employees to investigate the merits of the requests.

A person may be extradited for every act made punishable by a state, including misdemeanors. Actually misdemeanors account for most extradition requests. They are scrutinized no less closely than requests for persons who have committed more serious crimes.

In only one circumstance may a governor legally refuse to extradite, and that is when the person to be extradited is able to show clearly that he was not in the demanding state at the time of the crime. Except for that, no governor is required to consider any defense offered by the defendant; indeed, it is expressly improper to do so. If the defendant is innocent, or if the statute of limitations has run out, or if the defendant has any other defense, the time and place for these defenses is in court when he returns to the state where the crime was committed. Seldom does a defendant secure his release before extradition by *habeas corpus* (a court order to bring a person before a judge to determine if he is being held in custody legally). If the defendant requests a *writ of habeas corpus* to fight extradition, the court will not listen to any argument except the one that he was not in the demanding state at the time of the crime.

Suits between States

In colonial times disputes between colonies were settled in London by the Privy Council. The Articles of Confederation gave this job to Congress, but the Framers of the United States Constitution decided the Supreme Court should decide all controversies between states.[14] The Supreme Court has original jurisdiction in such cases: when states sue each other they do not begin in the lower federal

---

[13]Kentucky v. Dennison, 24 How. 66 (1861).
[14]*U.S. Const.*, Art. III, Sec. 2.

courts but file their suit directly with the Supreme Court. No other court has power to hear suits between states.

Most suits between states have been over boundaries. Ten of the 13 original states were having boundary disputes when the Constitution was written. During the first 60 years of our national existence nearly all disputes between states involved boundaries. More recently, however, states have found other things to sue each other about. A number of such suits have concerned water rights, particularly in the West, where water is a much fought over treasure. There have also been disputes over which state has a right to collect death taxes from someone's estate. In these disputes the court usually has to decide which of two or more states the dead person legally resided in. States have also sued each other for the enforcement of contracts between them. Virginia and West Virginia even had a dispute about the percentage of Virginia's public debt that West Virginia was obliged to assume after it separated from Virginia.

Privileges and Immunities

According to the Constitution, "the Citizens of each State shall be entitled to all Privileges and Immunities of Citizens in the Several States." What this means has so perplexed judges for 200 years now that very few cases have been decided under its authority. What are the **privileges and immunities** of, say, the citizens of Florida? Whatever they are, anyone from any other state who goes to Florida has the same privileges and immunities. In the search for a list of such privileges and immunities, judges have looked back to a similar but lengthier and more specific clause in the Articles of Confederation. No doubt the authors of the United States Constitution in 1787 had this general provision in mind. It states that out-of-staters have (1) the right to freely enter and leave the state, (2) the same rights to engage in trade and commerce that are enjoyed by the inhabitants of the state, and (3) the right to be subject to only those taxes and laws that citizens of the state are subject to.

If states cannot discriminate against out-of-staters, why do nonresidents have to pay higher tuition at state universities than residents? Why do nonresidents have to pay higher fees for hunting and fishing? Don't these things discriminate against nonresidents? Yes they do, but the United States Supreme Court has managed to throw a cloak of protection around such discriminations. Only hostile discrimination against out-of-staters is forbidden by the privileges and immunities clause, said the Court; reasonable discrimination is permissible![15]

SUMMARY

The Framers of the United States Constitution designed a system of government suitable for conditions in 1787 but not suitable in every detail for today. Since 1787 the nation has changed drastically. It is a fundamentally different nation today in size, population, wealth, power, and above all in economy and tech-

[15]Blake v. McClung, 172 U.S. 239 (1898); Travis v. Yale & Towne Mfg. Co., 252 U.S. 60 (1920).

nological development. Fortunately the Constitution was written in broad generalities. This has made its reinterpretation easy. The Constitution has been repeatedly bent to fit the nation's changing circumstances.

The Framers intended to divide power between two sovereignties: the central government and the states. The central government (which we call the *federal* government) was delegated a limited number of powers, such as regulating interstate commerce and providing for the common defense. Within the sphere of those delegated powers the central government was to be sovereign.

However, the central government immediately began to expand its sphere of sovereignty at the expense of state sovereignty. The Constitution has not been a great obstacle to this growth of federal power. Indeed, it has been used as legal justification for it. Broad interpretations of the federal government's delegated power has given legal sanction to a multitude of federal activities never dreamed of by the Framers. The loose style of the Constitution lent itself to these broad interpretations. The Constitution, for example, seems to have given the federal government unlimited spending powers, and this has allowed the federal government to buy up powers "reserved" to the states. Federal payments to states have regularly been made on condition that the money is spent on projects that the federal government wants.

Furthermore, the federal government is authorized by the Constitution not only to exercise its various delegated powers, but also to do whatever is "necessary and proper" in order to execute them. These *implied* powers seem almost indefinable and limitless. Broad interpretations of the commerce clause have been a particularly great source of growth in federal power at the expense of state power.

Wherever a valid exercise of federal power has collided with state power, the states have been forced to yield because the Constitution says federal law is the supreme law of the land. Furthermore, if there is a question of whether federal law is valid (constitutional), the issue is decided by the federal Supreme Court, not by states.

Adjectives that political scientists nowadays like to hang on the word *federalism—new, cooperative, creative*—are intended to tell us that today very little is accomplished by one government alone; most projects are joint efforts, sometimes by all three levels of government—federal, state, and local. Although federalism may have served a more useful function early in our national history, it continues to have important merits today.

The national government is supposed to have certain obligations to the states, the states are supposed to have certain obligations to the national government, and the states also supposedly have various obligations to each other.

SUGGESTIONS FOR FURTHER READING

BREAK, GEORGE,   *Financing Government in a Federal System.* Washington, D.C.: Brookings Institution, 1980.

GLENDENING, PARRIS N., and MAVIS M. REEVES,   *Pragmatic Federalism: An Intergovernmental View of American Government* (2nd ed.). Pacific Palisades, Calif.: Palisades Publishers, 1984.

HOWITT, ARNOLD M.,   *Managing Federalism.* Washington, D.C.: Congressional Quarterly Press, 1984.

NICE, DAVID C., *Federalism: The Politics of Intergovernmental Relations.* New York: St. Martin's Press, 1987.

PEIRCE, NEAL, "Federal Preemption and the State's Role," *State Government* (Summer 1978), 173–79.

Publius (Winter 1979). Entire issue devoted to the state of American federalism.

REAGAN, MICHAEL D., and JOHN G. SANZONE, *The New Federalism* (2nd ed.). New York: Oxford University Press, 1981.

ROSS, DOUGLAS, "Safeguarding Our Federalism: Lessons for the States from the Supreme Court," *Public Administration Review* 45 (November 1985, special issue):723–31.

THOMAS, ROBERT D., "Implementing Federal Programs at the Local Level," *Political Science Quarterly* (Fall 1979), 419–35.

U.S. Advisory Commission on Intergovernmental Relations, *The Significant Features of Fiscal Federalism.* Washington, D.C.: ACIR, 1985.

WALKER, DAVID B., *Toward a Functioning Federalism.* Cambridge, Mass.: Winthrop, 1981.

WRIGHT, DIEL S., *Understanding Intergovernmental Relations* (2nd ed.). Monterey, Calif.: Brooks/Cole, 1982.

4
election machinery

PREVIEW

AN ELECTION LAW

As faculty meetings go, this would be one of the more exciting ones. The biggest proposal of the year was on the agenda. Mut and Jeff would be on opposite sides. They were two senior full professors, both in their sixties, inseparable friends and allies in the endless stream of faculty wars. Today for the first time in anyone's memory they would be at odds.

The argument would not be over the proposal directly, but over who would have the right to vote on that proposal when it was put to ballot later. Should administrators be allowed to vote? Or should the right to vote on this issue be limited to nonadministrative faculty? That was the immediate question on today's agenda. Mut thought administrators should not be allowed to vote. "They're not faculty," he insisted. "Only faculty members should vote."

Jeff disagreed. "Sure they're faculty. They should vote."

Everybody knew the proposal would go down to defeat if administrators voted. Both Mut and Jeff were sure that most department heads, deans, vice-chancellors, and other administrators would vote against the proposal.

Everybody who showed up for the faculty meeting got their money's worth. Mut and Jeff were at their best that day—both were skilled performers, skilled phrase coiners, skilled word slingers. The debate was savage. Mut pounded his desk, spoke ponderously in his baritone voice, quoted Shakespeare more than once, shook his heavy jowls, looked darkly from beneath bushy eyebrows, and warned against regarding administrators as faculty. Jeff, a slender man with long legs and a great head of white hair, talked fast, waved his index finger, and delivered shrill broadsides. Both professors sprinkled their remarks with sarcasm, and the faculty broke into full-throated laughter six or seven times during the spectacle. It was at once the funniest meeting of the year, and the grimmest.

Many found it painful to think that one of them—Mut or Jeff—must go down to defeat. But the moment of decision finally came and the question was called. By show of hands the faculty split narrowly (49 to 50) in favor of regarding administrators as faculty for purposes of voting on the proposal.

Walking together out of the hall, Mut and Jeff could be seen smiling about something. "You old fox," said Mut. "You knew the election would turn on who is allowed to vote in it."

"Yes, old rascal, you knew it yourself better than I," Jeff said, patting his comrade on the back.

Two weeks later the proposal went down to defeat when it was put to a mail ballot. The result surprised no one.

THE SYSTEM DICTATES THE OUTCOME

If an election were called to determine whether children should have ice cream cones every day (to use a ridiculous example), the outcome might depend on whether you allow children to vote. It might also depend on when, where, and how you hold the election, because if you held it in the middle of the night by a graveyard some youngsters might skip voting. In short, the election system (the time, place, and manner of holding elections, and who you let vote) has a lot to do with the outcome of an election. Every cog, lever, and gear of that system produces a result[1]—often highly predictable. There has been a lot of tinkering with the election system by people trying to control the outcome of elections.

CONTROL OF ELECTIONS

Who Runs Elections?

Elections in the United States are run by local governments, not by the federal government. Not even elections for president, vice-president, and United States senators and representatives are run by the federal government. Nor do states have much to do with the day-to-day administration of the election system. States do make most of the election laws, but those laws are enforced and the election system is run at the local level, often by counties, which sometimes administer elections for cities, school districts, and special districts as well. In any case, local (not state or federal) officials control the machinery. They run elections without much supervision or training from the state. Many states do not even set performance standards. These local officials, many of whom are not college graduates and some of whom are swayed by prejudices that interfere with their work, are

---

[1]"Electoral regulations are continuously changing, and even small alterations can profoundly influence political behavior." Andrew D. McNitt, "The Impact of State Legislation on Political Campaigns," *State Government* (Summer 1980), p. 135.

supposed to read and apply the often complex, technical, lengthy, vague, and contradictory state election laws.

Elections are fundamentally important to republican government. Administration of elections is sometimes so poor and amateurish among the nation's local governments, however, that there have been calls for federal regulation of elections. Various members of Congress seem to think the whole system of voter registration should be handled by the federal government, at least the registration of those who vote for federal officers (president, vice-president, senator, and representative). This plan, however, would mean hiring many federal bureaucrats to run the system and would mean an even further erosion of state and local control.

Determining Who Shall Vote

State Power   The United States Constitution gives power to the states to determine who shall vote for federal officers. Keep in mind that the only federal officers popularly elected under the Constitution as it was written in 1787 were members of the lower house of Congress. The president, you will recall, was (and still is) elected by presidential electors, and senators were elected by the state legislatures. The Constitution tells in Article I, Section 2, just who shall vote for members of the House of Representatives (and now senators as well) and what their qualifications shall be. "The House of Representatives," it says, "shall be composed of Members chosen every second Year by the People of the several States, and the Electors in each State shall have the Qualifications requisite for Electors of the most numerous Branch of the State Legislature." Obviously since state law determines the qualifications of electors of the lower house of the state legislature, so also does state law determine the qualifications of electors of the lower house of Congress. When United States senators were made elective officers by adoption of the Seventeenth Amendment in 1913, the same voter qualifications were adopted.

The Constitution leaves the manner of choosing presidential electors entirely up to the states: "Each State shall appoint, in such Manner as the Legislature thereof may direct, a Number of Electors, equal to the whole Number of Senators and Representatives to which the State may be entitled in the Congress."[2]

Federal Power: Race, Sex, Age, Poll Taxes   All this would seem to tie the hands of Congress with regard to voter qualifications. The states seem totally free to set any qualifications they want—age, citizenship, literacy, residence, and so on—but this is not quite the case. Several constitutional amendments have superseded state law relating to voting by blacks, women, persons over 18, and persons who have not paid poll taxes. States (and the federal government) were forbidden by the Fifteenth Amendment (1870) to deny or abridge the right to vote on account of race, color, or previous condition of servitude. In 1920 states and the federal government were forbidden by the Nineteenth Amendment to deny or abridge the right to vote on account of sex. In 1964 the Twenty-fourth Amendment forbade states and the federal government to deny the right to vote for federal officers by reason of failure to pay any tax, specifically poll taxes.

[2]*U.S. Const.*, Art. II, Sec. 1.

(This amendment, by the way, affected only elections for federal officers—president, vice-president, senator, and representative.) Finally, in 1971 states and the federal government were forbidden by the Twenty-sixth Amendment to deny anyone 18 years of age or older the right to vote on account of age.

Thus, certain qualifications that used to be enforced by some states have been banned by the Constitution, but in each case it had to be done by constitutional amendment. Congress is not free to alter voter qualifications, but note that the amendments concerning race, sex, poll taxes, and age each include a small but meaningful clause giving Congress the power to enforce the amendment by appropriate legislation. Congress has used this power to strike down various voter qualifications (such as the literacy test) and various practices in the administration of elections that indirectly accomplish what the amendment was designed to prevent. The 1965 Voting Rights Act was based primarily on the right of Congress to enforce the Fifteenth Amendment (race) by appropriate legislation. That law requires the federal Department of Justice to approve or disapprove any voting rules change projected by state or local governments that have a history of discriminatory election practices—currently nine states and parts of seven others. Intent to discriminate does not have to be shown, only discriminatory results.

The Fourteenth Amendment   We must not overlook the Fourteenth Amendment in this discussion of the authority of Congress to interfere with the power of states to determine voter qualifications. The Fourteenth makes state and local acts unconstitutional if they are unfair; such is the presumed meaning of the due process clause of the amendment. Therefore, any voter qualification that strikes judges as unfair can be declared unconstitutional, even though the Constitution gives states exclusive power to determine voter qualifications. In other words, although the federal government cannot establish any voter qualifications, it is free under the Fourteenth Amendment to quash any state-mandated qualifications it considers unfair. This power extends not only to voter qualifications but to any state or local law affecting elections in any way. The equal protection clause of the Fourteenth Amendment is also commonly used in cases involving the election process. Furthermore, the Fourteenth Amendment puts states in jeopardy of losing representation in Congress if they wrongfully abridge the right of any of their citizens to vote.

Time, Place, and Manner of Elections   The Constitution gives power to state legislatures to prescribe the times, places, and manner of holding elections for United States senators and representatives, but adds that Congress may at any time make or alter such rules (except as to the place of choosing senators).[3] Since state and local election officials wish to make their jobs as simple as possible, federal election laws for members of Congress, such as the law setting the date of elections, tend to become the practice for state and local elections as well. It's simply too complicated to have one set of rules for United States Senate and House elections and another set of rules for other elections. However, all but about a dozen states hold their elections for state and local offices in non–presidential election years. This is to protect those elections from being overshadowed by presidential politics.

[3]*U.S. Const.*, Art. I, Sec. 4.

WHO MAY VOTE?

Age

Until fairly recently the age of 21 was both the **voting age** and the age one legally changes from a minor to an adult—the so-called age of majority. The proposal to allow voting at 18 was hailed by those who imagined younger voters would produce "good" election results; it was attacked by those who feared youthful voters could only do damage. Conservatives thought young people would flock to the polls and vote irresponsibly for all manner of wild proposals, would have little regard for private property or the work ethic, and would vote for welfare programs and giveaway schemes. Some liberals secretly agreed with this assessment but were less alarmed by the prospect. However, both liberals and conservatives were surprised when it developed that young people did not do what they were expected to do. Instead of flocking to the polls, they proved apathetic about voting. Many of those who did trouble to vote came from middle- and upper-class families who put a high value on the civic duty to vote, and a good many voted the conservative biases of their parents. In 1971 the Twenty-sixth Amendment lowered the voting age in all federal, state, and local elections to 18. Georgia, Kentucky, Alaska, and Hawaii permitted voting by those under 21 prior to the amendment.

Residency and Citizenship

Many people erroneously believe that one must reside in a state for a certain period of time to become a citizen of that state. Actually no period of residency is required for acquisition of citizenship (acquisition of the right to vote is another matter). Speaking now only of citizenship, one becomes a citizen of a state the instant one crosses into it with intent to reside permanently there. The Constitution says all citizens of the United States are citizens of the state "wherein they reside."[4] Just what constitutes residence is sometimes debated. Courts have often had to settle the issue. Some people are rather hard to pin down as to their residence—those, for example, who winter in Florida and summer in Minnesota and maintain homes in both states. (The question of residency is important to tax collectors and taxpayers because citizens have to pay a variety of taxes, such as the income tax, to their home state that they don't have to pay other states in which they might be visiting.)

In all states one must be a citizen of the United States and of the state itself in order to vote. However, in some 30 states one must also have resided in the state for a certain period of time, usually 30 days, to vote. The remaining states have no **residence requirement** per se but do prohibit registration of voters within a certain period of time before each election, again usually 30 days.

Not long ago most states had much longer residency requirements—one year was common. Lengthy residence in the state as a prerequisite for voting was defended as necessary to allow registration officials time to check whether a would-be voter was in fact a citizen of the state. It was also defended as a way to keep out-of-staters from swarming into a state just before a hotly contested election (as pro- and antislavery people did in bleeding Kansas just before the

---

[4]*U.S. Const.*, 14th Amendment.

Civil War). A further justification of lengthy residence requirements is that people ought to have a chance to become informed about the state's politics before they're allowed to vote.

Nevertheless, in recent years both Congress and the Supreme Court have assaulted the residency requirement. In its Voting Rights Act of 1970[5] Congress prescribed a 30-day residency period for those voting in presidential elections. Congress thought 30 days was long enough for election officials to get their work done. New arrivals would be as well informed about presidential candidates and national issues as anyone already in the state—a long residence requirement would hardly be justified if the purpose of such a requirement was to allow voters time to inform themselves about presidential candidates. Since 1970 most states have set their residence requirement at 30 days for *all* elections or have eliminated the residence requirement altogether, relying only on a system of stopping all new registrations a certain number of days before each election.

Basically the Supreme Court considers all voting requirements to be a burden on the right to vote but believes some requirements serve the public interest with sufficient force to justify the burden. A short residence requirement is a justifiable burden; a long residence requirement is not. Finally, long residence requirements also put a burden on the so-called right to travel, a right mentioned by the Supreme Court in its consideration of residence requirements.

Registration

In most places you can't vote unless you're registered to do so. Every state except North Dakota has some system of **voter registration.**[6]

Prior Registration: How Long? Supposedly the reason why states require registration before voting is to prevent confusion and fraud at the polls on election day. On that day election officials are allegedly too busy looking after voting machines and ballot boxes to be distracted with judging who among those who come to vote are legally qualified. Thus, almost everywhere, would-be voters are required to register no later than a certain number of days before a general election. Oklahoma and New Hampshire feel 10 days is long enough. South Dakota requires 15, Kansas 20, and most other states around 30. A few states, such as Minnesota, Maine, and Wisconsin, allow registration until election day itself. Various states, chiefly in the Midwest, have long permitted citizens in rural areas to vote without prior registration, and Minnesota and Wisconsin have experimented with no-registration voting in large cities as well as in rural areas.

Does Registration Impede Voting? All registration systems throw a roadblock between citizens and the polling booth. Thousands of people don't register and therefore can't vote on election day. The less seriously a person takes his or her civic duty to vote, the less likely he or she is to register, and hence to vote. One could argue that those are just the people who ought not vote. In fact, some registration systems may have been designed to complicate voting procedures

[5]84 *Statutes at Large* [hereafter abbreviated *Stat.*] 315.
[6]Council of State Governments, *The Book of the States 1986–87* (Lexington, Ky.: Council of State Governments, 1986), p. 208.

for those who are the least motivated. But such obstacles may impede voting by the poor and the uneducated more than anyone else. At any rate, some present-day defenders of complex voter-registration procedures seem to believe that it is not altogether bad to put up a few obstacles to voting.

Periodic or Permanent? **Periodic registration,** which requires voters to reregister before each election or after some other (usually short) period of time, is a greater hindrance to voting than is permanent registration. Under a system of periodic registration, which was quite common until recently, voters have to summon the energy and interest to register not once, but every couple of years. Besides being exceedingly inconvenient for voters, periodic registration has proved expensive and troublesome for county clerks and other election officials. Thus almost every state today has some form of **permanent registration,** in which persons, once registered, stay registered unless for some reason (failure to vote, change of residence) their names are purged from the registration list. The practice of periodically purging the lists is a remnant of periodic registration. Typically an individual who fails to vote within a certain period of time is notified through a nonforwardable postcard that his or her registration has been canceled. In some states the postcard includes a detachable mail-back form with which voters may reinstate their registration.

Making Registration Easier The chore of registration can be eased for citizens in a number of ways that do not open the system to fraud. One of these is the detachable mail-back form just mentioned. This is now a fairly common practice. The post office could also be used in other ways: people could, for example, be allowed to register or transfer their registration by mail. Actually about half the states have some form of voter registration by mail in effect.

Registration officials who want to reach out to the public and make it easy to register may, if allowed by law, take registration services to the people rather than making people come to the county courthouse to register. It is often hard for people to find the time and energy to go all the way downtown to government offices; registration is easier when branch offices are provided at firehouses, libraries, shopping centers, fairs, exhibitions, driver's-licence agencies, or anywhere people congregate. A deputy registration official can establish a "field office" wherever a card table and chair can be set down. It would be helpful if each polling place opened for several days just prior to elections so that people could register. A secretary in every high school and college could be deputized to register young people. City and county registration offices could be kept open after hours and on weekends to help people who can't leave their jobs to register. The closing date (the date prior to an election after which no one may register) could be brought as close as possible to election day. Thirty days before elections is now, as we have seen, the legal maximum closing date, but several states have earlier closing dates. Officials could conduct registration campaigns and cooperate with campaigns carried on from time to time by community groups. The purging of registration lists could be less frequent, perhaps every four or six years instead of every two.

How Convenient Should Registration Be? Many of these proposals to make registration more convenient are actually being practiced here and there across the country. But is there a limit to what these convenient mechanisms can accomplish? No matter how easy you make registration, the individual must still have sufficient civic consciousness to take advantage of the opportunities. Many people are "too busy" to put voter registration high on their list of priorities. The National Municipal League has suggested that city and county registration officials be responsible for registering all eligible voters; they could do this by a system of canvassing, using squads of paid or volunteer deputies to go house to house registering people on their doorsteps.[7] This would require a big bureaucracy, but to those who believe in universal registration, the benefits seem high. One is tempted, however, to ask an old question: Is there no value in retaining a registration system that requires some exhibition of civic consciousness, some desire and determination to register, some individual initiative as the price of registration? No matter how easy you make registration, or even if all registration is dispensed with, there remains the problem of motivating people to vote.

BLACKS AND THE ELECTION SYSTEM: A CASE STUDY

A perfect example of how the election system can be tinkered with is seen in the history of attempts in some states to preserve white supremacy by keeping blacks away from the ballot box. Of course, slaves in the pre-Civil War Days were regarded as property and had no more right to vote than houses, barns, or horses. When slavery ended, things didn't improve much for blacks. Though technically free, this "freedom" did not make them citizens. Several states excluded blacks from citizenship and therefore from voting. The Fourteenth and Fifteenth Amendments to the Constitution attempted to put a stop to laws excluding blacks from citizenship and voting. The Fourteenth Amendment, adopted in 1868, defined citizenship for the first time in American history. It made all persons born or naturalized in the United States and subject to its jurisdiction "citizens of the United States and of the State wherein they reside." This forced the authors of election laws to rely on something besides noncitizenship to bar black voting. The Fifteenth Amendment, passed in 1870, complicated things still further for white supremacists by stating flatly, "The right of citizens of the United States to vote shall not be denied or abridged by the United States or by any State on account of race, color, or previous condition of servitude." This only teased the ingenuity of election-law writers in some states.

Literacy Tests

One contrivance was the **literacy test** combined with a "grandfather clause" which appeared in several states around 1895. The clause exempted anyone from the literacy test who was a voter in 1867 or who was a descendant of a person who had voted in 1867. Since almost no blacks were voters in 1867, they could not claim exemption from the literacy test. Blacks, therefore, had to take the test, but most whites, many also illiterate, did not. Illiteracy or near illiteracy among blacks was common until well into the 1900s, partly because it had been a crime to teach a slave to read and write and also because it had been a severe and

---

[7]National Municipal League, *A Model Election System* (New York, 1973).

punishable misdeed for any slave to learn to read or write. Literacy among American blacks in our time is astonishingly high considering the obstacles they have had to overcome since the Civil War. In 1915 the United States Supreme Court found the grandfather clause unconstitutional.[8]

Literacy tests survived until recently, and many people still think there is every justification for denying illiterates the right to vote. Advocates of the literacy test doubt that illiterates can vote intelligently—they cannot even read the ballot, let alone a printed discussion of issues. Literacy tests are not unconstitutional as long as they are fairly administered, but in a number of states they were not fairly administered. Racial minorities were "failed" as a matter of course by some election officials. The story is told of a black Ph.D. who tried to register. A bigoted election official asked, "Can you read?" The black Ph.D. claimed he could. The official opened a copy of the *Rankin County News.* "Read that paragraph," he demanded. The black easily read the paragraph about a recent lynching in the county. The official then smiled and pulled out a French newspaper. "Read that." The black Ph.D. read several sentences aloud in faultless French and translated it for the astonished official, who then reached for a German newspaper, which the black also read easily. Finally the election official impatiently reached under the counter and got a Chinese newspaper. The black Ph.D. looked at the paper, then up at the official. "Dis say day ain't gonna be no Nigger vote in Rankin County." "You sho is illiterate," said the official, moving on to the next customer.

Although the United States Supreme Court has upheld the constitutionality of literacy tests administered in a nondiscriminatory way, it has also held that literacy tests administered with an intent to disenfranchise some group are unconstitutional.[9] Congress also tackled the literacy test, in the Civil Rights Acts of 1957[10] and 1960[11] and the Voting Rights Act of 1965.[12] In 1970 Congress suspended all literacy tests throughout the nation for five years,[13] and they have not reappeared.

Other Tests

White supremacists have devised several other "tests" designed to give election officials an excuse for not registering people they didn't want to register. There was a test to determine whether one could "understand" and "properly interpret" the state and federal constitutions. Interpreting constitutions is difficult enough for Supreme Court justices. Therefore it is highly presumptuous to suppose that election officials (some of whom are nearer to illiteracy than those who stand before them) have such a great capacity to interpret the Constitution that they are qualified to judge with finality who properly understands the Constitution. And then there is the "good character" test, which allows election officials to bar the registration of any person not of good character. Blackness of

---

[8]Guinn v. United States, 238 U.S. 347 (1915).

[9]Lassiter v. Northampton County Board of Elections, 360 U.S. 45 (1960); Davis v. Schnell, 336 U.S. 933 (1949).

[10]71 *Stat.* 634.

[11]74 *Stat.* 86.

[12]79 *Stat.* 437.

[13]Voting Rights Act of 1970, 84 *Stat.* 315; 42 *U.S.C.* Par. 1973aa.

character and blackness of skin were one and the same thing in the eyes of some officials.

White Primary

The **white primary** was not a test, but it was a momentarily successful way to shut blacks out of primary elections. Political parties in a number of states excluded blacks from membership by saying that a political party is a private association. Thus blacks were not allowed to vote in party elections held to select party nominees for public office—the so-called primary election. Defenders of this practice claim it was perfectly legal. Political parties, they said, are private associations. The United States Constitution does not bar discrimination by private associations: the Fourteenth Amendment is aimed at state action, not private action. Furthermore, these individuals claimed, primary elections are not really elections within the meaning of the Fifteenth Amendment, which forbids states to deny the right to vote on account of race or color; the primary is not a *state* election, but an election held by a private association.

The white primary survived until 1944, when it was struck down by the United States Supreme Court.[14] The Court had no difficulty arguing that primary elections are elections within the meaning of the Fifteenth Amendment and that political parties are state agencies when they are entrusted by state law to select candidates for public office. Every state of the Union has detailed laws regulating the conduct of primary elections and the organization of political parties. To say that parties (and their primaries) are merely private affairs contradicts the obvious fact that states employ parties as mechanisms of the electoral system.

Racial Gerrymandering

Drawing election-district boundaries so as to exclude, or include, people on the basis of race has also been attempted. The United States Supreme Court declared this **racial gerrymandering** unconstitutional after the Alabama legislature changed the boundaries of Tuskegee (home of world-famous Tuskegee Institute) from a simple 4-sided square to a 28-sided creation excluding practically every black resident formerly within the city limits.[15] More recently, when a large city tried to annex a predominantly white suburb, the United States Supreme Court ruled that the annexation would violate the 1965 Civil Rights Act. The Court said that the annexation would dilute the black vote and that the city had been unable to prove its purpose was not to deny the right to vote on account of race.

Poll Taxes

From the Civil War until the 1960s, voters in several states were required to pay a **poll tax** prior to voting. One's ability to pay the tax constituted a qualification for voting based on wealth. It rather effectively discouraged the less affluent from

[14]Smith v. Allwright, 321 U.S. 649 (1944).
[15]Gomillion v. Lightfoot, 364 U.S. 399 (1960).

voting, including large numbers of blacks, most of whom were poor. Blacks were not the only poor people, however: countless poor whites were also discouraged. The Twenty-fourth Amendment, adopted in 1964, outlawed the poll tax in federal elections for president, vice-president, senator, and representative. The amendment did not include state elections, but use of poll taxes in state elections was also ended in the mid 1960s by act of Congress and by decision of the United States Supreme Court. The Court said wealth has nothing to do with one's qualification to vote: "Wealth, like race, creed or color, is not germane to one's ability to participate intelligently in the electoral process."[16] Consequently, said the Court, poll taxes unreasonably discriminate between the affluent and the less affluent and therefore constitute a denial of equality contrary to the equal protection clause of the Fourteenth Amendment. The poll tax especially discriminated against blacks because a high proportion of them could not afford to pay the tax, and because in administration of the tax blacks might be asked for receipts, whites not.

Intimidation

Although intimidation was never a part of the official election machinery, it did lurk for many generations as a quasi-official policy in various parts of the country, and was a very effective deterrent to voting by blacks.

NON-RACIAL DISCRIMINATIONS

Most of these attempts to juggle the election system have been either outlawed or declared unconstitutional, insofar as they are aimed at racial discrimination. All sorts of discriminations remain, however, that are not racial. It would be hard to think of any election system, or of any feature thereof, that does not discriminate in some way against someone. Every election system is "stacked" in the sense that it includes or encourages some and excludes or discourages others. Every system gives advantages to some group, class, or social sector. The mere existence of mass popular elections may be viewed as an affront by some who think a narrower segment of the population should make decisions—white supremacists, for example, who think only whites should vote, or wealthy persons who think only people of property should vote, or male chauvinists who think only men should vote, or aristocrats who think only the nobility should vote, and so on.

An election system distributes power. It is not the only distributor of power, but it is one of the most important. The presence or absence of certain features in an election system can make or break a party. If the state election law makes it difficult for small political parties to get their candidates listed on the general-election ballot, this can doom small parties and preserve large parties. Many political scientists believe the two-party (rather than a multiparty) system in the United States owes itself to one critical feature of the election system—the single-member constituency (see p. 77). The design of a ballot or the way it is arranged can affect the outcome of an election—the grouping of candidates by party rather than by office on the ballot, or the listing of candidates in alphabetical order rather than in some other order. The ease (or difficulty) with which

---

[16]Harper v. Virginia Board of Elections, 383 U.S. 663 (1966).

one is able to register to vote may spell the fate of parties and social classes; some groups in society are more determined than others about voting. Everything concerning the time, place, and manner of voting has its impact on the outcome of elections. The slightest adjustment in the system is cause for alarm or cause for joy by those affected by elections. Every major group, party, and faction on the political scene is alert to proposed changes in the rules of the game.

WHO VOTES? NONVOTING IN AMERICA

Having discussed who may vote, let us now ask who actually does vote, who fails to vote, and why. For a country that fancies itself the greatest democracy on earth, it is astonishing how many people in the United States don't bother to vote. More vote in presidential elections than in any other sort of election, yet only about *half* of all eligible voters will journey to the polls in America to help pick a president. Other elections fare worse. The turnout may be only 25 to 30 percent in the typical state and local election.

Why do so many people not vote? A number of studies have probed this question,[17] but the minute we think we've got some causes pinned down, we find more causes behind those causes. The first cause of nonvoting is that most eligible voters who don't vote are people who simply don't want to vote badly enough to do it. Not wanting to vote is clearly a cause of nonvoting, but why do such a huge number not want to vote? Nonvoting is by no means confined to the uneducated, the poor, or to racial minorities, although those groups have a somewhat greater incidence of nonvoting than do the educated and the affluent. Yet there is massive nonvoting amont the educated, the affluent, and virtually every class of American society. Again, why? If it were only a tiny handful perhaps the question wouldn't be of such interest, but nonvoting is enormous.

Logic tells us that one big group of nonvoters is composed of people who are so muddled about the nation's political life that they may not even know it's election day, or how to vote, or what the issues are. No doubt some of these innocents are so wrapped up in their families, their jobs, their homes, their cars, and the great life, that politics passes over them like geese in the night sky.

Perhaps one reason many younger people don't vote is because they are too busy establishing careers, families, and homes. Another bloc of nonvoters probably don't see any point in voting. They don't think their one little vote will change anything, and consequently they go to the tennis court instead of to the polls. These people may also feel that it doesn't make much difference who is elected because anyone elected is going to end up facing the same problems with the same limited number of solutions.

There are, of course, a whole list of other possible reasons why people don't vote: some elections are less exciting than others (primaries tend to be less interesting than general elections); some persons of minority races might hesitate to vote because they don't identify with the mainline Americans on the ballot; some persons may not vote because they're newcomers and don't feel at home yet; some might not vote because they're sick or disabled; some simply haven't gotten into the habit of voting, or it isn't in the family tradition (mom and

[17]See, for example, Arthur T. Hadley, *The Empty Polling Booth* (Englewood Cliffs, N.J.: Prentice-Hall, 1978).

Box 4-1. Election Fervor

El Paso County was voting on an $18-million bond issue for a new jail. But in precinct 214 no one cared. Not a single person showed up to vote. Three election judges opened the polls in precinct 214 promptly at 7 A.M. and remained on duty, alert and expectant, until 7 P.M., when they turned in their empty ballot box to the county clerk. The bond issue passed.

---

pop never voted); some can't make up their minds who or what to vote for; some might not vote because even though they have a keen interest in politics, they are carrying some sort of chip on their shoulder against "the system"—their nonvoting is an act of defiance; some might not vote because they're too contented with life—why vote when everything, career, family, life, is so sweet? some might not vote because of the weather; some because their minds are boggled by candidates and issues, none of which they understand very well.

Of course, in addition to nonvoting by people eligible to vote, there is a very large number of persons who might like to vote but are legally ineligible: many of these people haven't lived in the state or community long enough to meet residence requirements or have not acquired citizenship. And then, of course, vast numbers never register to vote. The causes of nonregistering are identical to the causes for nonvoting.

What does this enormous disregard for voting say about democracy in America, about the attitudes of people toward the democratic system, and about the so-called sovereigns of that system?

DOES DEMOCRACY WORK?

A great many people are apathetic about voting. Their apathy stems not only from the reasons for nonvoting suggested before but also from a pessimism about the whole idea of democracy. It may not be a conscious pessimism—everybody's for "democracy," whatever it is. Nevertheless, there certainly are some questions that need to be asked about the meaning of elections.

What Is a Mandate?

Newly elected officeholders are fond of claiming a "mandate" to carry out their campaign promises: "I said I would reduce the size of the bureaucracy. My election is a mandate to do so." In truth, it's hard to know just what the people meant by electing one candidate over another. It may not have anything at all to do with what he advocated; it may have nothing at all to do with his platform, or his party's platform. Maybe the voters didn't really vote *for* him as much as they voted *against* his opponent. Suppose voters do vote *for* a candidate, and suppose none of the planks in a 10-plank program was individually responsible for the victory. Then where is the mandate? Maybe no plank attracted more than a small fraction. Election to office cannot be a mandate to act on planks that attracted only a fifth, or a tenth, of the voters. If the candidate won only a narrow victory, can it be said that he or she has a mandate for anything at all, except to be sworn into office?

The picture is complicated further by a truth we all instinctively recognize: even when we vote *for* someone, we do not always vote for "what he or she stands for." We often—perhaps more often than we dare admit—vote for the candidate as a personality. What pleases us may have nothing to do with planks, programs, or ideology. It may have more to do with physical attractiveness, with charm, with honesty, frankness, and general demeanor. Psychologists might have to probe the deepest and darkest corners of our inner selves to know just what makes us vote for somebody.

Although election analysis has been developed into a high art, it remains difficult to prove that any officeholder has a mandate from the people to do anything. It is exceedingly hard, if not impossible, to know what the people have really said on election day. If we cannot decipher what the sovereign people say on election day, how can we believe they are sovereign?

Furthermore, even if we are able to decipher what the people have said, is it valid to assume that they would say the same thing a week, a month, six months, or a year after election day? Does the mandate last longer than the will of the sovereign? Do officeholders have the same mandate in the fourth or sixth year of their term even though the people changed their mood three days after the election? The masses are notoriously unstable. Candidates know this full well. They approach an election with prayers for stability in mass opinion, as if they were aircraft bombardiers praying for stability in the crucial run over the target. Any event in the hours just before an election can trigger wild swings of mass opinion.

Finally, we all know—and it has often been pointed out by fascists and communists to our embarrassment—that the people (all of us) are terribly ignorant about the issues that face us on election day and about the candidates themselves and their positions.

OTHER FORMS OF POLITICAL PARTICIPATION

A rich world of politics thrives outside and beyond elections and political parties. Even dictatorships have politics. Reading *Inside the Third Reich*[18] by Albert Speer (Adolf Hitler's armaments minister), one sees the intensity of backstage struggles among leading figures of the dictatorship. Similar bureaucratic struggles go on in all countries, in all governments, in all agencies, and in all offices. Elections aren't the only avenue of political participation. Politics—or shall we say, political participation—in the United States occurs in many forms.

Anything one does to influence those in power, such as talking to them, is *political participation*. The process of influencing the actions of others is *politics*. There is politics in the family, in the corporation, in the fraternity, in the university, in the convent. Governments and their officers can be influenced a thousand ways. One way, of course, is to vote, but a nonvoter may bring his or her influence to bear through other avenues.

[18]Albert Speer, *Inside the Third Reich* (New York: Avon, 1970).

NOMINATIONS

Primary Elections

A **primary** (meaning "first") **election** comes before the general election. The purpose of a primary is to nominate candidates who will run against one another in the general election.

Not all nominations are done by a primary, but most of them are today. Nominations for some local offices are done by a process of self-nomination: anyone who wants to run simply goes down to the proper office and signs a paper declaring himself or herself a candidate. In some cases, nomination is done by petition. This amounts almost to self-nomination: one simply gets the required number of signatures (anywhere from a handful to several hundred) on a petition. Technically the people who sign your petition nominate you. Normally persons who do not seek nomination by a party, but wish to run as independents, may get on the general-election ballot by petition. In some states, "third-party" (minor-party) candidates may be required by state law to nominate their candidates by petition, whereas major parties use the primary election to nominate.

Caucuses

Primaries have been the preferred system of nomination for national, state, and many local offices since the early 1900s. Previously the preferred system was the party convention, which became predominant about 1830, and before conventions there was the caucus. A **caucus** was simply a group of influential individuals who met and put up candidates. Caucuses were informal meetings: in fact, the word itself comes to us from the Greek *kaukos*, which means drinking cup. In our early nationhood caucus clubs were in vogue. They were political social clubs, which put forward the names of persons they favored for public office.

Conventions

Decline of the Caucus In the days of "King Caucus" the right to vote was severely limited by property qualifications. Only the well-to-do could qualify to vote, and the nation was run by that oligarchy (government ruled by a few). As the political process became more democratic by gradual relaxation of property requirements, so did the process of nominating candidates. The **nominating-convention** system was more democratic because it removed the process from oligarchic caucus clubs. Convention delegates were chosen in a more or less orderly and fair manner from the rank and file of the party. From about 1830 nominations were done chiefly by party conventions. Conventions were a democratic reform of sorts but were replaced by a still more democratic reform later on.

Corruption The trouble with conventions was that they were too easily controlled by special interests. Many delegates to conventions could, and did, sell their vote to the highest bidder, and some bidders were very generous indeed, because the stakes were high. Governments could bestow contracts and other benefits upon favored private enterprises. Whoever controlled the offices of government also controlled that flow of government benefits. Conventions also fell victim to bossism: delegates knew it was in their interest to cooperate with the bosses through whom flowed the spoils of political victory. Rebellion against the convention system in the late 1800s and early 1900s was a rebellion against bossism and corruption.

Presidential Conventions   Why then do we still use conventions to select presidential candidates? Although presidential nominating conventions are now somewhat *pro forma* (a matter of form) because of the rise of presidential primaries in the states, they have until recently been a striking success. They have worked well, even magnificently. Why? Probably because the national spotlight has focused so glaringly on the presidency and upon national conventions. Thieves and corrupters prefer not to operate in the light. Neither state and local officials nor state and local conventions were illuminated by the media as fully as national conventions. The quickest way for a party to lose a presidential election is to nominate a candidate for president whose moral stature cannot stand close examination. It has proved too risky for any party to hold a corrupt national convention or to nominate a corrupt candidate.

Quite another picture prevailed at state and local conventions, and the cure was to abolish conventions and give the job of nominating candidates to the rank and file of the party. A primary election allows all registered members of the party to go freely to the polls and help choose candidates who have offered themselves for nomination. With the rank and file doing the nominating at primaries, some of the evils of conventions were avoided.

Primaries versus Conventions   Conventions aren't and weren't totally bad. They have their good points, one of which is that party leaders meeting together can settle on a candidate who more or less meets their mutual satisfaction, someone who can unite the party. Conventions can balance the ticket geographically, philosophically, and so on. A primary might nominate someone with whom the party cannot unite: this also happens at conventions, but less often. Conventions are not as divisive as primaries. Second, a convention of party activists is more likely to know the true character of persons offering themselves for nomination. Rank-and-file voters in a primary don't always know much about the candidates they vote for.

As for bossism, primary elections have not been a complete cure, although it is harder for bosses to control primaries than to control conventions. Party machines and party bosses do, however, still function under the primary system. Curiously this is because primaries tend to bore voters, so light voter turnouts are the rule rather than the exception. The lighter the turnout, the more likely the primary will be controlled by a steel core of party activists who do take the trouble to vote and who do tend to vote for the favorites of the party machine (because they themselves are the machine). We must be careful in using the terms *boss* and *machine*. The machine is often nothing more than a rather loose collection of party activists. Bosses are often nothing more than the mutually agreed-upon leaders of the activists. Such leaders are rarely bosses in any autocratic sense, although there are some notable exceptions. Occasionally our worst image of the boss and of the machine does exist in reality, but usually reality is much less sinister. Party leaders and party activists still, to repeat, do influence primaries chiefly because many nonactivists don't bother to vote in primaries. Only 25 to 30 percent of registered party members can be counted on to vote in a typical primary.

Where Conventions Still Function Conventions are not entirely dead at the state and local level. Some largely one-party southern states—Virginia, South Carolina, Georgia, and Alabama—allow officials in each party to decide whether they want to nominate candidates by convention or by primary. The minority party normally uses a convention. The majority party almost always uses a primary. Indiana nominates all state officers except the governor by convention. In Iowa a political party nominates its candidate for a particular office by convention if, and only if, no party candidate for that office receives 35 percent of the votes cast at the primary. The same rule prevails in South Dakota. Trustees of the University of Illinois are the only state officers in Illinois nominated by convention. In Michigan the lieutenant governor, secretary of state, and attorney general are the only state officers nominated by convention. Several states give minor parties the option of nominating by convention.

Preprimary Convention Endorsements Convention power over nominations still flickers in a few states[19] where party conventions make **preprimary endorsements.** In those states the rank and file of the party does the actual nominating of party candidates in the primary election, as elsewhere, but before primary-election day the party convention endorses one or more aspirants. This usually works a great hardship on those who seek the nomination without such a party blessing. Incumbents and front-runners have it easier: the greater the involvement of party conventions in the nominating process, the less likely that incumbents or front-runners will be challenged.[20]

Colorado's system of preprimary designations is an interesting example of the species. Each party holds conventions (technically called *assemblies*) before the primary election to "designate" one or more candidates to run in the primary. Aspirants to party nomination for a particular office who are not designated by the assembly may petition themselves onto the primary ballot, but that is a difficult procedure. Anyone who gets 30 percent of the vote at the party assembly is considered designated. If more than one candidate is designated, their names are listed on the primary ballot according to the size of their vote at the assembly: highest vote-getter at the top, second highest second from the top, and so on. The one who gets top-line designation has a good chance of winning the primary because for some reason about 10 to 20 percent of the voters will vote for the top name on the list simply because it is first. Designations for county officeholders are made by county assemblies, state senators by state-senatorial-district assemblies, representatives by congressional-district assemblies, and so on. Preprimary designations are an intriguing system that allows both the party organization and the rank and file a say in the nominating process. Basically it

---

[19]Colorado, Connecticut, New York, and Utah.

[20]See Andrew D. McNitt, "The Effect of Preprimary Endorsement on Competition for Nominations: An Examination of Different Nominating Systems," *Journal of Politics* (February 1980), pp. 257–66.

amounts to letting the rank and file pick among various persons acceptable to the party organization.

Runoff Primaries

Several states hold **runoff primaries** after the first primary. The runoff is between the two top candidates if the leading candidate does not get a majority in the first primary. States that provide runoff primaries—Alabama, Arkansas, Florida, Georgia, Louisiana, Mississippi, North Carolina, Oklahoma, and Texas—are fundamentally states in which the Democratic party has dominated state elections for many years. Since nomination by the Democratic party is often tantamount to election it seems sensible, when none of the several candidates gets a majority, to hold a second primary to take the place of the general election.

Most other states in the Union have no runoff and don't need one as long as there are two strong parties. Where there is no runoff, the candidate who gets the most votes in the primary is nominated. It is not necessary to get a majority—a plurality does it.

Open and Closed Primaries

The basic purpose of a primary is to allow the party rank and file to choose party nominees. A primary is party business; therefore, it makes sense to close a party primary to all except members of the party. People declare their party affiliation when they register, or in some states at the polls on primary-election day, or in several states in the secrecy of the voting booth. If you go to the polls on primary-election day and are handed only the ballot of the party for which you have previously declared an affiliation, then you are voting in what is known as a **closed primary**—closed to all except those who have thus affiliated. In the states that allow voters to decide their party affiliation *after* they go behind the curtain, each voter is handed the primary ballots of all parties and must decide which one to use and discard the others. This is known as an **open primary.** Two states (Alaska and Washington) do not require voters to choose a party in the primary election, either before or after going behind the curtain. Those two have what we call a **blanket primary:** only one ballot is used, and on it appear the names of all candidates of all parties and the office for which they are running. Voters in a blanket primary are free to help nominate, say, a Democratic candidate for state treasurer and a Republican candidate for attorney general, but may indicate only one preference for each office.

There is spirited debate between advocates of open and closed primaries. The main trouble with an open primary, say its enemies, is that it allows members of one party (in the secrecy of the voting booth) to use the ballot of the other party and vote for that party's weakest candidates. This practice is called raiding. The amount of raiding may be exaggerated.

Despite the danger of raiding, the open primary does have one overriding benefit according to its defenders: it protects the secrecy of the ballot. Many people do not want to declare their party affiliation; some fear to do so. One hesitates to announce to the world a party affiliation that conflicts with that of one's boss, and since most of us have a hierarchy of bosses above us, the proba-

---

Box 4-2. Finding a Nominee

Recently a major political party in Massachusetts had trouble finding a suitable candidate for governor. At first, only one candidate volunteered, but his hopes faded when he was accused of bizarre behavior, including being discovered naked in his office on several occasions and pretending to hold telephone conversations into a dead line. Furthermore, it was charged that widespread forgeries existed on his nominating petitions. After that, the party pressed another individual to run for governor, but he very quickly dropped out of the race after it was alleged that he falsely claimed on repeated occasions to be a Vietnam War Green Beret hero.

---

bility of pleasing everybody is slim indeed. One might also have a number of other reasons for not recording a party affiliation. People do, for example, change their minds about their choice of party, and by then it may be too late for them to change their registration. The blanket primary is said to have the added advantage of allowing voters to vote for the best candidate for every office, regardless of party.

Nonpartisan Primaries

Partisan primaries, of course, cannot be used to nominate candidates for nonpartisan offices. Most local elections are nonpartisan, although county elections are almost always partisan. In Nebraska even state legislators are elected on a nonpartisan basis. No candidate on a nonpartisan ballot is identified by a party label. The function of the **nonpartisan primary** is basically to reduce the number of candidates to two. The general election then selects the winner from among those two, although in many cases, if a candidate in the primary gets a majority vote, he or she is declared winner of the office; sometimes whoever gets a plurality is the winner.

THE GENERAL ELECTION

Ballots

Until almost 1900, secret ballots were rarely used in the United States. In the first decades of the Republic, oral voting was used: a voter (and remember, only the well-to-do voted) stepped before election officials in the presence of others and stated out loud who he voted for. Poll watchers representing the various candidates and sometimes even the candidates themselves were there to thank those who voted "right." Oral voting was thought to be the manly way to vote.

Eventually paper ballots were used, cast openly. Each party printed its own ballot on colored paper, listing only the names of its candidates. Voters were supplied these ballots at the polls by party workers, and the ballots deposited in plain sight. Finally around 1888 the **Australian ballot** (so called because of its use there) was introduced in this country. A paper ballot printed at public expense and supplied directly to each voter by official election judges, it listed the names of all candidate and was cast in secrecy. It was soon adopted in all states, South Carolina being the last to do so, in 1950.

Party Column versus Office Block Ballots

Party leaders often favor ballots designed to make it easy for voters to vote a straight party ticket. Thus they tend to favor a ballot that lists all candidates of a particular party for all offices in a column and that allows voters to vote for every name on the list by marking one box or moving one lever. A ballot designed that way is called a **party-column ballot** (Figure 4-1). Under such a system, voting a straight ticket is easy, although provision is made to vote for candidates of more than one party (in other words, to split the ticket). Party-column ballots are used in about half the states.

Ticket splitting is easier on the other main form of ballot, the **office-block ballot** (Figure 4-2). On such a ballot there is rarely any single place to vote a straight ticket; the candidates of all parties for a particular office are listed under the name of the office rather than in a party column. Usually the party affiliation of each candidate is shown after his or her name. This form of ballot is used in about half the states.

Voting Devices

Most states still use paper ballots to some extent but rely heavily on voting machines and punch cards (Figure 4-3). A few states also use optical scanning devices.

Whether paper ballots or other voting devices are used, elaborate and precise measures are almost always taken to protect the secrecy of the ballot. Although there are many variations in voting procedure, most systems share some fundamental patterns. If voting machines are used, state laws usually provide that they must afford voters an opportunity to vote in absolute secrecy, must be closed to view during the process of voting so that no one can know the number of votes cast, must prevent voters from voting on any candidate or issue they are not entitled to vote on, must allow voters to vote on all they are entitled to vote on, must prevent voters from voting more than once, and must allow write-ins. The law may also require election judges (people hired temporarily by the city or county to administer the voting process) in each precinct to inspect voting machines just before the polls open to make sure that no votes have been cast—that the machine registers zero. Laws also generally require that if a voter asks for instructions concerning the manner of voting after entering the voting-machine booth, two judges (of opposite political parties) are to give instructions. Each voter is usually allowed about three minutes in the booth, but judges are generally allowed the discretion to give more time.

Voting

Normally everybody within the geographic boundaries of a **precinct** votes at the same place—often at a school or some other public building. A precinct usually includes about 500 to 1000 people. To vote, voters must present themselves to an

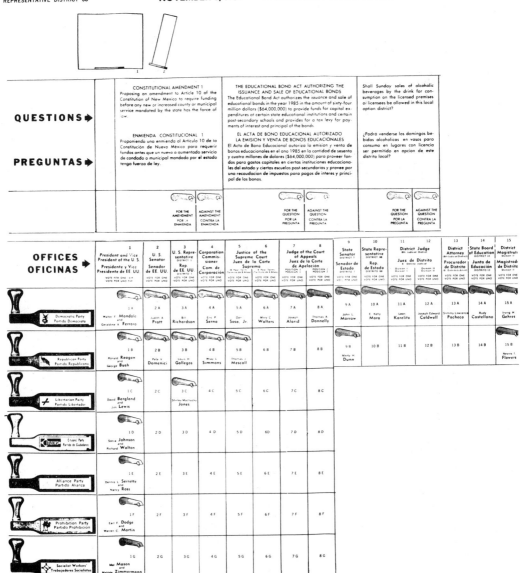

Figure 4-1 A portion of the party-column ballot used November 6, 1984, in Colfax County, New Mexico. Note lever at left for straight party voting.

OFFICIAL BALLOT — COUNTY OF SAN BERNARDINO
GENERAL ELECTION   NOVEMBER 4, 1986

STATE

Governor   Vote for One

TOM BRADLEY, Democratic
Mayor, City of Los Angeles   **3** ➡

MARIA ELIZABETH MUNOZ, Peace and Freedom
Educator   **4** ➡

GARY V. MILLER, American Independent
Governing Board Member, Mt. SAC Comm. College Dist.   **5** ➡

JOSEPH FUHRIG, Libertarian
Professor of Economics   **6** ➡

GEORGE 'DUKE' DEUKMEJIAN, Republican
Governor, State of California   **7** ➡

Lieutenant Governor   Vote for One

JAMES C. 'JIM' GRIFFIN, American Independent
Truck Driver   **9** ➡

LEO T. McCARTHY, Democratic
Lieutenant Governor   **10** ➡

MIKE CURB, Republican   **11** ➡

CLYDE KUHN, Peace and Freedom
College Instructor   **12** ➡

NORMA JEAN ALMODOVAR, Libertarian
Author   **13** ➡

Secretary of State   Vote for One

BRUCE NESTANDE, Republican
County Supervisor   **15** ➡

MARCH FONG EU, Democratic
Secretary of State of California   **16** ➡

GLORIA GARCIA, Peace and Freedom
Worker   **17** ➡

RICHARD WINGER, Libertarian
Election Law Consultant   **18** ➡

THERESA 'TENA' DIETRICH, American Independent
Printer   **19** ➡

Controller   Vote for One

JOHN HAAG, Peace and Freedom
Peace/Political Organizer   **21** ➡

BILL CAMPBELL, Republican
California State Senator   **22** ➡

NICHOLAS W. KUDROVZEFF, American Independent
Retired Electrical Director   **23** ➡

GRAY DAVIS, Democratic
Member of the State Assembly, California Legislature   **24** ➡

CAROLYN TREYNOR, Libertarian
Business Administrator   **25** ➡

Figure 4-2 A portion of an office-block ballot used on November 4, 1986 in San Bernardino, California.

VOTING INSTRUCTIONS

STEP 1 Remove the ballot card from the envelope.

STEP 2 Using both hands, slide the ballot card all the way into the Vote Recorder.

STEP 3 Be sure the two slots in the end of your card fit down **over the two red pins.**

STEP 4 To vote, hold the punch **straight up and push straight down** through the ballot card for each of your choices.

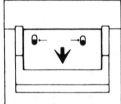

STEP 5 Turn the pages to continue voting.

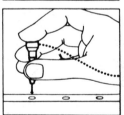

STEP 6 After voting, slide the card out of the Vote Recorder and place it **under the flap** of the envelope.

If you make a mistake, return the ballot card and envelope to obtain another.

INSTRUCCIONES PARA VOTAR

PASO 1 Saque la tarjeta-balota del sobre.

PASO 2 Usando las dos manos, meta la tarjeta-balota hasta el fondo en la Votomática.

PASO 3 Asegúrese que los dos hoyos en la parte superior de su tarjeta caigan **sobre los dos alfileres rojos.**

PASO 4 Para votar, detenga el picador **derecho para arriba y pique directamente para abajo** por la tarjeta-balota por cada una de sus selecciones.

PASO 5 Voltee las páginas para continuar votando.

PASO 6 Después de votar, saque la tarjeta de la Votomática y póngala **debajo de la tapa** del sobre.

Si hace un error, devuelva la tarjeta-balota y el sobre para obtener otra.

Figure 4-3 An automated vote-counting system. Instructions for California's punch-out ballot card.

Box 4-3. Why Not Vote by Mail?

San Diego voters did not have to go to the polls when they voted in 1981 on whether to build a new convention center. They voted by mail. Almost half a million ballots were mailed out on April 20, and 261,433 valid ballots were returned by the deadline, midnight May 5. The signature on each ballot was checked against signatures on registration records. Never had a higher percentage of eligible voters participated in a city election. Voting by mail saved the city about $200,000. The proposal to build a new convention center was defeated.

---

election judge, who either looks in the registration book to see if they're registered or determines in some other way whether they are legally qualified to vote. Election judges affiliated with each major party are usually on hand, supposedly to prevent election fraud. However, in rare cases election judges perpetrate rather than prevent fraud. Judges in collusion can produce some very unsavory results. For example, they could undercount votes for third-party candidates. Nor is it unheard of for judges of opposite parties to trade votes under a secret agreement that one party shall "win," say, state treasurer and the other party, say, attorney general.

Miscellaneous **poll watchers** are also commonly present. They represent the parties and sometimes the candidates themselves and can make it hard for judges to get away with dishonest practices. Watchers have a right to see everything done by election officials in connection with the election. Once a voter's identity and his or her legal right to cast a ballot is established by election judges, the voter is allowed to enter the immediate voting area and vote.

NONPARTISAN ELECTIONS

About three-fourths of American cities fill city offices by **nonpartisan elections.** Also, most school boards are elected on a nonpartisan basis, as are numerous special district governing boards. A nonpartisan ballot does not identify the party affiliation of candidates.

The basic argument for nonpartisan elections is that public officeholders should serve the public, not a party. Party interest is said to conflict with the public interest. A political party is only part of the community, not the whole community, and community officials should serve the whole and not be answerable to a party.

This idyllic theory may be attractive, but in fact people have differences of political philosophy and eventually associate themselves with others of like mind to voice their views. Nonpartisan elections cannot create a permanent vacuum of political organization. As we learn in physics, nature abhors a vacuum.

Many nonpartisan elections are nonpartisan in name only. Beneath the surface they may be intensely partisan. In some localities it is almost impossible to win any nonpartisan office unless backed by a party: candidates are either "nonpartisan Democrats" or "nonpartisan Republicans."

In some places local associations rather than political parties are active in nonpartisan elections. These associations may be one-issue groups that rise to fight a battle and then disappear, or they may be permanent associations. The purest of all nonpartisan systems are those in which candidates are not selected either by parties or by associations but rather by themselves and run their own campaigns.

Although a great many local governments use nonpartisan ballots, and although the idea of nonpartisan election is often championed as a faultless, pure, and intelligent way of running elections, there are those who do not see nonpartisanism in that rosy light. We began this chapter by noting how every election system benefits some and hurts others. But who could possibly be hurt by so innocent a thing as a nonpartisan election? And who helped? A good deal of howling about the evils of nonpartisan elections comes from political parties that cater to minorities and the poor. Some of the leaders of these parties claim that if elections aren't run by parties, then they will be run by civic associations. Civic associations are mostly businessmen's clubs. Thus nonpartisan elections, insofar as they are dominated by civic associations, decrease the role of the poor and exalt the role of the affluent. Also, it seems that the lower economic classes are less likely than the middle and upper classes to go to the polls when there is no party organization at the precinct level urging them to vote. Finally, it is difficult for some voters to pick out candidates with views similar to theirs without party labels to guide them.

Minorities sometimes complain that high-prestige civic associations rarely sponsor minority candidates in nonpartisan elections. In recent years, however, it has become more fashionable to sponsor a minority.

Some career politicians resent nonpartisan elections. They find it difficult to pursue a career in both partisan and nonpartisan politics. Once you commit yourself as a candidate to a party and run for office with a party label, it becomes an embarrassment to turn around and run for some other office that is supposed to be nonpartisan. How can you convince people you're truly nonpartisan when everybody remembers you as the Democratic or the Republican candidate for another office? Likewise, those who have risen in the nonpartisan world sometimes find it awkward to suddenly sprout partisan wings.

Voters also have trouble with nonpartisan elections: when candidates bear no party label, it's hard for some voters to identify the "good guys."

REFERENDUM AND INITIATIVE ELECTIONS

From 1890 through about 1920 the American people were awash in a great wave of distrust of government, and with good reason. Consequently, during that period many states amended their constitutions to give the people power to legislate directly—no longer would the public have to rely entirely upon elected state and local legislators. Of course, **direct legislation** was by no means new in the United States at the turn of the century. New England town meetings had long existed. The initiative and referendum—two of the new direct-legislation procedures—attempted not to duplicate the town meeting but to bring proposed laws directly to the people, bypassing or superceding the legislature.

Bringing issues directly to the people was thought to be a good way to thwart the special interests that were corrupting legislators. It did not occur to many people at the time that special interests would find ways of using and corrupting these new methods too.

The difference between *initiative* and *referendum* is that in an initiative, the people draft and enact their own legislation; in a referendum, measures being considered, or already passed, by the legislature are referred to the people for their approval before they become laws.

Referendum

In some states legislation is referred (or "submitted") to the people by the legislature itself. In other states the people may petition for a referendum. In still other states the constitution requires certain questions such as debt authorization and constitutional amendments to be referred to the people. And some states, such as Michigan, use all three systems of referendum.

Initiative

Some initiatives are direct and some indirect. Under direct initiative the people put questions directly on the ballot. Under indirect initiative the legislature must first be given an opportunity to enact the measure (or amend it) before it goes to the people. Depending on what the state constitution says, an initiative may propose either a constitutional amendment or an ordinary statutory law.

All initiatives and some referendums are started by people signing a petition in favor of initiating or referring some measure. State laws normally require a large number of signatures: usually 5 to 10 percent of the number of votes cast for governor in the last general election. Petitions for local initiatives and referendums likewise require the signatures of a certain percentage of those who voted within the local jurisdiction.

Acquiring the necessary signatures is often a long, tedious process; it usually requires the work of a large, well-heeled organization. The elections department then has the horrible job of checking the validity of signatures. After the signatures are verified, the matter is then put on the ballot. In some states the legislature is allowed on its own to refer proposals to the people. In that case, obviously, no petitions are required. Not surprisingly, initiative exists in fewer states than referendum.

Disadvantages of Direct Legislation

One criticism of all direct legislation is that it makes the ballot too long and asks people to vote on things they don't really know much about. Ballots are already long enough in the United States: voters are asked to choose among an army of candidates for numerous offices—offices that in most other nations are filled by appointment rather than by election. Adding several thought-provoking pieces of legislation to an already lengthy ballot makes voting a chore even for geniuses. Direct legislation also undermines legislative responsibility, encouraging legislatures to avoid hard questions. Moreover, turnout is light.

RECALL ELECTIONS

Recall is another reform that spread across the nation early in this century; it now exists in some 15 states. It is a system by which voters can remove an elected public officer before the end of his or her term. The procedure for conducting a recall election differs according to the laws of various jurisdictions (Table 4-1). The typical recall might go roughly as follows: First, the recall election (like an initiative or referendum) is initiated by petition. The number of signatures required is often set at a certain percentage, usually about 25 percent, of the total number of votes cast in the last election for candidates aspiring to the office whose incumbent is now the subject of a recall attempt. The recall petition may include a statement for signers to read. It presents reasons why the recall is sought, and the same statement (usually limited to about 300 words) may also appear on the ballot. The officer being recalled may also present his or her side of the story in an equal number of words, for publication on the ballot. The recall ballot is usually quite simple. It asks voters to decide two questions: (1) whether to recall the officer filed against, and (2) who should take his or her place. The recall and the election of a successor take place on the same ballot. The following question usually appears on the ballot: "Shall _____ be recalled from the office of _____?" Elsewhere on the ballot are the names of persons nominated to succeed the officer filed against. Normally it is not legal for the person filed against to be a candidate to succeed himself or herself.

Rarely is anyone removed from office by a recall election, although it is commonly threatened. The job of gathering enough signatures on a recall petition is staggering, not to mention the additional signatures needed to nominate a successor. Nor is there much point in going to all this effort inasmuch as most elected officeholders serve fairly short terms and could soon be on the ballot again. Furthermore, state laws may prohibit filing recall petitions against an officer during his or her first six months in office.

Some critics of recall argue that it makes officeholders too fearful of powerful, well-financed groups capable of mounting recall efforts. Also, recall presents a special problem for judges in that it may make them fearful of hand-

Table 4-1 States Where State Officials May Be Recalled

Alaska	*	Michigan	*
Arizona	**	Montana	***
California	**	Nevada	**
Colorado	**	North Dakota	**
Georgia	**	Oregon	**
Idaho	*	Washington	*
Kansas	*	Wisconsin	**
Louisiana	*		

***All public officials elected or appointed may be recalled.*
**All elected officials may be recalled.*
All elected officials except all or some judicial officers may be recalled.

Box 4-4. A Recall in Omaha

In 1987 the mayor of Omaha lost a recall vote in the middle of his second term. The recall was started after a tumultuous row between the mayor and his police department stemming from several alleged encounters between the police and individuals very close to the mayor. Allegedly, one person got some traffic citations, another was arrested for drunk driving, and two others were arrested on charges of soliciting prostitution. The mayor tried to have the arresting officers disciplined. But when the police chief strongly objected to this, he was fired by the mayor. Immediately a recall was activated.

This well-publicized recall seems to have touched off a series of other recall efforts in Nebraska, mostly in small towns where recalls can become bitterly divisive.

---

ing down unpopular decisions. But even though the effort necessary to stage a recall is so great that it is rarely attempted and even more rarely successful, the possibility of a recall, according to its defenders, does tend to make public officials more responsive to the public.

SUMMARY

An election system is a body of law pertaining to such things as the qualifications of voters and the time, place, and manner of holding elections. The rules of every election affect its outcome. Powerful classes and groups within a society usually see to it that the rules of the election system do not injure their cause. Most election systems are entirely compatible with the interests of those who have power to make the rules.

A perfect example of tinkering with the rules by people trying to control the outcome can be seen in the history of attempts to preserve white supremacy by keeping blacks from the ballot box. Contrivances such as grandfather clauses, literacy tests, tests to determine if would-be voters could "understand" and properly "interpret" the Constitution, good-character tests, the white primary, racial gerrymandering, and poll taxes effectively ensured white supremacy in a number of states for a considerable length of time.

Rarely may anyone vote in any American election who has not reached a certain age (usually 18), who is not a citizen of the state wherein he or she seeks to vote, who has not resided in the state for a certain length of time (usually 30 days), and who is not registered.

The states have exclusive power to determine who may vote. However, their laws must conform to the United States Constitution. The Constitution forbids denial of the right to vote on account of sex, race, and age (above 18). The power of states to set the qualifications of voters extends to election of federal officers as well as state and local officers. The federal government has nothing to say about who votes for president, vice-president, or United States senator or representative, except insofar as it enforces constitutional guarantees against discrimination. Nor does the federal government administer elections: this is done by local governments executing primarily state law.

In addition to establishing the qualifications that voters must have, states have power under the Constitution to regulate the time, place, and manner of holding elections. But the federal government may alter such regulations as they pertain to election of federal officers.

The question of who votes is quite different from the question of who may vote. A large number of people eligible to vote don't vote. Numerous reasons are offered for this.

If it is uncertain just why masses of people don't vote, it is equally uncertain just why those who do vote do so, or what they as a collectivity mean to express when they elect someone to office. Figuring out what "the people" have said on election day is tricky. Although many officeholders like to claim a mandate from the people to embark on certain programs, this mandate is much harder to prove than to claim.

Early in our history nominations for public office were made by caucus—an informal meeting of influential persons. A rather oligarchic way of nominating, King Caucus gave way to conventions of delegates chosen in a more or less orderly and fair manner from the rank and file of the party. State and local conventions became corrupt, however, and were largely replaced by a system of primary elections in which rank-and-file party members directly nominated party candidates.

Primaries come in two main varieties, open and closed. In an open primary voters can determine their party affiliation in the secrecy of the polling booth. In closed primaries voters must declare their party affiliation before entering the booth and are given only the ballot of the party with which they are affiliated. Each system has its pros and cons.

General-election ballots are generally of two kinds: the party-column ballot and the office-block ballot. The former makes it easier for voters to vote a straight party ticket, not an unblemished virtue.

Paper ballots are still used to some extent, but most states rely heavily on voting machines and punch cards.

About three-fourths of American cities fill city offices through nonpartisan elections. Also, most school boards are elected on a nonpartisan basis, as are numerous special district governing boards. A nonpartisan ballot does not identify the party affiliation of candidates. Nonpartisan elections are often nonpartisan in name only: beneath the surface they may be intensely partisan.

A number of states have initiative and referendum elections. In an initiative the people draft and enact their own legislation. A referendum, as its name implies, is a system for referring measures already passed by the legislature to the people for their approval before they become laws. About 15 states also have recall elections, whereby voters can remove an elected public officer before the end of his or her term. The merits of these systems are debated.

SUGGESTIONS FOR FURTHER READING

ALEXANDER, HERBERT E., "Financing Gubernatorial Election Campaigns," *State Government* (Summer 1980), 140–43.

COMER, JOHN C., *Nonpartisanship in the Legislative Process: Essays on the Nebraska Legislature.* Washington, D.C.: University Press of America, 1978.

COOK, RHODES, and STACY WEST, "Incumbents, Winners Hold Money Advantage," *State Government* (Summer 1980), 144–47.

JEWELL, MALCOLM, E., *Parties and Primaries: Nominating State Governors.* New York: Praeger, 1984.

RABINOVITZ, FRANCINE, and EDWARD K. HAMILTON, "Alternative Electoral Structures and Responsiveness to Minorities," *National Civic Review* (July 1980), 371–85.

RAE, DOUGLAS, *The Political Consequences of Electoral Laws* (rev. ed.). New Haven: Yale University Press, 1971.

ROSENSTONE, STEVEN J., and RAYMOND E. WOLFINGER, "The Effect of Registration Laws on Voter Turnout," *American Political Science Review* (1978), 22–55.

SMOLKA, RICHARD G., "Symposium: Gerrymandering and the Courts," *UCLA Law Review* (October 1985), 1–282.

WOO, LILLIAN C., *The Campaign Organizer's Manual.* Durham, N.C.: Academic Press, 1980.

ZIMMERMAN, JOSEPH F., "Local Representation: Designing a Fair System," *National Civic Review* (June 1980), 307–12.

5

parties, pressure groups, and elites

PREVIEW

PARTY FUNCTIONS

In gothic romances women are always swooning. I never realized a man could swoon until one afternoon when Bertha and I lay down on the grass in the park. She rolled half on top of me and brushed the hair back from my forehead. I nearly floated into oblivion.

She was president of a well-known campus political club. I guess they elected their prettiest member to the office. My own political club was more responsible: it elected someone like myself president.

What brought us together was serious business: the forthcoming Political Ball. The festivities were to begin with a 30-minute debate between the presidents of the two rival clubs. Bertha and I had already met three times to plan the affair. It was our third meeting when she whispered "I love you" in my ear. After a minute or two I said, "Ich liebe dich auch." Bertha was from Austria; she would understand. If there was ever love at first sight, this was it. It was incredible to me that I could feel this way about a member of her political party.

"Bertha," I said playfully on our fourth meeting, "I've got a bad idea for the debate." "Why don't you bowl everybody over at the debate by simply standing up and announcing right at the beginning that you've decided to join my party."

"No, sweet boy. We mustn't disappoint them." She grew serious. "It is our duty to clarify the issues between our parties, to clarify our different solutions to problems. That's one great service political parties can do for people. Parties do more than nominate candidates."

With a mischievous grin I pursued my proposal. "But, Bertha, it would clarify things if you simply came over to the good guys right off the bat."

I knew at once that I had pushed my joke too far. She drew back. Her owl eyes opened wide and focused directly at me. "I wouldn't join your party for fifty thousand dollars in cash." She was mad, and laid into me for ten or fifteen minutes. She stated just why she believed in her party. When she finally quieted down I realized she wasn't elected president just because of her looks. I also realized I had just heard the main thrust of what she would say in the debate, and that I better get my arguments ready.

Bertha and I didn't meet again until the fateful Political Ball. I was sure she didn't like me anymore.

Bertha's performance at the debate was wholly magnificent—her arguments were as nicely packaged as her body. When she finished, the applause was long and loud. It was my turn to perform. I proceeded to explain how parties can serve voters by helping clarify issues and answers, and by doing a number of things besides nominating candidates. I tried to explain why I was a member of my party. I wanted to say it well. I believed in my party as much as Bertha believed in hers. I wanted Bertha to know that I had reasons too. The words tumbled out of my mouth fast and earnestly. When I finished my oration there was a moment of silence as if everybody were too embarrassed to move. Then, suddenly, an outburst of applause.

Bertha came over to me. She threw both arms around my neck. "You were beautiful when you said parties do things besides nominate candidates," she whispered.

I grew faint again.

PARTY FUNCTIONS

One can hardly imagine a human group that lacks cliques, sects, factions, and subgroupings. Fraternities and sororities have their circles; churches, their rings; offices, their cabals and combinations. The division of groups into subgroups seems to be about as unavoidable as the division of rainbows into colors. This divisive tendency in human society gives us political parties.

Political parties do several things above and beyond their basic function of staffing and controlling the government. These many auxiliary functions of parties are sometimes discussed as if parties were consciously contrived for those purposes, but most party functions are no more contrived and planned than rainbows.

One of the great functions of political parties is to throw bridges across the many islands of political machinery in our fragmented system of government. The two houses of a legislature, for example, are sometimes brought together by the uniting threads of political party. The threads are not always there, of course, but usually if one house is controlled by a particular party, so is the other. Similar bridging occurs among cities, counties, states, districts, and all arms and agencies of government.

Another so-called function of political parties is to keep a close and critical eye on the other party when it is in power. Out-parties become watchdogs of the system.

Still another function of political parties is to generate interest in public affairs by stirring up fights over issues and candidates. Campaigns draw attention away from soap operas and ball games just long enough to give the public some slight understanding of what is going on in government. Parties through their campaigns help clarify issues for masses of voters. Parties also contribute to public affairs by designing and presenting programs of action, which prove useful whether the party wins or loses.

In some localities political parties also help individual citizens deal with the bewildering network of bureaucracy. This is particularly true in urban areas where large masses of poor, ignorant, and confused people are huddled together in city precincts and where precinct captains and ward leaders try to build political machines by offering help and service to the needy.

Of course, the central and official function of political parties is to nominate candidates for public office. The nominating function goes to the heart of what political parties are all about—to the heart of who will control the government and its vast powers.

THE TWO-PARTY SYSTEM

We have basically a **two-party system.** Even though we have more than two parties, rarely does any party other than Republican or Democratic win public office. Almost all members of Congress, state governors, and state legislators (except those of Nebraska, who are supposedly nonpartisan, and about a dozen independents elsewhere in the country) are either Democrats or Republicans,[1] as are nearly all other elected officers, except nonpartisan local officials. Some states are "one-party states," where the same party usually wins, but almost nowhere does one find more than two strong parties—that is, parties strong enough to have a genuine chance of winning office. However, a good many other nations do have numerous strong parties: France, Belgium, Holland, Italy, West Germany, and Japan each have four or five major parties, and some countries have dozens of lesser parties holding at least a few elective offices.

Party History

We have always been at core a two-party country. The present Democratic party is fond of tracing its ancestry back to the earliest hours of the Republic, particularly to a group backing Thomas Jefferson, which called itself the Democratic-Republican party to emphasize its antimonarchic sentiments. Around 1840 the Democratic-Republican party became known simply as the Democratic party and was opposed by a party known first as the National Republicans and later as the Whigs. The Whigs were in turn replaced by the Republican party, founded in 1856. The members of this new party were drawn partly from the Democratic

---

[1] Currently the only thing approaching third-party control of a state legislature is seen in Minnesota where every legislator generally belongs either to the Democratic Farmer-Labor Party or the Independent Republican Party. But these parties have strong ties with the national Democratic or Republican parties. Recently several Libertarian party members were elected to the Alabama legislature.

party itself (mainly those Democrats opposed to slavery) and partly from the ranks of the old Whig party. It was slavery that shook up the old parties.

The Republican party's first candidate for president was John C. Fremont, famous as an explorer of the American West. He was called the Pathfinder because of his expeditions into the central Rocky Mountains to find a route for a railroad to the Pacific, an enterprise that excited the whole nation. Fremont failed to win the presidency, but the Republican party's second candidate, Abraham Lincoln, won in 1860.

The present two parties are among the oldest continuously operating political parties in the world today.

Third parties have occasionally been formed in response to momentary excitements. The last time a third-party candidate got any votes in the electoral college was in 1968, when George C. Wallace, running on the American-party ticket, got 46. In 1924 Robert M. LaFollette, standard-bearer of the Progressive party, received 13 votes. From time to time third parties have enjoyed temporary success within certain states or cities,[2] but these successes have not lasted long.

Why Two Parties?

Why does the United States have a two-party system? And why do a good many other countries have multiple parties? When political science students are asked these questions, they offer all sorts of imaginative reasons. For example, there is the theory that we've always had two parties, and that's why we have two parties now: tradition. There's the theory that Americans are naturally less prone to divisions and factionalism and therefore less prone to multiple parties catering to those divisions and factions.

Many political scientists seem to think the two-party system in the United States is mainly the result of our single-member-district, winner-take-all electoral system. The multiple-party phenomenon in some parts of the world is explained (to the satisfaction of some political scientists) by multiple-member districts and proportional representation.

Most American election districts are **single-member districts.**[3] Most state legislators, for example, are elected from their own district. On the other hand, in many countries where multiple parties exist, each legislative district usually has several representatives in the parliament. In the United States, furthermore, no matter how many persons may be running for the legislature in a single-member district, there can be only one winner (since there is only one seat to be filled) and that is the person who gets the most votes. In Europe and wherever the **multiple-member constituency** is used, however, there can be more than one winner. If each legislative district is permitted to send, say, five representatives to parliament, then there can be five winners. If the system used for determining which five candidates are going to win is a system of **proportional representation** (PR, as it's called), then conceivably five different political parties may find their way into parliament from one district.

---

[2]The Farmer-Labor party of Minnesota elected Floyd B. Olson governor in 1930, 1932, and 1934 but then merged with the Democrats in 1944.

[3]The statistical accuracy of this statement is questionable, however, when one considers the vast number of local-government councils, commissions, and boards in which all or some seats are filled through at-large elections.

PR, you see, does not give all the spoils to one winner. PR would not give all five seats to the political party that gets the most votes, unless perchance that party took nearly all the votes in the election. Under PR, if one party gets three-fifths of all the votes cast, then that one party would get three of the five seats. If another party got one-fifth and a third party got another one-fifth, then each of those other parties would get one seat, making a total of five. In other words, seats are divided among parties according to what proportion of the total vote each party got.

In our American single-member, **winner-take-all system,** there can be no second prize, or a third, a fourth, or a fifth prize. In that sense our system is rather cruel because there can be only one winner no matter how close the others come to winning. In a sense the losing political party gets no mandate to represent the district at all, even if it took nearly half the votes.

We won't delve into the virtues of one system versus another; each has its merits, each its shortcomings. However, one of the results of our system is that it drives nearly all groups—blacks, laborers, farmers, Catholics, women, and so on—into one or the other party. Many of those with separate interests would form themselves into separate political parties if it were profitable to do so. But there are no rewards for third parties in America. Therefore, everybody who has a vested interest in winning wants to be allied with a party that does have some chance of winning.

Third Parties

Most so-called **third parties** in the United States are not really political parties, but mini-educational institutions trying to sell some particular philosophy to the public while pretending to run candidates for office. If they really wanted a share of power they would do what everybody else does—become Democrats or Republicans.

Third parties in America have a built-in **suicide mechanism.** Normally they advocate ideas that are not sufficiently popular to be advocated by the big parties. The instant a third party begins to succeed in popularizing its central program, both big parties seize it for their own platforms, as a hawk seizes a rabbit. This undercuts the third party, whose vitality and justification for exis-

---

Box 5-1. Some Third Parties

American Party of the United States
Communist Party of the United States
Conservative Party of New York State
Liberal Party of New York State
Libertarian Party
Prohibition National Committee
La Raza Unida Party
Socialist Labor Party
Socialist Workers Party
Socialist Party, U.S.A.

tence hang upon its exclusive possession of the idea. This further explains why our two-party system has been so durable: the two parties swallow and digest newcomers.

Party Ideology

Ideology As Strategy   By comparison with the ideological parties of Europe, America's Republican and Democratic parties are about as ideological as professional football teams. Both parties are willing to play any winning idea. The two parties are not exactly alike, not exactly Tweedledee and Tweedledum, but they generally have more in common than is popularly imagined. Curiously, the ideology of a state party organization may conflict with the ideology of its own national party organization on a number of feverish issues. A party at the state level is not always the same thing ideologically as the party at the national level. Sometimes the two levels are run by different tribes with different philosophies. These varying state parties try to get together as best they can every four years to capture the presidency. The national presidential conventions are meetings of a vast collection of slightly incongruous state party organizations to fulfill the one dream they all share.

Two Conglomerates   The two parties are two great conglomerations. One senses, however, that certain groups feel more at home in one party than in the other, although there are people from all groups in both parties. Many urban workers, Jews, Catholics, and blacks are, of course, Republicans, but more of them are Democrats. Likewise, many rural and small-town people, suburbanites, Protestants, businessmen, and professionals are, of course, Democrats, but more are Republicans. Generally the leadership of the Democratic party wears a "liberal" cloak, whereas the leadership of the Republican party wears a "conservative" cloak, although we hesitate to define those adjectives. We also hesitate to look beneath the cloak, because the labels people wear for external consumption are sometimes deceptive. The same person or party may be "liberal" about some things, such as civil rights for racial minorities, and "conservative" about others, such as economic matters. Furthermore, the public pronouncements of people and parties may not truly reflect their feelings, many totally camouflage a disturbed sea of feelings. Parties are split personalities: they freely advocate impossible contradictions, such as more spending by government and lower taxes. The Republican and Democratic parties find room for many diverse points of view: racists and nonracists, sexists and nonsexists, hawks and doves, leftists and rightists. A party that invites into its fold almost any collection of believers who can vote is forced to say everything to please everybody.

Middle of the Road   Most successful candidates for public office are **middle-of-the-roaders.** That is another reality of American politics, another product of the two-party system. Parties must pitch their appeal to virtually everybody, must say things on which everybody—from leftists to rightists, from atheists to believers, from blacks to whites, from rich to poor, from smart to dumb—can more or less agree. Candidates must speak in generalities—must speak for "God, mother, and love." The minute a candidate gets down to specifics, or begins to advocate something on which the great masses cannot agree, he or she begins to make people mad. And it doesn't pay to make people mad. Remember, there is no consolation prize in American politics. The purpose of a party is to win, and to win one must have the *most* votes, and to get the most votes one must usually stick to the middle of the road. Two classic examples of presidential candidates who lost elections partly because they based their campaigns on a point of view that was not middle of the road at the time were Republican Barry M. Goldwater in 1964 and Democratic George S. McGovern in 1972.

There is a certain vague, intangible quality about American political parties. Nobody seems to be able to say just exactly what a Democrat is supposed to believe, or what a Republican is supposed to believe. Because both parties must attract all types of people to win, both must believe everything and nothing. In Europe, where several parties can be victorious, most parties are identifiable by a rather clear set of political dogmas.

PARTY ORGANIZATION

The Organization Chart

On an organization chart America's two major parties look neat and hierarchical. Organization charts do not always reflect reality, however. Suffice it to say that if the Republican party were a platoon of soldiers and the captain said forward march, every person would march in a different direction. Democrats behave the same way. Perhaps we don't want disciplined parties of the European variety, but it is worth knowing why such a difference exists. One reason is that in Europe the leaders of the parties generally determine who runs for office and who doesn't. In the United States, primaries and conventions, not bosses, usually decide who runs for office.

An American political party is like a city street—it has little control over the candidates who drive on it. Political traffic gets hot and heavy at times, especially during the five o'clock traffic of election years, and there are collisions and terrible blazing accidents. A European party is more like a toll road—it determines which drivers or vehicles are allowed on it. These analogies, of course, overdraw the situation both here and in Europe, but not too seriously.

Hundreds of Parties

Someone has said we do not have two parties in the United States but rather hundreds of parties. According to this theory, there are 165 parties in the Kansas legislature because all members mount their own political campaign, build their own political machine, find their own financing, and do all this with very little help from the Republican or Democratic party on whose ticket they run. They in effect form their own party within a party. Still, candidates almost have to run on a party ticket (unless the election is nonpartisan). To run on the party ticket, however, candidates seldom wait for the party to pick them. They must prove to the party that they can win by organizing an army of political helpers, getting petitions signed to be put on the party's primary ballot, and fighting to win the primary.

Who Are Party Members?

In addition to the confusion about what a Democrat or a Republican is supposed to believe, there is also confusion about how one goes about determining who is a **party member.** To join a European political party you have to apply and be accepted: you even get a party card that certifies you're a member. You can be kicked out of the party for heresy or for disloyalty or for a number of other sins. Nothing is more peculiar about American political parties than their inability to control who joins and their inability to cleanse their ranks or kick anybody out. It is not even clear how membership in an American political party is determined. Are you a Democrat if you think you're a Democrat? Are you a Democrat if you vote Democratic? Are you a Democrat if you register Democratic? Are you a Democrat if you vote in a Democratic-party primary election? Does joining a Democratic club make you a Democrat? Does contributing to the Democratic party or to any of its candidates make you a Democrat? What is the yardstick, the measure, the ultimate thing that determines whether one is—or is not—a member of the Democratic or Republican party?

It seems to be generally accepted in this country that one is a member of the party with which one declares an affiliation at registration. That definition cannot be very helpful in North Dakota, where there is no registration or in states where no party affiliation is recorded on the registration form. Nor can registration be a very helpful definition of party membership in states having open primaries where voters are given the ballot for all parties and select the party of their choice in the secrecy of the polling booth or in the case of Washington and Alaska (the blanket-primary states) where voters may pick and choose among primary election candidates of various parties.

In states where one does register affiliation with one party or another, no party has power to refuse anyone. You could broadcast on the radio that you are a Marxist and still register Republican; you could confess a belief in Hitler's nazism and still register Democratic.

Parties as State Agencies

Within each state the formal structure of political parties, the exact manner in which they go about their formal business, the titles of their officers, the dates of their meetings, and all sorts of other major and minor matters are determined by state law.[4] Party rules may supplement but not contradict or change these laws. So thoroughly regulated is the structure and procedure of political parties within states that one could almost say they are not parties at all in the European sense, but simply quasi-state agencies that, like highways, serve to channel, systematize, regularize, and control political traffic within the state. Parties are really part of the state's election machinery. The Supreme Court correctly sensed this when it struck down the white primary on the grounds that political parties are not simply private clubs with freedom to include and exclude whomever they please. Parties were prohibited by that decision from excluding blacks from mem-

---

[4]However, national party procedures (for example, those of the national convention or national committee) do not appear subject to state law.

bership.[5] The decision rested on the same equal protection clause that prohibits states themselves from discriminating against blacks.

State law also defines which organizations are political parties. Usually such laws provide that any political organization whose candidate for governor received a certain percentage of the total votes cast for governor (say, 5 percent) in the last general election is officially deemed to be a political party and must organize itself and conduct its affairs according to state laws applicable to political parties.

Structure

Party organization differs somewhat from state to state. Our description of it must therefore be general. Basically party structure is designed after the political design of the nation: there are national, state, district (congressional district and state-legislative district), county, city, and, within urban (as well as some rural) areas, ward and precinct organizations (Figure 5-1).

Precinct Let us start from the bottom up and try to visualize what makes political parties tick—organizationally. At the bottom are precincts. The precinct is a small geographic area (especially small in urban areas) containing about 500 or 600 people, all of whom vote in the same place. The precinct is also the lowest level of party organization. In some states a **precinct caucus** occurs every two years. The time and place of this caucus is announced in the newspaper, and every party member is invited to attend. The caucus may be held in someone's living room, or it may be held in a school or public building. Normally the only people who bother to attend are a handful of party activists in the precinct. There may be hundreds of party members in the precinct, but perhaps only six or ten will show up for the caucus. Sometimes, of course, precinct caucuses are better attended. It depends, really, on how political the neighborhood is.

In many states each precinct caucus chooses a precinct captain (sometimes called a **committeeperson**). In some jurisdictions precinct captains are not elected but appointed by higher levels of the party.

The job of a precinct captain is to "deliver" the precinct on election day—to get acquainted with everyone in the precinct, to persuade as many of them as possible to become members of his or her political party, to make sure every "member" of the party is registered to vote, to peddle campaign literature, and to hustle voters to the polls on election day. Another function of the precinct captain is to serve on the ward and county committees and to participate in the election of a county party chairperson.

As political parties have declined in their power to control nominations and campaigns, and as more people desert political parties to register as Independents, the significance of precinct organization comes ever more in doubt. Across vast areas of the nation, party organization at the precinct level is nonexistent. This, of course, is especially true within minority parties in one-party states, but it is also true in countless other places where there is insufficient interest in a party to convene a caucus or to find anyone willing to serve as precinct captain.

[5]Smith v. Allwright, 321 U.S. 649 (1944)

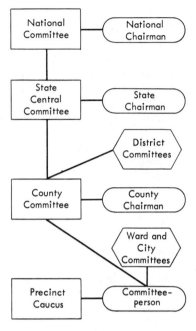

Figure 5-1 Typical party organization

County The precinct caucus is the seed from which the mighty party organization grows. The caucus, as we have seen, is presided over by a precinct captain who serves on the county committee.

The job of the county committee is to aid in the election of party nominees (actually, nominees are responsible for getting themselves elected for the most part). The county committee also raises and distributes as much money as it can, provides information useful to party candidates, and in general manages the affairs of the party. Since the county committee may be composed of several hundred people, it elects a county party chairperson and an executive committee to run the party when the committee is not meeting (which is most of the time). If the party has any money, it may rent a headquarters and hire a few secretaries to work there.

State The county party committee convenes every couple of years to elect delegates to the state central committee, which may include several thousand people. The state central committee acts like the county committee, except on a statewide rather than a countywide basis. The state central committee elects a state party chairperson and a state party executive committee. Together they manage the affairs of the party and do what they can to help the party's nominees, but, to repeat, those nominees usually have to rely primarily on themselves and their own political organization to get elected.

National Two national committeepersons from each state serve on the national committee of the party. They are often selected by the state central committee. The national committee is the supreme governing body of the party. It elects a national chairperson and an executive committee to run the party. Usually the national committee will gladly elect anyone to the post of national chairperson desired by the president of the United States if the president is of its party. The president is actually the *de facto* (unofficially recognized) head of his or her political party just as the governor is the *de facto* head of his or her party at the state level. Local officeholders as a group are more or less the *de facto* heads of their local party. Although the president would not want to rely solely on the party to get reelected, election of the president is the chief function of the national committee, the national chairperson, and the national party headquarters. The national party apparatus also does what it can to raise money and assist the candidacy of party candidates throughout the nation, but its resources are too limited to contribute much help to many.

The National Convention

In addition to the national committee, there exists at the national level another important piece of party machinery—the national convention, which nominates the party's candidates for president and vice-president every four years and adopts a platform. This great convention is a gathering place for a large part of the leadership of 50 state party organizations.

Presidential Primaries   With the spread of presidential primaries as a method for selecting delegates to the national convention, the convention has been reduced almost to a mere formality—it confirms a decision already made in the primaries and turns itself into a "Hallelujah" chorus for the nominee.

About 30 states now have **presidential primaries,** in which delegates to the national convention are chosen by the rank and file of the party from competing lists of would-be delegates representing competing presidential hopefuls. If the primary is only *preferential,* delegates chosen by party conventions are advised (according to the outcome of the primary) whom to support at the national convention. How long a delegate is required or expected to remain committed to a candidate depends on party rules and to some extent on the wishes of the candidate.

About 80 percent of all delegates to the Republican and Democratic national conventions are now selected or instructed by state presidential primaries. The other 20 percent are usually selected by state conventions, by district (usually congressional-district) conventions, or by a combination of state and district conventions. The state presidential primary first appeared in the early 1900s and rapidly spread to about half the states, then dropped back to about one-third of the states until the 1970s, when its popularity again surged. National conventions are now little more than a time, place, and manner of ratifying the will of rank-and-file party members as expressed in presidential primaries. Just enough uncertainty about the outcome of national party conventions remains to make them a worthy subject for television coverage. However, the networks are beginning to wonder whether national conventions are still important enough to blank out soap operas for three whole days. A number of southern states chose March 8, 1988, as their presidential primary date in hopes a unified primary would motivate presidential candidates to pay more attention to southern interests. Several other states outside the South have also chosen that fateful date, which is called "Super Tuesday."

More Loss of Party Discipline Presidential primaries, like all primaries, deprive party leaders and party activists of some control of the party. If party leaders can't control nominations, this interrupts their control of nearly everything else. This loss of control by party leaders may be the greatest reason American political parties are so uncoordinated and decentralized. The rise of primary elections was a blow to party leadership and therefore a blow to the cohesion of parties and to the role of political parties in our system of government.

Campaign Organizations

Although working for the election of the party's candidates is the central function of local, state, and national party committees, some candidates are wary of associating themselves with their own party, especially candidates of the weaker party, because they will need votes from the other party to win. But candidates who pitch their appeal to voters of both parties and to Independents cannot expect their own party to be an enthusiastic accomplice to this.

Ineffectual Parties Nor do candidates trust their own party machinery. They form their own **campaign organizations** rather than relying on the party apparatus. People in the party organization can't be counted on to run an efficient campaign—often they don't really know as much about campaigning as they should. Also, political parties are torn with factionalism. Frequently a candidate has won the nomination only after a long battle within the party against others who wanted it. Since many candidates fear disloyalty and inefficiency in the party organization, they form their own campaign organizations.

Urban Machines This picture of ineffectual parties does not necessarily apply to big-city **political machines,** some of which are highly disciplined and have an almost military hierarchy of command reaching from precinct to ward to city to county. Only a few of these machines still exist, however, such as the Democratic party machine of Chicago (which fell into considerable disarray following the death of Mayor Richard J. Daley in 1976).

Urban machines of a former era, such as those of Ed Flynn of Bronx County in New York, Boss Crump of Memphis, Tom Pendergast of Kansas City, and Mayor Hague of Jersey City, kept themselves in power by doing all sorts of favors for people in need—especially newly arrived immigrants—providing them with food, jobs, and other help. People who received these benefits gave their votes and their loyalty to the machine. Since the onset of modern welfare programs, government agencies have done a fair job of taking care of people in need. This robs political machines of some of their power. However, there are still enough good deeds and favors at the disposal of political organizations in big cities to keep a flicker of machine life burning.

Party Discipline

Because party leaders do not have firm control of nominations and because party machinery isn't very helpful to candidates in their battle to get elected and stay elected, parties are hardly in a position to demand obedience from members who have successfully run for public office. Therefore, very few party-line votes occur in state legislatures or in local councils. In a good many foreign countries, any member of parliament who fails to vote the party line cuts his political throat. **Party discipline** in England, for example, is nearly absolute. Rarely in the United States does any officeholder jump when his or her party snaps its fingers. In most legislatures there is only one occasion when a Democrat jolly well better vote Democratic and a Republican Republican. That's when they vote on how the senate and the house shall be organized: in other words, when they vote to determine how many Democrats and how many Republicans shall serve on each committee and who shall be speaker of the house and president pro tem of the senate. On that occasion (with some colorful exceptions, induced by party factionalism and bipartisan coalitions) any Democrat who doesn't vote to put all the machinery of his house into the hands of Democrats in effect resigns from the party; Republicans the same. The usual punishment for wavering at that crucial moment is to be left out of all committee assignments. (If a member of the legislature has no committee assignments, his effectiveness is very limited.)

Although party solidarity is the supreme consideration in organizing a legislative body, from then on it is far from being the supreme consideration. This is because every legislator knows he must vote in accordance with the political demands of his district to ensure his political survival—not in accordance with the musings of a political party that plays a rather small role in his survival even though he carries its banner.

This somewhat overstates the insignificance of party in the life of a legislator. After all, legislators do have a vested interest in the good name of their party and in the success of its candidates. They do wear the party label, and their power in the legislature does depend somewhat on whether their party controls that legislature and on how they get along with their fellow partisans. And so there are party caucuses in legislatures and a certain common interest among legislators of the same party to act in concert, to some modest degree at least.

CAMPAIGNS

Campaigning in large districts for important offices has changed dramatically since the end of World War II. A new politics has emerged that is highly technological and scientific and features professional campaign management. The net result of this new science has been to remove campaigning from the control of political parties and to give it to professional campaign managers employed by candidates. This has further contributed to the decline of party organizations. Neither party machinery nor party ideology plays a central role in the new politics. The candidate's private campaign organization plays the central role, and that organization may be quite distant from (and hostile to) the party's campaign organization. The personality and ideology of the candidate (not the party) are given top billing, and frequently the candidate's views are at odds with those of the party.

At the same time there has been a sharp decline in party affiliation among voters: about a third of them now identify themselves as Independents. Likewise there is a sharp increase in ticket splitting and party switching.

Campaign-Management Services

Although a few **campaign-management firms** have been on the scene since the 1930s, their numbers have vastly increased in recent years. Today nearly every candidate for an important elective office who has any expectation of winning will hire one or more professional campaign services.

Rarely will such a firm take on an entire campaign. Most firms specialize in one kind of service, such as polling public opinion, conducting advertising campaigns, consulting on the use of media, raising funds, arranging campaign trips, or making statistical analyses to determine the ethnic, religious, occupational, and other economic, social, and political characteristics of a district. Some firms also specialize by party—handling only Democratic candidates or only Republicans. Some firms go so far as to specialize ideologically, preferring to handle only conservatives, or only liberals, and so on. These firms are money making enterprises. They build their reputations by winning elections, and they do not like to associate themselves with candidates who have no realistic hope of winning.

Media Science

Media experts are probably the most numerous group among professional campaign managers. Some advertising agencies that promote soap and cereals also promote candidates. The same principles of salesmanship apply to all. The sales pitch is based on sophisticated sociological and psychological data about what makes people think positively or negatively about a candidate. These experts try not only to make the candidate fit the voting public but also to make the voting public fit the candidate (by changing its attitudes).

Voters are heavily influenced by their perceptions of the qualities of a candidate. Media experts therefore work hard to project a favorable image of the candidate as a personality. Television has reduced campaigns almost to battles of personality; political organizations today are built largely around personalities rather than ideologies. Personalism now dominates American politics. Media experts coach the candidate on how to make a favorable impression on and off camera during press conferences, interviews, talk shows, speeches, and all other appearances. They advise the candidate how to get as much free media coverage as possible and how to keep the press corps happy. Media experts also recommend the best use of all forms of communication, including billboards and direct mail as well as television, radio, and newspapers. Candidates for important offices may commit half their campaign budget for media expenditures, and it is extremely important to know how and where to spend it.

Polling

The next biggest expenditure in the realm of scientific campaigning is **public-opinion polling.** Such polling constitutes the eyes and ears of a campaign—it is a valuable source of intelligence about what the public is thinking as the campaign rolls from stage to stage. Some polls have been rigged to yield a predetermined result, and these have given polling a bad reputation. However, public-opinion polls can be extremely accurate if carefully conducted, properly structured, and correctly analyzed.

Polling is very expensive, especially if conducted in person. (Telephone polls are much cheaper but less accurate.) But if a candidate can afford it, he or she should by all means use it. Polls can help a candidate concentrate on the right issues, at the right time, in the right manner. They can dissect a candidate's constituency, revealing all sorts of economic and social patterns within a district.

Polls can tell candidates what the public thinks of them, their personality, their speaking ability, their ideas, and their opponents.

Computers

A third realm of scientific campaigning consists of electronic data processing. An effective campaign rests on the rapid analysis of myriad facts about myriad people. A computer is a machine designed to store and selectively retrieve and correlate masses of facts at lightning speed. Its function is essentially secretarial, but it can handle more in an hour than a secretary can handle in several life-times.

An example of the computer at work in elections is the computer-assisted direct-mail campaign. Campaign workers feed the computer information about masses of people gleaned from various sources, such as lists of members of groups, lists of subscribers to particular publications, voter-registration lists, occupational lists, and residential lists. From this mass of data the computer can tell who is likely to be receptive to a particular appeal. Candidates then design direct-mail communications aimed at a dozen or a hundred different shades of opinion, and the computer will send the right communication to the right people.

This kind of computer information about the economic, social, political, and ideological composition of the electorate is useful to candidates every step of the way. Wherever they go, whatever neighborhood or group they approach, the computer can virtually tell them what to say—can tell them what message will win the hearts and minds of that particular audience. Computers give candidates the information that precinct captains and county chairpersons used to supply, but they do it with greater speed, precision, and thoroughness.

Where Does the Old Style of Politics Still Survive?

Modern scientific campaign services are generally too expensive for small-scale campaigns. Candidates for the city council, county board, or state legislature are still generally (except in some metropolitan areas) conducted in the personal, intimate, **old-style politics.** Such campaigns are built upon handshakes, door-to-door solicitation, speeches before flesh-and-blood audiences, rallies, and other personal contact with the electorate. Political parties play a somewhat greater role in such campaigns, but again, the major burden falls on the candidate. Such campaigns are usually quite haphazard and unscientific.

CAMPAIGN FINANCE

Mother's Milk

Maybe it was Senator Everett M. Dirksen of Illinois who said, "Money is the mother's milk of politics." The average successful campaign for the United States Senate costs perhaps $2 million or $3 million; for the United States House of Representatives, perhaps $500,000; for governor, possibly $2 million or $3 million; for other statewide offices, such as secretary of state, maybe $75,000; for the state legislature, perhaps $20,000. Of course, campaign costs vary widely according to the population of the district (it's not going to cost as much to run for governor of Rhode Island as it does for governor of California). Costs also depend on the nature of the opposition and on a number of other circumstances.

Campaign Costs

Money does not always win elections, but when several relatively unknown people are running for office, the one who can finance the biggest propaganda onslaught is almost sure to win. However, when a candidate is already well known and already has a public image, it's hard for others to catch up.

Propaganda Costs   One prime-time national television commercial lasting a couple of minutes may cost $80,000. Commercials on local stations supporting state and local candidates aren't that expensive, of course, but they run hundreds of dollars per minute. Newspaper advertising is also high-priced. There are many other expenses.

Candidates for big offices like governor or United States senator need paid campaign managers, a campaign headquarters, advisors, advance men, research teams, speech writers, publicity people, communications specialists, photographers, stenographers. Meetings, parades, and rallies do not just happen spontaneously; they require expensive public-relations efforts and lots of spending for telephone calls, buses, and other crowd-raising procedures. Furthermore, candidates have to spend money on bumper stickers, buttons, baloons, posters, placards, straw hats, booklets, brochures, stamps, direct-mail advertising, and a thousand and one other trivia such as matchbooks, pencils, and pens, all suitably inscribed with the candidate's name. Air and surface transportation for the candidate and his or her staff is a big item.

The more expensive an election is, the more candidates have to sell themselves into political bondage to get money—unless, of course, they are wealthy enough to finance their own campaign. To run successfully for any big office that requires an expensive campaign, candidates must either be rich or have a pipeline to sources of great wealth elsewhere. This usually means they must have access to people and organizations willing to supply money in *large* chunks. Only a few candidates in the history of American politics have managed to collect lots of money from a mass of *small* contributors.

Consequences of Cost

Candidates who buy their way into office through expensive campaigns, and who do this with other people's money, are going to owe a big debt of gratitude after the election. Those who supply the money, the special interests, are not just playing Santa Claus: they expect the candidates to be smart enough to know how to repay the debt. Most candidates keenly understand from where the money comes and act accordingly.

It is sometimes said that as long as candidates are forced to become indebted to those who have money, the capitalist system will be secure from the schemes of reformers who, if they had their "harebrained" way, would make it almost impossible to run a private business in the United States. On the other hand, it is also said that elected officeholders cannot vote for what is in the "public interest" as long as they have to prostitute themselves to private special interests to get money for election campaigns. Capitalists answer that office-holders do serve the public interest when they serve the private interest, because "what is good for tobacco is good for Virginia"—private interests in America provide the jobs and the incomes that make the good life possible for millions of people. To that, reformers reply that special interests play too big a part in financing American elections. Candidates should be freed from this bondage, and elections should be funded at least in part by the government. At the very least, candidates should be forced to reveal the sources of their campaign money.

Campaign-Finance Laws

History   Over the years national and state governments have tried to compel candidates to disclose the source of their campaign money and how it was spent. Attempts have also been made to limit the amount received by candidates and the amount spent. But before 1971 none of these **campaign-finance laws** were very effective; often they were disregarded. Labor unions and corporations were forbidden by the Taft-Hartley Act of 1947[6] to make campaign contributions in federal elections, but it was ridiculously simple to get around the law by making back-door contributions. Corporations could do this by joining associations, paying "dues," then letting the association make political contributions and conduct propaganda. Or individual corporate officers could make hefty campaign contributions in full expectation of being repaid by an annual Christmas bonus. Labor unions found it easy to evade Taft-Hartley Act prohibitions on campaign contributions by simply organizing *political-action committees* (PACs) composed of union members who join "voluntarily" and pay dues. **PAC** treasuries support various kinds of political action, including the campaigns of favored candidates for public office.

In 1925 the Corrupt Practice Act was passed, requiring disclosure of campaign contributions. The act was notable for its exceptions. State and local elections were not included, nor were presidential elections. The only elections covered were those for the United States Senate and House of Representatives, but even in those races primary elections were excluded. The Hatch Act of 1939 and 1940, another toothless law, limited contributions from any individual or political committee to $5000. This law was easily bypassed by funneling contributions through individuals or political committees, which could be mobilized by the hundreds whenever needed for the purpose of donating a $5000 chunk of money. These laws were so hollow that they brought ridicule upon the *United States Code*. Candidates for Congress were forbidden to spend more than a certain amount of money on their campaigns, and political committees could not spend more than $3 million. Of course, there was no limit to the number of political committees confined to $3 million each. These apparent limitations on campaign funding did little to enhance respect for the electoral system. Futhermore, the whole attempt to limit campaign spending seemed slightly un-American to some people: it tended to limit freedom of speech and the press by limiting how much candidates could spend to express their views.

---

[6] *Stat.* 156 (1947), 29 *U.S.C.* Par. 185.

The Federal Election Campaign Act of 1971 Congress tried to tighten its campaign-finance laws in the 1970s. Its most effective new legislation concerned presidential-campaign financing. These laws applied only to elections for federal officers: president, vice-president, United States senator, and United States representative. Although congressional campaigns are largely state-based and state-oriented, they are regulated chiefly by federal, not state, campaign-finance laws. However, most states have enacted similar laws (to be discussed shortly) covering campaigns for state and local offices.

The main contribution of the **Federal Election Campaign Act** of 1971[7] was its inauguration of federal financing of presidential elections. The financing scheme runs like this: In the primaries the federal government will provide matching funds up to a certain limit to any candidate who raises a total of $5,000 in each of 20 states in amounts of $250 or less. In the general election, each party can receive a substantial amount of money—up to tens of millions of dollars adjustable for inflation each year. But to get this money, the party must agree not to receive or spend any other funds.

One intriguing aspect of the new law that ran into trouble was an attempt to limit the amount of money a candidate could contribute to his or her own campaign. It was one thing to limit what others could contribute, but quite another to limit what the candidate could spend. That part of the law was struck down as unconstitutional in 1976 by the United States Supreme Court in the case of *Buckley* v. *Valeo*.[8] Former United States senators James Buckley of New York and Eugene McCarthy of Minnesota, plus the Conservative party of New York and the New York Civil Liberties Union (an interesting combination of liberal and conservative plaintiffs), had brought suit alleging that the limitations Congress set on campaign expenditures, including those by the candidate, were an unconstitutional limitation of freedom of speech. The Court agreed that free speech involved the use of money to communicate. The Court did, however, uphold the limits on campaign spending by presidential candidates who accepted federal money to assist their campaign. The Court reasoned that no presidential candidate is forced to accept federal money, and that the federal government can make candidates promise not to use private financing as a condition of receiving the public financing.

State Laws Although *Buckley* v. *Valeo* concerned the constitutionality of a federal law (not a state law), the principles of the decision have been extended to state elections and affect the legality of state campaign-finance laws insofar as those laws affect freedom of speech. Today almost every state in the Union has a campaign-finance law. Most require some sort of reporting by campaign committees, political action committees, individuals and/or candidates. These statements are usually filed with the secretary of state and/or with the county clerk (or with the appropriate elections commission, if any exist). The statements are usually supposed to show campaign contributions and expenditures over a certain size. Many laws also attempt to limit the amount that may be contributed and spent.

There is considerable variation among states with regard to the specifics of their campaign-finance laws. For example, at last report Illinois required only

[7] 2 *U.S.C.* 431 et seq.
[8] 424 U.S. 1 (1976).

political committees to file, while Iowa required all candidates and committees receiving contributions or spending $250 or more to file. Illinois does not limit the size of contributions from corporations, labor unions, political action committees, regulated industries or political parties. The Iowa law is similar except that it prohibits contributions by corporations (including, specifically, insurance companies). Many states prohibit the assessment and/or solicitation of government employees, prohibit anonymous contributions, and prohibit the giving of contributions by one person in the name of another. Contributions by a candidate to his or her own campaign are unlimited in most states, and where limitations exist they are of doubtful constitutionality (because of the right of free speech and the press) except where they are preconditions a candidate must agree to in order to receive public funding.

TWO- AND ONE-PARTY STATES

States are often labeled **one-party states,** *modified one-party states* or *two-party states.* In some states, such as Georgia, one party regularly wins most of the elections and holds most public offices. In other states, such as New York and Pennsylvania, two strong parties compete vigorously and share the delights of victory and torments of defeat. Between the one-party and the two-party extremes, there are all shades of variation among the states.

Each of our 50 states has a political personality of its own, and the character of its parties is part of that personality. Among the states there is considerable variation in how people regard political parties, in how effective parties are as instruments for winning elections, and in how torn by factionalism parties are.

Where one party regularly wins most elections, there is a good deal of hand wringing (especially in the minority party) about the evils of a one-party system. But does it really make much difference whether a state has a one-party or a two-party system? Often it is claimed we don't need two parties because factionalism within the dominant party nicely takes its place: if you don't have competition between parties, you have it between the various cliques within the one top party. These **factions** become parties for all practical purposes.

Primary elections in one-party states are the central political drama; candidates from two or more wings of the party battle it out as if they were candidates of separate parties. The winner is considered elected even before the general election. In Georgia the Democratic party nominee for governor is called governor-elect as soon as he or she is nominated. Perhaps it can be argued that two parties are no better than one, as long as factions give voters a choice.

Still, there are those who say a faction isn't as good as a party: we get something from a party we don't get from a faction. A party, we are told, builds a record, and that record (for better or worse) sticks with the party, sometimes for generations. Parties may not be entirely responsible for what happens during their reign, but people hold parties responsible anyway, and this motivates parties to keep in mind that what they do might just be remembered a long time. Factions do not have the same permanency or the same concrete identity as parties. Factions may be temporary moths of the political summer. They flicker around issues, around personalities, and around momentary enthusiasms, and often live short and precarious lives. It's hard for voters to hold a faction responsible for anything. It's like trying to nail water to the wall. Nevertheless, in states such as Virginia, where factions last longer than usual, they are held responsible.

ELITES

Officeholders aren't the only people who determine what a government does. Of course, nothing happens without them. They are the gas pedal of government. But what foot pushes the pedal? Officeholders authorize whatever a government does—the building of a new street, for example—but who or what pushes them to think a new street should be built? Often the push comes from outside. Elected officeholders rarely act alone (nor do appointed officeholders). They are affected by the wants and desires of other persons; they are affected by influences, pressures, inducements, persuasions, motivations, biases, urgings and seductions of every sort. A legislator whose brother is employed by an architect may be powerfully influenced by the architect. A mayor may be influenced by a campaign contributor. A county commissioner may be influenced by the realtors' association that has a history of throwing lots of money around at election time. One cannot begin to list all the influences to which officeholders are susceptible, but it is a fact that public officials are influenced and could hardly stay in office if they were not. Being influenced is not always evil. After all, the whole idea of democracy is that officeholders will respond to the public. Hopefully, they will respond to influences arrayed on the side of "public good." Unfortunately, hardly any two persons can agree on what is a public good.

The Iron Law of Oligarchy

Some of the influences affecting officeholders lead us to wonder how democratic our democracy really is and whether officeholders are responsive to the many or to the few. Is government in America "of, by, and for" the many—or is it "of, by, and for" the few? Or is it sometimes one and sometimes the other? Or is it a mixture of the few and the many?

The **elite theory** is that all governments and in fact all organizations are run by the few. One analyst calls it the **iron law of oligarchy** rather than just a theory.[9] Wherever one looks—card clubs, fraternities, sororities, baseball teams, political parties, churches, labor unions, families, legislatures, appellate courts, universities, faculty senates, trade associations, conventions, cities, nations—the few, not the many, are in charge. Wherever there may be a facade of equality there is the reality of inequality—a tiny oligarchy of influential persons runs every organization. No matter how democratic the organization in its formal procedures, no matter how legally equal every member may be, no matter if one-man-one-vote is the law, no matter if praises to equality are sung at every gathering, rule by the few always and everywhere prevails. Political science comes close to being an exact science when it postulates the iron law of oligarchy. As a law of human behavior, the law of oligarchy is perhaps as certain and fixed as the law of gravitation.

[9]Robert Michels, *Political Parties* (Glencoe, Ill.: Free Press, 1949).

Who Are the Leaders?

When one says the few always rule, one is not necessarily saying anything about the character of those few or about how a person gets to be one of them. All that is quite another story. Oligarchies may be open, or they may be relatively closed. The titled aristocracies of Europe were closed. The American "aristocracy" is relatively open; the oligarchies of most organizations are more or less open. Leadership in a party is constantly changing, shifting, restructuring, rearranging, reshaping, as is leadership in most American organizations.

Party leadership often goes to those who have an active interest in the organization, who have the time to involve themselves, who have social and verbal skills, and who have energy and other resources to invest. In our society there is generally room at the top for those who have the will and the resources to reach the top.

Furthermore, individuals may be leaders in one organization and followers in another. Whether one is a party leader depends on the situation: the qualities possessed by each individual make him or her more likely to lead in some situations and in some types of organization than in others. Adolf Hitler's peculiar talents suited him more for leadership of a particular political party at a particular stage of history in a particular nation. Whether he would have been equally successful as youth director of a YMCA is doubtful. Hitler never exceeded the rank of private first class in the German Army during World War I, even after four years of service. That milieu, that situation, that combination of circumstances was not fertile for his leadership talents, although he apparently enjoyed the war. Likewise with each of us. Whether we are a leader in a given situation depends on whether that situation is fertile for our particular talents. Never is the same person suited for leadership in all organizations and in all situations.

A Divided Oligarchy

No single oligarchy monopolizes power. Numerous organizations and numerous sets of leaders attempt to influence public policy. The leadership of all organizations shifts and changes. As issues change, so does the primacy of one set of organizations and leaders versus others. Always and everywhere there is some sort of leadership, some sort of oligarchy, in control. The mass never leads.

Seldom does the oligarchy within any society agree on all issues. The oligarchy of a city—that is, the total collection of persons exercising leadership with regard to a particular issue at a particular time—is usually divided. Elite theory does not claim that all leaders are arrayed in one phalanx against a common enemy. Of course, alliances among leaders and among groups obviously exist at times, but warfare among them is just as common. It is said that competition among elites keeps us free from the tyranny of any single elite. This view is known as the *theory of countervailing power*—when organized labor walks up the steps of the capitol, for example, so does organized management.

Are Elites Antidemocratic?

Elite theory does not argue that all elites are joined together in one giant self-seeking conspiracy against the masses. First, elites are apt to be caught up in a general civil war among themselves. Second, elites are often public-spirited—

partly because most (or at least many) elites are just plain, ordinary people who because of their special interests and special energies have become leaders of various causes and organizations. They are not conspiring against the public, at least not consciously, as a general rule. In their self-image they are part of the public. Third, by education and by immersion in American democratic culture, most American elites, whether rich or poor, whether high or low in social status, are habitually public-spirited because they believe it's part of being American.

Elite theory does not assert, either, that elites are icy, remote, and unresponsive to public opinion. Honest elections and a free press help keep elites sensitive to public opinion.

Elite theory is not an antidemocratic theory but rather a theory about how democracy really works. It pictures American democracy as a competition among elites. The masses play a role in this competition much as fans in the stadium play a role in baseball games by rooting for this or that team. In politics, however, the fans do more than root—they also vote.

Political scientists debate about which elites are the most influential in community politics. To find out who really runs our cities, towns, and states, several authors[10] have tried to dissect the politics of certain communities, probing into how decisions are made, looking to see who is responsible for what, who defers to whom, who has leverage over whom, and what interactions among people and forces result in governmental decisions. In fact, a belief is now prevalent among political scientists that if you want to know what makes an organization tick, if you want to find out who plays what role in an organization, the way to do it is to trace the history of a recent decision, or of several recent decisions, and identify all the actors on stage as they played their role leading up to that decision.[11] This procedure has been elevated to the status of theory—*decision-making theory*—and is used for analyzing who has how much power and how that power is exercised and applied. A defect of decision-making theory is that different issues call forth different leaders, and it is therefore difficult to isolate the leaders of a community, except in relation to particular issues.

Those who play a decisive role in the decision-making process are called the *elite structure* of the organization. Cities, counties, states, and nations have elite structure that can be identified. Some of these elites influence decision making by virtue of their official positions, others do so by influencing those who have official positions and by influencing the process by which public officials are elected or appointed. Officeholders themselves are part of the elite.

In their attempt to find out which elites are most influential in city politics, political scientists have found cities in which one tiny elite representing one dominant special interest (perhaps the managers of an industry in a one-industry town) controls the town without any significant competition from other elites: Anaconda, Montana. Other towns are bipolar (dominated by two central and competing interests)—for example, a one-industry town in which that industry is strongly unionized: Dearborn, Michigan. Union and management may compete for power or strike a bargain. A third variation is the town with a diversified economy and a multiplicity of special interests, one of which is somewhat ascendant over the others but not clearly dominant: Pontiac, Michigan.

[10]Including Floyd Hunter, *Community Power Structure* (Chapel Hill: University of North Carolina Press, 1953); and Robert Dahl, *Who Governs?* (New Haven: Yale University Press, 1961).

[11]Herbert A. Simon, *Administrative Behavior* (New York: Macmillan, 1957).

Finally, a fourth variation is a town with a diversified economy in which many special economic interests as well as noneconomic interests and miscellaneous personages exercise influence, no one of which is clearly dominant within the city: Los Angeles.

The same variations in elite structure exist within states, some being essentially one-industry, one-elite states, and so on.

In states where a few economic interests predominate, such as the power, timber, and manufacturing interests in Maine, groups representing those interests tower over other groups in state politics. Similarly, copper interests in Montana, oil interests in Texas, and coal interests in West Virginia are reputed to be leaders among pressure groups in the politics of those states. In some states, such as Michigan, the leading interest groups (automobile manufacturing and organized labor) sharply compete for power. In other states, such as California, where the economy is highly diversified, it is hard to identify any single interest group that leads the others in influence.

Do Economic Elites Rule?

Yes, They Do A good deal of discussion is heard about the influence of business notables in community politics. Some observers[12] think the managers of major businesses constitute a community superelite that directs the government from behind the scenes. Is prostitution to be curbed? Is fire protection to be increased? Is a major street to be widened? Is a municipal auditorium to be built? Is a downtown mall to be constructed? Is the city to annex new territory? Is urban renewal desirable? All these kinds of questions—according to one view—are decided by the economic elite of the city; all other elites take their cue from the business elite.

Certainly it is true that the **economic elites** of a town are equipped to make themselves heard. Campaigns are expensive, and they have money. Few candidates for state and local office are members of the economic elite, and so they must rely on gifts to mount campaigns for election and reelection. Occasionally a wealthy person will run for state or local office, but most members of the economic elite are too busy to hold public office. Furthermore, the economic elite may consider public office beneath its station in life. Perhaps being governor squares with its self-image, but being a state legislator, or county commissioner, or city-council member, or even mayor is questionable except as amusement to fill one's retirement years. Of course, the economic elite does not have quite this same lofty attitude about federal elective offices—president, vice-president, or United States senator—or about cabinet appointments. Economic elites usually prefer, however, to control public affairs indirectly, insofar as possible.

Besides campaign contributions the economic elite of a state or community may influence officeholders by being their employer or by being the employer of their friends and relatives. This packs a wallop in small, one-industry towns. Even if officeholders and their friends and relatives do not work for that one industry, they are apt to work for some other employer who is more or less under its economic sway. Also, the economic elite—some of its members, at any rate—have control of business firms that could upon sufficient aggravation,

---

[12]For example, Hunter, *Community Power Structure.*

decide to move out of town. Threats to move can disturb lots of people who might lose their jobs or might have to start paying higher taxes if the firm moved. These threats can bring tremendous pressure on community officials and even on state officials.

Economic elites have other avenues of influence besides money. These other avenues are, admittedly, tied in some way to their wealth and economic power. A good example is their prestige. Our word *prestige* stems from Latin and French words that meant "illusion." Prestige is an illusion that someone has all sorts of qualities he or she doesn't really have. That illusion produces a feeling of subservience and awe in others. Prestigious people are listened to (even if they should happen to be a little muddled). They have no trouble getting an appointment to see the mayor or a state legislator or a city-council member. A public official is normally quite pleased to be seen in company with prestigious persons, is eager to associate with them, and hears their ideas sympathetically and attentively. John Q. and Mary Citizen and their ideas don't usually fare so splendidly.

In the routine course of business, economic elites will become acquainted with many community officials, thus opening more channels for the flow of ideas and influence into capitols, courthouses, and city halls. The personal touch helps and is made all the more effective by the social and verbal skills of many elites. Elites work with ideas more than ordinary people, are practiced in the expression of ideas, and schooled in the fine art of getting to know the right people and stroking them the right way.

No, They Don't There are many reasons to believe that economic elites run community and state affairs, yet there are also reasons to believe that they don't do so as completely as some people like to think. Economic elites are not the only elites. There are leaders whose leadership does not stem from wealth. As a matter of fact, most leaders in most communities may be people who become leaders chiefly because of their interest, enthusiasm, drive, ambition, and activity within groups that especially interest them. Also, the economic elite is not necessarily interested in every issue. Each separate issue calls forth its separate elite—calls forth the exertion of people interested in that issue, who may or may not be economic elites. A separate community elite exists for each issue—not one elite for all issues, although there is, of course, some overlap. The parent-teachers association and its elite may be more influential than any combination of wealthy persons in deciding whether there ought to be a special education program for exceptionally talented students. The issue of whether police officers ought to be allowed to bargain collectively with the city calls forth another elite—activists in the police protective association and leaders of employees' unions. In other words, power in communities (as in states and nations) is pluralistic: there is a separate elite for each issue, and those issue-elites may, or may not, be dominated by wealthy people.

An array of reasons explain why economic elites often prefer to stay out of community affairs. Strange as it may seem, community involvement is often too costly for the wealthy, not in money but in time and energy. To be effective in community affairs one has to plunge in with both feet, spend countless hours at meetings, and devote mental, physical, and psychic energy to the matter. Economic elites are usually too busy applying their energies to the firm. They are interested in their own progress in the firm and in their career and cannot be distracted by attention to community affairs. Furthermore, involvement in community affairs often means involvement in controversy, and it's often poor public relations for business firms (or their executives) to be taking sides in community battles. Therefore, many persons within the economic elite are stingy with their time when it comes to community involvement. This leaves the field open to other elites.

Even when economic elites do jump into community battles, they don't all jump onto the same side of every issue. By no means. In fact, their various economic interests clash as often as they mesh. Practically every single thing done by government benefits some business interests and harms others—affects different interests differently. One classic difference of opinion among business leaders is between downtown commercial interests and suburban commercial interests. Should the city spend tax money to make it easier for people to shop downtown—spend on freeways leading downtown—or should it focus on shopping-mall crime prevention? Hardly anything government does meets the universal approval of economic leaders. The economic elite often cancels itself out by taking opposite sides on issues. This therefore elevates the importance of other elites.

Finally, some economic elites don't really feel a very strong attachment to the community in which they live. This is sometimes true of executives in national firms. They are not owners, but high-level employees. They do not have the same vital concern for community affairs that the owner of a local business might have. New taxes on business do not have the same personal impact on a branch manager as on the proprietor of a local firm. Furthermore, executives of national firms tend to be somewhat nomadic, moving from branch office to branch office, never staying in one community very long. They may not even live in the city where their branch office does business. Their emotional involvement with the community is dampened by the gypsy character of their sojourn. For these and other reasons, the impact of economic elites on state and community politics may be much less than commonly thought.

PRESSURE GROUPS

Is there a difference between a political party and a **pressure group?** A party is an organization whose alleged immediate and exclusive purpose is to elect candidates to public office. Pressure groups, by contrast, are not mechanisms for staffing the elective offices of government. Rather than directly running candidates for office, they try to influence elections and officeholders. Another difference is that political parties want to manage the whole government across the total scope of public affairs. Pressure groups, on the other hand, are not usually interested in trying to run the whole government; they usually aim to influence government policies in a few matters of special interest to themselves.

Of course, these differences between pressure groups and parties are all a matter of degree: some pressure groups, such as Common Cause, also have a broad (rather than a narrow) range of interest; some do in effect run candidates for office, do conduct campaigns, and are in fact political parties in disguise. Likewise, some parties are so narrow in their interest, and so unlikely to win any office, that their whole stance as political parties is a masquerade: they are really pressure groups. This is true of a number of hopelessly small, narrow third parties, such as the Prohibition party. (They want to prohibit liquor.)

Box 5-2. Jimmy Carter on Special Interest Groups

"Today, as people have become more doubtful of the ability of the government to deal with our problems, we are increasingly drawn to single issue groups and special interest organizations to insure that whatever else happens our own personal views and our own private interests are protected. This is a disturbing factor in American political life. It tends to distort our purposes."

President Jimmy Carter
Farewell Address
January 14, 1981

Groups are usually more powerful than individuals in our political system, but every group, of course, is led by a few individuals. Influential individuals usually have something backing them up, quite often organized groups. Groups, and the leaders of groups, play such an important role in American politics that they are often discussed in basic American-government textbooks in the same chapter with political parties. Government officials pay attention to groups because groups have votes, money, political savvy, and the organizational strength to mobilize their resources.

The influence of a group dpends, of course, on how big and how united it is. Size alone is not decisive. A big group may be composed of people with such diverse points of view that it cannot bring itself to take united and forceful stands. A case in point may be the United States Chamber of Commerce. This group purports to speak for "business," but business is not at all united. What is good for one commercial interest may not be good for another—what is good for trucks may be bad for railroads. A giant conglomerate may be a lot less effective than a small united interest group, such as the National Federation of the Blind, the Disabled American Veterans, the Sierra Club, or the United Mine Workers Union.

Interests groups would be stronger if every individual belonged to only one of them. Most of us, however, belong to all sorts of groups. We divide our loyalties, and this further weakens the ability of any single group to fully mobilize its members. If you belong to the Cut Taxes League and to the Friends of the Library, and the Library wants higher taxes to buy books, you soon find you can't be on both sides.

Leaders of groups do not always reflect the attitude of the membership with absolute fidelity. Once in control of the group, leaders become something of a law unto themselves. Most public officials learn to take with a grain of salt the threats and declarations of those who purport to speak for groups.

ETHNIC POLITICS

America is said to be the "melting pot" where nationalities stop thinking of themselves as separate and blend one with another into a completely new community of people, happy in each others' company.

This cheerful picture is somewhat illusory—as is obvious to anyone who takes a drive through any large American city. Ethnic neighborhoods with razor-sharp boundaries are plain to see: white, black, Asian, Hispanic, and so on. Even the individual nationalities within broad ethnic groups hesitate to mix. Among

Asians there is a good deal of separateness between Chinese, Japanese, Vietnamese, and Koreans. On the other hand, fusion of nationalities occurs among whites—and yet in the larger cities one can readily find separate white nationality neighborhoods, Italian, Russian, Polish, Greek, and all the rest.

Voting statistics also show that we have a good deal further to go before everything in the melting pot has dissolved into a new American race. As Mayor Edward I. Koch of New York City wrote in the chapter on ethnic politics in his book *Politics*,[13] "A lot of people like to talk about the melting pot. It's all bull___. There is ethnic politics in this country, and in this city in particular, and it's okay. More Jews will vote for me than for an ordinary non-Jewish candidate."

Voting statistics in New York City show that Puerto Ricans tend to vote for Puerto Ricans, Italians for Italians, blacks for blacks, Jews for Jews, and so forth. This is born out by voting records in numerous other cities. For example, when Harold Washington, Chicago's black mayor, won reelection to a second four-year term in 1987, he had nearly unanimous black support, 97%, and only 15% support among whites. Likewise Edward R. Vrdolyck, Mayor Washington's Republican white opponent got 74% of the white votes. (Incidentally, Hispanic voters were by no means unanimous for the black mayor, but gave him 57% of their vote.)

The extent of ethnic voting at any given time or place depends no doubt upon many imponderables. Some candidates may arouse less race consciousness than others. Denver, Colorado, has a two-term Hispanic mayor even though Denver's Hispanic population is only about 18%. Most of the people who voted to elect Mayor Federico Peña over his non-Hispanic white Republican opponent were non-Hispanic. The election seemed more partisan[14] than racial, and almost nothing was said about ethnicity in the election. Peña made no ethnic appeals, and his first term apparently had not been ethnically biased to any remarkable degree. Peña himself possesses almost no outward personal characteristic that would distinguish him from Denver's Anglo majority other than his name, which, if it were Smith, Schultz, or Polanski, would seem just as plausible. Nevertheless, Peña's ethnic origins were certainly no secret, and a vast majority of Denver's Hispanic voters gave him their support, but they were not alone. Party affiliation may have been the pivotal force in Denver, yet elsewhere ethnicity has very often been among the most important catalysts.

Ethnic solidarity has its limits.[15] Social class, religion, and other forms of group identification sometimes exert more pull on voters than race. And occasionally ethnic groups are so politically divided that candidates of another race seem preferable to those of hostile factions.

LOBBYING

Lobbying is the process of trying to influence power holders. Sometimes lobbying is so sophisticated that nobody knows it's happening. Many techniques of lobbying are used. Wining and dining the target may not be the most efficient

---

[13]Edward I. Koch, *Politics* (New York: Warner Books, 1985), p. 213.

[14]Denver elections are nonpartisan, but the party affiliations of candidates were well known: Peña, Democrat.

[15]See Byran O. Jackson, "The Effects of Racial Group Consciousness on Political Mobilization in American Cities," *The Western Political Quarterly* (December 1987), pp. 631–646.

technique, but legislators and powerful administrators are human and are apt to do favors for people who show them some kindness. A great deal of lobbying, however, is in the form of education—education of the general public (propaganda) and education of power holders themselves. In the long run, this may be the most effective kind of lobbying.

All public officials in a democracy such as ours are influenced by public opinion—obviously legislators are. One of the best ways to influence public officials is to influence the public. Some special interest groups spend enormous amounts of money to convince the public of the rightness or wrongness of a particular course of action. The American Medical Association may, for example, consider it valuable to educate the general public on a certain plan for government-sponsored medical insurance. Interest groups also invest enormous amounts of time and money on the special education of particular officeholders. Most officials genuinely want to do what's right and welcome instruction from those most concerned with an issue, and once they have decided to support a certain course of action they want to be able to defend their decisions with facts. Facts are often supplied with great skill and thoroughness by special interest groups.

Regulation of Lobbying

Many states attempt to regulate lobbying to some extent by requiring lobbyists who contact legislators to register with the clerk of the house or secretary of the senate and to reveal whom they represent and how much money they spend in the effort. These laws are difficult to enforce, however, because the word *lobbying* is hard to define and the activity itself is difficult to distinguish from the efforts of individual citizens to communicate with legislators. The constitutional rights of freedom of speech and freedom of assembly render all lobby regulation somewhat toothless. Some organizations do not think what they are doing is lobbying; they say they are simply trying to "educate" legislators.

POLITICAL CORRUPTION

Bribery

On January 22, 1987, R. Budd Dwyer, Pennsylvania state treasurer, called a news conference in Harrisburg. As the television cameras rolled, he pulled a pistol, put it to his mouth, and pulled the trigger. He was scheduled to be sentenced the following day for awarding a $4.6 million contract to a computer firm in return for a $300,000 bribe.

In 1986 Donald R. Manes committed suicide by stabbing himself in the chest. He was an influential New York City political boss who had been forced to resign his post as president of the borough of Queens because of allegations of corruption. Apparently he was involved in an extortion scheme in which companies had been forced to make payoffs in return for getting contracts with the city for the parking ticket collection business.

Seldom do the recipients of bribes see fit to stab or shoot themselves. More often they go happily to the bank with their earnings.

How Common? Although the vast majority of American public officials are perfectly fine and honest citizens, political corruption nevertheless prowls the backstairs of all government. Possibly 99 percent of all political corruption is never uncovered. The cases we hear about—the indictments, convictions, and scandals—only hint at its true dimensions. In emphasizing the disease, we do not want to forget the great mainstream of people in government who are ethical and honorable, nor forget the countless local elected officials who practically donate their time to public service.

But a few cannot resist the allure of easy money—sometimes more money than they ever dreamed of having. And all they have to do is make a few "right" decisions. Even small bribes are attractive. One can easily imagine, say, a county purchasing agent, who in most matters is altogether trustworthy, but who thinks it would only be natural to receive a gift of several hundred dollars from a company that sells road graders to the county. Anyone in government who has power to give or withhold something is the possible target of a bribe.

News about Bribes Most news stories about bribe taking involve business deals of considerable sweep where thousands or millions of dollars might hinge on letting a government contract or issuing a license. Recently a deputy mayor of Washington, D.C., resigned from office after disclosure that he had accepted $3000 from an auditing firm doing business with the city. A party leader in Bronx County, New York, was indicted for bribery for his role in obtaining a $22 million city contract for a certain company. Not long ago in California the biggest political corruption scandal in 30 years was uncovered, which touched a number of city and county officials in Southern California. And recently in Louisiana there was a celebrated case involving charges that bribes were paid to assure successful pardon applications. The speaker pro tem of the Louisiana House of Representatives and the chairman of the state pardon board were indicted. The alleged bribes ranged from $15,000 to $130,000. These big cases that hit the front pages should not obscure the many small bribes that no one discovers or chooses to prosecute.

Modus Operandi A bribe can be given in many simple or sophisticated ways. Cash payment straight from giver to taker is probably the most primitive method. Cash generally leaves no trail and is good for both large and small transactions, although there are miscellaneous risks.

Bribes may be paid in a number of roundabout ways. One of the most convenient ways to "buy" an elected public official is to make contributions to his or her campaign chest. Laws restricting the sources and uses of campaign funds are wobbly at best.

Also, nearly any legitimate business can be used to hide a bribe. For example, bribe payments to realtors who are public officials involves letting them sell a piece of property and collect the commission. Or in the case of a lawyer-officeholder, retaining him or her for legal counsel is the way bribery can be hidden. Honorariums for giving speeches to clubs, businesses, and associations may, of course, be used as a form of bribe, as can consulting fees: anybody can be a "consultant." Again, we emphasize that this kind of thing is the exception, not the rule, among America's body of public officials.

Some bribery is so smooth that the target hardly knows he or she is being bribed. There is even such a thing as emotional bribery where one gives honor, comradeship, flattery, acclaim, applause, cheer, or anything psychological. Emotional bribery appears to be perfectly legal in any quantity no matter how given as long as there is no commercial transaction.

Culture and Bribery   In some foreign cultures, offering money to public officials is the normal way to get their attention. Rarely in those nations does any official do anything without payola. Every government service is bought and sold, even the offices themselves. It is not necessary to pay public officials any significant salary in some parts of the world because everything they do in office is sold for a price, and that's how they get paid. Everybody understands this. Prosecutors seldom prosecute it.

Bribery is certainly not routine practice in the United States. Most bureaucrats and elected officials in this country would be offended by any attempt to bribe them. However, a malignant subculture of political corruption does thrive in some places. Once a state or local political ring is infected, the disease runs its course. New York City had a long siege of it. For generations political corruption seemed to be a way of life with Tammany Hall (the dominant political organization). The word "Tammany" became virtually synonymous with corruption. In recent years the city seems to have cleansed itself considerably, yet total cleansing may be an impossible dream anywhere.

Investigating Corruption   The Federal Bureau of Investigation (FBI) has been very active in probing state and local corruption. This is particularly helpful for several reasons. First, it is not unusual for state and local bribery to involve activities that span state lines. Second, the FBI is better equipped to carry on clandestine investigations than most state and local bureaus. Thirdly, state and/or local law enforcement people may not have the courage to tackle crooked officials in their midst, and police and prosecutors themselves may be part of the crooked ring they are supposed to investigate.

Sting Operations and Entrapment   One approach to gathering evidence of bribery is to set up sting operations—offer bribes and see whether they are taken. An elaborate sting operation by the FBI made headlines in the Abscam cases a few years ago and resulted in the conviction of a New Jersey United States Senator and others. At that time the FBI was both applauded and condemned for its use of stings. Stings may be effective, but do they constitute entrapment? (Entrapment means inducing somebody to commit a crime he or she was not otherwise disposed to commit. Motivating people to do something they were disposed to do anyway does not constitute entrapement.) The debate continues. Meanwhile sting operations are used with spectacular success in hundreds of cases.

The Justice Department has issued guidelines under which the FBI may authorize undercover agents to offer bribes to public officials. No such undercover operation is to be approved without the specific written authorization of the director of the FBI and unless the undercover operations review committee of the Justice Department has reason to believe that the individual involved is engaging, has engaged, or is likely to engage in illegal activity or has found that the individual was predisposed to commit a crime.

In 1987 the FBI completed a sting operation that swept from New York to the Canadian border. Agents offered 106 bribes to public officials—105 were accepted. (One was refused because the bribe was too small.) The targeted officials—mostly local municipal purchasing agents and highway superintendents—were individuals previously fingered by FBI informants as corrupt. Thus the FBI was able to say that it had reason to believe the individuals were predisposed to commit the crime for which they were "stung".

Election Fraud

Massive vote fraud was reported in the Philippines during the last presidential election held under the regime of Ferdinand E. Marcos. Various world press reporters were on hand to cover the event. Our own American election system seemed squeaky clean by comparison. But one news commentator said Marcos could still learn a few lessons in vote fraud from Chicago.

Admittedly Chicago does often make news. Massive vote fraud is alleged to have occurred in a recent Chicago mayoral primary according to reviews conducted by Election Watch 87, a citizens' watchdog group headed by a former United States attorney. Election Watch 87 said that at least 50,000 people were allowed to illegally cast ballots. Some voters claimed nonexistent addresses, and some voted in the name of dead people. The basic validity of Mayor Harold Washington's 78,000-vote victory was not in doubt. However, dozens of key aldermanic contests had been decided by close margins.

About the same time, a federal grand jury in Indiana indicted several local party officials for paying between $15 and $35 to voters to vote a straight party ticket in that state.

Prosecutions of vote fraud occur most often where the magnitude of the crime and the political stakes at issue justify a court case. On the whole, American election administration is surrounded by all sorts of safeguards (discussed elsewhere), and these generally produce clean elections in most precincts. Yet there are some notable exceptions.

SUMMARY

A political party is an organization whose alleged immediate and exclusive purpose is to elect candidates affiliated with it to public office. Pressure groups are not normally interested in trying to staff the whole government; they usually want to influence officials and policies in a rather narrow range of matters of special interest to their members.

Basically we are, and always have been, a two-party country. Most other democracies in the world are multiparty countries. Why does the United States have a two-party rather than a multiparty system? Many political scientists think it is mainly the result of our election system: the single-member-district, winner-take-all system. Likewise the multiple-party phenomenon in other parts of the world could be explained mainly by the mechanics of their electoral systems, many of which are characterized by multiple-member districts and proportional representation. In our single-member, winner-take-all system, there can be no second prize, nor a third, fourth, or fifth prize—hence it is difficult for third parties to survive as serious parties. Most American third parties are more like interest groups than parties. By comparison with the ideological parties of Europe, America's Republican and Democratic parties are about as ideological as professional football teams. Since second best is no good, each party is willing to play any winning idea for the same reason football teams are willing to play any winning strategy. Our two major parties are not exactly alike ideologically, but they have more similarities than differences.

America does not have disciplined parties of the European variety. The leadership of American parties does not have the same degree of influence over party nominations that European party leaders have. Nor are American parties of much help in campaigning. Elected officeholders in the United States rarely owe much to their party except the party label. Each candidate gets the nomination largely through his or her own effort and has to mobilize his or her own campaign organization in order to get elected.

At one time party leaders had more to say about nominations than they do today. Nominations were once the work of party conventions. The convention system became corrupt, and nominations are now mostly the work of primary elections in which the rank and file of the party pick nominees. The convention system survives as the method for picking presidential nominees, although it is being weakened by presidential primaries preceding the convention.

So informal are American parties that no one can tell with absolute certainty what one has to do to become a member of the party, although one's party declaration at registration is often accepted as the ultimate proof.

So thoroughly regulated is the structure and procedure of American political parties by state law that one could almost say we have no parties at all in the European sense, but simply quasi-state agencies that, like highways, serve to channel political traffic within the states.

The basic structure of our two major parties is designed after the political design of the nation: there is the national organization; there are state organizations, district organizations, county organizations, city organizations. Within urban areas there are ward and precinct organizations.

Campaigns are very expensive. Candidates who have to buy their way into office through expensive campaigns, and who do this with other people's money, are going to owe a big debt of gratitude to those people.

Over the years, attempts have been made by national and state governments to compel candidates to disclose the source of their campaign money and how it was spent. Attempts have also been made to limit the amounts received and spent by candidates. Before 1971 these laws were not very effective. The Federal Election Campaign Act of 1971 revamped them and set up a system for federal funding of presidential elections. Every state in the Union also has a campaign-finance law.

States are one-party states, modified one-party states, two-party states, or somewhere in between. Often it is claimed we don't need two parties because if there is only one party, factionalism within that one party nicely takes the place of a second party. If you don't have competition between parties, you have it between factions. A faction does not build a record quite the same way that a regular party does, however, and a faction is not held responsible for its record quite like a party is.

Parties and officeholders aren't the only people who determine public policy. They are affected by the wants of other persons. Some influences affecting officeholders lead us to wonder how democratic our democracy really is, and whether officeholders respond to the many or to the few. According to elite theory, all governments and all organizations are run by the few, even governments and organizations that claim to be democratic. This "iron law of oligarchy" does not mean that the same few are running all organizations or influencing all public policies. Different sets of influential persons come forward to play their role as different sets of issues surface. Furthermore, the oligarchy of most American organizations is relatively open to newcomers and is constantly changing. Elite theory is not an antidemocratic theory, but rather a theory about how democracy really works. Political scientists argue about which elites are the most influential in community politics, and there is a good deal of discussion about whether business notables exercise more influence than other elites in community policy making.

Groups are usually more powerful than individuals in our political system. The influence of a group depends on how big it is and how united. Size alone is not decisive. A big group can be composed of people with such diverse points of view that it cannot take united and forceful stands.

The United States is said to be a great melting pot. Nevertheless ethnic politics occurs. Voting statistics show that ethnicity influences voting.

Lobbying is the process of trying to influence power holders. "Education" of the public and of individual power holders by interest groups may be the most effective lobbying technique.

Political corruption is not routine in the United States, but it is not exactly rare either. Anyone in government who has power to give or withhold something is the natural target of a bribe. Bribes are paid in a number of roundabout ways. The big cases that hit the front pages should not obscure the many small bribes that no one discovers or chooses to prosecute. On the whole, American elections are clean, but election fraud does in fact occur from time to time, as do prosecutions for vote fraud.

SUGGESTIONS FOR FURTHER READING

ALEXANDER, HERBERT E., *Financing Politics* (2nd ed.). Washington, D.C.: Congressional Quarterly Press, 1984.

BIBBY, JOHN, CORNELIUS COTTER, JAMES GIBSON, and ROBERT HUCKSHORN, "Parties in State Politics." in *Politics in the American States* (4th ed.), ed. Virginia Gray, Herbert Jacob, and Kenneth Vines, 59–96. Boston: Little, Brown, 1983.

COMMITTEE ON POLITICAL PARTIES OF THE AMERICAN POLITICAL SCIENCE ASSOCIATION, *Toward a More Responsible Two-Party System*. New York: Holt, Rinehart & Winston, 1950.

DYE, THOMAS R., and L. HARMON ZEIGLER, *The Irony of Democracy: An Uncommon Introduction to American Politics* (6th ed.). Monterey, Calif.: Brooks/Cole, 1986.

GOODMAN, WILLIAM, *The Party System in America*. Englewood Cliffs, N.J.: Prentice-Hall, 1980.

HAWLEY, WILLIS D., *Non-Partisan Elections and the Case for Party Politics*. New York: John Wiley, 1973.

HREBENAR, RONALD J., and RUTH K. SCOTT, *Interest Group Politics in America*. Englewood Cliffs, N.J.: Prentice-Hall, 1982.

JEWELL, MALCOLM E., and DAVID M. OLSON, *Political Parties and Elections in American States*. Chicago, Ill.: Dorsey, 1988.

KAYDEN, XANDRA, *Campaign Organization*. Lexington, Mass.: Heath, 1978.

KIRKPATRICK, JEANE JORDAN, *Dismantling the Parties: Reflections on Party Reform and Party Decomposition.* Washington, D.C.: American Enterprise Institute for Public Policy Research, 1978.

SABATO, LARRY, *The Rise of Political Consultants: New Ways of Winning Elections.* New York: Basic Books, 1983.

STILLMAN, RICHARD J., II, "Campaign Management in Transition or 'The Party's Over,'" *Public Administration Review* (January/February 1978), 93–97.

6
the governor

PREVIEW

JOYS AND SORROWS OF BEING GOVERNOR

I had the gall to ask a governor who happened to be a friend of mine whether it was fun being governor. That was after our second coke, and he almost shouted, "Heck yes, it's fun. But . . . on the other hand. . . ."

"On the other hand?" I prodded.

"On the other hand, I'm not running for a second term."

That was a bombshell he hadn't even released to the press yet. It took me totally by surprise.

"Why not?" I asked in disbelief. "You're the most popular governor in twenty years."

"No Bob, I've had enough. It's fun—in a way—being governor, but just between you and me, I can hardly wait for my successor to take the oath. Being governor isn't all fun. The part that isn't fun is getting to me."

"Is this a devious way of saying you're running for the United States Senate?"

"Absolutely not. I'm through with races and campaigns. And I'm not going to take an ambassadorship or a cabinet post. To be perfectly honest, I'm going back to Gem City and settle down to a normal life. I'm going to pick up the pieces of my law practice."

I had a doubting look on my face. I simply couldn't fathom this planned jump to obscurity.

"Look," he said earnestly. "I've got a twelve-year-old son and a fourteen-year-old daughter and a wife. I like to spend time with them. I really like my family. Also, I like mowing the lawn, keeping the garden, making candlesticks on my lathe, and sitting on the porch. The press reporters say I'm a hardworking governor. And I am. My professors in college said I was a hardworking student. And I was—made Phi Beta Kappa. I can work, but at heart I'm a lazy dog. Being governor is a day-and-night job. Talk about a rat race! This is it. I'm not going to make a career of it."

"Being a good lawyer in Gem City is a rat race, too," I ventured.

"Yes, but not like this one. You have no idea how driven a governor really is. It's almost a twenty-four-hour-a-day job. I have to fight for every spare minute. If my family wants to go on a picnic Sunday afternoon, it may mean I have to cancel my previously scheduled appearance at a highway ribbon cutting, or it may mean I have to cancel a television interview, or a speech, or a visit to the Boy Scout jamboree. I can't just up and do what I please on Sunday afternoon, or any other afternoon, or any time of day or night without canceling something. Governors are scheduled. When the schedule is violated, all sorts of people feel hurt and disappointed. I literally have to make an appointment to play baseball with my son or take my wife to lunch."[1]

"Sounds like you may have something else you should be doing right now besides fooling away time with me," I said a little sheepishly.

"To be perfectly honest, I really shouldn't be sitting here. Right at this moment," the governor said, looking at his watch, "my federal relations aide is cursing a blue streak because he's been waiting three days for an appointment with me—some kind of trouble we're having with the environmental protection agency about strip mining—and I'm missing the appointment. If I get back to the capital by three p.m. there'll be three state senators waiting to bawl me out for vetoing an appropriation for the State Tuberculosis Hospital. The hospital hasn't got any TB patients—the cure, you know, was found thirty years ago—but they still want money to keep forty employees on the payroll."

"Great balls of fire! I feel guilty keeping you here."

"Weg mit der Hunde!" the governor said, recalling the favorite expression of our German professor long ago when we were sophomores. "Let's get another drink." We did. And after that we had a leisurely steak supper. He didn't get back to the capitol until seven p.m. In one afternoon he had dashed the hopes of some thirteen people who waited in vain for their cherished appointments with his excellency. From the capitol he sped across town for a speech to one thousand members of the labor federation about the significance of Labor Day.

GOVERNORSHIP AS AN INSTITUTION

Overworked governors are sometimes asked, "Can't your staff take some of the load off your back?"

Certainly being governor of an average middle-sized state might be easier if a governor had a bigger personal staff. The governor of such a state may

---

[1]One survey found that former governors felt interference with their family life was the most difficult aspect of serving as governor. See Thad L. Beyle, "Governors' Views on Being Governor," *State Government* (Summer 1979), pp. 103–9. Note other aspects of the job of governor included in Beyle's survey.

have a staff of around 40—minuscule by comparison with the president's staff of some 500 White House aides grouped into agencies that take almost total charge of certain problem areas. When a **governor's staff** is small, this forces him or her to eventually get involved with practically everything the staff is doing. Perhaps governors of big states such as New York or California are not as overwhelmed as their counterparts in smaller states.[2] Big states can afford a more lavish governorship, an institutionalized governorship. Governors of these states, like the president, have entire agencies doing jobs that most other governors can't spare more than one or two aides for. The average governor, for example, may have only one or two intergovernmental-relations aides, whereas a big-state governor might have an entire bureau to deal with such matters. The bureau solves the problems, communicates with interested parties, and leaves the governor more or less out of it until some final stage when he or she might simply have to choose among several well-thought-out alternatives. In that respect, big-state governors have it easier than governors of small or middle-sized states. On average the governors of states with a small population will have personal staffs ranging from 10 to 25. The governors of Texas and New York have over 200. In other states it is not unusual to find staffs of 50 to 70.

SOME ADVICE FOR NEW GOVERNORS

What advice might a former governor give a new governor? Former governors could probably lecture for hours on that. First, they might tell the newly elected chief executive to read the handbook for new governors put out by the National Governors' Association.[3] The handbook helps new governors avoid some of the worst blunders lying in wait for them.

The Risks of Appointing Campaign Staff to Personal Staff

A new governor can do some terribly blind things right off the bat if he isn't careful. The first dangerous temptation is to appoint lots of hardworking **campaign staffers** to his personal staff in the governor's office. Unfortunately, chief lieutenants in a campaign may tend to harbor an exaggerated view of the role they played in the governor's victory. Consequently they may think the governor should now listen to their advice on how to run the state. If the new governor does not listen, they feel rejected, and if the governor ultimately has to fire some of them, they will surely become his bitterest enemies. Governors certainly need campaign-wise people on their personal staffs, but they must be very selective. Blunders can haunt them for years.

[2]Beyle speaks of "something akin to a continuum underlying the various governors' roles which runs from the personalized governorship to the institutionalized governorship." Ibid., p. 103.

[3]Center for Policy Research, *Governing the American States: A Handbook for New Governors* (Washington, D.C.: National Governor's Association, 1978).

Managerial Appointments

Any governor can prevent all kinds of headaches by taking care to hire good people. Here's where the old saying "An ounce of prevention is worth a pound of cure" holds very true. It is a mistake for a governor to choose appointees solely on the basis of their loyalty. Naturally, team players are needed, but so is competence. The governor should look for professionals, nationwide as well as in-state. If a governor needs, say, a director of prisons, he or she should look for someone with experience as director of prisons in some other state—someone perhaps with a graduate degree in corrections and with a decade of administrative experience. It's very important for a governor to be sure his cabinet members are people with proven track records—people who have dealt successfully with the press in their former posts, who have dealt successfully with politicians, with the public, with their own departments, and with their staff and their own superiors. Nobody can mess up the life of a governor more than a fool in a cabinet-level job. Every hour a governor spends sifting through applications, interviewing applicants, and checking their backgrounds is worth it. Governors should never make hasty appointments if they can avoid it.

Staying in Command

New governors should be warned against relying too heavily on the expert opinions of those high-quality cabinet officers they appoint, or letting themselves become the lackey of their own staffs or of so-called experts. A governor needs to remember that he is governor, not the staff or cabinet. They were not elected—he was. No member of the staff, no cabinet officer can view the job of governor with quite the same sense of responsibility that the governor does. It is a little like the difference between a homeowner and a renter. Staff and cabinet officers are somewhat like renters: the property isn't quite theirs. The governor, on the other hand, has a sense of responsibility that cannot dwell quite so deeply in the hearts of subordinates. Governors must therefore stay in command and make the decisions—albeit, of course, with advice.

Avoiding Splendid Isolation

New governors should also be warned against isolating themselves from their staff or management team. Staying in command does not mean trying to govern in splendid solitude. Governors simply have to hit a happy medium between being their own person and being at the mercy of their team. Governors should try to avoid acting on anything without first talking it over with the appropriate people. Others may have fresh viewpoints.

Guarding One's Time

There's always more to do than can possibly be done. New governors should not let the job make them into drudges. Maybe there is no way to avoid becoming a drudge, but governors should fight back. They need time alone—time away from the rat race. It might not be a bad idea for a new governor to take a

---

Box 6-1. Guarding Time

Governors may be busy, but this does not always excuse them from jury duty. At least not in Colorado, where Governor Richard Lamm was called in 1981. Denver District Court Judge Clifton Flowers refused to excuse him from jury duty. "I don't even excuse my own judges," said Flowers. "If the Governor is summoned, he's going to serve." The governor did inquire whether his jury service could be postponed, but "he didn't make a big issue of it," said Flowers. "It was just sort of an inquiry. But I said that if a person is 18 or older he has to serve." Lamm did willingly report for duty, but was not called for a case.

---

vacation the first week in office (rather than vowing to work like a horse). It might also be a good idea for governors to schedule one or two hours every day when they don't see anybody or schedule anything. Governors have to protect their own sanity—they simply have to escape all those people and their endless problems.

Trying To Do Everything

There is enough work to keep a governor busy 24 hours a day, and if the day were 72 hours, there would still be things to do. No governor can—or should— try to do everything. He or she simply must appoint good, intelligent, sensible, and trustworthy department heads and let them alone until they start messing up. The same with personal staff. Governors should, within the limits of their budget, try to **institutionalize the governorship** rather than to personalize it. Governors should let their staff run the governorship to the maximum degree consistent with their own determination to stay boss. If governors don't delegate, they'll never get a vacation and probably won't be especially efficient governors.

On the other hand, it's not a good idea to institutionalize the governorship excessively. It's hard to know how much delegation is too much or too little. A governor's management team can help if it is told that the governor doesn't want to be in on every trifle that hits the office. What is a trifle? A governor needs managers who can sense the difference between a trifle and a matter of high significance. A governor should try to get as much settled at lower levels as possible—not try to jump in on everything. Obviously he wants to know what's going on; a steady flow of information will help him judge what to intrude upon and what to leave to others.

Setting Priorities

Most governors get enough speaking invitations to keep them speaking all day and all night for the rest of their lives. The same with ribbon cutting and the like. Governors just have to say no as politely as possible from time to time. Governors ought to meet the public and be available but at the same time keep some private time. They need to determine what their most important priorities are. Their staff, appointments secretary, and entire management team should be taught to run interference.

Miscellaneous Advice

If one were to write a manual on how to be governor, there are all sorts of suggestions one might include, such as the importance of having a good press secretary and good press relations and of projecting one's best image through the mass media. One might discuss the importance of flattering the egos of legislators and keeping an office door open to them. One might also warn new governors about the horrors of working with the federal government, the horrors of internecine strife among government agencies (strife that governors have to referee), and the horrible times when it's as bad to do one thing as to do another.[4]

WHO BECOMES GOVERNOR?

Race, Religion, Sex, Party, Occupation, and Demeanor

Most governors in American history have been white, Protestant males. That remains so today although being of another race, religion, or sex is no longer as great a bar to the governorship. Judging by the party affiliation of today's governors, it is safe to say that one has a much better chance of becoming governor by being a Democrat than a Republican. And judging by the occupational background of governors today, a lawyer is more likely to become governor than a person having any other occupation. No doubt research would also show that it helps to look, dress, talk, and walk like a governor, although defining exactly what that consists of might require considerable analysis.

Pregubernatorial Public Office

What sort of political career have most governors had before they became governor? It is rare to find a governor today who has never served in any public office before. Most governors have previously held some kind of elective office, usually as state legislator, an elected statewide officer, a member of Congress, or a local elected officer. Some have held appointive office—director of a major state, federal, or local agency perhaps.[5]

Governors who have served in the legislature find their legislative experience extremely useful. Service in the legislature, especially if that service was immediately prior to their election as governor, gives them an understanding of state problems and issues, teaches them a lot about the political forces at work in the state, familiarizes them with the bureaucratic apparatus of the government, and acquaints them with many leading personalities with whom they, as governor, will have to work and deal.

[4]In his survey of advice given by incumbent and former governors to newly elected governors, Beyle, "Governor's Views," touched on these points.
[5]See Larry Sabato, "Governors' Office Careers: A New Breed Emerges," *State Government* (Summer 1979) pp. 95–102.

PEOPLE WHO WORK IN THE GOVERNOR'S OFFICE

Dangers of a Poor Appointment

After a candidate for governor has heard the election returns and knows he really made it after all, one of the first things he has to think about is the matter of appointments to key positions in his new administration, including appointments to a personal staff. No doubt he has been pondering these long before election day. Every appointment is a calculated risk. Even the most trusted associates may have skeletons in the closet—indiscretions, corner cuttings, even crimes—which if brought to light could be costly, if not catastrophic, for the governor. Furthermore, no governor can be absolutely certain which lieutenants may start taking graft or prove incompetent. Nor can a governor always be 100 percent sure about his or her political or ideological compatibility with those he or she appoints to office: sometimes the pressure cooker of power draws out hidden differences among associates.

Mistakes are expensive, sometimes disastrous, particularly mistakes in the form of poor appointments to the governor's immediate staff: the closer the staffer is to the governor, the worse it is. Still, governors must have a personal staff, for there is more work to be done than they can possibly do themselves. They must have assistant governors; the bigger the state, the more assistants. Once these people are appointed, it is difficult to get rid of them. Many governors (like most other employers) find it distasteful to fire anybody, and besides, it can be dangerous to fire someone who knows what goes on in the governor's office. A resentful former governor's aide could regale the press with all sorts of appetizing revelations. Thus, smart governors rarely fire anybody from their staff: the unwanted are promoted and transferred. If nothing suitable can be found in the bureaucracy, governors may have to draw on their connections in the private sector.

Turnover

Although in most states the governor is allowed complete latitude in hiring and firing members of his or her staff, **turnover** in that staff is normally very low. Few are fired, and few leave for better jobs. Most who have jobs in the governor's office find it captivating work on the whole. Hours may be long and hard, but job satisfaction runs high. There is a good deal of psychic income from being able to say "I work for the governor," or "I'm the governor's press secretary," or "governor's assistant," or "governor's switchboard operator." There is also the pleasure of being at the pivot of a perpetual political drama, of being an insider at the hub of many important events. And there is the satisfaction, even delight, of possessing behind-the-scenes knowledge of what is going on. Indeed a large part of the work of a governor's staff is to keep an eye on what is going on in the many sectors of activity interesting to the governor.

Furthermore, most members of a governor's staff are intensely loyal, in fact are hired in the first place partly because of that loyalty; this is another reason they do not leave his or her service for light causes. On top of that, there are some career benefits in working for the governor: it is a good recommendation for future employment. Working for the governor can pay off in other ways. One has, for example, an opportunity to meet and establish useful contacts with numerous influential people—legislators, publishers, corporation officers, and others. An up-and-coming staff officer may wish to cultivate these people not only for the governor's sake but for his or her own sake in anticipation of the day when the governor is no longer governor and the staff is no longer staff. Some staff members may have political ambitions of their own, may even dream of sitting in the governor's chair one day. In any case, a governor's assistant will surely want to keep one eye fixed on that day when a new employer must be found or a new career developed.

Who Works for the Governor?

Size of Staff   Some governors have more to do than others because some states are more perplexing than others. The size of the governor's staff and the size of a state's population are directly related.[6] The governor of a state small in population may not have much more than a few clerk-typists and an executive secretary, whereas the governor of a populous state may have a staff exceeding one hundred. The average American state governor will have at least an executive secretary, press secretary, legal advisor, legislative secretary, plus stenographers, receptionists, file clerks, mail clerks, police aides, and telephone operators.

Loyalty, Shared Attitudes, Good Sense   What does a governor look for in picking a personal staff? A governor's staff must have **loyalty:** their first thought must be the governor's interest, not some other interest. This is one reason a governor may hesitate to pick a party regular for his or her staff: party regulars are by definition loyal to the party, and the party's interest may not be the governor's interest. The party's stand on, say, abortion, legislative reapportionment, or appointments to the bureaucracy may be quite at odds with the needs of an ambitious governor, especially when a governor's hopes for relection lie with a broader segment of the public than is represented by the party. Nor, for the same reason, does a governor want staff members who fail to share his or her enthusiasms and attitudes or who alienate people and interests upon whom the governor depends for support. After all, a governor cannot accomplish anything, or hope to be reelected or advanced to higher glory, without the support of a collection of robust interests; therefore, staff members must radiate the same affection for those interests that the governor does. Nor does a governor want fools in his or her entourage; something more than loyalty, more than a mutuality of enthusiasm is required. That something is good sense—indefinable, but recognizable.

Insofar as party regularity has anything to do with staff appointments, it would most likely affect appointments in the secretarial staff because loyalty to the governor's policies is not always important in a secretarial job. However, even these positions are sometimes occupied by people doing important political work for the governor.

---

[6]Based on returns from a 1976 survey of governors' office managers from 34 states. National Governors' Association, "Managing the Governor's Office," *Governor's Office*, Vol. 8 (Washington, D.C., 1976), p. 9.

Public-Relations Know-How In addition to loyalty, shared attitudes, and good sense, most governors want a staff with **public-relations** know-how. In a sense, the staff is one big public-relations firm whose job is to sell the governor: it is his or her taxpayer-supported reelection and glorification committee. Thus it is common to find journalists (in addition to the press secretary) on the governor's staff. Governors of larger states also need staff specialists in various problems irritating the state: perhaps an environmental specialist, a forestry specialist, and so on.

Political Savvy Nor does a governor want people on his or her staff who lack political experience, lack an understanding of what one has to do to get elected and stay elected. Being governor means ceaseless practice of politics—politics to win elections and politics to advance programs. A governor's staff is an extension of the governor—it is his or her alter ego. Each staff member is a piece of the governor and is therefore perpetually involved in the practice of politics on behalf of the governor. The art of swimming political waters is something that cannot be learned except by practice. Thus, a governor will want to have aides who have learned through practice, either as candidates themselves or as star players in someone else's campaign, possibly the governor's own.

Lawyers Surveying the staff of a typical American governor, one generally finds a great many lawyers. This is not especially because the governor needs legal advice, although he or she needs that too. Lawyers may count for half a governor's professional staff. Most are there simply because lawyers as a class tend to dabble in politics and often, therefore, have just that combination of political sense and intellectual breeding desirable in a governor's office.

Few Merit-System Employees Few merit-system civil servants are found in the typical governor's office. Even if a merit system dominates the civil service, state legislatures have typically allowed the governor total freedom in appointments and dismissals within his or her immediate staff. Few merit appointees would possess that one characteristic demanded of a member of the governor's staff: loyalty to the governor above and beyond the call of ordinary bureaucratic duty.

Duties of the Staff

Handle the Trivial Basically the staff does almost everything the governor is supposed to do and helps him or her along every avenue of that work. In many matters the staff is a collection of semisecret minigovernors. They answer most of the mail, even though the governor signs the letters. Although the staff is by no means confined to handling such details, one of its central tasks is to defend the governor from harassment by details. It is a screen that allows the governor to spend time and energy on things he considers important. True, some of those "important" things may seem trivial, such as posing for pictures with a beauty queen, but "triviality" and "importance" are often weighed by their contribution to the governor's power.

Supply Information In some ways the staff is a miniuniversity whose star pupil is the governor. A governor needs to learn all sorts of information about all sorts of matters. Of course, he picks up lots of information from special interests that attempt to influence him on a multitude of issues, but he needs neutral sources, for there are times when a governor wants to do what's right rather than merely what's popular. A governor cannot even count on the various departments and agencies of the state bureaucracy to be neutral; agencies themselves are commonly under the spell of narrow and selfish interests. Thus a governor may want to use his or her staff to produce information, which if not neutral is at least highlighted to show the governor how his or her goals would be served by a particular course of action.

Screen Information   Governors commonly suffer from a glut of information rather than a shortage of it. Data, reports, letters, editorials, and every imaginable form of communication flood the governor's office, much in writing, much orally. The staff screens this flood, condenses it to essential points and issues, and presents the governor with a neat, manageable package, including a list of various courses of action the governor may wish to take (his or her "options"), and the pluses and minuses of each.

Help with Visitors   If you ask to visit the governor, it is normally a staff member who decides whether you may. Naturally governors want to see as many people as they possibly can, but the day is only so long. Many visitors are merely curious to see the person who symbolizes the state. There is no end of people, including many bureaucrats, politicians, legislators, judges, and prominent persons in all walks of life, who come to see the governor on real or contrived business and who, in the process, wish to introduce a wife, son, daughter, mother, father, sister, friend, or associate to the governor.

Visitors of that sort, usually more than the governor can possibly find time to see, are almost always hovering near the governor's office waiting their chance. The governor's appointments secretary or executive secretary frequently has to employ all the diplomatic arts at his or her command to turn some of these visitors away. Tired and hungry after a laborious morning, the governor of one state muttered that he simply could not face a delegation from the League of Women Voters waiting to see him. His executive secretary said, "Don't worry, Governor. I'll handle them for you. Just duck into your bathroom [it adjoined his office] and shut the door." After the governor disappeared his executive secretary suavely received the women and apologized that the governor had just been called away. Three hours later staff members began wondering where the governor was. No one saw him go out. Suddenly it dawned on the executive secretary—he had forgotten to tell the governor the women had left. Emerging from his bathroom after the ordeal, the governor said he was the only chief executive in the country with a desk that flushed.

Answer the Mail   Many of the governor's visitors have problems to discuss. Insofar as possible the staff will listen to those problems and settle them for the governor. Much of the governor's mail also comes from citizens with problems. People seem to think the governor can do something about almost anything: they complain about their landlord, about air pollution, about streetlights, about all kinds of things over which the governor may have no control whatsoever. The staff works hard to respond verbally or in writing to these complaints, generally referring distressed people to agencies and officers who they hope can do something. The staff tries to satisfy everybody and tries to make friends for the governor, not enemies. However, many people simply will not believe the governor isn't boss of everything in the state and suspect he is giving them the runaround when he sends them a letter suggesting they contact someone else about the problem. Some persistent letter writers are mentally disturbed, and consequently their letters are never answered. Nor are psychotic visitors to the governor's office encouraged.

Much of the governor's outgoing mail is signed by staffers, especially letters that may prove disappointing to the recipient. Thus, the governor is always in a position to reverse himself. If necessary, the governor can shift gears and lay blame on an "error" made by a staff assistant. Of course, letters bearing good news generally go out under the governor's own signature. All this squares with the fundamental duty of a governor's staff: to create a favorable image of the governor. It is their sometimes self-effacing duty to put a good face on everything the governor does, certainly on everything emanating from the governor's office.

Liaison with the Bureaucracy   In addition to being politicians, modern governors are expected to be in charge (at least nominally) of the bureaucracy. They therefore need to know what is going on in the bureaucracy, but sometimes bureaucrats withhold information. Part of a staff's duty is to keep in regular touch with activities of the executive branch so the governor can appear to be knowledgeable, handle problems before they become embarrassing, and take as much credit as possible for everything favorable happening or about to happen. Good liaison with the bureaucracy may require transferring some members of the governor's staff to this or that sensitive agency to act as spies. Such transfers are often viewed with suspicion by agency bureaucrats and are sometimes resisted by the staffer-spy who is about to be transferred. However, a person sufficiently loyal to be selected for the governor's staff is usually loyal enough to accept such a transfer obligingly and to supply the governor with a stream of secret and immensely useful intelligence. Some governors have special staff or cabinet officers whose primary duty is to keep an eye on the bureaucracy and to coordinate activities of the executive branch insofar as it is within the governor's power to do so. Such a coordinator may be called "director of administration" or some such title.

Dangers of a Staff   Governors have to beware of the staff that encircles them and screens them from trivia, edits information, decides who sees them, decides which letters and documents they see, and decides which problems are worthy of gubernatorial attention and which options for the solution of problems are feasible. Even if the staff does not have total power over these things, governors should never forget that to whatever degree their staff is a screen and a filter, to that same extent they are at its mercy. Staff members themselves, no matter how loyal, self-effacing, self-sacrificing, and seemingly devoted to the governor's welfare, remain human beings fully equipped with self-serving egos, imperfect morals, and flawed intelligence. A governor of New York is more likely to be victimized by his staff than a governor of Wyoming: the bigger the operation, the more helpless the governor without his staff.

THE WAR AGAINST GOVERNORS

One might say the American Revolution was a war against governors. It was they who had to enforce the unpopular laws and collect the oppressive taxes against which colonists rebelled. Royal governors, furthermore, represented a distant Crown that made laws to govern an American empire about which it had little firsthand knowledge and about which it was sometimes lavishly ignorant. Royal governors were not locally elected but were appointed by the king of England; too often they arrived fresh from England untutored in the ways of the New World. The Revolutionary War was a war against executive power in America, an executive power often commanded from London to take actions that the colonists thought outrageous.[7]

Therefore, when independence was declared the states hastened to write constitutions that severely curbed the power of the executive branch of government, particularly the power of governors. The idea of weak state governors has persisted in varying degrees and for various reasons up to the present.

THE GOVERNOR'S APPOINTMENT POWER

The Plural Executive

State constitutions commonly tell a falsehood when they gradiosely describe the governor as one who possesses "supreme executive power." Such descriptions are a gross overstatement, for in nearly every state there are other elected officers at the statewide level who share executive power (Table 6-1): there is a **plural executive.** Almost everywhere the secretary of state, attorney general, and treasurer are popularly elected, and about a third of the states have elected auditors or fiscal officers. These officers have a direct mandate from the voters and are quite independent of the governor. If the governor phones one of these individuals and says, "Would you please come to my office this afternoon?" the reply might be, "I'm busy. You come to my office."

Not only are these officers separately elected, they may also be of separate political parties and be motivated by a wish to embarrass and torpedo the governor rather than cooperate. Furthermore, whether of the same or a different party, these separately elected officials often aspire openly or secretly to be governor themselves one day; therefore, they are anxious to see the incumbent governor retire, or even be driven, from office so their turn will come sooner. Rather than enjoying the support of a loyal team of top executives, most governors have to spend a good deal of time pulling knives out of their backs that were put there by scheming secretaries of state, treasurers, attorneys general, au-

---

[7]For example, in 1761 the Crown decided to reserve all the Western Territory between the Alleghenies and the Mississippi for the Indians. The purpose of this seemed quite logical in London: to secure favor with Indians in the disputed area in order to secure defense of the territory against the French and Spanish. Colonial governors were instructed to prohibit future land purchases in the West—a most unpopular thing for governors to do, because its net result was to wipe out the vested interest of land speculators and fur traders and other holdings by colonists in the Western Territory.

Table 6-1 Elected State Officers

OFFICERS	NUMBER OF STATES
Governor	50
Lieutenant Governor	43
Attorney General	43
Treasurer	39
Secretary of State	36
Auditor	27
Education Officer	18
Agriculture Officer	12
Board of Education	12
Comptroller	11
Public Utilities Commission	9
Insurance Officer	8
University Board of Regents	5
Land Commissioner	5
Labor Officer	4
Corporation Commission	3
Railroad Commission	2
Executive Council	2
Board of Equalization	1
Mine Inspector	1
Highway Commission	1
Tax Commissioner	1
Adjutant General	1

ditors, and lieutenant governors. These individuals may also be shooting at each other. It may be a great show to watch, but it does impair the governor's ability to mobilize his administration and political party into accomplishing his goals.

Furthermore, states commonly provide for the appointment of some cabinet members and a few other high-level officials by a board or commission rather than by the governor. An elected state board of education might, for example, appoint the head of the department of education. A similar board might appoint the head of the department of higher education. A highway commission might appoint the head of the department of highways. Thus, a governor might live with the awful truth that he or she cannot control a third or a half of the major department heads.

Whom May the Governor Appoint?

Of course, there are numerous other important high-level officers whom the governor does appoint. In most cases he or she is free to appoint most cabinet members, that is, the heads of major departments, with the exceptions noted. Also the governor generally has power to appoint the members of many regulatory or advisory boards and commissions, but here again his or her power is qualified: most members serve for a fixed term of years and cannot be removed except for cause. Removal for cause means the governor has to prove (in court, if necessary) that the member was not doing his or her duty—that is, not showing up for work, was violating the law, or something of that nature. Officers who cannot be removed except for cause gain courage to defy the governor. This may have its benefits, but it makes it more difficult for a governor to control the administration, and it encourages high-level officers (and sometimes whole boards and commissions) to stray into the orbit of special interest groups.

The Legislature's Role in Appointments

To call a governor the supreme executive power also overlooks the power that legislative bodies wield over the executive branch: the power of oversight, power of the purse, power of confirmation, and so on. With regard to confirmation (approval), in many states the senate must consent to the appointment of most high-level state officials. In a few states both houses must confirm a number of appointees. In New Hampshire a council representing the legislature approves gubernatorial appointments, and in Maine many of the governor's appointments must be approved by the appropriate legislative committee and the senate. Thus, very few governors are free to make high-level appointments without some sort of legislative involvement in the process.

Impediments of the Merit System

In some states the **civil-service** merit system itself impedes the governor's ability to coordinate the state's bureaucracy. Merit systems are generally lauded by the "good government" lobby; one risks their displeasure by suggesting that too much application of "merit" can be unhealthy. But everything in excess is unhealthy, said Aristotle. Reformers fought for civil-service merit systems to combat the spoils system. But many reformers today question the value of merit systems that limit a governor's power to appoint subcabinet officers. Is it possible to have good management without giving the state's chief executive the power to coordinate the state's bureaucracy, to control the people who control the bureaucracy—the agency heads and the chiefs of major subunits within agencies?

What Positions Should Be Competitive?   In some states the merit system has run riot and embraced high-level officials, even agency heads themselves and their major subordinates. One can understand the desire of those who believe in good government to see such officials appointed according to their merit. At the same time, however, these officers must be appointed by the governor and serve at his or her pleasure if the governor is to have power to coordinate the bureaucracy. Just how deep into the bureaucracy a governor's power should extend is debatable, but many governors believe they should be able to appoint not only agency heads but also second- and third-level officers beneath the agency head. Advocates of this are sometimes charged with wanting to reintroduce the spoils system. Of course, no one likes to be charged with that, and it sometimes takes courage to advocate a partial rollback of merit procedures for filling high offices.

What Is Merit?   The trouble with the merit procedure for selecting high-level officials is not, of course, that it selects meritorious people but that their selection, promotion, and even dismissal is handled by an independent civil-service commission rather than by the chief executive. One can campaign for merit in high places without insisting that the only way to get merit is through a civil-service commission. Governors are fully able to appoint meritorious people to high office and indeed are in jeopardy if they don't. Furthermore, one element of merit in high-level positions may consist of an officer's willingness to support the policies of the chief executive. After all, when the voters go to the polls and elect a governor, they believe they are electing someone to direct the bureaucracy; a governor cannot do this without the power to hire and fire major subordinates in the bureaucracy.

Gubernatorial Powerlessness

Most people don't have the slightest idea how powerless their governors sometimes are to control the bureaucracy over which they are thought to be the "supreme executive." It is embarrassing and painful for a governor to have to tell a constituent who has a complaint about rude treatment at the hands of the state motor-vehicle bureau that he, the governor, has no power whatsoever over the bureau, whose head is selected not by the governor but by the civil-service commission independent of the governor. Governors usually solve this problem with a mild form of prevarication: they say they'll "investigate" the complaint, which, of course, is a far cry from doing anything about it. A governor's power over much of the bureaucracy is as frail as his or her power over a professor in a state university. In fact, the entire university system, plus the secondary school system, is largely beyond a governor's direct supervision, even though this is the biggest and most expensive function of state government. (Interestingly, professors at public colleges and universities are not selected by any civil-service merit system, and yet it is safe to say that merit more or less regularly governs their appointment.)

It must be emphasized that the typical governor is less impeded than the president of the United States by merit systems. On the whole, merit systems are less used among the states than in the federal government (although there are some remarkable exceptions); many state governors have a tighter grip over their state bureaucracy than the president has over the federal bureaucracy. Patronage is a much greater power for the typical state governor than for the president, simply because a greater swath of the typical state bureaucracy is filled by a spoils system. (The average American governor appoints some 400 persons to the state payroll.)

A Source of Leverage on the Legislature

Control of the bureaucracy gives the governor some degree of power over legislators because the bureaucracy is in a position to do a lot of things *for* and *to* people—to reward and to punish. Many opportunities for rewarding and punishing exist in what we call "executing the law." The executive branch of government, including the governor, is charged with enforcing the law, but there are so many laws that no one has time to enforce them all. Thus bureaucrats, like police officers, must pick and choose which among the myriad laws to enforce vigorously, which to enforce haphazardly, and which to ignore. Naturally, the more the governor actually controls the bureaucracy over which he is the symbolic head, the more he can manipulate this process of selective enforcement and therefore manipulate a variety of interests and their allied legislators. To the extent the governor controls the bureaucracy, he or she controls a vast sphere of rule making and policy making within the bureaucracy, activity that vitally affects countless special interests and numerous legislators coached by those interests.

THE GOVERNOR AS LEGISLATOR

There are many oddities in American government, and one of the most striking is that the executive branch—federal, state or local—is the chief *lawmaking* branch of government. The **chief legislators** are the governor and the bureaucracy, not members of the legislature. This is true even though every state constitution enshrines a separation-of-powers doctrine declaring that the legislative branch shall be the lawmaking branch. Some state constitutions flatly forbid the executive to make laws, thus following the example set by the first constitution of Massachusetts, which provided that "the executive shall never exercise the legislative . . . power."

Governors and bureaucrats legislate directly by making rules that have the force of law, and they legislate indirectly by influencing the legislature. We will not discuss here the vast rule-making authority that has been vested in the bureaucracy, especially in recent generations. (That will be discussed in Chapter 12.) The kind of legislating that concerns us here is that which the governor, and bureaucrats generally, accomplish by influencing the legislature. Every source and variety of gubernatorial strength is brought to bear on the legislature, and it is a mistake to think some of the governor's powers, such as the veto, are legislative powers, and that other powers, such as the appointment power, are not legislative powers. Perhaps it is true that the authors of state constitutions were not thinking of the governor's legislative powers when they gave him the power, say, to command the state militia. But power is not fastidious about where and how it is used. Power is like a gas that seeps under doors and through hallways and envelops every conceivable target, sometimes with a sudden and lethal effect, sometimes slowly or with a marginal effect.

We can get a pretty good idea what powers governors have by examining how they pressure the legislature to get what they want. Governors do not, of course, always get what they want from the legislature. Their power over the legislature (as over anything else) differs from state to state, governor to governor, legislature to legislature, year to year—it depends at any given moment upon countless circumstances. In no state does the governor get everything he or she wants, but in all states the governor is a potentially great influence upon the legislature.

The relationship between governors and legislators looks different depending on where you stand. One governor said, "When I was a member of the legislature I felt rather small and powerless and looked with envy at the governor's influence. Now that I am governor I see the legislature in a new light, and it towers as a mighty force."

THE GOVERNOR'S ABILITY TO INFLUENCE PUBLIC OPINION

Influencing Legislators through Public Opinion

A sizable bloc of legislators hope to be reelected and are therefore influenced by **public opinion.** Some consider it their duty to vote the opinions prevailing in their district. After all, a representative is supposed to *represent.* Therefore, obviously, if a governor can influence public opinion, he or she can influence legislators through public opinion.

Concentrating on Issues

There are limits to the ability of a governor to influence the public. He cannot hope to sway mass opinion about every bill before the legislature: there are hundreds, even thousands of bills. To mobilize mass public opinion, he must zero in on one or two major issues and concentrate on the pieces of legislation affecting those issues. This he can do better than any other politician in the state.

Addressing Segments of the Public

A governor need not always mobilize the mass public; in many instances it is necessary only to mobilize that segment of the public most sensitive to a given issue. If the bill concerns, say, a new tax on trucks, then the trucking industry is going to be wide awake to that issue and the rest of the public may be sound asleep. A governor may need only address those who are awake, for legislators tend to respond to that part of the public that is awake. For them public opinion is the opinion of that part of the public that cares. As long as only a fraction of the public is awake to an issue—that fraction being perhaps some small and narrow special interest—legislators are going to respond to that fraction. If the governor's purpose is to disarm that narrow minority, he has the power to do so by awakening the general public, thus forcing legislators to pay attention to that wider segment. Because the governor is known to nearly every voter in the state, he or she, better than anyone else, can sound an alarm that will be heard and listened to.

The Governor as a Celebrity

All governors are celebrities and therefore interesting to the mass media because they are interesting to the mass public; the more attention governors have, the more they get. Governors symbolize their state and are regarded with a certain awe by the general public. When governors speak, people listen. They are presented with endless opportunities to speak and always have more invitations than they can possibly accept.

Electronics Favor the Governor

Radio and television make modern governors more powerful than their predecessors. Television has wrought more changes in government than any other mechanical invention, and one of its most important effects is to strengthen the office of governor. All political chiefs—the president, the governor, the mayor—have been strengthened because electronics allow them to address countless thousands, and to address them repeatedly. Legislators may also use these electronic marvels, but the legislature speaks not with one voice but with as many voices as there are legislators. Legislators are seldom asked to appear on statewide hookups; few are known statewide, and few are elected from statewide districts. A state legislator from Pottawatomie County may be known and listened to in Pottawatomie, but not in many other places. Perhaps a handful of party leaders in the legislature enjoy some glimmer of statewide recognition, but rarely anything like the sun glare in which the governor stands. The governor not only has a statewide constituency but also personifies the state government itself. He reaffirms this role in the minds of the people whenever he dedicates a bridge, makes speeches on holidays, marches at the head of parades, welcomes dignitaries. The legislator from Pottawatomie cannot outshine the governor, nor can the legislature as an institution.

The visibility and persuasive powers of governors make them a power in the legislature for they can reach every legislator's district better and oftener than the legislator, and can even build waves of public opinion that no legislator can ignore.

Building a Legislative Record

A governor normally wants to influence the legislature, especially with regard to those things upon which his or her political future hangs. The governor is, of course, elected—indeed is the most conspicuous elected official in the state. A governor will have made campaign promises. Eventually he may want to run for a second term on his **record,** and even if not, his influence with the public during the present term may depend somewhat on his success at reaching the well-publicized goals of the campaign. Of course, failure to reach goals can sometimes be turned to advantage if the governor can blame enemies in the legislature who stand in the way of progress, but it is perhaps better to show a record of success than a record of failure. To that end, governors spend much time lobbying legislators, explaining and justifying their program, holding out whatever rewards for cooperation they have, and suggesting ever so subtly the punishments at their disposal for those who do not cooperate. Much of their staff is kept busy with liaison work of the same sort.

Governors generally avoid trying to cram too much down the throat of the legislature. A few major proposals each session are enough; there is a limit to how much change the public is willing to take all at once. There is also a limit to how much the public can understand all at once, and the same limitation applies to legislators, for they have only so much time for their duties and only so much willingness to study and comprehend important new measures. Furthermore, governors do not for one instant want to insult the legislature's image of independence by seeming to tell them everything.

The Disillusionment of New Governors

Newly elected governors with soaring visions of the things they are soon to accomplish soon hit the pavement of reality with a disillusioning thud. The two main reasons for this almost unavoidable fate are (1) almost everything governors want to accomplish will cost money, and there isn't enough money; (2) almost everything they want to accomplish will rock the boat, threaten empires, and disturb vested interests inside and outside the bureaucracy.

Of these, perhaps the money shortage is worse. Much of the available revenue is already earmarked by law. Most of the rest is, in a sense, earmarked politically. If governors want to inaugurate some major new program, they have to find money somewhere. This means they have to rob other equally important or powerfully supported programs, or ask the legislature to raise taxes. However, taxpayers don't like to pay taxes, governors don't like to suggest higher taxes, and legislators don't like to vote them. Therefore, most discussion of daring new programs bogs down sooner or later in debate over the funding for them. Even if money problems and political problems are overcome, there remains the fact that budgets are made some 18 months in advance, and it may take governors that long to make their impact on the budget.

THE GOVERNOR'S POWER TO CALL SPECIAL SESSIONS

Most governors have the power to call the legislature into special session. Of course, legislatures that meet year-round are not annoyed with **special sessions,** but most legislatures meet only a few weeks or months a year and members generally do not like to be called away from their homes and jobs for special sessions. It is just for that reason that governors can use the threat of a special session to win legislative cooperation during the regular session. Special sessions offer certain unique advantages for governors. First, the governor has the upper hand in public relations. By calling the session he is in effect accusing the legislature of not doing its duty during the regular session. Second, by calling the session he focuses public opinion on the issue that precipitated the call and upon his reasons for demanding action from the legislature. The special session is not normally permitted to consider anything not laid before it by the governor. Of course, if the legislature even under these extreme conditions fails to give the governor what he wants, that could be a damaging defeat for him. Furthermore, a governor runs the risk of antagonizing the legislature if he drags them away from home and job in the middle of the winter, and this may make relations with them difficult during the next regular session.

THE GOVERNOR AS PARTY LEADER

Dangers of Party Disunity

As his party's most conspicuous officeholder, a governor has power over his fellow partisans in the legislature. These legislators have a selfish interest in making the governor look good: if he looks good, they will all prosper. By the same token, if he looks bad, they may be dragged down as well. Naturally, it helps to have a majority in the legislature (providing it is not too large). If it is too large, then it may disgrace itself with family disputes, and the governor is likely to be the favorite of one party faction and the bitter enemy of another. This is commonly true in one-party states, but as we have seen, party factionalism is the substitute for a two-party system. Where there is a two-party system and both parties are in good health and substantially united, a majority of the governor's party in the legislature can, if they play it right, glorify their governor. Of course, governors who are faced with a legislature controlled (or partially controlled) by the opposition can be embarrassed, belittled, and smeared. Their administration can be made to look feeble and ineffectual, their proposals defeated, their nominees for office rejected, their budget ridiculed, their subordinates "investigated," their administration probed, their policies debated.

Maverick Governors

Some governors have trouble with their own party because they are **mavericks** who succeeded in winning their party's nomination against the passionate opposition of party regulars. Some mavericks eventually come to terms with the party regulars, and some don't. Where governors serve two-year terms, regulars may hope to drive out a maverick after 24 months before he or she takes over the party. However, all but three states[8] today provide four-year terms, and the party regulars may find it more profitable to join their maverick governor than to carry on four years of war against him. Every governor is to some degree a maverick; rarely does anyone win nomination for that office without some contest, colossal or puny, within his or her party.

Sources of the Governor's Influence in the Party

Normally governors are the leaders of their party, or become so, if for no other reason than their conspicuousness. With their fate goes the fate of the party, to some extent, and the fate of every officeholder wearing the party label. Governors are almost automatically crowned as **party leader.** The influence a governor acquires by being the most prestigious political figure in the state is reinforced by various "official" powers at his disposal, such as the power to make appointments and to give honors, which he can bestow upon friends or withhold from enemies or those of weak faith. Popular governors can sometimes reward their friends in the legislature by campaigning for them. Whether governors can motivate voters to vote for candidates other then themselves is highly questionable. Nevertheless, candidates often appreciate the "help" and, if victorious, will allow themselves to be influenced by the governor. Governors are prime speakers at political rallies and are a great attraction at fund-raisers. Perhaps a governor cannot influence people to vote for the state senator from Pottawatomie County, but he or she can help fill the senator's campaign treasury by appearing as the key attraction at a $50-a-plate fund-raiser.

THE VETO POWER

The word *veto* is a Latin verb meaning "I forbid." All American state governors except one have power to (temporarily) forbid enactments of the legislature from becoming law. In North Carolina there is no veto power at all (no formal power, that is). Elsewhere the veto comes in several sizes and shapes.

---

[8]New Hampshire, Rhode Island, and Vermont.

Item Veto

All but about a half dozen states[9] also allow the governor some sort of *item veto*. This is the power of the governor to veto a single item within an appropriations bill, as an alternative to vetoing the entire bill. Some states also allow the governor to *reduce* amounts if he or she does not wish to prohibit an item altogether. About 20 states allow governors to go beyond prohibiting or reducing amounts of money. In those states the governor may also veto *language* within appropriation bills which attempts to define the uses to which money may be put, and so forth.

Some states allow the governor a long time to sign or veto a bill during a session (Illinois allows 60 days). Others hardly allow the governor time to read the bill (Nebraska, 5 days).

After the legislative session ends, the governor is allowed a certain number of days to sign a bill. If he does not sign during this period, the bill in most states becomes law without his signature.

Several states allow a governor to **pocket veto** bills in his possession at session's end. This means that if he doesn't sign it within so many days after the legislature adjourns, the bill dies.

Some states allow the legislature, having passed a bill and sent it to the governor, to snatch it away from the governor when they find out about a possible veto and to change it to meet the governor's objections or perhaps to kill it. Some states allow the governor to return bills to the legislature in the hope they will take further action rather than forcing him to veto it. This is sometimes picturesquely called the *executive amendment*.

The Legislature's Power to Override

Some states make it easy and some make it difficult for the legislature to **override** a governor's veto. A very small percentage of bills vetoed by American governors are overridden by state legislatures. All states require more than a simple majority of those *present and voting* to override a veto, although some states do not require a great deal more than such a majority. For example, in six states it is possible to override a veto with only a majority of those *elected*. Some states require a vote of three-fifths of those elected, some three-fifths of those *present*. Some states require two-thirds of those elected, others two-thirds of those present.

To summarize, the typical procedure for vetoing is as follows: Most governors possess a veto power that includes the power to veto items of appropriation bills as well as entire measures. They have about ten days to sign or veto before the legislature adjourns; if they fail to sign or veto within that limit, the bill becomes law without their signature. They have roughly a like period of time after the legislature has adjourned to sign or veto bills passed at the end of the session, after which the bills become law without their signature. If they veto a bill, it will require two-thirds of those elected in each house to override the veto. The legislature (anticipating a veto) may withdraw a bill before it is vetoed.

---

[9]Indiana, Maine, Nevada, New Hampshire, North Carolina, Rhode Island, and Vermont.

> ***Box 6-2.*** Give Me the Line-Item Veto
>
> "The budget process is a sorry spectacle. The . . . nightmare of monstrous continuing resolutions packing hundreds of billions of dollars of spending into one bill must be stopped. We ask Congress, once again: Give us the same tool that 43 governors have, a line-item veto, so we can carve out the boondoggles and pork—those items that would never survive on their own."
> President Ronald Reagan
> State of the Union Address
> January 27, 1987

Governor and President Compared

The veto power of the typical American governor is stronger than that of the American president. The main source of this greater strength is the item veto. If a president wishes to veto any item within a bill, he must veto the entire bill, even if his objection is narrowly focused on particular items of general appropriation bills. The president shares this inability to veto items of appropriation bills with only seven governors. Furthermore, the president has ten days after receiving the bill (not counting Sundays) to decide whether to sign or veto. The president is not given any set number of days after adjournment to act, as are most governors, only those ten days. If Congress adjourns during that ten-day period, the president has what remains of it, except in that case the bill dies instead of becoming law if he fails to sign. Thus the president, like the governor of certain states, can veto a bill by sticking it in his pocket and forgetting about it after the lawmakers adjourn. About two-thirds of the governors do not have this pocket veto: they typically have a specific time after adjournment to sign or veto, after which bills become law even without their signature.

THE GOVERNOR'S TERM AS A POWER

Perhaps a governor's term is not, properly speaking, a power, but the length of that term undoubtedly affects the potency of his other powers. Obviously, the longer he is likely to be "in power," the longer his opponents (some of them at least) will delay provoking him. The best time to provoke a governor is when it will hurt you the least and him the most. That time is toward the end of his tenure in office. In some cases it is hard to know just exactly when the end will be; in other cases it is very easy to know. It is easiest (or at least most definite) where the state constitution forbids a second consecutive term. In those states governors begin to lose their power on their first day in office and progress toward impotency each successive year with particular acceleration in the latter years. They are **lame ducks** the minute they take office. Some states allow a second consecutive term but prohibit a third, thus postponing lame-duck status until the second term. At last report there were only four one-term states (Kentucky, Mississippi, New Mexico, and Virginia). Most of the rest were divided fairly evenly between a **two-term limitation** and no limitations at all.

Some states have lengthened the governor's term from two years to four years but at the same time added a one- or two-term limit. Lengthening the term is intended partly to "strengthen" the governor, but there is reason to believe the net result is to weaken the governor when the term limitation is added.

No doubt these term limitations have found their way into state constitutions with the enthusiastic support of prominent figures in state legislatures who want to see not only an embarrassment of the governor's power (so their own and that of the legislature will be glorified), but also a turnover in governors so their own opportunities for that office will be increased. One result of changing the terms from two years to four years has been less turnover in the office of governor—to the detriment of those legislators who are ambitious to become governor. The increased length of term stems largely from recognition that a governor simply can't accomplish much in two years: it takes a long time for new programs to move from the drawing board to implementation.

Term limitations, of course, have also grown out of the fear of future Huey Longs, state dictatorships, or political machines. But whether term limitations succeed in preventing political bosses from perpetuating themselves in office is questionable. Governors faced with a constitutional bar against serving a second or third consecutive term can arrange to install his or her spouse, or some other compliant helper, for an intervening term. The trouble with this is that compliant helpers, once in office, sometimes decide they don't want to be compliant any more.

THE GOVERNOR'S BUDGETARY POWER

The Governor's Budget

Governors in most states try to tell the legislature how much money it should appropriate for this and that purpose. Such behavior is not gubernatorial insolence. Quite the contrary. Legislatures almost everywhere invite the governor, indeed command him or her, to give recommendations. This certainly does not mean the legislature always accepts those recommendations. Nevertheless, the legislature welcomes them for at least one very good reason: the **governor's budget** in most states is the only place where legislators can see a single list of how much money every agency in the far-flung executive branch is asking for, and why. But that is not the most important part of a governor's budget. The most important part is, or should be, that the governor (actually, the budget office) weighs the needs of one agency against another in view of limited revenues and in view of political reality. In most states the legislature itself is not equipped with a professional staff to study in depth the needs of each agency or to evaluate the efficiency with which agencies are using the money they already have. Legislatures, of course, are not entirely helpless: some are less in need of a governor's budget and less respectful of a governor's budget than others.

The Weight of the Governor's Budget

Thus the governor's budget generally carries a good deal of weight if for no other reason than that it is generally the only coherent, systematic, "rational," "intelligent" overview of the state's financial needs available to the legislature. Of course, the governor's budget comes to the legislature in a suit of political armor:

it is armed with whatever other influence the governor has over the legislature. It is remarkable how similar the legislature's ultimate appropriations bill often is to the original requests in the governor's budget. This occurs partly because the budget has logic and partly because the legislature knows it is not equipped to dispute that logic.

Thus governors can sway legislatures by force of the superior expertise at their command. However, not all governors are equipped with well-staffed budget offices. Nor do all governors have absolute control over those offices: some are headed and staffed largely by merit-system appointees. Perhaps no American governor is armed with a budget-making agency comparable in expertise to the president's Office of Management and Budget. Some governors' budgets are prepared with such want of competence, such want of research into the real needs of the state, that they offer little intelligent guidance to the legislature. If the legislature is equally incompetent, and equally bereft of professional staff to research the needs of the state, then the state wanders on a desert of ignorance and inaction.

Earmarking

Of course, no governor, whether well staffed or ill staffed, can have much influence over that tremendous part of the budget of every state that is already earmarked, sometimes by statute, sometimes by the state constitution, and sometimes by custom. For example, many states **earmark** gasoline taxes for road repair and construction. Commonly, more than half a state's expenditures are already agreed upon by the time the legislature meets and thus are not dealt with, except perfunctorily, in the governor's budget. The governor's budget, in other words, pertains chiefly to the general fund—funds not already earmarked.

Incremental Budgeting

Furthermore, both the governor and the legislature work under the sway of politics. Most budgeting is done by politicians, and politicians do not like to rock the boat or make too many people mad. Thus to keep everybody more or less happy, they annually allocate most agencies approximately what they got the previous year, with perhaps a little extra. This is known as **incremental budgeting,** and it limits the likelihood that governors or legislators will fundamentally alter the pattern of state expenditures.

WHAT IS A "POWER"?

Duties versus Powers

It would be difficult and perhaps meaningless to list in one column the things governors *do* and in another column their powers. What do governors do? They exercise their powers. Nearly everything governors do is a dimension of their powers.

The Difficulty of Ranking the Governor's Powers

It is also difficult to arrange governors' powers in a list from greatest to least, strongest to weakest, or most effective to least effective. There are several reasons why one power cannot be mathematically and unshakably fixed above or below another power. First, all powers contribute to all other powers. Take, for example, the veto power and the so-called budget power. They are part of each other: the governor's power over state spending (the budget power) obviously includes the power to veto spending and revenue bills. Each of the governor's powers is really composed of all the other powers. None of these powers can be precisely defined. Of what does a governor's budget power consist? It consists obviously of all power available to the governor. Conceivably a governor could be ranked weak in formal budgetary powers yet be a virtual dictator over expenditures through sheer political influence in the state. It would be a miserably inadequate and unscholarly definition of the budget power to say that it consists of the governor's power to appoint whomever prepares the budget. Actually the budget power is the broad power to influence expenditures by the state. Thus, besides the veto, it would include every influence the governor holds over the legislature; it would include the governor's control over various departments of the bureaucracy receiving money under the budget; it would include whatever power the governor may have over the rank-and-file civil servants who prepare the budget; it would be affected by availability of revenues; it would be affected by the power or lack of power represented by the earmarking of funds; and it would be affected by the extent of the governor's power to impound appropriated funds. The governor's budget power is affected by every circumstance and by every gubernatorial power, or lack of power.

Another reason the powers of governors cannot be mathematically ranked is that the potency of any power depends heavily on the willingness and ability of the governor to use it. Formal veto power means nothing unless a governor is willing and able to use it. On the other hand, a governor with no formal veto power (and we have only one in the United States: the governor of North Carolina) could conceivably wield so much power over the legislature that he or she needs no veto.

Thus there are many variables affecting the potency, the importance, and the definition of every gubernatorial power—so many variables that not even computers could sort out which of the governor's powers is greatest, which second greatest, which third greatest. All the governor's powers contribute to one another, none of them can be precisely separated from the others, and each is influenced by a multitude of circumstances that differ from time to time, place to place, and governor to governor, such as the governor's own personality and political wallop.[10]

None of this necessarily nullifies the value of Joseph A. Schlesinger's attempt to rank the governors according to the potency of their *formal* powers—

[10]For a discussion of how "weak" governors can be strong, see Regina K. Brough, "Strategies for Leaders Who Do Not Have a Lot of Power," *State Government* (July–August 1987), pp. 157–161, and Richard C. Kearney, "How a 'Weak' Governor Can Be Strong: Dick Riley and Education Reform in South Carolina," *State Government* (July–August 1987), pp. 150–156. The same general problem has been discussed in relation to weak mayors. See James H. Svara, "The Mayor in Council-Manager Cities: Recognizing Leadership Potential," *National Civic Review* (September–October 1986), pp. 271–290.

that is, powers that stem from legal provisions concerning such things as budgeting, veto, appointments, length of term, and self-succession.[11] However, formal power is not always the same as actual power—various circumstances may inhibit a formal power or magnify it.[12]

HOW STRONG SHOULD GOVERNORS BE?

In recent years there has been much talk about strengthening the office of governor. This is a reform that seems to have won the hearts and minds of "good government" forces. Strong governors are visualized as good, not evil. But if the purpose of strengthening the office of governor is to make it easier for governors to govern, then this runs head-on into the theory that legislatures should legislate. "Governing," after all, involves legislating. Of course, times do change, and if we look deep into the hearts of the voting public we may discover that they feel the governor, not the legislature, is the proper leader in all things the state does or is about to do. If there is such an attitude, it may be in part because the public understands governors better than legislatures. The governor is a clear personality with a clear program. The legislature is a faceless (or multifaced) collectivity with no single voice and no single policy; in fact, it seems rather complex and mysterious. The governor's visibility through the mass media not only allows him to set the agenda for public debate but also establishes him in the eyes of millions as the one to do something about state problems if anything can be done.

Actually most governors do not have the power they are imagined to have by the general public. Nevertheless, the public holds governors responsible for nearly everything that happens in the state, no matter how helpless a governor may be to do anything about it. The president of the United States is in the same unhappy position. Herbert Hoover was blamed for the 1929–1939 depression although his role in it was minute by comparison with other forces. Likewise Franklin Roosevelt was acclaimed as the man who got us out of the depression, although his role was minute compared with that of Adolf Hitler, who involved the world in a total war that put everybody back to work. There are those who say governors (and presidents) should have power to match their public image: if the public believes governors are responsible for seeing to it that problems are solved, then governors should have power to solve problems without unreasonable interference by representatives and senators in the legislative branch. There are others, however, who say it is better to have unsolved problems than to have a gubernatorial or presidential dictatorship.

[11]Schlesinger devised an index of the governor's formal powers, giving each a numerical rating, and compared all the governors on that basis. See Joseph A. Schlesinger, "The Politics of the Executive," in *Politics in the American States,* ed. Herbert Jacob and Kenneth N. Vines (Boston: Little, Brown, 1971).

[12]One analyst concludes that "formal tools of power are useful to executives despite other features of state politics which might be assumed to threaten their utility." Nelson C. Dometrius, "The Efficacy of a Governor's Formal Powers," *State Government* (Summer 1979), p. 125. But another observer argues, "There is little evidence that a governor's formal powers significantly affect policy outcomes in the fifty states." Thomas R. Dye, "Executive Power and Public Policy in the States," *Western Political Quarterly* (December 1969), p. 936.

Some of those who advocate strengthening the position of governor do not see this as strengthening his power over the legislature but rather strengthening his power primarily over the bureaucracy of which he is nominally head. Increases of gubernatorial authority over the bureaucracy, however, come somewhat at the expense of other branches.

It may be carrying things too far to hoist the specter of managerial authoritarianism and to suggest that legislative power would be subverted if governors were given tools needed to manage the huge and burgeoning executive branch. The bureaucracy costs a lot of money, and it needs to be run by a chief executive equipped with the tools of management. A governor needs these powers not only to run an economical and efficient operation but also to ensure that the state services upon which we all depend are brought to us in a satisfactory manner. Since the legislature is composed largely of part-time, short-term amateurs, we depend heavily on the governor with the help of experts in the state bureaucracy to come forth with solutions to state problems. Therefore, we need to provide the governor with such professionals and such powers appropriate to good management.

Proposals for Strengthening Governors

What, basically, are the proposals for strengthening the office of governor? The following do not exhaust the list, but they include most of the major themes on the subject.

Terminate the Plural Executive   First of all, the plural executive (a system in which several top-level executives are popularly elected) should be terminated; governors and lieutenant governors should be the only statewide elected officials. The lieutenant governor should be an executive right hand to the governor, should be nominated and elected with the governor as a team, and should thereafter remain a part of that team.

Increase Appointment Power   Governors' appointment power should be increased in those states where it is unreasonably limited. Governors should have the power to appoint not only department heads but also policymaking officials deep within the bureaucracy, even if this involves a partial retreat of the civil-service merit system. Nor should governors have to clear these appointments with any board, not even with boards they appoint. Governors should fill by appointment the department headships now filled by popular election. Legislative confirmation of appointments should be limited to the heads of major state agencies.

Increase Removal Power   Governors should have absolute freedom to remove anyone they appoint, except judges and the heads of independent agencies that are justifiably independent.

Increase Power to Organize   Governors should have considerable freedom to organize and reorganize (subject, of course, to legislative veto within a specified period of time) the work of the executive branch so that its many missions can be accomplished without unreasonable organizational inefficiencies.

Reduce Span of Control The numerous agencies, offices, bureaus, boards, and commissions of the bureaucracy should be arranged into major departments that are sufficiently few to enable governors to supervise them all. In other words, the governor's span of control (the number of officers supervised by the governor) should be reduced to manageable proportions.

End Two-Year Terms, and Limits on Consecutive Terms The term of a governor should not be two years. Nor should lame-duck governors be manufactured by laws limiting the number of consecutive terms governors may serve.

Provide Adequate Staff Governors' offices should be adequately budgeted so that they can appoint a staff of sufficient quality and quantity to enable them to be effective managers, to keep on top of miscellaneous state problems as they unfold, and to anticipate them before they unfold.

Provide Adequate Budget Office Governors should be equipped with a well-staffed budget office headed by their own appointee. This will help enable them to study the money needs of each agency in view of the needs of other agencies and in view of available revenues, and to make sure that money appropriated to the bureaucracy is well spent.

Gubernatorial Competence

One thing none of these reforms can assure is that governors will be capable managers. Giving governors the power and the tools to be good managers does not insure they will have the talent to use that power or those tools in a fashion hoped for by the good government lobby. They may lack both the talent and the wish to use that power intelligently. Laurence Peter's principle[13] that people tend to rise to the level of their incompetence may accurately explain what's wrong with management in many states. Being a good state legislator, a common stepping-stone to the office of governor, does not necessarily make one a good executive. Nor does being a good campaigner, a good orator, a handsome man or woman, or having any of the qualities that make one successful as a candidate for governor.

Do We Need a State Manager?

Perhaps one further reform is needed: a reform that would not strengthen the office of governor but would weaken it and relegate it to a ceremonial office. The city-manager system could be transplanted to the state level. What if the legislature elected a "state manager" and gave him or her the same kind of power to run the state as a city manager has to run the city? What if the governor's power were limited to cutting ribbons and planting Arbor Day trees?

[13]Laurence J. Peter and Raymond Hull, *The Peter Principle* (New York: Morrow, 1969).

THE LIEUTENANT GOVERNOR

Should the Office Be Abolished?

Candidates for the office of lieutenant governor, and especially people who make speeches for such candidates, go overboard describing the importance of the office. It is called the second highest office in the state, second in importance only to that of governor. The holder of this office "stands next to the governor" and is "only a heartbeat" away from being governor. All this is technically true; still, in most states the office of lieutenant governor could perhaps be extinguished with no damage at all. Seldom is there much for a lieutenant governor to do. A recent candidate for lieutenant governor in Colorado ran on the promise that if she won and found the office had no substantial excuse for existence, she would propose its abolition. (She won and served her entire four-year term without saying much more about abolition.) Eight states of the Union have no elected lieutenant governor: Arizona, Maine, New Hampshire, New Jersey, Oregon, Tennessee,[14] West Virginia, and Wyoming. In three the secretary of state succeeds the governor; in five the presiding officer of the senate succeeds.

Constitutional Duties

Lieutenant governors customarily have three basic duties: (1) to succeed the governor if the governor dies, retires, is impeached, or is incapacitated, (2) to act as governor when the governor is out of state, and (3) to preside over the state senate, breaking roll-call ties if necessary and, in a few states, appointing committees and assigning bills to them. Lieutenant governors are, of course, assigned miscellaneous other duties, such as serving as state ombudsman or chairing this or that committee.

Running as a Team with the Governor

In some states the candidates for governor and lieutenant governor of each party run as a team—voters do not vote separately for governor and lieutenant governor but cast one vote for the team of their choice. The **team system** may apply only to the general election, or it may also apply to the primary election. If one favors the team system at all, then there is something to be said for the idea that candidates should run as a team in both the primary and general elections. Where the team system does not apply to primaries (that is, to the nominating stage), a candidate for lieutenant governor may be nominated who isn't compatible with the candidate for governor. The two of them might not run well together in the general election, and they might not work together if elected.

    Although the team system does not insure compatibility, it does assure that the lieutenant governor will belong to the same political party as the governor. This presumably makes it easier for the governor to use him or her as a true administrative assistant. Terrible disharmonies can exist within as well as between parties, and it often happens that a party's candidates for governor and lieutenant governor are rivals. The team system helps avoid this—providing the

---

[14]Tennessee gives its speaker of the senate the statutory title of lieutenant governor.

two members join up as a team in the primaries. If they don't, the team system may simply have locked two rivals together.

A compatible lieutenant governor can be helpful to a governor. The governor is more likely to give a compatible lieutenant governor jobs within the administration that he or she wouldn't dare give a rival.[15]

Some lieutenant governors complain, however, that the team system focuses all attention upon the candidate for governor, downgrades the lieutenant governor, and reduces the prestige of the position. Furthermore, if a lieutenant governor is supposed to play a strong role in the legislature, as some do, then perhaps it would be out of order to tie that officer too tightly with the governor.

Negation of Separation of Powers

Characteristically, lieutenant governors are split between two branches of government more than any other elected officer. In most states they are a curious negation of the concept of separation of powers. In some states the lieutenant governor is a key player in the executive-branch but in most states he or she is a high officer in the legislature—president of the senate.

Although most lieutenant governors have both legislative and executive functions, they tend to be involved primarily on one side or the other. Most have virtually no legislative duties except to preside, a duty they gladly neglect. When the lieutenant governor isn't there to preside, the president pro tem, or anyone who isn't doing anything more important, presides. On the other hand, some lieutenant governors, such as those of Texas, North Carolina, Mississippi, and Alabama, are heavily involved in the work of the senate, assigning bills to committee, appointing committee members, and a number of other things.

A lieutenant governor who is rooted mainly in the executive rather than the legislative side may be a member ex officio of a number of boards and commissions, may be in charge of such things as civil defense and intergovernmental relations, may be the state ombudsman, or may actually head a major department, as do the lieutenant governors of Florida and Indiana (each heads a commerce department). An executive-oriented lieutenant governor will probably sit as an active member of the governor's cabinet and will, if he or she is on good terms with the governor, be assigned miscellaneous duties, including, as Beyle and Dometrius point out, liaison, ceremonial, policy, and management assignments.[16]

Succession to the Governorship

As we have seen, one duty of a lieutenant governor is to succeed the governor if the governor dies, retires, is impeached, or is incapacitated. It is perfectly clear

[15]Beyle and Dometrius employed seven variables in their study of conditions that lead to a governor's greater or lesser use of his lieutenant governor: region, size of state, gubernatorial power, party affiliation of governor, length of gubernatorial tenure, length of gubernatorial service, and whether the governor has been a lieutenant governor. Thad L. Beyle and Nelson C. Dometrius, "Governors and Lieutenant Governors," *State Government* (Autumn 1979), p. 188.

[16]Ibid., pp. 191–92.

what the words *die, retire,* and *impeach*[17] mean, but it is not perfectly clear what *incapacitated* means. A governor may declare himself or herself incapacitated, but it is also possible that he or she may be unable or too irrational to do so. Several states have set up procedures for removing an incapacitated governor. Normally it is a two-stage process. First, there is an allegation that the governor is incapacitated. Second, there is a judgment on whether that allegation is correct. Some states designate in their constitutions who is responsible for bringing the allegation (usually legislative officers) and who is responsible for judging (often the state supreme court).

SUMMARY

The American Revolution was largely a war against governors because it was they who had to enforce the unpopular laws and collect the oppressive taxes against which colonists rebelled. When independence was achieved, the states wrote constitutions that severely curbed the power of governors. The idea of weak state governors has persisted in varying degrees and for various reasons until today.

It is difficult to arrange the governor's power in a list from greatest to weakest: all powers contribute to all other powers. No power can be surgically separated from any other. Nor can governors be ranked from strong to weak on the basis of their formal powers, because the potency of any formal power depends heavily on the willingness and ability of the governor to use it.

Governors exercise great influence over legislation. In many states their veto power includes the powerful item veto. Governors also influence legislation through their influence on public opinion, their influence as the party leader, their influence over the bureaucracy, their power to make appointments, their power to make a budget, their power to spend appropriated money, their power to call special sessions, and in fact every power at their disposal. The longer a governor's allotted term, and the less the limitation on consecutive terms, the greater a governor's power over the legislature is likely to be.

State constitutions commonly tell a falsehood when they grandiosely describe the governor as one who possesses "supreme executive power." Such descriptions are a gross overstatement, for in nearly every state there are other elected officers at the statewide level who share executive power. The governor's power to appoint even nonelected department heads may also be limited. In some states, independent boards control certain top-level appointments, and civil-service systems control others. The senate's power to confirm appointments is a further limitation on the governor's appointment power. Also, the governor's power to remove appointees is impeded in some states by civil-service merit systems and by laws that prohibit removal of officers except for "cause."

Every governor is assisted by a personal staff. The bigger the state, the bigger the staff is likely to be, and the more dependent the governor upon it. In a sense, the governor is not one person but a collection of persons. The governor's staff is a group of assistant governors. Most governors want a staff with

---

[17]Fewer than a dozen governors have been removed by the impeachment process. The most recent example is Governor Evan Mecham of Arizona, April 1988. See *The Book of the States, 1986–87 Edition* (Lexington, Ky.: The Council of State Governments, 1986), p. 26.

public relations know-how in addition to loyalty, shared attitudes, and good sense.

Newly elected governors with soaring visions of all they will accomplish soon hit the pavement of disillusioning reality. The two main reasons for this almost unavoidable fate are (1) almost everything a governor wants to accomplish will cost money, and there isn't enough money, and (2) almost everything he or she wants to accomplish will rock the boat, threaten empires, and disturb vested interests inside and outside the bureaucracy.

Actually governors do not have nearly the power they are imagined to have by the general public. Many people advocate strengthening the position of governor by increasing his power to appoint and remove top-level bureaucrats and his power to organize and reorganize the executive branch. Reformers who wish to strengthen the office of governor also favor lengthening the term, abolishing laws that limit the number of consecutive terms, strengthening the governor's personal staff, and establishing a strong budget office for the governor.

The importance of the office of lieutenant governor is often exaggerated. However, if a lieutenant governor is compatible with the governor, the governor can delegate many important jobs to him or her. Nominating and electing the governor and lieutenant governor as a team, rather than each separately, helps produce a compatible duo.

SUGGESTIONS FOR FURTHER READING

BEYLE, THAD L. and LYNN MUCHMORE, *Being Governor: The View from the Office.* Durham, N.C.: Duke Press Policy Studies, 1983.

DOMETRIUS, NELSON C., "Measuring Gubernatorial Power," *Journal of Politics* (May 1979), 589–610.

"THE GOVERNOR AS CEO," *State Government* (July–August 1986), entire issue.

MOREHOUSE, SARAH MCCALLY, "The State Political Party and the Policy-Making Process," *American Political Science Review* (March 1973), 55–72.

NATIONAL GOVERNORS' ASSOCIATION, *The Governor's Office.* Washington, D.C., 1976.

PRESCOTT, FRANK W., and JOSEPH F. ZIMMERMAN, *The Politics of the Veto of Legislation in New York State* (2 vols.). Washington, D.C.: University Press of America, 1980.

RANSONE, COLEMAN B., JR., *The American Governorship.* Westport, Conn.: Greenwood, 1982.

SABATO, LARRY, *Goodbye to Good-Time Charlie,* 2nd ed. Washington, D.C.: Congressional Quarterly Press, 1984.

WARREN, ROBERT PENN *All the King's Men.* New York: Harcourt, Brace, 1946.

WYNER, ALAN J., "Staffing the Governor's Office," *Public Administration Review* (January/February 1970), 17–24.

7

the legislature

PREVIEW

MAJESTY

Andy and I walked over to the State Capitol Building for lunch. He is a blunt and rather bilious newspaper reporter. I wanted to ask him what he really felt about the state legislature. "But that's an awful question," he said as we descended the once-palatial stairway to the ground floor. "What can one *feel* about a legislature?"

The cafeteria was dimly lit by bare bulbs. The marble floor was strewn with cigarette butts and crumpled napkins. Battered chairs were in disarray around plastic tables whose tops were sticky with mustard and pickle drippings. We bought cold ham sandwiches and cartons of milk from a blind man who ran the sandwich bar. The golden dome of the Capitol was several hundred feet straight up from us.

"How do I feel about the legislature? Feel?" Andy took a bite and chewed it as if it were the question I had put to him. "Well, you know," he said, "I guess you could say I feel the same way about the legislature as I feel about this cafeteria. Yes, that's it, that's actually how I feel."

"What do you mean?"

"The mingling of splendor and trash. The mixture of beauty and ugliness. Dignity and coarseness."

"Doesn't that mixture mirror the electorate itself—the people?" I asked as we got up to leave.

"Yes, I sup . . . Aw . . . now look what I did . . . stepped on a wad of gum."

THE TRIUMPH OF LEGISLATIVE POWER

State legislatures once symbolized America and America's democratic faith. Colonial legislatures led the epic struggle against an arbitrary British crown. For a quarter century after the Declaration of Independence, state legislatures were totally dominant, were in fact the government. Governors were barely tolerated. Judges, too, came under the shadow of the legislature, which in many states had acquired the power to appoint them. Although separation of powers was theoretically enthroned in state constitutions, legislatures towered above the other branches as a tree towers over ants. Even in Massachusetts, whose constitution bluntly said that "the legislative department shall never exercise the executive and judicial power," this was never fully observed. The American Revolution had been at heart a rebellion against executive power—a war between legislative and executive power. Legislative power triumphed.

DECLINE

Like all rebellions, however, the American Revolution went too far. Twenty-five years of legislative dominance were sufficient to demonstrate the need for executives. States gradually strengthened their governors and created a variety of new offices to be filled by election. Although these separately elected officials did not add to the governor's power, they did augment the role of the executive branch in state affairs. Slowly, as memory of autocratic royal governors faded and as experience with less frightening governors accumulated, legislatures relaxed their hostility to executive power and accepted executive power as a necessary ingredient of good government. One might say the decline of legislatures began with the lessening of hostility toward governors and with a growing trust in executives.

However, the decline of American state legislatures did not result solely from the resurrection of governors. Legislatures themselves fell into disgrace; it was particularly shameful since they had had such an exalted, honorable, and heroic role. It was as if the town preacher had been caught stealing sausages. Indeed it was theft and corruption that cost so dearly.

DEMOCRATIZATION

Democratization of state legislatures had something to do with their skid. **Jacksonian democracy** it was called. Property qualifications for voting were abandoned. Andrew Jackson, the crude, brawling, semiliterate from backwoods America, personified the new masses of propertyless voters. His opponent in the presidential election of 1828 was John Quincy Adams, a stiff and scrupulous candidate who represented the old order. The likes of Jackson and the likes of Adams were battling it out at every level of American government: it was a war of the new order versus the old order, of the semiliterate versus the literate, of the provident versus the improvident, of the discerning versus the indiscerning, of the rigid versus the reckless. Such a description overstates the contest, of course, but all over America a battle of contrasting breeds was going on: mini-

Jacksons fought mini-Adamses. With the rise of Jackson and his breed, the character of people serving in state legislatures was profoundly altered. The change did not come all at once, but continued throughout the nineteenth century.

CORRUPTION

As democratization progressed, service in the legislature ceased to be a favorite "community service" of the wealthy and the able. Many now shunned it. Furthermore, politics offered little financial reward, except, of course, for bribes. Most able men therefore preferred business or the professions. Thus, legislatures came to be populated by a lesser sort.

Buying Legislation

While those prone to take bribes were populating the legislature, those prone to give bribes were also thriving. The new business giants that were popping up all over the country—merchandising, investment, manufacturing, transportation, mining, oil, to mention a few—learned how greatly they could be hurt or helped by what state legislatures did. Many business leaders were as anxious about the legislature as they were about their factories and corporate offices. They bought legislation as if they were buying a ton of steel or a carload of fertilizer.

Many ingenious, indirect, and seemingly legal ways of buying legislation blossomed. Flat payment to legislators for votes was rare by comparison with the more sophisticated payments masquerading as ordinary business transactions. A legislator might be paid an "honorarium" for making a speech, or a "retainer" for supposed legal counsel; be allowed to "manage" the sale (at 6 percent commission) of expensive property, or to buy property at bargain prices; or simply be given generous campaign contributions. The bribers were really quite inventive.

Curbing the Legislature

Laws against the purchase of legislation are almost as useless as laws against breathing. The only sure way to stop corruption by public officials is to do away with public officials. Since that appears out of the question, our ancestors—harassed by rampant bribery—did everything short of doing away with the legislature, and that accounts for several of the worst "shortcomings" of legislatures today. Some of the shortcomings that are so piercingly condemned by today's reformers were put there by yesterday's reformers to curb legislative abuse of power.

REFORM

Muckrakers

One cannot say for certain whether corruption of legislatures was worse at the turn of the century or whether it only seemed worse because everybody was exposing it. In any case there is a period in American history called the *era of the muckrakers* so named because President Theodore Roosevelt in 1906 praised the people who **muckrake,** or expose alleged corruption by public officials. The press flourished on muckraking, digging up every little supposedly corrupt thing an officeholder ever did. It was the mainstay of numerous publications and grist for countless authors. Reporters did not by any means limit their attention to corruption in state legislatures but investigated all branches and levels of government and society. Their actions led to an attack on monopolies and upon extremes of wealth and poverty in the nation. A great book of the era dealing with political corruption was *The Shame of the Cities* by Lincoln Steffens.[1] All this was part of a larger phenomenon called the Progressive movement, led by William Jennings Bryan, Robert M. La Follette, Theodore Roosevelt, and Woodrow Wilson.

Progressive Movement

The **Progressive movement** brought many changes in state and local government. Between 1900 and 1920 state constitutions were revised by nearly a thousand constitutional amendments. The supposed cure for boss rule and corruption was to limit the power of legislatures and give more power to the people. The first years of the twentieth century saw the introduction of the referendum, the recall, and the initiative. Direct popular election of United States senators was introduced[2] (they were previously elected by the state legislatures.[3]) Municipal home rule was invented to free cities from the machinations of state political bosses, some new variations of city government were evolved to curb boss rule of cities, and civil-service merit systems were devised for the same purpose. Business regulation was expanded so that a collar could be put around some of the great financial interests that, while building the country, were also at times corrupting government and abusing the public. Limits were put on legislatures. Many states severely limited the frequency and duration of legislative sessions, assuming that the less they met, the less damage they could do. Debt limitations were introduced to civilize the financial power of legislatures. The pay of legislators was also limited. The stringency of many of these limits on state legislatures has been modified in recent years in numerous states.

SESSIONS

A Winter Pastime

Most state legislators in early America were farmers. Now if you were a farmer serving in the legislature, when would you like the legislature to meet, and for how long? You might say, "Let's not meet 'til the crops are harvested and Christmas and New Year's celebrated, then let's meet through January, February, and March until it's time to plow again." That's exactly the timetable that became traditional for state legislatures and was written into many state constitutions.

[1]Lincoln Steffens, *The Shame of the Cities* (New York: McClure, Phillips, 1904; New York: Sagamore, 1957).
[2]*U.S. Const.,* 17th Amendment.
[3]Ibid., Art. I, Sec. 3.

One might almost suspect that in early America the purpose of the legislature was to give its members something to do during the long winter months.

Frequency of Sessions

In the early nineteenth century most state legislatures convened every year, but toward the end of that century, as public trust in legislatures declined, sessions in many states were limited to one every two years (biennial sessions). By 1940 only four states had annual legislative sessions. Since then, though, the trend has been back to annual sessions, and today most states have regular annual sessions. However, several states with annual sessions operate somewhat biennially in that every other year the session is limited to such things as budget matters and items presented by the governor. The ten most populous states (except Texas) all have annual sessions. Why Texas with its great population, complexity, and size continues to limit its legislature to biennial meetings, and for only 140 calendar days at that, is hard to understand. California's legislature runs continuous two-year cycles from December each even-numbered year to November 30 of the next even-numbered year. Essentially the California legislature is in session all the time, except for an occasional recess.

Length of Regular Sessions

A large number of states severely limit how long their legislature may meet in regular session (another product of the age of suspicion), although 8 of the 10 most populous have no such limits. Florida's legislature is allowed to extend its sessions upon approval of a three-fifths vote of members of both houses. Texas remains the only top-ten state to hold a stopwatch on its legislature, but its time limit is fairly long compared with those in other states. All told, fewer than a dozen states set a limit on the legislature. At the other extreme, Wyoming imposes a limit of 20 legislative days in even years but allows its legislature to bask in an ocean of time (40 days) in odd-numbered years. North Dakota tells its legislature to get everything done in 80 days every other year. Iowa and a few other states ingeniously limit the length of sessions by limiting the number of days legislators may be paid for their labors.

Special Sessions

Special sessions, which may be called by the governor in most states (or by the legislature itself in some), offer a cushion of time to allow the legislature to deal with emergencies. Governors have to be frugal in their calls for special sessions: members of the legislature don't like their lives interrupted for light causes. Furthermore, the press never fails to ballyhoo just how much it is costing taxpayers per day for the legislature to convene in special session.

Should Frequency and Duration of Sessions Be Limited?

Although at one time it may have seemed the height of wisdom to limit the frequency and duration of legislative sessions, it has become increasingly popular to believe (especially among political scientists) that all such limits should be thrown off and the legislature given all the time it wants to do its job. Why, it is asked, should the legislature ever adjourn if it doesn't want to? These limitations make people think the legislature isn't very important; they are demeaning to the legislature. This in turn gives people the idea that members of the legislature shouldn't be paid very much, don't need offices, don't need any paid assistants, don't in fact need a very good place to work. The absence of all that accouterment feeds still further the idea that the legislature really isn't too important. Reformers say the legislature *is* important. What it does touches our lives in countless ways. Legislative bodies should not be told to get everything done in 20, 40, or any specific number of days. The complex problems legislatures have to deal with need to be studied, pondered, and discussed, and the legislature needs time for this. Reformers point to the end-of-session madhouse that prevails in so many state legislatures when hundreds of bills must be voted up or down before the clock strikes twelve—members vote wildly and blindly on countless measures they don't know a thing about.

Modification of Session Limitations

A number of states, not wanting to cast aside all limits on the frequency and length of sessions, have taken steps to modify the rigors of those **session limitations.** Some states, though allowing annual sessions of the legislature, restrict the

---

Box 7-1. The Case for Short Sessions

"Heck no!"

That was the answer I got from a gaunt and graying member of the Iowa general assembly when I asked him if he would like longer sessions of the legislature.

"Wouldn't the legislature do a better job if it had more time?"

"Maybe. Maybe not. But I've got a business to run back home. I can't afford to be here all year. We're not elected or paid to be full-time legislators. We're part-timers; sessions are already too long. I've been trying to shorten them. There aren't many members here who want longer sessions. We're doing all sorts of things to keep our sessions down to a reasonable length. And the more we speed up our work, the better job we do. That's a serendipity."

"Serendipity?"

"Yes, We farmers are using big words these days. It means a fortunate unexpected byproduct. Our attempts to shorten the session have made us more efficient. We work harder and pay better attention."

Another member of the Iowa legislature, Senator Lowell L. Junkins, wrote how the legislature attempts to shorten its sessions through improved efficiency in the use of committees, including budget subcommittees, and interim study groups, which "enhance the acceptability of legislation" such committees propose.[4] New York Senator Earl W. Brydges described how the legislature of that state achieved its "impossible dream" of passing bills earlier in the session by changing the rules to allow bills to stay alive for two years, unless killed. This makes better use of January and avoids the temptation of the press to call the legislature a "do-nothing legislature" when it doesn't start passing bills during that month.[5]

---

[4]Lowell L. Junkins, "Changes in Legislative Procedure: The Iowa Experiment," *State Government* (Winter 1978), p. 43.

[5]Earl W. Brydges, "The New York Legislature Gets Its Impossible Dream," *State Government* (Summer 1970), p. 163.

session every other year to budgetary matters and to matters presented by the governor. Some state legislatures, limited in the time they may meet each session and not wanting to crowd too much into too short a time, have adopted the practice of meeting twice each year; they hold *split sessions.* During the first session the legislature organizes itself and bills are introduced. Then it adjourns for a month or so while members collect their thoughts and consult interested parties in their district. Then the second part of the split session begins, and the members debate and act on proposed legislation. At present around 20 states use split sessions.

Interim Committees

Another mechanism now used widely and very effectively to avoid the rigors of short sessions is the interim committee. Although a legislature itself may not meet year-round, several of its committees may. Thus when the legislature convenes, these committees are ready to propose some well-researched bills.

LIMITATIONS ON LEGISLATIVE POWER

Legislatures are curtailed in many other ways besides having their sessions limited. They are also restricted in what they may do, especially where money is concerned. Many of these limitations are the direct result of past legislative abuses.

Debt Limits

Quite a few state governments today maintain balanced budgets, treasury surpluses, and **debt limits.** In this they shine brightly when compared with the federal government. But the states did not always shine. The horrors of past irresponsibility resulted in a tidal wave of state constitutional amendments limiting or prohibiting the legislature from incurring state debt and requiring state bond issues to be submitted to popular vote.

Earmarking

Although the "power of the purse" is said to be the greatest power of legislative bodies, all states have removed a sizable slice of that power from the legislature by earmarking funds. When a typical state legislature sits down to enact an appropriation bill, it finds it has little or nothing to say about a large piece of the state's annual outlay—the money has already been appropriated, so to speak, by constitutional provisions that command how the proceeds of a particular tax or fee shall be spent. In many cases the same result has been achieved through enactments by the legislature itself declaring the purpose for which certain sources of revenue shall be used. The amount of earmarking ranges from around 80 percent in some states to none in others. The average is about 30 to 40 percent. Perhaps the most commonly earmarked tax is the gasoline tax, which is generally reserved for highway construction and repair, but there are all sorts of earmarkings. For example, the Montana constitution says the property tax on livestock must be used to pay bounties for destruction of predatory animals. Commonly license charges and regulatory fees are to be used to cover costs of licensing and regulation. All this has its pros and cons, of course, but one obvious result of earmarking is that it removes funds from the annual scrutiny of the legislature. This is the secret purpose of some earmarking. Powerful interest groups have cornered the proceeds of various taxes for the precise purpose of avoiding the dangers of legislative scrutiny.

Miscellaneous Legal Limitations

Of course, there are all sorts of legal limitations on what the legislature may do. In fact, the entire state constitution is a mass of limitations. The legislature may not pass any law that runs counter to any provision of the state (or federal) constitution. For example, the legislature cannot pass a law abolishing the office of governor if that office was created by the constitution. Nor may the legislature enact laws violating the freedoms of speech, the press, religion, or assembly. Those freedoms are guaranteed by the federal and most state constitutions.

Special Legislation

Legislatures are forbidden by most state constitutions to enact **special legislation.** Legislation must not be directed at individuals, but at the general public or large groups. Thus a legislature may not pass a law granting a divorce to Mr. and Mrs. Smith but may pass a general divorce law. The legislature may not single out a specific city and pass a law concerning it, but may enact general laws applying to categories of cities. Sometimes special legislation masquerades as general legislation, as when the legislature passes a law applying to all cities with more than 500,000 inhabitants, knowing full well there is only one city in the state of that size.

BICAMERALISM

You might think a camera is something to take a picture with, but to early English lawyers a camera was a room or chamber. Even today lawyers use the term *in camera* to describe a hearing that goes on in the judge's office. The term **bicameral legislature** was drafted into the English language by Jeremy Bentham to describe a system wherein the legislature is divided into two chambers.

Because only a single one-house legislature exists among the 50 states, we sometimes hear that unicameralism is rare. But it is not rare among local governments. Almost all city councils and other local governing boards are unicameral (single-house) bodies.

Why Bicameralism?

Examples of Congress Possibly the reason most state legislatures have two houses is that Congress set the example. Constitution writers in most states used the federal constitution as their model. The necessity for two houses in most states is not as compelling, however, as the necessity for two houses at the national level. The Constitutional Convention of 1787 was about to disband because of the bickering between big states and little states when finally a solution was found—the Great Compromise. States with big populations such as New York and Pennsylvania naturally wanted representation in Congress based on population. Small states, of course, preferred equality—the states, being equally sovereign, should be equally represented in Congress. Eighty-year-old Benjamin Franklin broke the impasse with an ingenious suggestion. Let both the big and the little states have their way: let us have a Congress with two houses, one in which states are represented by population and another in which states are equally represented. Ultimately this great compromise was adopted. Without it there might have been no Union.

Can any state of the Union, however, honestly say that it established a two-house legislature because it would have been politically impossible to form the state without two houses? Two houses might be politically useful and politically convenient. But politically indispensable? In answering these questions the United States Supreme Court drew a distinction between the United States Senate and the senates of the various states and rejected the idea that both the federal government and the states could rely on the same argument for having one house of a legislative body based on arbitrary geographic units. Both houses of a state legislature must be based on population.[6]

Houses Check Each Other   Of course, there are some classic arguments for two houses other than that they can represent constituencies of different sizes. If both houses have to agree on every law, then neither can get away with precipitous and stupid behavior unless the other is prepared to be equally precipitous and stupid. Yet, sadly, it is also true that neither house can get away with being wise and sensible unless the other house can lift itself to a like brilliance. If careless, impetuous action is an evil to be avoided, there are plenty of brakes against speed in each house without multiplying the situation by two. In modern legislative bodies the main illness to be cured is inaction—not impetuosity. Nor are two houses a sure-fire guarantee against impetuosity, nor is impetuosity always bad. It took the two houses of Congress only minutes to declare war against Japan after President Franklin D. Roosevelt asked them to on December 8, 1941. The procedure through which bills have to pass in each house of the typical American legislative body is a wonderland of circumlocution, a fortress of complexity safe from the allurements of speed. One house of each bicameral legislature in America could disappear without causing any dangerous violations of the legislative speed limit.

Nebraska

Nebraska replaced its two-house system with a one-house legislature in the depression year of 1934 and seems to be getting along fairly well. The system's great champions, such as Senator George Norris, were not especially motivated by the notion that one house would be cheaper than two, but they guessed, and rightly so, that the economy argument might appeal to depression-poor voters.

A cardinal advantage of the one-house legislature, aside from economy and speed, is that it is much easier for observers to keep an eye on the progress

[6]Reynolds v. Sims, 377 U.S. 533 (1964); Baker v. Carr, 369 U.S. 186 (1962).

of bills through the legislature—much easier to watch the ball as it bounces across the legislative court. Special interests have one less house, one less procedural jungle, in which to assault and defeat legislation or to put over deals.

The less the public understands the legislative drama, the less it bothers to watch. Procedural complexity makes an apathetic public. In effect, this apathy removes the legislature from the people, makes it less democratic. The Nebraska reformers wished to make the legislature more visible and therefore more understandable and controllable by the public. Another concern was that parties, and the games they play in the legislature, further blur the picture. Therefore, the same constitutional amendment that made the Nebraska legislature unicameral also made it nonpartisan: let issues, rather than party alliances, govern voting patterns, said the reformers.

The supposed advantages of unicameralism had been advocated long before its adoption in Nebraska in 1934. In fact in 1920 the idea had achieved such popularity that the National Municipal League recommended it and offered a model state constitution embodying its principles.

Since the adoption of unicameralism in Nebraska, the idea has popped up all over the United States. Practically every year a smattering of legislators across the country make page-three headlines in the capital-city press by dropping a "unicameral" bill in the hopper. Jesse Unruh, treasurer of the state of California and once speaker of the California State Assembly, has championed unicameralism for years. Despite persuasive arguments, such efforts never get to first base against the force of tradition. Unicameralism has worked well in American local government: almost all local governing bodies are unicameral. Furthermore, there is ample evidence from Canada that unicameralism works fine at the "state" level: every province has a unicameral parliament.

Nomenclature

Nebraska calls its **one-house** legislature a *senate*. Most states call their legislature either the *general assembly* or simply the *legislature*. Massachusetts and New Hampshire use the term *general court*, whereas North Dakota and Oregon refer to the *legislative assembly*.

Every state calls its upper house the senate, and most states call their lower house the *house of representatives*. Several states (including California, New York, Nevada, and Wisconsin) call their lower house the *assembly;* New Jersey uses the term *general assembly;* Maryland has a *house of delegates*.

Upper and Lower Houses

The term *upper house* is somewhat insulting to the **lower house,** but neither term is official. Why is one house upper and one lower? What is upper or lower about them? Very little. The terminology is inherited from the British Parliament, where in earlier times the House of Lords, being composed of lords, was higher in a social sense as well as in power. The other house of Parliament, Commons, was, as its name implies, composed of commoners, who were obviously lower in status and power. Today the power relationship between the two houses of Parliament has reversed itself: Lords is almost powerless; Commons is all-powerful.

Although the two houses of our state legislatures are roughly equal in power, state senates do have certain characteristics that reveal a distant, almost forgotten, relationship to the House of Lords. First, a senator's term is longer—most state-senate terms are four years; most lower-house terms are two, although about a third of the states, such as New York and North Carolina, provide equal terms for members of both houses. The longer terms for those in the upper houses of most states is reminiscent of the longer terms for Lords (which are lifetime).

State senates also have some vestiges of judicial power. Lords has long been the supreme court of England. American senates are by no means courts in that sense, but they do serve as courts for trial of impeachments. Lower houses bring charges; upper houses try those charges. Impeachments are rare. An officer threatened with impeachment is likely to resign before impeachment actually occurs.[7]

State senates confirm the appointment of a wide variety of officials. This harks back to the role of Lords as an advisory council to the Crown. We see survivals of that advisory role in the power of senates to "give advice and consent" to appointments. The United States Senate gives its advice and consent to treaties as well as to appointments.[8] Furthermore, state senates are upper in that they are smaller and therefore more exclusive and "aristocratic." The smallness of senates gives each member more power than a crowded lower house gives its members.

SIZE OF THE LEGISLATURE

America has about 2000 state senators and 5500 members of lower houses, some 7500 state legislators in all. The average upper house has about 40 members; the average lower house about 113. New Hampshire has the biggest lower house—400 members, almost as many as the United States House of Representatives. There are so many New Hampshire representatives that they can't get acquainted with one another, especially since about 170 members disappear every two years and are replaced by a new set of strangers. Massachusetts also has a gigantic house of representatives—160 members—and Pennsylvania's lower house has 203. The smallest legislature is Alaska's—with 60 members. Alaska also has the smallest upper house, 20, as well as the smallest lower house, 40.

Is a Large Legislature More Representative?

Large Organizations Have Oligarchic Tendencies   These huge numbers do not necessarily make the legislature more representative or more democratic. In fact, the opposite may be true. The larger a body, the more oligarchic, disciplined, and even dictatorial it must become in its internal organization in order to get anything done. A clique of 10 or 15 people are apt to run the show. Of course, as Robert Michels has so eloquently pointed out, the iron law of

---

[7]See Malcolm B. Parsons, "Checking Abuse of Power: Does Impeachmet Work?" *National Civil Review* (July–August 1986), pp. 219–224.

[8]*U.S. Const.*, Art. II, Sec. 2.

oligarchy rules everywhere: every organization is run by the few.[9] It may also be an iron law, however, that the smaller the organization, the less oligarchic it is. Certainly small groups tend to be more personal and informal, and it is easier for a small group than a large group to discuss things. One would think a legislative body should be small enough to allow coherent discussion on the floor by those who want to say something. Certainly a legislative body that exceeds 50 is pushing the limits of toleration. Even so, there are only three states—Nevada, Delaware, and Alaska—with fewer than 50 in the lower house. However, it is encouraging that most *upper* houses do have fewer than 50 members.

Committees "Reduce" the Size of a Legislature

Legislatures generally do their work through committees, where most of the discussion and debate goes on—and committees tend to be about the size of university seminars. Committees are said to be necessary because no legislator can be an expert on everything that comes before the legislature. Committees are therefore set up to make themselves expert on various departments of knowledge. One suspects, however, that the larger a legislative body, the more it is driven to rely on committees. The sheer impossibility of carrying on much floor discussion leaves no alternative but to resort to committees. Probably a good deal could be discussed by an entire house, if the house were small enough to handle it. The United States Supreme Court grinds our great quantities of "judicial legislation" on highly complex subjects without resorting to committees. The court has only nine members, and one cannot help wondering if state legislatures might be improved if each house were reduced to that size.

Size Means Organizational Complexity

Clearly the larger a legislative body, the more it must organize itself to get anything done; size therefore means organizational complexity. Organizational complexity is the natural habitat of special interests, which lurk behind every tree and bush of the procedural jungle, ready to chop down any bill they don't like. Procedural complexity makes the legislature less responsive to the wide public and more subservient to narrow interests. Furthermore, the procedural complexity of this jungle leaves the public lost, dumbfounded, and apathetic. Under cover of this thick brush of procedure, all sorts of things go on that the public wouldn't stand for if they could see them. No doubt a great many people are convinced that the bigger the legislature, the more democratic it is, but appearances are deceiving. It's quite possible that the more democratic something looks, the less it is in fact.

It's Difficult to Reduce the Size of a Legislature

Why don't states simply reduce the size of their lower houses? Reducing is difficult. Trying to reduce the size of a house of representatives is like trying to reduce the size of the Pacific Ocean. Just how do you go about getting the waters to recede? Of course, it can be done by constitutional amendment. In most states, however, the legislature itself proposes most constitutional amendments, and you're not likely to catch legislators proposing their own doom. Members might vote for a smaller house if they were sure their own seat wouldn't be liquidated in the process, but when you talk about getting rid of three-fourths, or one-half, or even only one-fourth

---

[9]Robert Michels, *Political Parties* (Glencoe, Ill.: Free Press, 1949).

of the house, you're talking about a threat to the continued service of every member. It is fine to vote for good ideas, as long as one's own survival isn't threatened.

Of course, in many states people can amend their constitution without getting permission from the legislature, but this initiative procedure usually requires an astronomical number of signatures on a petition. Such signatures are especially hard to get because very few voters have the slightest idea there is anything at all wrong with having a larger legislature; seldom is any voter roused to indignation by the thought of it. Still, several states have managed to reduce the size of their legislature: Nebraska in 1934, Vermont in 1965, Iowa in 1971, and Illinois in 1980.

TERMS AND TURNOVER

All states except four now have two-year terms for members of the lower houses (those four have four-year terms). As for the upper house, most states provide four-year terms for senators; about a dozen cling to two-year terms. Short terms might be less objectionable if more members served several terms, but many do not come back—the turnover rate is astounding. A sizable chunk of every legislative body is composed of brand-new first-termers; consistently about a third of all American state legislators are in their first term. Sometimes as many as 60 or 70 percent of a particular legislative body will be new. This not only results in gross amateurism but also has some curious side effects. It gives tremendous power to old-timers who know the ropes, and it weakens the power of elected leaders of the house.

Reasons for High Turnover

Why are there so many new faces in every legislature? Some members are defeated, but this isn't the biggest cause of turnover. Many simply don't want another term—they either resign their seat or decline to run again. What dampens their spirit? What brings them to the point of abandoning that for which they once fought so ardently? Some members, of course, never intended to serve very long and in fact never had much interest in the job of legislator. Their candidacy may have been a publicity stunt to advance some other career. Lawyers, for example, find this an excellent way to advertise, an excellent way to acquire new clients. Being elected to the legislature not only puts a lawyer's name in the news but also surrounds him or her with an aura of success, power, and connections. Sometimes members of the legislature receive attractive job offers by virtue of a successful campaign. Even an unsuccessful campaign sometimes leads to opportunities in the public or private sector.

Occasionally members quit the legislature because it bores them. Their original romantic notion of the job may have been distant from the reality they collided with. Other members find public service frustrating. They may have gone to the legislature with heroic ideals and found they couldn't get anywhere without compromise. Other members quit because conscientious service there takes too much time. They may have thought the job was only part-time—just a couple months in the spring, then nothing until the following spring. They soon discover it's a whole lot more than that. Between sessions they have interim committee work; they find themselves serving as year-round lightning rods for unhappy constituents; they find themselves called upon year-round to help all sorts of people with all sorts of problems; they become the target of lobbying by public agencies, such as state universities and hospitals, and the target of more lobbying by private interests, such as truckers and farmers. This goes on all year, day and night; absorbs time; fractures days, weeks, and months; disrupts family life; harasses professional life. The life of plagued and perturbed legislators may be quite different from what they envisioned on that splendid day a few years before when they first pictured themselves seated under the majestic dome of the capitol. Some members dread the thought of another election, another campaign, another half year of meetings, coffees, fund-raisers, and evenings out. Some members abandon the attempt at reelection when their seat has been imperiled by reapportionment, and occasionally members leave the legislature to run for higher office.[10]

Very little can be done to curb turnover. Longer legislative terms might help. Short terms obviously increase the opportunities for defeat or retirement. Staggering the terms of legislators could help mitigate the ravages of turnover. Increasing the pay of legislators might sweeten the pot.

Are Short Terms More Democratic?

We hear that legislators should have short terms because it keeps them on a short leash and close to the people—it makes the system more democratic. But what is the price of this supposed benefit? The price may be loss of the very thing it allegedly produces, loss of responsiveness to voter opinion. How so?

First, the oftener anyone has to stand for election, the more he or she is at the mercy of those who have the money to finance those elections.

Second, is good government served by keeping legislators' necks constantly under the ax of voter disapproval? Voters don't always know what's good for them. Legislators don't either, but it might help if they had sufficient time in office to study the issues. Also, the longer the term, the freer legislators are to use their informed judgment.

Third, campaigns are very time-consuming. Do we want a legislative body composed of members who are forced to spend nearly all their time campaigning? We might be better off with a legislative body composed of people who have sufficient time between elections to legislate. Legislators are apt to be a total loss their first year: they arrive at the capitol not knowing much about legislative procedure, not knowing how to introduce a bill or who to see about what, not knowing their way around the capitol building itself, or around the bureaucracy, or around the city. Legislators do not begin to be effective until

---

[10]Among the several factors that may significantly affect the extent of voluntary retirement among state legislators are probability of electoral defeat, degree of interparty competition at the state legislative level, the opportunity for higher office, length of legislative session, average size of legislative district (number of people represented), size of the chamber, level of compensation, reapportionment, type of electoral district used (single-member or multimember), and the length of the term of office. Jerry Calvert, "Revolving Doors: Volunteerism in State Legislatures," *State Government* (Autumn 1979), pp. 174–81.

they get their bearings. Two-year terms really aren't very democratic: legislators might not really begin to represent anybody until their second year.

COMPENSATION

Differences among States

The pay of state legislators varies widely from state to state. California legislators (who serve full time) are currently among the best paid—at last report they were making about twice the average annual income of American workers. Michigan, New York, Illinois, and Massachusetts also give their legislators higher salaries than most other states. Thirty states pay legislators about what an average American worker makes. A few states pay almost nothing at all. New Hampshire legislators, after their most recent pay raise (the first in a century), now get $200 a year.

What is Pay?

The word **pay** is not easy to define. Lawmakers in most states get side benefits that look suspiciously like pay—per diem allowances (so much per day to cover living expenses while attending legislative sessions), insurance policies, pensions, a telephone, postage and travel privileges, district-office expenses, interim payments, and "leadership" allowances (for holding an office within the legislature). Thus it is rather tricky to calculate just what legislator's salary is, and one wonders if legislators don't deliberately make the calculation of their precise pay a mathematical challenge. In some states, legislators get a variety of freebies, such as free tickets to football games at the state university and immunity from speeding tickets issued while on state business. Private interests may also be generous with free memberships in clubs, free passes to ski areas, reduced prices for hotel rooms, and the like.

Proper Level of Pay

What should a state legislator be paid? It does, after all, cost money to campaign for the office, sometimes a lot of money. If legislators don't get paid enough to finance their campaign, they're liable to get the money from special interests. On the other hand, they may get it from special interests anyway. Competent people won't work for nothing, nor will they work for a little. So we hear. If you want competent people in the legislature, you have to pay them the going rate for competent people. On the other hand, some competent people seem willing to serve for practically nothing because there are other compensations besides pay—psychic income, power, prestige. Furthermore, some legislators can advance their other career by service in the legislature—lawyers, for example.

Voters resist high pay for part-time legislators. Whether higher pay would attract better legislators or free them from special interests or induce them to stay in the legislature for longer periods is uncertain. Higher pay would certainly make it easier for salaried people such as schoolteachers to serve.

IS THE LEGISLATURE REPRESENTATIVE?

Can a Legislature Mirror the Public?

Members of state legislatures in general are more prosperous and have more education than the public they serve. In that sense they do not mirror the general public, and it is therefore claimed they are not representative of the general public. State legislatures also fail to mirror certain other characteristics of the general public, such as sex and race, and on that account too are charged with being nonrepresentative. The list of ways in which state legislatures fail to mirror the public is very long. It would probably be impossible for any legislature to exactly mirror the public. Perhaps every group of human beings—whether a legislature, a fraternity, or a labor union—is nonrepresentative of the larger public simply because every group attracts persons with a select set of qualifications appropriate for that group. Bowling leagues attract people who like to bowl, and so on. Legislatures also attract people with special characteristics that make them likely candidates for the job, not the least of which is a certain awareness of social problems and a desire to do something about them. The quest for a representative legislature is perhaps noble, but not completely attainable.

Occupation, Gender, and Ethnicity

Lawyers may still be the biggest occupational group among state legislators, perhaps about 20 percent. Lawyers have a natural interest in the law, and service in the legislature can be helpful to their law practice. But their numbers in the legislature have been decreasing partly because other occupational groups are increasing. One might also assume that lawyers find the ever-lengthening sessions of the legislature so destructive to their law practice that it outweighs the benefits. This is particularly true in the larger states where legislatures are approaching the point of being in continuous session. Longer sessions may also be affecting the ability of other occupational groups to remain in the legislature and turnover rates. In states where legislative sessions are longest, many members (sometimes up to half of them) simply list their occupation as "legislator". The number of "business managers" has decreased. Service in the legislature requires lots of free time, unless, of course, one thinks of legislative service as a regular job.

Educators (mostly retired ones) are now a large and growing occupational group in state legislatures, numbering perhaps 10 percent today. This reflects the increasing organization and political aggressiveness of teachers. States spend about half their money on schools, and it is perhaps useful and natural to have teachers in the legislature. On the other hand, when teachers vote on school appropriations there is perhaps a conflict of interest—though no more so than when lawyers in the legislature vote on legal procedure, or truckers vote on highway legislation, or farmers vote on farm bills, or insurance agents vote on insurance legislation (farmers and insurance agents are two other very large occupational blocs in state legislatures). Conflict of interest is the rule, not the exception, in state legislatures.

A striking increase in the number of women in state legislatures is apparent in recent decades. Today more than a thousand of the nation's 7500 state legislators are women. Moreover, there has been a very great increase in the number of ethnic minorities in state legislatures.

THEORIES OF REPRESENTATION

Not long ago I asked a state senator, "Do you vote on bills the way you think your constituents want you to vote or the way you think you ought to vote on the basis of your own judgment?" He said he did both—that his votes are a mixture of his own judgment plus the wishes of his constituents.

Is There a Majority View?

One **theory of representation** is that legislators should simply vote the way the majority of their constituents want them to vote. This is a very popular view, but it suffers certain practical difficulties. There may not be a majority view. Most voters have never heard of most bills. Most bills touch obscure matters—so obscure that even the average legislator isn't very conscious of the issues involved. Most of the general public simply has no awareness of what the legislature is doing. If the legislature has before it a bill to transfer the office of financial analysis from the treasury department to the controller's office, chances are not one voter in ten thousand could venture an opinion and not one in a million would have any basis for an opinion. Legislatures deal with hundreds of bills every session, and it may well happen that none of them has received enough publicity to produce a majority view among voters.

If there is no majority view, then perhaps there is a view held by a majority of those who do have a view. Normally, however, those who have a view on any particular piece of legislation are a tiny slice of the public—those directly affected by the legislation, especially the leaders of pressure groups. Normally, then, a legislator has to choose between competing interest groups.

Insofar as the general public has a majority view of anything, its view is most likely broad and vague. A majority may clearly want clean rivers and blue skies, but there may be no majority view with regard to specific measures to reach those goals, such as putting a stop to automobile traffic or shutting down factories.

What Is a Mandate?

Some legislators seem to feel that their election is a **mandate** to do the things they said they would do if elected. Even this is questionable because no one really knows why anyone is elected to a particular office. People vote for candidates for all sorts of reasons that may have little to do with platforms or programs. Physical appearance, speaking voice, platform manner, race, religion, sex, age, behavior, and all sorts of circumstances may be involved. Is it justified to assume that voters are rational and have cast their ballot on a purely rational assessment of what a candidate will or won't do once elected? Voters sometimes, perhaps oftener than we think, vote against, rather than for. Candidates may be elected because of the objectionable qualities of their opponents rather than because of their own qualities. Or they may be elected because they had more money to spend on advertising. There is sufficient doubt about the rationality of elections to justify doubting whether any candidate under any circumstances can accurately claim to have a mandate to do anything. Also, does a candidate who has made many campaign promises acquire a mandate for all of them, even though voters may have been favorably influenced by only some of them? And if only some, which? The closer one examines the idea of representative democracy, the fuzzier the idea becomes; ultimately one begins to wonder whether there is or can be any such thing. The system seems to boil down to an arrangement whereby elected officials do whatever they want, until defeated.

The Legislator as Agent

If representation means anything, it may mean that voters acknowledge a legislator as their **agent,** whether or not he or she actually does what they want. An agent (according to the law of agency) holds power delegated to him or her by a principal as long as that principal agrees to let the agent hold that power. Agents can do anything they want within the circle of power delegated to them and may even do things the principal doesn't like. Still, agents remain agents until dismissed by the principal. Agents thus represent the principal, but only in the sense that they stand in place of the principal.

APPORTIONMENT AND REAPPORTIONMENT

Gerrymandering

Naturally we assume that a representative in the legislature represents everybody in his or her district. Technically this may be so, but all sorts of special interests want to be specially represented—urban people, rural people, teachers, farmers, upstaters, downstaters, eastern slopers, western slopers, and so on. Naturally every such group wants to maximize its strength in the legislature, whether by fair means or foul. **Gerrymandering** is one of the foul means. It is a technique by which legislative district lines are drawn in such a way as to magnify the power of one or another group of voters. Political parties are the main perpetrators, increasing their "representation" through astute line drawing and thereby cheating other parties out of their "fair" representation. Of course, when the cheated come to power they get their chance to draw lines. Besides serving party advantage, gerrymandering may also, of course, serve other purposes as well, such as racial gerrymandering (see p. 53) or gerrymandering by incumbent legislators to protect their own chances for re-election.

    The word *gerrymander* arose from the strange appearance of a district cleverly designed in Massachusetts long ago by Elbridge Gerry. The shape reminded someone of a salamander with arms and legs and a twisting torso—hence the combination *gerry-mander*. The boundaries were contrived so as to bring into the district just the right people, and exclude as many others as possible. Gerrymandering can be a great deal of fun and richly rewarding for the majority party. All parties, all factions, and all interests joyfully leap at the opportunity to gerrymander in their own favor. Suppose party X controls the legislature and wants to create a solidly X district. This is done very simply by drawing the district lines so that they include more X people than non-X people. Suppose now party X wants to continue controlling the state legislature. This is done by putting a majority of X people in a majority of the legislative districts. The problem is what to do with the non-X people, who may outnumber X people. You bottle as many of them as possible into the smallest number of districts possible. You'll probably have to concede a number of districts to the opposition, but the important thing is to draw lines giving X at least a slim majority in a majority of districts.

Reapportionment is a lurking threat to every member who happens to hold a seat at the time it occurs each decade. Periodically the boundaries of legislative districts must be redrawn so that all districts are kept more or less equal in population. Redrawing the lines may bring into a district (or exclude from it) certain categories of people that would make a member's reelection difficult. Normally the party in power conducts the districting processes in a highly partisan way—gerrymandering wherever possible in their own behalf. This can be fatal (and is so intended) for some minority-party legislators, and if not fatal, then troublesome beyond words. Even some majority-party legislators may bite the dust through the unfortunate mathematics of reapportionment.

Gerrymandering is an affront to fair representation. Some aspects of it have been successfully attacked in courts.

Geographic Representation Leads to Malapportionment

Sometimes unconscious gerrymandering occurs. Imbalances may be the innocent product of population shifts, although it is not so innocent to allow such imbalances to go uncorrected. Earlier in our history it was common for states to make legislative districts out of counties and other geographical areas but to do so with little regard for the population of those areas. This made sense at the time because counties were natural political units: the population was scattered rather evenly across the landscape in rural areas, and there were few really big towns. Eventually, however, multitudes of people moved into urban areas, and this gave some election districts many more people than others. A classic example of this was the county of Los Angeles, which on the eve of the 1964 reapportionment revolution had some six million people and only one representative in the 40-member state senate; another district, containing Death Valley, had few people but also had one representative. Los Angeles had 38 times as many people as the Death Valley district but the same representation. Such **malapportionment** was repeated on a lesser scale in scores of legislative districts across the nation. It clearly robbed people in populous areas of equality. It was discriminatory and unfair—a denial of equal protection of the law. Denials of equal protection are forbidden by the United States Constitution,[11] yet for many years the United States Supreme Court refused to hear lawsuits seeking to have such schemes of representation declared unconstitutional. The Court shunned those cases because it thought such essentially "political questions" should be left to the political process for settlement—that the state legislatures should simply amend their apportionment laws.[12] The Court felt it should reserve itself for legal controversies that lacked a political solution.

[11]*U.S. Const.,* 14th Amendment.
[12]Colgrove v. Green, 328 U.S. 549 (1946); South v. Peters, 339 U.S. 276 (1950).

Political versus Judicial Solutions

However, political solutions are easier to speak of than to accomplish, particularly solutions to legislative malapportionment. In some states they require an amendment to the state constitution, and many constitutions are difficult to amend (and deliberately so). Also, few legislators want to vote themselves (or their colleagues) out of a job.

Finally in 1962 a case came to the United States Supreme Court in which a plantiff charged that a Tennessee law apportioning seats in the general assembly among the state's 95 counties was a denial of equal protection of the laws.[13] The Tennessee apportionment law had been passed in 1901, and even then the arrangement was arbitrary and capricious and based on no logical formula whatsoever, except the convenience of using counties as legislative districts. Since 1901 the situation had worsened as the state's population redistributed itself. The Supreme Court agreed to hear the case, and in 1964 it handed down six decisions[14] that ultimately led to the redistricting of nearly every state legislature in the United States. Each state was required to "make an honest and good faith effort to construct districts, in both houses of its legislature, as nearly of equal population as is practicable."[15] The same principle applies to local governments[16] and to congressional districts.[17]

Has One-Man-One-Vote Improved Things?

City-Rural Split   Does it really make any difference whether anybody is overrepresented or underrepresented in the state legislature? Urban leaders used to say gross overrepresentation of rural people made the legislature insensitive to the needs of cities. Rural people tend to think big cities are dens of iniquity and that no amount of state aid can uplift them—just let the urban sores fester; better to pave a rural road than a city street; better to spend money on clean, honest, God-fearing rural people than on cities; city people aren't really worth as much as rural people; and there's no reason why the voting power of a block of slums in the city should equal the voting power of a whole town in the countryside. Just what effect such attitudes had on the output of rural-dominated legislatures is uncertain. Surely it must have had some effect, but it is hard to measure because we don't know how cities would have been treated by state legislatures if city people had had their fair share of representation.

City-Suburb Split   If cities were once afflicted by rural domination of legislatures, they are today afflicted by suburban power in the new **one-man-one-vote** legislatures. Nearly every major city is surrounded by collections of people outside the central city limits. Suburbanites are willing to tolerate the city

[13]Baker v. Carr, 396 U.S. 186 (1962).

[14]Reynolds v. Sims, 377 U.S. 533 (1964): WMCA, Inc. v. Lomenzo, 377 U.S. 633 (1964); Maryland Committee for Fair Representation v. Tawes, 377 U.S. 656 (1964); Donis v. Mann, 377 U.S. 678 (1964); Roman v. Sincock, 377 U.S. 695 (1964); Lucas v. Forty-fourth General Assembly of Colorado, 377 U.S. 713 (1964).

[15]Reynolds v. Sims, 377 U.S. 533 (1964).

[16]Avery v. Midland County, 390 U.S. 474 (1968).

[17]Wesberry v. Sanders, 376 U.S. 1 (1964).

Box 7-2. Where One-Man-One-Vote Isn't Necessary

In water districts the right to vote may be limited to those who own property. The property requirement in such districts can be perfectly constitutional, said the United States Supreme Court in 1981. The case, *Ball* v. *James,* involved the Salt River Agricultural Improvement and Power District in Arizona, a water district. Directors of the district are chosen by the voters, but state law permits only persons who own property within the district to vote—one full vote for each acre of land owned. A fractional vote is given to persons who own less than an acre.

A group of people who had been given fractional votes challenged the law in court on constitutional grounds. They pointed out that the Court in an earlier case, *Reynolds* v. *Sims* in 1964, had held that state legislative districts had to be apportioned in such a way as to make the vote of each voter approximately equal in weight—the so-called one-man-one-vote doctrine. However, the high court has now held that the one-man-one-vote principle does not extend to water districts that base voting on landholdings.

insofar as it provides football stadiums, opera houses, museums, quaint restaurants, and a place to earn a living. They do not, however, wish to be part of that city politically, nor do they wish to pay taxes to care for its wretchedness or even taxes for the opera, the zoo, the museum, the stadium, or any other attraction. They cluster around the central city like campers around a fire, just beyond its tax collectors and beyond its miserable schools, but still close enough to enjoy its warmth. Soon they outnumber and outvote the central city and become as hostile to its financial demands as rural folk in a former era ever were. One-man-one-vote has given suburbanites the full force of their numbers.

Is Gerrymandering Dead?

The one-man-one-vote decisions of the Supreme Court have not ended all gerrymandering. Just because districts have to be roughly equal in population does not mean they have to be the same shape. There is still plenty of opportunity to draw lines that include and exclude the people you want to include and exclude, as long as districts are **contiguous** (as long as adjacent districts are touching along all or most of one side). The Supreme Court may one day more vigorously attack party and incumbent gerrymandering even within districts that are equal and contiguous.[18]

STAFF SERVICES TO LEGISLATORS

Like a troupe of actors, the legislature requires stagehands to make things work right during the performance. Legislators are backed up by staff services. Before a bill is introduced there needs to be (or should be) research on what laws already exist on the subject; somebody to write the proposed bill in suitably legal language; printing presses and people to operate them; budget experts to calculate

[18]See Tony Stewart and Sydney Duncombe, "Gerrymandering in the Courts: Threshold of a New Reapportionment Revolution?" *National Civic Review* (March–April 1986), pp. 88–98.

the anticipated financial impact of bills; guards, secretaries, and clerks; and more.

Offices and Personal Staffs

Most state legislators have nowhere near the facilities or staff support enjoyed by members of Congress. But the situation is improving. Only a few years ago a typical state legislator had no office—only a minidesk on the house floor. Today a majority of states provide legislators with offices, and some states have built spacious new office buildings for that purpose. Yet in other states, office space is provided only for officers of the legislature, such as the speaker, the president pro tem, and the floor leaders.

Likewise, the idea of providing individual legislators with personal staffs was almost unheard of a generation ago. Today nearly all states furnish legislators some form of help. Certain states give year-round personal staff at the capitol, although in some cases this help must be shared by more than one legislator. Several states also endow legislators with staff help for use within their district, but in a few cases legislators are merely allowed to decide whether they want to use their staff at the capitol or in their district. A number of states do not provide personal staff except during actual sessions of the legislature. Four or five states grant senators a bit more staff help than representatives.

Some states are equipping legislators with personal computers to show off in new offices. Although some legislators may still be a little mystified by the tremendous powers of microcomputers, these machines are beginning to have a striking effect on legislative activity. Research might show that computers have done more to strengthen legislatures in recent years than anything else. Throughout this century one of the great deficiencies of legislative bodies has been their clumsiness (by comparison with the executive branch) in marshaling the facts they need to argue successfully with the administration, or even to go through the motions of legislation. When it comes to putting their hands on information, especially financial information, legislators can get a lot of critical facts through computers (for example, how much of his annual appropriation the attorney general has used up as of today) and can get those facts in short order, without having to dispatch letters, make telephone calls, or send a secretary running all over the capital. Computers also help legislators look up any law or track the progress of a bill through the legislative maze, saving them time and energy for other things. Word processing (typing by computer) also saves oceans of time, because once something has been typed it doesn't have to be retyped and retyped: staff can use their time on something more productive.

Committee Staffs

State legislatures do most of their work through committees in which the pros and cons of legislation are weighed. These committees need clerical and research assistance, but here too most legislative bodies operate on a shoestring. The trouble with giving committees the staff assistance they need is that the majority party is prone to use such staff for partisan work as well as committee work. (The same danger of misuse occurs when legislators are given personal assistants, as is evident in Washington, D.C., where taxpayers support lavish personal congressional staffs that spend much of their time working for reelection of their employer.) It is hard to keep politics out of anything as intensely political as a state legislature or a Congress. Elections are expensive, and many elected officials are eager to shift the expense of elections to taxpayers. One way to do this is to use committee (or personal) staff as campaign workers. For better or for worse, recent years have seen a trend toward increased committee staffs; some states have gone so far as to give staffs to party caucuses. This trend toward committee staffs has come partially at the expense of legislative councils.

The Legislative Council

How is it possible to equip a legislative body with a professional staff that will not be diverted, exploited, and manipulated for political purposes? Probably there is no fail-safe political chastity belt for staffs, but at least one fairly successful mechanism has been used in numerous states. It is commonly called the **legislative council**—a fact-finding, information-collecting agency for the legislature. Normally the legislative council is a bipartisan committee of the legislature; it hires a staff director, who in turn hires a professional staff. The professional staff itself has come to be called the legislative council. Insofar as possible the staff will help individual legislators acquire information. In a number of states the legislative council also provides temporary staff with which committees of the legislature can do research. The council may also assist committee chairpersons in administrative matters. In some states the legislative council supplies a good deal of leadership. But the future of legislative councils is uncertain because of the ongoing decentralization of the legislature, whereby more staff are being given to individual legislators and to legislative committees and party caucuses.

Bill-Drafting Service

Legislatures also commonly provide themselves with a staff of professional bill drafters—a **legislative drafting office.** Its job is to help committees or individual legislators draft bills. A legislator may have only a general idea what he or she wants a bill to say. The drafting office will translate that general idea into specific language. This is basically a legal service. The drafting office therefore maintains an attorney-client relationship with any legislator who comes for help.

Bill drafting involves, first, a search of existing law to see whether part (or all) of the proposed bill is already on the books or would require repeal of any existing law. New bills must be written in view of existing law and in language to which judges and lawyers are accustomed. Furthermore, bill drafting involves some skill at writing—not the kind of writing one finds in best-selling novels, but the kind that nails down everything that is to be nailed down. Few legislators have the time, the knowledge, or the talent to write their legislative proposals in language suitable for publication as a state law. The legislative bill-drafting service can make any member of the legislature look very smart.

Revisor of Statutes

Revised Code   Another service every legislature needs is a staff whose job is to keep track of what the legislature has enacted over the years. This year's law may modify or repeal last year's law. Somebody has to keep track of every action ever taken by the legislature since the state was admitted to the Union. An up-to-date **revised code** is needed so that the general public, as well as members of the legislature, can know all of that accumulation of law. To accomplish this vital work, many state legislatures appoint a **revisor of statutes.** Many revisors make their work easier by computerizing the law, that is, by exhaustively indexing all the laws passed by the legislature—by idea, by key word, and by every other way imaginable—so that all they have to do is push a few buttons to find out whether any new law conflicts with or impinges upon any prior law. Obviously the legislative bill-drafting service will want to keep on good terms with the revisor of statutes, who can supply information on how a proposed new bill may impinge on existing law.

Session Laws   Normally the revisor is in charge of publishing the **session laws,** a book that lists (often chronologically) all the laws enacted during a particular session of the legislature. The revisor is also normally in charge of publishing the state code, in which all the laws of the state currently in force are arranged by subject matter. It costs a lot of money to publish a state code, and most states do it only once a decade, each new issue perhaps labeled the *Revised Code of the State of X.* The revised code, of course, immediately becomes obsolete at the very next session of the legislature, when a mass of new laws are passed. Thus, after each session the revisor prints a booklet of revisions for each volume of the code. There is a pocket in the cover of each volume in which the revisions (sometimes called a *pocket part*) may be inserted.

Postauditor

Nearly every state legislature arms itself with a staff whose central duty is to audit the books of state agencies to see whether appropriated money is being spent for purposes stated in the appropriation. The officer responsible for such auditing is normally called the **state auditor,** and the kind of audit he or she performs is a postaudit, not a preaudit—that is, he or she looks at what has been spent rather than what is about to be spent. Normally preaudits (which determine the legality of money *about* to be spent) are done in the executive branch, perhaps by a person called a controller who in some cases must countersign drafts written on the state treasury. Legislative postaudits, however, are a check on the controller and on the entire state governmental apparatus, a check that often probes beyond whether money is being spent for proper purposes and inquires into whether power is being used for purposes intended by the legislature. Sometimes the audit function becomes an almost boundless license to investigate everything being done by any arm of the state government in order to uncover inefficiencies as well as wanderings from the intent of the law. This broad *performance auditing* obviously runs parallel with the so-called oversight function of the legislature: the legislature not only makes laws and sets up agencies to carry them out, but it also keeps an eye on those agencies to see how well they are doing. Oversight is done by the various standing committees of the legislature.

State auditors are chosen in a variety of ways. In some states they are elected by the people and do not have a particularly close relationship with the legislature. In other states they are appointed by the legislature, often from among candidates nominated by a committee of legislators sometimes called the *legislative audit committee.*

State Library

Numerous legislatures are served by state libraries that offer legislators a number of reference services, including information on subjects of special interest; research materials for articles or speeches; bibliographies and reading lists on specific subjects; commercial, vital, financial, and other statistics; information from public agencies (particularly useful when the legislator prefers not to deal directly with the agency); information on educational, medical, scientific, religious, and other institutions; and information from published federal and state documents.

Commission on Uniform State Law

Within the various staff arms of the typical state legislature are found a collection of other services that help the legislature do its job. There may, for example, be a commission on **uniform state law.** The first function of such a commission is to keep informed on what the national conference of commissioners on uniform state laws is doing. The national conference promotes uniformity of state laws on all subjects where uniformity seems desirable and practical. To that end it drafts model acts and recommends them for consideration by state legislatures. Since 1914 the national conference has proposed dozens of laws that have been adopted by many states. Some of these proposals are more popular than others. Only six states have enacted the uniform adoption law, but the uniform child custody law has been enacted verbatim by almost every state in the Union. Occasionally states will revise a "uniform" law to meet their own needs and adopt the revision.

Within each state the job of the state commission on uniform state laws is to study the suggestions of the national conference and recommend whether or not the legislature should adopt them.

Compensation Commission

To help the legislators set a proper level of pay for themselves and other elected or appointed officials outside the competitive merit system, the legislature may have a compensation commission. This commission makes a continuing study of salaries, retirement benefits, expense allowances, and other payments and reports periodically on the results of its studies to the legislature.

Clerk of the House and Secretary of the Senate

The **clerk of the house** and the **secretary of the senate** also provide a variety of important services for a typical state legislature. They are the chief administrative officers of their respective houses and have general supervision over a number of things important to the daily existence of the legislature, such as ensuring that employees of the legislature get paid, keeping custody of a great many documents and records important to the legislature, preparing a daily journal, making sure that the media have proper accommodations, and running a message center for members. The clerk of the house and the secretary of the senate perform many jobs connected with the mechanics of passing bills. These include keeping a record (called a *docket*) of the numbers and titles of all bills (or other actions) and every action taken on them; distributing copies of bills to the various committees and officers who need them; keeping a record of everything that should be included in the official journal; reading aloud—or having somebody read—from the rostrum all matters that come before the two houses; operating a printing room to reproduce copies of all bills, resolutions, and so on and distributing them to members of the legislature at the proper time and place. A legislature could not function without its chief clerk and its secretary of the senate.

Sergeant at Arms

Another functionary in the legislature is the **sergeant at arms,** who is comparable to an ordinary police officer. The sergeant at arms is responsible for keeping unauthorized people off the floor of either house, ensuring that visitors are seated in the right place, making sure the lights are turned on and the windows open, and so on. Sometimes the legislature or one of its committees may wish to serve subpoenas on people, in which case the sergeant at arms will do it.

Budget Staff

A number of state legislatures have special committees and staffs that help prepare appropriations bills. These we discuss at greater length elsewhere.

STANDING COMMITTEES

A visitor to the state capitol who climbs to the gallery overlooking the senate or the house and gazes down upon the legislators does not see the whole picture of lawmaking. It may well be some *pro forma* stage of lawmaking, the dotting of an "i," so to speak. The floor is not center stage for the dance of legislation, but a remote wing. The drama, the dance, the opera begins long before and far away; its most dramatic moments, its high points, and its climaxes may be elsewhere.

Importance

State legislatures work through committees. Committees are the basic building blocks of the legislature. Why? Because no member of the legislature can know everything. A legislative body simply must divide itself into subject specialities so that every matter receives at least some degree of expert treatment.

Committees have long been the core of legislative procedure, but today they are more important than ever. Our complex, technological world requires ever more expertise by those who would govern it. Specialized committees are therefore necessary. Committee members acquire knowledge through service on a committee. Often certain members hold seats on particular committees because of their expert knowledge. A teacher-legislator may be assigned to the education committee, a trucker-legislator to the transportation committee, a farmer-legislator to the agriculture committee.

However, committees don't rely entirely on their own expertise. They invite expert testimony from the bureaucracy and from any and every source. The bureaucracy is intimately acquainted with what is being done and what needs to be done, so committees often take much guidance from its experts. In most states a legislative council and a state library also help committees acquire information. Some committees may also have a staff that helps them acquire information. A great deal of information is also given to committees by lobbyists. Their views are rarely neutral, but the conflicting views of competing lobbyists give legislators a fairly balanced picture of issues. Even information from the bureaucracy is biased, because government agencies, who also compete with each other, want things from the legislature—generally more money and more power—and slant their testimony to justify their acquisition. The danger of relying on such outside sources for expertise is that the legislature then allows these experts to influence legislation from behind the scene.

Number

Normally each house will have around 15 permanently established bodies called **standing committees.** In different states they go by different labels, but generally there is a standing committee in each house for each of the following broad subjects: agriculture, energy, natural resources, environment, business, labor, education, health, welfare, judiciary, local government, transportation, appropriations, taxes, and state affairs (a catchall committee). Many committees are divided into subcommittees.

Joint Committees

In addition to the standing committees of each house, there is usually a collection of **joint committees** composed of members of both houses. Joint committees generally provide some service to both houses—for example, the research service provided by a legislative council. Sometimes standing committees are joint or at least hold joint meetings so that witnesses won't have to give the same testimony twice and staff won't have to do research twice. In some state legislatures nearly all standing committees are joint. A recent example of a joint hearing was the House-Senate Iran-Contra hearings in the United States Congress. (The hearings were joint, not the committee.) These joint hearings conveniently spared witnesses like Lieutenant Colonel Oliver North from having to give their testimony twice and speeded things along.

Power

Generally every bill has to receive the blessing of a standing committee before the legislature votes on it. The power of standing committees varies from state to state, but in general they have the power to kill or modify bills before the full house ever gets a chance to vote on them. In some cases committees simply give their recommendation, positive or negative, to the legislature.

Because committees are so powerful, it is very important to a member of the legislature which committee he or she sits on. It is customary to appoint every member to at least one committee, and many serve on two or more committees, especially state senators, because the senate is smaller and each member has to cover more bases. A considerable portion of each member's power over legislation stems from his or her membership on committees.

Some committees are more powerful and prestigious than others. In fact, a legislature may give almost everything important to only three or four of its many committees. When that happens, the ruling clique of the legislature serves on those select committees. Other legislative committees may do almost nothing except provide impressive titles for their members. Senators and representatives like to impress the public by listing important committees on which they serve, as if to say, "My colleagues in the senate (or house) think highly of me, and depend on me, and have therefore put me on these important committees." The most powerful committees in every legislature are those that write spending bills. The power of the purse is the legislature's greatest power because money is the key to almost everything.

Chairpersons

Chairpersons of standing committees generally have quite a bit to say about the fate of bills that come before their committee, and sometimes the power of life and death over them. Committee chairpersons are almost always members of the majority party, handpicked by the majority leadership. In the lower house of most state legislatures, committee chairpersons are appointed by the speaker. The speaker, you will recall, is elected by the house and is generally a leader of the majority party.

The system in the senate is normally somewhat similar: chairs are picked by leaders of the majority party (usually by the majority leader of the senate, the president of the senate, or the president pro tem of the senate). Sometimes the job is done by a committee on committees or by the rules committee, as in the California Senate.

Membership

Other committee members get their assignments basically the same way chairpersons do: appointment by the leadership—primarily the leadership of the majority party. Normally the minority-party leadership is consulted about the assignment of minority-party members to committees.

It is generally assumed that once appointed to a committee one has at least some moral right to be reappointed, providing there has been no change of party strength in the legislature that would require some removals from committees. The same applies to reappointment of committee chairpersons. Of course, there is no ironclad assurance of reappointment under any circumstances. The various legislatures are ruled by various customs with regard to these matters.

State Legislative Committees versus Congressional Committees

Powerful as committee chairpersons might be in the state legislatures, they are not usually as powerful as the chairpersons of congressional committees, who in a sense aren't appointed by anyone. Congressional-committee chairpersons almost always get their job by virtue of seniority on the committee among those in the majority party, serve until death, retirement, defeat, or reduction of their party to minority status, and are therefore answerable to almost no one. Nor do the rank-and-file committee members in the state legislatures have the permanency of assignment enjoyed by their congressional brethren. Once appointed to a committee, a member of Congress may continue to serve on the committee as long as he or she wishes, unless forced off by the mathematical imperative that the majority party in each house have a majority on every committee thereof. State legislators, by contrast, are more dependent on the continuing good will of the party leadership for their continuance as a member of a particular committee. The near-total independence of members of Congress from their "leadership," except for the initial appointment as a member of the committee, was intended to be a reform when the system was introduced in 1910—a reform to end boss rule in the house and senate. The reform produced a kind of leaderless chaos in Congress, which one sees less often in state legislatures.

Interim Committees

No state legislature meets year-round, although more than a dozen states, such as California, New York, Illinois, Ohio, and Michigan, are free to do so if they wish. The California and New York legislatures spend about 200 days a year in session. Many states, of course, are constitutionally limited to fairly short sessions. For business that must be conducted between sessions, when the legislature as a whole may not be meeting, most legislatures establish **interim committees** that study problems and prepare bills. Some legislatures simply allow their regular standing committees to meet during the interim. However, since most state legislatures appoint their standing committees for only two or four years, it isn't always clear just who is to meet in the interim. Sometimes both interim and regular standing committees meet between sessions.

SPEAKER AND PRESIDENT PRO TEM

Power in most state legislatures is generally controlled by the speaker of the house, the president pro tem of the senate, and a circle of other leaders, including the chairpersons of the most important committees. Probably the most crucial job of the **speaker** and the **president pro tem** is that of appointing committees and their chairpersons. Of course, these two presiding officers and the inner circle of party leadership also have a lot to say about what bills are passed and how much money is spent; they are, in effect, lords of the legislature.

Strong leadership in legislatures is good for several reasons. First, the leaders are generally persons in whom the majority party has confidence: they are usually competent and responsible. Second, the leaders have usually been around quite a while; thoroughly understand the state, its problems, its aspirations, its internecine disagreements, its far-flung governmental apparatus and bureaucracy; and know the legislators and their varying talents and shortcomings.

Besides appointing committees and being in general charge of the flow of business, the speaker and the president pro tem generally have a collection of other jobs, including, of course, presiding over meetings of the house and senate, administering oaths, and signing papers.

OTHER OFFICERS

Legislatures have four kinds of officers: (1) those elected by the whole membership of each house, (2) those elected by each party of each house, (3) those appointed by the president pro tem or the speaker, and (4) those who are not members of the legislature but employees.

The speaker of the house and president pro tem of the senate are the two most conspicuous officers elected by the whole membership of each house.

Members of each party in each house elect a leader. The leader of the majority party is called, logically, the *majority leader;* the leader of the minority party, the *minority leader.* They are assisted by party officers called **whips.** Each house has a majority and a minority whip. These officers—the leaders and the whips—sometimes have assistants. The job of a whip is to mobilize the members of his or her party to support measures upon which the party takes a stand. Most matters before the legislature are not partisan issues, but some are. A whip is something like a lobbyist for the party on partisan issues; so is the leader.

The president pro tem and the speaker of the house appoint various assistants, some of whom are members of the legislature and some of whom are employees. Certain employees of the two houses might be considered officers— the secretary of the senate, the clerk of the house, the auditor, the sergeant at arms—but most employees are clerical workers.

HOW TO KILL A BILL

The enemies of a bill have many opportunities during its passage through the legislative jungle to wound and kill it. So great are those opportunities that successful passage of any significant piece of legislation is as uncertain as the successful passage of a chicken through a pack of hyenas. The mortality rate of bills is high. During a recent session of the New York legislature 15,021 out of 15,916 bills died: 94 percent. It took only six months to accomplish that slaughter. Meanwhile, it was taking the Massachusetts General Court about a year to kill 8282 out of 9100 bills: 90 percent. In most state legislatures the mortality rate of bills is possibly in the neighborhood of 70 percent. It would be a strikingly healthy year for bills if 50 percent should survive. These statistics do not tell us whether an important bill is more likely to perish than an unimportant bill (there isn't any standard of importance that satisfies everyone), but it seems likely (perhaps someday someone can prove it) that the more controversial a proposal, the greater the danger to its survival. The term *controversial* is also foggy. A bill may be controversial only in narrow circles, but that narrow circle may be influential and skilled at killing legislation in the legislative wilderness. One thing is clear: when a bill has active and determined enemies, there are many places in the procedure of most state legislatures to bring that bill to destruction, or at least to maul, modify, or maim it.

The Idea

Let us imagine we are a group trying to stop passage of a bill. How shall we do it? Where shall we strike? How shall we attack? Suppose it is a bill to require every automobile owner to have his or her vehicle inspected for safety every year by an official state inspector who would have the power to order any repairs necessary to put the vehicle in safe condition. The bill would not require the state itself to hire any inspectors but would allow the state to license gas-station operators to serve as inspectors. The bill would authorize the arrest and prosecution of any driver of an automobile that does not bear an up-to-date inspection sticker. The alleged purpose of this bill is to reduce the number of auto accidents caused by unsafe vehicles.

The Interests

Who could object to highway safety? What better inspectors are there than the people who deal in auto repairs? They stand ready at the first sight of anything unsafe to sell the necessary repairs. In fact, the State Association of Service Station and Garage Mechanics is the main group pushing the safety-inspection bill, so great is its concern for auto safety.

The bill would provide that each motorist pay $20 for the inspection. Inspectors would pocket $19 as their payment; the state would get the other dollar for administering the program. Repairs required as a result of the inspection could be undertaken by anyone chosen by the automobile owner, but if these repairs were not done by the inspector, the owner would have to bring his or her vehicle back to the inspector to see that repairs were done right. It would, of course, be easier and more diplomatic to simply let the inspector make whatever safety repairs he or she finds necessary.

The Association of Service Station and Garage Mechanics is elated by the new safety-inspection bill and has appointed a full-time lobbyist to convince legislators how important this bill is to automobile safety. The association has also launched an expensive publicity campaign by radio, television, and press to depict how dangerous it is to drive unsafe cars and to impress upon the public how risky bad brakes, bad shock absorbers, bad wheel alignment, bad windshield wipers, bad tires, and faulty lights can be. The association let it be known that its many mechanics and service-station operators are ready, willing, and able to make sure that all the state's one million plus cars are kept in safe running order, and that $20 for the inspection is modest.

The bill is instantly opposed—by us. We are accused of being against auto safety and probably against motherhood as well. Our group is the Society of Consumers against Rip-offs. We're not a very big society, or very rich, because it's hard to organize consumers, to keep them organized, and to keep them paying dues, but we do have a respectable group of right-thinking people, organized into small but exciting chapters in 40 or 50 towns across the state. We see this bill as a gigantic rip-off of the consumer by gas-station operators and garage mechanics. Yes, we see the safety value of regular auto inspections, but we also see that the bill puts every motorist at the mercy of people who have an incentive to find something wrong during the inspection so that they can fix it. Auto repairers are put in charge of determining whether you need auto repairs and are elevated to the status of official state inspectors so that their determinations are imposed on consumers with all the force and majesty of the law. Imagine! Every gas station operator a licensed inspector. It's like putting the fox in charge of the chicken coop.

The Leg Men

The first thing the gas-station operators do is find a likely legislator to introduce the bill, one member in each house. Representative Beatrice Broohaha in the house of representatives and Senator Rufus Ruffle in the upper house agree to do it. Broohaha owns an auto dealership in a northeastern county, and Ruffle is a minister from the capital city whose only son was killed about three years ago in a tragic automobile accident. Both agree to sponsor the bill in their respective houses. Lobbyists for the gas-station operators also succeed in getting 15 other representatives to cosponsor the bill in the lower house and 9 other senators to cosponsor the bill in the upper house. It's useful to have cosponsors; they are like godparents who help the bill along its treacherous legislative path. The gas-station lobbyists have also tried to win the governor's support, but she remains quiet. Both sides in the struggle supported her in the last election, and she has no wish to make either the consumers or the gas-station people mad at her. Many legislators have the same problem; they will try to stay on both sides of the issue and look for compromises.

The Drafting Service

Representative Broohaha sits down with the gas-station leaders. Together they scribble out roughly everything they want in their bill. Broohaha takes this draft to the legislative drafting office. The lawyers there look to see just where in the code the bill would fit, to what laws it would relate, and with what laws it might conflict, and then rewrite the rough draft into a finished proposal couched in legalese and ready for introduction as a bill. Ruffle does the same thing to get his senate bill ready. As a matter of fact, almost everything Broohaha does, Ruffle also does in the other house.

There's really not much we can do at this stage except mobilize our own lobbying effort, try to prevail on the governor, try to prevail on all sorts of other influentials in and out of the legislature. Our opponents have already reached influential bureaucrats. They've gone to the department of revenue and told its bosses that in all likelihood the inspection program would be administered by them (since money is involved—the inspection fee). The executive director of the department of revenue realizes that this vast new program would make his department bigger—would add to his empire. He said he was one thousand percent in favor of auto safety but would have to withhold his public support for this bill until the governor makes her position clear (the executive director serves at the pleasure of the governor).

So far, we cannot attack the bill anywhere in legislative procedure. The action until now is mostly a gathering of forces.

Introduction of the Bill

Representative Broohaha is now ready to introduce her bill. She makes four copies of it and takes them with her to a meeting of the house. At a certain point in the legislative day reserved for introduction of bills she reads her bill to the members (or has it read by the clerk). This **reading** consists only of reading the title of the bill, not the whole bill, and is called the *first reading*. Early in the history of legislatures, bills were actually read aloud in their entirety. Even though this took time, it was necessary because some legislators were illiterate. Today it is presumed every legislator can read, and so the oral readings (there are three) have been shortened. Today the terms *first reading, second reading,* and *third reading* are used by legislators to signify a certain point in legislative procedure. When a legislator says, "The auto-inspection bill hasn't even reached first reading," that means it hasn't been introduced yet. Second reading occurs when the bill reaches the committee of the whole (a committee composed of all the members of the house) after the standing committees have completed action. Thus when a legislator says, "The bill is about to have its second reading," that means the standing committee is about to finish its consideration of the bill and send it forward to the committee of the whole. Third reading is the very last stage when the house takes up a bill for final action.

Delivery to the Clerk

After introduction Broohaha delivers a copy of her bill to the clerk of the house, who gives it a number (*dockets* the bill). It will be the thirty-third bill introduced in the house of representatives this session and HR-33.

Which Committee?

Next, the speaker of the house will refer the bill to a standing committee within 48 hours. Here at last we—the opposition—fire a shot: we try to convince him to refer the bill to a hostile committee. The speaker, of course, is supposed to refer bills to standing committees specializing in whatever the bills concern. Transportation bills go to the transportation committee, health bills to the health committee, and so on. However, bills often concern several subjects and might logically be referred to any of several committees. The auto-safety-inspection bill could rationally go to the transportation committee (the bill concerns vehicles), to the health committee (safety and health are related), to the highway committee (vehicles to be inspected travel on highways), to the revenue committee (the bill requires payment of a fee by motorists), to the business-affairs committee (the bill affects the auto-repair business), or to the state-affairs committee (everything is a state affair).

We try to convince the speaker he ought to refer the safety-inspection bill to the health committee. We like the health committee. Its members are consumer-oriented and can be counted on to bury this bill deeper than a dead whale. We've sized up the probable attitude of every committee toward the inspection bill. If the speaker won't give us our first choice, we have a second, third, fourth, and fifth choice for committee assignment.

Also, since the bill logically falls into the subject-matter orbit of several committees, we ask the speaker to refer the bill to *all* relevant committees one after the other, so that when the first committee is through, the second takes it up, then the third, then the fourth, and so on. Somewhere along this murderous line we might win. If the bill is studied by successive committees, it will surely be studied to death and never reported out in time for passage.

Now when we say we try to convince the speaker to do these things, we really mean we try to convince various people close to the speaker as well as the speaker himself. Most speakers are simply one among a circle of house leaders. The speaker represents the leadership of the majority party, and it is that circle we address ourselves to. We do likewise when we lobby any point in the power structure: what we lobby is the ring of power surrounding that point.

In Committee

We neither lose nor win with the speaker: he refers HR-33 to the highway committee, which we have identified as neither friendly nor unfriendly. We shift our guns to that front. Our immediate target is the chairperson of the committee. She sets the committee's agenda and decides when, where, and if the committee will meet. She has the power to put this bill at the bottom of the agenda, a place reserved for unwanted bills because the chairperson never allows the committee to reach the bottom of the agenda. How do we lobby the chairperson? It is not necessary to tell her how many members we have in our society or how determined they can be when they become dissatisfied with a legislator. She already knows that, so it is necessary only to convey our sincere belief that the auto-safety-inspection bill is a consumer rip-off by service-station operators. Her reaction is likely to flow from a mixture of concern for the public welfare and for her personal political welfare. Our adversaries will also be speaking to the chairperson, and it will not be necessary for them to say how many service-station operators, garage owners, and auto mechanics there are in her district or how deeply people believe in auto safety. Legislators not only want to know who is for and against a bill and how powerful these people are in their district but also the arguments for and against a bill, because, despite all cynicism, it helps in politics to be right. Not right versus left, but right versus wrong. Although right may be a matter of dispute, power still drifts to those who are perceived to be in the right, wherever that may be. Legislators like to be right, especially when it doesn't conflict with their chances of reelection.

We do not concentrate our lobbying effort on wining and dining our target or on bribing her. We concentrate on convincing our target that we are right and supplying evidence to prove it. Of course, it does no harm to be friendly at the same time.

Unfortunately the chairperson of the highway committee cannot agree to bury the auto-safety-inspection bill. But all is not lost. She agrees to support an amendment limiting inspections to once every two years rather than once a year. The other side wishes to strengthen the bill by requiring two inspections every year rather than one. Furthermore, the chairperson agrees to support an amendment reducing the inspection fee from $20 to $10 but warns this may be self-defeating because the mechanics will simply find more things wrong that require repair if they aren't paid enough the inspection.

The bill is put high on the committee's agenda. We now turn our guns on the 15 members of the committee. We lobby every one of them, and 6 of the 15 agree to vote no. One member is uncertain how to vote. The other 8 vote yes, but we do find support on the committee to reduce the fee to $10 and to reduce the frequency of inspection to once every other year. In winning those amendments we have a partial victory. We carve up the bill a little, we butcher it a little, but we're not through. We will shoot to kill.

The Rules Committee

The bill now moves on to the **rules committee,** which has the power to do almost anything its heart desires with any bill. The rules committee is a major power cluster in the house of representatives—the leadership of the house sits on it, or controls it. The rules committee is the traffic cop of the house. It makes a rule for every bill, stating among other things when the bill will be heard in the house. It can derail a bill altogether; it can decide the bill needs further study and send it to another committee for consideration or back to the same committee for reconsideration; it can amend the bill. When HR-33 comes to the rules committee, we lobby the chairperson but make no particular headway. He frankly doesn't have a strong opinion one way or another about the auto-safety-inspection bill and leaves it to the mercy of committee members. We lobby the 15 members and to our immense pleasure discover that 9 think the bill should be referred to the health committee (our favorite committee) for further consideration.

Another Committee

When HR-33 gets to the health committee, we think we've won the battle. The chairperson is 200 percent with us but decides to let the bill come before the committee because he knows they will vote against it. They simply bury the bill and do not return it to the house. We are happy as mice in the pantry.

One week later we have a setback. The bill's advocates outside the health committee are trying to "blast the bill out of committee." To do this they use the **demand procedure** provided for in the rules of the house. All they have to do is get a majority of the house to vote for a motion demanding that the standing committee in possession of a bill return the bill to the house. To our distress this happens.

The Committee of the Whole

Having been blasted out of committee, the bill lands once again in the lap of the rules committee, which refers it to the **committee of the whole** for its *second reading.* The committee of the whole is a new battlefield for us. It is a committee composed of all members of the house; it meets in the house chamber. Casual observers might not be able to tell whether they are seeing a meeting of the house of representatives or a meeting of the committee of the whole. It is a strange committee. Why a committee composed of the whole house?

The committee of the whole is an escape from rules that govern meetings of the house. Take, for example, the matter of quorum. To do business most legislative bodies require a **quorum,** a word stemming from the Latin pronoun *qui,* meaning "who." The word *quorum* as used today means the minimum number of members who must be present at an assembly before it can validly transact business. The quorum in most legislative bodies is a majority of the members: one over half, or 51 members of a 100-member house of representatives. A quorum for the committee of the whole is much smaller, perhaps only 25 percent.

Second, the committee of the whole typically takes no roll-call votes. No one's vote is recorded, and voting is generally *viva voce* (Latin: "living voice"), which speeds things up and allows a member to vote no in the committee of the whole (where votes are unrecorded) and yes in other forums on the same issue.

Third, the rules of debate are relaxed in terms of how often a member may speak and for how long. There may be no mechanism for cutting off debate in the committee of the whole—no possibility of moving the previous question. Furthermore, debate may go on without interruptions caused by wrangles over procedural questions, because in the committee of the whole there is normally no appealing the decisions of the chair on questions of parliamentary procedure. In general, besides these "advantages," the committee of the whole enables the whole house to exchange views, to discuss and debate bills, and even to vote on bills without such action being in any way binding on the house.

We hack away at the inspection bill in the committee of the whole, and end up with some victories. First, we succeed in amending the bill to require inspections only once every three years. Second, we get an amendment providing a way for motorists to appeal the decisions of licensed inspectors. Third, we get the inspection fee knocked down to $5 and tack on a provision that allows the department of revenue to revoke the license of any inspector who orders unnecessary repairs on a motor vehicle.

Thus amended, the bill goes to *third reading*—to the house of representatives, where as usual it is passed in the form received from the committee of the whole. We have lost the battle in the house, yet through our amendments we have made some important gains. The bill is not law yet. It must still go through the senate, and we fight the same battles all over again at many points along its journey there. The bill also passes the senate, but we have won amendments there too. And still the bill is not law.

The Conference Committee

The bill has passed the senate and the house, but in different forms. There are still opportunities to assault the bill, for it must now go to a **conference committee,** a committee composed of members of both the house and the senate drawn from the standing committees in each house that considered the bill originally. Now we shift our assault to that forum. Conference committees generally work out a compromise between the senate and the house versions and send the compromise bill back to the two houses. We lobby for compromises that lean in our favor, and when the compromise bill reaches the two houses, we fight to kill it in each house, although our chances are slim.

The Governor

Once the auto-safety-inspection bill is passed by the two houses, it is still only a bill. To become law it must go to the governor, who may sign it into law, let it become law without her signature after so many days, or veto it. Naturally we do our best to prevail upon her to veto the bill, and to our joy and relief she does so.

The battle is still not over, however. A vetoed bill goes back to the two houses, which may override the veto by a two-thirds vote of the membership of each house. The governor's veto is overridden in the house of representatives but sustained in the senate. At long last we have won.

Suppose the governor had not vetoed the auto-safety-inspection bill and it had become law. Still the battle would not be over. We could continue to attack it in the appropriations bill. The inspection program could not exist without an appropriation to finance its administration.

SUMMARY

In the years immediately after the American Revolution, legislatures were in full ascendancy over the other two branches of government. The Revolution had been at heart a rebellion against executive power. However, as memory of autocratic royal governors faded and as experience with less frightening governors accumulated, legislatures relaxed their hostility to executive power. In a sense, the decline of legislatures began with the decline of their hostility toward executives and with growing dependence upon them. However, legislatures themselves became corrupt, abused their power, and fell into disgrace. Corruption was partly the result of democratization of American society in the nineteenth century and the election of a less noble breed to state legislatures. Harrassed by rampant bribery of state legislators, our ancestors severely curbed the ability of legislatures to abuse their power. That accounts for several of the worst shortcomings and weaknesses of today's legislatures.

A large number of states limit how long their legislature may meet, reasoning that the less it meets, the less damage it can do. Most legislatures hold annual regular sessions that last from January to about May. Legislatures are curtailed in many other ways besides having their sessions limited. They are also restricted in what they may do, especially where money is concerned.

All state legislatures except one (Nebraska) have two houses. In part this is because state legislatures are patterned somewhat after Congress. However, a two-house Congress was established because formation of the Union would have been politically impossible otherwise. Such was not true for states, but the tradition had been established.

Most states call their legislature either the *general assembly* or simply the *legislature.* Each upper house is called a *senate,* and most lower houses are labeled *house of representatives.* The terms *upper house* and *lower house* are inherited from the British Parliament. The average upper house has about 40 members, the average lower house about 113. In most states the term of a member of the state senate is four years and a member of the house of representatives two years. Turnover in the typical state legislature is high. The pay of state legislators varies widely from state to state.

In their membership, legislatures fail in many ways to mirror the general public. Legislators tend to be more prosperous and better educated, for example. Therefore, it is sometimes charged that legislatures are not truly representative of the general public. The meaning of *representative* is subject to debate.

Votes cast by legislators are a mixture of their own judgment and the wishes of their constituents. It is hard for a legislator to cast his or her vote the way the majority of his or her constituents feel about an issue because normally there is no majority view. Furthermore, it is questionable whether any legislator can justifiably claim to have a mandate from the people to do anything—it is never very clear just why voters elect a certain candidate to the legislature.

Gerrymandering state legislatures has been made much more difficult by the United States Supreme Court's one-man-one-vote ruling, which requires all legislative districts represented in each house to be roughly equal in population.

Legislators are backed up by various staff services, including personal staffs, committee staffs, legislative councils, bill-drafting services, libraries, an auditor, a compensation commission, a commission on uniform state law, clerks, secretaries, a sergeant at arms, a revisor of statutes, and a budget staff. The extent of this staff support differs widely among the states.

State legislatures work through committees. Committees are the right hand of every legislature. A legislative body simply must divide itself into subject-matter specialties. Normally each house will have around 15 standing committees, which are permanently established. Generally every bill has to receive the blessing of one of them before the legislature votes on it. The chairperson of a standing committee generally has quite a bit to say about the fate of bills that come before his or her committee, and sometimes the power of life and death over them. Basically the chairperson and the members of each committee get their assignments through appointment by the leadership.

Much power in state legislatures is gathered into the hands of the speaker of the house and the president pro tem of the senate and their entourage.

The enemies of a bill have many opportunities during its passage through the maze of legislative procedure to wound or kill it. So great are those opportunities that successful passage of any significant piece of legislation is highly uncertain.

SUGGESTIONS FOR FURTHER READING

CITIZENS CONFERENCE ON STATE LEGISLATURES, *The Sometime Governments: A Critical Study of the 50 American Legislatures.* New York: Bantam, 1971.

CRANE, WILDER, JR., and MEREDITH W. WATTS, JR., *State Legislative Systems.* Englewood Cliffs, N.J.: Prentice-Hall, 1968.

EPSTEIN, LEON B., *Political Parties in Western Democracies* (2nd ed.). New Brunswick, N.J.: Transactions Books, 1980.

HARDY, LEROY C., "Considering the Gerrymander," Pepperdine *Law Review* (1977), 243–84.

HEARD, ALEXANDER, ed., *State Legislatures in American Politics.* Englewood Cliffs, N.J.: Prentice-Hall, 1966.

HOWE, CHARLES B., "The Case for the Professional Legislator," *State Government* (Summer 1974), 130–34.

JEWELL, MALCOLM E., and SAMUEL C. PATTERSON, *The Legislative Process in the United States* (3rd ed.). New York: Random House, 1977.

ROSENTHAL, ALAN, *Legislative Life: People, Process and Performance in the States.* New York: Harper & Row, Pub., 1981.

———, and MAUREEN W. MOAKLEY, *The Political Life of American States.* New York: Praeger, 1984.

SHUMATE, ROBERT V., "The Nebraska Unicameral Legislature," *Western Political Quarterly* (September 1952), 504–12.

8

courts
and
law

PREVIEW

CHAIN OF COMMAND

She had slender legs and a provocative voice. He had wavy hair and a sensitive mouth. She was the youngest judge ever appointed to the county court. He was the youngest judge ever appointed to the state court of appeals. They were newlyweds.

"In my capacity as a judge of the appeals court," he said, buttoning his shirt, "I command you to cook me two eggs for breakfast."

She yawned and searched for her slipper. "And as a county judge in this county, I'm telling you to go straight to you-know-where."

"But," he said, tying his shoes, "if you don't cook me two eggs (and I'll have a small glass of orange juice too) then I shall have to remove your honor from the bench."

She stood close to the mirror and applied lipstick. "You, my lord, can't remove me from the county court any more than you can remove God from heaven."

"Then I'll reverse your decisions," he shouted into a bureau drawer where he searched for a cuff link.

She stood in front of him now and straightened his necktie, "Would you really reverse me, handsome boy?"

He held her head gently with both hands and kissed her nose. "Please, sweet girl, do boil me some eggs."

They had breakfast at the Point of Law Cafe, and hurried off to court.

GENERAL ORGANIZATION OF THE COURT SYSTEM

State court systems are not typically organized like an ordinary department of government—say, a department of agriculture—with a chain of command. Lower-court judges do not report to higher-court judges like captains to majors, or like bureau chiefs to department chiefs. However, lower courts may be reversed by higher courts, and lower courts often must follow procedures set forth by higher courts. Lower-court judges can't be fired for insubordination if they refuse to follow the policies of their higher-court brethren—the higher judges are not bosses.

Most states have a four-level court system. These courts have different names in different states. *Local courts,* which hear only minor cases and have severely limited jurisdiction, constitute the bottom level—justice-of-the-peace courts, municipal courts, and possibly county courts. At the next level are *trial courts of general jurisdiction,* which hear more important cases. Above them are *intermediate appellate courts.* Finally comes the *state supreme court*—the highest state court of appeals. We will start at the bottom of this heap and work upwards.

LOCAL COURTS

Casting one's eye across the system of local courts in America, one sees a nightmare of confusion. Even the term *local court* is unclear, for in reality all courts (except federal) are *state courts* inasmuch as all of them, including local courts, are established by state authority. States, of course, do generally allow municipalities to establish certain courts to enforce municipal ordinances. Basically what we mean by the term **local court** is a court with a fairly small territorial jurisdiction (perhaps a city, a town, a township, or a county) that is permitted to take only minor criminal or civil (noncriminal) cases. Local courts are called by a variety of different names and have a variety of powers. Local courts rarely hear felony cases or civil cases where the stakes are high. They normally hear only misdemeanor cases and small civil disputes. A **misdemeanor** is a minor crime, such as overparking, letting your dog run without a leash, or disturbing the peace. Ninety percent of local-court business concerns traffic offenses.

Many local courts are not courts of record. (That is, they do not keep a formal record of all testimony and other proceedings of the trial.) Appeals from them are therefore usually heard *de novo* ("anew," "afresh") by the state's trial courts of general jurisdiction. Some local courts are, however, courts of record and their findings of fact are considered final unless they are clearly erroneous (as revealed by the record). Of course, their findings of law and the legality of their procedures are subject to review by the appellate court. Courts that review local-court decisions aren't usually considered appeallate courts if the review is (or may be) *de novo.*

Some local-court judges are not legally trained. The more rural the area served by a local court, the more likely the judge has never seen the inside of a law school.

In large metropolitan areas local courts tend to be specialized. There may be a collection of courts, each specializing in a different kind of case: small-claims, juvenile, housing, traffic, and so forth. Elsewhere local courts may consist simply of county courts, although in some areas there are justice-of-the-peace courts and municipal courts. (Specialized courts are discussed further shortly.)

Municipal Courts

Municipal courts are commonly established and paid for by municipalities to try persons accused of violating municipal ordinances and certain state laws (mostly traffic) within the municipality. Most municipal ordinances are minor criminal laws—misdemeanors such as overparking. Ordinarily municipal courts are exclusively criminal courts and don't handle civil disputes. The biggest part of their business is traffic offenses. Most criminal and civil cases arising under state law (rather than municipal ordinances) go to state courts of general jurisdiction. Many municipalities do not wish to pay for a municipal court even if they are authorized to have one. Where there is no municipal court, violations of municipal ordinances are tried in the lowest state courts—often before a county court.

Justices of the Peace

From time to time we see justices of the peace portrayed in the movies. The scenario may go something like this: A young couple driving somewhere in rural America suddenly decide to get married. It is the middle of the night. They inquire for the nearest justice of the peace. They are directed to a ramshackle home with an equally ramshackle sign nailed to a porch pillar: "Justice of the Peace." The groom-to-be hammers at the front door. A disheveled man opens an upstairs window and demands to know what the commotion is. After some impatient conversation the justice agrees to marry the couple. This takes place in his living room. His wife, still in nightgown and hairnet, helps with the ceremony. The groom pays a fee, readily accepted. The happy newlyweds drive away. The justice and his wife shamble off to bed after depositing the fee in a cookie jar. Later in the day our justice of the peace has a brisk business in traffic cases. He and a local police officer are in cahoots. They operate a speed trap; the officer brings them in fast as he can; the justice convicts them and splits his fee with the officer. The fee is paid only by the guilty. Everyone is found guilty.

Although exaggerated, this rather sordid picture accurately suggests the haphazard, slipshod, unprofessional character of service offered by many justices of the peace.

Very few justices of the peace are lawyers. Most are local politicians. The original purpose of justice courts was to handle minor quarrels informally and to keep them out of the regular courts. Common sense rather than legal training was thought to be sufficient qualification for the job. A **justice of the peace** was to operate out of his or her living room. He or she needed no courtroom and no clerical help. These conditions still prevail, except in a few places where attempts have been made to set standards for justices and for their manner of dispensing justice. One particular area of concern is the way justices of the peace are paid. Under the fee system they are paid solely by fees they charge for their services. That's what leads to speed traps and other fee-splitting devices.

Reforming the position of justice of the peace is hard. Abolishing it is perhaps easier, and that has happened in many states, particularly in urban areas. Justices of the peace are not extinct, or even endangered, but they are a declining species.

TRIAL AND APPEALS COURTS OF GENERAL JURISDICTION

Original and Appellate Jurisdiction

Obviously every case, big or little, civil or criminal, has to start in some tribunal somewhere. Courts that specialize in giving a first hearing to cases are called *courts of first instance* or **courts of original jurisdiction.** As we have seen, minor offenses are often handled by local courts. Serious offenses, called **felonies,** and the more important private disputes are heard for the first time in the trial courts of general jurisdiction. In most states there are three steps on the ladder of courts above local courts: (1) courts of original jurisdiction (the so-called trial courts[1]), (2) an intermediate appellate court,[2] and (3) a state supreme court.[3] The first of these, the **trial courts,** specialize in hearing cases on original jurisdiction. The second and third steps are appeals courts.

Trial courts do at least two things that appellate courts generally do not: (1) they hear cases on original jurisdiction (for the first time), and (2) they decide questions of fact as well as questions of law.

Fact and Law

One thing happens at the first step that does not happen above the first step: facts are found and issues of fact are settled. **Appeals courts** do not find facts, except when the trial court has made a clear or substantial error in its finding of fact or has based a finding of fact on too little evidence. Rarely does an appellate court disturb a finding of fact made by a trial court.

The reason you don't see juries in appeals courts is that the main function of juries is to answer questions of fact. The only place you see juries is in courts of original jurisdiction—in trial courts—where facts are decided. If an appeals court thinks there isn't enough evidence supporting a crucial finding of fact or thinks the finding was clearly erroneous, it will reverse the trial court or send the case back for further consideration rather than attempt to determine the facts itself. If you are convicted of murder, and appeal, you have to convince the appeals court that there was a legal error in your trial. You cannot expect an appeals court to retry the question of whether you did in fact commit murder. It will focus its attention on whether your trial was fair and legal. It might find any one of a long list of possible errors of law—perhaps the law itself under which you were convicted was vaguely written or unconstitutional, perhaps the judge was biased, perhaps you were forced to confess under torture, and so on.

The case of rapist-kidnapper Caryl Chessman is an example of this. In 1960 he was executed in the California gas chamber. He had been sentenced to

---

[1]The major trial courts are generally called *superior courts, circuit courts,* or *district courts.* Ohio and Pennyslvania use the term *court of common pleas,* Massachusetts simply uses *trial courts,* and New York insists on *supreme courts.*

[2]The intermediate courts are generally called *courts of appeal.* Pennsylvania uses the terms *superior court* and *commonwealth court.*

[3]The court of last resort in all but two states is called the *supreme court;* the two exceptions are Maryland and New York, which use the term *court of appeals.* Since New York labels its major trial courts *supreme courts,* one has to remember that supreme-court decisions in New York are not edicts of the highest court.

death ten years earlier but had staved off his execution by appeals. In his final appeal, which ultimately went to the United States Supreme Court, he did not claim to be innocent. Nor did he confess. Chessman merely argued that his original trial was faulty because the stenographer who made a verbatim record of the trial (as is required in courts of record) died before she could transcribe her shorthand notes. She had used her own unique brand of shorthand, which was unlike anything taught in stenographers' school. It was undecipherable after her death. Thus, argued Chessman, there was no accurate record of the trial upon which to base his appeal. Without a verbatim record of the proceedings, how could the appeals court know if there were any legal errors in the original trial? The Supreme Court was not asked to determine guilt but only to determine the legal sufficiency of the trial. That was a law question, not a fact question. Chessman lost.

Appeals courts were formerly sometimes called *courts of error*. This was logical because the job of appellate courts is to determine if lower courts made errors. One reason why lawyers are always jumping to their feet with "objections" as a trial progresses is that every time one of those objections is overruled by the judge, the judge may commit a legal error that may later form the basis of an appeal to the court of errors. Of course, not every error justifies an appeal; some are harmless. Only errors that affect the merits of the case justify review of the case on appeal.

SPECIALIZATION OF COURTS AND JUDGES

A personable 55-year-old judge in Florida said, "People think we judges know everything there is to know about law. We don't. There's too much law for anybody to know it all. I would rather specialize in something like probate or juvenile or tax than be a jack-of-all-trades."

Courts in metropolitan areas with huge case loads and numerous judges do usually arrange some sort of division of labor among judges so that each can specialize at least a little. One judge may hear nothing but probate cases, another nothing but juvenile, another nothing but divorce, and so on.

It isn't necessary to have **specialized courts** if there is specialization within courts. Probably it's cheaper to specialize judges than courts. Specialization of courts leads to proliferation of courts, each requiring a small bureaucracy to back it up—a clerk, a recorder, secretaries. Specialization of judges in the same court avoids all that and gives judges more freedom and flexibility of assignment. A judge may get tired of probate work after several years. If he (or she) is seated permanently on a probate court there may be no escape short of resignation, but if he were specializing in probate cases on a court of general jurisdiction he could simply change specialties.

County and district judges in most areas have little opportunity for specialization. They preside over whatever case appears on the docket and muddle through as best they can with the help of whatever general information they may have in their heads or can find in the law library or in lawyers' briefs (the written statements with which lawyers summarize their arguments in cases). Undoubtedly the quality of justice is better where judges or courts, or both, are specialized.

SOME SPECIALIZED COURTS

Small-Claims Courts

The furious 22-year-old college senior with long blond hair said, "I'm gonna sue the guy. I really am. I'm gonna sue."

His roommate mumbled, "And pay a lawyer an arm and a leg to collect $28?"

The boy sued and collected his $28. Cost him $7. It all concerned some books he sold another student, who promised to pay but didn't. Without a small-claims court such a suit would be impractical. It would cost too much and take too long. The whole purpose of a **small-claims court** is to make lawsuits over small claims cheap, simple, and quick—lawyers, juries, rules of evidence, and a great deal of procedure are dispensed with. Some states even go so far as to forbid lawyers to appear in small-claims court (except as a party). The judge supplies such legal advice as is necessary and takes responsibility for asking the right questions of both parties and bringing out the necessary facts. No rules of evidence (or lawyers) impede the parties from telling their story naturally and coherently. The *inquisitorial* rather than *adversary* system is employed in small-claims court. When the judge has heard enough, he or she decides the case without jury and often does so as soon as the "trial" is over. Trials may last only 15 or 20 minutes.

How to Sue   If you are going to sue someone in small-claims court, your claim must obviously be small. The exact upper limit is set by law and differs from state to state but rarely exceeds $2000. Starting a case is usually simple. All you do is go to the clerk of the small-claims court and say you want to file a claim against someone. The clerk will explain how to do it or give you a set of written instructions. At the same time the clerk will tell you to fill in the blanks of a complaint form, and will request a small filing fee, perhaps $5 to $10, depending on what state you're in. A copy of the complaint is sent by registered mail to the defendant, who is required to answer within a few days and to appear in court at a certain time and place, usually within three months. If the defendant fails to show up, he or she loses by default. Most cases are settled by default. Defendants who *do* show up to defend themselves usually win—not because they show up, but because they probably wouldn't trouble to appear unless they have a good case. However, some defendants with a good case don't appear if it's cheaper to lose than to fight, or if they would rather fight at the appeals stage.

Appeals   Victory or defeat in small-claims court does not necessarily end the case. Either party may appeal, although this is seldom done. When done, the appeals court hears the case *de novo*, and parties have all the normal judicial procedural rights—attorney, jury, adversary procedure, rules of evidence, and so on. A respondent at the appeals stage may choose to abandon the fight rather than suffer the expense of fighting. The availability of appeal, with trial *de novo*, makes it constitutional to deny counsel, jury, and other procedural rights in the small-claims court.

A Disappointment to Reformers   Small-claims courts are a fairly recent development. In some ways they have disappointed those who fought for their establishment. Some reformers thought small-claims courts would help "have-nots" get quick, cheap, and simple justice in their small claims against "haves." In practice, it has worked just the reverse. Most defendants in small claims courts are not "haves" but "have-nots." Most cases involve attempts by small businesses to collect unpaid bills from the poor. Once again, theory is tricked by practice.

Family Courts

A **family court** handles divorces plus an assortment of cases pertaining primarily to children—paternity, adoption, support, custody, supervision, neglect, and juvenile delinquency. Family courts are a fairly recent development, most of them established since the 1960s. Divorce courts and juvenile courts are not needed where family courts exist.

Is It a Court? Family courts, like juvenile courts, deal with subjects only partially within the customary realm of courts. When one thinks of a court, one generally thinks of fines, imprisonments, and awards of money damages, but family courts deal with problems for which fines, imprisonments, and damages are seldom appropriate. Some critics denounce the idea of using courts at all, even family courts, for most family problems: a velvet glove is more appropriate than an iron fist. The equity power of courts (the power of a judge to decide a case according to his or her own sense of justice) is useful, however, in ordering an array of social-service solutions to family problems. A judge's power to fine and imprison those who flout his suggestions is the fist within the velvet glove. The family-court judge conducts much of his or her work in an informal consultantlike manner with the help of a staff of social workers. Marital problems are not solved by jail sentences, but (if solvable at all) by marriage counseling, mental examinations, physical examinations, and so forth. Family courts are essentially social-service agencies armed with equity powers. It is utter nonsense to establish a family court without staffing it with psychologists, social workers, physicians, psychiatrists, probation officers, and persons of that stamp.

Pretrial Disposition A large part of the function of family courts is to settle cases so that a trial can be avoided. The staff of the court, with help from police, spend (or should spend) a lot of time investigating the background of cases, interviewing people, and trying to find out what the problems are and how they can be treated. This type of investigation becomes in itself a kind of treatment: in the process of investigation the investigators informally suggest various courses of action to the parties involved. Probably half of all juvenile cases are disposed of in that manner, long before the judge is involved. When and if a case does reach the judge, the hearing is not strictly adversary, although of course there are always adverse parties, such as the prosecutor versus a juvenile delinquent, or a husband versus a wife. During the hearing the judge tries to get the whole story from witnesses and from the parties themselves, usually in a very informal manner.

Juvenile Courts

Everything just said about the manner in which family courts operate is also true of **juvenile courts.** However, the jurisdiction of juvenile courts is usually limited to juveniles—persons between the ages of about 7 to 18. Some juvenile courts also have jurisdiction to hear cases involving persons who do certain prohibited things *to* juveniles—contribute to their delinquency, neglect them, and so on.

Juvenile courts do have the power to punish: a juvenile can be sent to an institution, for example. Juveniles no less than adults are protected by the United States Constitution, which guarantees that no one shall be denied liberty without due process of law.[4] Due process means, among other things, a fair trial with the right to have counsel, confront accusers, cross-examine witnesses, present and rebut evidence, be heard orally, and not be compelled to incriminate oneself. However, juveniles all too often have found themselves sentenced to institutions without a hearing that could by any measure be called fair from their point of view. This has been an unfortunate byproduct not only of the informality of juvenile proceedings but of the age and ignorance of the "accused." In 1967 the Supreme Court held that juveniles have a constitutional right to most elements of a due process hearing in any proceeding that might lead to their institutionalization.[5]

Domestic-Relations Courts

Domestic-relations courts generally have two functions: one is to grant divorces; the other is to prevent divorce and encourage reconciliation where possible. Conciliation efforts do not lend themselves to adversary judicial proceedings. In pursuing conciliation, courts must act more like social-service agencies; they should be staffed with persons skilled at probing the difficulties between spouses and suggesting solutions.

Adversary procedure accommodates itself much better to divorce. In many states marriage is based on the theory of contract. If a marriage is a contract, then divorce is an action by one or both parties to have the state nullify the contract on grounds that its terms have been violated. Thus in many states the law specifies several violations (the grounds) for which a divorce will be granted. However, several states no longer require proof of fault; in those states it is necessary only to prove that the marriage has broken down or that there are irreconcilable differences.

Probate Courts

On his deathbed a 95-year-old makes a will excluding his son from any inheritance. After the old man dies, his son challenges the will. "My father was not of sound mind in his last hours," says the son. The case is heard in probate court, but the judge upholds the will. The old man, says the court, retained his faculties to the end and knew what he was doing.

Probate Defined The word *probate* stems from the Latin *probatio,* meaning "proof," and *approbatio,* meaning the "approbation given by a judge to proof." In Anglo-American legal language the word *probate* refers to the proof of wills—that is, proof that the document alleged to be the last will and testament of a deceased person is such in reality. In more recent times a *probate matter* has

---

[4]*U.S. Const.,* 5th and 14th Amendments.

[5]In re Gault, 387 U.S. 1 (1967). However, in McKeiver v. Pennsylvania, 403 U.S. 528, the U.S. Supreme Court held that juveniles don't have the right to a jury trial in juvenile-court proceedings.

come to mean a matter pertaining to settlement of the estate of a deceased person or any other matter customarily handled by **probate courts.**

Probate Work is Mostly Clerical Rarely is there any excitement in probate court. The vast majority of wills go uncontested; estates are usually distributed among heirs without any disputes whatsoever. One wonders why it is necessary to have a probate court (or any other court) involved in the step-by-step clerical process of distributing estates when there is no dispute. The function of courts should be judicial, not executive. Occasionally, of course, there is controversy: wills may be challenged, the claims of creditors against the estate may be challenged, or the priority of one claim in relation to other claims against the estate may be disputed. When controversies erupt, then a court is needed to settle them. But when there is no controversy and the only work that needs to be done is the routine administrative work of notifying people, paying off creditors, and filing papers, then what is needed is an administrative officer, not a court. The American Bar Association has, in fact, proposed a Uniform Probate Code[6] (called *uniform* in the hope it will become uniform among all the states—a hope far from realization at present) that would remove the processing of uncontested wills from courts to a registrar. Under this scheme the court would still have to give its blessing to the transfer of an estate even if it is handled by a registrar, and the court would handle all estates in which there are contests. However, most of the probate court's time and effort would be spent on controversy settling rather than on clerical work and paper shuffling.

In addition to its work with people's estates, a probate court sometimes has authority over living persons and their property. This is because probate courts are commonly given jurisdiction to determine if a person is mentally incompetent to manage his or her property, power to administer the property of persons declared incompetent, and authority to assign guardians to mental incompetents and to review the guardianship. Probate courts often have similar authority over the property and guardianship of certain children, such as orphans.

ADMINISTRATIVE TRIBUNALS

Number of Cases

Most Americans do not realize that many trials, called *hearings,* are conducted within the bureaucracy by bureaucrats. Strange as it may seem, more judicial business is transacted within the bureaucracy than in regular courts of law. In fact, the amount of judicial work going on within the administration dwarfs the amount going on in courts of law—not only in the sheer number of cases heard but also in the amount of money involved.

Hearings

Anyone summoned by a state or federal revenue service to answer questions about his income tax is being subjected to a low-level informal "trial." If the taxpayer is told as a result of this initial contact that he owes more taxes, he may

[6]American Bar Association, *Uniform Probate Code* (St. Paul: West, 1969).

challenge that finding and ask for a hearing at the next level within the service. Usually there are several levels of appeal within a revenue service, and at some point the taxpayer is entitled to a full formal hearing that is almost identical to a proceeding in a regular court of law, with a hearing officer presiding, with lawyers, witnesses, and cross-examination—the whole panoply of judicial procedure. After the taxpayer exhausts all levels of appeal within the revenue service, he or she may try to appeal the case to a court.

All agencies, at all levels of government, are likely to have numerous disputes with citizens. The process of settling them within the agency is called *quasi adjudication.* In such administrative "trials," the agency acts as both prosecutor and judge. A typical case might go like this: A barber violates a rule of the state barber board by failing to put his comb in disinfectant. An inspector of the board observes this and accuses the barber. The barber board holds a hearing to determine if the barber should be punished by suspension of his license for, say, 90 days. Hundreds of federal, state, and local agencies are making and executing rules that have the force of law and "trying" violators. That's why the amount of administrative adjudication is so massive. The most prolific courts of original jurisdiction in the United States today are not courts at all, but administrative agencies.

Only Limited Appeal to Court

Perhaps you think appeals of the decisions of **administrative tribunals** should go to appeals courts, not to trial courts. That is exactly what usually happens. Appeals courts treat the adjudicatory decisions of administrative agencies much like they treat the decisions of regular trial courts in civil cases. They review chiefly law questions, rarely fact questions. Thus if the barber wants to appeal his 90-day suspension, he cannot go to the appeals court simply to reassert his innocence unless he alleges the agency's finding was not based on substantial evidence. The barber board has found it to be a fact that he did fail to put his comb in the disinfectant. Thus the suspended barber has to find some legal error in the board's action if he wants to appeal to a court. The barber might allege that his hearing before the board was unfair, that the board had no legal power to make a rule on the subject of combs and disinfectants, and so on. Those would be legal arguments. The fact that appeals from administrative agencies go to appeals courts rather than to trial courts is evidence that the judicial system recognizes administrative agencies as a sort of trial court.

THE RELATIONSHIP OF FEDERAL AND STATE COURTS

Parallel Ladders

Federal courts stand not above state courts but rather beside them. The two systems are parallel ladders: cases involving federal law normally go to federal courts and cases involving only state law go to state courts (Figure 8-1).

Constitutional Cases: Either Ladder

The United States Constitution is not exclusively a federal law, nor is it exclusively state law: it is simply the supreme law of the land that all courts and all

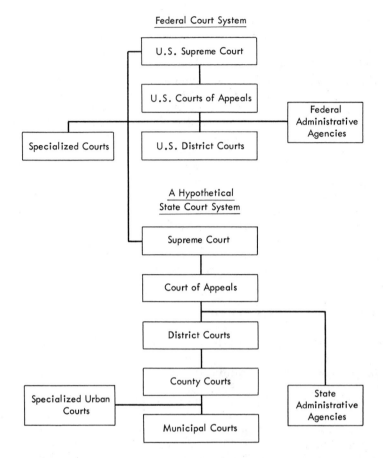

Figure 8-1 Federal and state court systems. In order to get this chart on one page, state and federal court systems appear vertically, rather than as parallel systems.

governmental officials in the nation—local, state, or national—are obligated to uphold. Thus if a plaintiff goes to court claiming that a state law runs counter to the United States Constitution, he or she may take the case to *either* a federal or a state court.

In the great segregation case of 1954,[7] Oliver Brown claimed the school-segregation laws violated the clause of the United States Constitution that says no state shall deny equal protection of the laws to any of its citizens.[8] The case was started in federal court but could have been started in a Kansas state court because Kansas courts, no less than federal courts, are obligated to enforce the United States Constitution. The choice of courts in cases involving the United States Constitution is up to the plaintiff. Had plaintiffs in the Brown case chosen Kansas courts, and had they ultimately reached the supreme court of that state and lost, they could then have appealed to the United States Supreme Court. In

[7]Brown v. Board of Education, 347 U.S. 483 (1954).
[8]*U.S. Const.*, 14th Amendment.

cases involving the United States Constitution, the United States Supreme Court is the final arbiter and stands above state courts.

Additional Powers of Federal Courts

Normally cases involving only state law go to state courts, but this rule has several exceptions. First, if two states are locked in legal combat over some issue (perhaps over the location of a state line), then the case must be heard by the United States Supreme Court. Second, disputes between citizens of different states may go to federal court if the amount of money involved exceeds a certain amount. Such a case might occur, for example, if a citizen of New York and a citizen of New Jersey have an automobile accident and one sues the other for a large sum of money. Third, ambassadors and diplomatic personnel from other countries who run afoul of state laws must be tried (if they are tried at all) before the United States Supreme Court. The same is true if they violate federal law. However, because the Supreme Court is busy it never hears such cases—offending foreign dignitaries are usually asked to leave the country if they repeatedly violate American laws or if they commit serious crimes. Since many foreigners find life in the United States quite pleasant, going home can be punishment enough for them.

JUDGES

Methods of Selection

The four most common methods for selecting state court judges (not including municipal-court judges) are as follows:

1. *Election:* either by partisan or nonpartisan ballot.
2. *Appointment:* by the governor with consent of the senate.[9]
3. *Combined appointment and election:* appointment by the governor from a list of candidates considered qualified by a judicial nominating commission, followed by approval or rejection by voters.
4. *Mixed:* some judges selected by one of the preceding methods and some by another.

The second of these methods was once a great deal more common than it is today. That system, which for the moment we shall call the appointment system, has steadily given ground to the Missouri system,[10] in which the governor's choice is limited to a short list of candidates submitted by a commission on judicial nominations.[11]

---

[9]Likewise, all federal judges on courts created under Article III of the U.S. Constitution are appointed by the president with the consent of the U.S. Senate.

[10]Missouri itself does not use the Missouri system exclusively.

[11]The Missouri system has also, of course, replaced some election systems as well as some appointment systems.

Election The election of judges has its frailties. Its main trouble is that the election process forces judges to be more political than perhaps they should. It raises the suspicion that judges may have a cautious eye on the next election when they are deciding cases, especially cases touching influential persons; even if an elected judge is determined not to be influenced by such things, subconscious bias can creep in. Furthermore, the spectacle of judges on the campaign trail drumming up votes demeans the office and reinforces suspicions of future bias. Hardly anything is more important to the cause of law and order than the reputation of courts. If judges themselves are doubted, if the idea is circulated that courts of justice are not really courts of justice, then all is lost. It is as important for a judge to seem fair as to be fair, to seem unbiased as to be unbiased, to seem above suspicion as to be above suspicion. When a judge goes on the campaign trail, all that is put in question.

Yet if judges are not elected, if they do not have to submit themselves to the electorate for periodic approval, then how can we be sure they will pay attention to the ideas of justice held by that electorate? The public certainly has thoughts about right and wrong, justice and injustice. The public has lively opinions about the death penalty, abortion, prostitution, about all sorts of things that come before courts. Still, "judicial legislation" of those and other matters goes on all the time. Judges in effect legislate by deciding what the law means. They legislate on a grand scale when they decide what the Constitution means: courts can outlaw something by simply saying the Constitution forbids it. Not long ago, as we saw in Chapter 7, the United States Supreme Court outlawed the practice common in most states of creating legislative districts grossly unequal in population.[12] As a result of that decision, the complexion of practically every state legislature in America has been changed. Judicial legislation by state supreme courts, and by the lesser courts, is not as well known as that of the United States Supreme Court, but it goes on wherever there are courts of law. For example, not long ago the supreme court of California decided that financing school districts primarily by the real-property tax results in a denial of equality to schoolchildren and is therefore unconstitutional under the equal protection clause of the California constitution. In short, the California court outlawed the practice of relying primarily on property taxes for school finance in California.[13]

If courts are going to legislate judicially on matters about which voters have definite ideas, then why shouldn't voters elect judges just as they elect legislators?

There are good arguments for *not* electing judges. A case can be made that judges should *not* mirror the prevailing attitudes of the general public as to what is right or wrong, just and unjust. From time to time the public is swept by passion. It can love; it can hate. The public can be a lynch mob, or it can sing the praises of a thief, such as Robin Hood or Jesse James. If courts were duty-bound to mirror the public's sense of justice, it would string people up from time to time without trial. Courts of justice are supposed to operate under a concept of justice somewhat more rational and deliberate than that which normally rules the

[12]Baker v. Carr, 369 U.S. 186 (1962) and Reynolds v. Sims, 377 U.S. 533 (1964).

[13]Seranno v. Priest, 487 P. 2nd 1241 (1971). The United States Supreme Court later held that such a method of school finance did not violate the equal protection clause of the United States Constitution. See San Antonio School District v. Rodriguez, 411 U.S. 1 (1973).

Box 8-1. Judicial Duties

In the midst of a trial in Golden, Colorado, Judge Gaspar Perricone was alarmed at the sight of a juror convulsing in her chair. He dashed to the jury box. "I figured she'd swallowed her tongue," said the judge, "and she did. I could tell she wasn't breathing. I had the best view of her from the bench." Judge Perricone revived the juror and ordered a new trial. Another day in the life of a judge.

---

hearts of ordinary citizens. The whole idea of a court is to dispense justice, not prejudice. The public's so-called sense of justice with regard to any given case is often formed by inadequate knowledge of the facts. The fundamental job of a court is to get the facts and weigh them dispassionately.

Another argument for not electing judges is that voters don't know what professional qualifications candidates have or ought to have. The same argument, however, could apply to any public office.

Appointment The appointment system has not been a perfect blessing. When governors appoint judges, politics often plays a bigger role than professional qualifications. "A judge is a lawyer who knows a governor," someone said. The appointment system has produced more bad state judges than bad federal judges. Actually appointment has worked very well in the federal government,[14] partly because most presidents are heavily influenced by the American Bar Association, which rates prospective appointees to the bench. Thus, in addition to their political qualifications federal judges must normally possess the high confidence of the legal profession. The role of bar associations seems less beneficial in state and local judicial appointments. Of course, the quality of applicants for judicial posts in many states is lower than the quality of applicants for federal judicial posts. Federal judges receive higher prestige and higher pay than the judges of most states.

The appointment system probably attracts higher-quality applicants than the election system. Many professionals have a distaste for election politics. However, the distinction between election and appointment may not be as great as imagined. Elected judges often get their jobs by being temporarily appointed to fill a vacancy. Once in the job they run as incumbents, and, as everybody knows, incumbents usually win elections.

The Missouri System Both the election system and the appointment system are in some ways terribly bad, yet each has certain good features. A new system was developed several years ago that combines appointment and election—the **Missouri system.** It corrects some of the evils of both. Basically the Missouri system works this way: Committees composed of both lawyers and nonlawyers recommend several candidates to the governor for each judicial vacancy. The governor must fill the vacancy with one of those nominees. After a short period of time—perhaps two years—the judge thus appointed must stand for election to a full term. When that full term ends (after perhaps four, six,

---

[14]Federal judges are appointed for life (technically they serve during "good behavior") —*U.S. Const.*, Art. III.

eight, or ten years) the judge must again receive an affirmative vote of the voters in order to serve another term. And so on until retirement. These elections are not competitive—no one runs against the judge. Voters are merely asked to vote yes or no on the question "Shall Judge X be retained in office?" Normally it requires a majority yes vote to retain the office.

Under the Missouri system, judicial nominating committees are usually appointed by the governor and are usually bipartisan in addition to being composed of both lawyers and laypersons. They normally do a careful job of sifting candidates for judicial appointment and usually present the governor with a list of competent persons. The governor can apply political criteria in his or her choice, but is limited to the names on the list—about three. Thus the best features of the appointment system are preserved: judges can be picked after careful screening on the basis of professional competence. The best features of the election system are also preserved: voters can periodically express their satisfaction or dissatisfaction with judges. No system of picking judges is perfect, but the Missouri system comes close. A few judges complain, however, that when judges are taken out of politics they lose their political power and much of their influence with state and local politicians.

Removal of Judges

Judges are not saints, and some are less saintly than others. Recently a judge in Mississippi was convicted of perjury for lying to a grand jury, and in Chicago another judge was sentenced to 12 years in prison for accepting a bribe. A justice of the Texas supreme court was the subject of an 87-count disbarment petition that included counts for soliciting a murder, obstructing justice, and forgery. A county judge in New York lost his job after mistreating a street vendor who sold him a "bad" cup of coffee: the judge had the vendor handcuffed and brought into court for a tongue lashing. A Michigan judge went to prison not long ago for taking an $8000 bribe, and a federal judge in Nevada was convicted of income-tax evasion. Some judges simply get lazy and neglect their work. Some judges get old and senile and can't remember anything. Some judges behave like tyrants in their courtroom. Some judges consort with parties in litigation before the court, take kickbacks, and do a variety of other fiendish things. Obviously there has to be a way to get rid of bad or ill judges.

Getting rid of judges presents a problem, however. If you want fair judges, then you have to give them job security. The less secure the judge, the less courageous he or she will be about making unpopular decisions. It may be better to let a few bad judges stay on the bench than to jeopardize the security of all judges by making it easy to unseat them.

Mechanisms for Removal   Judges usually have a good deal of independence and cannot easily be removed before the end of their term. However, removal can be done when necessary, and by several routes in many states. In many states a judge may be removed by impeachment for wrongdoing; generally this requires a two-thirds vote of the state senate. In many states the state supreme court also has the power to remove, retire, suspend, or censure judges. Less common methods of removal found in a scattering of states include removal by recall, removal by the governor when petitioned to do so by the legislature, removal by the legislature itself for incapacity (this is not quite the same thing as impeachment, which usually implies some sort of willful transgression), and removal by special courts for trial if complaints have been brought. Also, disbarment can usually accomplish the removal of a judge if he or she must be licensed to practice law in order to hold office as judge.

Where the state supreme court has the power to discipline judges, it is usually assisted by a **commission on judicial qualifications,** which investigates judges against whom complaints have been made and recommends a course of action to the court—perhaps removal, retirement, suspension, or censure, or perhaps nothing. Such a commission must operate in secrecy to protect the reputation of the judges being investigated. In addition to investigating judges suspected of wrongful behavior, these commissions also investigate cases of alleged judicial incompetence or illness. Removals are usually accomplished by prevailing on the target judge to resign. Of course, not every resignation is the result of such an investigation.

JURIES

Their Function

The jury could not agree. Eleven thought the man killed his wife and was guilty of first-degree murder. One lone holdout, a 55-year-old nurse, voted not guilty. Her reason: the wife deserved to be killed. The man escaped conviction.

We are often told that the main function of a jury is to find the facts. Yet the nurse who voted not guilty in this case had her mind fixed on something beside the narrow fact at issue. Was her action an affront to the jury system? Perhaps not, because after all, the jury system has very little justification for existence if it does not provide an average citizen's check on the rigidities of law. Indeed, one of the historic functions of juries is to reflect the spirit of the community in trials and to nullify prosecutions that run contrary to the feelings of the community. The nurse voted her feelings, which may also have been the feelings of a considerable sector of public opinion.

Juries are almost always told by judges that their only legitimate duty is to find facts and apply the law to the facts. One wonders whether such an instruction to a jury should be made, for to some degree it deprives juries of their single most important function in a democracy—to nullify unreasonable prosecutions and unreasonable laws, whatever the facts may be. Sometimes whole juries disregard their official charge and address a question supposedly foreign to their purpose, such as "Is the law itself just?" or "Is the prosecutor being vindictive?" or "Is the crime justified under the circumstances?" Some laws are so offensive that prosecutors have trouble convicting anybody under them no matter how great the evidence of guilt. For example, it was very difficult to prevail on juries in northern states before the Civil War to convict runaway slaves under the fugitive-slave acts. Likewise, it was hard to convict people for violating prohibition laws in the 1920s, no matter how clear the guilt. Today it is sometimes difficult to find a jury that will convict mercy killers of terminally ill relatives who are in pain and agony. And in 1987 a New York jury was in no mood to convict Bernhard Goetz who shot four young men whom he allegedly believed were about to assault him on a Manhattan subway.

Box 8-2. How to Kill

Alabama	Electrocution
Arizona	Lethal gas
Arkansas	Lethal injection
California	Lethal gas
Colorado	Lethal gas
Delaware	Hanging
Florida	Electrocution
Georgia	Electrocution
Idaho	Lethal injection or firing squad
Illinois	Lethal injection
Indiana	Electrocution
Kentucky	Electrocution
Louisiana	Electrocution
Maryland	Lethal gas
Mississippi	Lethal gas or lethal injection
Missouri	Lethal gas
Montana	Hanging or lethal injection
Nebraska	Electrocution
Nevada	Lethal injection
New Jersey	Lethal injection
New Mexico	Lethal injection
North Carolina	Lethal gas or injection
Ohio	Electrocution
Oklahoma	Lethal injection
Pennsylvania	Electrocution
South Carolina	Electrocution
Tennessee	Electrocution
Texas	Lethal injection
Utah	Firing squad or lethal injection
Virginia	Electrocution
Washington	Hanging or lethal injection
Wyoming	Lethal injection

States not listed have no death penalty or are not applying it.

Must a Jury Be Unanimous?

Juries have been part of the Anglo-American legal system for 600 years and were considered a great improvement over the system for determining guilt that preceded them. That system featured trial by combat and various other trials such as dunking in water (if after a certain period you sank, you were innocent). Early juries were impatient with dissenters: if the vote were 11 to 1, the 11 had the right to punish the dissenter. This almost guaranteed unanimous findings. It was also common to withhold food and water from juries until they reached a unanimous verdict. No one knows how it came to pass that unanimous verdicts were required. The United States Constitution does not require unanimous verdicts, but most states require it for conviction in criminal cases. Unanimity is now under attack, and several states, including Louisiana and Oregon, have rejected the requirement. Louisiana has used 9 of 12 to convict; Oregon, 10 of 12. The United States Supreme Court upheld the constitutionality of both the Oregon and Louisiana laws in 1972.[15] However, the unanimous-verdict requirement at least forces every juror to pay attention to the views of every other juror. Of course, majority (rather than unanimous) verdicts help protect a jury from the juror who just wants to be different. In civil cases unanimous verdicts have generally not been required.

Size of Juries

Nobody knows why the size of juries has been commonly set at 12. The reasons are lost in the mists of time. Some say it is because Jesus had 12 apostles; others say it was because Israel has 12 tribes; others give other equally intelligent reasons. Whatever the reason, a great many people are coming to the conclusion that 12 is too many. Nothing in the United States Constitution says juries have to number 12. There is now a trend away from 12 to smaller numbers in both civil and criminal cases. Six seems to be a currently popular number. Large juries are expensive (they have to be paid) and are more time-consuming in every way. It takes more time to find people for a jury of 12; it takes more time during trials for lawyers to agree on a jury; it takes more time for 12 people than for 6 to arrive at a verdict, and so on.[16] Abolition of juries altogether in civil cases wouldn't be a totally bad idea. However, the United States Constitution guarantees the right to jury trial in all civil cases exceeding $20 and in all criminal cases.[17]

Jury Duty

One source of dissatisfaction with the jury system is the unpleasantness of being called for jury duty and then having to sit in a room with dozens of other prospective jurors for several days waiting to be called—and often not being called. These long periods of useless waiting make people mad. Furthermore, it is expensive to pay people for doing nothing. Ways are now being explored to end this practice and to make the utilization of jurors more efficient. Reducing the size of juries helps. Allowing jurors to keep in touch with the court by phone also helps.

Jury Selection

Jury Stacking   Lawyers consider jury selection an art. It is such an art that the fairness of juries is now more than ever in question. Social scientists have developed ways of predicting who among a panel of prospective jurors would most likely be sympathetic to the defense or sympathetic to the prosecution. This

---

[15]Apodaca v. Oregon, 406 U.S. 404 (1972); Johnson v. Louisiana, 406 U.S. 356 (1972).

[16]Despite the trend toward smaller juries, the 12-member jury may have some elusive merits. Judging by such yardsticks as verdict outcomes, the nature of jury deliberations, jury representativeness of the public, and jury accuracy, one analyst concludes that "a strong case for the superiority of 12-member juries over 6-member juries can be made." Bernard Grofman, "The Slippery Slope," *Law and Policy Quarterly* (July 1980), p. 301.

[17]*U.S. Const.*, 7th and 6th Amendments, respectively.

> **Box 8-3.** Mom
>
> In Fresno, California, Ruby Ardaiz was summoned for jury duty and found herself assigned to a civil trial being presided over by her son, Judge James Ardaiz. The judge informed the parties that one of the prospective jurors was his mother, but neither side objected. Thus, he could not under California law exclude her from the jury. It is alleged that Judge Ardaiz was "nervous and squirmy" all through the trial.

has lately come to be known as social-science **jury stacking.** Juries so stacked are called "sociologically loaded dice." Of course, defense attorneys have from time immemorial practiced a good deal of common sense about these things. So have prosecutors. Each side is permitted to reject a certain number of prospective jurors without explaining why: the so-called peremptory challenge. Both defense attorneys and prosecutors have used their peremptory challenges astutely. Each side may also reject "for cause" any juror clearly biased about persons or issues involved in the case.

The most reliable jurors for the prosecution are people who have a stake in society: middle- and upper-class people who believe deep down in law and order because they have a lot to lose by disorder. Prosecutors want jurors who hold (or have held) managerial positions. Retired military officers, especially colonels, make dandy prosecution jurors. Defense attorneys in criminal cases, on the other hand, may look for jurors with a permissive outlook or irresponsible types. Large law firms have been known to keep card files of information about thousands of persons who have previously served on juries. Some firms conduct extensive undercover investigations to gather sociological data about persons who have been drawn for possible jury duty in a particular case. Prosecutors may also do some research. In fact, prosecutors often have sources of information about potential jurors not always conveniently available to defense attorneys: police records and government documents of all sorts, including, perhaps, information from supposedly private records, such as income-tax returns. Prosecutors usually have connections with officers in charge of drawing citizens for jury duty, and it is not unheard-of for prosecutors to encourage these officers (if they need encouragement) to select only "solid citizens" for jury service—in other words, to select from among the middle and upper classes. This, of course, is flatly unconstitutional but goes on anyway in a number of places because no one has challenged it. Somewhat the same result can be achieved by drawing people for jury service from the list of registered voters. Presumably those who take the trouble to register are solid citizens more committed to law and order than those who do not register.

Equal Protection in Jury Selection   The United States Supreme Court seems to have held that it is a denial of equal protection of the laws to try someone with a jury from which his or her peers have been excluded. As long ago as 1880 the Supreme Court held that the trial of a black defendant by a jury from which all blacks were by law excluded is a violation of equal protection.[18] Other convictions have been overturned in recent years because of exclusion of

[18]Strauder v. West Virginia, 100 U.S. 303 (1880).

representatives of the defendant's peer groups.[19] The Constitution requires that people called for jury duty represent a fair cross-section of the community. This can be frustrated by the exclusion of certain groups, such as women and blacks. Courts do not demand that persons basically like the defendant be on the jury— only that there be no discriminatory practice resulting in their exclusion.[20] Now that 18-year-olds can vote, the issue has been raised whether it is a denial of equal protection to try an 18-year-old by a jury from which 18-year-olds are excluded. Federal law now makes 18-year-olds eligible for service on juries in federal courts.[21]

Whatever the shortcomings of juries, they do serve as a democratic check on prosecutions, and they do make the general public a participating part of the judicial system by giving them a stake in the system and a personal relationship to it in some capacity other than that of defendant or plaintiff. Juries may also help prevent feelings of hostility toward and alienation from the court system by the public: it's hard to be alienated from something in which you're participating.

LAW

A Lawyer's Secret

It is the first day of the semester. Sixty new law students wait in a lecture hall for the professor's arrival. The door opens. You could hear a pin drop. A graying man steps to the lectern and disdainfully surveys the class. "I presume," he said, "you are here to learn the law. Well, let me tell you a secret. We lawyers have a secret. Our secret is that no one knows what the law *is*. Yes, we know what the law *was*. But we do not know what the law *is*. That is our secret."

Judge-Made Law

Why would a law professor say a thing like that? It all has to do with the doctrine of *stare decisis*—the policy of law that requires American courts to abide by laws and precedents previously laid down as being applicable to a similar set of facts. **Stare decisis** is the North Star of American law, the principle by which all compass headings in the law are set. By following this principle, courts give us **judge-made law.** How do judges make law? They make it by following their own precedents, by deciding today's case involving similar facts and situations the same way they decided yesterday's, or yesteryear's, or yestercentury's.

Why do we call those precedents *law*? Because if judges decide today's case by referring to yesterday's case, then the principle by which yesterday's case was decided is the law for today's case. Yesterday's decision influences today's decision and is therefore called law.

---

[19]Peters v. Kiff, 407 U.S. 493 (1972); Taylor v. Louisiana, 419 U.S. 522 (1975).

[20]Strauder v. West Virginia, 100 U.S. 303 (1880); Alexander v. Louisiana, 405 U.S. 625 (1972); and Peters v. Kiff, 407 U.S. 493 (1972).

[21]The Jury Selection and Service Act of 1968, as amended November 2, 1978, 28 U.S.C.A. § 1865.

No principle of law is more important than the principle of *stare decisis*. What exactly does it mean? Like so much legal jargon, it is a Latin phrase that would be less mystifying if it were simply said in English, but lawyers seemingly do not like the English language, especially plain English. In English *stare decisis* means "let the decision stand"; to abide by, to adhere to, decided cases; not to unsettle things that are established.[22] Thus once a case is decided it becomes law, so to speak, for identical cases in the future: it becomes judge-made law.

Of course, no two cases are exactly the same. One can never be sure how a court will decide today's case, but lawyers can make a pretty good guess by looking at how courts, especially appeals courts, have decided similar cases in the past. That's the lawyer's secret. Clients think lawyers know the law, but lawyers only know what the law was and have to guess what it might be for their client's case.

The most important judge-made law consists of the decisions of federal and state supreme courts. Cases decided by those courts constitute precedent that overrides the precedents of lower courts. Law students study mainly the decisions of supreme courts.

Most law in the United States is judge-made law, perhaps 90 percent of it (to pick a number rather haphazardly). A great deal of this law has built up around statutes and constitutions, like a pearl builds up around a grain of sand. Thousands of court decisions have explained the meaning of the United States Constitution (which is only a few pages long). Countless disputes have occurred over the meaning of such phrases as "due process of law,"[23] "equal protection of the law,"[24] "free speech,"[25] "free exercise of religion,"[26] "free press,"[27] and "freedom of assembly."[28] Hardly a word of the Constitution has escaped judicial interpretation. If you want to know what the United States Constitution means, it is almost dangerous to read the document itself. Its real meaning (as the courts see it) lies hidden in several hundred volumes of Supreme Court decisions. The same is true of state constitutions.

Similar judicial encrustment surrounds most statutes. A **statute** is a formal enactment of a legislative body that has become law. Many of these statutes are similarly vague and subject to judicial interpretation. If a statute says there shall be no saloon closer than six blocks from a school, the police may interpret that to mean six blocks as the sidewalk runs, whereas the owner of a new saloon may have set up business on the assumption that six blocks means six as the crow flies. The law being vague on this point, a dispute between the city and the saloon operator calls for judicial interpretation of the meaning of the word "block." The decision would become judge-made law for future cases in which the meaning of that word is at issue.

Courts are free to ignore their past decisions, free to abandon *stare decisis,* free to set new precedent, but their general practice is to avoid setting new precedent unless there are compelling reasons for doing so. Let us examine two

[22]Henry C. Black, *Black's Law Dictionary,* 5th ed. (St. Paul: West, 1979), p. 1261.

[23]*U.S. Const.,* 5th and 14th Amendments.

[24]*U.S. Const.,* 14th Amendment.

[25]*U.S. Const.,* 1st Amendment.

[26]Ibid.

[27]Ibid.

[28]Ibid.

leading cases that show not only how courts occasionally break their own precedents but also how they follow precedent.

Plessy and *Brown*

In the case of *Brown* v. *Board of Education,* the United States Supreme Court broke with its own precedent. You may remember that the *Brown* case was the great segregation case of 1954, but there were segregation cases before 1954. The first to be decided under the equal protection clause of the Fourteenth Amendment was *Plessy* v. *Ferguson* in 1896.[29] In that case a very light skinned "black" named Homer Adolph Plessy got aboard a train in Louisiana and took his seat in a car reserved for whites. Louisiana law required train companies to provide separate accommodations for whites and blacks. Although asked repeatedly and forcefully by the conductor to go to the car for blacks, Plessy refused. Finally an officer came to the scene and arrested Plessy for violation of the Louisiana segregation law. Plessy defended himself in court with the argument that Louisiana's segregation law was contrary to the equal protection clause of the United States Constitution because it implied the inferiority of the black race. The State of Louisiana argued that separation of the races did not imply inferiority of the black race any more than of the white race and that the railroad car for blacks was as good as the car for whites.

The United States Supreme Court agreed with Louisiana's argument, and the Court's decision in the case of *Plessy* v. *Ferguson* became the "leading case" that all courts in the land followed from then on when similar or roughly similar cases arose. *Plessy* v. *Ferguson* established the **separate but equal doctrine** as the yardstick for determining whether a given segregation law squared with the equal protection clause of the United States Constitution: separateness is legal and constitutional as long as the separate facilities are equal. For nearly 60 years "separate but equal" was the judge-made law on the subject of racial-segregation laws. Countless lawsuits concerning racial segregation under the equal protection clause were all decided according to the principle of *stare decisis.* Precedent was followed, and that precedent was the *Plessy* decision. For most of those 60 years, however, courts did not apparently look very closely to see how equal the so-called equal facilities were. Separateness passed almost unchallenged as long as some attempt was made at providing similar facilities for blacks.

In the 1940s courts began looking closer to see whether the so-called equal facilities were really equal. More and more segregation laws were struck down as unconstitutional violations of the equal protection clause on grounds that separateness of facilities was not accompanied by equality of facilities.

Finally in 1954 the United States Supreme Court broke with its own precedent, broke with the doctrine of *Plessy,* broke with the doctrine of separate but equal. Fifty-eight years after the *Plessy* case the Supreme Court finally agreed with Homer Plessy, by then, of course, long in his grave. Oliver Brown went to court in Topeka, Kansas, and used Plessy's argument to support the theory that Topeka's segregated school system was a violation of the equal protection clause. When the case finally reached the Supreme Court, Brown was upheld, and the

---

[29]Plessy v. Ferguson, 163 U.S. 537 (1896).

Court announced a new interpretation of the Constitution. It said the policy of separating the races is usually interpreted as denoting the inferiority of the Negro group. This creates a sense of inferiority in the Negro child and affects motivation to learn. Therefore, all racial segregation produces inequality and is a violation of the equal protection clause of the Constitution.

Since 1954 the *Brown* case has been the law of the land, the leading case, the judge-made law for similar cases. These two cases, *Plessy* and *Brown*, are treated here to illustrate how the doctrine of *stare decisis* creates judge-made law. This body of judge-made law is sometimes called *common law*.

The term **common law** comes to us, like so much in American law, from the British, whose system of law was planted on this continent. As the term was originally used in England 800 years ago, two things were intended to be common about the common law. First, it was to be built from the common practices and customs of the realm. Second, it was to be common to the entire realm. Very few court decisions today are based on custom, except insofar as judges look upon their own past decisions as customs to be followed. Occasionally, when there is no judicial precedent and no legislative act controlling the matter, courts will base their decisions on custom. This is a rarity, however, because practically everything by now has either been the subject of a prior law case or the subject of a statute.

The Civil-Law World

We in the common-law world are really not the whole world by any means. In fact, we are something of an island in a much larger world. Our common-law system, the system in which judges make most of the law, is usually found wherever the British flag flies or has flown. It is the British system of law, a system that spread across the seas with the empire. The system of judge-made law is most pervasive in lands such as the United States, Canada, and Australia, where British culture grew in lightly populated virgin lands. But where British culture encountered well-established legal systems, as in India and Africa, the common-law system took root somewhat superficially and was used chiefly in cases involving certain kinds of commercial transactions. Anyone who sticks a finger very deeply into the law of India soon encounters legal methods and legal rules strange to the common law.

But in most of the world common law is utterly unknown. A greater system prevails almost everywhere: the civil-law system. The chief difference between the civil-law world and the common-law world is simply that civil-law judges do not as a rule look to the decisions of their colleagues in previous cases for guidance in deciding today's case. Instead they look almost exclusively to statutory law—to the detailed codes of law enacted by legislative bodies. Almost no tradition in the civil-law world would motivate a civil-law judge to pay much attention to past judicial decisions.

When one speaks of the civil-law world, there is danger of confusing that civil law with our civil law. As you will see, our civil law is used in contrast with criminal law. The reason the civil-law world uses the term *civil law* to describe itself is that one of the first civil-law codes was called the *Corpus Juris Civilis*. Thus, the whole system was nicknamed the "civil" law system. It is also sometimes called Roman Law (or the Romanist system) because the *Corpus Juris Civilis* was compiled during the reign of Justinian and his successors, and was used throughout the Roman Empire.

There are, of course, codes of statutory law in the common-law world, but they play a much less stellar role than statutory law in the civil-law world.

Statutory Law

Statutory law encompasses administrative rules, constitutions, and enactments of legislative bodies. Youngsters confuse *statutes* with *statues,* but once over that hurdle, one wonders whether a constitution is a statute and whether an administrative rule is a statute. Here even adults are in a quandary. The term *statutory law* in its most common usage simply means law enacted by legislative bodies. Constitutions, however, are also counted as statutory law because they are enacted, so to speak, by the whole electorate. Administrative rules are counted as statutory law because they too are enactments of administrative agencies acting as quasi-legislative bodies.

Congress publishes its statutes in chronological order every two years in a big book called the *Statutes at Large* (abbreviated *Stat.*). Periodically these statutes are again published in the form of a *United States Code* (abbreviated *U.S.C.*), in which they are arranged by subject matter. Each state of the Union has similar publications (for example, the *Session Laws of Colorado* and the *Colorado Revised Statutes*). An *annotated* code includes a mass of notes citing court decisions that have interpreted the code, plus other materials useful to lawyers and judges.

Administrative Rules

Many administrative agencies make **rules** elaborating the laws they enforce. Administrative rules outnumber the acts of Congress, state legislatures, and local governing boards by perhaps a hundred to one or even a thousand to one. This is a little-known fact—little known at least to the general public. A city building department, for example, whose job is to regulate the way houses are constructed, makes a whole code of rules governing almost every detail of construction: exterior siding on housing shall have a minimum thickness of ⅜ inch; all exterior wall frames shall be braced at each end; nails shall not be driven closer together than one-half their length, and so on endlessly. A similar mass of rules govern electrical wiring; others, plumbing. Rules made by a typical building department exceed by many times the total legislative output of the city council. Other departments also make rules affecting the public. Fire departments make fire regulations, health departments make health regulations, and so on. Nor are these rules confined to detail. Nor is rule making confined to agencies of local government. State and federal agencies make thousands of rules. The number of regulations made every year by the typical state health department alone may exceed the number of laws passed annually by the typical state legislature. Federal rule making is also massive. A special daily newspaper has been founded to announce each day's output of rules and rule changes by federal agencies. The *Federal Register* is for administrative rules what the *Statutes at Large* is for acts of Congress. Periodically all federal rules are codified into a *Code of Federal Regulations* (abbreviated *C.F.R.*). *C.F.R.* is for regulations what the *United States*

Code is for acts of Congress. Few, if any, state or local governments have as excellent a system for announcing and codifying rules. Administrative agencies today are the chief lawmakers of America. Their rules must be considered the major part of statutory law.

Civil and Criminal Law

What is a crime? Is it a crime if you fail to pay a debt? If you hit a lamppost with your car? If you violate the zoning ordinance? The answer is probably not, yet in each of those cases you have committed a wrong. For some wrongs there is no punishment, although there may be *remedies*. Any law that does not provide punishment but does make a remedy available to the wronged party is called a **civil law.** Any law that does provide punishment for violators is called a **criminal law.**

Civil and Criminal Cases

Sometimes it is said that a **civil case** is a private dispute between private parties whereas a **criminal case** is always between the government and a wrongdoer. That is not entirely correct, although a vast number of civil disputes are between private parties other than the government, and all criminal cases do involve the government (which prosecutes them). However, a government may also be a party in a civil case. In fact, if you count all the quasi adjudication by government agencies in which the agencies themselves are a party, you would have to say that most civil cases in the United States do actually involve government as a party. If you have a dispute with the Internal Revenue Service about how much your tax bill should be, it will be a civil case in which the government appears very much like a private party. The tax case will be civil if the government is not accusing you of trying to cheat. Cheating implies intention to do wrong, which is the essential ingredient of every crime. If there is no intent to do wrong but merely a dispute over the meaning of the tax law, then it is a civil dispute. If you are found to have violated a civil law, then you are said to have committed a *tort,* a non-criminal wrong. The court will ask you to remedy the situation by paying money or by doing whatever the court considers a reasonable remedy. The remedy is not considered a punishment, although you may privately think it is punishment. A remedy is a remedy, not a punishment.

A civil case is obviously one in which a plaintiff is accusing a defendant of committing a civil wrong against the plaintiff. A criminal case is obviously one in which the defendant is being tried for violation of a criminal law. Although the crime may have been committed against an individual, all crimes are prosecuted by government on behalf of society. It is not the aggrieved individual but the aggrieved society that prosecutes. If a kidnapping has occurred, the criminal case against the kidnapper is prosecuted by the government that made the law against kidnapping. The victim, however, may also wish to bring a civil suit for damages against the kidnapper—the same kidnapping may be both a criminal and a civil wrong. Most, perhaps all, crimes are also civil wrongs, but the reverse is not true. (It is easier to win a civil suit after the defendant has been found guilty of the same wrongful act in a criminal trial.)

Equity

Occasionally judges are faced with cases (or aspects of cases) that they cannot decide fairly by application of any statute or judicial principle. In those cases judges apply their **equity power**—their power to decide such cases according to their own sense of fairness. For example, they may be faced with a situation in which no wrong at all has been committed as yet but has only been threatened—perhaps a threat by someone to kill my dog. Courts generally shy away from controversies in which no wrong has been committed. Courts prefer to deal with past wrongs, not threatened future wrongs. Perhaps 99 percent of all court cases concern past wrongs: attempts to punish crimes or to remedy civil wrongs. However, sometimes someone will ask the court to prevent a threatened wrong. Judges usually prefer to let the wrong happen and remedy it afterwards, but if they think that the wrong cannot be remedied afterward, that the threatened wrong would be irreparable, they can resort to their equity powers. Suppose I have an apple tree in my back yard whose branches spread high over my neighbor's property. Ripe apples drop on his driveway and car. He runs over this fruit and squashes it on the concrete. Gradually this produces a slick, slimy mess, to the distress of my neighbor. He asks me to trim the branches over his property. I refuse. It would ruin the beauty and symmetry of the tree. "All right," he says angrily, "if you won't trim your tree, I'm going to come over and chop it down." "You better not!" "Well, just you wait!" "He really means business," I think to myself. "Such a magnificent tree! So irreplaceable. How irreparable the damage if it were axed down."

Having taken a course in state and local government at the university, I remembered something about *writs of injunction*. Courts will issue writs of injunction to stop someone from doing something wrong that cannot be remedied later by a civil action. Certainly it would be an irreparable injury to me if my neighbor chopped down my apple tree. An apple tree takes a generation to grow. Only God can make a tree.

With these wild thoughts in my head, I go down to my lawyer and tell him the problem. He gently suggests that I trim the tree. I refuse. He says my neighbor has the right to trim that part of the tree over his property. "Maybe so," I answer, "but right now he's threatening to chop the whole tree down on my property." My lawyer concedes a point. My neighbor has no right to do this and is, indeed, threatening irreparable harm. My lawyer goes to the county judge and asks for a court order commanding my neighbor not to do what he has threatened. The judge issues an **injunction** but makes it temporary. She orders my neighbor and me to appear in court to explain everything. If after the explanation the judge thinks the injunction should be lifted, or made permanent, she will act accordingly. If while the injunction is in effect, my neighbor comes over anyway and chops the tree down, he is in *contempt of court,* and the judge can summarily punish him by jail or fine without trial.

The word *injunction* stems from the Latin *injunctio* meaning "to enjoin or prohibit." The most celebrated injunctions in recent years have been those issued under the Taft-Hartley Act[30] prohibiting labor strikes for a period of 80 days, the so-called 80-day injunction.

[30]Taft-Hartley Act, 61 *Stat.* 156 (1947), 29 *U.S.C.* Par. 185.

There are other equitable writs besides injunction, the most notable of which is **mandamus.** A *writ of mandamus* is just the opposite of injunction. It commands the recipient to do something. It is applicable only to nondiscretionary duties of public officials. Suppose the registrar of your state university has the duty of printing diplomas and delivering them to persons eligible to graduate. His duty is purely mechanical and nondiscretionary (or, as lawyers say, *ministerial*). He has no discretion over whether you ought to graduate; his only duty is to do what he is told. Suppose, however, that he refuses to deliver your diploma because he thinks you've been a troublemaker and shouldn't graduate. Your ultimate recourse would be to ask the nearest court for a *writ of mandamus* commanding the registrar to deliver the diploma. If he still refuses after receiving the writ, he is in contempt of court and subject to summary punishment.

CRIMINAL AND CIVIL PROCEDURE

Criminal procedure is the procedure by which a person who has committed, or is thought to have committed, an offense is brought to the point of being found guilty or innocent.

Indictment; Information

The word **indictment** stems from the Latin *indictio* meaning "a declaration or proclamation." An indictment is an accusation in writing presented by a grand jury charging a person with a punishable public offense. An **information** resembles an indictment but is filed at the discretion of the prosecutor rather than at the discretion of the grand jury.

Arrest

An officer may without a warrant **arrest** anyone who has committed a punishable offense in the officer's presence. If an offense is committed not in the officer's presence, the person may be arrested without a warrant only if the officer has probable cause to believe that an offense has been committed and that the person is the offender. In cases in which a warrant is required, a judge issues a written order (a warrant) directing a peace officer or other specifically named person to arrest the person named in it who is accused of an offense. However, suspects may be briefly detained without a warrant.

When arresting someone, the police should tell the suspect that he or she has certain constitutional rights. If the arresting officer fails to do this, statements made in the presence of the officer by the defendant may not be admitted in court for use against the defendant. The United States Supreme Court in *Miranda* v. *Arizona*[31] said that if statements made by defendants after arrest are to be used against them, they must have been told prior to making those statements that (1) they have a right to remain silent; (2) whatever they say can and will be used against them in court; (3) they have a right to consult with counsel prior to questioning and to have counsel present during questioning if they

[31]Miranda v. Arizona, 384 U.S. 436 (1966). Warnings must be given whenever there is custodial interrogation, which may or may not occur at the time of arrest.

desire; (4) if they fail to request counsel their failure does not constitute a waiver of the right to have counsel at any time; and (5) if they are unable to secure a lawyer, one will be appointed for them.

A summons such as one gets in most traffic violations is a noncustodial arrest. More precisely, it is an order issued by some representative of the court, such as a police officer, commanding the person named in the summons to appear at a certain time in court and answer the charges against him or her.

Right to Counsel

Any person in custody must be allowed to consult with an attorney as often as he or she wishes, and for as long as he or she wishes, within reason. The right to counsel applies at what the courts call the *critical stages* of the criminal process—interrogations, lineups, preliminary hearings, and the like. Indigent accused persons who cannot afford counsel must be provided counsel by the court.

Preliminary Hearing

After being arrested a person may have a **preliminary hearing** before a judge to determine whether there is probable cause that he or she committed the offense alleged. If there is no probable cause, the person is released. On this occasion the court again advises the defendant of his or her right to counsel and other procedural rights.

Bail

Any person in custody prior to conviction, unless he or she is charged with a capital offense in which the presumption of guilt is great, has a right to be released on **bail,** which is a deposit of money to secure the release. The money is forfeited to the court if the arrestee fails to appear in court when commanded.

Arraignment

After an indictment (or information) is filed, the defendant is brought to court to answer the matter charged. This is **arraignment.** The accused is called; the indictment, information, or complaint is read to him; and he is asked whether he wishes to plead (1) guilty, (2) not guilty, (3) *nolo contendere* (no contest), or (4) not guilty by reason of insanity. Refusal to plead is considered a plea of not guilty. If the defendant pleads guilty and if the court accepts this plea (after satisfying itself that it was not made under duress and is justified), the guilty plea is equal to conviction for the offense and constitutes a waiver of the right to trial. Sentencing follows the plea of guilty.

Jury Selection

Every person charged with a public offense has a right to trial by jury, although no one is required to be tried by jury. The right to a trial by jury may be waived, except by someone accused of an offense punishable by death. The jury usually consists of 12 persons if the offense charged is a felony. In matters involving misdemeanors the accused may be entitled to a jury of less than 12, perhaps 6. If the matter involves a petty offense, some states allow as few as 3 on the jury.

Those persons eligible for jury duty are chosen at random, ideally from a list of everyone who lives in the county. The list is, ideally, updated once a year. Courts serving populous districts usually employ a jury commissioner to maintain the list and draw persons from the list as needed for potential jury duty. This work is done in less populous districts by the clerk of the court. At such times as directed by the judge, the jury commissioner or the clerk, using an impartial method, will summon to court a certain number of those persons qualified to serve as jurors.

The bailiff seats the requisite number of prospective jurors in the jury box. Then begins the so-called **voir dire** (meaning in Latin and French "to speak the truth"). This is the process in which the court examines prospective jurors in order to select a jury reasonably satisfactory to both the prosecution and the defense. Attorneys for each side are entitled to a certain number of peremptory challenges, meaning they may challenge and cause to be removed from the jury a certain number of prospective jurors without offering any reason, relying on intuition if nothing else. Also the attorney for each side may challenge for cause an unlimited number of prospective jurors; any facts indicating bias are sufficient to excuse a juror for cause.

Opening Speeches and Presentation of Evidence by the Prosecutor

The trial opens with statements by the two opposing attorneys outlining what they will try to prove during the proceedings. Then the prosecutor presents evidence, calling witnesses one at a time. Each witness may be cross-examined by the defense attorney, who probes his or her honesty and accuracy. It is the responsibility of the prosecutor to make what is known in legal circles as a *prima facie* case (Latin, meaning "at first view"). The prosecutor must, in other words, present sufficient proof of the guilt of the accused to support a finding of guilt if evidence to the contrary is disregarded. Since at this stage the defense has not yet begun to present its proof, the judge has a clear view of the prosecution's case. If the prosecution's case looks weak, the defense attorney may move at this stage that the accused be acquitted on grounds that the evidence was not sufficient to make a *prima facie* case. If the judge agrees, the trial may be concluded and the defendant released.

Presentation of Evidence for the Defense

If the prosecution has made a *prima facie* case, the trial continues. The defense now presents evidence and calls witnesses. The accused may decline to take the stand inasmuch as the Constitution of the United States and that of most states guarantee that no persons shall be compelled to testify against themselves in a criminal case.[32] However, the accused may testify if he or she wishes.

---

[32]*U.S. Const.*, 5th Amendment.

Final Arguments

After the prosecution and the defense have presented their evidence, each side has an opportunity to make closing statements, summarize the evidence, and comment on its significance.

Instructions to the Jury

When the prosecuting attorney and the defense attorney have finished their concluding statements, the judge has a chance to "instruct" the jury on certain matters of law that should affect their deliberations, such as reminding them that in criminal cases an accused is presumed innocent until proven guilty. Other matters of law may be mentioned, such as the legal definition of the crime of which the defendant is accused. This is a touchy moment in the course of a trial because lawyers resent it when the judge's instructions to the jury seem to lean toward one party or the other. Many court decisions have been reversed on appeal because judge's instructions were unfair. To help avoid the pitfalls of biased or ambiguous jury instructions, judges refer to a large book of sample jury instructions that they are likely (and in some states required) to use in routine cases.

Jury Deliberations and Verdict

After jurors receive their instructions from the judge, they retire to a jury room (taking a written copy of their instructions with them), where they discuss the case and vote. In most states the verdict must be unanimous in criminal cases. Some juries cannot agree, even after numerous ballots. In that case they come out and tell the judge. The judge will probably tell them to go back and deliberate some more. If they still fail to reach a verdict, the judge declares a **mistrial** and ends the proceedings. The prosecutor may then institute a new trial on the same grounds as before, with a different jury.

The jury decides only fact questions—that is, whether the accused actually did what he or she was accused of doing. All law questions, on the other hand, must be decided by the judge.

Sentencing

If the accused is found innocent by the jury, the trial ends. If found guilty, the next step is sentencing. In this the law generally allows some discretion to the judge. Before deciding on the sentence, the judge will hold a hearing for the purpose of gathering medical, psychiatric, and sociological data about the accused that will help him or her arrive at a sentence that is appropriate to the accused and that serves the best interests of society.

Motion for New Trial and Appeal

Only a small percentage of all convictions are appealed. A case cannot be appealed solely on the grounds that defendants feel they are innocent and that the jury made a mistake. The finding of the jury is a finding of fact considered final unless it can be clearly shown to be in error. Seldom can it be shown that the jury made a clear error. Appeals almost always rest on grounds that there was some sort of legal (as opposed to factual) error in the trial, an error in selection of the jury, for example, or in admission of evidence, or in the instructions to the jury. An appellate court does not have a jury since it does not review fact questions. Appellate courts try to stick to law questions insofar as law and fact can be untangled. An appeals court bases its decision largely on the record—that is, on what is found in documents such as the indictment, the minutes of the proceedings, and the transcript of the trial. Lawyers also present arguments to the appellate court. If the appeals court sustains the conviction, there is still the possibility, however remote, of appeal to the governor for a *reprieve* (delay), a *commutation* (reduction of penalty), or a *pardon* (release from punishment). In the eyes of the law a pardon leaves the offender innocent, as if he or she had never committed the offense.

Civil Procedure

A civil case is an action, usually brought by a private party, to enforce, redress, or protect private rights. The defendant in a civil case is not charged with commission of a punishable public offense but with a private personal wrong, such as failure to pay a debt or to honor a contract. A civil case begins with (1) a summons and (2) a complaint. If A is suing B for nonpayment of a debt, A goes to court (usually through a lawyer, except in small-claims court) and asks the court to issue an order (*summons*) directing the defendant to appear at a certain time and to defend. The summons names the parties and includes a brief statement of the sum of money or other relief demanded by the plaintiff. If a copy of the complaint does not accompany the summons, then the defendant must be supplied with a copy within a short period of time. The summons may be delivered by the sheriff or by any person at least 18 years old who is not a party to the action. There are detailed rules about what constitutes actual service of the summons.

When the *complainant,* or *plaintiff* (the person who starts the suit), asks for a summons, he or she also files a *complaint* that informs the defendant of all material facts supporting the plaintiff's demands. The defendant is then entitled to ask for a *bill of particulars* describing the complaint in greater detail. After a set period of time, the defendant must answer the complaint or lose the suit by default.

If either party wants a jury trial, a jury will be called in much the same manner as in criminal cases. The trial proceeds in essentially the same way as a criminal trial, although there are several key differences. First, in a civil case, since there is no crime involved the defendant must (if called) take the stand and testify (although he or she has a right not to answer incriminating questions). Second, in a civil case proof of the charges need not show the defendant's fault beyond a reasonable doubt; the standard of proof is less rigid. Proof supporting a civil complaint need only add up to a "preponderance of evidence"—that is, the evidence must make it look more probable than not that the demands of the complainant are justified. Third, the findings of juries in civil cases need not be unanimous. The verdict of a majority of the jurors is sufficient unless the parties stipulate some number greater than a majority. The jury in a civil case usually consists of fewer than 12, usually 6. The jury does not have the right to decide everything: they may decide only fact questions, not law questions, a distinction never easy to make. If neither party wants a jury, then all issues are decided by the judge.

COURT REFORM

All courts have some degree of freedom to administer their business by procedures of their own choosing—subject, of course, to state laws and supreme-court directives. But court reformers often see virtue in standardization and centralization. For example, they advocate standardized court practices throughout the state, not only for trial procedures but also for administrative procedures preceding and following trials, and other court business. The idea is to give the state supreme court, assisted by a professional state-court administrator, the power to prescribe uniform procedures for all courts. This is, however, annoying to a good many lawyers and legal secretaries, who, once they are familiar with the ropes—how to file a suit, for example—don't want to reeducate themselves to satisfy reformers smitten with a passion for neatness and uniformity.

Many court reformers want a state court system, in fact as well as in name, and one that is more professional and less political. They want to equip courts with professional court administrators with master's degrees in the subject. They want a system of merit staffing of courts, and schools where the art of judicial administration may be taught. They want a uniform body of knowledge on the subject of judicial administration applicable throughout the state. They want all the jobs in the judicial system to be classified—given job descriptions—so that exams to determine eligibility can be given to applicants for those jobs. Only then can a merit system for court employees be introduced. Of course, this process would transfer hiring power away from local political rings to a central judicial-administration office at the state capital.

Some states have adopted these centralization techniques. Populous, big-spending states are more likely to have a properly staffed and budgeted central office of judicial administration,[33] partly because they are more likely to think they can afford it.

Some court reformers also like to think the court system itself would be more manageable if there were fewer types of courts—they favor consolidation of some courts and streamlining (simplification) of the court system. This is motivated partly by a wish for standardized jobs, standardized tests, standardized procedures, and so on.

Judges who are elected, and therefore owe their jobs to political forces, become part of the political establishment and are apt to oppose any "reform" that might upset the establishment, especially a reform that would change the system of selecting judges. They are also likely to oppose reforms that would sever political influence over the appointment of court employees.

[33]See Henry R. Glick, "State Government and Judicial Administration: A Political Analysis," *State Government* (Winter 1980), pp. 44–49.

THE OMBUDSMAN

Every day all of us are the victims of injustices that cannot be remedied in any court. It is perhaps unjust and wrong and hurtful if someone passes us in the hall without saying hello. Countless hurts and injustices are wholly beyond the reach of the legal system. And many of these wrongs are committed by government agencies: things like the failure of the government to answer a letter a distressed mother has written inquiring about the treatment of her son in the army; or some unspeakably rude behavior by an official at the driver's-license bureau; or the failure of the government to send out scholarship checks on time; or the failure of a professor to give reasonably correct advice and counsel to a student who has sought it. An endless variety of negligent, slovenly, below-par behavior by public officials can happen—none of it constituting a legal wrong, none of it redressable in court, but all of it nevertheless wrong.

Long ago the Scandinavian countries pioneered something called the ombudsman to handle such wrongs committed by government bureaucrats. The ombudsman in Norway, Sweden, and Denmark is an individual of high integrity appointed by the government to receive complaints of bad treatment by bureaucrats and to do something about it. Of course, if the complaint reveals illegal behavior, the ombudsman turns it over at once to the prosecutor. But if it is a wrong that is not a legal wrong, the ombudsman uses all his or her persuasion and influence to correct the situation, and is usually very effective. Often the wrongdoers are not fully conscious of their own behavior, and are eager to correct the problem when it is pointed out to them.

The ombudsman idea has caught on in much of the world in recent years. In the United States one finds ombudsmen, or individuals with other titles but similar roles, serving state governments—perhaps working out of the governor's or lieutenant governor's office. A number of cities and even agencies of the state bureaucracy have set up ombudsmen. Some universities have ombudsmen to whom students may go with miscellaneous complaints about their treatment.

Sometimes state legislators feel they are being upstaged by ombudsmen who attempt to solve citizen-state problems: legislators like to get the credit. Nevertheless, the office of ombudsman is an increasingly important adjunct to the system of dispute settling within many state and local governments. As a matter of fact, citizen complaining, whether through ombudsmen or by other means, is emerging as an important form of political participation.[34]

TORT LIABILITY OF GOVERNMENTS

At first it seems ridiculous that a state cannot be sued without its consent. But if you remember that each state is supposed to be sovereign (has no legal superior) in certain matters,[35] then how can anyone, even the courts, make it do what it does not choose to do with regard to those matters? Where it has no legal

[34]See Robert D. Miewald and John C. Comer, "The Complaint Function of Government and the Ombudsman," *State and Local Government Review* (Winter 1984), pp. 22–26.

[35]A state is sovereign in matters that are simultaneously within its geographic boundaries and within its exclusive subject matter authority as set forth in the United States Constitution.

superior, the state does not have to let itself be sued. This exemption from lawsuits is sometimes referred to as "sovereign immunity."

But states do chivalrously allow themselves to be sued. Why? Because it is just and fair to do so. Governments do after all commit civil wrongs (torts) from time to time. It is wrong for a health department doctor to pour carbolic acid into the ear of a patient. It is wrong for state highway workers to roll a twenty-ton boulder down the side of a mountain onto the top of a passing bus. It is wrong for police officers to shoot innocent people.

Thus, states have **tort liability acts,** which in a certain sense give people the right to sue the state (and by extension, to sue any instrumentality of the state, such as a local government). The federal government also has a tort liability act.

In recent years, many state courts have refused to recognize any overarching sovereign immunity by the state except when such immunity is affirmatively asserted by the state in a law declaring that the state henceforth is expressly immune from certain specific categories of tort claims. Thus, the so-called tort liability acts no longer focus on when the state can be sued, but rather on when it cannot be sued. One might call them "nonliability" acts. Thus, to repeat, many appellate courts now operate on the principle that in the absence of such a law establishing areas of nonliability, anybody can sue the state like they can sue anyone else, because the state by its silence is presumed to have given its consent to be sued.

Clearly, the general thrust of state appellate courts in recent years has been to increase, not decrease, the scope of state (and local) liability for torts. Furthermore, state legislatures have acquiesced in this pattern and have not been terribly vigorous about laying down limits to the state's liability. This, combined with the vastly increased number of acquisitive lawyers and with a seemingly insatiable public thirst for litigation, has led to a rise in damage suits against governments at all levels.

Many governments, especially local governments, take out insurance policies against damage suits. But insurance companies are not blind to the dangers of insuring governments these days. They have raised rates. In fact, insurance rates have soared, and in numerous instances the companies have simply refused to write policies for governments. This has blossomed into a major financial crisis, especially for local governments that aren't big enough to run the risk of living without insurance. Just imagine what a $10 million judgment against a town of 1500 people would do! Or even a judgment one-twentieth of that. The only answer for counties, towns, townships, cities, and school districts is to get what little insurance they can afford and be careful as possible not to incite a lawsuit. Many local governments have decided to cut back or abandon all sorts of things that might cause somebody to be injured—swimming pools, physical contact sports, and even patrolling the streets with motor vehicles.

Meanwhile, people are scratching their heads for a solution.[36] Assuming that insurance companies are not making excessive profits on liability policies, then the most obvious solution is for the state to limit the amount of money anybody may collect against a local government, or against the state itself. But the price of that is the old injustice of denying a fair settlement to people injured

[36]See Lanny Proffer, "Weathering the Storm of Liability Litigation," *State Legislatures* (November–December 1985), pp. 11–15.

by the state's negligence. Yet, juries seem to have the idea that the public treasury is bottomless and that whatever sum they award a plaintiff cannot cost any individual citizen very much. And so awards against governments tend to be excessive. Furthermore, lawyers have zeroed in on governments as the ultimate "deep pocket," the ultimate rich turkey to be plucked. Also, governments (being solvent) too often end up as the only defendant able to pay a judgment when perhaps the government was only one of several joint defendants and when perhaps its own part in the negligence was minor. (Under the doctrine of joint and several liability, a plaintiff may recover the full amount of the damages from any of multiple defendants if the others cannot pay.) States should not feel frightfully guilty about putting some sort of limitation on their liability considering these facts.

The state might also make an effort to fine-tune various technical aspects of the law of tort liability to soften the law's impact on governments. For example, one wonders if pain and suffering awards are out of control. There is no way under the sun to repay with money the pain and suffering caused by some torts, nor is there really any way to measure what an hour or a week or a year of pain and suffering is worth. Pain and suffering is an eight-lane highway directly into the public treasury. Perhaps awards in this area need to be arbitrarily limited, not only for government but also for doctors and everybody else. Yet, is it not an awful thing if a drunken police officer cripples someone for life with a reckless bullet? Should government be excused from paying the full price of the victim's agony, misery, and woe?

Also, the matter of holding governments liable for nonfeasance (neglect of duty, nonperformance, or omission to perform a duty) needs to be studied. There is no such thing as perfect performance of duty. All performance of duty is tainted with nonfeasance. To allow people to sue governments for imperfection (and that, by the way, is what many of the most expensive lawsuits against governments are about) invites financial disaster. Ought we to allow people to sue the city for not putting out a fire fast enough, for not installing a stop sign, for not catching a burglar, for not preventing the escape of a hatchet murderer from the local jail? Yet, what if your parent or child is the next victim of that murderer?

Surely, the subject of governmental tort liability is one that brings forth powerful competing concepts of right and wrong. Can we go on with a system of liability that leaves government unwilling to govern courageously, and hesitant to provide basic services, for fear of a lawsuit?

BARRIERS TO JUSTICE

Perhaps there is no perfect justice. Many people cannot even start a lawsuit or see a lawyer because they don't have the money. On the other hand, the more money one has, the better lawyers one can hire, the better justice one can buy. Some say everybody should have equal access to justice. At first glance this seems to be a gorgeous ideal. In fact, some attempt is made to give indigent felony defendants free defense counsel (the public-defender system). But the quality of that defense is variable, and very little has been done to give free legal counsel to indigents in civil cases. And what about those who are not indigent, but just poor or just making ends meet? Should the state also provide them with legal counsel?

If everyone who has the slightest urge to litigate were promised full financial backing by the state, the resulting waves of litigation would swamp the courts, drain treasuries, and bring down the political and social order—we would become a nation of lawyers and judges to handle the teeming litigation. Already the case load of courts in this contentious land is alarming, having increased, according to one estimate, 1000 percent since 1955, in part because of simplification of judicial procedure.[37] Justice for all may be totally unrealistic, yet this does not mean we should abandon efforts to alleviate the worst denials of access to justice, such as the inability of senile people to pursue their legal rights under the medicaid system: they don't have the wit (or perhaps the money) to hire a lawyer or even to ask for help.

Poverty is certainly not the only barrier to justice. Simple ignorance of the law and of the legal system keeps millions of people from using what is available to them. Add to that the psychological barrier—the awe of courtrooms and law offices—that makes many people (especially the poor and the uneducated) reluctant to enter such solemn and stately places. Yet is justice served by making courts less solemn and stately, by having pictures of clowns on the wall rather than pictures of Washington and Lincoln, by putting judges in blue jeans instead of black robes? Either choice is a barrier to justice.

Of course, complexity of procedure is another alleged barrier to justice, yet procedural exactness is also an avenue to justice. Someone has said procedure is 90 percent of justice, but perhaps some progress can be made—Chief Justice Warren E. Burger said not long ago that some procedure has been "constructed by the courts themselves as a defense mechanism against the hordes of litigants and lawyers that presumably otherwise would inundate the judiciary."[38]

A report issued recently at a conference on the judiciary listed several barriers to justice—economic, procedural, psychological, knowledge, geographic, language.[39] To that list one might suggest another, which is perhaps the greatest of all barriers to justice: the elusive character of justice itself. Justice cannot be defined. Justice may not exist. Justice certainly means different things to different people. All sides of a dispute may be right and just—as viewed from each side. Access to dispute-settling machinery may help settle disputes, but settling disputes is no guarantee of justice. Such a mysterious thing as justice may not be of this world, may be only of the next.

SUMMARY

Because no judge can possibly be an expert in all phases of law, it is helpful for judges to specialize. Courts themselves may be specialized, or specialization may occur within courts having numerous judges. Among the most common spe-

---

[37]Jag C. Uppal, "The State of the Judiciary," in *The Book of the States, 1980–81* (Lexington, Ky.: Council of State Governments, 1980), p. 143.

[38]Warren E. Burger, "Agenda for 2000 A.D.: The Need for Systematic Anticipation" (address delivered at the National Conference on the Causes of Population Dissatisfaction with the Administration of Justice, St. Paul, Minnesota, 1976).

[39]Task Force on Courts and the Community, *State Courts: A Blueprint for the Future.* Proceedings of the Second National Conference on the Judiciary, March 19–22, 1978 (Williamsburg, Va.: National Center for State Courts, 1978).

cialized state courts are small-claims courts, family courts, juvenile courts, domestic-relations courts, and probate courts. The typical state court system includes local courts (that is, municipal courts and justice-of-the-peace courts), trial courts of general jurisdiction, intermediate appellate courts, and a state supreme court. Cases involving only state law go to state courts, cases involving federal law go to federal courts, and cases involving the United States Constitution may go to either a state court or a federal court. However, the federal Supreme Court has final say, or at least a right to a final say, in all cases involving the United States Constitution. All cases are heard in the first instance by a court of original jurisdiction or by an administrative agency, where both fact and law questions are decided. A case may be appealed from an agency or from a court of original jurisdiction only on an issue of law. Fact findings cannot be appealed unless a clear error or substantial error has been made in the first instance. A great part of the judicial work in America is done by administrative agencies whose decisions in disputes between themselves and citizens are treated by appellate courts just like the decisions of trial courts.

Some state judges are appointed (usually by the governor), some are popularly elected, and some get their jobs by a process involving both appointment and election. Neither election nor appointment of judges is satisfactory, yet both have their advantages. The Missouri system is a compromise, combining the best features of both appointment and election. All states have systems for removing incompetent, ill, or dishonest judges.

The virtues and vices of the jury system are often debated. We are sometimes told that the sole function of juries is to find facts, yet juries are often defended as mechanisms for nullifying prosecutions (and laws) that run counter to the spirit of the community. The size of juries has historically been 12, but smaller juries are now in vogue. Most states require a unanimous jury in order to convict in a criminal case, but often only a majority vote is required for a jury finding in a civil case. A jury is supposed to consist of one's peers, and this has been the subject of litigation in recent years. Social-science jury stacking has become a fine art.

Lawyers do not know what the law *is*. They can only know (under a system of *stare decisis*) what the law *was*. They predict what the law *will be* by looking at what the law was. Common law is judge-made law. It consists of court decisions in past cases, which are law because judges habitually follow precedent in deciding cases. Statutory law includes the law enacted by legislative bodies. It is also interpreted by courts, and these interpretations become part of the common law. Administrative rules are part of the statutory law. There are many more rules than acts of legislatures. Most rules are made pursuant to (in accordance with) acts of legislatures and have the force of law.

Criminal laws make certain acts punishable. Civil laws establish certain acts as wrongful but not punishable. The remedy for a civil wrong is any legal remedy (often money damages) deemed appropriate by the court or established by law, but may not include punishment. (Punitive damages are, however, sometimes imposed.) Equity is commonly used as a system for preventing threatened irreparable wrongful damage. Injunction and mandamus are equity writs.

Criminal procedure begins with a grand-jury indictment, with an indictment or information filed by the prosecutor, or with an arrest. This is followed by a preliminary hearing, arraignment, and trial. Most defendants have a right to bail, and all have a right to counsel, among other procedural rights. Civil and criminal trials are much the same except that civil plaintiffs do not need to prove their case beyond a reasonable doubt (only a preponderance of evidence is necessary), nor does a civil jury need to be unanimous (majority votes are usually acceptable).

Recently court reform in many states has centered around standardization of court practices and procedures throughout the state, the employment of professional court administrators with degrees in the subject, a merit system for court personnel, consolidation of courts, and centralization of control over the state court system.

For many generations each Scandinavian country has had a judicial officer called the ombudsman, whose function is to do something about injustices committed by governments that are wrong but not illegal. This idea has been adopted by some state and local governments in the United States.

The doctrine of "sovereign immunity" gives each sovereign state (and its local governments as well) immunity from being sued for civil wrongs (torts). But each state can and does allow itself to be sued. For this purpose states enact tort liability laws that define the wrongs they will not allow themselves to be sued for. The general thrust of state appellate courts in recent years has been to increase the scope of state and local liability for torts. This, plus other forces, has greatly increased the number of lawsuits against governments, has increased insurance rates, and has made governments hesitant to provide certain services for fear of a lawsuit.

There are many barriers to justice. These include poverty (can't afford a lawyer), ignorance of the legal system, psychological barriers (fear and awe of law offices), complexity of legal procedure, and the elusive character of justice itself.

SUGGESTIONS FOR FURTHER READING

CANNON, BRADLEY C., and DEAN JAROS, "State Supreme Courts: Some Comparative Data," *State Government* (Autumn 1969), 260–64.

CHAMELIN, NEIL C., VERNON B. FOX, and PAUL M. WHISENAND, *Introduction to Criminal Justice* (2nd ed.). Englewood Cliffs, N.J.: Prentice-Hall, 1979.

COHEN, MORRIS L., ed., *How To Find the Law* (7th ed.). St. Paul: West, 1976.

EISENSTEIN, JAMES, and HERBERT JACOB, *Felony Justice: An Organizational Analysis of Criminal Courts.* Boston: Little, Brown, 1977.

GLICK, HENRY R., "State Government and Judicial Administration: A Political Analysis," *State Government* (Winter 1980), 44–49.

———, and KENNETH N. VINES, *State Court Systems.* Englewood Cliffs, N.J.: Prentice-Hall, 1971.

GOULDEN, JOSEPH, *The Superlawyers.* New York: Dell Pub. Co., Inc., 1973.

GRILLIOT, HAROLD J., *Introduction to Law and the Legal System.* Dallas: Houghton Mifflin, 1983.

HANDBERG, ROGER, "Engine of Injustice: The Criminal Justice System in Theory and Practice," *American Public Administration Review* (January/February 1979), 99–102.

JACOB, HERBERT, *Justice in America: Courts, Lawyers and the Judicial Process* (4th ed.). Boston: Little, Brown, 1983.

WATSON, RICHARD A., and RONDAL G. DOWNING, *The Politics of the Bench and Bar: Judicial Selection under the Missouri Nonpartisan Court Plan.* New York: John Wiley, 1969.

9

counties, towns, townships, and special districts

PREVIEW

DON'T WORRY, LITTLE GIRL

My high school civics teacher said, "You young people ought to get involved in politics." I did, the year after graduation. I didn't think I could win. Not as a candidate of my party. My party hadn't won an election in these parts for 20 years. It can't even get people to run for office. So when I said I would run for county assessor, they just threw their arms around me. They knew I couldn't win but were glad to have someone try. I went all over the county shaking hands and pretending everything was fine. You won't believe it, but I was elected. The other party had nominated a man who had been assessor 16 years. Two weeks before election day he was arrested for theft of public money. I was the only alternative on the ballot.

I don't know whether being a girl hurt me or helped me, or whether being queen of the senior prom last year helped or hurt. All I know is this: About midnight after the polls closed I was at election headquarters when a great big cigar-smoking man named Jake Jacobson came up and kissed me and said I was the new assessor. Jake is county chairman of the party. The news made me dizzy. I just sank back in a folding chair. Everybody was crowding around, congratulating and whooping and shouting.

"Jake," I called through the noise. "Jake, come here a minute. Jake, how does somebody be an assessor?"

"Don't worry, little girl. Just do what I tell you."

"Little girl? Doggone if I'll be his little girl," I said to myself.

"Flushed with victory," I believe they call it. I was so excited I couldn't get to sleep that night 'til four in the morning. Then I woke up at seven and jumped out of bed pleased at being the new assessor. No, it wasn't a dream. Mom and Dad were excited, too, and we had scrambled eggs and bacon and toast and jelly for breakfast. It was wonderful.

Jake Jacobson phoned about eight-thirty that morning and said two things. First, fire everybody who works in the assessor's office. Second, appoint people who helped you get elected.

"But those folks down there are the only people who know anything about assessing," I said. "Anyway, firing people is cruel."

"That's politics, little girl."

"Next time you call me "little girl" I'm going to change parties. Good-bye."

That afternoon I went down to the assessor's office. I never saw so many gloomy people in my life. One little old lady with tears came up to me and said, "I've worked here 16 years. I contributed 10 percent of my salary every year to my employer's campaign chest. I worked in his campaign organization every election. That's how I kept my job. Now I will help you. There's lots to learn." I patted her on the arm and said, "Thank you very much."

I wouldn't take office for six weeks, and I spent almost all that time worrying how to be an assessor. I checked books out of the library. I talked to everybody in the assessor's office and got to know them. I even went to see Jake Jacobson, who called me Karen this time. He said all I needed to know about assessment was not to raise anybody's assessment, not to rock the boat, and to keep everybody as happy as possible until the next election. "Fooey," I said to myself.

The date of my swearing in loomed like a range of mountains. I dreaded taking over a job I didn't know anything about. Should I go to Jake and just tell him I couldn't handle it? No, darn it, I'll face up to it. But how?

In the midst of my despair I got a mimeographed letter from the State Department of Local Affairs. It was addressed to all local assessors in the state. It announced a class for newly elected assessors. Incumbent assessors and their employees could also attend. It was absolutely free. It would be held at the state capitol and would last one week. My heart leaped. I telephoned the man who wrote the letter and said I wanted to attend. We talked a long while. He said the main job of the Department of Local Affairs was to help local officials do their jobs professionally. The department, he said, puts on classes, sends experts out to help local officials with their problems, and does a lot of other things. I could have kissed him.

When I was sworn in on January 2, I stood tall. Daddy said I looked like a bride on her wedding day. And the little old lady from the assessor's office had tears in her eyes again. She would be my assistant.

LOCAL GOVERNMENT IN GENERAL

Mother and Child

Local governments in America are children of the state. All local governments (except Washington, D.C.) are created by state law and may be dissolved by state law. The 50 states have been prolific: they have brought forth some 82,000 local governments (Figure 9-1). A few of these "youngsters" aren't so young—Boston is as old as Massachusetts, and Massachusetts is older than the Republic.

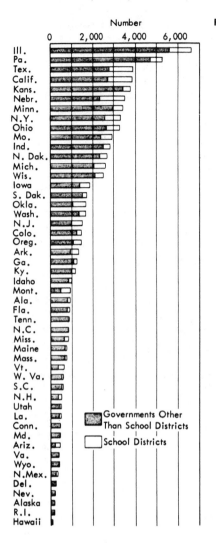

Figure 9-1 *Local governments, by states: 1977.* (Source: U.S. Bureau of the Census, Chartbook of Governmental Data: Organization, Finance, and Employment: 1976, Series GF 76, No. 7, p. 3.)

Oddly, the most common type of local government is a type most people have never heard of: special districts, some 28,000 of them. There are also about 19,000 municipalities. 15,000 townships, 15,000 school districts, 1500 New England towns, and 3000 counties.[1]

Neglect and Renewed Interest Child neglect has been rampant in state–local relations. Local governments, once brought into the world, were until recently left in the streets to fend for themselves. Actually they did a pretty good job of caring for themselves, relying primarily on the property tax for money.

[1]U.S. Bureau of Census, *Statistical Abstract of the United States: 1987* (Washington, D.C., 1986), p. 272.

In recent generations, however, especially since World War II, local governments have found life increasingly difficult, increasingly expensive. States have lately begun to take parenthood more seriously, and today they give massive aid to local governments for such things as education, welfare, and highways. Help has gone beyond money. States are now playing the full role of parenthood, acting as teacher, collaborator, leader, consultant, regulator, and gadfly—holding their children back from evil, spurring them on to good. One of the most inspiring sights of modern American government is the new tribal closeness between state and local governments.

Federal Involvement with Local Governments

As states take a new interest in local governments, so does the federal government, which now roams the neighborhood with revenue sharing, grants-in-aid, block grants, project grants, and a thousand and one pieces of hard candy. Today the federal government is a powerful rival for the affection of local governments. States have occasionally tried to insert themselves between the federal government and local governments, but local governments value their newfound direct relationship with well-heeled federal bureaucrats and do not want federal money to be always channeled through the state government. However, state governments usually prefer receiving all money intended for local governments. Some federal grants to local governments are, in fact, channeled through the state government—transportation grants, for example—but many federal grants go direct to local governments, bypassing the state altogether—community-development grants, for example.

State Departments of Local Affairs

The new outpouring of state assistance to local governments has motivated some states to create cabinet-level departments to look after and fuss over local governments. These new agencies are sometimes called *departments of community affairs* or *departments of local affairs*. They are supposed to hover over local governments in a maternal fashion, offering all sorts of help, advice, and encouragement.

Most local governments welcome this state help, especially the smaller towns that are run by part-time amateurs and lack either enough money to hire professional bureaucrats or enough work to keep them busy. One problem for small-town officials is the multiplicity of federal and state grant-in-aid programs. Local officials can't keep track of them all, don't know where to apply or how to apply, and haven't got the time or the skill to write applications (which often require as much research as a Ph.D. dissertation). Even the larger local governments have trouble with this. A state department of local affairs can help in this area: it can be a central source of expertise as to what "aid" is available and how to go about getting it. Local governments welcome help from the state in this matter as long as the state confines itself to giving advice and assistance and avoids trying to sever the *direct* relationship between local governments and the federal government, a relationship many local officials find attractive.

State departments of local affairs often busy themselves with letting local governments know about the existence of various aid programs and inspiring local officials to take advantage of them. When a specific local project requires coordination of numerous state and federal aid programs, the state department of local affairs will also try to midwife the necessary coordination.

Local officials can, as a matter of fact, use help in everything they do. Professional help can make the difference between muddling through and waltzing through their work. It takes a lot of knowledge to issue bonds; keep books,[2] plan and zone; build streets; lay sewers; revise charters; provide human services for the young, the old, the ill, and others; calculate how to spur economic development and deal with its numerous impacts; figure how best to protect the public from fire and crime; assess property; and so on. Besides helping local governments with these tasks, a state department of local affairs can publish how-to-do-it manuals; hold seminars, clinics, and short courses; provide research assistance; and coordinate the planning efforts of various local governments within a region. In addition, states are now supplying local governments with vast amounts of money for roads, education, welfare, and a multitude of other things. This accounts for the new intimacy, the new closeness between states and their small fry.

Legal Status

What is the legal status of local governments? We know that the legal status of states is set forth in the United States Constitution, which draws boundaries between state authority and federal authority. But what does the Constitution say about local governments? It says nothing! A man from Mars reading the Constitution would get no idea at all that such a thing as local government exists. The Constitution recognizes only two powers: the central government and the state. The Constitution does not bother to define how states shall subdivide their quota of power. The Constitution is entirely blind to that: states are totally free to organize themselves any way they want as long as they remain "republican,"[3] a word that baffles even the Supreme Court.[4] No state is required to have any local governments at all. Every local government is the creature of the state, an "instrumentality" of the state, and has no right to exist except insofar as such a "right" is bestowed by the state. Every right bestowed by the state may also be terminated by the state. States can (and have) abolished cities, counties, school districts, and special districts. Sometimes it takes an amendment of the state constitution to do so, and sometimes it takes only an act of the state legislature, but in any case it can be (and is) done. The most commonly abolished governments in recent years have been school districts: perhaps 20,000 of them have bitten the dust since World War II, most of them consolidated with other districts. Cities and towns are rarely dissolved unless everybody has moved away. (On average about a dozen disincorporations of cities occur every year.) It makes

---

[2]Inflation, and a Proposition 13 mentality, have put local governments in a financial vise that makes it especially important for them to strengthen their fiscal practices. States can greatly help local governments improve their financial management. Local-government accounts may not be professionally kept or professionally and regularly audited. See Paul Moore and Alan G. Billingsley, "Financial Monitoring of Local Governments," *State Government* (Autumn 1979), pp. 155–60.

[3]*U.S. Const.*, Art. IV, Sec. 4.

[4]Luthur v. Borden, 7 How. 1 (1849).

no difference, however, how rarely the state's power to abolish local governments is used; our concern here is with the state's legal authority.

What the state is forbidden to do by the United States Constitution, so also is every arm, agency, instrumentality, and local government of the state. The Constitution forbids states, for example, to deny liberty to any of its citizens without due process of law. That applies to every city, town, county, school district, or special district as well. Therefore if Liberal, Kansas, should set up a city censor and forbid any newspaper in Liberal to publish anything without first receiving the censor's approval, this would bring the city (which is part of the state) into conflict with the Fourteenth Amendment, which forbids states to do things like that. Nor may Liberal, Kansas, coin money—the Constitution says no state may do so.[5] Nor may Liberal grant titles of nobility,[6] pass *ex post facto* (retroactive) laws,[7] or do any other thing that the Constitution forbids states to do. In the eyes of the United States Constitution, whatever Liberal does, the state does.

As parents, the states cannot be described as permissive in their legal relationship with local governments. Except where a local government has been granted home rule (see p. 254), states keep their political subdivisions on a short leash, legally. Legislation giving power to local governments is strictly construed by courts. If there is any doubt about what power a law allows a local government to exercise, courts customarily take the narrowest possible view. This is in accordance with the famous **Dillon's rule:** a municipal corporation may possess only powers "granted in express words," those powers "necessarily or fairly implied in or incident to the powers expressly granted," and those powers "essential to the accomplishment of declared objects and purposes of the corporation—not simply convenient, but indispensable."[8] The author of this rule also declared that "any fair, reasonable, substantial doubt concerning the existence of power is resolved by the courts against the corporation, and the power is denied."[9] The same general principle governs the legal relationship of states with all local governments, not just with cities.

COUNTIES

What Is a County?

In the word *county* we see the glowing ember of ancient happenings in one of the lands of our cultural ancestors. Owing to the invasion of England in 1066 by French-speaking Normans, who proceeded to rule England for 300 years, most English words having to do with law and government have French origins. *County* is just such a word. In Norman England the principal divisions of the nation were headed by counts, and hence were called *counties*. Today counties

[5]*U.S. Const.*, Art. I, Sec. 10.

[6]Ibid.

[7]Ibid.

[8]John F. Dillon, *Commentaries on the Law of Municipal Corporations*, 5th ed. (Boston: Little, Brown, 1911), I, Sec. 237.

[9]Ibid.

are the principal divisions of all states except Louisiana and Alaska (and New England, where counties are overshadowed by towns). Louisiana calls such divisions *parishes*. The word *parish*, incidentally, stems from the Old French word *parroche*, which in Middle England became *parissche*, meaning "the district served by a church," which ultimately became a governmental district in Britain. The principal subdivisions of Alaska are called *boroughs*, a word of German origin stemming from the Middle English word *burgh* and from the German word *burg*, meaning "fortified place."

How Do Counties and Cities Differ?

A **county** differs from a city in one important legal way: it is not created at the behest of its inhabitants, nor is it intended to serve their unique governmental needs. On the contrary, counties are set up by the state on the state's own initiative to serve as a kind of political outpost of state government, applying state laws and administering state business at the local level.[10] However, counties have become to some degree a vehicle for local self-government. But technically a county is not a municipal corporation—it is not a public corporation created at the request of its inhabitants. Insofar as a county does actually provide its inhabitants with a vehicle for local self-government, it comes closer to being a municipal corporation—one imposed, so to speak, on the people, not one for which the people have asked in any legal or formal sense. In some states the law treats counties as *involuntary* quasi-municipal corporations. In fact, some counties have home rule and perform municipal functions.

Most counties concern themselves with such things as public safety, zoning, building regulation, welfare, health, hospitals, parks, recreation, highways, justice, assessment, and record keeping. The importance of a county to the average citizen usually depends on whether he or she lives in a city. Cities normally supply their inhabitants with most of the services for which rural people look to the county, plus a good many other services. When a city is established within a county, the county normally withdraws most of its services from the city: city police will enforce state law within municipal boundaries; county police, outside. However, counties often find themselves supplying all sorts of urban services in densely populated areas that elect not to incorporate. Sometimes the urbanized areas of counties resist incorporation because they believe a city government would cost more and because the county seems to be doing everything a city could do. To avoid the unnecessary piling up of levels of government, some highly urban counties are also cities—that is, they are city-counties: Denver, San Francisco, and Honolulu, among others.

Some New England counties, on the other hand, have very little county government at all. They are mainly geographical areas and court jurisdictions.

Particularities of Counties

It is hard to describe the "average" county, because counties differ radically from one another. On the other hand, most counties fulfill basically the same roles, but some, because of their large population, operate on a much more

[10]New counties are occasionally created today. Two fairly new ones are Cibola County, New Mexico (1981), and La Paz County, Arizona (1983).

elaborate scale than others. Counties range in population and geography from giants to midgets. Geographic giants are not always population giants, although America's most spacious county—San Bernardino, California—is both. San Bernardino County is larger than Vermont and New Hampshire combined; traveling 55 miles per hour, one needs more than four hours to get across it from east to west. Its population is nearly a million. But Inyo County just to the north (which includes Death Valley and is larger than New Jersey) has only some 20,000 people. On the other hand, Arlington County, Virginia, with only 24 square miles, has some 200,000 inhabitants. Most counties have between 10,000 and 50,000 people. However, more than a hundred counties have more than 250,000 residents, while another 150 or so counties have between 100,000 and 200,000. And there are a few monsters, including:[11]

Los Angeles County, California	8.0 million
Cook County (Chicago), Illinois	5.3 million
Harris County (Houston), Texas	2.7 million
Kings County (one of the five boroughs of New York City), New York	2.3 million
Orange County (Santa Ana), California	2.1 million
San Diego County, California	2.1 million
Wayne County (Detroit), Michigan	2.1 million
Queens County (one of the five boroughs of New York City), New York	1.9 million
Dallas County, Texas	1.8 million
Maricopa County (Phoenix), Arizona	1.8 million
Dade County (Miami), Florida	1.7 million

On the other hand, a sprinkling of America's 3080 counties have fewer than 1000 people: Loving County, Texas; Hinsdale County, Colorado; Petroleum County, Montana; Esmeralda County, Nevada.

Of course, counties differ in many ways: some are rich, some poor; some are rural, some urban; some are industrial, some agricultural; some are fertile, some arid; some are mountainous, some flat; some are dominated by the few, some by more than a few; and so on.

The number of counties within states differs greatly. Western states tend to have fewer but larger counties than states in the rest of the country. Georgia has 159 counties to accommodate five million people spread over about 60,000 square miles; Michigan, which is about the same size but shelters twice as many people, has only 83 counties. Texas is the champion: 254 counties. Delaware has only 3 counties, but of course you could put Delaware into Texas 132 times. The average size of a Texas county is about 1032 square miles, of a California county 2695 square miles, of a New York county 771 square miles. The size of most counties was determined in the horse-and-buggy era: they tend to be about the right size to allow anyone within their boundaries to get to the county seat and back within a day, or within several hours by horse. Many of the western counties are larger than that because no one dreamed the outlying areas would be inhabited. Who would have guessed that towns would one day grace the Mohave Desert?

[11]International City Management Association, *Municipal Year Book: 1987* (Washington, D.C., 1987), p. xiv.

The Tangle of County Government

Henry S. Gilbertson called counties "the dark continent of American politics."[12] The chief reason counties are considered a "dark continent" is their hodgepodge governmental structure. The typical county is an organizational snarl of the worst sort. It normally consists of numerous separately elected officials who run their own departments without much coordination with one another. Among these are the sheriff, the clerk, the treasurer, the assessor, the coroner, the attorney, and the board of supervisors. A surveyor, a recorder, and a superintendent of schools may also be elected. Still other elected officers are found in some counties: collectors of taxes, registrars of wills, public administrators, constables, and judges. The typical county elects a row of major officials who manage their own departments without any supervision by a higher authority in the county. Seldom does any higher authority exist, except, of course, the voting public. Elected officials are czars of their own little semiautonomous government. The sheriff, for example, is not answerable to anyone, not even to the so-called county board, which is often erroneously believed to govern the county. Some exceptions to this chaotic picture exist. A few counties have been streamlined, but it is not easy to streamline a county or indeed to reorganize any governmental apparatus. Each such apparatus is a nucleus of political power, and each has a robust instinct for survival (Figure 9-2).

This mincemeat structure of county government was invented in the era of Jacksonian democracy—the 1820s and 1830s. Prior to that, most county officers were appointed by the state. Jacksonian democracy was a political trend that supposedly brought a government closer to the people. Property qualifications for voting were abolished, and the new voting masses elected as president Andrew Jackson, a "man of the people." In the eyes of Jackson and Jacksonians, the common people were qualified not only to vote but also to staff the government. Major state and local officials should therefore be elected rather than appointed. Furthermore, their terms should be short and elections frequent to constantly remind officials that they are servants, not masters, of the people.

County Boards

Functions If **county boards** cannot control the numerous elected department heads, then what function if any, do they have? Well, they are not completely powerless or useless. They have more to do in urban counties than in rural counties. Many counties today do things that counties hardly ever imagined doing in the last century. In that earlier era counties did almost nothing over and above what the elected "row" officers, such as the sheriff or clerk, did. Today, however, there are numerous departments or agencies not headed by elected officials because those functions did not exist in the 1800s, when major offices were being made elective. Therefore, whenever a county sets up a department (such as a department of planning) that does not fall within the orbit of any traditional elected official, it comes under the county board.

Counties, remember, were originally set up as administrative divisions of the state for the purpose of localizing the administration of state functions. The

[12]Henry S. Gilbertson, *The County: The "Dark Continent" of American Politics* (New York: National Short Ballot Association, 1917).

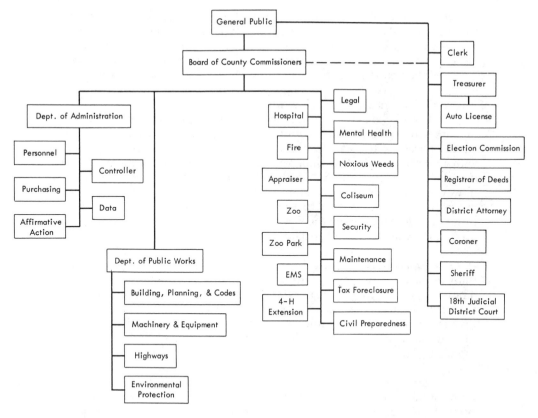

Figure 9-2 *Organizational chart, Sedgwick County, Kansas.* (Source: Sedgwick County, Kansas.)

sheriff, although locally elected, enforced state law primarily; the clerk helped the state run elections and kept records deemed important by the state; and so on through the whole list of elected county officials. Today, however, counties carry on numerous activities largely unknown in the 1800s. Many of these new functions are of local, rather than state, concern. County park and recreation programs, for example, are usually run on a far grander scale today than yesterday. Counties run libraries, airports, health services, utility systems, and numerous other programs seldom dreamed of by counties in the 1800s. The more densely populated a county, the more such services are offered. Therefore, many departments today come under the county board rather than other elected officials.

The county board is not entirely without influence over elected officials. The board does, after all, have the power to make the county budget. The sheriff may not be answerable to the county board through any chain of command, but the sheriff still must get his or her money from the county board, and the board will probably also have the power to revoke, amend, or shift appropriations once made. Furthermore, the board will probably have the power, rarely exercised though it may be, to approve every expenditure made by county officials (elected or appointed), a further fiscal "hook" that gives the board some degree of influence over wayward elected officials. However, the board still has to be wary of "punishing" a defiant sheriff: if the sheriff doesn't get enough money to enforce the law, he or she can blame every crime on the board. Other elected officials have similar strategies for resisting the board's dollar power.

The board sets county tax rates, chiefly the property-tax levy. The board also lets contracts for various things, buys and sells county land, and can (within severe limits) arrange for the county to borrow money.

County boards are often thought to be legislative bodies like city councils or state legislatures, but few county boards do much legislating. Counties, being "field offices" of the state, are more concerned with carrying out state law than with making new law of their own. The ordinance-making power of county boards is narrowly limited and almost nonexistent in some states. Counties do, however, generally adopt zoning ordinances, subdivision regulations, and building regulations. According to Dillon's rule, counties may not legislate on anything except those things the state legislature or the state constitution explicitly gives them the power to legislate on.

Supervision   County boards spend most of their time supervising rather than legislating—indeed, many county boards are called *boards of supervisors*. They "supervise" the officials whom they have appointed and attempt as best they can to supervise those they don't appoint. They supervise the county's property, and in some counties members of the board (as individuals) take direct managerial charge of one or more county agencies. If they are not directly managing, they sometimes try to oversee those who do.

Licensing   States very often permit their counties to license various kinds of businesses, especially businesses that need to be carefully and constantly policed, such as bars, dance halls, amusement parks, and massage parlors. The power to license usually includes the power to revoke or suspend licenses—a quasi-judicial power. Before a license can be revoked or suspended, the board must allow the accused to defend himself or herself—to present evidence, to rebut evidence, to cross-examine witnesses, and so forth. If the board's revocation or suspension is to be sustained by the courts, their action must rest on substantial evidence of wrongdoing by the licensee. All this thrusts the county board into a judicial role.

Board of Assessment Appeals   The county board may be the place where unhappy property owners can go when they are aggrieved by the valuation put upon their real estate by the county assessor. In other words, the county board may also be the county board of assessment appeals. This, too, is a highly judicial function.

Size   Most county boards are small, usually three members, perhaps five, but some boards are quite large. Typically all counties within a state have the same number, or roughly the same number, of board members.

Name   County boards are usually called *boards of commissioners*, but in a number of states they are called *boards of supervisors*. Use of the term *supervisor* stems from the fact that the board in some states is composed of one supervisor from each organized township within the county. He or she is the chief executive (or supervisor) of the township. However, county boards in some states are called *boards of supervisors* even if they are not composed of township supervisors.

A considerable handful of America's county boards are called *courts*. Most of these go by the name *county court* or *commissioner's court* and have judicial power (or remains of judicial power) and perhaps some involvement in the county court system. In Alabama, for instance, the board is called the *court of county commissioners* and has the power to subpoena persons and papers and to punish for contempt.

Election Except in counties in which the board is made up of township supervisors, board members are elected. Some counties elect commissioners at large, other counties elect commissioners from districts, depending on state law. Occasionally commissioners elected at large are required nevertheless to live in a certain district (a compromise between the two systems). *Election at large* means election by all the voters in the county; *election by district* means the county is divided into districts, each of which elects a commissioner. The merits and liabilities of these methods of electing local councils and boards are discussed on pages 267–70. Commissioners usually serve two-year or four-year terms, which are usually staggered to provide some degree of continuity in county affairs: no more than two members of a three-member board will be elected at the same time.

Meetings The degree of formality observed by county boards during their meetings depends, it seems, on the population of the county. County boards in some of the more populous counties meet in grandiose chambers spacious enough to accommodate press and public. They have carpeted floors, elegantly draped windows, walnut paneling, silver service, sophisticated sound systems, and every accounterment befitting the role of potentate. Large-county boards follow rigid parliamentary procedure, as if they were a state legislature or the British House of Lords.

At the other extreme we find county boards in small rural counties trying to be as folksy as possible. Members may attend board meetings in their blue jeans, sit in battered chairs around a battered table, disregard *Robert's Rule of Order* as dogs disregard fire hydrants, and freely interrupt their meetings if any local resident happens to wander in with a problem. However, most county boards function with at least a modicum of formality, meeting perhaps one day a week in the board room of the county courthouse.

Pay Board members in populous counties that require full-time service may be paid a full-time salary, often a substantial amount. Board members in medium-sized counties may get only a modest fee for their part-time work. In sparsely populated counties board members may be paid by the day—enough to cover travel and expenses when the board meets.

County Clerk

The **county clerk** is the chief paper shuffler of the county. He or she will, among other things, serve as a secretary to the county board, assemble items for the board's agenda, and publish the agenda. The clerk keeps track of actions taken by the board and officially records them. If letters need to be written or other clerical functions done as a result of board action, the clerk may be responsible. The clerk may also help the board make the county budget. Normally the clerk also has charge of registering voters, conducting elections, designing and distributing ballots, and recording the results of elections. Records of births, deaths, marriages, and divorces are kept in the clerk's office, and the clerk may also keep records of deeds, mortgages, and certain other business transactions, although there may be a separate county recorder to do this.

Recorder or Registrar of Deeds

The recorder of deeds does just what the title suggests, but why are deeds recorded, and what does *record* mean? By *record* we simply mean making an entry in official county books that such and such a piece of property was bought, along with the conditions of the deal. These books are open to the public and constitute official evidence that the purchase occurred.

It is in the selfish interest of anyone who intends to buy a piece of real estate to check the records in the recorder's office to be sure that every prior sale and purchase of the property from the beginning of time has been recorded. This involves searching the recorded history of the property. If a search reveals that any seller has in the past sold the property without there being any record of his having purchased it in the first place, this clouds the title—that is, it raises uncertainties as to whether he ever really owned it. If any prior seller's title (record of ownership) is clouded, then every subsequent title is also clouded. It behooves a would-be purchaser not only to search the title but also to make sure his own purchase is recorded. If it is not recorded, this failure may at some awkward moment in the future raise questions about his title.

Very few purchasers of real estate do their own title searching. That can be a tedious job and is best done (and usually is done) by title-insurance companies. A title-insurance company is in the business of selling insurance to the owners of property, guaranteeing their title. If after you buy a piece of property you discover that the person you bought it from really didn't own it, then the title-insurance company will pay you for your loss, providing, of course, you have a policy. Obviously a title-insurance company will make constant use of the recorder's records.

Recorders also record a variety of other documents. In fact, they will record almost anything you want, such as marriages, divorces, wills, liens, and bonds. In counties that have no recorder, these functions are usually handled by the county clerk.

Clerk of the Court

Courts require the assistance of a secretary who will record actions taken by the court; prepare necessary papers when the court wants to issue an order of some kind; and collect and make note of fines, forfeitures, penalties, and assessments of court costs. These are the functions of the clerk of the court.

County Treasurer

The treasurer collects taxes, keeping the money in safe storage, and pays it out upon proper authorization. In the process of paying it out, he may also be thrust into the role of an accountant because it is necessary to keep track of what has been spent and how much of each appropriation remains. The treasurer does not keep county funds under a mattress. One of his duties is to deposit the money in banks. This can touch off competition among banks for the privilege of holding funds and may also touch off a public debate whether it is better to deposit the money locally (although at a lower interest rate) or to deposit it elsewhere, even out of state, to reap higher returns. In some states the county treasurer is given the latitude to invest county money where he thinks it will earn the most, rather than merely depositing it in a bank. Some treasurers are worth their weight in gold as shrewd investors of the taxpayers' money. Unfortunately, most taxpayers don't have any idea whether their treasurer is doing a good job or not.

County Auditor

The auditor keeps the treasurer and other officials who handle money honest. Basically the job of the auditor is to see that expenditures are legal. By *legal* we mean that the agency has the money to buy what it has contracted to buy, that it is authorized to buy what it wants to buy, and that the goods and services bought are actually delivered. Since it is often the auditor who actually writes checks for purchases, she will not pay unless the transaction is in every way legal. Auditors sometimes do most of their auditing after payment is made rather than before, in which case they are said to *postaudit*. Audits taken prior to payment are called *preaudits*. Sometimes postaudits are done when the auditor doesn't have time to preaudit.

County Assessor

Importance   Counties used to depend almost totally on the property tax for their revenue. Today they depend somewhat less on that one source of revenue because of state and federal aid, but still the property tax (discussed in detail on pp. 308–311) is a principal source of county revenue and of city, school-district, and special-district revenue as well. There can be no tax on property until the value of that property is determined—the property tax is, after all, a tax on the value of property, an *ad valorem* (meaning "in proportion to value") tax.

The county assessor's assessments are often relied on by other governments within the county—cities, special districts, and school districts—as the assessment upon which they base their own property tax. In addition to relying on the assessor's assessments, these other governments within the county also commonly rely on the county treasurer to collect their property tax and deliver the money.

Putting a value on property is not an exact science; rather it is a judgment, and every government using the property tax must rely on someone's judgment of the value of each piece of property taxed. The assessor has that important and touchy job. It is a touchy job because property owners resent having a value put on their property that is higher than the value put on other comparable property—their property tax increases proportionately.

Appeals   Property owners dissatisfied with their assessment should try to prevail on the assessor to change the assessment. If the assessor refuses, then the owners can appeal their assessment to the county **board of assessment ap-**

peals (normally the county board of commissioners or supervisors), which has the power to reassess the appellant's property. If the board of assessment appeals upholds the assessor, the owners may have recourse to a state board of assessment appeals, and if they fail there, they may take their appeal to court.

Underassessment Sometimes the amount of state aid given to a local government is determined by the assessed valuation of the property held by the citizens of that government. State aid is commonly given on the basis of "need." This is commonly determined by a mathematical formula: total assessed value of property divided by population. Obviously such a formula motivates assessors to assess property below true value. The poorer any local government is made to look by this tactic, the more aid it gets. However, states using such formulas are not altogether duped. Many have a state board of equalization whose duty is to compel all assessors within the state to assess at the same (that is, at an equal) percentage of true value. Most assessors try to preserve their popularity with the voters by assessing at a percentage far short of true value—often around 20 or 30 percent. State boards of equalization are often willing to play along with such undervaluations as long as all assessors undervalue to exactly the same degree. Equality of assessments is what the state board of equalization wants.

Sometimes this competitive undervaluation goes on within counties (as well as between them). Within counties the game is between the county itself and the incorporated cities. This is likely to be played in cases where the county assessor assesses only property outside the corporate limits of cities and where each city has its own assessor to assess property inside the city. The city assessor may compete with the county assessor to see who can assess at the lowest percentage of true value. The lower your percentage of total county property value, the lower your percentage of total county taxes. See?

Mills The amount of money raised from a property tax is determined by multiplying the assessed valuation by the tax rate. Thus, if a piece of property is assessed at $10,000 and the tax rate is two mills, the tax is $10,000 × .002 (a **mill** is one-thousandth of a dollar—ten mills to the penny), or $20. It makes no difference mathematically whether the tax levy is high and the assessed value low, or vice versa. The result is the same. If more money is needed from the property tax, it can be gotten without raising taxes: all the assessor has to do is raise assessments across the board. This endangers his or her political career, however. To raise taxes endangers the political careers of members of the governing board. Obviously the county assessor stands at the vortex of a neverending storm over who is going to pay how much property tax.

County Sheriff

The sheriff heads the county's police force and, with his deputies, is in charge mainly of law enforcement outside the limits of incorporated areas. In urban counties the sheriff's role may be larger than usual or smaller than usual, depending on how much of the urban area is incorporated. If much is incorporated, the resulting cities will handle law enforcement within the city limits. However, numerous unincorporated urban areas across the nation resist incorporation because they don't want to pay taxes to support a separate police force or a separate set of city bureaucrats. Residents of unincorporated urban areas are sometimes delighted to let the county supply whatever limited services it can supply. They wish no more.

The sheriff usually runs a county jail. In addition, he and his deputies help courts by serving arrest warrants to suspected perpetrators of crimes, summonses to jurors, and subpoenas to witnesses. The sheriff's department also commonly helps in civil cases by serving summonses to defendants. Since a summons instructs the defendant to appear in court and answer complaints, serving such a summons can be difficult, especially when a defendant suspects he or she is about to be served and tries to avoid it. Plaintiffs in civil actions are normally free to use expert summons servers (other than the sheriff) if they wish.

Prosecuting Attorney

The **prosecuting attorney** does more than prosecute: she is the county's lawyer and advises the county board and other county officers on legal problems related to their duties. She looks at contracts to see that they say what they are supposed to say. She may be asked to advise a county official on whether a proposed action is within that official's legal powers or whether the procedure by which that power will be used is legally correct. When the county sues or is sued, the prosecuting attorney represents the county. Sometimes a prosecuting attorney is too busy prosecuting to give much time to her functions as attorney for the county. In that case the county may wish to hire an additional lawyer or perhaps a whole staff of lawyers to work full time on county legal problems. These additional lawyers are not elected but are simply retained for an appropriate fee or hired as members of the county civil service.

The prosecuting attorney's central function is, of course, to prosecute criminal suspects. The prosecutor may initiate a criminal case by charging someone with an offense or may ask a grand jury to bring charges if it thinks there is probable cause that the suspect is actually guilty of the offense. However, the grand jury does not have to wait for the prosecutor to ask it to indict: it can investigate suspects and bring indictments on its own initiative. However, it is the prosecutor who prepares a case against the defendant and represents the state, or the "people." Prosecuting attorneys in the larger counties are assisted by deputies, sometimes a dozen or more of them.

The prosecutor (who is also sometimes known as the *district attorney,* or DA) can be a great force for good or evil in a county. She has almost total freedom to prosecute or not prosecute as she sees fit. She can either be diligent in investigating and prosecuting certain kinds or crime or (like the police) choose to look the other way. Little can be done about, say, prostitution in a county when the DA prefers to spend time on other types of cases. The same with almost any species of crime. Opportunities for collusion between the DA and criminal organizations are ever present, nor is collusion a rarity. On the other hand, we needn't think all DAs are in cahoots with the underworld. Many have won fame as courageous prosecutors and have gone on to higher political office because of their vigorous prosecutions; some have been dispatched to the next world by the bullets of irate criminal gangs.

County Coroner

Coroners investigate deaths that occur under suspicious circumstances. To do this job well, one ought to be both a medical doctor and a legally trained criminal investigator. Many coroners are neither. Some have never been to high school. This has inspired a good many people to call for abolishing the office of coroner altogether and splitting its duties between a medical examiner and the prosecuting attorney. The medical examiner would handle the medical side and the prosecutor the legal side, aided by the facts reported by the examiner. Coroners commonly have the power to summon a special jury to determine the cause of a suspicious death. The jury's finding after such an *inquest,* plus the evidence on which it is based, is then turned over to the county prosecutor or a grand jury.

County Superintendent of Schools

In some states there really isn't much for a county superintendent of schools to do anymore. Numerous counties have done away with the office. The superintendent's basic job in recent years has been to make reports to the state school board concerning schools within the county. But the school districts themselves are usually capable of making these reports, often with little help from the county superintendent. Sometimes the superintendent's job is simply to help school districts make their own reports, but again, the districts don't ordinarily need the help. The office of county superintendent of schools is a relic of the days when most schools were run by the county, or by cities within the county, or by a flock of very tiny school districts. The office continues to have much importance where those conditions still prevail.

County Surveyor

Typically the surveyor represents the county in boundary disputes; establishes the boundaries of county property, including road rights-of-way; keeps a record of all survey monuments in the county; examines all maps and plots before they are recorded; and files in his office all surveys pertaining to work authorized by the county board.

Property owners often have disputes over the exact location of their property lines. The county **surveyor** may be available upon request to make an official determination of boundary lines—not only the lines of privately owned property but also the lines of county property and the property of school disticts, special districts, and cities within the county.

Reforming the County

Fossils? County government has been amazingly resistant to change. The county is a dinosaur lumbering across the political landscape. If one didn't know that Henry S. Gilbertson's description of the shortcomings of county government was written in 1917, one might think it were written just this year by some lively and eager political science student. Of course, there has been progress here and there since 1917, but the basic chaos of county government still prevails.

Centralization The multiheadedness of counties causes all sorts of major problems. For example, it makes a competitive civil service nearly impossible. How can a county hire employees on a basis of merit after competitive examinations when each elected department head has sole authority to hire and fire the people in his or her department? How can the county government "as a whole" have a merit system when there really isn't a county government "as a whole"? Attempts can be made to persuade the county board and the elected department heads to voluntarily submit to a merit system, but most elected county officers prefer the spoils system, prefer to use the personnel of their department as a private political machine ready for the next campaign. Perhaps the only way to have a county merit system is to eliminate the independently elected department heads or to trim their power to hire, promote, and fire their own subordinates.

Decentralized multiheadedness makes it difficult, sometimes impossible, to coordinate the work of various departments so that they mesh and assist one another. Instead of working together, county officials often ignore one another, each wanting to build an empire unto himself or herself. Or they may fall into habitual conflict and jealousy. It is not at all unusual for the various elected officers to hold different party affiliations or to belong to different factions within the same party, with obvious results.

Decentralization can be fearfully uneconomical, not only because departments are ignoring one another or warring with one another, but also because county work is done piecemeal, department by department, with no overarching direction. Work can be done more economically if done centrally, though admittedly there may be higher values than economy. Yet there is something to be said for economy. Take purchasing, for example. Everybody knows that purchasing in large quantity can be cheaper (per unit) than purchasing in small quantity: you can get a better buy on typewriters if you buy them by the hundred rather than one at a time. Almost everything—planning, organizing, staffing, directing, coordinating, reporting, budgeting—can be done cheaper, and perhaps better, if done centrally rather than in bits and pieces.

Home Rule? The idea is gaining ground that counties should be run like city-manager cities and furthermore should be given the constitutional **home rule** that cities enjoy. Under a county-manager system no one would be elected in the county government except the county board. The board would then appoint a professional manager, who would appoint all department heads. The number of department heads, in fact the whole organization of the county, would be determined by the county itself—on the basis of its own home-rule charter. Counties would have broad power under home rule to organize and reorganize themselves, but not have as much power to add or delete services as home-rule cities. Remember that counties are "field offices" of the state whose central duty is to do what the state wants them to do. Thus, county home rule would be the freedom to organize but would not be the unrestricted freedom to determine what services the county should perform. Home-rule counties might, however, be allowed to add whatever services they want over and above those required by the state. However, this might displease some county residents because for all practical purposes it would make municipal corporations out of counties. Many people live beyond the city limits because they specifically do not want to live within a municipal corporation that has the power to add services and costs. One of the alleged virtues of living in unincorporated county territory is that most counties are severely limited in what they are allowed to do and are therefore cheaper than cities. Furthermore, some people value freedom from government—a freedom they find more of under county government than under city government.

Is Chaos a Virtue?   Of course, there is something to be said for the chaos of county government. Political philosophers tell us that one of the things saving us from governmental tyranny is the confusion, awkwardness, and bungling of government. If government could really get its act together, really run as smoothly and flawlessly as a Rolls Royce engine, then we would all be lost to its unerring power. It is erring government, amateurish government, clumsy government that saves us from being enslaved by government.

Furthermore, perhaps there is something to be said for the old idea of the Jacksonians that a long ballot—electing many rather than few officers—keeps government close to the people, especially when elections are frequent and terms short. There is a certain efficiency in inefficiency. If we cannot be democratic without practicing certain inefficiencies and if, above all, we are trying to run a democracy, then those inefficiencies contribute to the efficient practice of democracy.

County Managers   Some counties, without making all department heads subject to appointment by the county manager, have nevertheless hired county managers. This is a growing practice. The main job of these limited county managers is to help the county board manage functions that fall under its direct jurisdiction. Such county managers have more to do in populous counties than in rural counties, simply because in populous urban counties the board supervises a large number of services that do not fall under the various departments headed by independently elected officers.

COUNTY SERVICES

What are the services offered by counties? We saw some of them as we looked at the duties of independently elected county officers. However, counties perform many other jobs. In fact, if we were to look at all the counties in the nation and search in all their dark corners, we might be able to count 300 or maybe 500 separate functions ranging all the way from fairs to social centers to clinics to waterworks. Let us take a look at some of the paramount operations of most counties. Keep in mind that some of these so-called county services, such as zoning, are supplied wholly or in part by cities within city limits, by towns in New England, by townships, occasionally special districts, or sometimes by the state itself.

Health

Most counties try to prevent the outbreak of disease. To do this they need statistics: data about births, deaths, and the existence of known cases of diseases. Therefore, collection and study of these data is a prime function of a county health department. Most counties employ a sanitarian to patrol swimming pools, restaurants, food stores, dairies, sewage- and garbage-disposal facilities, water supplies, and other potential sources of disease. Counties may also employ a public-health nurse to visit chronically ill persons and offer advice to the public about health and nutrition.

Counties may also run hospitals (or rent wards in private hospitals) and operate clinics of various sorts, such as child-guidance clinics and psychiatric clinics. Air pollution is a growing concern of county health departments. Most of the county's health functions are carried on in close cooperation with state health-department officials and with health officials of schools, cities, and towns within the county.

Welfare

Welfare (like health) is an intensely intergovernmental function supported by federal, state, and local money. The main categories of people helped by welfare are needy people over 65 (old-age assistance); needy blind persons (aid to the blind); needy disabled persons who can't completely support themselves by work (aid to the permanently and totally disabled); aid to children who have been deprived of a certain degree of parental support because of the death, absence, or incapacity of one or both parents (aid to families with dependent children); needy persons requiring medical care (medicaid); and other needy persons requiring general assistance. Counties often run homes for the elderly and for children. Most counties employ a number of caseworkers who screen applicants for various welfare programs and keep a watchful and helpful eye on those who receive welfare.

Parks and Recreation

Counties are drawn into the park and recreation business partly because open land for parks is mostly outside city limits—mostly, that is, within unincorporated county territory. In highly urbanized areas composed of numerous towns and suburbs, the county is an appropriate governmental vehicle to provide parks for the whole area. Of course, counties also provide parks for folks in the county who do not live in any city, especially counties that have densely populated but unincorporated areas.

Planning

What Is It? Sometimes it is claimed that city and county **planning** relates only to physical development, not social development. However, planning the future location of factories, schools, or parks is not entirely divorced from future social development. If you plan to locate a school next to a commercial district, you are in effect planning the future social environment of the school. County planning is therefore both physical and social.

The Comprehensive Plan Here's how county planning works. The heart of it is something called a *comprehensive plan,* which designates areas for residential, business, and industrial use and that indicates the location of playgrounds, parks, open spaces, golf courses, arboretums, zoos, cemeteries, highways, transit systems, railroads, ports, waterways, airports, utility systems, water and sewage systems, power lines, pipelines, shopping centers, off-street parking, fire stations, and every public facility. A comprehensive plan isn't cast in concrete; it's constantly changing—or should be.

The Planning Department   The making and continual updating of a comprehensive plan is the county board's job, but board members often rely on a county planning commission and a county planning department. The planning department is staffed with several workers—sometimes a dozen, sometimes a hundred, depending on the size of the county. The planning department studies proposals made by interest groups for changes in the plan; it also develops ideas of its own. However, the planning department has no power to enact a plan.

The Planning Commission   Proposals from the department go to the **planning commission,** whose members are appointed by the county board and whose duty is to decide what, if any, of the proposed changes to recommend to the board for enactment. A busy county board will rely heavily on its planning commission. A negative or a positive vote by the commission carries a lot of weight with the board. Many of the great battles over the location of roads, fire stations, parks, or whatever are fought before the planning commission.

The Politics of Planning   The commission is essentially a political body and should include representatives from major interests and neighborhoods of the county. Planning in a democracy is a highly political process and must be done with due regard to what people want. Otherwise the plan will be disregarded and viewed as an enemy rather than a friend. Fortunately the preponderance of political force is often on the side of sensible growth, because sensible growth—city beautiful—makes good business sense. It is not uncommon for major business firms to support scholarships for the education of city planners. This does not mean that every act of every company always contributes to sensible growth, nor does it mean that everybody agrees on what constitutes sensible growth. Nevertheless, the business community, taken as a whole, wants an attractive neighborhood in which to do business.

Attractiveness means physical beauty as well as economic rationality. Chambers of commerce are often keen to these matters and will support development of city and county comprehensive plans. If community planning does no more than make the area a nicer place to live, that in itself is good for business. Many business firms especially want to be located in "nice places to live." Executives want nice places for themselves and their families, and they want nice places for their employees so that they can keep a stable work force (if for no other reason). Nobody wants to live in an overgrown junkyard, and that is what an unplanned city or county will certainly become.

The comprehensive (or "master") plan must not become an iron mask or a steel vice, thwarting all deviation from its rule. The plan should, of course, be adopted by the county board, and the board should try to follow it. Nor should the plan be disregarded once adopted. It should be kept up to date, revised, kept flexible and sensible, and kept in front of the county board so they won't forget it. The plan needs the continuous attention of a planning commission and a planning department.

Consultants   It is better to have a fifth-rate self-developed plan than to hire a consultant to make one. The trouble with consultants is that once they've made a plan and departed, the plan is liable to be filed away and forgotten because no one really understands the research that went into its construction, nor is anyone on hand to keep updating it, nor (in all probability) were community leaders sufficiently involved in its construction. It's better for a local government to make its own plan, to hire whatever staff it can afford to do the job, or, if nothing else, to appoint a planning commission with enough savvy and spare time to develop a plan and keep it current.

Zoning

Many parts of the comprehensive plan concern the use of private property. **Zoning** is one of the legal teeth governing that use. The zoning ordinance (which includes a map) describes exactly what areas may be put to what use. Normally there are about eight or ten categories: industry, highway commerce, central business, neighborhood shopping, agriculture, and three or four categories of residential districts. These zones are explained in the zoning ordinance. The ordinance is enforced by a building department that issues building permits. The department is forbidden to issue a permit for any structure not conforming with the zoning ordinance. Certain structures, however, may already exist that conflict with the ordinance when it is adopted. In that case the ordinance might forbid any improvements on the nonconforming structures or might require cessation of that unauthorized use within so many years.

The zoning ordinance can be amended at any time. Unfortunately the county board (or city council) may fall into the habit of allowing so many exceptions to the ordinance by amendment that zoning becomes a farce. Political pressures are brought to "spot-zone" this or that piece of property. A city with too many spot zones is like a child with too many freckles. Zoning may be a good idea, but it often falls into the maelstrom of politics. The temptation is great to bribe county boards into making changes in the zoning ordinance that would highly profit particular individuals. More than one lawmaker has gone to jail for it, and for every one jailed, countless others go undetected. Bribes can come in many forms, from money payments to all sorts of direct and indirect favors. Naturally, the zoning ordinance should be somewhat flexible, but there are limits.

Most planning departments are so busy administering the zoning ordinance—studying proposed changes in it and tinkering with it—that they have little time for planning. Their creative energies are exhausted when they finally get around to studying the future development of traffic, parking and transit, parks and recreation, utilities, and so forth. Those things often find a permanent place at the bottom of the list of priorities.

Subdivision Regulation

One of the greatest benefits of planning comes from doing first things first. Take something like laying a sewer. Laying sewers is expensive. Now suppose the county (or city) installs a multimillion-dollar sewer to serve present needs and five years later that sewer proves too small. The whole expensive process has to be done over again. If a sewer is to be laid—or, for that matter, any utility installed or anything big built—the county (or city) should make certain the job won't have to be done over five or ten years later, especially if laying new pipes involves digging up streets. Planning can save a lot of money by predicting the future and constructing utilities adequate for future needs.

This is also one of the central purposes of **subdivision regulation.** A subdivider is a person (or firm) that buys a large tract of land and divides it into residential lots for sale to home builders. (Sometimes subdividers also build the homes.) Subdivision regulations require subdividers to do many things. First, the lots themselves must be a certain depth and width. Second, subdividers are required to give (*dedicate*) land to the county (or city) for streets, parks, schools, fire stations, and other public uses. Normally the amount of land for such purposes is determined by a set formula—perhaps 15 percent of all land in the subdivision. Third, the subdivider must pave the streets and install curbs, gutters, sidewalks, storm drains, streetlights, street-name signs, and perhaps even trees. Subdividers are required to do numerous other things as well.

When you go out to a subdivision to buy a lot or a house, don't forget (if the price seems high) that you are paying for all this in the price of your property. Subdivision regulations require this of subdividers in order to prevent the construction of brand-new slums, and also because it's much cheaper to make streets the proper width the first time rather than trying to widen them later on, and much cheaper to set aside land for parks and schools before that land is covered by houses. Furthermore, there are esthetic values gained by subdivision regulation—the whole area becomes more suitable for human habitation. Buyers are also protected by subdivision regulations. Buyers can be woefully ignorant of what it takes to make a neighborhood livable and workable. Few buyers ever appreciate or comprehend how subdivision regulation improves the likelihood that their investment in property will be a sound one.

Building Codes

Almost everywhere in urban America one must get a building permit from the county (or city) before constructing anything sizable. Almost everywhere there are also at least some regulations (**building codes**) governing how you construct whatever it is you want to build. Safety is one reason for these codes. Buildings can collapse unless they're properly framed. Walls need bracing and anchoring. The size of nails, the thickness of beams, the strength of trusses, the character of shingles, and a thousand other details of construction are regulated by the building code. There are detailed electrical codes regulating exactly how wiring should be done. There are detailed heating codes regulating exactly how furnaces should be installed, heating ducts built, chimneys constructed. There are also precise housing codes regulating the minimum space per occupant, minimum amounts of light, ventilation, fire safety, and sanitation. All these are controlled by a system that requires builders to submit detailed plans to the county (or city) building department before construction begins. If plans conform to all these building, electrical, heating, and housing regulations, and if the proposed structure conforms to the zoning ordinance and other laws, a building permit is issued. Periodically during construction at stated intervals of progress, a county (or city) building inspector will drop by the construction site to investigate whether the original plan is being followed and whether the work is being done in conformance with building regulations. At any point along the way a building inspector can halt construction.

Housing codes pertaining to space, light, ventilation, fire safety, sanitation, and so on, are also applied to structures previously built. Inspectors from various departments may order the owners of defective buildings to correct the defects or stop using the buildings.

Obviously large investments of money can be jeopardized by the adverse finding of a building inspector or housing inspector. It is not unheard of to offer inspectors bribes to divert their attention from violations of building and housing codes. There seems to be more of this corruption in large cities than in small ones. On the other hand, inspectors in towns and rural areas are more likely to be swayed by their personal relationship with violators. In some areas housing codes are simply not enforced.

Counties also carry on many other functions—urban renewal, industrial development, transportation, road building, water distribution, sewage disposal, garbage collection, airport building, and numerous other fascinating endeavors.

County Finance

To pay for all these operations, counties have to raise money. The main tax used by counties is the property tax, but counties also get revenue from other sources, including substantial amounts from the state and federal governments. The property tax is discussed on pages 308–311; intergovernmental revenues are discussed on pages 28–29; and public finance in general is discussed in Chapter 11.

THE NEW ENGLAND TOWN

Don't confuse the word *town* as it is used in New England with the word *town* as it is used elsewhere. A **New England town** is a unique political creation found only in Maine, Massachusetts, New Hampshire, Vermont, Rhode Island, and Connecticut. It is a unit of government that combines the role of both city and county as they function elsewhere in the nation, and it usually consists of one or more urban settlements plus surrounding rural areas. City incorporation is far less common in New England than in the rest of the nation because incorporation is not really necessary where town government has all the powers customarily held by incorporated cities. Some larger urban areas have, however, incorporated and withdrawn from town government.

Counties in New England do less work than counties in other states. This is because New England towns do things customarily done by counties elsewhere. Most towns are smaller than counties: Vermont, for example, fits some 237 towns into 14 counties.

New England towns are perhaps most famous for their annual town meetings, where direct democracy is practiced. Every resident of the town is summoned to these meetings in the town hall (or in an open space somewhere) once a year, although attendance is often sparse. Those who trouble to attend proceed to elect town officers, pass laws, levy taxes, and appropriate money for roads, welfare, education, and whatever else they feel is needed. The officers usually consist of a justice of the peace, an assessor, a clerk, one or two constables (law officers), a tax collector, a treasurer, and a board of selectmen who more or less run the town between town meetings and who appoint any administrative officers or boards needed (Figure 9-3).

New England towns are said to be the last remaining stronghold of direct democracy in the United States where citizens meet together as a deliberative body. The town's great redeeming feature is said to be its closeness to the people. However, direct democracy is apparently not as redeeming today as it once was—very few residents show up for town meetings, unless, of course, something pertaining to liquor, sex, or vice is on the agenda. Town meetings normally take all day, and sometimes all night if something exciting is under discussion. Most people don't consider it worth taking a day off to attend. The vision of town halls packed wall to wall with alert citizens does not square with reality very often. Sometimes nobody comes to a town meeting but the town officers and their families. They promptly reelect themselves, flip through the agenda, and go home, not to return for another year. Such is the frenzy for direct democracy. For this reason some towns have turned to a system of representative town meetings.

Towns in New England are generally too small to hire professionals and are therefore sometimes run in a highly amateurish and bumbling fashion. The more populous towns have simply had to adopt a town-manager system (Figure 9-4), in which the voters confine themselves to electing the three selectmen (and perhaps a clerk and a tax collector), leaving it to the selectmen to appoint a professional town manager (comparable to a city manager), who in turn appoints all the other officers. Some towns, finding themselves unable in town meetings to

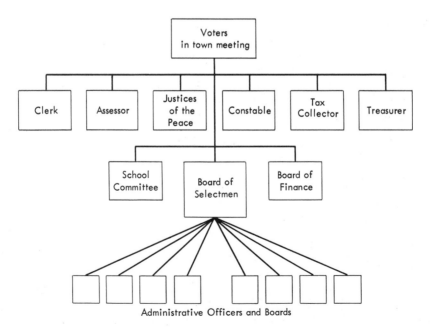

Figure 9-3 *Organization chart of New England town government.* (In many towns, the selectmen may perform the functions of at least some of the offices listed.)

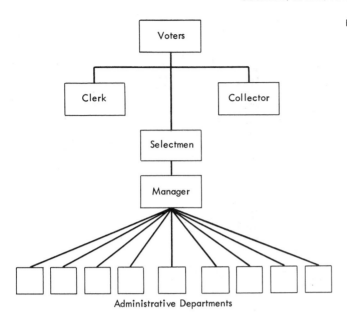

Figure 9-4 *Organization chart of town-manager government.*

decide how much money to appropriate for what functions (or sometimes appropriating all their money before they get to the bottom of the list of important things to be funded), have elected finance committees to present them with a proposed budget or have asked the town manager to prepare such a budget.

TOWNSHIPS

Townships are somewhat akin to counties in function. Where townships exist, there may be a dozen or two of them within each county, doing work that the county could probably be doing itself (depending on state law). Townships do not exist in all states, or in all parts of those states that have townships. Much of Indiana, Iowa, Kansas, Michigan, Minnesota, New Jersey, New York, Ohio, Pennsylvania, and Wisconsin are covered with townships. Parts of Illinois, Nebraska, Missouri, and the Dakotas also have townships. (In some other places certain administrative districts called *townships* exist but have no political organization.)

A **township** is not the same thing as a New England *town,* although in New York State townships are called *towns,* and elsewhere townships are occasionally nicknamed *towns.* There are several distinct differences between townships and New England towns. First, a township is intended primarily to be rural government, not city government, whereas a New England town is intended to provide government for both urban and rural areas within it boundaries. Second, townships are by no means the principal unit of local government, as are the New England towns. Third, townships do not practice direct democracy in the New England town-hall fashion, except in some isolated places. Fourth, the boundaries of most townships are arbitrary squares, six miles to a side, no at-

---

Box 9-1. How Many Townships?

Illinois	1434
Indiana	1008
Kansas	1367
Michigan	1245
Minnesota	1795
Missouri	325
Nebraska	470
New Jersey	245
New York	928
North Dakota	1360
Ohio	1318
Pennsylvania	1549
South Dakota	996
Wisconsin	1269

Source: U.S. Bureau of the Census, *Census of Governments: 1982.*

tempt having been made to encompass natural communities in the way New England towns do. The New England towns are irregular in shape because they were originally laid out to include a settlement and its environs. Township boundaries are for the most part (except in New York, New Jersey, and Pennsylvania) the result of a monumental effort to survey the vast territory acquired by the Louisiana Purchase.

In colonial times the surveying and disposal of government land was rather slipshod. After the Revolutionary War, when the nation began to grow by huge acquisitions such as the Louisiana Purchase, the federal land managers were determined not to repeat the slovenly survey practices of the colonial era. Beginning with Ohio in the 1780s, most federal land was carefully surveyed, numbered, and mapped before it was deeded to settlers. A system of neat squares was laid out, six miles on each side, and each of these squares was called a *township;* each such township was subdivided into 36 blocks of one square mile called *sections.* Along the boundaries of each of these sections a road was built. Today, as one flies across Iowa, Illinois, and numerous other areas of the nation, one can almost count the miles by counting the roads along section lines. The vista below is a great mass of rectangles, like a huge checkerboard. The word *township* as the surveyor uses it has no political meaning. In spite of this, states generally used the surveyor's township as a political unit also called a *township.*

Township government today is the least glorious of all government; the most local of all government; the most obscure of all government; and probably the most trivial, homely, and provincial of all government. Townships are being slowly extinguished by counties except, curiously, in some urban areas where they are being used as a vehicle of metropolitan-wide government.[13] Most of the functions of townships (which are basically identical to those of counties) are simply being transferred to counties.

---

[13]In Michigan, for example, Battle Creek Township merged with Battle Creek in 1983.

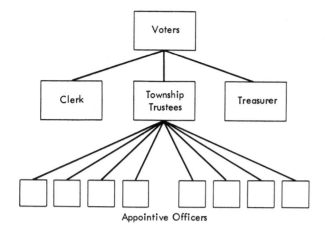

Figure 9-5 *Township government.*

Most townships are governed and administered by township boards (Figure 9-5). Many townships, unlike New England towns, elect a chief executive commonly known as a *supervisor*. Other township officers bear titles identical to those of the New England town. The most important things townships do today is construct and repair roads, but they may also involve themselves with education, welfare, law enforcement, fire protection, parks and recreation, public health, cemeteries, business licensing, sewers, disposal plants, waterworks, planning, and zoning. To repeat, however, counties have taken over most of this. Today it is possible to pick up a basic text on American government and find no mention whatsoever of townships, as if they have already passed from existence.

SPECIAL DISTRICTS

How Many?

Special districts are the most numerous form of local government existing in the United States. Counting school districts, about half of all units of local government are special districts. Even excluding the nation's 15,000 school districts, the remaining 29,000 special districts are still more numerous than counties, municipalities, or townships. Yet special districts are a vast unknown, a terra incognita, for most Americans: they are the most numerous and the least visible of all species of local government.

Definition

Most special districts are one-function governments. A mosquito-control district does one thing: it tries to control mosquitoes. A school district does one thing: it tries to run schools. A cemetery district does another, a park district another, a transit district another. There are special districts to do almost everything imaginable.

Special districts go by a variety of names; some are called *authorities* (Massachusetts Bay Transit Authority), some are called *boards* (Detroit Board of Education), some are called *corporations* (New York City Health and Hospitals Corporation), and, of course, many are called *districts* (Chicago Park District).

Not counting school districts, the most common type of special district is the fire protection district (about 4500 of them). Next are the drainage and flood control districts (about 2700), water supply districts (about 2600), soil conservation districts (about 2400), sewerage districts (about 1600), and cemetery districts (also about 1500). Other common types of special districts are for libraries, highways, hospitals, parks, school buildings, airports, and housing.[14]

Organization

Most special districts are run by boards consisting of about five members, but there is great variation in how those board members are chosen. In some cases they are popularly elected, as are nearly all school boards. However, the boards of most special districts (other than school boards) are not elected. Most are appointed for fixed terms by some other unit of government, usually by the county governing board. Appointment of their governing boards by other governments is a queer feature of special districts that puts them somewhat under the control of those other governments. Despite this hint of subordination, board members, once appointed, are usually secure and cannot be removed any more easily than the members of independent commissions. Once appointed (or elected), the governing boards of special districts are as independent (within their narrow circle of power) as the governing boards of counties or cities.

The Need for Special Districts

Cost to Users Why do we need special districts at all when we have general-purpose cities and counties to do everything that needs to be done? One answer is that special districts are a mechanism for doing what other governments won't or can't do. For example, residents in a certain neighborhood of the county may want a water system. The county board may not wish to tax the entire county just to supply a small area with this special service—let the neighborhood form itself into a water district and pay for its own service. A special district is therefore a tool for laying the cost of special services on those who want the service. How precisely it does this depends on how the district finances itself. Many special districts raise their revenue from the sale of a service—say, the sale of water. That focuses the cost on users very precisely. However, some special districts, such as library districts, raise revenue by taxing residents, some of whom may not want the service. But even where revenue is raised by taxes rather than by sale of service, the consent of at least a majority of the residents within the district is normally necessary in order to set up the district in the first place.

Detour Another reason for the existence of special districts is that sometimes cities and counties are forbidden by the state to provide certain services. A special district may be able to do what other local governments have no power to do. Furthermore, most states limit the amount of debt that local gov-

---

[14]U.S. Bureau of the Census, *Census of Governments, 1982*.

Box 9-2. Run, Eric, Run

Eric Salem, a 14-year-old ninth grader at Irving Junior High School near Lincoln, Nebraska, wants to be elected to the governing board of the Lancaster County Weed District. The district is a small, one-function government whose only job is to control weeds within its boundaries. The Nebraska Attorney General issued an opinion in January 1982 saying Eric's age cannot keep him from being elected to the five-member board.

Eric became interested in running for the board after reading about a fatal traffic accident in which weeds may have been a contriubting factor. He learned there was such a thing as a weed-control board that was supposed to do something for such things and decided to run for it. He doesn't think his age will work against him in the election. "I'm certain that I'm as serious about the job as any other candidate could be, and if I'm elected I'll take the responsibility seriously," he said.

---

ernments may acquire and also the millage rate of local property taxes. Local governments may therefore be quite willing to supply a needed service but be unable to do it because they've reached their debt and tax limits. Special districts are magnificent vehicles for skirting tax and debt limits. If these limits prevent a city from building new parks, then simply establish a park district. Even when tax, debt, and power limits have not been reached, the members of city and county governing boards may be reluctant (for political reasons) to vote new tax levies to support a service. They may be quite willing, however to set up special districts. Special districts often have fiscal autonomy—that is, they can levy taxes, impose service charges, and borrow money.

Across Boundaries   Sometimes special districts are set up because the job to be done extends across the boundaries of several governments. For example, a metropolitan transit district may give bus service to dozens of cities and to a collection of counties within a heavily populated area. Sometimes the job to be done extends even across state lines: the Port of New York Authority is a multipurpose special district established by interstate compact between New York and New Jersey to operate ports, tunnels, bridges, airports, and mass transit in and around New York City.

Politics   Sometimes special districts (especially school districts) are set up to take a particular activity "out of politics." Most people don't want schools run by the spoils system: they don't want teachers hired merely because they supported the winning party or fired because they didn't. To insulate schools from the ordinary run of partisan politics, most school systems in the United States have separated themselves from city and county governments and set themselves up as special districts—independent one-purpose governments with a popularly elected nonpartisan governing board. Although some 1300 public school systems still operate as part of county, municipal, or township government in the United States, more than 15,000 others (90 percent of all public school systems) operate as special districts.[15]

---

[15]U.S. Bureau of the Census, *Statistical Abstract of the United States: 1987* (Washington, D.C., 1986), p. 272.

Halfway Houses There are, in fact, a multitude of motives that produce special districts. In some ways a special district is a halfway house between cityhood and noncityhood, between incorporation and nonincorporation. Communities that don't want to go the whole way to incorporation sometimes settle for one or two special districts to carry on one or two fundamental services. Some special districts are also set up to run utilities (government-owned businesses); this frees managers of those utilities to hire, fire, and promote employees without the usual civil-service red tape.

Cheap Government Most special districts are "cheap" governments. Members of their governing boards are seldom paid. Most special districts are exceedingly small: a water district may have no more than one full-time employee to keep the water pump going, repair breaks in the line, and hook up new customers. On the other hand, some special districts are giants that spend more money than some states. The Chicago Transit Authority employs some 12,000 persons (about the same number employed by the state of Vermont) and spends some $200 million a year.

Faults of Special Districts

Cost As a species of government, special districts have several frailties and defects. Some of these stem directly from the fact that most special districts are small operations. They suffer the disadvantages of smallness—as do small towns and small departments. They reap none of the advantages of bigness: they don't, for example, do enough purchasing to get discounts for buying in large volume. They are not big enough to have a full-time lawyer and must resort to consulting a private lawyer, paying by the minute for advice. Thus although the typical special district is bargain-basement government in that it has almost no full-time bureaucracy, the hidden costs of smallness can make the services offered by it very expensive. Furthermore, because there is usually no sizable bureaucracy and therefore no professional managers, the administration and record keeping of many special districts is often casual to say the least.

Fragmentation Government by special district is government by bits and pieces—fragmented government. This is bad because government should, to some degree at least, be a single machine in which each part contributes to the success of other parts. The various departments of a city government cooperate with one another—police with fire, for example—and plan their development with reference to one another. Each part of city government contributes to the whole and is made more effective by interaction with the whole. When a single function, such as fire protection, parks, libraries, cemeteries, water supply, or trash collection, tries to stand alone as a separate government, it garners none of the rewards of familial interaction with other functions. All planning becomes difficult when separate functions such as police and fire are under separate governments. Aggressive coordination with adjacent governments is not likely to come forth from the directors of most special districts. Their management practices are often listless and negligent, if not downright blundering. Nor do the officials of adjacent governments always have the stamina to coordinate everything with the directors of diverse special districts.

Investments   Still another costly byproduct of special districts is their frequent inability to invest wisely the revenues they receive from selling their service. Since a special district is normally forbidden to do anything but one particular thing (such as provide water), that means it has to plow back any profit it may receive into expanding or improving that service or else give the money back to subscribers. A tendency to expand and improve exists, whether expanding and improving is needed or not. If the service were part of a multipurpose city or county government, the profits might be spent on higher-priority items. Why have a Cadillac water system next to a horse-and-buggy sewer system? If both were under the same government, one might be able to support the other.

Invisibility   Special districts often operate in dim light at the outermost fringes of public consciousness. This is not necessarily true of school districts, which usually have popularly elected governing boards, but the directors of most special districts are appointed. Lacking the ballyhoo of elections, the appointment of most special-district officers eludes public attention entirely. Both they and the district itself hardly exist in the minds of voters. Many voters don't have the slightest idea that their water supply, electric service, or whatever comes from some unit of government separate from the county or city. Even if they did know, their control over such districts and over the appointed directors thereof would still be faint. Furthermore, the existence of numerous overlapping governments puts government beyond the comprehension of ordinary voters. It adds to the untidiness of government and to the bewilderment of voters, and consequently to their apathy. If perchance a citizen should be up in arms about something pertaining to a special district, he or she may regretfully discover that officers of the district are appointed (not elected) and that they hold terms lasting several years. Even special-district officers who are elected are usually appointed to the board of directors initially and therefore run, even for their first term, as incumbents. Incumbents are always hard to beat.

Although special districts can at times be useful, we might not want to give that form of government an E for excellence.

SUMMARY

All local governments in the United States (except Washington, D.C.) are created by the states. There are some 82,000 of them, including about 3000 counties, 19,000 municipalities, 15,000 townships, 29,000 nonschool special districts, 1000 New England towns, and 15,000 school districts.[16] Until fairly recently, local governments had to fend for themselves without much help. Today they receive considerable help from state and federal governments, much of it in the form of grants with strings attached, although federal general revenue sharing has been largely free of stipulations. Some federal aid is funneled to local governments through state governments, and some is given directly to local governments. State aid to local governments is given either in money (primarily grants for education, welfare, and highways) or in professional assistance. Many states have established departments of local affairs that advise local governments in practically everything they do.

[16]Ibid.

The United States Constitution does not mention local government. All power is divided by the Constitution between the central government and the state governments. Local governments are instrumentalities of the state and are an extension of state power. State grants of power to local governments are narrowly construed by courts, according to Dillon's rule.

Counties are the principal divisions of all states except in New England, where town government prevails. In Louisiana counties are called *parishes;* in Alaska, *boroughs.* A county differs from a city in one important legal way: it is not created at the behest of its inhabitants, nor is it intended to serve their unique governmental needs. Counties are set up by the state itself to serve as a kind of political outpost of state government, applying state laws and administering state business at the local level. A county is not a municipal corporation.

Most counties handle such things as public safety, zoning, building regulation, welfare, health, hospitals, parks and recreation, highways, justice, assessment, and record keeping. The typical county government includes numerous separately elected officials, each running his or her department separately; there is little central coordination of one department with another. There is usually a sheriff, clerk, treasurer, assessor, coroner, attorney, and board of supervisors. A surveyor, recorder, and superintendent of schools may also be elected, as well as a collector of taxes, registrar of deeds, public administrator, constable, and judge. Usually each elected official (except members of the county board) is czar of his or her own little semiautonomous government. The county board is in charge of departments not supervised by any other elected officials. The board has only faint (if any) control of departments headed by elected officials. County services other than those provided by the standard row of elected officials commonly include health, welfare, parks and recreation, planning, zoning, subdivision regulation, and building codes. Counties rely heavily on the property tax and on substantial aid from state and federal governments. The major current proposal for reforming county government is to establish a county-manager system similar to the city-manager system.

A New England town is both a county and a city in the sense that it does essentially everything counties and cities do elsewhere. However, towns, not counties, are the cardinal units of local government in New England, even though towns are technically subdivisions of counties. New England towns are known for their unique annual town meetings where direct democracy is practiced.

Townships (not to be confused with New England towns) exist in some 15 states, mostly in the Midwest. Originally townships did nearly everything a county did—they were in fact small-scale counties—but they have never played the central role in local government that New England towns have played. Nor do many townships practice direct democracy. Counties are gradually taking over the duties once performed by townships. The most important jobs townships do today is construct and repair roads, but they may involve themselves in a number of other things as well.

Special districts are the most numerous form of local government in the United States. A special district is a one-function government: it is limited to only one role, such as operating cemeteries, transit systems, ports, parks, hospitals, or schools. Special districts exist to do what other governments won't or can't do, but they suffer many hidden disadvantages.

SUGGESTIONS FOR FURTHER READING

BOLLENS, JOHN C., *American County Government.* Beverly Hills, Calif.: Sage Publications, Inc., 1969.

————, *Special District Government in the United States.* Berkeley and Los Angeles: University of California Press, 1957.

DANIELS, BRUCE C., ed., *Town and County.* Middletown, Conn.: Wesleyan University Press, 1978.

DUNCOMBE, HERBERT SYDNEY, *Modern County Government.* Washington, D.C.: National Association of Counties, 1977.

KAMMERER, GLADYS M., *The Changing Urban County.* Gainesville: Public Administration Clearing Service, University of Florida, 1963.

LANCASTER, LANE W., *Government in Rural America.* New York: D. Van Nostrand, 1952.

LOPACH, JAMES J., and LAUREN S. MCKINSEY, "Local Government Reform by Referendum: Lessons from Montana's Voter Review Experience," *State and Local Government Review* (January 1979), 35–39.

LYONS, W. E., *The Politics of City-County Merger.* Lexington: University Press of Kentucky, 1977.

MOORE, PAUL, and ALAN G. BILLINGSLEY, "Financial Monitoring of Local Governments," *State Government* (Autumn 1979), 155–60.

SMITH, ROBERT G., *Public Authorities, Special Districts and Local Government.* Washington, D.C.: National Association of Counties, 1964.

STEPHENS, G. ROSS, "State Centralization and the Erosion of Local Autonomy," *Journal of Politics* (February 1974), 44–76.

10

cities
and
metropolitan areas

PREVIEW

CREATURE OF THE STATE

How hot it was that summer! But the mornings were cool, and I signed up for an 8 A.M. class in business law. One morning the white-haired professor gave a rambling lecture on the meaning of the word *corporation.* He said it was an "artificial person."

I raised my hand. "Who is the God and Creator of this artificial person?"

"The state is its creator. Not God. It has no soul."

"Can artificial persons vote?"

"No. They cannot vote. But they can do almost anything else a citizen can do under the law. They are even covered by the Bill of Rights. They have freedom of speech, they have equal protection of the laws, they have a right to counsel, they can own property, they can sue, they can. . . ."

"Wow," I thought. "An artificial person! What would it feel like to be an artificial person? A person with no soul?"

"Yes," mused the professor, "when a group of people go to the state and say they want to carry on a business and would like to be considered as a new and separate person for purposes of that business, the state waves a wand and declares them to be a new and separate person."

"Is it hard to form a corporation?" I asked just as the bell rang.

"Son," said the professor, "why don't you try it?"

You know, I did try.

"How much did the lawyer charge you?" asked my friend.

"Oh, I did it all myself. First thing I did was go to the public library and look up the state law on corporations. It tells how to set one up—step by step."

"Then what?"

"Then I wrote a letter to the secretary of state of my state and asked for a blank form on which to file 'articles of incorporation.' This one-page form came by return mail. It was free. I filled it out: things like the name of the proposed corporation (I called it the T I Corporation—for 'try it'), how many shares of stock (one-thousand was a good round number), the name and address of at least three incorporators (I got my mother and sister to volunteer). I sent the form back to the secretary of state together with a forty-dollar fee. After about a month the secretary of state mailed me an impressive document called a Certificate of Incorporation. That document gave birth to T I Corporation. My mother, my sister, and I were transformed into a new fourth person."

"What did the professor think of your feat?"

"I met him one day on the sidewalk and told him I had created a corporation."

"No, you didn't son. Only the state can create a corporation. But bully for you, son," he smiled, patting me on the back. "Now try setting up a *municipal* corporation."

MUNICIPAL CORPORATIONS

An Artificial Person

Lawyers tend to think of cities as municipal corporations. A **municipal corporation** has much in common with private business corporations. Both are created (chartered) by the state. Their certificate of incorporation is their birth certificate, so to speak.

Cities begin like private corporations: a group of people go to the state and ask to be officially declared a corporation. A corporation is an "artificial person."[1] It can own property, sell property, sue and be sued, borrow money, loan money, enter into contracts, and carry on similar business operations. If you sue a corporation, you aren't suing the members thereof—a corporation is something different and apart from its members.

Stockholders of a private business corporation are its members. Membership in a private business corporation has no geographic limits—stockholders may live anywhere in the world. Members of a municipal corporation, in contrast, are the residents within its borders—the people who live inside the city.

A private corporation is a convenient vehicle for carrying on business operations in which its members are jointly interested. Municipal corporations likewise are created to carry on operations of special interest to their members. Towns incorporate to supply themselves with more services than surrounding governments (primarily the county) are willing or able to supply—more and better police, for example. Or they incorporate to give themselves closer control of such services. Thus a municipal corporation is formed to provide something special for its members, something over and above what the state, the county,

---

[1]Henry C. Black, *Black's Law Dictionary,* 5th ed. (St. Paul: West, 1979), p. 307.

and special districts are supplying. The process of incorporation begins when a certain proportion of the residents sign a petition to incorporate.

Compared with Counties

Most counties are not municipal corporations—not technically. They are not created as a result of a petition to the state by residents thereof. Counties are generally created by the state on its own volition to deliver state services locally. The central legal difference between a city and most counties is that a city is a corporation and most counties are not. Whatever their legal differences, counties and cities often do much the same work. Both, for example, provide police service.

Size

Some 19,000 municipalities exist in the United States, most of them very small.[2] Only about 6000 municipalities have more than 2500 people. However, at the other extreme, Chicago, New York, Los Angeles, Philadelphia, Detroit, and Houston exceed one million. Cities are about as equal as creatures of the jungle—there are municipal elephants and municipal mice—yet most cities have certain things in common. Both the village and the big city have legislative bodies. Both have chief executives. Both usually give fire protection, collect garbage, run sewer systems, build streets, supply police protection, and take at least some steps to prevent disease. Of course, the larger cities provide these on a more grandiose scale. The larger the city, the greater the chance it will supply a collection of other services as well, such as libraries, museums, parks, playgrounds, auditoriums, swimming pools, hospitals, and zoning. Since the problems of unemployment, poverty, blighted housing, racial discrimination, drug addiction, juvenile delinquency, crime, and an assortment of other afflictions are bigger in big cities, services in those matters also increase geometrically with the size of the city. However, these problems also exist to some degree in all cities, even in villages. Every village is a small-scale model of a big city, and for that reason many political-science students doing field study or internships in local government often learn more about city government by interning in small cities rather than big cities. Interns in small towns are not limited to a single department but get to see the whole picture of city functions from their perch in the mayor's office, the clerk's office, or wherever.

CITY CHARTERS

The basic governmental structure and the basic powers of each city are set forth in a **charter** provided by the state. Every city is a creature of the state. Even though the cities are created at the request of their inhabitants to serve their

---

[2]International City Management Association, *Municipal Year Book: 1987* (Washington, D.C., 1987), p. xiv.

special wants and needs, cities are created by state power and may not do anything the state prohibits. Much of what the state allows is written in the charter.

The idea of having a city charter stems (as so many things do) from colonial times, when royal governors created cities by issuing them a charter (a written grant of specified rights). The word *charter* is sometimes used as if it meant *constitution* (for example, the Charter of the United Nations). A city charter indeed is in a sense the constitution of the city: it lists major city officers and describes their method of selection, their powers, and their relationship with one another; it sets forth what the city may do and perhaps may not do. The charter also states the geographic boundaries of the city and normally describes how the charter itself may be amended.

General-Law Charters

Not many generations ago state legislatures created cities one by one. A separate law establishing each and stating its structure, powers, and boundaries was passed, and a special charter was issued. This practice largely stopped in the late 1800s, when there was a hue and cry against "special legislation." Legislatures had fallen into the sometimes corrupt habit of passing special laws granting favors to named individuals or corporations. Today most state constitutions forbid special legislation; laws must now usually apply *generally*. Thus legislatures are now usually forbidden by their state constitutions to enact a special law saying "such and such a city is hereby created." Instead general laws are now passed establishing regular procedures by which cities are created. Such general laws may classify cities by size, may provide a different pattern of government for each class (through *classified charters*), and may even provide an assortment of charters (*optional charters*) from which prospective cities may pick. Cities chartered under such general laws are often referred to as **general-law cities.**

Whether the state legislates a separate charter for each city, as the states used to do, or deals with them generally, the charter remains in state law: everything it says is sanctioned by legislation. However, the charter of a city is not the only state legislation affecting that city. Many other laws require, or allow, or forbid cities to do various things. Probably the charter won't say anything about speed limits within cities, but state law often does and might require cities to enforce that law. As creatures of the state, cities are expected to serve the state and obey its laws.

How liberally are state grants of power to cities interpreted by courts? If state law says a city may operate a bus system, does that mean it may also operate a railroad system? Probably not, because the powers of cities (like the powers of all local governments) are narrowly construed by judges. All doubts about whether a city has legal power to do something are generally decided against the city if the matter is brought to court. This rule of narrow construction is known as Dillon's rule[3] (see p. 221).

---

[3]John F. Dillon, *Commentaries on the Law of Municipal Corporations*, 5th ed. (Boston: Little, Brown, 1911), I, Sec. 237.

Home-Rule Charters

Why not let each city decide for itself how it should be organized and what functions it should perform? Since the turn of the century about four-fifths of the states have decided to give cities that very freedom, called *municipal home rule*. Of course, no state can afford to give cities complete freedom. All cities continue to be instrumentalities of the state and are therefore obliged to do (or refrain from doing) what the state requests in matters wherein the state has a paramount interest. The purpose of home rule is to allow cities freedom to do largely what they want within the realm of local concerns wherein there is no paramount statewide interest. Unfortunately the line between *statewide* and *local* is very fuzzy; that is the fundamental flaw in the whole concept of municipal home rule. Home-rule power is power of self-determination solely within the realm of local matters, not statewide matters.

An example of a matter usually considered local rather than statewide is the internal organization of cities. In the realm of organization, home-rule cities have great freedom. Disputes about what is statewide and what is local usually center on powers claimed by home-rule cities. A city might, for example, think it is purely a matter of local interest whether it levies a sales tax, but in many states the kind of taxes levied within the state is considered a matter of statewide interest. The manner in which cities annex adjacent territory is also usually considered statewide, since annexation involves people beyond a city's boundaries. States also usually consider the regulation of public utilities, even local utilities, to be a matter of statewide interest. Just where the line between statewide and local lies is often decided in court battles between home-rule cities and the state when their separate claims to power collide. Courts in every state decide case by case whether the state or the city has a paramount interest in a certain matter.

There is one kind of home rule that home-rule advocates do not recognize as true home rule: the kind authorized by act of the state legislature rather than by provision of the state constitution. Home rule should be rooted in the state constitution, not in ordinary legislation, say its advocates: it should be constitutional home rule, not statutory home rule. If the freedom of a city to draft its own list of powers and design its own form of government is merely a freedom granted by ordinary legislation, then what is to prevent the legislature from nibbling away at that freedom, from overriding it and disregarding it? If, on the other hand, home rule is granted by the state constitution itself, then the legislature would be acting unconstitutionally if it attempted to reduce the home-rule power of cities.

No city is forced to be a home-rule city. Home rule is a privilege offered to those who want it. A city can always incorporate as a general-law city. Most home-rule cities begin, in fact, as general-law cities. To switch from general law to home rule usually involves first the circulation of a petition among city voters. The petition asks that city voters be polled at the next election on whether they wish to establish a commission to draft a home-rule charter for the city. If voters at such an election agree to a commission, the commission thus elected goes to work drafting a proposed charter. The proposed home-rule charter is then put to a vote of the people. If they vote for the charter, it becomes the city charter, and the city is promptly reorganized according to its provisions. If voters refuse the charter, then everything remains as it was.

Quite a few states limit the privilege of home rule to cities of a certain size, perhaps to those over 2500.

FORMS OF CITY GOVERNMENT

Among America's cities about half use the *mayor-council* form of city government and about 40 percent use the *council-manager* form. A tiny fraction (perhaps about 3 percent) use the *commission* form. The remaining fraction use some variety of town meeting. The city-manager form is most popular among cities ranging in population from 10,000 to 100,000. The mayor-council system is most popular among very small and very large cities.[4] Each of these forms comes in as many variations as Campbell's soup. We can only hope to discuss the archetype of every form. Your imagination will have to take over from there.

The Commission Form

Where Used One wonders if the **commission form** of city government might finally disappear altogether if professors would quit giving it so much space in textbooks. Only about a hundred cities use the commission system—a system that never was very popular and is losing ground steadily. Even Galveston, Texas, which gained fame of sorts in 1901 when it adopted the commission form of government after its previous government seemingly failed to cope with the chaotic situation following a tidal wave, has now abandoned the commission form. Still there remain a number of cities—Mobile, Topeka, Shreveport, Atlantic City, Tulsa, Portland (Oregon), Chattanooga, Salt Lake City, and others—that at last report still use the commission form with reasonably good results. The commission form seems to have found some popularity in several states, whereas in others it is all but unheard of. A considerable handful of cities in such states as New Jersey, Mississippi, Alabama, Florida, Illinois, and the Dakotas use the commission system, whereas California and Ohio, to mention only two, have no commission cities at all, and Michigan and New York have almost none at last count.[5]

Features The basic feature of commission government is its union of legislative and executive power: each member of the city council (or *commission*, as it is called) also serves as head of a major city department. The typical city commission has five commissioners and five departments. Those five departments might be public safety, public works, finance, social service, and parks and recreation.

Advantages The advantage of this unique arrangement is said to be that the persons who make city policy (the commission) are also in charge of carrying it out. City legislators don't have to wonder whether department heads understand what they're supposed to do—legislators are the departments heads.

[4]International City Management Association, *The Municipal Year Book: 1987* (Washington, D.C., 1987), Table 3, p. xv.

[5]International City Management Association, *The Municipal Year Book: 1987* (Washington, D.C., 1987).

Legislators don't have to wonder whether departments heads are getting too much political power—legislators are department heads. Legislators don't have to wonder whether departments heads are competent—legislators are department heads and, of course, totally competent. Everything is supposedly very simple and very efficient—no department heads to hassle the commission, no lapse between word and deed. It is at first glance the perfect union of legislative and executive power, no less intimate, no less enchanting than the perfect union of husband and wife. Still, not all conjugality is made in heaven.

Disadvantages What could possibly be wrong? Perhaps the worst problem with making department heads out of elected commissioners is that commissioners aren't always competent to be department heads. High-level administration is a science and an art that very few people have—that's one reason why top administrators get so much money. Furthermore, anyone who's going to be head of, say, the public-works department should probably have a degree in engineering, ought to know something about accounting, computers, public relations, planning, management, budgeting, and personnel administration, and ought to have had some management experience. Normally people with that kind of talent are too busy to serve on city commissions. Quite commonly people elected to city commissions are ill equipped to serve as head of any department. Furthermore, most commissioners are part-time amateurs in government who may spend no more than one day a week on city business.

Nor does anyone have general overall charge of the city's administration. Departments are divvied up among the commissioners, but no one coordinates the various departments with one another. There is, of course, a mayor, but usually the mayor in a commission system of government is elected by the commission—one of the commissioners is simply given the title of mayor by the other commissioners. Being also a commissioner, the mayor has charge of one department (or several) but typically he or she has no power over the other commissioners or over the other departments. The mayor, in other words is "weak." There is no city manager, or strong mayor, to knit the city administration into a coherent whole.

True, the commissioners themselves sitting together as a commission are theoretically supposed to be coordinating with one another. This coordination may be feeble, however, because (1) the individual commissioners may have only a feeble grasp on their own departments, and (2) rather than coordinate with one another, commissioners may try to butter one another's bread in anticipation of future elections. Logrolling is apt to be the name of the game among commissioners: "I'll give your department what you want, if you'll give my department what I want." This makes it especially hard to put a brake on spending. The commission system also saturates administration with politics, more perhaps than in other forms of city government. Of course, we know there can be no complete separation of politics and administration in any form of government because administrators must enter the political arena in some disguised or open way to get what they want, no matter what the form of government. However, the commission system drags administration into the political thicket excessively. This is because the head of every department is also a political figure, always on the lookout for reelection, and always playing ball with the other commissioners.

Finally, if you're going to cram everything the city does into five departments so that each commissioner can be in charge of one, this immediately causes administrative problems. First, it means every department is going to be a conglomeration of incompatible functions, each function being a specialty requiring professional and specialized knowledge. A department of public works might include everything from A to Z. No one but a universal genius could intelligently administer such a vast array of activities, certainly not a part-time amateur whose only reason for wanting the commissioner's post may have been for amusement. Nor is there any freedom to add or delete departments: the system is set in concrete—five commissioners, five departments, and that's that. If more departments than commissioners exist, then each commissioner may head several departments. This produces the same problems described before. If each commissioner is elected from a district or ward, then the department he or she heads becomes a property of the ward, so to speak.

If by some lucky fate the voters elect five top-flight commissioners experienced in administration, learned in technology, and endowed with oceans of spare time to bestow on their duties, then perhaps the commission system might have some tremendous advantages.

The commission form of government comes in many variations. Some variations mitigate the problems described before. For example, in some commission cities a mayor is elected at large and can thus apply a measure of central direction, which is lacking when all commissioners, including the mayor, are elected by districts.

Council-Manager Form

The Manager   A **city manager** is somebody appointed by a city council to administer the city. In theory, the council makes policy—that is, it sets general directions—and the manager sees that those general policies or directions are carried out by the city administration. For example, the council may say, "Build a road from point A to point B." The manager then gets the road built. Now, of course, the manager and the city bureaucrats may have been responsible for suggesting that new road in the first place. Thus the city manager often does make policy and does set general directions behind the scenes through his or her influence over the council. In theory, however, the council makes policy, and the manager carries it out.

The manager is hired by the council and can be fired at any time. The manager, in turn, hires and can fire the heads of all departments—he or she is the ultimate boss of nearly everyone who works for the city except judges and elected officials (Figure 10-1).

The Mayor   The mayor's job in this picture is largely ceremonial. He or she presides over the council and represents the city in various ways but rarely has the power to hire or fire anybody, not even the manager. The manager works for the council, not the mayor, except insofar as the mayor may be a member of the council. The mayor is the ritual head of the city; the manager is the administrative head. If they are smart, they will try to remember their separate roles and not get into each other's hair. However, weak mayors do have considerable leadership potential.[6]

[6]See James H. Savas, "The Mayor in Council-Manager Cities: Recognizing Leadership Potential, *National Civic Review* (September–October 1986), pp. 271–290.

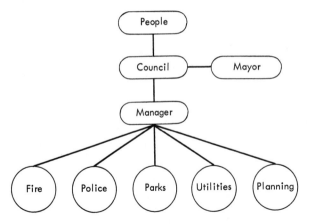

Figure 10-1 Council-manager form of city government.

Advantages The supposed central advantage of having a city manager is that he or she gives full-time professional overall management to city business. In most cities, the council and the mayor are really part-time amateurs, although admittedly some council members work endless hours on city business. But even when they do have time and knowledge to set general policy for the city, they often haven't time or knowledge to supervise the detailed execution of those policies. A good city manager can do those things. Part of a professional city manager's skill should be an ability to pick competent chiefs for the other departments of city government. By having a professional city manager, a city also gets professional department heads who in turn will appoint professional subordinates, and so on down the line. Professionalization at the top seeps down through the whole bureaucracy. Not every city manager is a professional, but many are.[7] An increasing number are graduates of public-administration degree programs.

Where Used Small towns under 5000 may not be able to afford a city manager or fully employ his or her talents, although sometimes a group of small towns will get together and hire a joint manager who "rides circuit" among them. Large cities exceeding a million don't use the city manager system either. New York, Chicago, Los Angeles, Philadelphia, Detroit, and Houston (our six largest cities) do not have city managers. Why? Most big cities seem to need strong mayors armed with power to hire and fire department heads and handle most of a manager's functions. Such a mayor combines political power with administrative power—he or she is both the political leader and the administrative leader of the city. This is said to be the kind of cement needed to hold a big city together. The bigger the city, the more vulnerable its departments, bureaus, offices, and branches to capture by special interest groups. A city manager has trouble dealing with these gigantic forces because he or she is not a political figure, only an appointee. A mayor, on the other hand, who is elected at large in a great city, becomes politically powerful and thus can deal with the city's other great political powers much better than an appointed manager can.

---

[7]The International City Management Association is a professional organization for chief appointed management executives in cities, counties, towns, and other local governments.

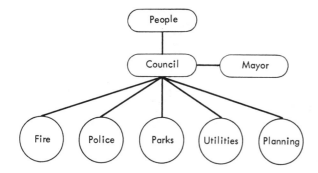

Figure 10-2 Mayor-council form of city government (with weak mayor).

The centrifugal forces of most medium-sized cities seem to be more manageable than those of the big city, and that is one reason why the city-manager form of government is more workable and more popular in medium-sized cities.

Mayor-Council Form

In the **mayor-council form** of city government, there is no city manager. The mayor and council are saddled with executing their own policies. Mayor and council appoint department heads and coordinate the work of agencies. Without a manager they themselves must tend to the details of administration and are left without professional guidance in policy making. In a "weak"-mayor system (Figure 10-2), the council makes appointments; in a "strong"-mayor system, the mayor makes appointments and has many of the powers of a city manager. In large cities a strong mayor will hire a professional assistant who may become somewhat like a city manager.

MAYORS

Is There a Future in Being Mayor?

"Being mayor is fun and exciting," said Boston's mayor James Michael Curley, "but there is no future in it."[8] In so saying, Mayor Curley reflected the long-standing political axiom that the mayoralty is a dead-end job. Many local politicians aspire to be mayor, but once they make it to the mayor's office and finish their term, what other office can feed their ambition? None in the city. Perhaps a state job? Governor? Being mayor of only a small town is not sufficient to propel one into statewide politics. Being identified with a large city could hurt a politician's chances for state office, as Mayor Edward Koch of New York City may learn if he should be a candidate for governor of his state. Would it then be proper to carve in granite over the courthouse portals Dante's despairing counsel, "All hope abandon, ye who enter here"?

[8]John T. Galvin, *Twelve Mayors of Boston 1900–1970* (Boston: Boston Public Library, 1970), n.p.

Perhaps not. Despite the well-publicized problems experienced by ex-mayors seeking higher and more glorious office, statistics seem to show that former mayors do about as well in continuing their political career as the holders of other major offices.[9] Of course, putting mayors in company with other major officeholders does not necessarily mean that mayors have a brighter future, only that both have a similar plight. The probability that any major public officeholder can improve his or her station by winning a still higher post is slim at best. We leave the phrase *higher office* undefined.

Strong and Weak Mayors

Some mayors are strong and some weak. In the jargon of political science the terms *weak* and *strong* when applied to mayors refer to their power of appointment. Essentially a **weak mayor** has virtually no power of appointment; a **strong mayor** has wide appointment authority. Where weak mayors exist, power to appoint is vested either in the council or in a city manager. Of course, a mayor may be strong in political power as well as strong in formal appointment power. This is usually the case in big cities, where the power to appoint department heads is usually given to the mayor, who is also usually elected directly by the people (rather than by the council) and therefore has a strong citywide political base. Many of the sources of a mayor's political power are identical to sources of gubernatorial power—media centrality, ability to dominate political organizations, budgetary power, veto power, and so forth.

Election

In more than 90 percent of all cities the people directly elect the mayor. However, a few cities let the city council choose one of its members as mayor. Such council-elected mayors are usually weak in the political sense because their power base may rest only in one district of the city and because everyone knows they were not elected mayor by the people. Mayors elected by the council seldom have any significant power to appoint department heads, such power usually being vested either in the council as a whole or in a city manager.

On the other hand, many big-city mayors are politically powerful because they are elected at large and are also technically strong because they have vast powers of appointment. Yet some big-city mayors have little appointive power despite their political power, and are therefore technically classified as weak mayors. Sometimes these technically weak mayors are able to influence appointments indirectly through their political weight. Politically powerful mayors may get their way whether they have formal powers of appointment or not.

In about 20 percent of America's cities, being mayor gives one almost no power except the privilege of saying "I am the mayor." These are mostly small communities. But in most smaller cities the mayor at least has the "power" to preside over the council, but casts a vote only when necessary to break ties. In medium-sized cities the mayor is likely to have "direct voice and vote"—that is, he or she is expected to participate in debate and cast a vote just like any member

[9]See Russell D. Murphy, "Whither the Mayors? A Note on Mayoral Careers," *Journal of Politics* (February 1980), pp. 277–290.

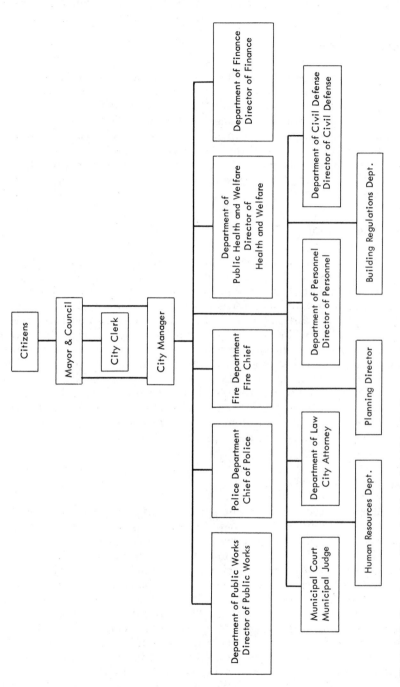

Figure 10-3 Departments of the city of Springfield, Missouri.* (*Source:* City of Springfield, public document.)

*The director of public health and welfare is appointed with the approval of the County Court and functions as the head of both the city and county health programs.

The municipal judge is nominated by the city manager and elected by the City Council for a term of four years. Other department heads are appointed by the city manager for indefinite terms.

The *Springfield City Code* establishes a Department of Civil Defense. However, since October 1969, based on an agreement between the city and the county, it is the Springfield-Greene County Civil Defense Agency. The directors of the agency are the presiding judge of the county and the city manager. In practice, they have agreed upon the appointment of a director of the joint agency so that the Department of Civil Defense of the City does not function as such.

The planning director is appointed by the city manager with the concurrence of the Planning Commission.

of the council. Perhaps half such mayors have a veto power as well, and many are charged with making a budget for the council to consider.

The Symbol of the City

Strong or weak, every mayor is the city's chief representative. Hardly a major gathering in the city occurs without the mayor's presence to make a speech, cut a ribbon, or lay a cornerstone and thus symbolize the city's official recognition of the event. This symbolic role is especially useful in public emergencies, when mayors may be looked to for leadership even when they have no formal power to do anything at all. Also their "headship" of the city makes them ambassadors of sorts, representing their city in Washington, D.C., at the state capitol, or at miscellaneous places where the city's voice is to be heard or its representative seen.

The Chief Administrator

Of course, a strong mayor must also be a chief administrator, a role for which he may or may not be fitted. His political talents may not entirely qualify him for his administrative role, although political talent is surely among the arts of a good administrator. Being an administrator is never easy, and city mayors are beset with a large collection of difficulties. Although strong mayors have the power to appoint major department heads, this power is blemished if all such appointments must be approved by the city council. Likewise all dismissals. When this is the case, a department head cannot always afford to view the mayor as his or her sole boss. Furthermore, some city officials may be appointed by neither the mayor nor the council, but by an "independent" board of citizens that may also have the sole power to remove such appointees. The actual strength of strong mayors in the area of appointments may range from very strong to almost weak, depending on what agency heads they appoint and on what interferences with their power exists.

Controlling the Civil Service

The Merit System Intrudes The appointment powers of mayors may be limited to the appointment of department heads, or it may extend deep into the bureaucracy. A good many large cities use a **merit system** to appoint most employees. This, of course, limits the mayor's appointment powers. Merit systems are usually run by independent civil-service commissions. Much is to be said for merit systems, but such a system does limit the ability of a mayor to manage the executive branch. He or she cannot freely hire and fire the mass of employees who do the work of government. They are hired, fired, promoted, or rewarded under rules of an independent civil-service commission, which the mayor is not supposed to control. A mayor cannot under such a system simply hire someone who shares his or her aspirations for the city. Nor can the mayor fire those who do not. Employees in a merit system are not measured by that kind of merit. A typist is hired for merit in typing, not for "political merit." Sometimes the merit system covers employees fairly high up in the bureaucracy—middle-level managers and sometimes even high-level managers only a few steps from department head. The more managers within the merit system and therefore beyond the mayor's power to hire and fire, the less control the mayor has over the system. Officials who don't like the mayor or don't share his or her enthusiasm for certain goals can sabotage the mayor's plans. If a mayor wants to put an end to open prostitution but is not supported by certain police officers and if these officers cannot be removed except for "cause," it is doubtful the mayor will get far with his or her campaign to end prostitution. The same principle applies in every other department of city government where merit-system employees don't share the mayor's wish to accomplish this or that goal. Mayors, especially big-city mayors, are busy with a multitude of things and don't have enough hours or basal metabolism to do everything they might want. They are also hampered by their limited knowledge of the complex nature of most city agencies. This further limits their ability to control the bureaucracy.

Innovators

Mayors (like presidents and governors) may be aggressive innovators of new policy or they may, once elected, sit back and handle routine business without trying to lead the city toward new goals. The safest role to play is usually the inactive "caretaker" role: it makes no waves. A mayor who simply wants to enjoy the glory of office will find the caretaker role comfortable, peaceful, and satisfying. However, a mayor who wants to attack problems, make changes, and start new programs must expect a turbulent career.

Power   Certainly the office of mayor is an ideal platform for proclaiming the need for change. However, mayors who come to office with high hopes of accomplishing great things soon collide with a few unexpected realities of public life. First of all, they may be surprised by their lack of real power—they have less authority than they imagined. They quickly and painfully discover the limits on their power to hire and fire people. They learn that they have to clear a lot of things with the council, and that the failures of merit-system employees whom they may want to remove must be proven legalistically. They may discover that whole sectors of "their" government are under the control of independent boards. Schools, the most expensive activity on the political landscape, are almost surely beyond their power and probably aren't even part of the city government at all, but run by separate governments called school districts. They find they can't even remove people they have the authority to remove, without upsetting powerful groups. Bureaucrats often take care to arm themselves with political support, especially the support of those who benefit from the service rendered by the agency they run.

Mayors discover that everything they want to accomplish involves first changing things to make room for those accomplishments. But changing things means colliding with every interest satisfied with the status quo.

Money   Even if a mayor succeeds in clearing the way for new programs, there remains the problem of paying for them. Every grand idea carries a dollar sign, and local governments have nearly exhausted every source of new revenue. If you want a new program, it's probably going to mean shutting down or reducing other programs, or levying unpopular new taxes. Any new "progressive" mayor who expects to eliminate some existing programs to help pay for new ones soon learns that every existing program has its defenders who will shout at the slightest threat. It is, of course, possible for a determined mayor to overcome these obstacles and to attack some terrible problems that need attacking. Such mayors deserve our applause, but they are not likely to get much applause, because it's human nature to be noisier in criticizing than in praising.

CITY COUNCILS

Size

City councils are elected and usually have around five to nine members, but on average the larger the city the larger the council. The average size of councils in cities of 500,000 to 1 million is about 13 members, and the average for cities of more than 1 million is about 22. Some cities like Nashville, New York, Cleveland, Chicago and St. Louis have councils ranging into the 30s and 40s. Yet large cities do not always have large councils: Dallas, Boston, New Orleans and a number of other cities of similar size have councils of only seven or nine members.[10] Curiously, city councils in New England are slightly larger on average than councils in other parts of the country.

Influence of Bureaucrats

Part of the mythology of our time is that legislative bodies do all the legislating. Actually most legislation in this country (at all levels of government) is done by administrators. Granted, city councils and other legislative bodies do pass laws, but most of those laws are recommended by agencies, offices, and bureaus within the executive branch of government. The bureaucracy has frontline contact with problems that require legislation and is better able than the city council, because it has the time and expertise, to analyze those problems and consider alternative solutions. Thus city councils spend much of their time considering proposals from bureaucrats. In effect, the executive branch legislates. The bigger the city, the bigger the role of executives in legislation. The smaller the town, the more its council is forced to do for itself.

   Why are city councils so docile in the face of city managers, agency heads, and strong mayors? One can easily understand why councils would want to leave the details of administration to administrators. But councils routinely enact the policy recommendations of administrators, generally without much deliberation and without inserting many changes. Why? First, we have to remember how much study goes into a major policy or program recommendation before it is made. Most local-government projects are a lot more complicated than people imagine. Take sewage disposal. To set up a sophisticated and safe sewage-disposal system requires application of many branches of science and technology. Council members aren't likely to challenge the findings of engineers with regard to sewer-system planning because most council members have neither the time nor the professional skill to investigate those findings.

   Any major question that comes before the council—sewage, water supply, street cleaning, police service, parks, finance, zoning, or whatever—requires

---

[10]International City Management Association, *The Municipal Year Book: 1987*, Table 3/7.

specialized knowledge. A 7-member council, or even a 50-member council cannot possibly know as much as the experts and bureaucrats working in the various city agencies about the practical questions it faces every day. This is not a sign that council members are ignorant; it is merely a sign that no single individual—or any 7-member council—can hope to know everything in this era of technology. On many issues the council simply must listen to experts. Otherwise it will bumble into stupid decisions that can prove very costly.

It would not be truthful to say that councils make no policy whatever. They do make policy, especially in smaller towns, but their ability to do this effectively without the aid of experts in the bureaucracy is limited, and their limitation increases with the size and complexity of the city.

Part-Time Members

Another reason city councils delegate authority is that most council members are part-timers who share their time between the city and their own means of livelihood. What time they can afford to spend on city business is often taken up with routine. Most city councils meet once a week, and by the time they have dealt with such things as approving the names of new streets, adopting variations to the city building code, approving sales of city property, and other miscellany, the meeting is nearly over. Little time is left for pondering the obscurities of large issues. Nor is there much other time during the week for deep thought about city problems. Naturally, there are some laudable exceptions among council members. Some, elected to what they thought would be part-time unpaid duty, end up working full time on city business, still without pay. Occasionally city councils are dominated by people who put city business before private business, but most councils simply thank their lucky stars that there are people over in the executive departments who are paid to study the city's problems full time.

Pay

Few cities pay council members enough to warrant their full-time attention to city business. Vast numbers of cities pay nothing; others pay a nominal amount. Some big cities, such as Los Angeles, New York, Detroit, Philadelphia, Boston, Pittsburgh, and Seattle, where council members meet often and work full time, pay a substantial salary to members, but rarely is that salary higher than the average income of American wage earners.

Box 10-1. Getting Elected Alderman

In Puxico, Missouri, Ronnie Loonie and John Roach were in a race for city alderman. Some people wondered if the race would ever end. The two candidates tied in the first election—87 to 87. A tie-breaking second election for the $25-a-month position was held at a cost of $250. The outcome was again a tie—96 each. The 877 residents of Puxico were again called to the polls, and a third tie occurred—96 to 96. Finally, after grumbling and threats of rebellion against the cost of these elections, the harassed voters of Puxico reelected John Roach by a thundering margin of 103 to 92.

Office and Staff

It is indicative of the low level of work expected of council members that they generally have no offices in city hall or any staff to research questions before the council. Nor does the council as a whole, or any of its committees, generally have staff assistance. In a sense the city council regards the bureaucracy as its staff, and this again is evidence of the dependency of the council on city bureaucrats.

Attitudes

Strange as it may seem, a large number of council members—perhaps even most of them—have no great inclination to belabor themselves solving the city's problems. This may simply be a personality characteristic of some council members, but often this reluctance to jump feet first into problem solving goes beyond personality, beyond disinterest, beyond laziness, beyond stupidity, and owes itself to simple fear.

Why would a council member fear to challenge proposals made by city bureaucrats? Well, in big cities—and we will confine ourselves for the moment to big cities that have mayors elected at large—the bureaucracy often speaks to the council through the mayor, who is usually a political force far greater than any single council member. The mayor huddles with his or her political and bureaucratic team and brings forth proposals to the council. Council members rarely see profit in fighting these proposals: to do so is to fight the mayor. The mayor's tremendous influence can be used to punish enemies and reward friends. The greater the mayor's power to punish and reward, the greater his or her gravitational pull upon each member of the council. One of the dirty tricks mayors can play on an uncooperative council member is to field an opponent against that member in the next council race. Uncooperative council members seldom run uncontested, and a contest costs a fortune in campaign expenses and a fortune in time, trauma, and sweat. No council member who has become a thorn in the side of the city's most influential politician can expect an easy time renewing his or her term on the council.

Furthermore, several (if not most) members of the council may be politically indebted to the mayor—may owe their seat to political support by the mayor. Some members of the council may also have economic ties with the mayor. Mayors control a lot of city spending and are not always above arranging for the city to place substantial orders with firms in which this or that member (or member's relatives or friends) has an economic interest. Mayors can also find jobs for people—sometimes inside and sometimes outside the city government—and can therefore influence council members by getting their friends and relatives hired. No complete list of a mayor's (or of anybody else's) influence can be made: influence works in wondrous and mysterious ways in a multitude of unsuspecting quarters.

Council–Mayor Disharmony

Still, the council is not powerless, nor is every member servile to the mayor. Mayors and council members do have their disputes. Sometimes clashes of ego and personality drive politicians to feud with each other. These feuds may range from mild competition to murderous hatreds. In 1978 a former member of the San Francisco board of supervisors killed Mayor George R. Moscone. Sometimes disputes are simply the result of party competition. Even local elections that are officially nonpartisan may be cuttingly partisan beneath the surface. Sometimes disharmony occurs between a mayor elected by the entire city and a council member elected by a district. In that case each has to keep a different set of constituents happy. What is good for the member's district may not be good for the city as a whole. The array of special interests backing a council member may be quite different from those backing a mayor: the mayor may, for example, be the favorite of downtown merchants, whereas a member of the council may get backing from merchants in outlying shopping centers.

Sometimes a mayor may, for all the above reasons, be a swords' point with the entire council. However, forces dictating cooperation with the mayor often exceed the forces of discord.

Unicameralism

Earlier in American history two-chambered city legislative bodies were common. Today city councils rarely have two houses; they are typically unicameral (*uni* means "one," *camera* means "chamber"). New York City's "two-house" legislative body is an exception.[11] Possible reasons for the decline of two chambers are the complexity of doing business when everything has to be cleared through two houses and the impracticality of having such a complex legislative system for small political units. Furthermore, in early American history cities seldom had any executive officers at all—the council was all there was to city government. Now, instead of separation between two houses of the council, we have separation between the council and the executive branch.

ELECTIONS

At-Large versus District Elections

Should each city council member be elected by voters of a separate district or by voters of the whole city (by **at-large elections** or by **district elections**)? This question is oft debated.[12] Some cities do it one way, some another, and some compromise by doing it both ways.

For At-Large An argument against electing council members by district (or ward) is that candidates are forced to emphasize what they will do for their

---

[11]New York has a city council and a board of estimate—not quite a two-house system, but the board of estimate does have budgetary, planning, and franchising functions.

[12]The National Municipal League has established a clearing house to assist state and local officials, as well as private citizens, who are studying and designing state and local representation systems. See *National Civic Review* (June 1980), p. 300. "An ideal local government electoral system should maximize effectiveness of ballots cast, voter participation at the polls, responsiveness of elected officials, access to decision makers, equity in representation and legitimization of the governing body," says Joseph F. Zimmerman in "The Single-Member District System: Can It Be Reformed?" *National Civic Review* (May 1981), p. 255.

district rather than what they will do for the city as a whole. This emphasis on district comes at the expense of emphasis on the city: what is good for a district may not be good for the whole city. For example, it may be good for a certain district to have an extra fire station, but as viewed from a larger perspective that station should possibly be somewhere else. When a council is made up of members from separate districts, they all too easily fall into the habit of logrolling. Rarely is anyone motivated to vote because "it's good for the city." This was the central argument used by the Chamber of Commerce in its successful effort in 1980 to change from a district system to an at-large system for electing supervisors in the city and county of San Francisco. The Chamber thought an at-large system would make supervisors accountable to the city as a whole and less subject to pressure from neighborhood groups.[13]

For Districts   Therefore, at first blush, at-large (rather than district) election of council members may seem better. But at-large election also has its faults. One of these faults is the impossible political position in which it puts minorities. Ethnic minorities and the poor often reside in well-defined areas of the city. Being minorities, they are outnumbered and outvoted in the typical city; therefore rarely does anybody from their area get elected to public office in at-large elections. In district elections—depending on the size of the districts—major minorities will generally be able to elect a council member. Within a particular district a minority, such as blacks, may be a majority and thus easily be able to elect a council member. Rigging the electoral system to allow minorities a chance to elect someone might give them a stronger sense of participation in public affairs, a stronger sense that government is at least partly theirs because one of them is elected to help run it. At-large elections can be a form of gerrymandering against minorities; conversely, election by districts can amount to gerrymandering in favor of minorities.

The Wealthy   There is one particular "minority," however, that does not always prefer the district system: it does not want its share of representation—it wants more than its share. That is the minority of the well-to-do. Although they commonly live in their own posh quarter of town, they are fond of at-large elections because they don't want to be limited to representation from one district. They have the money and often the spare time and motivation to become candidates. They do not wish to be limited to one seat on the council. They wish to have a crack at all seats, and in fact they often end up with most of the at-large seats. Furthermore, it must be conceded that their neighborhood includes a high proportion of the city's well-educated people, who often make unusually good public servants.

Districts Bring Government Close to the Voter   Election of council members by district helps bring government closer to all people, not just to minorities. Any council member who is elected from a district or ward is going to work hard to keep in contact with the people of his or her district—will attend all sorts of meetings within the district and do everything possible to get acquainted. This

---

[13]Proposition A, favoring at-large districts, passed by a narrow majority of 50.57 percent in the August 1980 election. From the *Colorado Springs Gazette Telegraph*, August 21, 1980, p. 9E.

helps bring city government close to home. A council member elected at large, who has no district, cannot possibly (except in a small town) hope to establish the same rapport with the entire city as he or she could with a narrower district. Civic leaders have decried the **alienation** or people from their government—the apathy of voters. This alienation and apathy must surely be caused in part by the increasing distance between citizen and government—not just geographic distance, but social distance. The bigger the city, the less likely anyone will have personal contact with officials. It is the absence of personal contact between citizen and government that germinates feelings among citizens that the government is something apart from them, alien and even hostile to them. Election of council members by district does not necessarily produce an intimate relationship between the people and their government, but it helps.

Apathy and At-Large Elections The kind of campaigning in at-large elections leaves the public somewhat listless. Of course, sadly, so does campaigning in most American elections. At-large elections do, however, exceed district elections in cultivation of stupor. Why? Partly because no candidate runs against a specific opponent: each runs against a whole field of semifaceless opponents. If you have, say, four vacant seats on the council, there might be eight or ten candidates running in one big scramble. The four who get the most votes are elected. You don't have issues drawn between two leading candidates for a specific seat, as you might in a district election where only one seat is up for grabs. When several at-large seats are to be filled and a platoon of candidates are rioting for those seats, the contest among them is more like a barroom brawl than a prizefight. It's hard for the voter-spectator to make sense out of the barroom scene with chairs and tables and bodies flying everywhere. It's easier to follow prizefights, where there are usually only two main combatants—it is easier to assess their merits as they square off one to one in district elections.

We mustn't make too much of this comparison, because both barroom brawls and prizefights are a lot more interesting to most voters than the average municipal election. As an election process, at-large elections are rather suffocating—so many candidates one can't keep them distinct. It's a blur of names, a blur of total strangers asking for your vote. Serious campaigning may last only a week or so. Election day stealthily approaches, and one fine day John Q. and Mary Citizen suddenly realize, by golly there's going to be a city election day after tomorrow. About 70 percent of them won't bother to vote, unless, of course, there's something about sex or race on the ballot.

At-large council elections featuring a great smudge of names asks too much of voters. No one, not even political science professors, can sort it all out and cast an intelligent ballot. Casting an intelligent ballot is hard enough anyway.

The blur of names in at-large elections maximizes the importance of name recognition and therefore maximizes the chance that incumbents will be reelected. Of course, incumbents always have an advantage in all elections because they are known, and people tend to vote for familiar names even if those names have become familiar through wrongdoing ("Better to be infamous than unknown"). When a crowd of people are running for office, name recognition spells victory. Therefore at-large elections degenerate into relentless gimmickry whose purpose is to momentarily sear the names (not the merits) of candidates into the dull consciousness of voters. Incumbents have it easier because they're already known. One wonders whether incumbents should be given so great an advantage that only death or resignation can remove them from office under normal circumstances. Election by district at least opens the possibility that challengers can make themselves as well known as incumbents.

Identical Mayor-Council Constituency   Finally, at-large election of council members gives every member the same constituency as the mayor, who (when elected by the people) also runs at-large. The well-known tendency of city councils to fall under the influence of strong mayors may be all the more pronounced where both the mayor and the council represent the same citywide combination of forces. If the council were elected by districts and the mayor elected at large, a certain useful tension between mayor and council might result.

Mix of At-Large and District Seats   Given the competing values of at-large versus district elections, some cities (about 60 of them) compromise by electing some of their council at large and some by districts.[14] Kansas City, for example, uses a six-six mix: six district-based and six at-large; the New Orleans council has five district seats and two at-large; the Buffalo council has nine district-based seats, five at-large seats, and a president elected at large. Two authors note that this mix of at-large and district seats "seems to have achieved a movement toward black representation equal to or exceeding their mathematical proportion" in the population of each of these three cities.[15] No doubt it also helps each sizable minority—whether racial, ethnic, religious, or economic—to elect one of its members to the governing body, if such a minority occupies a geographic "ghetto."

Federal Involvement

Because the system by which city-council members are elected can have a direct impact on the representation of racial minorities, federal lawmakers have concerned themselves with those systems. In fact, as one analyst says, "Congress and the United States Supreme Court in effect have imposed a federal 'Dillon's Rule' on state and local governments subject to the Voting Rights Act, since they must secure federal permission to make any change, no matter how minor or desirable, in electoral systems. . . ."[16] An interesting case of federal involvement occurred in the 1970s when the constitutionality of a New Orleans plan for council districts was litigated. The districts were laid out in a north–south pattern; the city's blacks lived mostly in a belt running east and west across the city.[17]

Nonpartisan Elections

In a nonpartisan election the ballot shows no party affiliations for the candidates.

---

[14]The sixth edition of the Model City Charter 1964 drafted by the National Municipal League included a mixed-district/at-large provision, the first time such a provision had appeared in the charter.

[15]Francine F. Rabinovitz and Edward K. Hamilton, "Alternative Electoral Structures and Responsiveness to Minorities," *National Civic Review* (July 1980), p. 384.

[16]Joseph F. Zimmerman, "Local Representation: Designing a Fair System," *National Civic Review* (June 1980), p. 307.

[17]Beer v. United States, 425 U.S. 130 (1975).

Class Bias? One might speculate that the affluent and the educated as a class tend to favor nonpartisan elections. Perhaps this is because nonpartisan elections discourage participation by lower-class voters. Since nonpartisan elections are often less exciting than partisan elections, bored lower-class voters are thought to be less likely to vote than bored middle-class and upper-class voters. Nonpartisan elections, by being more tedious and confusing, may also discourage the lower economic classes from voting: their interest in civic affairs is flickering at best. This leaves the political field clear for the "better" part of society and might explain why "solid citizens" as a class prefer nonpartisan elections.

Why Parties? Of course, nonpartisan elections are not always a plot to disenfranchise the poor and the ignorant. Those who favor nonpartisan elections may not always be exactly aware why they feel as they do. If anything, "solid citizens" probably have only a vague feeling that the razzmatazz of party politics is not necessary in local affairs—that "responsible people" do not need the help (or intrusion) of political parties when it comes to running municipal affairs. Furthermore, "responsible people" have little wish to be split among themselves by parties. It's enough to be split by differing views on civic problems, let alone by senseless partisan loyalties. Some opponents of local partisanism say there is no Democratic or Republican way of collecting garbage. Of course, the same argument could be applied to nearly everything government does. Differences between Republican and Democrats are hazy at best, no matter what the issue. Some party zealots insist, however, that there is, by Jove, a Democratic way of collecting garbage and a Republican way.

Where? Elections in about three-fourths of the cities are nonpartisan. Small cities are more likely than very large cities to have nonpartisan elections, although the ratio of partisan to nonpartisan elections remains remarkably constant across the board from large to small cities. Many supposedly nonpartisan elections are highly partisan beneath the surface.

When? Municipalities often hold elections in odd-number years, when there are no state or national elections. This helps voters concentrate on local issues, undistracted by the hoopla of those larger elections. It also helps isolate nonpartisan municipal elections from the partisan zeal of state and national elections. For further discussion of nonpartisan elections, see pages 67–68.

RURAL GOVERNMENT

In our classrooms and in our textbooks, political science professors tend to discuss topics that pertain mainly to big governments. Quite a bit of what we teach, therefore, does not really square with what is seen in small governments.[18] For example, we discuss city managers, but city managers are seldom seen in

[18]For a recent study of small government administration see Jim Seroka, ed., *Rural Public Administration: Problems and Prospects* (New York: Greenwood Press, 1986). This study includes writings by Jim Seroka, Frank Bryan, Cal Clark, Janet Clark, Garrey Carruthers, Clyde Eastman, Kathryn Renner Hansen, Terri Jeffrey, Alvin D. Sokolow, Edward B. Lewis, Keith Snavely, Lewis G. Bender, Thaddeus C. Zolty, J. Dixon Esseks, Robert B. McCallister, R. D. Sloan, Jr., and Ken Hibbeln.

"rural" government. They are found mostly in medium-sized cities. Many other big-city activities are completely missing in rural government or exist only at a primitive level, such as zoning, city planning, personnel administration, budgeting, air pollution control, parks and recreation, family social services, public information, central purchasing, data processing, and public housing. Even discussions of political parties, interest groups, and elections need to be qualified when applied to rural areas.

Diversity of Rural Government

"Rural governments" will be defined here as governments serving a population of anywhere from a handful up to 10,000 or so and situated well away from metropolitan areas. We tend to think they are all alike and extremely dull. But certainly they are not all alike. Some are counties; some are cities; some are towns, townships, or even special districts. Furthermore, no matter which type they are, rural governments may differ greatly in other ways: some are rich and some are poor; some are growing, some are shrinking; some are "liberal," some "conservative"; some are of this race and culture, some are of that race and culture; some are within "progressive" states and some are within slumberous states where change is not in vogue.

Despite their differences, most rural governments have two characteristics that seem chiefly the product of smallness: (1) a certain informality and (2) a stick-to-the-basics sparseness of function.

Sticking to the Basics

One reason rural governments stick to the basics is that their governing bodies are not generally in a mood to spend money on nonessentials. Rural voters may be more acutely aware than their big-city brethren that higher government spending results in higher taxes. One is not likely to find many people in small town America who think their town government has an inexhaustible source of money sufficient to satisfy any want. The relationship between what a city gives and what a city takes may be a good deal clearer in Sundance, Wyoming, than in Boston. When a rural government is deciding what to spend money on, it cannot assume that a huge portion of the public is entirely foggy about the source of that money. Also, when rural governments find themselves with a few extra dollars, they do not tend to embark on new services, but rather to spend more on basic services already in place.

What rural voters want mainly from their local governments are road maintenance, sewers, garbage disposal, education, public health, ambulance service, law enforcement, fire protection, libraries, welfare, agricultural extension, and whatever administrative services, assessment, and tax collection is necessary. In extremely small towns, fire protection is usually a volunteer activity, and the need for police is not quite what it would be in hoodlum-ridden cities. Nor is welfare likely to be as important as road maintenance in a county with more miles of road than inhabitants.

Of course, another reason (perhaps the main one) for the rather narrow scope of activities in rural government is simply the absence of a severe need for much else. The number of mental patients in Big Timber, Montana, would hardly justify a mental clinic there. Nor is parking such a problem that Big Timber must tackle it with a major government program. And so forth.

Management

Management within rural governments is often accomplished without hired managers. Generally the town council oversees everything collegially, and the mayor does not become chief administrator of the city. In many cases a small-town mayor is simply a member of the council who is elected to preside and thus to hold the ceremonial title, and the same is usually true of the presiding officer of a board of county commissioners in a rural county. Even where the mayor is separately elected by the town's voters, his or her administrative powers may not be great.

Usually the members of a small-town council or a small-county board of commissioners will do most of the administrative work themselves. Some of it they may do collectively (hiring new employees), some of it they will delegate on a continuing or temporary basis to individual members of the council. Just how work is divided will vary from place to place depending on the habits of the council and talents of its members. Naturally, when assignments are passed around, the particular expertise of the members is taken into account. If someone has experience in police work, that member will no doubt become "police commissioner" or "head of the police department." Such informal titles are commonly bestowed on members. The term "commissioner" is used even where the so-called commission form of government (see p. 255) is not used. If there are no specifically organized departments—only an employee or two in several different "policy areas," such as streets, water, sewer, garbage disposal, zoning, animal control, and liaison with other governments, then each of these would be put under the general supervision of one member, or perhaps of a committee of members. As in all human groups, the informal authority and influence of any council member over an activity of government really depends on how much confidence he or she inspires among the council members. Also, some of the larger governments do have full-time or part-time employees who serve as department heads, and the degree of authority they have in relation to the commissioner and to the council at large depends on all sorts of variables affecting human relations.

Commissioners in charge of these things often have considerable personal involvement with them on a daily basis; this may mean merely keeping an eye on the activity for the council, or it may mean actual management of the activity. The commissioner may become the spokesperson and advocate for activities under his or her wing (which, of course, raises the specter of logrolling among members—you vote for my things and I'll vote for yours).

Rural counties generally have bigger budgets and more employees than rural towns, and they tend to be more formally structured into departments. Thus rural-county commissioners generally are less intimately involved in day-to-day operations—their administrative duty might be described as loose oversight or simply as review of operations.

Personnel Administration

Personnel management in rural governments is generally very unstructured and informal. It is still quite rare to find anything similar to the elaborate personnel procedures found in big cities and big counties. Very few rural governments bother with any sort of formal recruitment and selection procedures. Job classification systems and job descriptions are seldom seen. Nor does one often find a merit system for making appointments—that is, basing appointments on competitive examinations. Independent civil service commissions rarely exist. Formal performance evaluations seldom happen, and there is generally no formal grievance procedure or established method of dealing with employee organizations, which in any case rarely exist.

When job vacancies occur in rural governments, recruitment (the effort to attract applicants) is not likely to be very strenuous. While most rural governments do publish vacancy announcements in a local newspaper, only rarely will such announcements be placed in professional job-finder publications with national or statewide circulation or even placed in the want ads of nearby large-city newspapers. Quite likely most people who learn of a vacancy will have heard about it by word of mouth.

Selection (the actual appointment of an applicant to the job) is usually done by the local legislative body (city council or county board), and the appointee is usually somebody well known to them who may already be on the payroll in some other capacity. Promotions from within seem to be preferred. Some states have laws that limit the freedom of local governments by imposing training standards for certain employees, such as police and firefighters. Also some states require all levels of government to follow certain equal-opportunity procedures. In addition, the federal government in some instances requires local governments to follow formal personnel procedures in those departments receiving federal aid. These state and federal mandates have introduced a certain level of "professionalism and formality" into the personnel practices of rural governments in some areas of activity, which has not been met with universal hostility by rural legislative bodies. As a matter of fact, many city and county elected officials are glad to have an excuse for not hiring those who clamor to be hired. State mandates for standards and procedures get them off the hook. Also the mandating of training standards and equal opportunity has motivated some rural governments to recruit more energetically beyond their own borders.

Promotions and pay raises in rural government rarely involve moving from one carefully defined position to another in a career development ladder. Position classification, job descriptions, and career development ladders hardly ever exist in rural governments that have only a small number of employees and that operate with a high degree of informality. The precise responsibilities of employees are apt to be rather vague and fluid. Employees' jobs expand and contract with the level of their competence and the nature of their personality. If the local legislative body likes an employee, it may cross their minds to give him or her a pay raise. When the council sits down to make its annual budget, it is not unusual for them to consider pay adjustments last after everything else is budgeted. Any uncommitted anticipated revenue visible at that stage might be applied to pay raises.

Formal grievance procedures hardly ever exist because individuals usually handle their differences informally, face-to-face, as problems come up. If formal procedures should happen to exist, they are frequently ignored; this is likewise the fate of formal procedures touching many other aspects of employment in rural governments. Life is too short to fool with them—it's easier to ignore them where possible. Employee unions and associations are also a rarity in rural government. Those that exist are usually composed of police officers in the larger places. If there should happen to be paid firefighters (but most are

Box 10-2. The Maze

"A maze of interlocking jurisdictions and levels of governments confronts average citizens in trying to solve even the simplest of problems. They do not know where to turn for answers, who to hold accountable, who to praise, who to blame, who to vote for or against."
President Ronald Reagan
State of the Union Address
January 26, 1982

volunteer), they too may be organized. The remaining public employees are normally bunched together into a single separate bargaining organization, if per chance they are organized at all. Public employee organizations are encouraged in some states, such as California, more than in others. In California local governments are required by state law to meet and confer with employee bargaining units.

METROPOLITAN GOVERNMENT

The multiplicity of governments in **metropolitan areas** makes government all the more difficult. Take the St. Paul–Minneapolis metropolitan area. A recent survey found some 273 governments there, including 7 counties, 140 cities, 49 townships, 49 school districts, 22 other special districts, and miscellaneous other governing bodies.[19] A similar glut of government afflicts every large center of population in North America. Some areas have managed to achieve a semblance of order: Nashville, Jacksonville, Indianapolis, Miami, Toronto, St. Paul–Minneapolis, to mention a few notable examples. Most others wallow in a nightmarish entanglement of political jurisdictions.

Probably none of the local governments in a typical metropolitan area covers the entire area geographically. Nor is it likely that any single local government has the power to perform all the functions that need performing in the area. Thus to cover the entire area with an entire range of services, a collection of separate governments piles up. Several methods are used to overcome this chaos of government within metropolitan areas.[20] None of them is an easy solution: each has its difficulties and shortcomings.

Annexation

The Old English word *annexen* meant "to bind." Today the word *annex* means "to add a smaller thing to a larger thing." **Annexation** as we use the term means the process of adding a piece of territory to a city. Normally annexation occurs only after both sides—the city on the one hand, the people living in the territory

---

[19]John J. Harrigan and William C. Johnson, *Governing the Twin Cities Region* (Minneapolis: University of Minnesota Press, 1978), p. 4.

[20]For a review of several interlocal approaches to regional governance see David B. Walker, "Snow White and the 17 Dwarfs: From Metro Cooperation to Governance," *National Civic Review* (January–February 1987), pp. 14–28.

to be annexed on the other—have given their consent. Commonly the city council gives consent on behalf of the city; people living in the territory to be annexed give their consent by popular vote. Sometimes a popular vote on both sides is required.

Annexation is not a major method of dealing with the chaos of metropolitan government in most places in the United States. It has had only limited value in dealing with the basic problem, but annexations do take place and it is worth knowing something about the process.

Encircling Suburbs   Annexation of the entire metropolitan area by the central city would give the area coherent government. However, this is not possible for most great central cities because they are already surrounded by incorporated suburbs. Cities cannot annex each other, unless one of them first decides to disincorporate, an extremely rare occurrence—many suburbs incorporated in the first place just to avoid annexation by their giant neighbor. Most big cities are imprisoned by a solid wall of **suburbs** on all borders. As a city grows in population the people along its outskirts become alarmed by the threat of annexation. They don't want to become involved in the social, economic, and political evils of the big city. Suburbanites living in identifiable neighborhoods also fear loss of identity if swallowed up by the metropolis, and some fear higher taxes. Taxes could be higher because big cities have all sorts of problems that suburbs have until recently been spared. Most of the crime and poverty in metropolitan areas is located in the core city, where more police, more fire fighters, more welfare workers, more welfare money, more judges, more urban renewal, more of nearly everything done by government is needed. Thousands, even millions, of people have moved beyond city limits to avoid the crowding, corruption, filth, poverty, crime, laws, and high taxes of mammoth cities. Suburbanites usually fight like tigers against annexation, and as a last resort they incorporate themselves into independent towns.

Unilateral Annexation   Some states have laws that allow cities to annex neighboring unincorporated areas even when the inhabitants of those areas don't want to be annexed. Usually these laws allowing **unilateral annexation** apply only to areas completely or nearly surrounded by the city. These islands and peninsulas of unincorporated territory impede the orderly delivery of city services. Streets run through them, and yet the city cannot regulate their width or look after their upkeep: a wide boulevard might suddenly degenerate into a narrow battleground of potholes and mud. Similar impediments to water lines, sewers, fire protection, and so on, exist. Such islands are like permanent guests in one's home: they aren't quite members of the family, yet they never go away. They benefit from being within the family but are not full dues-paying members of it. People in such areas about to be annexed against their will often cry that their "democratic right to vote" is being denied. Perhaps so. Yet without annexation the city would be forced undemocratically and against its will to serve as permanent host to enclaves of people who use the city, drive on its streets, fill its parks, attend its auditoriums, visit its museums, roam its galleries, and in general profit from being within a great city while not paying city taxes to support any of these benefits.

Box 10-3. The Ten Largest Metropolitan Areas

(1987 Population in round numbers)

1. New York	18.0 million
2. Los Angeles-Long Beach	13.0 million
3. Chicago	8.1 million
4. San Francisco	5.9 million
5. Philadelphia	5.8 million
6. Detroit	4.6 million
7. Boston	4.0 million
8. Dallas	3.7 million
9. Houston	3.6 million
10. Washington, D.C.	3.5 million

Cost Cities aren't always eager to annex every piece of property they can get their hands on. State laws or city charters commonly require cities to offer equal service to all their residents. Annexation of unincorporated territory might stagger the city budget: sewers and waterlines would have to be laid; streets paved, lighted, and policed; parks built; the poor looked after, and so on. To get these benefits, a few suburban neighborhoods have eagerly petitioned for annexation and been refused. However, the most common attitude of suburbs is to resist annexation and to acquire, meanwhile, at least a few essential city services by purchasing them, by forming low-cost special districts, or by incorporating themselves.

To help overcome the reluctance of suburbanites to be annexed, some states have laws freezing tax rates within newly annexed territory for a certain number of years, usually two or three. Thus residents of a newly annexed area would not have to start paying higher city taxes immediately. At the same time, such a freeze gives the city time to install all services before imposing its taxes.

Extraterritorial Jurisdiction

Another partial answer to the need for metropolitan-wide government is to give cities certain powers beyond their boundaries. This is at heart a form of limited annexation and suffers many of the same shortcomings. It is a wholly inadequate answer to the need for metropolitan-wide government. **Extraterritorial jurisdiction** does, however, help cities regulate developments on their edge and prevent undesirable things from happening there. Extraterritorial jurisdiction usually gives a city the power to zone beyond its boundaries for a certain distance, to apply building and subdivision regulation, to enforce health and safety laws in the area, and to control nuisances. Cities with extraterritorial jurisdiction are also usually allowed to extend various city services, such as water, beyond their boundaries. In fact, extension of services is the most common form of extraterritoriality.

The main complaint against extraterritorial jurisdiction is that it fails to grant residents subject to extraterritorial jurisdiction the right to vote in the government that has jurisdictions. Although this may seem unfair, it would perhaps also be unfair to force cities to suffer nuisances, health risks, and threats to safety adjacent to their borders and to helplessly watch the growth of cheaply built subdivisions that may (together with their problems) soon come within the city through annexation.

City-County Mergers

One way to simplify governments is to get rid of several by uniting them into one government. **City-county mergers** exist to one degree or another in about a dozen major metropolitan areas: Baltimore, Denver, St. Louis, San Francisco, Boston, Philadelphia, New Orleans, New York, Baton Rouge, Jacksonville, Nashville, and Honolulu. New York City is actually composed of five counties.[21] Technically some of these unions were brought about by the *separation* of the city from the county: separated cities then acquire county power within their borders and thus become city-counties. The city-counties of Baltimore, Denver, San Francisco, and St. Louis were formed that way.

Annexation The growing population of city-counties very often spills over their borders. When a city-county then decides to expand by annexation, a legal question may rise whether a county can annex at all. Does a city-county acquire new territory the way cities acquire new territories or the way counties acquire new territory? A city-county is neither a city nor a county, but both—a separate breed. When a city annexes, a vote of the people in the annexed areas is usually required, but when a county strikes off a piece of neighboring county, then normally the entire electorate of the neighboring county votes, not just the electorate of the territory being stricken off. For a long time the city and county of Denver was allowed to take pieces of abutting counties by citylike annexation procedures. To stop Denver's "aggression," suburban voters managed to place a constitutional amendment on the ballot requiring Denver to annex like a county rather than a city, thus requiring the vote of the entire abutting county before any part of its territory could be annexed to Denver. The amendment passed.

The ideal city-county consolidation may be that of Honolulu, which includes the entire island of Oahu—ideal in the sense that metropolitan Honolulu is not likely to spread beyond the city-county "line" unless people are prepared to drive their cars on the Pacific Ocean.

Partial Unions of Cities and Counties Some city-county unions are only partial, such as Baton Rouge with East Baton Rouge Parish. The city of Baton Rouge still exists, but most of its powers were transferred to the parish when the parish acquired home-rule powers. Both a city council and a parish council remain, but all seven members of the city council serve on the parish council, which also includes two members from areas of the parish beyond the city limits. The two governments share the same "mayor-president," who supervises the administrations of the two governments, prepares their budgets, presides over their meetings, and so on. City functions are limited to such things as garbage collection, street lighting, sidewalk maintenance, and police and fire protection.

[21]Bronx, Kings (Brooklyn), New York (Manhattan), Queens, Richmond (Staten Island).

Dade County, Florida, is another example of partial city-county consolidation. Actually Dade is not as much an example of consolidation as of how a county can be strengthened to the point where the cities within it are left with a good deal less reason for existence. This strengthening of the county happened in 1956, when Florida voters amended their state constitution to give Dade County home-rule powers. County voters then adopted a home-rule charter that gave the county vast new power to perform most municipal functions throughout the county, both inside and outside cities. Any such function the county doesn't want to tackle, it can let cities carry out under performance standards set by the county. The county can take any such function away from a city that fails to meet those standards. Cities are allowed to provide police and fire protection and do a variety of other things.

Dade County does not have the power to abolish cities or to alter their boundaries. Besides Miami there are some 22 other towns. The county is governed by a nine-member board of county commissioners, eight of whom are elected at large, although each of the eight must live in a different district of the county. A ninth member of the board (also elected at large) is mayor and chairperson of the board. The board appoints a county manager who administers the county much like a city manager, appointing the heads of such departments as finance, personnel, planning, and law and creating other departments as he or she sees fit.

All is not peace and harmony between Dade County and its cities. A continuous clash of wills goes on between those who want their cities to have more power and those who want the county to virtually extinguish the cities. The division of responsibilities between cities and the county is not perfectly efficient; cities clutch for a piece of the action.

In some metropolitan areas city-county unity is sought through an attempt to establish a third unit of government to handle areawide functions. This has been done in Toronto, to be discussed shortly.

Opposition Resistence to city-county consolidation comes in part from the same people who resist annexations—often from suburbanies who don't want to be swallowed up by the city. Rural people living in the county also look with apprehension upon city-county consolidation: it would rob them of their county government, which is closer to them psychologically than any big-city government could be.

How Often Does City-County Consolidation Occur? Rarely. Before there can be any such consolidation it usually has to be preceded by an amendment to the state constitution permitting it. This in itself is a great hurdle. If such an amendment should pass, then at least two more votes are usually required—that of the city electorate and that of the county electorate. Some 50 or 60 city-county consolidations have been attempted since World War II, but the vast majority of them have failed at the polls. Only one city-county consolidation has occurred since 1980: Houma with Terrebonne Parish in Louisiana, January 1984.

City-States

Why not solve the problem of multiple governments by simply turning our great metropolitan areas into states—**city-states?** That would get rid of the city, the county, the special districts, and—importantly—the state itself. By creating a new state consisting only of metro, the metro area could be free to legislate answers to its own problems without too much external interference. This, of course, is a slightly whimsical idea, offered from time to time as an "ideal" solution by college professors to stimulate classroom discussion. It is a truly "academic" (impractical) solution.

Why impractical? Because the United States Constitution does not permit the dismemberment of any state without the consent of that state, and it seems highly unlikely that Illinois would let go of Chicago, or Texas Houston, for example. Still, the day may come when a state might gladly rid itself of its great metropolitan sores, rid itself of the constant and growing demands for financial aid from such places. The state of New York might one day say to itself, "Maybe New York City would, after all, make a fine state all by itself." However, when a city realizes it gets more from the state than it gives, it may lose all passion to be separate. If Washington, D.C., were to achieve statehood, the result would be a city-state, and obviously it would not be necessary to detach the city from any existing state.

Certainly the top 20 or so metropolitan areas would make substantial states. About half the states have smaller annual budgets than the city of New York. Finding suitable names for these new states might be a headache. Could we call New York City the "state of New York"? We already have one of those.

Metropolitan Districts

A New Level   One way to restore order in metropolitan areas is to create still one more government—a supergovernment that spans the entire area. Give this supergovernment all or some of the powers possessed by the dozens or hundreds of other governments within the area. This new level of government might be totally independent of other governments in the area, or it might be their agent. The agent system—that is, the "federal" arrangement whereby existing governments jointly control a new areawide level of government—has been proposed and defeated in Boston, Oakland, Pittsburgh, and St. Louis. The system is working however, in Toronto, Canada.

Toronto   The municipality of Metropolitan Toronto, as the new level of government is named, has a 33-member legislative body called the *metropolitan council.* Twelve of the 33 represent the city of Toronto. The remaining 21 are distributed among five other areas into which the municipality of Metropolitan Toronto is divided. These five divide the 21 seats proportionally according to the population. No council members are elected specifically for the purpose of sitting on the metropolitan council. All get their seats by virtue of holding some office in the city of Toronto or in the other five areas of metro. For example, the mayor of each member unit is a member of the metropolitan council. Others become members by virtue of their election by a certain margin of vote to the city councils or member cities. Still others become members because they are controllers of member cities. (A *controller* is a financial officer.) This indirect election is criticized because it leaves the total electorate of metro, acting as one body of voters, without any direct role in picking members of the metro council. The dual role and divided loyalties of council members are also criticized.

The chairperson of the metropolitan council is a full-time official appointed by the council. He has little formal power other than to preside over meetings, but being a full-time employee, he exercises influence over the council because he is conversant with matters with which the council deals.

Metro does not by any means exercise all governmental power within its territory. Functions are divided between metro and the member cities. Some functions are dealt with by both metro and the cities. Metro has exclusive jurisdiction over such things as assessment of property, borrowing of money, regional parks, libraries, golf courses, zoos, expressways, arterial roads, traffic lights, public transit, water distribution, sewage-disposal plants, air pollution, welfare, police, administration of justice, business licensing, and civil defense. Area municipalities, however, retain control of such things as zoning, local parks, local roads, sidewalks, street lighting, local distribution of water, collection of water bills, garbage collection, operation of the school system, public health service, fire protection, dog and marriage licensing, and building codes. Many basic functions are, as you can see, curiously divided between the cities and metro—for example, police (metro) and fire (city).

Disturbing the Status Quo Special districts, you will recall, are often defined as "one-purpose" governments. Most **metropolitan districts** are exactly that—they are special districts whose boundaries cover the entire metro area, and they usually confine themselves to one function, such as transportation, parks, or sewage disposal. But multipurpose (as well as single-purpose) special districts are possible and might be clapped on top of an entire metro area like a lid on a can of worms. Such a special district would do all or part of what the preexisting governments were doing. The idea may sound good in theory and might work well in practice but, like so many other solutions to metropolitan government, requires a considerable rocking of the political boat to establish. The status quo has its defenders. No plan that involves disturbing powerful political vested interests stands much chance of being adopted. Many officeholders and their friends and allies wildly resist any proposal to upset their niche of power. This is one fundamental reason why all proposals to change the formal structure of government in metropolitan areas encounter trouble. The most practical solutions to metropolitan problems are often those that retain existing power structures and existing governments but encourage cooperation among them. This seems pallid compared with other solutions, but it is better than nothing. Nothing is apt to result from more Draconian proposals.

Cooperation

Council of Governments If the multiplicity of governments in metropolitan areas is the main problem, and if all those myriad governments have enough political support to keep themselves alive, and if all else fails to curb them, then the next best solution is to get them to cooperate—to set up some kind of formal machinery to help them cooperate. There are thousands of examples of cooperation among governments, and there are dozens of places where quasi governments have been set up in metropolitan areas to foster metropolitan-wide cooperation. Such a quasi government is often called a **council of governments.**

The typical council of governments is composed of representatives from the various governments within the metropolitan area. Sometimes the number of representatives from each government depends on population: a large central city would have more representatives on the council than a small suburb. Participation is almost always voluntary; any government can withdraw at any time. The typical council has almost no independent source of revenue, and depends almost entirely on contributions from member governments. (Councils of government have occasionally received some federal and state revenue.)

Power Typically a council of governments has no power to order anyone to do anything; it is a recommending body, a research body. The council staff might, for example, study the transportation system of the entire metro area, devise a transportation plan, and recommend it to the council. If the council adopts it, then it is hoped the member governments will carry out their part of the plan. However, execution remains entirely optional; member governments all too often don't carry through, may grow disenchanted with the council and withhold financial support, or may drop out entirely. That is why the major thrust of a council of governments is likely to be in the direction of "idea spawning" rather than concrete action. Thinking is safer than doing.

Twin Cities The Metropolitan Council of the Twin Cities Area is different from the typical council of governments. First of all, it was not created by the voluntary and joint action of cities and counties in the area. On the contrary, it was created by the state legislature of Minnesota in 1967—was imposed, one might say. Voters of the region did not have a chance to vote the plan up or down, although the legislature had within it at the time a large number of Twin Cities–area members. The Metropolitan Council of the Twin Cities Area is also different from the typical council of governments in that the Twin Cities council is not made up of representatives of governments within its boundaries. The council is composed of 16 members appointed from districts established by the Minnesota legislature. Nor does the Metropolitan Council of the Twin Cities Area depend wholly on financial contributions by member cities—there are no member cities. Instead it is financed by a property tax.

Nevertheless, the Metropolitan Council of the Twin Cities Area is intended to be primarily an agency for planning policies rather than executing them, although it does have some indirect control over the Metropolitan Sewer Board and the Metropolitan Transit Commission and possesses some other powers that make it almost like a new level of government. Areas to which the council directs its attention include air pollution, regional parks and open space, water pollution, solid-waste disposal, tax-assessment practices, storm-drainage facilities, and so on. The council also helps local governments within its boundaries get federal grants by reviewing their applications.

Contracts

Another well-known form of cooperation among governments is the selling of services by one government to another. The most famous case of such buying and selling has been that of Lakewood, California, and the county of Los Angeles: Lakewood buys almost everything from the county—police, fire, planning, and so on.

TWO CITIES

Denver: Mile High Metropolis

If today General James W. Denver were to rise from his grave in Ohio and return to Colorado he might be surprised to see what the city named after him has become. Actually, the founding and naming of Denver was a rather trivial event at the time. Only a sprinkling of people inhabited what is now Colorado: a few Indian tribes and some scattered hunters, trappers, and gold seekers. In fact, much of the so-called Pikes Peak region was considered virtually uninhabitable. The state of Colorado did not yet exist: much of the area was merely a distant zone of the Kansas Territory.

However, in 1858 several hundred dollars worth of gold was panned from Cherry Creek where it joins the South Platte River. Word of this discovery quickly spread east. A group of Kansans arrived and prepared to get rich. They established their camp on land that was not exactly theirs, but nevertheless they laid claim to it and called it Denver after Governor James W. Denver of the Kansas Territory. (Some say they wanted the governor's blessing for their disputed claim.)

On the other side of Cherry Creek, the group who made the original gold strike had set up the town of Auraria. For about a year there was considerable rivalry between Denver and Auraria, but soon the two settlements merged as Denver. Auraria survives today chiefly as the name of a college campus in Denver.

In 1859 the full force of Colorado's gold rush hit. Many diggings were in the mountains just west of Denver. Thousands flocked to the region. Denver quickly became a transportation and supply hub and remains so today.

Today almost 2 million of Colorado's 3.3 million people live in the Denver metropolitan area. Colorado is often equated with Denver. The successes and failures of Denver become those of Colorado. That is why the entire state today keeps a wary eye on Denver's air pollution problem. It is not good for the ski business in Aspen, the tourist business in Estes Park, or the space enterprises of Colorado Springs if Denver has a brown cloud. After all, the trade mark of Colorado is pristine air, blue skies, snow-capped peaks, and scenery galore. If that image is broken in Denver, all Colorado suffers.

Colorado and Denver are locked into an uneasy marriage. Across the decades, each has tried to rule the other. Around the turn of the century most Denver residents were convinced that politicians in the state capitol were trying to dominate their city. As proof of this, they pointed to the Denver Fire and Police Board established by the legislature in 1891 to run the public safety departments in Denver and grant saloon licenses there. Members of the board were appointed by the governor, not by anybody in Denver. The governor's manipulation of this board led to one of the strangest chapters in Colorado history: an actual military confrontation between the governor of Colorado and city officials in Denver. To subdue Denver's resistance against state control, the governor ordered the First Regiment of Colorado Infantry and the Chaffee Light Artillery with 400 militiamen, two field pieces, and two Gatling guns drawn up in front of the Denver City Hall to quell the dissidents inside.

Many Denverites felt harassed by state politicians and also by vice, corruption, and bossism fostered by those politicians. Denver found a solution to its woes in the Progressive Movement that brought a wave of state and local reform across America in the early 1900s. Political corruption was the main target of Progressives. They saw municipal home rule as a splendid remedy against the intrusions of corrupt state legislatures into local affairs. To Denver home rule could mean freedom from the state legislature, freedom from the governor, and even to some extent freedom from state courts. The idea was joyfully embraced by Denver. And shortly a combination of political forces in 1902 succeeded in amending the state constitution to give home rule to Denver.

The city not only gained constitutional home rule (freedom from state laws except those of statewide concern), but also achieved liberation from Arapahoe County of which it was previously an unhappy part. Denver was made both a city and a county. It remains today the only city-county in the state.

As a county, Denver today carries on the usual functions of county government, serving as a field office of state government to bring various state services to the people within its boundaries. Thus many Denver officials act both in a county capacity and in a city capacity—the chief of police not only does what a city chief of police does, but also what a typical county sheriff does.

Possessing home rule, Denver was free to write and adopt a charter organizing itself as it saw fit. Denver chose a mayor-council system and endowed its elected mayor with power to appoint most key executives of the city, such as the chief of police.

Although Denver is a city-county, it has more of the trappings of a city than of a county. For example, it has a mayor, which obviously counties do not have. It has a board of council members (popularly known as the city council) rather than a board of county commissioners. It has no independently elected sheriff, clerk, coroner, assessor, treasurer, or surveyor such as one finds in almost all Colorado counties. Rather, these functions are done by officials with various titles appointed by the mayor. Denver has no partisan elections. Like all Colorado cities its elections are nonpartisan (county elections are partisan).

In the process of setting Denver up as a county as well as a city, it was given a sizable chunk of rural territory extending well beyond the populated area of the city. This was hailed as a solution to the metropolitan problem—no independent suburbs could crowd the edges of Denver. But that was long ago when the population of Denver was only 140,000, a fraction what it is today. To make a long story short, the city grew to its boundaries, and other cities blossomed around its edges. Today Denver itself has about 518,000 residents, but the Denver metropolitan area has about 1,847,000. Thus, more than two-thirds of area residents do not live in Denver but in numerous adjacent cities, such as Aurora (over 200,000) and Lakewood (over 100,000), which completely encircle and imprison Denver.

Originally the city and county of Denver was allowed to annex like a city rather than like a county. The difference is this: when a county wishes to annex a piece of another county, it has to get the prior consent of a majority of all the voters in the other county, not just the voters in the area to be annexed. A city has it much easier: basically all it needs is consent of the voters in the area being annexed.

Over the decades the city and county of Denver, using its city-like powers, did increase its area by one-third, annexing sparsely settled lands. Then it started bumping up against densely populated neighbors who valued their independence from Denver and its problems. Fear of annexation was especially passionate in the 1970's when various controversial problems afflicted Denver's school district. The city-county has only one school district, whose boundaries are coterminous with it. Thus any area annexed by Denver, automatically becomes part of Denver's single district. This fact generated more resistance to any possible annexation by Denver. A drive was successfully mounted to amend Colorado's constitution changing the way Denver annexes from that of a city to that of a county. It is now virtually impossible for Denver, acting as a county, to annex new territory.

One of the great riddles of modern America is how to efficiently govern large metropolitan areas. Denver, like so many other metropolitan areas, is a fermenting brew of cities, towns, counties, special districts, and school districts. Efforts have been made to bring forth some sort of metropolitan-wide government, and Colorado's Service Authority Act of 1972 invites this. But in 1973 a proposed urban service authority for the area was defeated by Denver voters. There is, however, a metropolitan Denver sewage disposal district that provides sewage treatment for about 75 percent of the area. Also, a regional transportation district was created by the legislature to operate a mass transit system. An urban drainage and flood control district was established by the state legislature. And there is a Denver regional council of governments representing the various counties and cities in the Denver metropolitan area. The council studies regional problems and makes recommendations. Denver itself provides water service to number of surrounding areas.

It has been said that creation of the city and county of Denver is a reform that failed. Certainly this would be true if its sole purpose was to create one single regional government.

New York: The Imperial City

Some residents of New York City might be saddened to see their town ultimately surpassed in population by Los Angeles, Chicago, or some other Johnny-come-lately place. Right now there is nothing to worry about: New York's 8 million easily outstrips the combined population of Chicago and Los Angeles, which claim only about 3 million apiece. New York has long been America's biggest city. Even when its population was only 30,000 about 200 years age, it was a great metropolis of the new nation.

Eventually some challengers appeared upon the horizon. The 1890 census showed that the four largest cities in America were New York City (1.5 million), Chicago (1.1 million), Philadelphia (1 million), and Brooklyn (0.8 million). Chicago was rising fast, and Brooklyn, just across the East River, was growing.

Ten years later, however, the 1900 census showed New York City more than twice as big as it was in the previous census and twice as big as its nearest rival Chicago. By a monumental consolidation of local governments in the vicinity of New York Harbor, the state legislature made New York City into a colossus. This consolidation didn't come to pass easily or quickly. For half a century advocates of consolidation had been hard at work on the project. They included the Municipal Union Society, Andrew Haswell Green (it was his life-long hobby), and much of the New York press. Several events across the decades were harbingers of consolidation. For example, part of the Bronx, an area north of Manhattan Island on the "mainland" just across the Harlem River, was annexed by New York City in 1874. The Bronx (a corruption of Bronck, the family name of some early settlers in the region) was then a rural district of scattered villages, and no one dreamed there would be a Yankee Stadium. Still more of the Bronx, the part east of the Bronx River, was annexed in 1895.

And there were other happenings that pointed to the future. When Brooklyn was incorporated as a city in 1834, the incorporation was opposed by New York City's mayor and board of aldermen. Having lost that battle, the city prevailed upon the state legislature in 1857 to create a metropolitan police board, with boundaries including both New York City and Brooklyn and most other areas that are included in today's city. In 1866 a board of health and a board of excise were created with comparable boundaries.

But this was not enough. The advocates of metropolitan union labored in every political arena, especially within the state legislature to achieve their goal. There were many defeats before, finally, in 1898 Thomas C. Platt, a long-time state party leader, persuaded the legislature in Albany to pass a consolidation law. In that law, all of Queens, Brooklyn, and Staten Island were added to New York City. In total, five counties now comprised the enlarged city: New York County, Bronx County, Queens County, Kings County, and Richmond County. And each of these counties, in addition to being a county, also became a borough (semiautonomous neighborhood) of the city of New York. The county governments were stripped of almost all functions and left with only a skeleton crew. The boroughs were allowed a few officers (including a president) and possessed several independent powers, but most of the authority in the City of New York became vested in a highly centralized city government.

Three of these five boroughs have names different from the names of the counties they overlap. Manhattan Borough is coterminous with New York County, Staten Island Borough is coterminous with Richmond County, and the Brooklyn Borough is coterminous with Kings County. Queens Borough and Bronx Borough have the same names as their coterminous counties.

Of the five boroughs, Brooklyn is by far the most populous with some 2.5 million inhabitants. Manhattan (the original New York City) has about 1.5 million, as does the Bronx. Queens has about 2 million. However, Staten Island is "almost rural" with only about 300,000 residents.

And that is how the imperial city grew.

SUMMARY

Cities are municipal corporations created by the state at the request of a certain percentage of local residents. Municipal corporations are somewhat comparable to private business corporations in that they are both chartered by the state and are both "artificial persons" in a legal sense: they can own property, sell property, sue and be sued, borrow money, loan money, enter into contracts, and carry on similar business operations. Both are created to serve the special needs of their members. The members of a municipal corporation are the residents within its boundaries (Members of private corporations are their stockholders.) Although created primarily to serve the special governmental needs of its inhabitants, every city remains an instrumentality of the state and must obey state laws, many of which require cities to do, or refrain from doing, various things. The power of cities is narrowly construed by the courts according to Dillon's rule.

States enact general laws providing for the incorporation of cities. To be incorporated and to receive a city charter, groups of residents petitioning for municipal incorporation simply follow the procedures set forth in laws that pertain to general classes of cities rather than to any specific city. Cities incorporated under such general laws are called *general-law cities.* These general laws provide for certain specific forms of governmental organization and grant certain specific powers to cities. Some states also allow cities home-rule powers to write their own charter, design their own form of government, and draft their own list of functions. Cities organized that way are called *home-rule cities.* Sometimes home rule is granted to cities by ordinary legislation (statutory home rule), and sometimes by the state constitution (constitutional home rule).

About half of America's cities use the mayor-council form of government, about 40 percent use the council-manager form, and about 3 percent use the commission form. In the commission form each member of the city council (or *commission,* as it is called) also serves as head of a major city department. In the council-manager form the city council appoints a city manager to administer the city; the mayor's job is usually ceremonial. In the mayor-council form there is no city manager; the city council either attempts to manage the bureaucracy itself or has a strong mayor who does so.

Mayors are classified as *strong* or *weak* depending on how much appointive power they have. A weak mayor has virtually no power of appointment. A strong mayor usually has considerable power to appoint major agency heads within the government. A mayor may be classified as weak yet be strong in a political sense. All mayors act as a symbol of their city at many ceremonial occasions, but strong mayors also act as chief administrators. Big-city mayors often have trouble controlling the bureaucracy upon which they rely so heavily. Mayors who wish to guide the city along innovative paths encounter resistance from those in the community and the bureaucracy who have vested interest in the status quo.

Most city councils have around six members. City councils are commonly thought of as legislative bodies, but their legislative activity is greatly influenced by the municipal bureaucracy. This is partly because the bureaucracy possesses facts relevant to issues before the council and partly because most city councils are composed of part-time amateurs. Strong mayors, agency heads, city managers, and the bureaucracy are deeply involved in city policy making.

Members of city councils may be elected at large or by districts. Each method has its advantages and disadvantages. Some cities compromise by electing half of the council at large and half by districts. Most city elections are nonpartisan.

In our classrooms and in our textbooks, political science professors tend to discuss topics that pertain mainly to big governments. Quite a bit of what we have to teach, therefore, does not really square with what is seen in small governments. For example, we discuss city managers, but in general city managers do not exist in "rural" government. They are found mostly in medium-sized cities. Many other big-city activities are completely missing in rural government or exist only at a primitive level, such as zoning, city planning, personnel administration, budgeting, air pollution control, parks and recreation, family social services, public information, central purchasing, data processing, and public housing.

Governing metropolitan areas is made particularly difficult by the multiplicity of governments. Great metro areas may have more than a hundred governments operating within them. Several methods are used to overcome this chaos of government. They include annexation, extraterritorial jurisdiction, city-county mergers, metropolitan districts, and cooperation. No solution is easy to accomplish, and each has its shortcomings.

Denver and New York are examples of big cities that have tried at one or another time in their histories to incorporate within their borders as much of the surrounding suburbia as possible. In this they have been only temporarily successful.

SUGGESTIONS FOR FURTHER READING

BANFIELD, EDWARD, C., *The Unheavenly City Revisited*. Boston: Little, Brown, 1974.
———, and JAMES Q. WILSON, *City Politics*. New York: Random House, 1963.
BOLLENS, JOHN C., and HENRY J. SCHMANDT, *The Metropolis: Its People, Politics and Economic Life* (4th ed.). New York: Harper & Row, Pub., 1981.
BROWNSTONE, MEYER, and T. J. PLUNKETT, *Politics and the Reform of Local Government in Metropolitan Winnipeg*. Berkeley and Los Angeles: University of California Press, 1983.
CARALEY, DEMETRIOS, *City Governments and Urban Problems: A New Introduction to Urban Politics*. Englewood Cliffs, N.J.: Prentice-Hall, 1977.
HORAN, JAMES F., and G. THOMAS TAYLOR, JR., *Experiments in Metropolitan Government*. New York: Holt, Rinehart & Winston, 1977.
JOHNSON, WILLIAM, and JOHN J. HARRIGAN, "Innovation by Increments: The Twin Cities as a Case Study in Metropolitan Reform," *Western Political Quarterly* (June 1978), 206–18.
KOCH, EDWARD I., *Mayor*. New York: Warner Books, Inc., 1985.
MORGAN, DAVID G. *Managing Urban America: The Politics and Administration of American Cities* (2nd ed.). Monterey, Calif.: Brooks/Cole Publishing Co., 1984.
NATIONAL MUNICIPAL LEAGUE, *Model City Charter* (New York ed. 1964).
ROYKO, MIKE, *Boss: Richard J. Daley of Chicago*. New York: Dutton, 1971.
SEROKA, JIM, *Rural Public Administration*. Westport, Conn.: Greenwood Press, 1986.
"SYMPOSIUM: THE AMERICAN CITY MANAGER," *Public Administration Review* (January/February 1971), 6–46.

11
money

PREVIEW

WHAT'S IN A BUDGET?

The professor decided to exterminate his persecutors—the three individuals who for a generation had held up his promotions and stopped his pay raises and who now had submitted a budget to the University Board of Directors omitting all funding for his program. To terminate the program was to terminate the professor, who held its only budgeted position.

The professor may have deserved his fate. His classes were magnets for everyone who needed an easy A. He gave no lectures and did nothing in class but preside over seemingly aimless bull sessions. His colleagues thought he was a disgrace to the teaching profession. The president, the dean, and the department head had been trying for years to get rid of him. But nothing worked—the professor was tenured and couldn't easily be fired. He also had lots of friends among students and alumni.

This year the three administrators felt they had to act. Revenues had fallen. There was a financial crisis. They could save money by eliminating the professor's program (and the professor himself) from the budget. They acted on that plan and sent the new budget to the Board of Directors.

Very quickly the professor learned of this plot hatched by his old enemies. He decided to settle the problem once and for all. He would simply remove them from the university payroll. He cleaned his .45 caliber automatic pistol and put nine rounds in the clip. Early Monday morning he phoned and made an appointment with each of the three, separated by five minutes. Their offices were on three floors of the same building—the president's on the third, the dean's on the second, the department head's on the first. They all thought they knew what was coming—another tongue-lashing from the professor.

But this time the professor's tongue was quiet. He walked into the president's office, shut the door behind him, and fired three well-aimed shots directly at his tormentor. He opened the door, walked quietly past a shrieking secretary, descended the stairs, entered the dean's office, and fired three more expert shots. He calmly descended one more flight of stairs and entered the department head's office, where the last three rounds found their target. The professor tossed his gun into a wastebasket as he strolled out of the building onto the broad green campus. He sat on a bench under a spreading oak where he so often relaxed, and where for years an endless succession of students had visited with him.

"Professor!" cried a middle-aged woman.

He looked up. "Vera, It's been several days since we talked." Sirens grew louder in the distance.

"Professor, it has been twenty years since I saw you last. I graduated long ago. Today I am back for my first visit. How wonderful to see you. Professor, I remember your course as though it were yesterday. I loved it. I learned more from you than from all the rest."

City police frisked the professor, put handcuffs securely on his wrists, and drove him to jail.

"But Professor," said an acquaintance on the Board of Directors who years ago had sat in his classes and who now paid a visit to his cell. "Professor, it was only a budget, only a proposal. The Board never would have accepted the president's budget. Never, Professor. When our alumni return to the campus you're the one they ask about first, you're the one they love most. No, no Professor. We would never accept that budget."

"Well, it's all academic now."

THE BUDGET

Chloroform

Nothing shuts the eyes of bored students faster than the word *budgeting*. Yet nothing would open a student's eyes faster than being given a $100 bill. Money can be the dreariest of all subjects, and the liveliest of all subjects. Students seldom find budget documents published by governments very exicting or the methods and procedures by which those budgets are prepared very stirring. Dollar signs in government budgets don't have much impact on them: the sums and totals don't signify any personal triumph, any personal defeat, any personal gain or loss—at least none acutely sensed.

Some people, however, do acutely sense the impact of dollar signs in budgets. To them budgets are exciting. For certain bureaucrats a governmental budget can be the central fact of life. Its columns tell whether one's empire is growing or shrinking, strong or weak, healthy or ailing.

What Is a Budget?

The word **budget** stems from the Latin *bulga*, meaning "leather bag." Romans carried the word to Gaul, where it became *bouge*, also meaning "bag." The

French carried it to England in 1066, where the word *bougette* (a diminutive of *bouge*) took its place in Middle English and came to mean "purse" or "the contents of a purse."

Today the word *budget* means "a plan for spending money." A budget is not the same as an appropriation. An **appropriation** is a determination by the legislature of how much money shall be spent for various purposes—it is an authorization to spend. The legislature may be guided, but is not bound, by a budget when it makes an appropriation. A budget is a suggestion, a proposal. Sometimes one hears bureaucrats say, "My budget was cut" or "I got a bigger budget this year," by which they usually mean their appropriation was cut or raised. Technically that's a misuse of the word *budget.*

Who Makes a Budget?

The Governor Most budgeting in state governments is done by the governor, his or her personal staff, the budget office, and the entire bureaucracy. Budgets are put together slowly and painstakingly throughout the **budget calendar.** The needs of every agency and office of the bureaucracy are forwarded from level to level and debated at each level: the requests of each agency are weighed against the requests of others. This weighing is not done in the light of any objective standard of worth but in the light of political backing for each demand. By *political backing* we are not referring solely to partisan politics but to all sources of influence. Partisan politics may be the least important of all forms of politics influencing the budget process. Pressure-group politics and contests among influentials is most important. The tug of war for money continues step by step upward through the bureaucracy. Finally each major department forwards its detailed requests to the governor, who with a personal political staff and a budget office makes final budget decisions, publishes a *governor's budget,* and delivers it to the legislature.

The Legislature Rarely do state legislatures do much budgeting. For the most part they rely on the governor's plans. Legislatures do not always hew to the governor's plans for spending, but in the absence of any other systematic plan, they find it convenient to use.

The fact that state legislatures are so influenced by the governor's budget, and so dependent upon it, disturbs some people. The power of the purse is a legislature's greatest power, and when a legislature abdicates that power, it abdicates too much. Of course, legislators are perfectly free to ignore the governor's budget, but in fact they do not—not in most states. The state government in most states is a very big enterprise, perhaps the biggest business in the state. Money is limited; demands of the bureaucracy are unlimited. Much study, much analysis, is required to weigh the demands of any one agency against the demands of all the other agencies. The bureaucracy spends a year developing the budget document that the governor ultimately hands to the legislature in January.[1]

Most legislatures simply do not have the staff to duplicate that long, drawn-out effort in the executive branch. In a former era when state governments were smaller and simpler, perhaps legislatures could pass appropriation bills without the guidance of any systematic financial plan, but this is rarely done

---

[1]More than a dozen states use biennial rather than annual budgets.

today. Some state legislatures are better equipped to participate in budgeting than others. Colorado is an outstanding example of a state where the legislature attempts to take charge of budgeting, where the governor's budget is regarded no more reverentially than any other suggestion for spending that may come to the legislature's joint budget committee.[2] However, Colorado is an exception, not the rule. The rule is legislative dependence on the governor's budget.[3]

Incremental Budgeting

Both the process of making budgets and the process of making appropriations is incremental in the United States (and perhaps in all the world) at all levels of government. *Incremental* is another of our words stemming from Latin, meaning in English about what it meant in Latin, "something added." The budget, and ultimately the appropriation, for each agency is usually based on last year's appropriation, with a little something added to match inflation. Now and again departures occur—new programs, new thrusts, and some shrinkages here and there—but change seldom comes in great leaps. It is slow, evolutionary, building upon the past. Thus it is called incremental budgeting. Perhaps 95 percent of all budgeting is incremental.

Nonrational? Incremental budgeting is hotly criticized by those who view it as a rather mindless way to go about deciding where to spend money. What could be less rational than to justify this year's appropriation on the grounds that last year's appropriation was substantially the same? Why not ask every agency to justify itself from the ground up, to justify its very existence—not merely its increment? Why not lay out all the various things the state needs to do, arrange them in a list of their importance, give money to the most important, and let the rest go? Why assume that a program or agency already in existence should stay in existence or should be stressed to its present degree in the budget? Why not ax the less imporatant and stress the more important? In other words, why not make the budget process and the appropriations process rational? Incremental budgeting is lazy, inefficient, wasteful, and above all nonrational. So say its critics.

Politics But the critics themselves have lapses from rationality. What they sometimes do not understand, will not understand, refuse to understand is that budgeting is a political process at its core. Budgeting is a contest of powers. Power attracts money like iron filings to a magnet. At every stage of budgeting, step by step up the bureaucratic ladder, money goes to those who, like a magnet, can pull it in.

Budgeting as a Power Struggle

Special Interests Most voters haven't the foggiest idea how much money any particular office or agency of the bureaucracy should get. Budget makers and legislators normally operate in a public-opinion brownout and therefore

---

[2]The Colorado joint budget committee treats the governor's budget so cavalierly that one governor recently neglected to submit a complete budget.

[3]The governor's budget is often referred to as the *executive budget* because it is made by the chief executive and the executive branch.

respond to narrow, sometimes well-heeled special interests that are fully alive to every move affecting them in the money-doling-out process.

Bureaucrats The bureaucracy itself is among the most active and powerful of all special interests. Each agency, each office, each suboffice, each individual of the bureaucracy has a will to grow. A person rises in the bureaucracy by growing bigger, not by growing smaller. By *bigness* we mean bigness of budget, bigness in program, bigness in number of subordinates. No one is fighting to grow smaller; everyone is fighting to grow bigger, richer, more powerful. To achieve this, every agency of the bureaucracy mobilizes its clients, those who benefit by its existence—farmers to support the department of agriculture, doctors for the board of medical examiners, and so on. The burearcracy and the other special interests have a mutually beneficial relationship.

Budgetary battles reveal what an armed camp the bureaucracy really is. Each agency jealously guards its borders, its field of authority, its power, its jurisdiction, its physical turf, its offices, its personnel—its budget. Each also conspires to rip off a piece of another's territory or to grow by selling new programs to budget makers and legislators.

Budgeting is first, last, and always a political process. Expert budget readers can have as much fun reading a budget as you or I might have reading a gossip column. To them a budget (and likewise an appropriations bill) is an up-to-the-minute report on who is shafting who in the bureaucratic wars.

Rationality in Budgeting

Rationality in budget making is elusive. Rationality, like soup, comes in 57 varieties. Not everyone has precisely the same taste in rationality. Incremental budgeting is said to be nonrational, but to a politician it is the highest form of rationality. A legislator wandering among the armed camps of special-interest groups—knives, armor, explosives on all sides—is being perfectly rational when he or she tries to avoid startling or annoying anyone too much. Incremental budgeting pushes no one, shoves no one, and leaves every camp in a state of armed coexistence. It makes no one insanely happy. At the same time it makes no one insanely mad. Incremantal budgeting is the politician's rationality, not the professor's rationality.

The politician's rationality has been condemned as nonrational. A bush corps of enlightened people demand an end to incremental budgeting and the substitution of a "new era" of rational budgeting. Thus we bathers in the academic surf are assaulted by wave after wave of highly cerebral ideas for bringing "sense"to budgeting.

Zero-Based Budgeting

The current wave foaming across the beach, sweeping everything and everybody along with giddy force, is called **zero-based budgeting** (ZBB). No self-respecting bureaucrat or legislator or professor of public administration dares confess ignorance of zero-based budgeting. Simply letting the phrase roll off the tongue in the right company is worth points. But when you demand a precise definition of zero-based budgeting, no one seems able to say exactly what it is. Its many advocates fail to agree on any single definition.

Zero-based budgeting was preceded by the planning, programming, budgeting system (PPBS), which was preceded by program budgeting, and so on backward in time. All are vaguely related, vaguely interested in bringing "rationality" to budgeting, somewhat imprecise, somewhat impractical and foggy, yet all have seemingly one single enemy. That enemy is politics. Advocates of these new waves of budget philosophy are accused of wanting to substitute their own (supposedly rational) opinions for the (supposedly nonrational) opinions of politicians about how to spend the people's money.

In zero-based budgeting, budgeters supposedly must answer the question of why an agency should receive any money at all and, if so, how much—why, in other words, it should get more than zero dollars. Some of the dreadful entanglements of answering that question are described in the following section.

Very little zero-based budgeting lives up to its name. Rarely do those who claim to practice zero-based budgeting actually do it. Rarely do they attempt to apply ZBB to all agencies, and rarely do they try to make agencies justify themselves from the ground up every year, or at any time. Nobody has time to make such colossal studies, and nobody has time to comprehend the results. Montana's short-lived romance with zero-based budgeting in the late 1970s is an example of how hard it is to make ZBB work and of how far a so-called system of ZBB can be from true ZBB. The Montana legislature was at least modest enough to call its new scheme the Priority Budgeting System, rather than ZBB. The system applied only to seven Montana agencies. Each of the seven was required for budget purposes to subdivide itself into a collection of separate "activity packages" or functions, to prepare three alternative budget levels for each function, and to explain the programmatic impact on each function of these three levels. The alternative levels were (1) the current level of funding, (2) a level 20 percent below current, and (3) the level requested by the agency. Then the budgeters were required to rank in order of priority the functions within each agency and present the budget to the legislature in that fashion.[4]

Thus we see there was no *zero*-based budgeting in Montana. Eighty percent of current funding was as close to zero as the Montana budgeters got.

Zero-based budgeting, of course, is also attempted in local governments here and there across the country, and their experience with it has been roughly identical to the experiences of the states. Local-government officials object to the time and paper work it involves and often do not see much improvement in budgeting as a result of their efforts. At the same time, however, local officials, like their state-level colleagues, have found that zero-based budgeting—as a procedure—has the beneficial effect of involving middle-level managers to a greater degree in budgeting and likewise helps top city officials understand the operations of all municipal departments.[5]

Cost-Benefit Analysis

Politicians versus the "Experts"   Experts sometimes wish to substitute their own view of right and wrong for the politician's view. This worries politicians and makes them suspicious of these tides of budget reform that rise every

[4]See John S. Fitzpatrick, "Montana's Experiment with Zero-Base Budgeting," *State Government* (Winter 1980), pp. 11–16.

[5]See Perry Moore, "Zero-Base Budgeting in American Cities," *Public Administration Review* (May–June 1980), pp. 253–58. Moore investigates the benefits and problems associated with the application of zero-base budgeting in 35 American cities.

decade or so: it boils down to a political struggle between the politicians and the "experts." Experts claim to know best how the people's money should be spent. They claim to have a simple mechanism—cost-benefit analysis—for determining what to spend money for.

How It Works **Cost-benefit analysis** is almost laughably easy to contemplate. The system works this way. All you do is decide basically what you want, say, long-range air defense. Then you list all the different forms of long-range air defense. Then you quantify all the advantages and disadvantages of each. You feed this mass of figures into a computer. Push a button and the computer tells you which form of long-range air defense is the best buy, which form gives the most defense at the least cost, which form gives the biggest bang for the buck. This information may be rather influential with politicians. Facts are persuasive.

Political Costs and Benefits However, certain forms of long-range defense may have political benefits or shortcomings not related at all to defense. There may be tremendous political support for the long-range bomber because thousands of workers and huge financial investments are committed to it. With such political support legislators might reap rewards for advocating bombers even if the facts were to show that the bomber isn't the best long-range defense.

State governments, of course, don't have to wrestle with long-range defense, but they do have to wrestle with such things as highway safety. Do you get more highway safety by buying patrol cars or by improving highways? Budget makers have to contend with the political clout of the highway patrol itself, of road-building contractors, and of other groups such as truckers who also have a vested interest in the presence or absence of certain forms of highway safety. Truckers may prefer good roads to good police. Rarely is highway safety the sole consideration. Safety may ultimately be lost in the dust of other considerations. Selfish interests of various sorts intrude—contractors, bureaucrats, truckers, anyone who in any way might profit or lose by a particular approach to highway safety. They all exercise muscle. Politics hovers around all budgeting and has more impact on it than any system, such as cost-benefit analysis, for identifying the best buy. The best buy in one sense may not be the best buy in another, and politicians are often interested in the best political buy above all else. The best buy as determined by cost-benefit analysis may not be politically satisfactory.

Clarity of Budgets

One contribution to rationality would be to make budgets clear, understandable, and interesting to the average person who might wish to read such documents. Rationality cannot prevail unless legislators know what they are doing when they vote money. Part of knowing what they're doing is knowing what they're buying—not just knowing how many pencils and typewriters, but for what programs those pencils and typewriters are to be used. In other words, a legislator should receive a budget document that explains in plain (even interesting) language what programs he or she is being asked to support, the exact nature of each program, and the total cost of each.

Programs? Often the appropriation for a program is confusingly strewn through separate appropriations for a variety of agencies and bureaus. If a legislature could receive a budget that tells it, for example, just how much it costs to run the state parks, then the legislature could judge whether it really wants to spend all that much on parks. The cost of parks may far exceed the cost of the state parks department. A whole collection of agencies may have a hand in keeping parks: the state highway patrol may be involved, the fish and wildlife service may be involved, the department of agriculture may be involved, and so on. If the budget makers would add all this up and present the true bill for parks, it might be enlightening. If rationality is what we want, then a budget that presents a lucid picture of just what the full cost of every program is would be useful.

Plain Language   Here and there some budget makers try to write lucid budgets and try to provide readers with plain-language explanations of what programs the budget supports. However, judging by the style of budget writing prevalent across America, one can only wonder whether budgets (and appropriation bills) are not deliberately designed to confuse and hide rather than to clarify and make lucid. There is, after all, some danger in being too clear. It's hard to hide anything in a lucid budget. If you keep everything shrouded in a mysterious and authoritative fog, then who can ever learn enough about what you're doing to denounce it? Clarity opens you to attack. Combatants on bureaucratic and legislative battlefields, like combatants in shooting wars, prefer to wear protective camouflage calculated to confuse and mislead the enemy.

THE FISCAL YEAR

The word *fiscal* comes to us from the Latin *fiscus*, meaning "purse." Today *fiscal* means "financial." Anything financial is fiscal—anything pertaining to the income and outgo of money. The **fiscal year** is a financial year. The word *year* does not necessarily mean a calendar year beginning in January. All but four state governments begin their fiscal year on July 1, six months before the calendar year begins. Thus the fateful year 2000 will come six months early for fiscal matters in most states. The federal fiscal year used to begin July 1 and end June 30, but the Congressional Budget Act of 1974 changed it to October 1 through September 30 to give Congress more time to enact the annual appropriations. Similar reasoning may have motivated Alabama and Michigan to set the beginning of their fiscal year at October 1, and Texas to September 1. New York's April 1 date for the fiscal year probably was not intended to be a joke. A good many local governments simply use the calendar year as the fiscal year, and a good many others use July 1.

How does one account for the common practice of beginning the state fiscal year on July 1? No doubt it was calculated to coincide roughly with the annual adjournment of state legislatures. Legislatures usually meet in the winter because in a former era most members of state legislatures were farmers. The best time for farmers to meet was after Christmas and before planting time. Thus legislatures convened in early January, did what they had to do, and adjourned in time for spring plowing. Early summer, July 1, was a suitable date for bureaucrats to begin spending money given them by the legislature. Not so many of our legislators today have to get home for spring plowing, but the traditional dates for legislative sessions and fiscal years remain.

When it sits down to consider appropriations for the next fiscal year, the legislature normally has before it the governor's suggestions (that is, the governor's budget). The governor's suggestions are based on long study begun in the executive branch about one year before the legislature is handed the budget. That means, if you stop to think about it, that money being spent on projects in the final hours of a fiscal year was being mulled over and planned two years earlier.

APPROPRIATIONS

Appropriation bills are handled basically like any other bill introduced into the legislature. First stop is the appropriations committee of either house. Appropriations committees consider only bills to appropriate (spend). Tax bills are not generally considered by appropriations committees; separate finance committees consider revenue measures.

After the legislature has given permission to spend (that is, after it has appropriated money), then begins the actual spending, just as soon as the new fiscal year is born. Once spending begins, how does one prevent an agency from spending its entire appropriation in the first six months and then coming back to the legislature for a "supplemental" appropriation? This can, as you might suspect, be a good roundabout tactic for securing a larger appropriation. The usual procedure for combating quick-spending tactics is to allot the money on a quarterly basis. The state controller or other appropriate agency is instructed by the legislature (or by the governor) not to allow more than one-fourth the agency's money to be spent before the end of the first quarter, not more than half before the end of the second quarter, and so on. Supplemental appropriations may still be needed (and granted) for unanticipated expenses, however.

AUDITING

Auditing is important because it is an effort to determine whether public servants are doing what they are supposed to be doing. In its broadest sense auditing is a system for looking at the performance of public officers and agencies to see if that performance squares with the intent of the law. On the other hand, auditing in its narrowest sense means to look at every expenditure to be sure it is legal and to look at the books to see that they are accurate. Good auditing lies at the heart of good government.

The Controller

Various states vest responsibility for establishing accounting systems, for pre-auditing expenditures, for checking the accuracy and honesty of bookkeeping, and for making periodic allotments of money in the hands of an officer commonly called a **controller** (sometimes spelled *comptroller*). The word obviously stems from the word *control*. Some states vest these control functions in officers or agencies that go by other names, such as *director of finance* or *director of accounting*. Many states scatter control function among several different officers.

The Treasurer

Normally the **treasurer** is not involved in controlling as much as keeping and investing the state's funds. Treasurers cash checks (called *warrants*) written on the state by officers of agencies that have appropriations from the legislature. Generally state treasurers will not cash any check unless its legality has first been preaudited by the controller. A check is illegal if it exceeds the agency's appropriation, or if it is paid for purposes not intended by the legislature when it made the appropriation, or if the check is for more money than required by the vendor's statement.

Pre- and Postaudits

All states have an officer who conducts postaudits (as distinct from preaudits). The **preaudit** comes before expenditure; the **postaudit** comes after. Usually the person who preaudits is not the same person who postaudits: they are two entirely different officials who generally represent entirely different points of view. The preauditor, who is often the controller, is within the executive branch and is usually appointed by the governor. The postauditor (often called the auditor) is usually elected by the people or appointed by the legislature. Those in charge of preauditing will normally be sympathetic to the administrator's problems, will interpret the laws in ways that make the most sense to the governor and his or her administration, and will sanction accounting practices most useful to administrators in conducting their business. The postauditor will most likely have a somewhat less proadministration bias.

The Auditor

The word **auditor** stems from the Latin *audire* ("to hear") and *auditus* ("a hearing"). Although auditors probably use their eyes more than their ears, auditors do "hear" when they listen to the explanations given by public officers whose expenditures of public money seem strange.

To be a perfect auditor one should have several attributes of God. An auditor should be all-knowing, all-good, and all-wise. The perfect auditor would be absolutely independent and absolutely unbiased. Unfortunately no one on earth has these qualities to perfection.

Elected or Appointed?

In about a dozen states the auditor is popularly elected. He or she may be called *auditor, auditor general, comptroller,* or *examiner.* One of the great debates among students of state government is whether the auditor should be elected directly by the people or appointed by the legislature. The fundamental question is which of the two systems is likely to produce the most independent, the least biased, and the most competent auditor. In some cases the elected auditor only checks the correctness of payments and financial statements, whereas the auditor appointed by the legislature serves that body by determining whether the will of the legislature has been followed by agencies receiving appropriations and whether those agencies are being efficient and economical in pursuit of their mission.

Legislative Audit Committees

A classic argument against filling almost any office by election is that voters seldom know whether their chosen candidate is qualified for the office and seldom know with any great precision what the duties of the office are. How many voters know what an auditor does?

This problem is solved by a system in which the legislature picks the auditor from a panel of candidates chosen by the **legislative audit committee.** However, even that system has its severe shortcomings. An auditor appointed by the legislature and working in close cooperation with a legislative audit committee may not be as independent as he (or she) ought to be. If you are nominated by such a committee, you hate to turn around and bite its members. The audit committee is bound to include members who have close relationships with the very agencies you're going to be auditing. A legislative audit committee is composed of perhaps 10 or 15 members of the legislature, all of whom sit on several other committees. These other committees usually have a warm alliance with the agencies they supposedly oversee. Therefore if the auditor were to examine a certain agency and find it wanting, he would indirectly offend the oversight committee, which presumably should have found the deficiencies itself. He would annoy and embarass one or more members of the audit committee who may also sit on the oversight committee.

What if the auditor appointed by the legislature decides to investigate the legislature itself? The legislature probably needs auditing, investigating, and reforming as much as any other "agency" of government. An auditor elected by the people would be largely free to investigate wherever he or she wanted without fear of the legislature and would possibly have more freedom. Remember, nothing is more important to an auditor than independence and objectivity.

Yet, as we have seen, election of auditors by the people also has its problems. There seems to be no perfect way to choose an auditor.

Legislative Oversight

The concept of auditing has been expanded in recent years, an expansion that further heats up the question of whether auditors should be elected by the people or appointed by the legislature. Actually legislatures have always tried to "audit" the performance of the other two branches of government by means of their so-called oversight function. Oversight has long been one of the more salient and exciting functions of the legislature. Commonly each agency of the executive branch falls within the oversight of one standing committee in the house and one in the senate. Since these agencies are created and supplied with money by the legislature, it has a perfect right to look over their shoulders to see if they're doing what the legislature had in mind and whether they're doing it aptly and adequately.

Oversight sometimes ends up being more like meddling. Furthermore, a cozy and incestuous relationship often exists among the oversight committee, the overseen agency, and various special interest groups. Oversight is intended to be a form of auditing, but more often it degenerates into a form of special interest politics. For that reason, and also because oversight committees are often poorly staffed and often do not function year-round, some legislatures have decided to professionalize and broaden the auditor's function to include checking up on agencies to see whether they are doing what the legislature intends they should do and doing it well. This is called performance auditing.

Performance Auditing

Performance auditing involves what we call *organization-and-management* (O & M) studies. An O & M study probes whether an agency is properly organized and managed to do its job efficiently—that is, whether it is achieving the greatest output with the least input. This general snooping within agencies to see how they're doing has become a high-prestige profession. O & M is one of the glittering new specialties of our time, and lots of officials make a hobby of it. Oversight committees, appropriations committees, legislative councils, the governor's budget office, the controller, the department of administration, the auditor, and a variety of others pursue O & M studies of a sort. Organization-and-management studies are often accompanied by a good deal of hocus-pocus, pseudoprofessionalism, and mystifying jargon.

Performance auditing (sometimes known also as *functional auditing* or *operational auditing*) is now well within the orbit of approved and recommended activities for auditors. Some people ask, "How can we imagine that an auditor (who is presumably trained in accounting) has enough information about, say, a hospital to know whether it is being run efficiently, economically, and according to the best standards of medical science?" This is a good question. Those who defend performance auditing by postauditors argue that anybody, including auditors, can learn a good deal about anything by reading and by exercising a little inquisitiveness. Auditors learn quite a bit about everything they audit in the process of examining purchase orders, contracts, and books for accuracy. Specialists, such as doctors, lawyers, and engineers, like to believe that outsiders cannot hope to understand the mysteries of their specialty, but in fact practically anyone can acquire enough knowledge about almost anything after a couple weeks' inquiry to make some pretty shrewd judgments.

Not all state auditors do performance auditing. The level of auditing varies widely from state to state. Many auditors, frankly, do not venture beyond checking for honesty, accuracy, and legality in financial transactions. Some auditors don't have the staff support to go further. Some don't have the ambition. Some auditors are discouraged—or at least not encouraged—to go further. And some auditors fear to go further. Others, however, have the ability, the will, and the staff to do a fine job of performance auditing.

Performance auditing depends upon establishment of performance standards by the legislature for agencies to follow. An agency's efficiency can be measured only against goals. Without clearly stated goals, no one can possibly measure efficiency.

EXPENDITURES

State Expenditures

The combined annual outlay of all the states of the Union has been around $360 billion in recent years (see Table 11-1). This represents about 20 percent of total governmental expenditures in the United States.

Table 11-1 State Expenditures

California	44.5 billion
New York	35.9 billion
Texas	16.9 billion
Pennsylvania	16.6 billion
Ohio	16.3 billion
Michigan	15.4 billion
Illinois	15.0 billion
New Jersey	12.6 billion
Florida	10.4 billion
Massachusetts	9.7 billion
Washington	8.1 billion
Louisiana	7.7 billion
North Carolina	7.6 billion
Wisconsin	7.5 billion
Minnesota	7.5 billion
Virginia	7.1 billion
Maryland	6.9 billion
Georgia	6.7 billion
Indiana	6.4 billion
Kentucky	5.4 billion
Missouri	5.3 billion
Alabama	5.2 billion
Connecticut	4.9 billion
Tennessee	4.8 billion
Oklahoma	4.7 billion
Colorado	4.6 billion
South Carolina	4.4 billion
Oregon	4.4 billion
Iowa	4.3 billion
Arizona	4.0 billion
Alaska	4.0 billion
Mississippi	3.4 billion
West Virginia	3.1 billion
Kansas	3.0 billion
New Mexico	2.8 billion
Arkansas	2.6 billion
Utah	2.4 billion
Hawaii	2.2 billion
Nebraska	1.9 billion
Rhode Island	1.8 billion
Maine	1.8 billion
Nevada	1.5 billion
Wyoming	1.4 billion
North Dakota	1.4 billion
Montana	1.4 billion
Idaho	1.3 billion
Delaware	1.2 billion
New Hampshire	1.1 billion
South Dakota	1.0 billion
Vermont	.9 billion

Source: U.S. Bureau of the Census, *Statistical Abstract of the United States: 1987*, (Washington, D.C., 1986), p. 261.

Table 11-2   State Expenditures by Function

Education	32.10%
Public Welfare	17.37
Miscellaneous	11.72
Insurance Trust Expenditure	9.57
Highways	8.00
Health and Hospitals	6.90
Interest	3.63
Debt Redemption	2.86
Corrections	2.13
Natural Resources	1.64
General Control	1.28
Financial Administration	1.24
Police	.86
Employment Security Administration	.70

Source: U.S. Bureau of the Census, *State Government Finances, 1984.*

Table 11-2 shows the functions carried out by state governments and what percentage of all money spent by states is spent on each. It does not include what states give to other governments to spend on those functions or what states pay out to the beneficiaries of state-run insurance systems.

Local Expenditures

Local expenditure, as shown in Table 11-3, includes the spending of all forms of local government including cities, towns, counties, and school districts and other special districts. Each expenditure is shown as a percentage of the total 1981–1982 expenditure of local governments which was about $311 billion.

States and local governments spend money on many things, but three-fourths of their money goes for education, public welfare, highways, and health. Those are the big four of state and local spending. Education is the biggest of the big: states typically spend a quarter of their revenue on it, and nearly half of all local spending is for schools. Of course, if you look at the budget of a typical American city, you may find nothing at all for schools. That's because local school spending is done chiefly by school districts, which are one-purpose governments separate from cities and counties but overlapping them. A typical school district is likely to spend as much as all other local governments combined within its boundaries.

Growth of Spending

Another noteworthy characteristic of spending by state and local governments has been its growth. Because federal spending has grown still more than state and local spending and has become so gargantuan, we sometimes fail to notice that state and local spending has also grown. Seeing the growth of federal expenditures, some people have jumped to the conclusion that state and local governments are withering away. They are not. They have been growing—not power as much as in size—but the growth of state and local spending has not

Table 11-3 Local Expenditures

Education	36.06%
Utilities	13.30
Health and Hospitals	6.70
Welfare	4.74
Sewerage and Sanitation	4.68
Highways	4.64
Police	4.52
Government Administration	4.47
Interest on Debt	3.52
Housing and Urban Renewal	2.44
Fire Protection	2.22
Parks and Recreation	1.94
Insurance Trust	1.54
Corrections	.95
Libraries	.59
Natural Resources	.43
Other	7.26

Source: U.S. Bureau of the Census, *Governmental Finances in 1981–82.*

been quite as feverish as the growth one has seen at the top of our political system.

This swelling of government outlay is, as everyone knows, caused partly by our population growth. When the American government started in 1789, the nation had only four million people. That's fewer than the present population of Los Angeles County. The biggest city had only about 40,000.

Government spending has grown for many reasons. Government has waxed faster than the population. One basic reason for this is that we've changed from a society of family farms and businesses to a less self-reliant kind of world in which most of us are employees of large operations. Many people feel rather at the mercy of these giant organizations for which they work and turn not only to unions but to government for help. Many people have changed their attitude about what they want government to do and to be. Earlier in our history people did not see government as their cradle-to-grave provider. To most, government meant law and order—courts, police, army, and so on. But today, for better or worse, a great many people see government as a great provider. Voters, even while condemning big government, ask for new programs and new agencies to cope with all sorts of personal problems.

As our society has become increasingly technological and sophisticated, it has increasingly needed an equally technological and sophisticated government to preside over it. For instance, we all have radios and television, but we couldn't have them unless somebody decided who could broadcast on the few existing channels. We also have cars and love to drive them, but we need roads and rules for using them. Government seems to be the logical choice for controlling such functions that affect most people.

Some people suspect that this growth in government is a conspiracy of some sort. It is not a conspiracy. It is the fault of each and every one of us who wants anything from government. It is the sum total of everybody's attempt to get something from government. Bureaucrats, of course, are only too eager to satisfy our every want. All we have to do to slow the growth of government is to decide if we want less government more than we want more services. But where is the voter who is ready to give up his or her automobile so the government won't have to build roads or police them? Where is the voter who is willing to give up his or her TV set so the government won't have to regulate the air waves? Where is the voter willing to give up anything?

REVENUE AND TAXATION

State Revenue

Table 11-4 lists the sources from which state governments receive their general revenue; each source is shown as a percentage of the total general revenue received by all states in 1986. Although total revenue may change over time, these percentages are likely to remain fairly stable for several years.

Miscellaneous General Revenue: Lotteries   State lotteries are among the more intriguing sources of miscellaneous state revenue. Although only about a quarter of the states are operating lotteries, they include a number of very populous states, such as New York, Massachusetts, Pennsylvania, Illinois, and Ohio. Nearly half the nation's population live in lottery states. The state may glean 1 or 2 percent of its general revenue from a lottery. Although not a tremendous percentage, it represents millions of dollars, all collected in a rather joyful way—unlike most taxes. So successful and popular have state lotteries been that most lottery states have expanded into the daily numbers game, competing with organized crime for a piece of the action.

State lotteries are, of course, bitterly opposed by many people for many reasons. One objection to a lottery is that it tends to be most attractive to lower-income people, who can least afford to throw their money away on it. It becomes an expensive vice, diverting money from essentials. The dream of striking it rich with a $2 investment is irresistible—especially to those who hardly have enough money to buy food for the table. Some individuals do strike it rich—Wilfred Madelle, Jr., while an inmate at the Worcester County House of Correction, acquired a million dollars in September 1980 when he won the big prize in a

Table 11-4   Sources of State Revenue

General Sales Tax	25.21%
From Federal Government	24.64
Charges and Miscellaneous	20.29
Individual Income Tax	17.82
Corporation Income Tax	4.70
Motor Fuels Tax	3.74
Licenses	3.60

Source: U.S. Bureau of the Census, *Statistical Abstract of the United States: 1987* (Washington, D.C., 1986), p. 252.

drawing of the Massachusetts Lottery Commission's Big Money Game. Madelle is entitled to payments of $50,000 a year for 20 years, if he wants the million to come slowly.

Local Revenue by Source

Local revenue, as shown in Table 11-5, includes the revenue taken in by all forms of local government including cities, towns, counties, and school districts and other special districts. Each source is shown as a percentage of the revenue of all local governments put together.

Who Levies What Tax?

State governments today get more of their revenue from the federal government (almost 20 percent) than from any single form of taxation. Local governments now get more than a third of their income from the state and federal governments. Every indication suggests that states will fall more into the financial grip of the federal government and that local governments will fall ever more into the joint grip of state and federal governments. Most intergovernmental gifts of money carry instructions on how it shall be used. These gifts (they're called *grants*) are disguised purchases of power.

Each level of government has its favorite form of tax; the federal government likes income taxes, state governments like general sales taxes, local governments like the property tax. Of course, all levels use a variety of taxes, but each level of government more or less respects the special claims laid by other levels to their favorite tax. The federal government does not use a general sales tax, although it does levy specific "excise" taxes on selected items such as gasoline, cigarettes, and liquor. Nor does the federal government make much use of the property tax. State governments, for their part, try to be somewhat modest in their use of the income tax and generally avoid the property tax. Local governments honor the state's primacy in sales taxes and could hardly administer a graduated income tax if they wanted to, although several cities do have low flat-rate (not graduated) income taxes.

Table 11-5   Local Revenue

From State and Federal Governments	34.61%
Property Tax	25.28
Charges	11.82
Utility Revenue	9.48
Miscellaneous Nontax General Revenue	8.53
Sales Tax	4.99
Insurance Trust Revenue	2.10
Individual Income Tax	1.55
Other Taxes	1.23
Corporation Income Tax	.41

Source: U.S. Bureau of the Census, *Statistical Abstract of the United States: 1987* (Washington, D.C., 1986), p. 252.

What Is a Good Tax?

Each form of taxation has its strong points and its weak points. Professors of economics like to lecture on what they called the **canons of taxation,** which set forth the characteristics of a "good" tax. Actually the virtue or vice of a tax is in the eye of the beholder. There can be no universal and objective standard: all things political and economic are measured by the standards of the one who measures. Every tax hurts some more than others, benefits some more than others. A thousand-dollar tax on the purchase of machine guns might delight the law-and-order crowd more than the bank-robber crowd.

The word *canon* comes to us from the Greek *kanon,* meaning "rod." Hence a canon is a measuring rod, a rule. One of the supposed canons of taxation is that every tax should be designed so that its weight is felt equally by all. The key word is *felt.* If a rich person and a poor person are each taxed $100, they do not feel the tax equally, even though they equally pay $100. Thus it is said a tax cannot be fair unless it is equally felt. This, of course, assumes there is something inherently, naturally, and spontaneously good about equality. Certain kinds of inequality may possibly benefit us more than equality. For example, we may all be benefited by a tax that gives breaks to producers of jobs and wealth because we may benefit by the jobs and wealth thus produced. We will not delve further into the question of whether so-called canons of taxation are indeed sensible or whether they are simply "prejudices of taxation."

Income Taxes

The **progressive income tax** is intended to be a tax that weighs equally on all, is felt equally by all: the higher your income, the more tax you pay. One reason an income tax is so complicated is that it tries to take into account everybody's ability to pay. One's ability to pay depends on just what one's income really is, and a good part of the income-tax return is a series of questions and calculations designed to isolate ability to pay by deducting things (such as costs of doing business) that do not represent income. Those who cry for a *simple* progressive income tax are asking the impossible. It cannot be progressive and simple at the same time. A progressive income tax demands a whole series of complicated mathematical computations to determine exactly what each taxpayer's income really is and to relate that to size of family and other variables. Certainly there are loopholes that if closed would simplify the income tax form, but many people who complain about the complexity of the tax form are not willing to sacrifice their own favorite loophole just to simplify the form. One popular loophole excuses people from paying income tax on the money they pay out in interest. This is a great boon to people—most of us—with mortgages on their home. As a good many people see it, a little complexity on the income tax form is better than paying tax on interest.

State income-tax forms could be simplified if the state would merely ask taxpayers to pay an amount equal to a certain fixed percentage of their federal income tax.

One great deterrent to use of the income tax by local governments is their inability to administer the tax. They don't have a bureaucracy comparable to the federal Internal Revenue Service to check the accuracy of returns. Another reason local governments don't use the income tax is that taxpayers are already fed up with state and federal income taxes and might feel unkindly toward any set of local politicians who advocate still more income taxation.

A third reason why local governments avoid use of income taxes has to do with the debate over whether the tax should be levied only on residents of the local jurisdiction that imposes the tax or on all people who earn money within the jurisdiction, whether they are residents or not.

The Sales Tax

Most Americans come face to face with the **sales tax** several times a day. It is the few extra pennies merchants ask from you when you buy just about anything. The tax may be levied exclusively at the point of retail exchange. Or it may be levied on wholesale and other transactions prior to retail, in which case it is often called a *gross-receipts tax*. The tax may be levied on sales of all items (a *general sales tax*), or it may be levied only on certain items (an *excise tax*). Usually the general sales tax is supplemented by special sales taxes (excises) on selected items, such as motor fuels, alcoholic beverages, and cigarettes. Sales taxes remain the largest source of state tax revenue, although the income tax is steadily rising.

Advantages There are many objections to the sales tax as a means of raising revenue—it is a failure by nearly every canon. Experts in the field of taxation condemn the sales tax, yet are forced to admit it has one mighty advantage no matter how inadequate it may be otherwise—it is the most convenient, painless, and simple method of taxing small incomes. It is also an admirable way of taxing tourists and suburbanites.

Disadvantages On the negative side local sales taxes tend to drive trade to the borders and are therefore detested by merchants: the higher the tax, the more it motivates people to get in their cars and go to the city limits to do their shopping. Politically this is perhaps its worst feature. Only the smallest sales tax can be imposed without business being threatened. State sales taxes do not suffer this disability as seriously. It's not as convenient or economical to go clear out of state to evade a sales tax, except for those along the state line.

The sales tax is said to be unfair and inequitable because it taxes the poor more than the rich—that is, it is regressive. It has been termed an *inverted income tax*. Although the rich may consume more than the poor and therefore pay more sales tax, the amount of a rich person's consumption will not reflect precisely the amount of his wealth. Both the rich and the poor eat two eggs for breakfast. Some attempt is made to lessen the regressiveness of sales taxes by omitting certain basic items, such as food, from the tax.[6]

The sales tax is somewhat unpredictable because there are no means of accurately estimating from one year to the next what the tax will yield—yield fluctuates with the business cycle and with inflation. Fraud and evasion in administration of sales taxes are common because the chief burden of collecting the

---

[6]Among the points made by the Joint Economic Committee in a recent study, *Trends in the Fiscal Condition of Cities: 1978–1980,* is that increased use of sales taxes (and user charges) by cities is likely to put a greater burden on the lower-income population than on the middle- or upper-income population.

tax is turned over to sellers. States do, of course, need a bureaucracy to administer the sales tax. Having that machinery, states could make a good case for administering all locally imposed sales taxes.

The Real-Property Tax

The **real-property tax** is levied annually on the value[7] of real estate. Owners must pay. If they do not pay, the government that levies the tax may seize their property. States hardly use the property tax at all—it is a tax exploited almost exclusively by local governments and is by far the greatest source of local tax revenue. Despite its terrible problems, the real-property tax is appealing in some important ways. It is relatively easy to enforce: land and buildings cannot be hidden under a mattress or in a bank box. In that respect the real-property tax differs from its sister, the personal-property tax, which is an often futile levy against easily hidden jewelry, cash, clothing, and comparable small and movable items. Immovability is the definition of real estate: land and the structures thereon. Furthermore, the property tax is not as complicated or as expensive to administer as sales taxes, income taxes, or almost any other tax.[8]

Real Estate Is Not an Accurate Measure of Wealth However, critics assail nearly everything else about the property tax. First, real estate simply isn't an accurate measure of wealth anymore. Perhaps it was long ago in the era of small one-owner stores, farms, and enterprises, when a person's income and total wealth could be roughly estimated by the real property he or she owned. Today, however, mass production and huge corporations have changed things. Modern managers rarely own the corporation they manage. Their wealth (and many are highly paid) is not in real property, but in personal property—stocks, bonds, and interests—that do not fall under the real-property tax. Their home and the land it sits on may be the only real estate they own, but that is by no means a true measure of their wealth, even if they live in a mansion.

Rigidity Another defect of the property tax is its rigidity. Rate increases have become a raw wound to the property-owning public. Nothing is as likely to register outcries from the public than news of a possible higher millage rate. In a sense the property tax isn't itself rigid, but its intended victims are. Of course, the property-tax yield rides up and down with the price of real estate, providing assessments keep pace with changes in value.

Regressiveness Among the ugliest alleged evils of the real-property tax is its **regressiveness,** meaning it burdens the poor more than the rich. Lodging is a necessity of life, but the cost of housing weighs heavier on the poor than on the

[7]*Value* may mean full market value (the amount a willing buyer would pay a willing seller), or it may mean only a percentage of full market value, or it may mean reproduction cost (cost to reproduce the structure at today's prices), or it may mean the value of the property as it is currently used (not as it might be used), or it may mean various other things. The laws and practices from jurisdiction to jurisdiction differ with regard to the definition of value.

[8]For a history of property taxes, see Jens Peter Jensen's classic work *Property Taxation in the United States* (Chicago: University of Chicago Press, 1931).

rich, and so do taxes on it. The well-to-do have a smaller slice of their wealth tied up in homes and therefore expose a lower percentage of their wealth to this form of tax. If people in modest circumstances own a home, they lay nearly their entire worldly possessions naked before the tax assessor.

Equal Taxation of Unequal Property　It is also claimed that the property tax does not adequately distinguish between income-producing property, such as an apartment house, and nonproductive property, such as owner-occupied homes. The property tax treats them equally: both are taxed according to their assessed valuation. In some areas homestead exemptions moderate that problem by giving partial exemptions from the property tax to people who own the homes in which they live. Laudable as that may be, it is unfair to people who rent, especially to people who rent because they're too poor to buy. If landlords who rent out their property are denied the homestead exemption, they are obviously forced to pay higher property taxes, which they promptly shift to their tenants in the form of higher rent. This amounts to a tax on being poor and is the essence of regressivism.

Reciprocal Immunity　Another problem with the property tax results from federalism. Some serious difficulties flow from the inability of state and local governments to tax federal property, and vice versa. The doctrine of **reciprocal immunity** from taxation prohibits either side of the federal equation from taxing the other. The power to tax is the power to kill. If the two partners in the federal system could tax each other, they could put each other out of business and destroy the federal system, as Chief Justice John Marshall surmised long ago.

Post offices, veterans' hospitals, military installations, and so forth, often occupy choice locations in a community. They are immune from taxation, and their existence blocks construction of private buildings that would be taxable. Nearly every major city has some federal property, sometimes so much (as in Alexandria, Virginia, across the Potomac River from Washington, D.C.) that the local tax base is wrecked. The more a local government depends on its property tax, the more the rule of reciprocal immunity hurts. In certain circumstances the federal government contributes money to local treasuries in lieu of taxes. School districts near military installations often receive such assistance because many children who live on the installation attend public schools.

Other Exemptions　Exemptions are also customarily granted to various kinds of private institutions, including libraries, museums, cemeteries, churches, hospitals, orphanages, and colleges. These exemptions cut another gash in the property-tax base and result in high taxes on remaining property holders.

Assessment　Assessment is the first and most important step in property-tax administration—and is sometimes the point of almost ludicrous failures. **Assessment** is the process by which government finds out the value of property. The person who does that complex job is the assessor. The overwhelming majority of local governments have neither enough people to warrant a full-time professional assessor, nor enough money to pay for one. This may be the worst assessment problem.[9] It takes more than 10,000 people to give full-time work to an assessor.

Most jurisdictions that have an assessor elect him or her for two or perhaps four years. Anyone qualified to vote is usually qualified to hold the office. Most assessors are therefore short-term amateurs. Yet even in those small, poor districts where the assessor is appointed, an amateur part-timer will normally get the job because no one else would take it. Where the work amounts to only three or four hours a week, the assessor may be paid a modest hourly wage.

All this means that in many thousands of jurisdictions the assessment system, which is the foundation of a good property tax, is designed and run by amateurs rather than by professionals. This can result in incompetent and inaccurate assessments. Many of these amateurs have fallen into the lazy habit of copying previous assessments rather than systematically and frequently reviewing the market value of property. Thus it often happens that new construction is assessed at market value while previous construction is allowed to go underassessed because the assessor doesn't bother to change assessments as property values change. This results in unequal taxation of equal property. Most states have laws requiring that property be assessed uniformly. These laws are outrageously broken, partly because of incompetence and partly because of a deliberate and illegal policy of assessing different kinds of property at different rates. In some areas property valuations are a mockery of uniformity laws. Someone has said, "Never has so much money been raised from so many people so inequitably as in the current administration of the local property tax on real estate." Assessors sometimes deliberately create inequalities by assessing certain kinds of property, usually corporate property, at a higher percentage of true value than other property.

Furthermore, in counties where the county assessor relies on assessments made by city assessors, the practice of competitive undervaluation occurs: the various cities in a county may compete with one another to have the lowest assessment rate in order to pay less county tax. This same competition sometimes occurs between counties when state financial aid for schools and other purposes is based on the lowness of a county's assessed valuation.

Some valuations of property are difficult to make, even by experts. Property owners may make important improvements indoors that escape the assessor's eyes yet greatly increase property value. The assessor cannot see everything. The valuation of certain kinds of property is also extremely vexing—for example, a railroad roundhouse whose market value is nil because nobody wants to buy it. If market value cannot be determined, original cost or replacement cost is used as a standard. Neither is satisfactory. Suppose the roundhouse was con-

---

[9]"Geographical fragmentation of the assessment function results in many assessing offices which are too small to realize the economies of larger scale operations and often cannot even support a single full-time assessor," says Kenneth Back in "Potential for Organization Improvement of Property Tax Administration," in *The Property Tax and Its Administration,* ed. Arthur D. Lynn, Jr. (Madison: University of Wisconsin Press, 1969), p. 33. However, for an argument that assessment quality may not be significantly related to the size of the assessing unit in Virginia, see John H. Bowman and John L. Mikesell, "Uniform Assessment of Property: Returns from Institutional Remedies," *National Tax Journal* (June 1978), pp. 137–53. One reason why small assessing units are not always inefficient is the availability of private mass-appraisal firms whose services may be contracted and the availability of state aid in assessment.

structed 75 years ago during a depression. Why tax the roundhouse on the basis of those cheap prices? On the other hand, replacement cost might be equally unfair because the railroad might not consider the roundhouse worth what it would cost to replace it today.

In most states some sort of supervision, control, guidance, and assistance is given local assessors by a state tax commission or comparable agency.[10] The state agency may take over assessment of certain kinds of property, such as railroads, gas and electric companies, or other utilities. The agency may also enter upon a campaign to educate assessors by holding clinics and meetings, providing tax manuals, sending out representatives to visit local assessors, and so forth. Or the agency may require reports, make rules and regulations, and in some drastic cases remove local assessors from office. States commonly have assessment-appeals boards to hear appeals from the decisions of county appeals boards, which in turn hear appeals from the decisions of local assessors in cases in which property owners appeal the assessor's assessment. That's a lot of appeals, but the machinery is there. Property owners may ultimately appeal to courts.

Efforts to improve administration of the real-property tax have not been overwhelmingly successful. Professionalization of the assessor is high on the list of desirable reforms, and some progress is being made in that direction. Yet taxpaxers seem to get some strange pleasure from a botched, bungled, and floundering collection system and seem willing to go along with their elected amateur assessor. However, in some localities the assessor has been put under a merit system, the local residence requirement has been waived, and arrangements made for appointment rather than election of the assessor.

One contribution to professionalization is the enlargement of assessment districts to the point where they will support a full-time assessor. Abolition of city assessors (leaving only the county assessor) and consolidation of assessment districts are probably steps in the right direction.

The Personal-Property Tax

Although the **personal-property tax** lingers on in all but a few states, it has faded to the borders of extinction.[11] No state today taxes all classes of personal property. Enforcement of the remaining personal-property taxes is often careless. The classic shortcoming of all personal-property taxes is the ease with which people can evade them by simply hiding the property. The harder it is to locate and assess a particular class of property, the less likely a state will persist in trying to tax it. Cash, stocks, and bonds, for example, are very easy to hide; only about half a dozen states attempt to tax them anymore. Likewise the tax on household items and personal effects has all but disappeared, partly because people resent intrusions of the tax collector into the privacy of the home.

---

[10]For a discussion of Florida's efforts to improve assessment, see J. Edwin Benton, "Tax Assessment and the Role of State Government," *State Government,* Vol. 57, No. 1, 1984, 22–31.

[11]For a discussion of the status of the personal-property tax in the states, see Steven J. Zellmer and Calvin A. Kent, "Trends in the Taxation of Personal Property," *State Government* (Winter 1979), pp. 12–18.

The personal-property taxes that remain in force attach things less intimate and less concealable—agricultural items such as livestock, machinery, and supplies of feed, seed, and fertilizer; business items such as construction equipment, inventories, and retail fixtures. As for motor vehicles, about half the states tax them as personal property, and a dozen more consider part of the annual license fee to be in lieu of a property tax. Boats, planes, and snowmobiles are treated about like motor vehicles.

In 1968 the Advisory Commission on Intergovernmental Relations advocated abolition of personal-property taxes.[12]

Federal–State Reciprocal Tax Immunity

Dual Sovereignty Again   When you set up two sovereigns and give them both the power to tax, sooner or later they will try to tax each other. This, of course, happened early in our national history when Maryland tried to tax a United States bank. After deciding that the United States government had a constitutional right to establish a bank, the United States Supreme Court went on to the question of whether Maryland could tax that bank. The answer was no.[13] Nowhere, of course, does the United States Constitution specifically say that a state may not tax the federal government (or conversely that the federal government may not tax the states), but Chief Justice John Marshall concluded that a federal system of government could not exist if the central government were able to tax the states out of existence, or if the states were able to tax the central government out of existence, or if either could cripple the other's operations. "The power to tax involves the power to destroy," said Marshall.[14] States do not have the power to pull down through taxation what the central government has an acknowledged right to build up. In later cases the Supreme Court declared that state instrumentalities were likewise immune from federal taxation.

Doctrine of Nondiscriminatory Taxation   A quick-witted county judge in Massachusetts who had been forced to pay federal income taxes sued in 1871 to get his money back on the grounds that when the federal government taxes his salary it is in effect taxing the state itself. He won his case and got his money back.[15] Carrying a good thing still further, a federal official tried some years later to claim immunity from state income taxes on grounds that the state tax on his salary was in effect a state tax on a federal function and therefore unconstitutional. However, he lost,[16] and in losing he lost for millions of local, state, and federal employees, who were no longer exempt from nondiscriminatory taxation by "the other government." The Court pointed out that technically, at least, the state income tax was not a tax on the federal government but a tax on private property: an employee's income becomes the employee's private property. The Court did admit that a government could kill another government by deliber-

---

[12]Advisory Commission on Intergovernmental Relations, *State Legislative Program, 1968* (Washington, D.C.: Government Printing Office, 1967), p. 159.

[13] *Wheat.* 316 (1819).

[14]Ibid.

[15]Collector v. Day, 11 Wall. 113 (1871).

[16]Graves v. New York ex rel. O'Keefe, 306 U.S. 466 (1939).

ately aiming a killing tax at the pay received by the employees of that other government. However, the state income tax involved in this case was not deliberately intended to burden the federal governments, nor are federal income taxes intended to burden state governments. These taxes are nondiscriminatory: they apply to all taxpayers of a certain income level who are within the boundaries of the government applying the tax. Just because federal employees have to pay a state income tax does not mean the state is trying to drive the federal government out of business or in any way impair its services. The same is true of federal income taxes on state employees. In that sense these taxes are nondiscriminatory.

The doctrine of reciprocal immunity from taxation is now therefore qualified by the doctrine of nondiscriminatory taxation. It is really reciprocal immunity from *discriminatory* taxation that governs the constitutionality of all taxes that have an *indirect* impact on "the other government."

Voluntary reciprocal tax immunity is also commonly practiced among local governments. The county tends not to tax the city, and vice versa. Likewise state and local governments forbear taxing each other: it would be like parents taxing children and children taxing parents.

State Debt Limits

Most states have some sort of legal limitation on their bonded indebtedness and on their deficit spending. Upper limits are put on both.[17] Furthermore, bond issues in most states are permitted only for the construction of *capital* items, such as office buildings, highways, and parks.

Spending more for ongoing programs (payment of salaries, purchase of goods and so on) than is taken in from the state's various sources—a practice called *deficit spending*—is also severely limited by law in many states. These legal provisions sometimes require the governor to submit a balanced budget, sometimes a balanced appropriations act, and sometimes both. All this adds up to treasury surpluses in most states. Surpluses come from efforts to stand well back from the danger of deficit spending. Some states have amassed colossal oversupplies of money. California's $5 billion came in handy to soften the blow of Proposition 13, which made paupers out of local governments by slicing their property-tax revenues.

Local Debt Limits

Most states put a legal bridle on the borrowing impulse of local governments. Many debt limits prohibit borrowing more than an amount equal to 5 percent of assessed valuation; others set the limit at from 5 to 10 percent. These limits may be found either enshrined in the state constitution or set forth in ordinary legislation. Some say debt limits are too rigidly established by the constitution: legitimate occasions may arise when a local government ought to be allowed to exceed the limit. If limits were statutory, the legislature could easily relax them when necessary. On the other hand, it is just this ease of legislative "relief" that

---

[17]The federal government does not maintain separate capital and operating budgets, nor are there any federal debt limits whatsoever, except the futile lid Congress puts on the size of the debt periodically.

makes the constitutional debt limit desirable. It may be wiser to put up with the evils of a rigid constitutional debt limit than with the still greater evil of a legislative limit that too often boils down to no effective limit at all in the face of pressure.

One can easily understand the motives of those who wrote debt limits into law. One has only to look at the extravagances of the 1870s, 1880s, and 1890s. During this era states and municipalities were exceedingly free-spending. They racked up debts with such abandon that one wonders if they had forgotten that borrowed money is supposed to be paid back. Some local governments buried themselves under debts amounting to 50 percent, 75 percent, and even 100 percent of their assessed value. Without going into the questionable motives that guided political "leaders" of that day in their financial decisions, the inevitable reform reaction took place and left a monument to itself in the form of debt limits. These limits were given further support by the default of about 10 percent of all municipal bonds during the 1930s.

Over and above limits on size of debt, some states also limit the purposes for which local governments may borrow, and some limit the time span over which bonds may be retired. In a few states local government must receive approval by vote of the people before incurring bonded indebtedness.

These legal limits usually restrict only borrowing through sale of *general-obligation bonds,* which are a charge against general revenues. *Revenue bonds,* on the other hand, are frequently exempted because they are merely a charge against the revenue of some particular revenue-producing government enterprise, such as a water department or a transit authority, for whose benefit the bond was issued. Buyers of revenue bonds gamble on the ability of the enterprise to repay them, whereas buyers of a general-obligation bond have a claim on the general credit and taxing power of the community.

Evading Debt Limits

An ingenious batch of evasions have been invented to combat debt limits. Laws limiting maximum debt have been circumvented by the multiplication of special districts, each with the power to incur bonded indebtedness and most of them doing special jobs that might better be done by cities or counties. There may be special water districts, sewer districts, park districts, lighting districts, fire-protection districts, parking authorities, air-pollution districts, garbage-disposal districts, drainage districts, mosquito-control districts, and others. Special districts may indeed be erected for any conceivable function, each operating as an independent government with the power to levy taxes and borrow money. Of course, special districts are set up for many reasons and aren't solely debt-evasion gimmicks. This galaxy of special districts contributes to the ramshackle character of American local government.

Another evasion of debt limits is a contrivance called *lease purchase,* which is a form of borrowing masquerading as mere rental. It wears various costumes. In one form it could work like this: the city needs a new city hall and conveys this information to a contractor, who borrows from the bank and constructs the building. The city then leases its new city hall for 20 years at a rent high enough for the contractor to pay back with interest the money borrowed and make a profit. The lease carries with it an option to purchase the building for one dollar after the lease expires.

Contractors and other lobbyists who stand to profit by relaxation of debt limits have pressured legislatures to exempt all sorts of things from the debt limit. Even when debt limits are written into the state constitution, special interests have prevailed on state courts to interpret the term *debt* in such a way as to allow some intriguing exceptions. Many states don't count certain kinds of debt as debt. Often excepted are current bills, short-term loans, revenue bonds, and special assessment bonds.

New York City's celebrated financial crisis of the late 1970s was partly caused by the New York State's debt limit on municipalities, according to Jon A. Baer.[18] In an effort to evade the debt limit, New York City was drawn into a collection of deceptive bookkeeping practices (such as borrowing against tax revenues due the city but uncollectable). These revenues brutally caught up with the city.

Tax Limits

Most states also put limits on the amount of taxes that may be levied on real estate. These **tax limits** take several forms. Some states have laws requiring assessors to assess property at only a limited percentage of true value, say 30 percent. (This represents a tax limit only as long as nobody raises the tax rate.) Some states prohibit an increase of property taxes beyond a certain percentage of increase from one year to the next. Some states put a limit on the per capita levy on real estate. Some states use a combination of limits.

The most famous tax limitation in recent years was the Jarvis-Gann Initiative (**Proposition 13**) adopted by California voters in 1978. It rolled back property taxes, limited future increases in the property tax, and made it difficult to increase other kinds of taxes. Proposition 13 led to similar attempts in a number of other states. In 1980 Massachusetts voters adopted Proposition $2\frac{1}{2}$, which required gradual reduction of local property taxes to $2\frac{1}{2}$ percent of market value. The Massachusetts proposition, like California's, precipitated a cash-flow crisis in school districts, cities, and other local governments.

SUMMARY

A budget is a plan for spending money. An appropriation, on the other hand, is a determination by the legislature of how much money shall be spent for various purposes—it is an authorization to spend. The legislature may be guided by a budget when it makes an appropriation, but no legislature is compelled to adhere to a budget. Most budgeting in state governments is done by the governor and his or her budget office, aided by the entire bureaucracy. Rarely do state legislatures do much budgeting. Legislatures generally rely heavily on the executive budget. Most legislatures simply do not have the staff to duplicate the long drawn-out budget-making process of the executive branch.

Most budgeting is incremental, as is most appropriating. An increment is an addition. Basically the budget, and ultimately the appropriation for each agency, is based on last year's appropriation, with a little something added. To

[18]Jon A. Baer, "Municipal Debt and Tax Limits: Constraints on Home Rule," *National Civic Review* (April 1981), pp. 204–10.

many people incremental budgeting seem nonrational, but it has great political rationality: incremental budgeting does not make many agencies or interests deliriously happy, but it does not rock the boat or make anybody terribly mad.

Budgeting is first, last, and always a political process. It is a struggle for power among agencies and interests. During the past generation a number of new methods of budgeting have been invented and advocated by "experts" who believe more "rationality" should be brought into the budget process. Among budgeting systems that are said to be more rational are program budgeting; the planning, programming, budgeting system (PPBS); and zero-based budgeting (ZBB). All are more or less based on the theory that decisions about spending should be grounded in cost-benefit analysis, which is simply a process of studying how to get the most for your money. This is said to make spending rational. However, cost-benefit analysis is useful only in selecting the best means to a goal, not for selecting goals. A choice of goals is made on the basis of nonrational desire. However, the choice of means to a goal may lend itself to quantitative analysis, especially if the means involve hardware. Zero-based budgeting begins by assuming that no agency should get any (hence *zero*) money unless it proves its worth. But *worth* is a political measure and therefore cannot be proven except politically. The political clout of an agency makes it worthy. Power has its own rationality.

One contribution to "rationality" in budgeting would be to make budgets clear, understandable, and interesting to the average person who might want to read such documents, especially legislators.

Fiscal means "financial." The fiscal year is a financial year. Many governments use the period July 1 to June 31 as their fiscal year. Most legislatures have passed their appropriation bills by then and have adjourned well before July 1.

Appropriation bills are handled in the legislature basically like any other bill. Once the appropriation bill is passed, the process of spending and auditing expenditures begins. Many states have a controller to audit each proposed expenditure *before* the seller is paid. Most states also have a state auditor to again audit expenditures *after* they have been made. The controller is usually appointed by the governor, whereas the auditor is usually elected by the people or appointed by the state legislature.

The purpose of both pre- and postauditing is to determine whether expenditures are legal and whether books are being kept accurately and honestly. In recent years a good many state auditors have also begun auditing to determine whether agencies are performing in the way the legislature intended they should perform when it established them and gave them money.

The perfect auditor would be absolutely independent, absolutely unbiased, and competent. There seems to be no perfect way to pick a person with such qualities. The voting public rarely knows enough about candidates or about the duties of the office to elect a good auditor. The legislature may know more about it, but an auditor appointed by the legislature may lack independence.

States spend about 20 percent of all money spent by all governments in the United States. Local governments spend about 33 percent, and the federal government about 47 percent. Most state and local spending is for education, public welfare, highways, and health. Although state and local spending has increased by leaps and bounds in recent generations, federal spending has increased still more. All government spending has increased because of the increase in population and for various other reasons, including the public's habit of demanding ever more services from government.

The main sources of state revenue are federal aid, sales taxes, and individual income taxes. The greatest sources of local revenue are state aid and property taxes. According to some experts, a "good" tax is a tax that weighs equally upon all—that is, a tax felt equally by all. Each form of tax, including the income tax, sales tax, and real-property tax, have their pluses and minuses. The progressive income tax is intended to be related to the taxpayer's ability to pay, but the tax is very difficult to administer. The sales tax is fairly easy to administer but is regressive. The property tax is also regressive, but since real estate cannot be hidden, it is a fairly easy target for local governments to tax.

States attempt in one way or another to put legal limits on the size of debts that the state government itself, or local governments, may acquire. Although debt limits have succeeded in putting a bridle on the borrowing impulse of governments, those limits have often been successfully evaded.

SUGGESTIONS FOR FURTHER READING

BAHL, ROY, *Financing State and Local Government in the 1980s.* New York: Oxford University Press, 1983.

BOTNER, STANLEY B., "The Use of Budgeting/Management Tools by State Governments," *Public Administration Review* (September/October, 1985), 616–620.

ECKSTEIN, O., *Public Finance* (4th ed.). Englewood Cliffs, N.J.: Prentice-Hall, 1979.

"THE IMPACT OF RESOURCE SCARCITY ON URBAN PUBLIC FINANCE," *Public Administration Review* (January 1981), entire issue.

KNIGHTON, LENNIS M., and ROBERT W. GRAHAM, "Is Auditing a Fourth Power?" *State Government* (Autumn 1970), 258–70.

LYDEN, FREMONT J., and ERNEST G. MILLER, eds., *Public Budgeting: Program Planning and Implementation* (4th ed.). Englewood Cliffs, N.J.: Prentice-Hall, 1982.

LYNCH, THOMAS D., *Public Budgeting in America* (2nd ed.). Englewood Cliffs, N.J.: Prentice-Hall, 1985.

PETERSEN, JOHN E., and CATHERINE LAVIGNE SPAIN, eds., *Essays in Public Finance and Financial Management: State and Local Perspectives.* Chatham, N.J.: Chatham House, 1980.

"SYMPOSIUM: BUDGETING IN AN ERA OF RESOURCE SCARCITY," *Public Administration Review* (November/December 1978), 510–44.

WILDAVSKY, AARON, *The Politics of the Budgetary Process* (4th ed.). Boston: Little, Brown, 1983.

12
civil
servants

PREVIEW

HOW I WAS FIRED

I thought I had a secure civil-service job. I had gotten it by taking a civil-service exam and had done my job well. I was a "merit system" employee, and couldn't be fired unless I failed to do my job well. They couldn't fire me just for political reasons. But I soon learned they could force me to resign, even if they couldn't fire me.

It happened this way. There was a change of party control, and I got a new boss. She was a political appointee. My own job was, of course, not political, but I worked directly under this political appointee. Unfortunately I disagreed with her whole approach to running the agency. She wanted the agency to emphasize certain goals and objectives that I was philosophically opposed to. My boss knew perfectly well that we were at odds over policy. She had no basis for firing me—no legal case against me. I came to work on time. I did everything I was supposed to do. But I did much of it rather reluctantly. She wanted an enthusiastic subordinate, not a reluctant subordinate. I didn't blame her for that.

One day she called me into her office. "You're fired," she said.

"I'm what?"

"Yes, Dave, I've decided to let you go. I'm sorry. I like you personally very much, but you're just not getting the job done."

"Don't you realize," I answered, "that I am a merit-system appointee and that you can't fire me unless you are able to prove to the Civil Service Commission that I am not doing my job properly?"

She ignored my comment, and said, "I'm not going to give you a formal letter of dismissal until about ten days from now. Meanwhile, you might want to consider whether to resign before the dismissal comes. If you resign, I'll do everything to help you find another job; I'll give you strong letters of recommendation."

I responded without hesitation. "The last thing I intend to do is resign. You have no case against me."

"Well, just think it over anyway," she said quietly as I turned to leave.

I couldn't believe this was happening. It was like being hit by a car. I walked hastily back to my office, shut the door, and picked up the phone. My hands were shaking. I could hardly dial my lawyer. When I finally reached him and related the story he said, "Don't worry, Dave, you'll win." He outlined a battle strategy that would involve a series of hearings before various boards and officers, a series of documents to be filed and appeals to be made, a series of witnesses to be called and arguments to be used.

When I hung up, my head was throbbing. I walked over to see my good friend in another agency. I told him what was happening. We spent a long time talking. Incredibly, he advised me to resign. "Don't try to fight it, Dave. It's not worth it. The fight will destroy you. She's probably dug up enough dirt to make a case against you. Any boss can make some kind of case against any subordinate. She may not win, but on the other hand she just may. If she does, and you're fired, you lose more than just a job. You lose your pension rights, you lose your insurance rights, you lose your right to hold another job with the government, you have it on your record that you were fired, and you lose your boss's help in getting relocated. It will be a two-year battle. Going through all those hearings will be a terrible psychological strain on you. You'll be filled with hate. You'll take out your fears and frustrations on your family. Meanwhile, you'll be suspended and without a pay check. Legal expenses will pile up. You'll have to pay witnesses, lawyers, and secretaries."

"Yes, but I can't just give up without a fight. I'm a merit employee, and I've done my job well."

"Think it over anyway," he said. Those were my boss's words, too.

I did think it over. Gradually I began to see the wisdom of a resignation. By the time I did finally hand in my resignation, I had acquired a new and deeper understanding of how merit systems sometimes fail.

HOW MANY AND HOW HIRED?

Every tenth worker in the United States works for state and local government. This includes teachers, fire fighters, police officers and an endless variety of others. More than 10 million (out of a national work force of some 100 million) are directly employed by state and local governments today.[1] Of this number about 3 million work for states, and well over 7 million for local governments (Table 12-1).

---

[1]Many others work indirectly for government either by contract or by employment with firms doing business chiefly with government.

Table 12-1 Full-Time Equivalent Employees of
State Governments

California	260,536
New York	259,648
Texas	185,486
Pennsylvania	121,881
Illinois	116,890
Michigan	113,426
Ohio	113,314
Florida	112,286
Virginia	94,849
North Carolina	88,276
New Jersey	88,066
Louisiana	86,193
Georgia	82,220
Maryland	79,358
Massachusetts	75,340
Washington	71,702
Indiana	65,661
Tennessee	64,991
Alabama	64,007
Wisconsin	61,540
South Carolina	61,509
Missouri	61,497
Oklahoma	60,714
Kentucky	59,247
Minnesota	54,406
Connecticut	48,461
Iowa	45,544
Mississippi	42,432
Colorado	42,122
Oregon	41,292
Kansas	38,848
Hawaii	37,763
Arkansas	36,288
Arizona	36,091
West Virginia	34,798
New Mexico	32,254
Nebraska	29,255
Utah	29,092
Alaska	20,866
Rhode Island	20,484
Maine	18,718
Delaware	16,173
New Hampshire	15,323
Montana	15,182
Idaho	14,636
North Dakota	13,484
Nevada	12,559
South Dakota	11,874
Vermont	10,496
Wyoming	9,921

Source: U.S. Bureau of the Census, *Public Employment in 1984.*

Basically these millions are hired and dealt with by one of three systems: (1) the spoils system, (2) the merit system, and (3) the fitness system. Under the **spoils system** elected officials fill government jobs with people who supported their election: "to the victor belong the spoils." In a merit system, on the other hand, workers are selected for employment by competitive exams. Finally, the **fitness system** is something short of being a formal merit system but is not entirely a spoils system either: employees generally get their jobs by possessing some degree of competence (fitness) while also being acceptable politically. Sometimes it is hard to say which of these three systems is operating in any particular jurisdiction—appearances are deceiving, especially the appearance of some merit systems.

THE MERIT SYSTEM

The merit system for hiring public employees did not spring as much from love of merit as from hate of politics. Even today most merit systems suffer an excess of negative purpose; rather than affirmatively trying to attract the best, they negatively try to block political intrusion. But political intrusion into the personnel system continues in many of America's 82,000 governments. Most of them, as a matter of fact, lack any systematic, formal merit system. However, since the federal government and most populous states and cities have a **competitive civil service,** most American public servants work within some kind of merit system.

Most states, even those operating basically as spoils systems, maintain at least part of their civil service within a merit system. The federal government will not give funds for certain purposes unless the state (or local) agencies administering those funds operate under a competitive merit system.[2] This has insured that at least part of every state's civil service is under a merit system.

The Case for Spoils

Before we look at how merit systems work, let's see how spoils works and ask ourselves, "Can there be merit in spoils?" Suppose the county sheriff, clerk, treasurer, assessor, coroner, and surveyor—all popularly elected officials—are free to hire anybody they wish to fill jobs in the agencies they head. As elected officials they will want to pay political debts by offering posts to those who helped in the campaign or to friends and relatives. Most of these appointees will, of course, want to keep their jobs. Therefore the staff of, say, the county clerk will have good reason to see that the clerk is reelected when the time comes. All are joined by a common interest in seeing that the clerk's office is well run, seeing that every "customer" is well treated, and avoiding corruption and scandal that might embarrass the clerk in the next campaign. There may be no tension between employees and employer—certainly no need for a labor union, certainly no strikes—because the employees and their employer have one com-

---

[2]Social Security Act of 1939, *U.S.C.* Par. 301 et seq.

mon purpose, and that purpose is to stay on the payroll.[3] No one connected with the operation would want to see the clerk put in jeopardy by poor performance. All this oneness of purpose may be a plus for the spoils system.

There is also something to be said for President Andrew Jackson's argument that if we want elected executives to do what we elected them to do—to carry out policies we elected them to carry out—then we have to give those elected executives the power to hire and fire. If a candidate for sheriff who promises to crack down on prostitution is elected by the voters to do just that, how can he really do it if subordinates in the sheriff's department oppose the policy? President Jackson said in his inaugural address that if the people want him to do what they elected him for, he would have to appoint people to office who share his views and toss out those who don't. That is not an altogether unmeritorious view. It is a view being accepted more and more by those who may have forgotten the dangers of political domination of the civil service. Such a view is one of many reasons why the federal Hatch Act,[4] the state "Little Hatch Acts,"[5] and the county and city "Littler Hatch Acts"[6] limiting political activity by public employees are all under attack.

What are the dangers of political domination of the civil service? One of the greatest in the minds of merit-system advocates is that the civil service will become one vast political machine beholden to a single party or faction. So large is the modern civil service that it can nearly muster the votes to control city, county, state, and national elections—especially when the votes of spouses, mothers, fathers, brothers, and sisters are added. Another alleged danger is that the unlimited supply of civil-service jobs can (under a spoils system) become an unlimited supply of paid party workers. This, of course, does not begin to exhaust the list of things people don't like about a politicized civil service.

Classification of Jobs

What Is It?   How does a formalized merit system work? The first thing you have to do if you want to install a merit system is classify all the jobs. **Job**

[3]Staying on the payroll may be easier in the future. The United States Supreme Court in *Branti* v. *Finkel*, 445 U.S. 507 (1979), held that it is a violation of due process of law to fire a politically appointed civil servant purely for partisan reasons unless party membership is shown to be "essential to the discharge of the employee's governmental responsibilities." The case involved two Republican assistant public defenders who had been discharged by a newly appointed public defender in Rockland County, New York. The court said patronage has a chilling effect on the exercise of freedom of expression and freedom of association because it has a tendency to coerce public employees into compromising their beliefs in order to keep their jobs. The less an employee has to do with policy making, the more suspect will be his or her dismissal for political reasons.

[4]5 *U.S.C.* Par. 7324 (1939). In 1940 state and local employees whose principal employment was in connection with an activity financed in whole or in part by federal funds were covered by the Hatch Act. See 4 *U.S.C.* Par 1501 et seq.

[5]The Commission on Political Activity of Government Personnel made a study of federal and state laws limiting political participation by public employees. See the Commission's *Commission Report: Research*, Volume 11 (Washington, D.C., Government Printing Office, 1967), pp. 91–154.

[6]Although all states have followed the federal lead and adopted "Little Hatch Acts," fewer than half the states have laws governing the political activity of local government employees. See Melvin Hill, Jr., "The 'Little Hatch Acts': State Laws Regulating Political Activities of Local Government Employees," *State Government* (Autumn 1979), pp. 161–68.

classification is so important to every merit system that the system itself is commonly called the **classified service.** (It is also called the *competitive service.*) What is classification? It is simply the grouping of similar jobs into classes (or categories) and the arranging of those classes into a hierarchy according to the level of skill, responsibility, and training necessary to carry them out.

Importance   Why is job classification so important to the existence of a merit system? It is important first because the whole idea of a merit system is that people will be paid according to the work they are doing and not according to the political pull they have. Thus each job needs to be studied so we can determine exactly what work is involved, and then put into a pay category along with similar jobs so that equal pay for equal work will prevail. A second reason for studying the duties of each job and putting like jobs into like categories is that it makes it possible to design tests for groups of similar jobs. One can't have a merit system without some means to find out who has merit, and how much. This is done, obviously, with tests of some sort. Written tests or practical tests, or both, are usually given for jobs involving specific skills, such as typing or welding. Candidates for appointment to jobs such as doctor or lawyer or manager "take" what is called an **unassembled test**—they are simply asked to supply a dossier with information about their schooling, experience, and so forth.

The Civil-Service Commission

A merit system is normally run by a nonpartisan independent board, commonly called a **civil-service commission.** Members of the board are usually appointed by the chief executive (mayor or governor), but each appointment must usually be approved by the legislative body. Members normally serve overlapping terms of several years. Their function is to arrange jobs into classifications, write descriptions for all jobs, design tests, and make rules for promotion, retirement, layoffs, dismissals, discipline, and other personnel matters. If the board does not do these itself, it supervises and sets standards for those who do. The board is also a quasi court for hearing appeals from civil servants who think they have been dealt with wrongfully under the rules. Of course, the civil-service commission has jurisdiction only over the classified civil service—that part that is within the merit system.

Centralization versus Decentralization of Personnel Management

Merit systems tend to centralize control of personnel administration in the hands of civil-service commissions and their professional staffs. In other words, power over promotions, pay raises, discipline, recruitment, and many other personnel matters is placed in considerable degree beyond the control of managers. As managers see it, this is a major fault of the typical merit system. They find management rather awkward without power over subordinates—that is, without possession of sticks and carrots that supposedly motivate work. Of course, merit systems do not totally strip line managers of their power over personnel. However, managers often find it so difficult to fire people that they usually don't even try; managers may also find it so difficult to give special rewards to devoted and competent subordinates that the deserving usually go unrewarded. Furthermore, in a large government where the merit system is centrally controlled by a civil-service commission, the effort to tailor the system to the special needs of each department becomes a nightmare, even though departments may sharply differ in their special needs. Uniformity of rules, procedures, and forms is too often imposed on those who require diversity, not uniformity. Furthermore, civil-service commissions and other central personnel agencies in large jurisdictions are finding the job of running the whole merit system singlehandedly too much work for their staff.

For these and other reasons some state and local governments have attempted to decentralize their merit system. "There is a movement away from committing major resources to centralized legalized procedures, toward delegating the process to the operating departments and agencies."[7] The new role of the central personnel agency becomes that of policy maker. But the policy maker is also armed with inspectors who see to it that the departments hew to the central policy line. If the central personnel agency declares, for example, that examinations for typists must be practical rather than written, the agency may then be left the job of designing and grading the practical exam. This relieves the central personnel agency of a lot of work and also allows departments to tailor exams to their own needs. By *tailor* we mean, for example, that a department may want to rig up selection and promotion exams that—although fair—stress the qualities uniquely needed by the department. In its test for typists a budget agency may want to stress the ability to type numbers.

Noncompetitive Jobs

Governor's Office   Never are all the jobs in a government under a merit system. Even where a state has a thoroughgoing competitive system, certain groups of employees are excluded. They hold **noncompetitive jobs.** The personal staff of the governor is almost always excluded. The governor may simply be given a block of money to run his office; the governor can use it to create jobs as he or she sees fit and can hire or fire anyone for any reason. The governor's office in almost every state is a small bastion of spoils, sometimes isolated in a sea of merit.

Department Heads   Merit systems also exclude the heads of most major departments, who at the state level are normally appointed by the governor and serve at his or her pleasure. A few department heads in most states are elected—officers such as the secretary of state, attorney general, and treasurer. They are, of course, excluded from the merit system. Some agency heads, such as the heads of universities, are appointed by boards. Furthermore, most merit systems exclude a certain number of high-level bureaucrats beneath the department head; these are usually appointed by the department head or by the governor without competitive examination.

Legislature and Courts   Employees of the legislature are usually outside the competitive system—clerks, secretaries, staff. Such appointments are normally highly political. Jobs in the judicial branch are also normally outside the competitive system. Some court systems establish their own merit system; others

---

[7]Norman Beckman and William Chadwick, "Making Personnel Administration Relevant to Management," *National Civic Review* (May 1980), p. 258.

leave appointments to the discretion of judges. Many judges are elected or appointed on a partisan basis, and this is reflected in the clerks, secretaries, and staff they appoint.

Thus a competitive merit system at the state level is usually confined to the executive branch and to the middle- and low-level employees therein.

Local Governments Some local governments, for reasons of their own, attempt to run only part of their bureaucracy under a competitive system. In some cases only police and fire personnel are covered. County governments often find it especially hard to run a merit system. This difficulty arises from the decentralized character of county government in many states. Separately elected county officers may not be answerable to any central governing body of the county. There simply may be no central county authority with sufficient power to set up a countywide competitive service. In some states the legislature could legislate a modern personnel system for counties, but the details of county government in many states are set in the state constitution. The county governing board may have no interest in a merit system. Even if it does there might be little it could do to accomplish it beyond persuading the separately elected county officials to establish voluntarily some sort of competitive system within their separate jurisdictions.

The Growth of State and Local Merit Systems

Federal Leadership Major changes in state and local personnel administration have more or less mirrored changes in federal personnel administration. Certainly this is true of the greatest change of all—the shift from spoils to merit. However, state governments did not suddenly switch from spoils to merit after passage of the federal **Pendleton Act of 1883.**[8] In fact, it wasn't until the 1960s that half the states had merit systems covering most of their employees (that is, comprehensive systems). Today only three-fourths of the states have comprehensive systems. Of course, the federal government itself did not suddenly switch from spoils to an across-the-board merit system. The changeover was a slow process: federal comprehensive coverage was not really achieved until after World War II.

Reform Long before the Pendleton Act was passed, civil-service leagues and other groups were campaigning against the spoils system. By the time James A. Garfield was assassinated in 1881 by a disappointed office seeker, the time was ripe for civil-service reform. The assassination produced an outcry against spoils that led directly to passage of the Pendleton Act, which established a federal merit system (or at least the framework of it). New York State immediately jumped on the bandwagon and enacted the first state civil-service law in 1883; the cities of Albany, Buffalo, New York, Syracuse, Chicago, Evanston, Seattle, and Boston had all adopted municipal merit systems by the end of the century. In 1895 Cook County, Illinois became the first county to adopt a merit system.

None of these early merit systems covered the whole civil service within their respective jurisdictions. Coverage was commonly limited to police, fire, and

[8]22 *Stat.* 27 (1883); 5 *U.S.C.* 1101. Formal title: An Act to Regulate and Improve the Civil Service of the United States.

clerical employees. There was still much room for patronage at all levels of government, still much room for spoils and corruption in government, especially in state and local government. In 1902 and 1903. for example, Lincoln Steffens published a series of articles in *McClure's Magazine* exposing corruption in St. Louis, Minneapolis, Pittsburgh, and Philadelphia. Steffens also examined attempts at reform in Chicago and New York. These exposures helped nudge state and local governments toward civil-service reform. A steady stream of states and cities adopted merit systems for some or all of their employees over the years, and the process is still under way.

The Social Security Act In 1939 Congress shoved state and local governments still further toward the merit system when it wrote a provision into the federal Social Security Act[9] requiring governments receiving federal-aid money to use a merit system for staffing agencies that execute programs supported by that money. In the 1930s there was a great expansion of federal aid to state and local governments for such things as public assistance, unemployment insurance, crippled children, and maternal and child health. To execute those programs every state government and many local governments were forced (if they wanted the federal-aid money) to go through the laborious process of setting up competitive personnel systems.

Federal Technical Assistance Establishing merit systems where none had existed before was a difficult challenge for state and local governments. Some really didn't know how to go about it. The federal government, having been largely responsible for this frenzy of activity, therefore provided manuals, test service, field consultation. and technical assistance to state and local governments. It also set forth merit-system standards for their guidance.

Today Many state and local governments did not extend their merit systems beyond those agencies supported by federal funds. Although today the majority of states do have comprehensive merit systems covering most state employees, the same cannot be said for local governments. Nearly all large cities over 250,000 do have comprehensive merit systems, as do most cities between 100,000 and 250,000, but the number of cities (and other local governments) with merit systems declines as one goes down the population ladder. In towns below 100,000, merit systems are often limited to police officers and fire fighters.

It is worth noting that state and local governments have occasionally introduced useful and important innovations, later adopted by the federal government. Chicago introduced the first position-classification plan in the nation, and New York City established the first retirement system for public employees.

A Meritless System? Adoption of a merit system does not by any means carry with it the guarantee that the system will be run with perfect integrity or with perfect skill and intelligence. As we shall see in the following sections, merit systems can be corrupted by politics. They can become fronts for spoils systems. Albany, New York, one of the first cities in America to adopt a merit system, also

---

[9] *42 U.S.C. 301 et seq.*

became one of the first whose merit system was ravaged and undermined by partisan influence (a problem hopefully corrected by now). The same thing has happened many times elsewhere across the country. Even merit systems that are able to keep their integrity may be administered by persons poorly trained to do the job or by unimaginative people so enraptured by the mechanics of a merit system that they neglect its broader purpose of attracting and selecting the best persons for government work.[10] Technique can triumph over purpose. Some-one has said, "The only thing worse than a merit system is no merit system." All merit systems have fundamental built-in weaknesses. Classification of positions, a procedure fundamental to all merit systems, is almost impossible to do well. Classification depends on accurate **job descriptions,** but very few positions can be described with any precision or permanency. Nor are valid examinations easy to invent, especially where jobs are hard to define. The list of fatal problems is very long.[11]

Illegal Patronage

There is so much **illegal patronage** in *some* so-called merit systems that they may as well be called spoils systems. Just because a town, county, or state has a civil-service commission and claims to run a merit system does not always mean that it does. Spoils can exist behind the facade of merit. The integrity of merit systems differs from place to place.

Temporary Appointments   One noteworthy form of illegal patronage is the temporary appointment. Civil-service rules allow employers to make tempo-rary appointments without the usual competitive procedures while the search goes on for a permanent appointee. Temporary appointments are limited to a certain number of months, usually three or six, but may be renewed if a perma-nent appointee has not been selected. Some temporaries have stayed on the job 20 or more years, renewal after renewal. People who get a temporary appoint-ment have an inside track for the permanent appointment if they want it: they learn how to do the job, and this gives them an advantage on the competitive exam. They may also make useful personal contacts within the agency that could favor their ultimate appointment to the permanent job.

Job Description   Another way you can corrupt the merit system is to write a job description to fit the talents of your favorite candidate like a glove. Design the job just for a particular person. If it is a job for a lawyer and the favored candidate has experience prosecuting consumer-fraud cases, write "must have had experience prosecuting consumer-fraud cases." By carefully designing the job description, you can exclude nearly everyone in the world except the one you have in mind.

[10]"The quality of administration depends upon such factors as top executive, legislative, and public support, broad gauged personnel leadership, competent professional staff, and adequate appropriations." Albert H. Aronson, "State and Local Personnel Administra-tion," in *Classics of Public Personnel Policy,* ed. Frank J. Thompson (Oak Park, Ill.: Moore, 1979), p. 111.

[11]See E. S. Savas and Sigmund G. Ginsburg, "The Civil Service: A Meritless System?" *Public Interest* (Summer 1973), pp. 70–85.

Ignoring the Description   The merit system can also be defeated by total disregard for the job description. Rather than trying to fit the description around your favorite candidate, you can save yourself that trouble by bringing your favorite into another job, perhaps a lower-level job for which he or she is qualified and then giving him or her the duties of the job you really want him or her to have. This, of course, is against the rules. Each job has its description. A person holding a merit-system job is not supposed to do anything but what's on the description of the job he or she holds. To give a clerk the duties of an administrative assistant offends the merit system. Not every violation of the merit system is discovered immediately. There aren't enough classifiers working for the typical civil-service commission to check whether everybody in the system is doing what they are supposed to be doing. The diligence and frequency with which jobs are audited varies from place to place: it may be several years before a violation is discovered. There are no criminal penalties for ignoring the job description. An erring employer is simply informed of the violation and told to correct it.

Tests   Another way to defeat the merit system is to stack the test in favor of one particular candidate you want to hire. This is easier to do if the position is a high-level one for which tests are unassembled, consisting mainly of oral exams and consideration of dossiers. It is always more difficult to define just what consititutes merit for high-level positions than to do so for low-level positions. Merit in typists is much more precisely understood and measurable than merit in, say, managers. No one really knows for sure what qualities make a good manager. Thus there is much room for judgment, and therefore much room for political favoritism. This is a very difficult gap in the merit system to close because there should be flexible qualifications for high-level positions. Yet that very flexibility invites favoritism.

The Register   Another way to put a political favorite into a particular job despite the merit system is simply to "wait out the register." The **register** is a list of people who have passed the exam for a particular kind of job. Names are arranged from top to bottom by scores on the exam. When there is a job vacancy, the civil-service commission refers the top names (usually three) to the employer. The employer can choose anyone referred; the others go back on the list and are referred again and again, until ultimately the list expires (usually after one year) or is completely used up. If your favorite, the one you want to hire, is somewhere on the register, you simply wait for those above him or her to be hired elsewhere. Then at just the right moment you announce your job. Three names including the one you want are referred, and you've got your favorite.

Consultants   Sometimes the appointment of consultants is patronage in disguise. A **consultant** is not a temporary occupant of a permanent position but is someone hired temporarily to fill a temporary need. Formal competitive procedures of the merit system do not apply, and the employer's choice of consultants is limited chiefly by money. Opportunities for appointment of political favorites are too obvious to explain.

Commission   Of course, the best way to defeat the merit system is to capture its civil-service commission. The commission is the ultimate enforcer of merit procedures. If captured by a political faction, clique, ring, or party, then one could guess the consequences. Capturing a local civil-service commission may be easier than capturing a state commission.

Firing People

The Complications of Tenure As we have seen, it is possible to hire political favorites by twisting and manipulating the merit system. Likewise it is possible to fire or get rid of people by twisting the system. Under most merit systems, appointees get *tenure* once they've held a job for a certain (probationary) length of time. Tenure means they can't be fired except for "cause." Cause has to be proved. The system deliberately makes firings difficult, deliberately forces managers to show the alleged failures of performance. If firing were easy and required no show of cause, then people could be fired for political reasons. The main idea, remember, is to keep politics out of hiring and firing and out of all other personnel actions of the system. Fired employees have many opportunities to appeal. The ultimate appeal is to the civil-service commission. It is so hard to dismiss a tenured merit-system employee, so laborious, so time-consuming for the manager, that most managers would rather do anything than try to fire anybody. The dismissal process often becomes a trial of the employer rather than of the employee.

Justification Consequently an employer who wants to get rid of a sub-ordinate doing poor work can use a variety of cagey techniques to accomplish the desired result without having to slog through dismissal procedures. The same cagey techniques can also be turned against political undesirables. Persons doing their job perfectly well can be subjected to unendurable harassments that will drive them away or shunt them aside. High-ranking people who hold tenure in policy-making jobs are especially vulnerable to these cunning tactics if they happen to hold political ideas different from those of the politically appointed agency head. The elected **political high command** of a government—federal, state, or local—often feels it has a right to run the executive branch according to its own political outlook. To do this effectively it needs the cooperation of key managers in the bureaucracy. Foot dragging by key people could bog down programs. If the politically appointed head of a welfare department believes welfare fraud should be ferreted out, but the major tenured merit-system subordinates don't agree, then it's going to be tough for the agency head to get his way. His orders will be quietly ignored. What is the agency head to do? He cannot easily fire the subordinates. They're tenured and probably doing a "good job" and not overtly refusing any orders. Nor does the agency head want to become involved in a long struggle to dismiss anybody. So he may resort to some fancy footwork that is technically within the civil-service rules in order to get rid of one or more of the disloyal subordinates. Such techniques may include threatening dismissal, abolishing the job, "layering" the job by hiring someone else to do it without dismissing the disloyal subordinate, or assigning the unwanted employee to an unpleasant duty station, unpleasant duties, or an unpleasant workplace.

Some civil-service managers say merit-system employees have too much protection, too many opportunities to appeal, and that managers simply have to use under-the-table methods to discipline and terminate employees.

Is Merit a Fraud?

All these techniques are clearly at odds with basic principles of the merit system. They exist beneath the facade of most merit systems. This does not mean that all merit systems are frauds. Many merit systems work surprisingly well for most employees most of the time. The sly tactics just described for getting rid of unwanted employees are usually reserved for high-level policy-making officials who are in conflict with their still higher ranking bosses. Sometimes these tactics are turned against ordinary rank-and-file employees, but not often.[12]

PUBLIC-SERVICE UNIONISM

Some History

Public-service unionism is by no means new in the United States, nor are strikes by public servants. More than 150 years ago there was a walkout by workers at the Philadelphia Navy Yard. Even though it has long been unlawful to strike against most governments, this has not prevented unions from organizing and fighting for their members through political channels and by miscellaneous other tactics. Among the first to organize were postal workers: the National Association of Letter Carriers was established in 1890.

Unions Today

Some 75 percent of all civilians who work for government in the United States work for state and local government. Numerous unions and associations representing state and local employees now flourish. Perhaps the greatest of these is the American Federation of State, County, and Municipal Employees (**AFSCME**). Two other unions enroll numerous state and local employees: Service-Employees International Union (SEIU), which caters primarily to white-collar and hospital employees, and Laborers International Union (LIU), which caters mainly to unskilled labor. Other unions, such as the Teamsters and various building-trades unions, have also been aggressively recruiting state and local employees. Over half of all police, fire, school, sanitation, highway, welfare, and hospital workers are now represented in negotiations with employers by unions or associations. AFSCME has well over a million members, the National Education Association represents more than two million teachers, and the American Federation of Teachers represents another million teachers. There has been not only a surge of union (or association) membership but also a surge in their militancy.

[12]For a sophisticated study of how the president can achieve a "loyal" chain of command in the federal service despite civil-service rules and regulations, see *The Malek Manual,* in *Executive Session Hearings before the Select Committee on Presidential Campaign Activities of the United States Senate, Watergate and Related Activities, Book 19* (Washington, D.C.: Government Printing Office, 1974). Although *The Malek Manual* pertains to the federal civil service, many of the observations it makes are equally pertinent to state and local merit systems. Frederic V. Malek was deputy director of the Office of Management and Budget in the Nixon administration.

Growth of Unions

Why this surge? No doubt fashion had something to do with it. The idea of organizing and demanding rights did indeed catch on. Militancy was in the air. Militancy by public servants was perhaps encouraged by that of women, Chicanos, and blacks.

Trade unions in the private sector had seemingly struck a stone wall in their attempts to advance unionism: for decades the private sector had remained about 25 percent unionized, less in recent years. Looking across to the workers in the public sector, union leaders saw an attractive vacuum to be filled and commenced forthwith to convert and recruit.

Perhaps the very size of the bureaucracy has invited collective bargaining. In recent decades a tremendous growth in state and local bureaucracies has occurred. The larger an organization, the more impersonal it becomes. Communication between bosses and workers becomes more difficult, more distant, more formal. Workers feel more at the mercy of employers in large organizations. They begin to feel the only way to communicate with management is to gang up and talk through employee organizations.[13] The larger the city, the more likely its civil servants will be organized. America's largest city, New York City, is America's most unionized city in the public sector. Almost all its 350,000 public employees belong to unions. As one goes down the population scale, one encounters less and less public-service union activity. Remember that most of America's 82,000 governments are rather tiny enterprises. Only some 15,000 of them employ more than 50 persons. Intimacy discourages formal collective bargaining.

Of course, big cities are also the site of big private manufacturing firms, citadels of private-sector unionism. The spirit of unionism roams freely in big cities and has roamed into the offices of the public bureaucracy.

Difficulties Unions Face

Although public-service unionism has increased by leaps and bounds lately, it has not been as useful to its members as they may have dreamed, although unions have undeniably won benefits, sometimes great benefits. Public-service unions encounter some problems that their private-sector counterparts do not. With whom, for example, does a public-service union negotiate? What's the point of bargaining and negotiating and painfully working out agreements with the administrative-agency heads when they are only employees themselves, answerable to others who have the final say? In the private sector unions deal with the ultimate authority—the owners or their agents. In the public sector the ultimate authority is not generally at the bargaining table—the ultimate authori-

---

[13]Economists debate whether unionization actually has any effect on wages over the short or long term and if so, how much. A study of the effect of unionization on the salaries of state employees presents evidence that "when state employees organize, increased salaries and retirement benefits should result." See Richard C. Kearney and David R. Morgan, "Unions and State Employee Compensation," *State and Local Government Review* (September 1980), pp. 115–19.

ty being the legislature, the city council, the county board,[14] the school board, or the sovereign people who in due time through the ballot have a final word. Public-service unions therefore may put less faith in bargaining with management than in lobbying and political action.

Another "problem" is that governments can survive strikes better than private firms can. The government cannot be driven out of business. When the employees of a brewery go on strike and shut the flow of beer from that firm, customers go to another brand. The firm's managers know this, fear it, and want to negotiate an agreement before their business is injured. But government is a monopoly. If police go on strike, the city doesn't have to worry about the police department "losing business."

On the other hand, the very fact that public-service unions know full well their adversary is not likely to go broke—that governments are financed by "inexhaustible" tax sources—makes them unusually demanding.

Since no strike is likely to drive the government out of business, public-service managers can get away with being hardheaded and unyielding in their negotiations with unions. They can also get away with being softheaded and too yielding—the government is in little danger of going broke. Of course, elected officials risk their political future by yielding too much. Sometimes they solve this problem by giving high pension benefits in lieu of immediate wage increases. Let the next generation pay the bill!

Public-Service Strikes

It continues, as these pages are written, to be illegal for federal and most state and local civil servants to strike. These antistrike laws are ticklish and awkward to enforce. Illegal strikes happen all the time. Laws against them are treated with the same respect that laws against drinking were treated in the twenties. That in itself is sometimes presented as an argument for legalizing public-service strikes—better to revoke unenforceable laws than to invite disregard for the law, better to prepare for strikes than to outlaw them, better to erase the law than pretend it's working.

Antistrike laws are almost unenforceable. If a thousand teachers illegally strike one fine morning, what can anyone do about it? Technically they could all be arrested. But what jail would hold them? What police department has the time to arrest them all? What elected city official would want to suggest arresting a thousand teachers? What court has time to process them all? What elected judge would want to sentence a thousand teachers to jail, or fine them? The spectacle would only make martyrs of them. Even if it's only 25 teachers, getting rough with them could cost more than the strike. Likewise with any other category of public worker. Nor does arresting and fining union officers help much: it makes martyrs of them, heats up emotions and adds fuel to the strike, and probably won't end the strike because employees may not obey a back-to-work

---

[14]"Increased teacher influence has not been at the expense of school boards; instead, by bringing boards into direct confrontation with organized teachers over educational and personnel policy, collective bargaining has revitalized their policymaking role." Nolan J. Argyle, "The Impact of Collective Bargaining on Public School Governance," *Public Policy* (Winter 1980), p. 139.

order given by leaders under duress. Nor do fines against the union treasury always work. They generate the same resentment as fines against officers.

The right to strike is said to be the ultimate weapon of any union, but it is not by any means the only weapon. Public-service unions have managed to represent their members with a good deal of success without calling strikes. Possibly the right to lobby, the right to propagandize, the right to condemn and praise, and the right to play politics are more powerful "rights" than the right to strike. Strikes, after all, can be expensive. In fact they often cost more than they yield. Anyone who goes on strike is at least temporarily out of a job and out of a pay check for the duration. Also, there is cost in good will as well as in dollars. Public servants who strike may make large parts of the public mad at them. Public servants depend on a cooperative public. Police need a sympathetic and supportive public to do their job. A teachers' strike can cause deep and bitter resentment among parents that may express itself in defeated school-bond issues and in other forms of public sullenness. Thus the political weapon may be more effective than strikes.

Unions versus Merit

Muscle Whether the weapon be strikes or politics, one occasionally hears all public-service unionism condemned by those who think it runs head-on into every concept of merit. The argument is this: a merit system should be run by merit and merit alone; hiring should be by merit; promotions, tenure, dismissal, and every personnel action should rest on merit, not on power. Unionism is said to substitute muscle for merit. How much pay should postal workers get? Is that a question to be decided by the character of postal work, or by the power of the postal union? Equal work for equal pay—that's the guiding principle of a merit system, not might makes right.

Seniority Another alleged conflict between merit systems and unions is the habitual use of **seniority** by unions for determining who should be promoted, laid off, recalled, transferred, given job or work assignments, given shift preference, granted days off, allowed overtime, and so on. Merit-system advocates hate to see such things determined by seniority rather than merit.

Union defenders answer that merit is difficult to measure, that seniority and merit are related, and that seniority is a clearly understood basis for decid-

---

Box 12-1. Even Medics Strike

Some 2000 medical interns and residents went on strike March 17, 1981, against six municipal hospitals in New York City to protest inadequate staffing and equipment. After one week the medics ended their strike and issued a statement saying they had "lost this battle." New York State's Taylor Law, which prohibits strikes by public employees, had something to do with the decision to end the strike. The Taylor Law penalizes striking public employees by taking away two days' pay for each day on strike. Mayor Edward Koch also had warned the strikers that they risked loss of their certification as doctors, and the city sought a fine of $100,000 a day against the union.

ing touchy questions that if decided by foggy definitions of merit would lead to suspicion of favoritism.

Politics Critics of public-service unionism accuse the unions of dragging the bureaucracy back into partisan politics from where it (in some areas) so laboriously struggled. The whole idea of a merit system is to take personnel decisions—especially hiring and firing—out of politics. Unions are deep in politics and practice it vigorously. Insofar as members of the civil service are loyal members of their union, they are propelled into the politics practiced by that union. So it is claimed.

A Nonmerit Condition of Employment Another collision of unionism with merit principles occurs because unions normally demand a **union shop:** they require everybody in an agency represented by a union to join the union if they want to keep their job. Winning union-shop contracts is a cardinal thrust of nearly every union. Unions argue that every employee benefits by union representation and therefore should be required to pay dues to support the union that wins those benefits. But defenders of merit argue that there should be no conditions attached to getting a merit-system job other than merit itself.

At present, union shops and **closed shops** are outlawed almost everywhere in the public sector.[15] The closed shop is even more restrictive than the union shop. Under a closed-shop contract no one may be hired who is not already a member of the union at the time he or she is hired. A union shop allows a new employee a period of time to join the union.

Right of Nonassociation

The United States Constitution guarantees freedom of association,[16] and many constitutional lawyers contend that if there is a freedom of association, there must also be a freedom of "nonassociation." Freedom to associate implies freedom not to associate. A union shop (and certainly a closed shop) seems to conflict with that right of nonassociation. The essential feature of a union shop or closed shop is forced association with a union—forced, that is, if you want to keep your job. Unions answer that no one is forced to keep his or her job. But many workers can't just pack up and find another job—they have no choice but to accept the alleged benefits of union membership. They may be justified in saying to the union, "Although I appreciate your help, I didn't ask for it. I especially did not ask for it because I knew that the price of your help would be forced membership in your organization and forced submission to its rules and leadership."

To avoid violation of this alleged constitutional right of nonassociation, a compromise has been invented called the **agency shop.** In an agency shop every employee must pay union dues to help finance the cost of union representation, but no employee is forced to "join" the union. Thus there is a fine line between paying dues and being a member. Where agency shops are permitted, unions are forbidden to use the money of nonmembers for any purpose but representa-

[15]Taft-Hartley Act, 61 *Stat.* 156 (1947), 29 *U.S.C.* 185.
[16]*U.S. Const.*, 1st Amendment.

tion. However, it is difficult to prevent unions from playing shell games with money.

A National Labor Law?

Public-service unionism is on the rise in America, the number of strikes is increasing, and there is perhaps a need to systematize and regularize the relations of unions with America's governments. Sometimes we hear, "Why not have one single national labor law pertaining to public-service unions—a law that would apply to all governments—national, state, and local?" Such a question betrays some degree of ignorance about our federal system. It is hard to have a national law on anything—labor, divorce, murder, or whatever. The federal government cannot make laws that apply nationally except in those matters that the Constitution specifies. Of course, the federal government can and often does pay states to do things it has no constitutional power to make them do, and perhaps states could be paid to enact a uniform national public-service labor law.

Such a law might govern the way unions treat governmental employers, and the way governmental employers treat unions. It might (1) regulate the procedures by which one particular union achieves the privilege of representing workers in a particular agency; (2) set forth subjects appropriate for bargaining (for example, should some subjects, such as pay and promotions, be off limits?); (3) forbid a variety of "unfair" labor practices—below-the-belt behavior that neither side may exhibit toward the other—such as firing people for belonging to a union, or using threatening language; (4) legalize strikes, but even if it didn't, it could provide a system for settling them as rapidly as possible if they occurred; (5) establish a national office to supply the services of mediators, fact finders, and arbitrators for those governments requesting such services. A uniform law of that sort would replace a large variety of laws now governing labor–management relations at the state, local, and national levels of government.

Such a national law already exists for the private sector (interstate commerce): the **National Labor Relations Act of 1935**,[17] which has been amended and reinterpreted over the last several decades. That law does not apply to public employees, however.

The idea of a national labor-relations law for public employees has its opponents. They say the very existence of such a law would encourage unionism where none exists and where none is wanted by either labor or management. Furthermore, they point out that it would force all 82,000 governments into the same labor–management mold. These thousands of governments differ in how employees and employers get along. It would be a mistake, they insist, to force a uniform set of labor-relations policies on so many diverse jurisdictions.

PRIVATIZATION OF PUBLIC SERVICES

Several hundred federal maintenance workers at military bases near Colorado Springs are in danger of losing their jobs because the Defense Department wants to "privatize" maintenance work. Private firms would be hired to do the work.

---

[17]49 *Stat.* 449 as amended, 29 *U.S.C.* 151 et seq.

Privatization[18] is a trend especially disturbing to labor unions representing government employees who see the "contracting-out epidemic" as their number one problem.

Of course, governments have always contracted with private firms to provide numerous services, such as road and building construction. Yet, as we all know, government provides many services itself. Most of the 15 or 30 million people who work for 80,000 governments in the United States are providing some kind of service. They are teachers, firefighters, police, bus drivers, trash collectors, street cleaners, park workers, and so on. Just go down the list of agencies and you will be reminded of the wide array of services provided directly to the public by government. And to keep those services going—for example, to keep a school running—you need plumbers, carpenters, lawyers, nurses, doctors, and an endless list of specialists of all kinds.

Advocates of privatization say that government should quit trying to do all this work with its own employees but should make a greater effort to contract it out to private companies. Do school nurses need to be civil servants? Why not contract with a private nursing service? Do governments need to run hospitals? Why not lease hospitals to private corporations that specialize in running hospitals? Does government need to employ civil servants to make movies, run medical laboratories, do geological surveys, operate laundries, run cafeterias, do data processing, landscape public property, stand guard duty, and do a thousand other things that are easily obtained by contract, without adding any civil servants to the bureaucracy?

More and more attempts at privatization have been started recently. One state now contracts with private parties to run community correctional facilities that look after certain convicted felons and to guide and supervise parolees. Another state is contracting with a company to locate people who have left the state without paying taxes they owe. Similarly a certain city now hires a company to track down people who have ignored traffic citations. An increasing number of towns have been contracting out garbage collection and electric, gas, water, and transportation services. At present the most controversial form of privatization pertains to prisons. One or two states and localities have experimented with this on a limited scale, but the debate goes on.

The privatization trend is partly motivated by ideas akin to Ralph Waldo Emerson's dictum, "The less government we have the better." And yet the advocates of privatization do not always want government to govern less. Often they merely want government to employ fewer people. The cutback in federal aid to cities and states may also have prompted a search for ways to get government work done cheaper than civil servants could do it. And finally there is the legend that private enterprise always does things better than civil servants.

Whatever may be the arguments for privatization, certainly there is reason for caution.[19] Trying to strike a separate deal with thousands of individual workers or with legions of different companies supplying separate services seems to be the sort of morass one might wish to avoid. The utility of having one

---

[18]See Keon S. Chi, "Privatization: A Public Option?" *State Government News* (June 1985), pp. 4–10.

[19]See Eugene Garaventa, "Private Delivery of Public Services May Have a Few Hidden Barriers," *National Civic Review* (May–June 1986), pp. 153–157.

body of civil servants subject to one uniform set of employment rules and owing allegiance to the government they serve cannot be overlooked. Nor can one overlook the danger that once a government has divested itself of the ability to supply a service, resuming that service, if necessary, might be a real headache. Finding competing contractors might be another headache. Furthermore, with regard to prisons, the legality and propriety of turning citizens over to private corporations for custody or punishment is questionable.

OUR RULING SERVANTS: BUREAUCRATS AS JUDGES AND LEGISLATORS

It might come as a stunning surprise to most people to learn that bureaucrats make more laws than legislators and decide more cases than judges. The **bureaucracy** is more powerful than many imagine. Civics courses often give a misleading picture of who runs America. Children are taught that legislators make laws and the president, governor, or mayor carry out these laws with the help of civil servants. State constitutions reinforce this picture by declaring in weighty language that the powers of government shall be divided into three branches—legislative, executive, and judicial—and that all legislative power shall be vested in one branch, all executive power in another, and all judicial power in a third, and that none shall exercise any power belonging to the other two. This doctrine of separation of powers is well rooted in American thinking—so well rooted that even when the doctrine is flagrantly and constantly violated few but experts see it, or if they see it they don't realize what they are seeing. Undoubtedly the most colossal development in American government this century has been the acquisition of measureless legislative and judicial power by bureaucrats.

Much of this growth of legislative and judicial power in the bureaucracy has been willingly accepted by legislators and judges who realize they do not have the time or knowledge to do all the legislative and judicial work they are theoretically supposed to do. Bureaucrats have become powerful partly because of the inabilities of legislators and judges and partly because of the unique capabilities of the bureaucracy. Much of the trouble afflicting legislatures and courts is caused by the complexity of life in our technological society. The heyday of legislatures was when there really wasn't as much to be legislated about, and the heyday of courts was when disputes weren't as numerous or as complex. Every government has to be as informed and as enlightened as the society over which it seeks to rule, however. If medical science has developed new drugs, and if government wishes to police the manufacture and sale of drugs, then government must employ people with medical and pharmaceutical knowledge equal to that possessed by those it would police. Thus the more elaborate and technological the society, the more elaborate and technological the government—the more baffling the society, the more baffling the government. Most people have no greater understanding of what goes on inside their government than they do of what goes on inside their television set. You and I may not know much about radiowaves or how to manage them, but the Federal Communications Commission does and makes rules and regulations based on their knowledge. The reason for those rules may surpass our understanding, and that of legislators, but that's the nature of modern government.

ADMINISTRATIVE LAWMAKING

One of the greatest reasons for the growth of **rule making** by administrative agencies is the inability of legislatures to understand what laws need to be made with regard to various bewildering subjects. No doubt a state legislature could, if every member became an expert on pharmacy and medicine, do all the work of the state department of health. However, legislators do not want to drop everything else and go to medical school, and they do not want to spend all their time studying the virtues and vices of drugs. They have other things to do. So they create a department of health. They give it money to hire experts and power to make rules having the force of law. The "legislative" output of the typical state department of health exceeds the legislative output of the state legislature in volume and very possibly in usefulness and significance.

Here is the job description of the health department of one state. It does not make exciting reading, but look at the scope of regulatory (lawmaking) power it possesses! The department of public health has the authority to investigate and control the causes of epidemic and communicable diseases; to establish and enforce isolation and quarantine; to close theaters, schools, and other public places and to forbid gatherings of people when necessary to protect the public health; to abate nuisances in order to eliminate the sources of epidemic and communicable disease; to establish and enforce minimum general sanitary standards as to the quality of water supplied to the public; to establish and enforce minimum sanitary standards as to the quality of wastes discharged upon land and as to the quality of fertilizer derived from human excreta or from the sludge of sewage-disposal plants; to collect reports of marriages, divorces and annulments, births, deaths, and morbidity; to regulate the disposal, transportation, interment, and disinterment of the dead; to approve chemical, bacteriological, and biological laboratories; to establish standards for diagnostic tests by chemical, bacteriological, and biological laboratories; to impound any vegetables and other edible crops and meat and animal products intended for and unfit for human consumption, and to condemn and destroy the same if necessary; to annually license and to establish and enforce standards for the operation of hospitals, clinics, health centers, and so forth, and to issue, suspend, renew, revoke, annul, or enforce standards for the operation and maintenance of such health institutions as hospitals, clinics, and health centers; to establish and enforce sanitary standards for the operation and maintenance of all buildings and places used for public gatherings; to establish sanitary standards and make sanitary, sewerage, and health inspections for charitable, penal, and other public institutions; to promulgate rules and regulations for the grading, labeling, and classification of milk and milk products; to establish minimum general sanitary standards for all dairy products sold for human consumption; to inspect and supervise the sanitation of production, processing, and distribution of all dairy products sold for human consumption; to issue licenses to operate milk plants and receiving stations; to establish and enforce sanitary standards for the operation of slaughtering, packing, canning, and rendering establishments and for stores, shops, and vehicles wherein meat and animal products intended for human consumption may be offered for sale or transported; to disseminate public-health information; to examine sanitary-engineering features of all proposed construction of community water facilities; to establish and enforce standards for exposure to toxic materials and radiation; to study the problem of alcoholism.

To carry out all those duties, the state department of health is authorized to issue orders, adopt rules and regulations, and establish standards.

The department of health is a prime example of an agency up to its ears in lawmaking. Almost every major department and agency of the bureaucracy makes some sort of rules and regulations affecting the public. Not only the so-called regulatory agencies but also every corner of the bureaucracy is involved in rule making and regulation. Agencies that concern themselves with social services, higher education, secondary education, highways, labor, natural resources, revenue, agriculture, personnel, law, and many other areas make rules. At the local level, police departments, fire departments, building departments, public-works departments, election departments, and others make rules affecting the public. So universal is administrative rule making that probably 90 percent of all lawmaking in America is done directly by bureaucrats through their rule-making power.

It is true, of course, that legislative bodies usually have the power to nullify rules, but so vast is the rule-making power of the bureaucracy and so overwhelming is its flood of rules and regulations that the legislature simply cannot cope with it—its members have neither the time nor the knowledge to do so, and that is the very reason administrative agencies have been given such vast rule-making power in the first place. Nevertheless, bitten by public criticism of their failure to supervise the rule-making powers of bureaucrats, some legislatures have attempted to make a show of being boss of the agencies. During the past decade more than two-thirds of the state legislatures have established **regulation-review committees** that screen new rules as they flood from agencies and refer any questionable rule to the regular standing committee of the legislature that has oversight of the agency that made the rule. The oversight committee can either take the matter up with the agency or refer the rule to the legislature with a request what a bill be passed specifically quashing or altering it. This procedure, called the legislative veto, has been declared an unconstitutional violation of the doctrine of separation of powers at the federal level by the United States Supreme Court.[20] It has also been under attack in several state courts. In some cases the committee has the power to suspend a rule pending further study, and in some cases rules do not become effective until they have lain before the legislature for a certain period of time: if the legislature does nothing, the rule becomes effective. Few, if any, review committees are adequately staffed to study the merits of rules that often touch highly technical matters.

They Ask for It

A good bit of business regulation is, believe it or not, asked for by those who are regulated. Most boards that license the various occupations, businesses, and professions have been created at the insistence of those same groups. Why do they ask to be regulated? In part it is an attempt to protect the integrity of their profession by excluding undesirables. The way to keep out quacks or people not

---

[20]*Immigration and Naturalization Service* v. *Chadha*, 462 U.S. 919 (1983).

really qualified to practice the profession is to require everybody practicing to have a license issued by a **licensing board** set up to review the qualifications of those who petition for a license. Such regulation gives consumers a degree of certainty that a dentist, a doctor, a lawyer, or any other regulated professional that they patronize has at least the minimum qualifications.

However, maintenance of their integrity isn't the only reason occupational groups ask to be regulated. There are some economic reasons, chief among them a desire to keep prices high and competition low. Take barbers. Anyone could probably learn to trim hair in a matter of hours. If no barber's license were required, a world of people would set up shops. The price of haircuts would be a half or a fourth of what they are now. So barbers in every state have clamored to be regulated, clamored to be saved from the rigors of the capitalist system. They assert it is dangerous to the health of customers to have their hair cut by people poorly educated in barbering. A state barber board should be set up, they say, to license barbers. Only barbers should sit on this board. The board should require people wishing to be barbers to go to barber school, perhaps for six months, and learn not only how to cut hair but also what a hair is, why it grows, and a whole lot of things to fill up six months. This would stop many people from going into the barber business. The barber board should also have the power to set the minimum price of a haircut and the power to revoke the license of any barber who charges less than the minimum price.

Most occupational licensing seeks occupational self-protection by trying to keep charlatans out and by maintaining an artificially low number of practitioners and an artificially high price. Agencies having the power to license occupations and professions also generally have the power to regulate the practice of those professions by a series of rules. Barbers are required to do such things as sweep up hair and put combs in disinfectant.

Monopolies

A good deal of business regulation occurs because of the monopolistic nature of some kinds of business. Certain businesses are unavoidably monopolistic: they are natural monopolies. Most public utilities are natural monopolies. It's hardly feasible to run competing electric utility lines, or competing telephone lines, or competing gas lines up and down the streets. When there is competition, the danger of price gouging exists. A telephone company could, if it wanted, probably get ten times as much for telephone service, if it were free to demand it. Most states have public-utility commissions to regulate utility rates and make rules touching many other aspects of the utility business.

Influencing Legislators

We are discussing why civil servants have acquired lawmaking power. We've touched only the formal rule-making power possessed by nearly every agency of government, but civil servants also make law indirectly by influencing legislative bodies. Lawmakers often wish to act on subjects they don't know much about. Even with the aid of standing committees, legislative councils, and other staff agencies, the typical legislature is woefully outclassed by the executive branch in possession of technical knowledge. The legislature turns to those who have knowledge for advice and guidance. It turns to the bureaucracy—not solely, not always, but often. The bureaucracy, like a patrol on the battlefield, is in contact with the problem and is aware of its dimensions and possible solutions long before the problem reaches the legislature.

Bureaucrats are not the only source of expert advice, but they may be the most influential in many cases, for in addition to their expertise, they generally speak for a collection of special interest groups allied to their function. Administrative agencies commonly have snug relationships with their clientele—that is, with the people they serve—and especially with the organizations representing their clientele. Farmers' organizations work hand in glove with the department of agriculture, labor unions with the department of labor, and so on. Before the department of agriculture makes a recommendation to the legislature, the department will almost surely have a powwow with client groups and will speak with their backing and with the backing of various members of the legislature, including possibly the agriculture committee itself, which is no doubt responsive to organized agriculture. Furthermore, the bureaucracy often has the backing of the governor when it speaks. Thus because of the expertise that is within the bureaucracy and because of the political power enjoyed by the bureaucracy, the various agencies of government are highly influential with the legislature. And that is how the bureaucracy makes law indirectly.

ADMINISTRATIVE ADJUDICATION

Judicial Power

Bureaucrats also have judicial power, a power they use to decide more cases and controversies than are decided by the courts of law. Why do agencies possess judicial power? Why is it tolerated by courts? Is it an unconstitutional violation of separation of powers for the executive branch to do work reserved to the judicial branch? Courts have willingly yielded judicial power to agencies. Courts find modern technology and the complexities of our era more than they can conveniently cope with. Furthermore, the number of disputes between citizens and government agencies has increased as the number of those agencies and the scope of their duties has increased. Rather than fight the growing adjudicatory power of agencies, courts have in fact formed an alliance with agencies and have encouraged them to become courts and to initially decide disputes arising from their own actions.

The Primary Jurisdiction Doctrine

How do courts make quasi courts out of administrative agencies? It is not difficult. Courts can (and do) refuse to hear any controversy between an agency and a citizen until the agency has first decided the case. This routine refusal has been elevated to the status of a doctrine—the **primary jurisdiction doctrine.** The agency has primary jurisdiction over disputes between itself and others. Courts will not accept jurisdiction of such a dispute until the agency has been given a chance to decide it. The agency has greater knowledge of the complex issues than the court could have. Also the volume of disputes between agencies and citizens is so vast that courts could not hope to deal with it all themselves.

The Exhaustion of Remedies Doctrine

Courts not only give agencies first crack at the case but also insist that anyone who has a dispute with an agency must exhaust every channel of appeal within the agency before coming to court. This flows from the **exhaustion of remedies doctrine.** Courts do not want to see or hear a case until the agency is entirely done with it and has had every opportunity to apply its wisdom to a settlement. Some agencies have three or four steps in their appeals process: people in conflict with some agencies can find it exhausting to exhaust all the remedies.

Appeal Only Law

A third way that courts force agencies to be courts is by treating agency decisions just like they treat decisions of lower courts. Appeals from agencies go straight to courts of appeals, bypassing the lower court. If a dentist has had her license to practice dentistry revoked by the state dental board and wants to carry the issue to court, she does not begin in the so-called court of original jurisdiction, because the agency was the court of original jurisdiction. She goes to the appeals court. However, appeals courts normally won't listen to appeals against findings of fact. (Neither do appeals courts listen to appeals from lower courts against the findings of fact made there.) Findings of fact are usually considered final and nonappealable except in unusual circumstances. If the dental board found it to be a fact that our dentist sold drugs to a pusher, the court of appeals would not reconsider that fact. Only one exception to that general rule exists: when the appelant (in this case, the dentist) is able to show that the agency's findings of fact was not based on substantial evidence. To determine whether the agency decision was based on substantial evidence, the appeals court generally has only to make a cursory glance at evidence supporting the finding of fact. If the finding obviously and glaringly lacks supporting evidence, then the court of appeals may either declare the finding unfair and send the case back to the agency for further hearing or hear additional evidence itself.

Judges, after all, are trained chiefly in law, and it makes sense for them to confine their judgments to legal questions rather than attempt to evaluate the correctness or incorrectness of a million and one possible fact questions in specialized areas. Our dentist may base her appeal on any kind of law question—she may claim, for example, that the dental board had no legal authority to make a rule concerning sale of drugs to pushers, or that she was denied a right to an attorney during the hearing held by the dental board, or that she was not allowed to cross-examine witnesses, or that the agency hearing that resulted in her loss of license was in one way or another unfair procedurally.

Thus through regular adherence to the doctrines of primary jurisdiction, exhaustion of remedies, and the finality of fact findings, the regular courts of record have elevated agencies to the status of courts of original jurisdiction. The courtlike action of agencies is called **administrative adjudication.** Because the role of administrative adjudication now looms so large in our legal system and continues to grow, many states (following the federal government's lead)[21] have adopted an **administrative-procedure act** (APA) setting forth (1) the procedures that agencies must follow when they are adjudicating cases and (2) the circumstances under which the final decisions of agencies may be appealed to regular courts of law. Many APAs also set forth the rule-making procedures.

Constitutionality

There have been many lawsuits claiming that the rule-making and adjudicatory activities of agencies are unconstitutional exercises of powers belonging to the legislative and judicial branches.[22] However, courts long ago upheld the constitutionality of these legislative and judicial activities of agencies[23] on the amusing theory that agencies do not really have legislative power, but only **quasi-legislative power,** and do not really have judicial power, but only **quasi-judicial power.** Quasi-legislative power is supposedly subordinate to legislative power: agencies make rules only after being allowed to do so by the legislative body. A legislative body cannot lawfully give such power to an agency without first defining exactly how it is to be used.[24] The Supreme Court asserts that it would be an illegal and unconstitutional abandonment of legislative power if the legislature were to simply give a certain power to an agency and tell the agency to do as it pleases.

Delegations of power to agencies are supposed to be "channeled." However, even this so-called channeling is rarely demanded anymore, except where agencies are given the power to make rules and regulations that would limit freedom of speech, the press, religion, or assembly. In areas not touching the First Amendment, however, courts are notoriously lax nowadays about the preciseness of standards in laws granting quasi-legislative power to agencies. Often there are really no standards worth mentioning, and agencies are free to make whatever rules they want as long as they stick to the general subject matter properly under their supervision and as long as the rules are more or less reasonable.

On the other hand, any law passed by a legislative body that gives an agency the power to make rules limiting any First Amendment freedom is likely to be declared void if there is any degree of vagueness about exactly what bureaucrats may or may not do with that power. This is why it is almost impossible to give a police department, or any other agency, the power to prohibit the sale of pornography—it seems impossible to write a crystal-clear definition of pornography. Therefore any law giving power to an agency to make rules for the distribution of pornography must necessarily lack precise standards because the very definition of pornography lacks precision.

[21]Federal Administrative Procedure Act, 60 *Stat.* 237 (1946), as amended by 80 *Stat.* 378 (1966), 81 *Stat.* 54 (1967), 88 *Stat.* 1561 (1974), 90 *Stat.* 1241, 2721 (1976).

[22]Schechter Poultry Corp. v. United States, 295 U.S. 495 (1935).

[23]State of Minnesota v. Chicago, M. & St. P. R. Co., 38 Minn. 281 (1888).

[24]Schechter Poultry Corp. v. Unites States, op. cit.

SUMMARY

Perhaps there is something to be said for Andrew Jackson's argument that if we want elected executives to do what we elected them to do, then we have to give those elected executives the power to hire and fire their subordinates. He defended the spoils system, but the spoils system was soon blamed for much corruption. The merit system for hiring public employees did not spring as much from love of merit as from hate of politics and corruption.

The first thing you have to do if you want to install a merit system is to classify all jobs according to the level of skill, training, and responsibility necessary to carry them out. This is a necessary first step to achieve equal pay for equal work and to design fair appointment and promotion exams. Few, if any, merit systems cover all government jobs. Even the most thoroughgoing merit systems usually exclude employees of the legislature, the governor's staff, and top-level bureaucrats. Despite the growth of merit systems in the United States, numerous state and local governments still operate under a spoils system.

Wherever there is a merit system, there is normally a nonpartisan independent board, commonly called a civil-service commission, to run it.

There is so much illegal patronage in some so-called merit systems that they may as well be called spoils systems. It is possible to hire political favorites by twisting and manipulating merit-system rules. Likewise it is possible to fire or drive away people you don't want by subverting merit-system rules. Some systems are more vulnerable to this than others.

Public-service unionism is by no means new in the United States. In 1890 the National Association of Letter Carriers was formed, and since then many other unions and associations have been established. A large percentage of all public employees are organized. Public-service unions have undeniably won benefits, sometimes great benefits, for members, but the public-service unions encounter some problems that their counterparts in the private sector do not. Although it is against the law for public employees to strike, these laws are difficult to enforce. The right to strike is said to be the ultimate weapon of any union, but it is not by any means the only weapon. Public-service unions have managed to represent their members with a good deal of success without calling strikes. Whether the weapon be strikes or politics, one occasionally hears all public-service unionism condemned by those who think it runs head-on into every concept of merit.

Rarely is the union shop or the closed shop permitted in the public sector. Both are said to violate the constitutional right of nonassociation insofar as they compel public servants to join unions. Agency shops are sometimes permitted. At present there is no national labor law for public servants comparable to the National Labor Relations Act for the private sector.

Privatization of government services is a trend especially disturbing to labor unions representing government employees who see the "contracting-out epidemic" as their number one problem.

Bureaucrats serve as judges and legislators through the exercise of their quasi-judicial and quasi-legislative powers and through their influence over the output of legislative bodies. Bureaucrats have become powerful in legislation and adjudication partly because of the inabilities of legislators and judges to cope with the complexities of our era and partly because of the unique abilities of the bureaucracy. Much government regulation of the private sector is requested by those who are regulated.

SUGGESTIONS FOR FURTHER READING

BAUM, BERNARD H., "The Upward Pressures of Position Classification," in *Classics of Public Personnel Policy*, ed. Frank J. Thompson. Oak Park, Ill.: Moore, 1979.

DRESANG, DENNIS L., *Public Personnel Management and Public Policy*. Boston: Little, Brown, 1984.

GERSHENFELD, WALTER, J. JOSEPH LOEWENBERG, and BERNARD INGSTER, eds., *The Scope of Public-Sector Bargaining*. Lexington, Mass.: Heath, 1977.

KRISLOV, SAMUEL, and DAVID H. ROSENBLOOM, *Representative Bureaucracy and the American Political System*. New York: Praeger, 1981.

LANE, FREDERICK S., *Managing State and Local Government: Cases and Readings*. New York: St. Martin's Press, 1980.

LORCH, ROBERT S., *Democratic Process and Administrative Law*. Detroit: Wayne State University Press, 1980.

MILWARD, H. BRINTON, "Politics, Personnel and Public Policy," *Public Administration Review* (July/August 1978), 391–96.

SAVAS, E. S., *Privatizing the Public Sector*. Chatham, N.J.: Chatham House Publishers, Inc., 1982.

"SYMPOSIUM: COLLECTIVE BARGAINING," *Public Administration Review* (March/April 1972), 97–126.

THOMPSON, FRANK J., *Personnel Policy in the City: The Politics of Jobs in Oakland*. Berkeley and Los Angeles: University of California Press, 1975.

TOLCHIN, MARTIN, and SUSAN TOLCHIN, *To the Victor . . . Political Patronage from the Clubhouse to the White House*. New York: Random House, Vintage Books, 1971.

13

agencies
and functions

PREVIEW

THE POLITICS OF ORGANIZING

The relationship between two professors, Jane and Crane, was not love at first sight. Nor was it even toleration at first sight. Jane took offense immediately at Crane's hairstyle. She warned against hiring him for the department's vacancy because "anyone with a crew cut is bound to be a conservative." Crane was also guilty of dressing as if he were on his way to a wedding—necktie, suit coat, creased pants, shiny shoes. Nevertheless, Crane was hired. He became very popular on campus despite his sartorial grandeur. But he never succeeded in winning over Jane.

Crane found it difficult to love Jane. There were lots of things he didn't like about her. She was short and fat, and had a hatchet face. She walked like a prizefighter, and was fond of wearing tight shorts, even on campus. She was belligerent with everybody and loved to play the role of campus rebel. Crane tried to get along with Jane, but no charm seemed to work. Soon the two were not speaking except in department meetings, where they constantly quarreled. She opposed everything he wanted for his program. "If that program grows," she argued, "it will soon dominate the entire department." With this argument she won reluctant allies, and soon Crane was unable to do anything for his program.

One day the shining shoes, the necktie, and the crew cut stood before the dean. "And you say," said the dean. "that you want to separate your program from the department—that you want to form a new department?"

"Yes, sir, that's about it."

"But, according to an article you wrote recently, all decisions about organizing an organization should be based entirely on rationality. Now you're telling me to organize a new department because you can't stand the sight of one of your colleagues."

"Yes sir."

"Is this an amendment to your rationality theory?"

"Yes sir, you might say so, sir."

Thus began a new academic department.

THE BUREAUCRACY

On average, each American state employs some 60,000 people full time and another 12,000 part time. However, averages don't tell us much; the states are widely different. New York's full-time state employees number some 216,000; North Dakota's, only 12,000.

These bureaucrats are organized into a cryptic maze of departments, divisions, bureaus, agencies, and offices. The size of that maze in any particular state depends on how populous the state is and therefore how big a bureaucracy it needs and can afford.

Despite enormous differences among states in the size of their civil service, all state governments do fundamentally the same kind of work. In broad outline most states are organized roughly the same. That structure sometimes looks vaguely like the one in Figure 13-1.

THE POLITICS OF ORGANIZATION

All organizational structure is the handiwork of politics. The birth of every department, division, bureau, agency, and office is a political act—the act of those who have the power to bring it about. No piece of governmental structure ever sprang forth spontaneously. Each is caused, politically.

Organizational dissimilarity between states is chiefly the product of differing political developments in each state. If state A has no department of transportation but instead retains multiple agencies to oversee various forms of transportation (a railway commission, a highway commission, an aviation agency, and so on), the reason is political—forces supporting a single department of transportation do not yet outgun forces defending the old multiagency system. Nothing in state government is more political than the organizational design into which its thousands of bureaucrats are arranged.

"Reason" does play a role in the politics of organizing: the reasonableness of a plan obviously gives it immense appeal and therefore immense political power. "Reason" is a slippery commodity, however. What is reasonable to one person is not necessarily reasonable to another. Furthermore, tradition colors our vision of reason. Having a highway commission rather than a department of transportation may seen more reasonable because highway commissions are traditional.

Any attempt to change the organizational structure of state government (or of any government) runs headlong into politics. Each piece of the bureau-

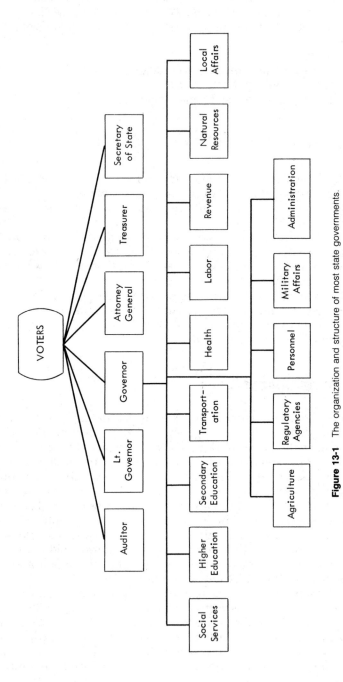

Figure 13-1 The organization and structure of most state governments.

cracy is a political strong point, an armed camp, a brigade ready for political action to defend its own interests. Reason, therefore, can be very parochial.

Sunset and the Licensing Boards

What Is Sunset?   In the last decade over half the states have put **sunset laws** on the books requiring the termination of certain agencies after a given length of time unless they can prove their worth. (Do not confuse *sunset* laws with *sunshine* laws that exist in most states requiring that the meetings of most boards, commissions, and legislative bodies be open to the public.)

Those in charge of weighing and judging the agencies subject to sunset and recommending their fate to the legislatures meet stiff opposition from those agencies, as would be expected. Generally the only agencies subject to sunset laws are regulatory agencies involved in occupational licensing.

Over the years there has been a great proliferation of occupational-licensing boards. Among the 50 states some 300 occupations are now licensed, such as doctors, lawyers, dentists, accountants, architects, optometrists, barbers, cosmetologists, morticians, harbor pilots, court therapists, polygraphers, watch-makers, escort-agency operators, photography-studio operators, land surveyors, abstractors, psychologists, social workers, mobile-home dealers, plumbers, and electricians.

Occupational licensing is defended as a form of consumer protection: consumers (it is said) are unable without this licensing to distinguish between competent and incompetent sellers of services. We assume that licensed massage-parlor operators know what they are doing or they wouldn't have been given a license. However, economists often see occupational licensing as giving licensed practitioners a monopoly on the practice. As we saw in the previous chapter, practitioners often control the licensing board and are motivated to artificially limit the number of licensed practitioners and therefore to raise the price.

Whatever the value of licensing boards, one thing is certain. Each such board has a strong will to live, and friends who want to help it live. Its friends include consumers (usually unorganized and weak) as well as most practitioners licensed by the board. The practitioners are usually well organized, vocal, well funded, and powerful.

How Many Sunsets?   Study groups have often declared that one or another occupational-licensing board lacks sufficient public purpose to warrant continued existence as a state agency, but very few agencies have been abolished. The friends of every board rally around the flag when sunsetters go to work. Lobbyists are hired by threatened groups to quash sunset efforts in the legislature. So many lobbyists find employment in this work that one of them called the sunset act "a lobbyists' relief bill."[1]

Five years of sunset activity has hardly produced a sunset. Sunset reviews have put several hundred such boards on trial for their lives, but only a tiny fraction have been recommended for termination, and only a tinier fraction still

[1]See Ronald E. Gregson, "Sunset in Colorado: The Second Round," *State Government* (Spring 1980), p. 61.

have actually been terminated. We have yet to learn how many of those agencies that died under the ax of sunsetters were later resurrected.

The entire sunset effort has demonstrated once again the determination of agencies to live, no matter how questionable their function. So few agencies have been dismantled that one wonders whether a cost-benefit analysis of the sunset effort itself would suggest its demise.

Byproducts   Sunset has a byproduct, however, that may make the whole effort useful even if very few sunsets occur. That byproduct is a vastly increased awareness by legislators about what is really going on among the myriad regulatory agencies. Still another byproduct is a greater awareness among consumer groups of how consumer-oriented their state legislators really are. As one observer points out, "One benefit of sunset legislation may thus be the information it generates about the voting records of legislators. . . ."[2]

The Attempt to Reorganize

Threats to Security   Attempts to reorganize governmental bureaucracies encounter the same sort of resistance that sunsetters encounter. Reorganization can disturb the security of every agency. Reorganization talk makes every bureaucratic dog clamp down on his bone and growl.

Is Neatness Efficient?   The growth of administrative agencies in state government has been somewhat like the growth of weeds in a patch. Weeds do not grow in neat patterns, and "good government" people like to think a neater bureaucracy would be more economical and efficient. Thus since 1965 about two dozen states have uprooted the weed patch and rearranged the bureaucracy more "geometrically" and "rationally." Agencies have been consolidated, bureaus moved, divisions created, offices abolished. The pruning and replanting has gone forward with considerable gusto. New Mexico recently consolidated 395 such government entities into 12 departments.[3]

Supposedly the governmental machine works better when organizational lines are groomed and prim, but the beneficial effect of all this is simply assumed, hardly questioned. We have very little hard evidence that immaculate organization charts are better than clumsy ones. "There seems to be a lack of interest in finding out" what has actually been accomplished by reorganization, said one analyst about the results of the reorganization of Connecticut state government.[4]

[2]Donald L. Martin, "Will the Sun Set on Occupational Licensing?" *State Government* (Spring 1980), p. 66.

[3]The Council of State Governments publishes data on state organization, listing which departments and divisions there are in each state, which officials are elected or appointed, who appoints them, and so forth. See *State Government Organization: A Preliminary Compilation* (Lexington, Ky.: Council of State Governments). The publication is kept up to date with supplements, which are sent to subscribers.

[4]Douglas M. Fox, "Reorganizing Connecticut State Government," *State Government* (Spring 1979), p. 80.

Tactics for the Reorganizer   New governors often like to embark on vast reorganization schemes. No doubt it is the natural tendency of anyone with a new toy to play with it. However, governors soon learn the political liabilities of playing with the bureaucracy—of rocking it too much—and soon quietly scale down their grandiose reorganization dreams. If a governor is determined to reorganize, the best time to press forward is immediately after the election, during the honeymoon that many new governors enjoy with the legislature during their first year. Another approach is to sneak up on reorganization, tackling it piece by piece, agency by agency, over the course of four or eight years—the incremental approach. Other strategies for governors who want to reorganize have been cataloged.[5]

WHAT DOES THE BUREAUCRACY DO?

What do the thousands of civil servants employed by state and local governments do? Most people know roughly what courts do and roughly what legislatures do, but the executive branch is a great dismaying blur to them. We have already discussed many state and local functions in this book and will not attempt to repeat it all here. The following discussion hits a smattering of functions not dealt with elsewhere. By no means is this intended to be an all-inclusive catalog. That would require another volume. Nor do we attempt to survey those public services that are delivered by private contractors.

Public Schools

Most grade and high schools are run by local school districts, not by state or municipal governments. However, states do help pay for those schools and do make numerous rules regulating how schools shall be run, what shall be taught, what qualifications teachers shall have, how schools shall be constructed, and so forth. Most states have an independent **state board of education** (usually appointed by the governor, sometimes elected) that, with the help of a department of education, carries out the state's relationship with schools. The chief state school officer, often called the **state superintendent of schools,** may be appointed by the state board of education (as in Texas), elected (as in Florida), or appointed by the governor (as in Maine), to act as head of the state department of education.

Collective Bargaining and Strikes   Among the public-school issues now debated is whether states should allow school districts to engage in collective bargaining with teacher unions. Well over half the states do allow such **collective bargaining,** but even in those states there remains strife about what is and is not negotiable at bargaining sessions, and what to do when the teachers and the school board cannot agree. **Binding arbitration** is resisted by school boards because it tends to put final authority into the hands of unelected arbitrators, but about a dozen states do allow some form of binding arbitration.

[5]See James L. Garnett, "Strategies for Governors Who Want to Reorganize," *State Government* (Summer 1979), pp. 135–43.

Although strikes by public employees are illegal in most jurisdictions, dozens of illegal strikes occur every year, mostly over pay but sometimes over working conditions and such things as dismissal and grievance procedures.

School Finance   Another major public-school issue has to do with real-property taxes as a method of school finance. Should the children who live in districts where property values are low be forced to suffer the ill effects of poorly financed schools, while children in high-property-value districts do not suffer the same handicap? Can there be equal opportunity under such circumstances? Must state governments, through their state aid to public education, attempt to equalize school districts? Where states themselves differ in resources, should the federal government attempt to equalize education among the states?

Public schools in the United States are financed jointly by local (48 percent), state (44 percent), and national (8 percent) governments.

Minimum-Competency Testing of Students   The shocking realization that a large number of virtual illiterates are graduating from high school has led to a demand for a **minimum-competency test.** Students would have to pass such a test before getting their diploma. The test would focus mainly on basic reading, writing, and arithmetic. Most states now have some form of minimum competency testing, but the test is vehemently opposed in some quarters because it works a greater hardship on culturally deprived races and groups than on mainstream Americans. Some teachers are also concerned that minimum competency testing can diminish an element of their academic freedom because the content of the exam dictates the content of what they must teach.

Competency Testing for Teachers   If students have to take a minimum-competency test, why not teachers? Sometimes the learning problems of students result from the incompetency of their teachers. Thus a number of states have set up systems in which persons applying for teacher certificates must pass a state-developed test as one requirement for certification. Certain legal problems make it difficult to force a teacher who already holds a certificate to pass the test. Attention is therefore focused on entering teachers.

Truth in Testing   Tests such as the Scholastic Aptitude Test (SAT) and the American College Test (ACT), which are weighed heavily by college-admissions officers, and tests such as the Law School Admissions Test (LSAT) and the Graduate Management Admissions Test (GMAT), which are weighed heavily by professional schools, can greatly affect an individual's future. What if the tests are not valid? What if they are erroneously scored? Should the organizations that design and score those tests be required to tell each person who took such a test what the correct answer to each question was, how each answer given by the person was graded, and just what evidence exists that the test is a valid measure of what it is supposed to be measuring? Some states, such as New York and California, have recently passed laws requiring testing agencies to give that kind of information. The agencies protest that to do so would be prohibitively expensive—no question could be used twice—but a growing number of people want the veil of secrecy removed. State legislatures seem to be responding to that wish.

Colleges and Universities

The most expensive thing states do is run colleges and universities. As other demands for state money increase—demands for welfare and health, for example—there are sidelong glances in the direction of dollar-eating institutions of higher education to see whether they need so much and whether they are wisely using what they get. Colleges, of course, hate to be thought unwise about anything, especially about academic questions such as whether this or that academic program is worthwhile. But academic institutions are afflicted with empire building no less than any other sector of the bureaucracy. There is no limit to the ambition of university administrators and faculty to run a bigger show. If they were given their every wish, no institution would be without a law school, a medical school, an engineering school, and so forth: every college would have every imaginable academic program.

That drive to be the biggest and the best is entirely human and is not necessarily to be condemned (although at many colleges "biggest" is valued more highly than "best"). Nevertheless, the wishes of colleges and universities would drive every state bankrupt if they were all granted. Of course, they are never fully granted, but now with declining enrollments, taxpayers' revolts, and other demands on the state treasury, the cost of higher education and its effectiveness are under closer scrutiny. This has led to some new organizational arrangements designed not only to stop the multiplication of law schools, medical schools, and dental schools but also to stop the duplication and overlapping of all sorts of other academic programs in the state. If a state has a dozen or so institutions of higher education ranging from junior colleges to state universities, there is every justification for insisting that there be some degree of specialization among them so they don't all try to do the same thing. Of course, there needs to be some duplication of effort because, obviously, certain basic courses, such as a course in state government, need to be offered nearly everywhere, but some other programs do not, certainly not the more expensive professional programs such as medicine and engineering.

Most states now have some sort of organizational arrangement for central clearance of new academic programs. In about 20 states all institutions of higher education are under one central governing board that has the authority to approve or disapprove new academic degree programs. Another 20 or so states have established some other kind of central agency with power over proposals for new academic degree programs but leaves the various institutions under their various governing boards. Sometimes these centralized higher-education agencies are well staffed and capable of doing their task, and sometimes they are woefully inadequate. It is not uncommon for a state's central budget bureau, usually located in the governor's office, to involve itself and to become a decision maker about what is worthwhile academically and what is worth funding. This tendency of nonacademic people in central budget offices to make academic decisions about such things as optimum class size, design of university buildings, pay of professors, need for travel money, need for this or that master's degree, the relative important of teaching versus research, and a host of other academic questions is highly offensive to a great many professors, who think academic questions should be decided by the faculty of each institution, not by budget officers at the state capitol.

The question of whether legislators, college administrators, or statewide coordinating agencies should have the primary role in determining higher-education policy is briskly disputed. Legislators, of course, are apt to feel they have every right to decide what institutions and what programs should receive state money. After all, it is their job to appropriate. But many people think legislatures, governors, state budget offices, and other statewide agencies are politically too timid to make hard decisions about school closings, terminations of programs, and the like. Even statewide coordinating agencies are not as courageous or as effective as they should be in a period of retrenchment. They seem better suited for planning growth than for managing retrenchment. Most such agencies were established in the 1960s to plan the frenzied growth of that frenzied decade, when practically everyone believed that such growth would never end. George B. Weathersby, commissioner of higher education in Indiana, said recently, "The alacrity with which governments avoid politically difficult decisions, such as school closings, leaves me with little hope for effective state governance of higher education in the future."[6]

The State Library

All states have a state library, and some have several. We do not mean the libraries at state colleges, but special libraries, such as a state historical library, a state law library, and a state general-purpose library. These are often located near the state capitol and sometimes offer an amazing list of services. We have already mentioned how state libraries help legislators. State libraries also commonly attempt to provide some degree of reference service for the state bureaucracy in general as well as local officials. State libraries generally keep a good collection of federal, state, and local documents and maintain state archives (records). State librarians, assigned the task of doing what they can to improve library service throughout the state, often develop statewide **information networks** that enable librarians throughout the state (perhaps with the help of computer hookups) to find out which libraries hold which books and documents.

Transportation

Department of Transportation   Most states now have a major department of government called a *department of transportation* to deal with highway, air, rail, and water transportation, as well as mass transit in cities. The main function of a department of transportation is to centralize most of the state's concerns with public transportation under one roof. Normally these departments do not regulate common carriers. That is usually done by independent public-utility commissions.

Not too many years ago, the central transportation concern of most states was highways and motor vehicles. That, of course, remains a great concern of every state and is still one of the greatest objects of spending. But with the tremendous increase in air transportation and a rising demand for urban mass

[6]Lorenzo Middleton, "Who Should Set State Policy in an Era of Retrenchment?" *Chronicle of Higher Education* (June 23, 1980), p. 7.

transportation, states have needed to consider the broader picture of transportation, *all* forms of transportation, and the coordination, planning, financing, and encouragement thereof.

Highways   States are deeply involved with the construction and maintenance of thousands of miles of highway. There are some four million miles of roads in the United States, and state governments, either alone or cooperatively with other governments, maintain or fund about a million of them. Local governments are responsible for the remaining three million. Looking after this huge network of highways has become a greater financial problem in recent years because revenue from gasoline taxes and other highway-user taxes has not increased as fast as the rising cost of building and maintaining highways. Fuel-efficient vehicles have reduced the consumption of gasoline and therefore the payment of gasoline taxes. Increasing numbers are riding mass transit, encouraged incidentally, by the technical assistance and financial support given to mass transit by some states.

Air   States also have an interest in doing what they can to improve air service by encouraging service to small communities, construction of airports, and improvements of flight safety and noise control.

Rail   States try to preserve their railway system and participate in studies to determine which segments of track should receive federal and state support for their improvement. All states, with the possible exception of Hawaii, which has few railroads, are involved in railroad planning. This has been spurred by the Federal Railroad Revitalization and Regulatory Reform Act of 1976.

Health

In the previous chapter we described the vast regulatory powers of the typical state department of health. States regulate and often directly sponsor a vast array of health programs touching maternal and child health, crippled children, communicable disease, dental health, chronic disease, sanitation, water- and air-quality control, solid-waste management, occupational safety, radiation control, and other concerns. Some state health departments do what they can to reduce the cost of health care and to improve its accessibility and quality. States also directly provide emergency medical and laboratory services. By comparison with local health departments, state departments do not provide many health services directly to the state's population. Basically the state's role is to coordinate, plan, and regulate delivery of health services rather than to undertake such delivery itself. A state health department may also have charge of medicaid, a multi-billion-dollar activity jointly financed by the state and national governments.

Every state in the Union licenses chiropractors, dentists, dental hygienists, practical nurses, professional nurses, optometrists, pharmacists, physical therapists, physicians, podiatrists, and veterinarians. Most also license psychologists, sanitarians, and nursing-home administrators.

Welfare

What Is Welfare?   We are said to have a welfare mess in the United States. The word *welfare* is itself a mess, for no two people seem to agree what it means. Let us try to define *welfare* and surround it with boundaries, for without boundaries one might justifiably say everything government does is for the welfare of somebody. Indeed the United States Constitution dedicates itself to promoting the general welfare[7] and gives the federal government the power to collect taxes in order (among other things) to provide for the general welfare.[8] Not all this welfare is for the poor. Any law that helps people solve problems or improve their lot is welfare, and it isn't only the poor who have problems and want their lot improved. However, in the following paragraphs we are going to talk chiefly about welfare for the poor. There are all sorts of laws designed to help the poor—too many to discuss here—so we are going to limit our attention to a few laws (or programs) that fall near the heart of what we generally call *welfare*. Some of these programs are basically federal, some basically state and/or local, and some are joint.

> *Federal programs*
> Old-age insurance
> Survivors' insurance
> Disability insurance
> Aid to the blind
> Food-stamp program
> Medicare
> *State and/or local programs*
> Unemployment compensation
> Assistance supplementing federal aid to the old, the disabled, the poor
> Institutions for the destitute, alone, and ill
> *Joint federal-state (or federal-local) programs*
> Medicaid
> Aid to families with dependent children
> Public housing

Federal Programs

INSURANCE   It is perhaps an insult to insurance to call it *welfare*. The whole idea of social-security insurance is to prevent the need for charity. Technically insurance is the reverse of welfare. Employees pay into the social-insurance system; their payments entitle them as a matter of right to draw the benefits of that insurance after age 65. Social-security checks received by some 33 million Americans are not a public charity—not in theory. The federal social-security program[9] was supposed to be actuarially sound—payments out of the fund were to be balanced by payments into it. This is no longer the case; more is going out than coming in. Politics is partly to blame. Pressures by those 33 million beneficiaries have caused Congress to increase benefits and broaden entitlements; pres-

---

[7]*U.S. Const.,* Preamble.
[8]*U.S. Const.,* Art. I, Sec. 8.
[9]Established by the Society Security Act of 1935, 42 *U.S.C.* 301 et seq.

sures from other quarters have deterred Congress from increasing "taxes" supporting the fund. Furthermore, the population is aging, and the proportion of nonworking people is increasing.

Persons covered by OASDHI (old-age, survivors', disability, and health insurance) may receive a certain payment after age 65. If an insured worker dies, his or her spouse receives benefit payments if there are dependent children; if there are no dependent children, payments to the spouse do not begin until age 65. Any insured worker who is prevented from working because of permanent and total disabilities is also entitled to benefit payments. Recently health insurance (medicare) has been attached to the insurance system. This vast federal "insurance company" is one step from bankruptcy and will become something other than insurance if the federal government is forced to dip into general tax revenues to keep the company afloat.

NEEDS TEST   Since insurance payments are given as a matter of right (entitlement), it is not necessary to have a staff of welfare workers looking into whether persons over 65 are in financial need of their social-security checks, or whether their survivors are in need, or whether the disabled are in need. It is the abominable **needs test** that complicates so many welfare programs. The process of deciding who is eligible for social-security payments is fairly simple and mechanical. Medicare, too, is a matter of right, not of need. Furthermore, aid to the blind, although a charity (instead of a right), is comparatively simple to administer insofar as separating the blind from the seeing is concerned. The food-stamp program, however, wallows in the needs test. To get food stamps (they can be used like money to buy food), recipients have to show they are eligible; eligibility is based on one's income and family size, both of which are somewhat difficult for administrators to verify.

MEDICARE   **Medicare,** the federal government's hospital-insurance program for persons over 65, is rather simple in concept. It is supposedly financed through payroll taxes collected under the social-security system. Persons covered by medicare may also enroll in a supplemental program that pays doctor bills and other medical costs; for this they must pay an additional fee. This supplemental program is financed partly by general tax revenues and partly by contributions from the aged. A multitude of problems afflict medicare. We don't have space to detail them all, but one problem is that medicare encourages people to seek treatment in hospitals rather than in clinics because certain types of care are reimbursed only if treatment occurs in a hospital. Hospitals are guaranteed all their expenses for medicare patients and therefore have little motive to be frugal. Certain individuals (thousands of them) in the medical industry—doctors, dentists, pharmacists, laboratory technicians—have conspired to give people service they don't need and have even fraudulently collected for services not rendered. For this and other reasons the cost of medicare has become a budgetary Frankenstein. The food-stamp program has become a similar Frankenstein, costing billions more than anyone dreamed.

Joint Federal-State (or Federal-Local) Programs

MEDICAID   Similar corruption, unfrugalities, and ballooning costs afflict medicaid (different from medicare). **Medicaid** is a federally sponsored program under which the states can obtain much of their cost of providing free

---

Box 13-1. Can This Offer Be Refused?

President Ronald Reagan proposed the biggest swap in history. His idea: the federal government would assume all costs of the fast-growing $30 billion medicaid program if the states would take over the full burden of aid to families with dependent children (which costs about $13 billion a year) and pick up the entire tab for the $11 billion food-stamp program. Most governors seemd to be in basic agreement with the idea of shifting programs to the states. As Governor Richard Lamm, Democrat of Colorado, put it, "We are tired of playing 'Mother, may I?' with federal bureaucrats." But he and many other governors wondered where the states would get the money to finance their new burdens if the swap were made. In March 1982 the nation's governors met in Washington, D.C., for their annual winter meeting and voted 36 to 5 to reject the idea that states would assume full responsibility for the AFDC and food-stamp programs. However, they seemed willing enough for the federal government to finance all of medicaid.

---

medical care for the poor. This is basically a charity, given mostly to persons who are already on some other kind of state or local welfare, and thus is somewhat difficult to administer, especially the matter of determining who is eligible and who is not.

AFDC   One of the most troublesome of all welfare programs is called aid to families with dependent children (**AFDC**). AFDC is supported partly by federal grants to the states, but states decide who needs this aid, how much they will get, and under what conditions they will get it. The states themselves have to pay part of the cost of AFDC. Among the states there is wide variety in benefits and in eligibility rules. Basically the program provides aid to needy mothers who are responsible for young children and either do not have a husband or have a husband who is not living in the home and not supporting the family. AFDC is riddled with problems. First, there are so many applicants whose need and circumstances must be investigated and so many recipients of aid whose continuing need must be continually monitored that there simply aren't enough welfare workers to do the job. Money is often paid to ineligible recipients.

AFDC is a target of criticism from every direction. It is said to encourage illegitimacy because the more children, the more aid. The suggestion has been made that only one, possibly two, illegitimate children should be aided—to stop unwed mothers from having children just to receive more aid. AFDC is said to break up families by offering a financial reward, in effect, to mothers without husbands. Thus it doesn't take much imagination for a poor family to see the advantages of breaking up, or for a husband to temporarily disappear or move away to some secret location nearby. Welfare workers have a hard time keeping on top of all these games. Another criticism is that AFDC makes too little effort to provide jobs for recipients. However, mothers with dependent children are not likely to go to work unless they can find a job that pays a good deal more than their AFDC check. Many mothers have no training and are not likely to find a job or adequate child-care for their children while they work. Good caring mothers are sometimes penalized for wanting to take care of their children. AFDC recipients are now required to sign up for work-training programs unless they are mothers of preschool children or fall into one or another excluded category. To discourage fathers from deserting their families, the federal government has offered matching funds to states that give benefits to families with unemployed fathers. Only about half the states have availed themselves of this option. So great is fhe financial burden of AFDC upon states that there has been a call for federal takeover. A federal takeover would not only free states of a crushing burden but would also equalize benefits among the states. At present AFDC families can roam the nation looking for the best benefits. Average benefits range from a low in Mississippi to a high in Hawaii.

HOUSING Another joint federal-state effort to help the poor is **public housing.** Since the 1930s the federal government has given money to local governments to build apartment houses for rental to the working poor.[10] The amount of rent paid for these units usually depends on income and size of family. The whole idea of public housing is often more beautiful in the abstract than in reality. The realities of life in public-housing units are often grim: large apartment complexes for the poor seem to incubate crime and perversion. Teenage gangs terrorize the area; robberies and vandalism are an everyday occurrence.[11] The greater the density of population in public-housing projects, the greater the hotbed of wrongdoing. Small apartment units or single-family dwellings would obviously be better, but they are more expensive. The attempt to economize leads planners to design high-rise, high-density public-housing projects. Whether it is worse to suffer the evils of rat-infested, dilapidated tenements or the evils of crime-ridden high-rise public housing is difficult to say. Such public housing has its vociferous opponents, including those who are forced to live near it. Some real-estate interests also oppose public housing because they prefer a system for housing the poor that would not compete with private-sector housing. There also continues to be a stigma associated with living in public housing.

In the 1960s attempts were made to involve the private sector in housing the poor. Low-interest federal loans were given to nonprofit groups interested in providing low-cost apartments for the poor. Congress also attempted to involve the private sector in low-cost housing through a **rent-supplement program** in which the government paid part of the rent of low-income families living in government-approved apartment houses. It was easier and cheaper for the government to give rent supplements than to bear the cost of building and managing public-housing complexes. Rent supplements also spared tenants the stigma of living in public housing and the need to move out when their income rose above a certain level.

In addition to its rent-subsidy program, the federal government also began a mortgage-subsidy program in 1968, designed to capitalize on the well-known fact that people take better care of property they own than property they rent. Thus the idea was to make it possible for low-income people to own the homes they lived in by helping them to pay the mortgage rather than helping them to pay rent. Unfortunately the mortgage-subsidy program was injured by corruption: certain real-estate operators were in the habit of bribing FHA appraisers, causing them to appraise houses at twice what they were worth. Low-

[10]As provided for by the U.S. Housing Act of 1937, P.L., 75-412 (as amended).

[11]For a study that, among other things, seems to suggest that tenant behavior is not really as bad as sometimes perceived, see Elton C. Smith, Laurence J. O'toole, Jr., and Beverly G. Burke, "Managing Public Housing: A Case Study of Myths and Reality," *State and Local Government Review* (Spring 1984), pp. 75–83.

income buyers, having faith in the honesty of the appraisal and therefore in the fairness of the price, would buy the home with help of a subsidized mortgage only to discover the awful truth after taking possession.

A recent development in federal support of housing for low-income persons is **urban homesteading.** Do-it-yourselfers can buy a structurally sound but deteriorated piece of property in a declining neighborhood for a nominal fee from the government, perhaps for as little as one dollar. Within a certain period of time they are required to bring the property into compliance with building codes. Homesteading helps prevent urban decay and puts property back on the tax rolls.

Also the federal government has tried to help certain property owners whose income is below a given level to rehabilitate their properties and make them more livable. This has been done by making loans available to such people at a very low interest rate.

In recent years the federal government has scaled down its involvement in housing programs. Most construction and rehabilitation programs have been terminated. Also tax reform has removed many incentives for individuals to invest in new rental housing. This has motivated some states to set up their own programs to help low-income people obtain at least minimum housing.

We see states embarking upon housing programs quite similar to those abandoned or scaled back by the federal government. This new state involvement seems to be exactly what presidential policy in the 80s has desired: state rather than federal responsibility for welfare.

State and local governments are not complete strangers to this field of endeavor. For decades they have been chiefly responsible for administering federal housing programs. The federal government invented the programs, supplied the money, and then turned it all over to state and local governments to administer subject to certain principles, policies, and guidelines.

Many state and local housing programs devloped lately are clones of federal programs being cut back or phased out, including:

1. Long term loans given at below-market interest rates to owner-occupants and investors in small rental properties. The money is for rehabilitating their properties.
2. Programs to give money to low- and moderate-income families to buy homes.
3. Programs to encourage new construction of rental properties for low-income people. The state or local government commits itself to help low-income occupants of those projects pay their rent.
4. Grants and other front-end one-time assistance given for the purpose of rehabilitating low-income housing or building new low-income housing. (The "but for" test is used: but for this assistance the project would not go forward.)
5. Programs to help low-income families pay their rent if they can find a place meeting the legal quality standards and if the rent charged is within legal limits of the program.

Considerable creativity has been exhibited by state and local governments in their efforts to design "look-alikes" for federal housing programs.

Support for low-income housing is not the only form of government aid for housing. There is another stream of support that almost equals the housing programs. It consists of state and local welfare programs that provide welfare recipients with a certain amount every month to pay their rent. These two streams—housing programs and welfare—are not always coordinated well enough to prevent what might be called "double-dipping" by recipients.

State and/or Local Programs   Several welfare programs are carried on exclusively by states or by local governments without federal involvement. One of these is **unemployment compensation.** However, the federal government has a law[12] that says in effect, "If any state doesn't run an unemployment-compensation insurance system, we (the federal government) will run it ourselves in the state." Every state has chosen to run its own program. It is insurance, not charity. Payments into the unemployment-insurance fund are made, however, by the employer, not the employee. An involuntarily unemployed worker may draw so many weeks of unemployment compensation. The amount and duration of payments varies from state to state. The program is fairly cut-and-dried and easy to administer. The most frequent disputes over eligibility for payment arise over whether an unemployed person is voluntarily or involuntarily unemployed. One can't collect unemployment-insurance compensation for voluntarily leaving a job.

Local Charities   Local governments commonly provide charitable welfare for the destitute, the alone, and the ill. Often money payment is not enough for such groups, and local governments establish orphanages and homes for the ill and the aged.

Agriculture

The Farm Problem   A cartoon appeared in the press not long ago showing the Russian minister of agriculture surrounded by his top assistants. He demanded to know why Russia can't have a "farm problem" like America's. The American farm problem for several generations has been a problem of overproduction and low prices. The federal government as well as state governments have lavished their attention on this problem, but curiously, government has been in a sense a cause of the problem, a cause of overproduction.

Agriculture Colleges   How can government be responsible for overproduction? Certainly we cannot accuse government of having any premeditated intent to afflict farmers. Surely the reverse has been true—state and federal governments have showered benefits on farmers, and among those benefits have been the creation of agriculture colleges in nearly every state.

Within those agriculture colleges (and in other colleges and universities as well) phenomenal discoveries have made possible an increased yield per acre of nearly every crop and an increased yield per animal of nearly every creature in the barnyard from cows to chickens. Chickens were bred that put all previous chickens to shame. Cows were bred that would mortify all previous cows. Pigs were bred that would humiliate all previous pigs. Hybrid seeds were laboriously nurtured that produced ears of corn so large, so golden, so beautiful, so bountiful that our forefathers would have been utterly stunned. Agronomists and botanists working at Iowa State College in effect doubled the size of Iowa by

[12]The Federal Unemployment Compensation Law, Social Security Act of 1935.

doubling the yield per acre of corn. State legislators are often insensitive to the value of research. Every dollar given to agricultural research has been returned a thousandfold. Almost everything farmers do from dawn to dusk has been the subject of research, not in one state but in all 50 states. The flood of agricultural products from American farms is, of course, due partly to the abundance of rich land in America, but to that abundance has been added an abundance of research that has brought forth the most efficient system of agriculture on this planet.

Technology   The technological revolution has also led to increased agricultural productivity. Tractors, trucks, grain combines, mechanical corn and cotton pickers, gang plows, and an array of other machines have made farming easier and more efficient. The extension of electric power lines to millions of farms (rural electrification) has added a still greater array of machines powered by electricity to the farmer's arsenal of equipment: milking machines, feed mills, grain dryers, and so on.

Consolidation of Farms   All this technology has created a problem: the farm problem, a problem that has driven millions of people out of farming and brought fundamental changes to the management of American agriculture. Since 1920 about two-thirds of the farms have disappeared or, more accurately, been absorbed into larger farms. The average size of an American farm is about 437 acres, but 14 percent of the farms account for half of America's more than one billion acres of farmland. Most of our farm production is accomplished by only a third of the farms. About half of the lowest-producing two-thirds are "farmed" by part-time gentleman farmers who get the major part of their income from other jobs. The other half of the lowest-producing two-thirds are the site of what we call "farm poverty."

The Political Power of Agriculture   The power of agriculture in American politics is not what it used to be but is still great. Most present-day farm programs were started several generations ago when there were two or three times as many farmers as there are now. The United States Supreme Court's one-man-one-vote decisions[13] sharply reduced rural representation in the lower house of Congress and in all state legislatures, but there remains a battalion of rural legislators in Congress and in state legislatures.

Most of the nation's great agriculture legislation comes, of course, from Congress rather than from state legislatures, but a considerable number of those programs, especially those supporting research, are carried out through state departments of agriculture and state colleges and universities. Many of those colleges and universities, in fact, were created with the help of the federal **Morrill Act,** passed during the Civil War, which donated lands to the states for the purpose of establishing colleges devoted to giving instruction in agriculture and engineering. Many of the prominent colleges in the Midwest and Far West owe their existence to the power of agriculture in Congress and in state legislatures.

Farm Bloc?   It would be a mistake, however, to visualize the *farm bloc* as a monolith: farmers are not all alike. Some farm groups are downright hostile to others: some have special interests and concerns not shared by others or in fact

---

[13]Baker v. Carr, 390 U.S. 186 (1962).

opposed to others. The National Milk Producers Federation and the National Grain Growers Association are more likely to be at one another's throat than linked arm in arm. What's good for grain farmers (high grain prices) may be anathema to dairy farmers, who have to buy that high-priced grain to feed their cows.

Farmers differ in many crucial ways: some run small and struggling operations and want government price supports, some run middle-sized operations, and some run enormous farms and ranches and have no present need for price supports or other programs designed to save small farmers. These differences are mirrored in the four general farm organizations that try to speak for agriculture as a whole rather than for the interests of some particular commodity. The American Farm Bureau Federation, most powerful of them all, speaks for the successful and prosperous farmer, for those who run large farms, and for the agricorporations. Three others—the Grange, the National Farmers' Union, and the National Farmers' Organization—speak for small and middle-sized farmers and tend to favor price supports. Of course, these characterizations of the membership of the four organizations are only general.

Department of Agriculture   Most states have a department of agriculture that carries on a world of activities related to farming, including consumer protection and promotion of agribusiness. Consumer protection includes such things as inspecting poultry products and eggs; assuring the accuracy of weights and measures; eradicating and suppressing animal disease, especially diseases transmittable to humans, such as tuberculosis and brucellosis; enforcing state law designed to prevent the spread of numerous plant diseases, weeds, and insects; and regulating the use of agricultural chemicals and pesticides by licensing commercial applicators and dealers and by prohibiting the use of certain chemicals. Some of these activities are carried out by other departments, such as the department of health, in some states.

Environmental Protection

Until a few years ago very little concern for the environment was exhibited. But today, if God were to consider remaking the world and re-creating the land and the waters and all the earthly creatures and the great ball of fire above, He might be required to submit an environmental-impact statement to a council on environmental quality before starting work.

Our Oasis in Space   Perhaps it was those photos of the moon and of Mars and of desolation everywhere among the planets that brought us to our senses and convinced us how incredibly unique this blue and white dot in space really is, and how alone we are in the solar system, and how fragile our environment is, and how irreplaceable. We begin to appreciate the beauty of our planet and to realize that the blue sky, the fresh air, the crystalline waters, the forests are all perishable. Smog in Los Angeles alarmed us. We soon learned that Los Angeles was not the only place in the world where such a thing could occur—that there could be repulsive brown clouds over Tucson, Phoenix, Denver, to say nothing of St. Louis, Chicago, New York, and the great cities of the North, South, East, and West, and in Europe, and across the whole world. Scientists standing on Wyoming's wide-open plains found air pollution in their test tubes.

ENVIRONMENT AND POLLUTION DEFINED By **environmental protection** we usually mean protection of land, air, and water from pollution; by *pollution* we usually mean that which is unhealthy for humans and the resources upon which they depend. Attempts are made to defend the land from indiscriminate disposal of America's 144 million tons of residential and commercial waste generated every year and to protect the land from some of the worst effects of strip mining and from the intrusion of roads and construction. However, the major thrust of environmental protection thus far has concerned air and water.

The *environment* actually includes everything. All creation is part of the environment—even ideas, philosophies, attitudes, and patterns of behavior. An environmentally perfect world would have to be "mentally" as well as physically pure. However, purity is a debatable concept. One person's purity is another's pollution.

What Is Pollution? Differing views about what constitutes pollution can lead to hideous fights. Take pesticides. Part of a healthful environment is a healthy population. Part of being healthy is being well fed, part of being well fed is fighting the insects that prey on agricultural products, and part of fighting insects is application of pesticides. Pesticides are, however, condemned by some people as pollution. Yet pesticides are the very reverse of pollution insofar as they foster a healthy, well-fed population.

Just what constitutes pollution is highly debatable. Environmentalists are always bumping into one another with conflicting ideas of a good environment. Some of them, for instance, believe wild and scenic rivers should be kept wild and scenic. But power companies would like to put dams across a few of those streams, such as Idaho's Snake River where it cuts a deep gorge called Hell's Canyon. Power companies have to fight Sierra Clubs and others who rise savagely to the defense of wild and scenic rivers. Power companies have become a favorite target of environmentalists, especially those who want to preserve wild and scenic rivers just the way God made them. Power companies say there is also something wild and beautiful about being able to turn on electric lights, and furthermore, they point out that electricity can be generated by water power with absolutely no air pollution or atomic waste—it's the cleanest power on earth. The alternative to a dam at Hell's Canyon is a smoke-belching plant somewhere else. The power companies that want to dam up rivers may themselves deserve to be called environmentalists as much as those who want to stop the dams.

Federal Role Most environmental legislation is national, not state. This doesn't mean states are apathetic about pure water and clean air. By no means.[14] Politicians in more than one state have found it useful to portray themselves as persons deeply concerned about environment. It is doubtful whether any candidate for governor of a state like Colorado could be elected without a solid commitment to environmental protection. States do have laws, dozens of laws, maybe hundreds, regulating the environment: zoning ordinances, land-use laws,

[14]For a discussion of federal–state clashes over nuclear-waste policy, see Stephen A. Graham, "The Nuclear Waste Policy Act of 1982: A Case Study in American Federalism," *State Government*, Vol. 57, No. 1, 1984, pp. 7–12.

and rules about trash disposal, nuisances, air pollution, water pollution, and a multitude of other things. But in all this, states operate under a thorny handicap: each is afraid to enforce severe environmental-protection laws lest they drive certain businesses out of state and deter others from coming in. Political pressures against environmental regulation can be powerful. Environmentalists seem less well organized and less well financed than certain enterprises that pollute the air and water. Those enterprises may pay taxes in the millions and employ workers by the thousands.

Water Nor does the federal government like to enact laws leaving much discretion to states to set standards of air and water pollution. States often use their discretion in such a way as to preserve business growth and development whatever the environmental consequences.

Congress has now largely quit relying on state standards and state action and has set some national standards. The goal was to make all streams safe for fish and for human swimming by 1983 and to stop all discharges of pollution into navigable streams by 1985. By 1983 private concerns and public agencies discharging wastes into streams were supposed to adopt the "best available technology" to clean it up. Federal money has been appropriated to help municipalities build sewage-treatment facilities. The federal government will pay up to 75 percent of the cost.

Air The federal government has had the same kind of trouble trying to get states to set air-pollution standards as it had trying to get them to set water-pollution standards: states fear economic consequences if their standards are higher than those of other states. Therefore, under present law the Environmental Protection Agency (EPA) sets emission standards for new plants in some 20 industries, including those manufacturing cement, nitric acid, sulfuric acid, and electricity. Such new plants must employ the "best feasible technology" for control of emissions and must meet specific standards for emission of certain substances, such as carbon monoxide, hydrocarbons, nitrogen oxides, sulfur oxides, and photochemical oxidants. Emission of asbestos, beryllium, and mercury are prohibited altogether.

EPA air-quality standards are not identical everywhere in the nation. The EPA divides the United States into several hundred air-quality-control regions and sets a separate level for each, but it is forbidden to allow the air quality of a given region to decline by setting a standard lower than that already prevailing. This, of course, condemns certain areas that have pristine air from attracting much industry and also makes it impossible for industries in some that have low air-pollution standards to find places with equally low standards to relocate.

With regard to the emissions of automobiles (which account for two-thirds of all air pollution), the federal government has tried to set standards but is constantly having to postpone them to avoid economic disaster and unemployment in the auto industry.

Energy Conservation

States have encouraged conservation of energy by subsidizing weatherization loans, giving income-tax credits for the cost of conservation measures, giving rebates for part of the cost of alternative energy systems, requiring deposits on all beverage containers to discourage use of nonreturnable containers which require more energy to produce than returnable containers, promulgating appliance-efficiency standards, and promulgating vehicle-efficiency standards.[15]

Corrections

Is Correction Possible? **Corrections** includes every state activity that has anything to do with handling persons convicted of crimes. Primarily this means the prison and parole system. To call all this *corrections* is perhaps inaccurate. There are those who doubt whether any such thing as correction is possible. Eighty percent of all felonies are committed by repeaters who were previously in contact with the corrections system and were not corrected by it. Some criminologists insist that criminals can be corrected, that very often criminals themselves are victims—of poor education and inadequate job training—and that they can be rehabilitated through a true corrections system that tries to educate and train rather than punish. Other criminologists say this is nonsense, that although a few prisoners might be rehabilitated through education or being taught a trade, all statistics point to an astronomically high **recidivism rate:** most prisoners return to a life of crime, made all the more criminal-minded by their sojourn in prison among other criminal-minded inmates. Even those who emphasize parole as a method of supervising the lives of prisoners for a certain period after their release have found to their dismay that it has little effect on the recidivism rate. Nothing seems to reduce recidivism, not the amount of money spent on corrections systems, not sentencing policies, not parole systems. To speak of corrections is perhaps only a concession to the high hopes of those who believe correction ought to be possible, even if it isn't.

Do Prisons Remove Wrongdoers from Society? Prisons do, of course, remove some wrongdoers from society and do for a time protect the public, but the number of wrongdoers who ever see the inside of a prison is only a drop in the bucket. The ratio of crime to punishment is fearfully low—only one in 50 perpetrators of serious crime go to jail for their crime. To begin with, most crimes are not reported. When a crime is reported, the police seldom succeed in arresting the offender, and when they do arrest and charge an offender, chances are three to one he or she will not be tried for the offense or will be handled as a juvenile. Prosecutors don't have the resources to prosecute every person arrested by the police, and those they do prosecute are often induced to plead guilty to some lesser charge to avoid the necessity of a trial. Some offenders are tried and erroneously found innocent. Thus prisons are very dull tools for segregating the law-abiding from the lawless, and this is true primarily because only an infinitesimally small number of wrongdoers are ever segregated in the first place. Of course, the idea works fine for those few who do reach prison, but they generally aren't segregated for long. Most continue to prey on society once released.

Punishment and Deterrence Besides the theory of segregation and the theory of corrections, there remain two other theories: (1) punishment and (2) deterrence. *Punishment* rests on the proposition that wrongdoers owe a debt to

[15]*State Legislatures* (July/August 1980), p. 14.

society that they should be forced to pay. Whatever merit that proposition may have affects only a tiny fraction of wrongdoers who are caught and convicted. *Deterrence,* on the other hand, may be the greatest benefit of prisons and of punishment. Of course, it would be next to impossible to measure just how effective prisons and punishment are as deterrents. We can, however, look into our own hearts and ask whether we ourselves might not at times be tempted to commit crimes if there were no punishment for breaking the law. Possibly some would-be murderers and other felons are circulating within our immediate company who are deterred from bashing heads or stealing diamonds by the danger of being put in prison. Some criminal acts are less subject to deterrence than others. Murders committed in the "heat of passion" will occur no matter how ghastly the penalty: they are committed on the spur of the moment by people in a blind rage who haven't the slightest thought or concern for penalties.

If deterrence is the main value to be gained from punishing criminals, then clearly we have much to gain by ensuring that such punishment is speedy, conspicuous, sure, and commensurate with the crime. Unfortunately American criminal justice is anything but speedy and is conspicuous only for the painful difficulty with which anybody is convicted for anything. At times our criminal-justice system appears to be an open invitation to break the law, not a deterrent. Because of plea bargaining, the punishment is often not at all commensurate with the crime, nor is it very sure, even for those few who are apprehended. If punishment and deterrence are the main job of prisons, then the argument for spending lots of money on prisons may be very unsound.

Crime-Rate Statistics and Their Validity   Perhaps it is worth mentioning here that anyone reading **crime-rate statistics** should be suspicious of them. Police can report only specific crimes they know about, and unfortunately they don't know about them all. In fact, the vast majority of crimes are never reported, especially rapes and thefts. Furthermore, the crime rate depends not only on reports received by police but also on the diligence of police in keeping accurate records of such reports, as well as their diligence in detecting the occurrence of crimes. Fluctuations in a city's crime rate may be only a fluctuation in the reporting of crime by police. Aside from being just sloppy at reporting, police departments at times find it to their benefit to report a declining crime rate and at other times (especially when their budget is under consideration) to report an increasing crime rate.

The Federal Bureau of Investigation does try to gather information from state and local police departments on the number of crimes per 100,000 people, broken down by various categories, such as murder, manslaughter, rape, robbery, assault, burglary, and larceny. The FBI publishes this information in its *Uniform Crime Reports.*

Police

Decentralization   America may have the most decentralized police system on the planet. In dictatorships, of course, and even among some of the world's great democracies, police are tightly controlled from the capitol. The United States government does, as we all know, have some national police to enforce federal law: the Federal Bureau of Investigation, federal marshals, Internal Revenue Service investigators, the Secret Service, the Narcotics Bureau, the postal inspectors, and various others. But we are unique among the democracies in having a mass of semiindependent state and local governments that run a mass of separate police departments that aren't under any command higher than the government of which they are part. Most of America's 3000 counties have county police headed by a sheriff. Thousands of municipalities maintain police forces ranging from highly sophisticated operations in the great cities to the almost comical one- or two-member part-time forces of villages. Furthermore, each of the 50 states has a police force (state troops or patrols) and various investigative agencies.

These approximately 4000 police forces do commonly cooperate with one another. The Federal Bureau of Investigation runs a national police academy that many hundreds of state and local police have attended, and also keeps a stupendous file of fingerprints that state and local police are invited to use. Perhaps the finest police laboratory in the world is run by the FBI, and this also serves state and local police when possible. Many states also maintain "little FBIs" (some aren't so little) with agents, fingerprint files, laboratories, and police academies to serve state and local police.

Police Education   During the 1970s, when federal assistance to police education peaked, more than a thousand colleges added police-science programs to their curriculum. Everybody wanted to help educate police officers, and some colleges did (and continue to do) a high-quality job of it, depending, of course, on how one defines *quality*. But quality did not prevail everywhere.

The main criticism of police-education programs seems to be that they teach too much "how to" information: how to write reports, how to use firearms, how to obey police-department regulations. One program offered a course called Handcuffs 101. Although this sort of technology is certainly useful to police, something more is needed. "Less than 30 percent of a police officer's tour of duty has anything to do with crime," said Gerald W. Lynch, president of the John Jay College of Criminal Justice. "The vast majority of an officer's responsibilities relate to a whole range of human encounters, from family-crisis interventions, to dealing with psychotic individuals, to defusing arguments and fights, to a whole range of other activities requiring physical courage, good judgment and understanding of human behavior and the law."[16]

Police, it is said, should be given a professional education, not merely a vocational education. Police are very important people: they handle many touchy situations and are in the midst of many controversies. They need something beyond Handcuffs 101. What they need, in fact, is a general education—an education that gives them an understanding of the sea of social forces in which they have to navigate as keepers of the peace. They need to understand, to fathom, to grasp what makes the social system tick: the economic system, the political system. They need to understand human psychology and group psychology. In short, they need economics, political science, public administration, psychology, sociology, philosophy, and, indeed, they need the fundamentals of what we call letters, arts, and sciences—they need an education over and above "how to" courses. So goes the argument of those who are critical of present-day vocational education for police.

[16]*New York Times*, September 19, 1984, p. A26.

Is crime actually reduced by giving a liberal arts education to police? Money to support that education has been voted by Congress under laws passed to "control crime" and "make the streets safe." It is hard to prove whether a liberal arts education serves that end. One analyst assures us, however, that "regardless of the absence of evidence that college-educated police are better police, in an increasingly educated, complex, and contentious society, officers obviously need the broader cultural understandings and improved analytical and communicative skills that can be expected from university education."[17]

Whatever the value of a liberal arts education, some police administrators seem to find it threatening when their subordinates start learning about such things as psychology, social issues, and management. Some chiefs may not feel as threatened by a *trained* subordinate as by an *educated* subordinate.

Today the minimum educational standard in 80 percent of the police and sheriff's departments is no more than high school graduation: another 10 percent of the departments have no minimum at all. The National Advisory Commission on Criminal Justice Standards and Goals once recommended that by 1982 four years of college should be a condition of employment for all police officers.[18]

Fire Protection and Emergency Help

Much of what has just been said concerning police officers also applies to members of fire departments. Fire fighters today do more than put out fires. They also investigate the causes of fires and enforce building codes and fire-hazard laws. For millions of people the fire station is the closest and most immediate source of emergency help no matter what the problem. Professional fire fighters are not actually part of the medical profession and are often trained to rescue people from dangerous situations of all sorts. It is probably time to consider changing the name of "fire" departments to something more descriptive of what they really do.

The state government itself has very little to do with fire fighting, but there are state laws on the subject of arson and fire hazards that fire fighters help enforce. Primary responsibility for fire protection is obviously local, not state.

The Militia

Each state had a militia before the United States Constitution was written, and the Constitution simply assumes that states will continue to have their militia. Since the purpose of the Constitution was to change the sovereign states into something less sovereign than before and to form states into one nation rather than leaving them as an alliance of independent nations, the Constitution naturally had to put some limits on state armies. The Constitution says states can't keep troops in time of peace without the consent of Congress.[19] The militia is evidently supposed to be something other than troops. One senses that "militia"

---

[17]David T. Stanley, "Higher Education for Police Officers: A Look at Federal Policies," *State Government* (Winter 1979), p. 41.

[18]National Advisory Commission on Criminal Justice, Standards, and Goals, *Police* (Washington, D.C.: Government Printing Office, 1973).

[19]*U.S. Const.*, Art. I, Sec. 10.

are less than troops and more than police—something midway. The Constitution gives Congress a variety of powers over the militia.[20]

The national government looks upon the state militia as a kind of ready reserve available for action in case of war. During World War I Congress formed the active militia of each state into what is known as the **national guard.** Congress had the power to do this because the Constitution writers of 1787 gave Congress the authority to pass laws organizing, arming, and governing the militia and the authority to call it out when necessary to enforce law, repel invasions, or put down rebellions. The basic pattern for organizing the national guard established in 1916 prevails today. The governor commands the state's guard and usually appoints an **adjutant general** to help with this. The governor also appoints commissioned officers of the guard, but all those appointments must be approved by the national government. Almost every detail of the guard is regulated by federal law—its size, types of units, qualifications of officers, salaries, periods of enlistment, and equipment. For all practical purposes, the national guard of each state is a part of the nation's armed forces.

State Police and Highway Patrols

Some states have state police, some have highway patrols, and some have both. State police commonly do a broader range of police work than the typical highway patrol, which may be limited to policing the highways. The main function of state police and patrols is to cope with the high mobility that motor vehicles give lawbreakers. Normally state police and highway patrols try not to annoy local police by patrolling streets within communities or by doing other things that local police are already doing, although state officers usually help local officers when asked. State assistance to local police also commonly includes supplying the services of crime laboratories, identification units, investigators, a communications network, and a police academy.

State law enforcement is not limited to highway patrols and state police. Universities, parks, and other state facilities often maintain uniformed security police. Fish and game officers roam the state. States also employ nonuniformed investigators to hunt down violators of the rules made by the state's many regulatory agencies. The states' "little FBIs" also employ nonuniformed investigators.

Labor

By giving the federal government the power to regulate commerce between states, the United States Constitution also (by implication) gives the federal government the power to regulate almost everything pertaining to labor in firms engaged in interstate commerce. States are excluded from regulating interstate commerce (as well as labor in such commerce) unless their regulations do not burden interstate commerce. Thus much, if not most, labor law is federal rather than state. States do, however, have jurisdiction over commerce within their borders that is not commerce between states and have enacted many laws affecting such commerce.

[20]*U.S. Const.*, Art. I, Sec. 8.

Health and Safety Laws   Most states have a great deal of law regulating in minute detail the physical conditions under which workers may work in factories, mines, stores, and various other places. These laws touch a multitude of things, such as fire escapes, sprinkler systems, protective devices, lighting, ventilation, dust, and restrooms. These laws have done a great deal to improve safety and health at the workplace.

Workmen's Compensation   Despite all the efforts of make conditions of labor safe, workers do get hurt on the job. Who should pay for these on-the-job injuries? Before the era of **workmen's-compensation laws,** the burden of injury usually fell on the injured worker unless he or she could successfully sue the employer, a process that was difficult and expensive. The employer could often avoid liability by proving the accident was caused by the worker's negligence (the *contributory-negligence doctrine*) or that the accident was caused by the carelessness of a fellow worker (the *fellow-servant doctrine*). If those two lines of defense failed, the employer could always fall back on the argument that the employee knew the job was dangerous when he or she took it and therefore assumed the risk (the *assumption-of-risk doctrine*). Whatever the merit of those arguments, they overlooked and ignored the theory that all industrial accidents are a part of the cost of production no matter who is at fault and should be paid for by the producer and ultimately by the consumer just like any other cost of production. Workmen's-compensation laws are based on that theory. Under such laws the three defenses described before are denied; employers are put under what is known as *strict liability* (liability without fault). At the same time employers are required to insure themselves either with private firms or with the state itself against accidents to their employees. Any employee injured on the job receives prompt compensation at rates determined by state law. The system is administered by state officials.

Unemployment Insurance   States are strongly encouraged by the federal government to pass laws requiring employers to purchase unemployment insurance for workers. Under such insurance former employees who have lost their jobs through no fault of their own and who cannot after a certain period of registration with the state employment service find other suitable work are entitled to receive compensation for a certain number of weeks. Both the employee and employer pay into an unemployment-insurance fund, which is administered by the state.

Miscellaneous Other Labor Laws   States have child-labor laws that prohibit the employment of children under a certain age (usually age 14 or 16) and that establish the daily and weekly working hours of children and limit their employment in various kinds of occupations that are morally or physically hazardous.

States also have laws touching such subjects as minimum wages, maximum hours of labor, discrimination in employment, relations between unions and management, tactics that may be employed in labor–management disputes, and the legality of various kinds of labor–management contracts.

States also provide services to assist the settlement of labor-management disputes: arbitration, mediation, and fact-finding services, for example.

Most states have a department of labor to administer many of the laws and services described above, although relations between government and labor also fall into the orbit of other departments as well, such as the health department or the agriculture department.

One of the liveliest labor-management issues today is whether states ought to pass "right-to-work" laws, which prohibit employers from requiring employees to join a union. Another hot issue is whether public employees should have the right to strike, or even to bargain collectively.

SUMMARY

Although most state governments are organized into vaguely similar patterns, there are nevertheless many organizational differences among them. Bureaucratic structure is the handiwork of politics—organizing is a political act. "Reason" affects the design of organizations only insofar as reason has political influence.

Each bureau in the bureaucracy is a political strong point, armed with clientele support and other political weapons for self-defense and expansion. Any attempt to reorganize and streamline the governmental bureaucracy encounters resistance from these strong points. Bureaucrats seldom appreciate any attempt to change the status quo. This is illustrated by the failure of "sunset" laws, an effort to terminate the existence of unnecessary agencies. There have been very few sunsets despite the apparent popularity of sunset as a theory.

Some of the major functions of state and local government not discussed elsewhere in this book are examined in this chapter, including elementary and secondary education, higher education, state libraries, transportation, health, welfare, corrections, police, fire protection, emergency help, the militia, state police and highway patrols, agriculture, and environmental protection.

SUGGESTIONS FOR FURTHER READING

FRIEDEN, BERNARD J., and MARSHALL KAPLAN, *The Politics of Neglect: Urban Aid from Model Cities to Revenue Sharing.* Cambridge, Mass.: M.I.T. Press, 1977.

FROHOCK, FRED M., *Public Policy: Scope and Logic.* Englewood Cliffs, N.J.: Prentice-Hall, 1979.

GARNETT, JAMES L., *Reorganizing State Government: The Executive Branch.* Boulder, Colo.: Westview, 1980.

GOODALL, LEONARD E., *State Politics and Higher Education.* Dearborn, Mich.: LGM Associates, 1976.

HENRY, NICHOLAS, *Public Administration and Public Affairs* (3rd ed.). Englewood Cliffs, N.J.: Prentice-Hall, 1986.

LEFTWICH, RICHARD H., and ANSEL M. SHARP, *The Economics of Social Issues* (5th ed.). Dallas: Business Publications, 1984.

LEHNE, RICHARD, *The Quest for Justice: The Politics of School Finance Reform.* New York: Longman, 1978.

"PUBLIC HOUSING: PUBLIC POLICY IN NEED OF REPAIR," *State Government* (May/June 1987), entire issue.

SCHILLER, BRADLEY R., *The Economics of Poverty and Discrimination* (4th ed.). Englewood Cliffs, N.J.: Prentice-Hall, 1984.

WEINBERG, MARTHA WAGNER, *Managing the State*. Cambridge, Mass.: M.I.T. Press, 1977.

ZIEGLER, HARMON, and M. KENT JENNINGS, *Governing American Schools: Political Interaction in Local School Districts*. North Scituate, Mass.: Duxbury, 1974.

14
epilog

Flying from Los Angeles to Boston one sunny day, I couldn't keep my eyes off the ground 30,000 feet below. From my window seat I gazed down on the Grand Canyon, which looked like a rather puny gash in the earth from that height. Being a political scientist, my thoughts wandered to the great entanglement of government beneath—the canyon itself a national park run by the federal government, within Coconino County, which also contains a piece of the Havasupai Indian Reservation, plus parts of the vast Navajo Reservation, as well as part of the Hopi Reservation (which is surrounded by the Navajo). And how many school districts, police districts, fire districts, cemetery districts, and municipal corporations of one kind or another were interlaced below? All this under the banner of a state government. Even amidst the loneliness and grandeur of the Painted Desert there is government galore.

Our progress across the continent continued. I searched for Colorado Springs as we crossed Pikes Peak and found it at the foot of the mountain. Our plane was so high no one could hear it or see it; only the long condensation cloud trailing us was visible. From my window I saw the great front wall of the Rocky Mountains suddenly drop off; then there was an endless flatness until finally the checkerboard pastures of eastern Kansas. I could not help thinking about the hundred or so counties in Kansas, all of them nearly square, set neatly in rows back and forth across the flattest state on earth. Think of it: only 2.5 million people, served by hundreds of municipalities, more than a thousand townships, countless school districts and other special districts, by counties, and by a state government with 165 legislators. Such a magnificent glut of government. Such an opportunity to practice democracy. Such government of, by, and for the people. Such prosperity and economic freedom by global standards, such great colleges, such great newspapers, such a glowing example of democratic self-government.

And so, across Missouri, Indiana, Ohio, Pennsylvania, New York—all political commonwealths greater than most nations of this earth, all of them awash in democratic local self-government, all with freedom of speech, freedom of the press, freedom of assembly, freedom of religion, and with stupendous economic freedom and security—all splendid and lovely societies by comparison with almost any other place in the solar system.

And finally into Boston, where in a sense it all began. I did truly want to see the State House, built in 1799 on John Hancock's cow pasture; I did want to see the blood-stained battle flags of the Revolutionary War and the spot where the Declaration of Independence was first read to the applause of the colonial legislature. But most of all I wanted to see something even more wondrous to an Iowan—I wanted to see a New England town, a town meeting, and direct democracy in action.

Flying back to Los Angeles, I had to confess—it isn't a perfect system, all this entanglement of government, nor is it a perfect democracy. But where is perfection on this planet? Clearly a speedier and smoother way of getting public business done could be invented. We could sweep the thousand townships of Kansas away, maybe even sweep Kansas itself away, and Colorado, too, and Massachusetts and 89 percent of the rest of state and local government. But all this abundance of government is a gymnasium—democracy's gymnasium—where the art and practice of self-government is exercised and kept in tone like the shining bodies of Olympic athletes.

appendix

JOURNALS

American Journal of Political Science.   Published quarterly by the Midwest Political Science Association.

American Political Science Review.   Published quarterly by the American Political Science Association.

Comparative State Politics Newsletter.   Published bimonthly by the Legislative Studies Center, Sangamon State University.

County News.   Published weekly by the National Association of Counties.

Journal of Politics.   Published quarterly by the Southern Political Science Association.

Mayor.   Published monthly by the United States Conference of Mayors.

National Civic Review.   Published monthly by the National Municipal League. Articles focus on urban affairs.

Nation's Cities Weekly.   Published weekly by the National League of Cities.

Polity.   Published quarterly by the Northeastern Political Science Association.

Public Administration Review.   Published bimonthly by the American Society for Public Administration.

Public Administration Times.   Published biweekly by the American Society for Public Administration.

State and Local Government Review.   Published three times a year by the Institute of Government, University of Georgia.

State Government.   Published quarterly by the Council of State Governments.

State Government News.   Published quarterly by the Council of State Governments.

State Legislatures.   Published monthly by the National Conference of State Legislatures.

Western City.   Published monthly by the League of California Cities.

Western Political Science Quarterly.   Published jointly by the Western Political Science Association, the Pacific Northwest Political Science Association, and the Southern California Political Science Association.

376

OTHER REFERENCE SOURCES

ABC Pol Sci.   A bibliography of publications in the fields of political science and government, published every two months by ABC–Clio, Inc.

Book of the States.   Published biennially by the Council of State Governments.

Management Information Service.   Published monthly by the International City Management Association.

Monthly Checklist of State publications.   Published monthly by the U.S. Government Printing Office.

The Municipal Year Book.   Published annually by the International City Management Association.

Public Affairs Information Service Index.   Published weekly with quarterly and annual cumulations by the Public Affairs Information Service. Lists books, pamphlets, periodicals, and government documents from a wide variety of sources.

Sage Public Administration Abstracts.   Published quarterly by Sage Publications, Inc.

Urban Affairs Abstracts.   Published weekly by the National League of Cities.

Urban Affairs Quarterly.   Published quarterly by Sage Publications.

U.S. Bureau of the Census.   Publishes various collections of statistical data pertaining to state and local government.

glossary

Adjutant general An officer appointed by the governor to help him or her command the state's National Guard.

Administrative adjudication The courtlike functions of administrative agencies.

Administrative-procedure act A law that exists in many states that sets forth procedures which agencies must follow when making rules or adjudicating cases.

Administrative tribunals Seats of judgment within agencies of the executive branch of government where disputes between the agency and citizens are settled.

Ad valorem According to value. An *ad valorem* tax (a property tax, for example) taxes something according to its value.

AFDC Aid to families with dependent children. A joint federal-state welfare program.

AFSCME American Federation of State, County, and Municipal Employees. A large union of civil servants.

Agency shop An agency of government that will not hire anyone who does not agree to either join a union, or pay union dues.

Agent One who holds power delegated to him or her by another.

Alienation A feeling of detachment, estrangement, distance, and unfriendliness.

Annexation The political and legal process by which cities acquire new territory.

Appeals courts Courts that hear appeals from the decisions of trial courts and usually confine themselves to issues of law (not fact).

Appropriation An enactment by a legislative body authorizing expenditure of specific amounts of public money for specific purposes.

Arraignment The process of bringing a person accused of a criminal offense before a court so that he or she can enter a plea of guilty, not guilty, not guilty by reason of insanity, or no contest.

Arrest To take custody of a person and detain him or her to answer charges of a criminal offense.

Assessment The process by which the value of property is determined for application of a property tax.

At-large elections Elections to fill seats on the governing boards of political units that are not divided into smaller election districts. All candidates run in a single large election district covering the entire area of the political unit; if elected, they represent the entire unit.

Auditing Attempting to determine whether

money is being spent for the purposes for which it was appropriated.

Auditor An officer whose duty it is to determine the legality of expenditures of public monies.

Australian ballot A system of voting by secret ballot, used originally in Australia.

Bail A deposit of money (or surety thereof) to release a person under arrest. The money is forfeited to the court if the arrestee fails to appear when commanded.

Bicameral legislature A two-house legislature.

Bill of rights A list of certain basic rights of citizens found in most constitutions.

Binding arbitration The settlement of labor–management disputes by a mutually agreed upon third party whose decision both sides agree in advance to accept.

Blanket primary A primary election in which voters of either party may participate in choosing the candidates of either party.

Block grant A federal grant of money to a subnational government. The subnational government is free to use the money as it sees fit within a broad subject-matter area.

Board of assessment appeals A county board to which appeals from the county assessor's assessments of the value of property may be taken.

Budget A proposal detailing how much money ought to be appropriated for various purposes.

Budget calendar A chronological series of stages through which the process of making a budget for a specific fiscal years goes.

Building code Detailed laws requiring buildings to be constructed in certain ways.

Bureaucracy An agency in which bureaucrats (civil servants) work.

Campaign-finance laws Laws that attempt to limit and publicize campaign contributions and expenditures.

Campaign-management firm A company that sells services, such as advertising, to candidates for office.

Campaign organizations Organizations established outside the regular party organization to work for the election of particular candidates.

Campaign staffers Paid and/or volunteer workers who hold key positions in a political campaign.

Canons of taxation The characteristics of a "good" tax.

Categorical aid Federal grants of money to subnational governments for the accomplishment of specific and narrowly defined programs.

Caucus A private meeting of party leaders to pick party candidates to run in elections.

Charter A state law conferring governmental powers upon a local agency of the state.

Checks and balances An aspect of separation of powers in which each branch of government—executive, legislative, and judicial—exercises some power over the others' activities, preventing a concentration of power in any one branch.

Chief legislator A term commonly applied to chief executives because of their influence over legislative bodies.

City-county mergers The uniting of a city and a county into one single political body having a single government.

City manager A person appointed by a city council who in turn appoints and supervises the heads of most city departments.

City-state The entity created by separating certain large metropolitan areas from the states they are presently in, and establishing them as states of the Union. A somewhat fanciful notion.

Civil case Any case involving civil law. Usually but not always a controversy between private parties.

Civil law Any law that provides no punishment for violators but opens the violator to a suit for damages or some other noncriminal remedy by the party wronged by the violation.

Civil rights The rights of individuals and minorities against majorities in the political system.

Civil service Employees of government, excluding elected officials, judges, and members of the armed forces.

Civil-service commission In some state and local governments, a nonpartisan independent board in charge of administering the merit system.

Classified service That part of the civil service selected by a merit system.

Clerk of the house Chief administrator of the lower house of a legislature.

Closed primary A primary election in which only registered party affiliates may vote.

Closed shop An agency (or company) that will not hire anyone who is not a member of a certain union.

Collective bargaining Union negotiations with management on behalf of union members.

Commerce clause A clause of the U.S. Constitution giving the federal government power to regulate commerce between the states.

Commission form A form of city government in which each member of the city commission (comparable to a city council) is also head of one of more city departments.

Commission on judicial qualifications The name commonly given to committees that investigate complaints against judges and recommend to the state supreme court a course of action.

Committee of the whole A committee composed of all members of one house of a legislative body.

Committeeperson The chief party official at the precinct level, often known as precinct captain.

Common law The body of judge-made law.

Competitive civil service That part of the civil service composed of persons appointed by a merit system based on competitive examinations.

Confederacy A system of government in which the national government has only such power as the states are willing from time to time to loan it.

Conference committee A joint house and senate committee charged with designing a compromise version of a bill passed in different forms in the two houses.

Constitutional amendment An addition to a constitution that adds to, deletes, or alters one of its provisions, or that adds a new provision.

Constitutional convention A gathering of delegates who represent the sovereign people for the purpose of drafting a new constitution or revising an existing constitution.

Constitutional law A constitution and various judicial interpretations of it.

Consultant Someone hired temporarily by a government to fill a temporary need.

Contiguous districts Adjacent legislative districts that touch along all or most of one side.

Controller An officer in the executive branch of government who establishes accounting systems and checks the legality of proposed expenditures of appropriated money.

Cooperative federalism A policy emphasizing cooperation between federal and state governments, rather than a division of power between them.

Coroner A public official who investigates deaths occurring under suspicious circumstances.

Corrections All state activities that have anything to do with handling persons convicted of crime.

Cost-benefit analysis Quantification of the costs and benefits of each of several methods of reaching a goal.

Council of governments A council composed of representatives of the various governments within a metropolitan area. Its power is usually advisory.

County The major administrative division within most states. Established for the convenience of the state in carrying out state functions at the local level.

County board In most states, the central legislative and administrative organ of county government.

County clerk A county officeholder whose chief duty is to keep county records.

Courts of original jurisdiction Courts that hear cases for the first time and decide issues of both fact and law.

Crime-rate statistics Information fathered by the FBI and other agencies about the number of crimes per 100,000 people, broken down by various categories.

Criminal case Any case involving criminal law. The plaintiff is always the government.

Criminal law Any law that provides for fining or imprisonment of violators.

Debt limits Laws prohibiting state legislatures and/or local governments from incurring certain kinds of debt beyond a certain amount.

Delegated power Power given to the federal government by the U.S. Constitution.

Demand procedure A procedure by which an assembly may withdraw a bill from a committee.

Dillon's rule A rule emphasizing narrow and strict interpretation of laws granting authority to local governments.

Direct legislation The enactment of laws directly by the people, rather than by representatives of the people.

District elections Elections to fill seats on the governing board of political units that are divided into election districts, each of which elects one representative to the board.

Domestic-relations court A court that grants divorces but is also charged with trying to encourage reconciliation.

Dual sovereignty The doctrine that neither the federal government nor the states have any legal superiority over the other when exercising functions within their exclusive sphere of constitutional authority.

Earmark Appropriate in advance the revenue to be raised in the future by a specific tax.

Economic elite Those among the most influential in a political entity whose influence stems largely from their business activity.

Elite theory The theory that the few rule, even in a democracy.

Environmental protection Protection of land, air, and water from that which is unhealthy to people and to the resources upon which they depend.

Equity power The power of a judge to decide a case according to his or her own sense of justice, where no common or statutory law compels otherwise.

Exhaustion of remedies doctrine The principle followed by most courts that they will refuse to hear a controversy between an agency and a citizen until the citizen has exhausted every channel of appeal within the agency.

Extradition Surrender by one state to another of fugitives from justice.

Extraterritorial jurisdiction Authority of cities in some states to extend certain of their powers, such as zoning, beyond their boundaries for a certain distance.

Factions As used here, the political groupings within the dominant political party in one-party states.

Family court A specialized court that handles cases pertaining to children and divorce.

Federal Election Campaign Act A 1971 federal law that attempts to limit and publicize campaign contributions and expenditures, and authorizes public financing of presidential elections.

Federalism The division of power between a central government and the state governments by a constitution that cannot be changed by either party without the consent of the other.

Felonies Crimes that are more serious than misdemeanors.

Fiscal year A financial year used for accounting purposes. It may or may not coincide with the calendar year.

Fitness system A system for selecting persons for government employment that falls short of being a merit system but is not entirely a spoils system.

Full faith and credit The policy whereby each state enforces various rights acquired by citizens under the laws and judicial proceedings of other states.

General-law city A city whose charter is in the form of a legislative enactment applicable to all cities of the same class.

General revenue sharing Grants of money from the federal government to subnational governments carrying few restrictions on how it must be spent.

Gerrymandering Drawing legislative-district lines in such a way as to magnify the power of one or another group of voters.

Governor's budget A detailed proposal for expenditure of public money during a fiscal year made to the legislature by the governor. Also known as an executive budget.

Governor's staff State employees working in the governor's office under his or her immediate supervision.

Grantsmanship The art of obtaining gifts of money from public or private sources.

Home rule The power granted cities and/or counties in some states to design their own governmental structure in place of a design set forth by state law.

Illegal patronage Patronage (appointments to civil-service jobs as a reward for political service) that violates merit-system laws.

Implied powers Powers of the federal government not directly given by the Constitution but inferred from those directly given.

Incremental budgeting Usually the practice of setting the annual appropriation for most agencies at a percentage (increment) of increase over the agency's previous year's appropriation.

Indictment A grand-jury accusation charging a person with a punishable offense.

Information An accusation made by a prosecutor charging a person with a punishable offense.

Information network A system enabling librarians throughout a state to find out quickly which libraries hold certain books and documents.

Initiative A process by which voters propose constitutional amendments or other laws for adoption by popular vote.

Injunction A writ (court order) commanding the recipient not to do something.

Institutionalize the governorship Accomplish as much of the governor's work as possible through professional aides and/or staff agencies.

Interim committees Legislative committees established for the purpose of meeting between sessions of the legislature.

Interpretation of constitutions Opinions about the meaning of a constitution given by legislators, judges, and bureaucrats—most importantly by judges.

Iron law of oligarchy The theory that in every organization a tiny minority of people are extremely influential in the affairs of the organization.

Item veto The power of the governor in some states to veto one element of a bill without vetoing the entire bill.

Jacksonian democracy An era (1820s and 1830s) of democratization in American political life when the right to vote was extended to propertyless people.

Job classification The grouping of similar government jobs into categories (classes) so that those in each category can be treated similarly under merit-system procedures.

Job description A written statement of the duties and responsibilities of a particular position.

Joint committees Committees composed of members of both houses of a legislative body and reporting to both houses.

Judge-made law The body of law created when judges decide cases by reference to past decisions: the past decisions become, in effect, law.

Judicial review The power of courts to rule on the constitutionality of legislative and executive acts.

Jury stacking The use of peremptory challenges by an attorney in such a way as to produce a jury slanted toward his or her client.

Justice of the peace Judge of a minor local court whose jurisdiction is limited to petty civil and criminal cases.

Juvenile court A court that handles only cases pertaining to children.

Lame duck An elected official who is known to be unwilling or ineligible to hold the office beyond his present term.

Legislative audit committee A committee of the legislature that helps choose an auditor and oversees his or her work.

Legislative council A fact-finding, information-collecting agency for the legislature.

Legislative drafting office An agency of the legislature that helps members translate their ideas into the specific language of bills.

Licensing board A board whose duty it is to make rules for the practice of a certain profession or occupation and to license practitioners.

Literacy test A test requiring voters to be able to read. Once used in some states primarily to limit voting by blacks.

Lobbying The attempt, usually by representatives of interest groups, to influence the actions of officeholders.

Local court A court with a small territorial jurisdiction that handles only minor civil and criminal cases.

Lower house In a two-house legislature, the house with the most members.

Loyalty Readiness to serve the interests of another.

Malapportionment Gross inequalities of population among legislative districts of the same house.

Mandamus A writ (court order) commanding an officer of government to perform a ministerial (nondiscretionary) duty.

Mandate A command given by voters to those whom they elect, sometimes alleged to be based on the campaign promises of victorious candidates.

Maverick One who takes an independent stand, refusing to conform—a strayed calf.

Mayor-council form A form of local government in which the mayor and council attempt to administer the city without a city manager.

Media Any means of communication that reach the general public.

Medicaid A joint federal-state program for providing free medical care to the poor.

Medicare The federal government's hospital-insurance program for persons over 65.

Merit system A system in which persons are selected for government employment by competitive examination.

Metropolitan area A large urban area that

may consist of numerous cities and other governmental units packed together.

Metropolitan district A special district whose boundaries enclose an entire metropolitan area.

Middle-of-the-roaders Politicians who take moderate positions on controversial issues.

Minimum-competency test A test that graduating high school seniors in some jurisdictions must pass before receiving their diploma.

Mill One-tenth of a penny, or one dollar per thousand dollars.

Misdemeanor A minor crime, such as overparking.

Missouri system A system of selecting judges that features elements of both appointment and election.

Mistrial A jury trial in which the jury cannot make up its mind. The accused may be retried before another jury.

Morrill Act A federal law passed in 1862 donating land to the states for the purpose of establishing colleges devoted to teaching agriculture and engineering.

Muckrake Ceaselessly dig up and publish evidence of supposed corruption by officeholders.

Multiple-member constituency An election district from which two or more representatives to a certain legislative body can be elected simultaneously.

Municipal corporation A legal institution formed by the state enabling a populous community to operate as a subordinate self-governing political entity.

Municipal court A court established by a city to try violators of city ordinances.

National economy Economic activity among the several states rather than solely within particular states.

National Guard The active militia in each state, organized, armed and governed by federal law.

National Labor Relations Act of 1935 A federal law governing labor-management relations within the private sector.

Necessary and proper clause A clause of the U.S. Constitution allowing the federal government to exercise powers implied from other powers explicitly given the federal government.

Needs test A test that requires recipients of welfare to show they are eligible for welfare.

New England town The principal unit of local government in New England. Has characteristics of both a city and a county.

Nominating convention A meeting of party delegates to select party candidates to run in the general election.

Noncompetitive jobs Civil-service jobs that are not under a merit system.

Nonpartisan election An election in which the ballot does not show the party affiliation of candidates.

Nonpartisan primary A nonpartisan election that narrows the number of candidates to two if no one receives an absolute majority.

Office-block ballot General ballot in which candidates are grouped by the office sought.

Old-style politics The attempt to win elections by personal contact rather than by reliance on the media and scientific campaigning.

One-man-one-vote The policy of making legislative districts of the same house roughly equal in population, thereby giving each voter equal weight.

One-party state A state in which only one party regularly wins elections.

Open primary A primary election in which voters decide in the secrecy of the polling booth which party they wish to be affiliated with for purposes of choosing party candidates.

Original 13 states The states that became states by ratifying the Constitution.

Override Make a bill law despite a veto. Requires an extraordinary majority vote of a legislative body.

PAC Acronym for political action committee.

Party-column ballot General-election ballot in which candidates are grouped by party affiliation.

Party discipline The control by a political party of the votes, words, and actions of its members who hold public office. Very weak in the United States.

Party leader A person who influences a party, either because of his or her prestige or because of formal election to high party office.

Party member In the United States, commonly defined as one who at registration declares a party affiliation.

Pay As used here, compensation for service as a member of the state legislature—often based on a complex formula not readily understandable by the public.

Pendleton Act of 1883 A law that established the federal merit system.

Per capita income All the personal income earned by all the people of a particular area or category, divided by the population of that area or category.

Performance auditing Auditing that goes beyond a narrow check on legality of expenditures to include a check on whether money is being efficiently spent for purposes intended by the appropriation.

Periodic registration A procedure by which a voter must reregister periodically in order to maintain certification as an eligible voter.

Permanent registration A procedure that allows voters to remain certified as eligible voters until they change parties, change addresses, or fail to vote.

Personal-property tax A tax on the value of personal property (property that is not real estate).

Planning Developing a program for the physical (and social) development of an area—hence county planning, city planning, urban planning, and so on.

Planning commission A committee appointed by a local governing body to study proposals to change the comprehensive plan and make recommendations.

Plural executive An executive branch of government that has more than one popularly elected administrator.

Pluralism A political system characterized by numerous centers of influence over government action.

Pocket veto In some states, the power of a governor to prevent a bill passed by the legislature from becoming law by declining to sign it within a specified period after the legislature adjourns.

Political culture The attitudes and customs of a people concerning how their government should be organized and run.

Political high command The top-level elected or politically appointed officers of government.

Political machine A successful political organization; a term often applied to the ruling political organization of a large city.

Poll tax A tax to be paid by voters before they are allowed to vote. Declared unconstitutional by the Twenty-fourth Amendment.

Poll watcher A person representing a candidate or political party who stands duty near the polls on election day to insure the integrity of voting procedures.

Popular sovereignty The doctrine that all legal authority comes from the people.

Postaudit A determination of the legality of expenditures of appropriated money after payment.

Power The ability to act, or to influence.

Preaudit A determination of the legality of proposed expenditures of appropriated money before payment.

Precinct An area in which all voters vote at the same location. Also, the lowest unit of party organization.

Precinct caucus A meeting of the registered voters of a particular party within a precinct to conduct party business.

Preliminary hearing A hearing before a judge, immediately after arrest, to determine if there is probable cause for believing the arrestee committed the offense for which he or she was arrested.

Preprimary endorsement Endorsement of one or more primary-election candidates by assemblies of party delegates prior to the primary election.

Presidential primary An election at which rank-and-file party members of a state express their preference among candidates for the party's presidential nomination.

President pro tem An officer elected to preside over the senate in absence of the lieutenant governor in states where the lieutenant governor serves as president of the senate.

Pressure group An organization that attempts to influence the actions of public officeholders.

Primary election Most commonly, an election in which rank-and-file party members select party candidates to run in the general election.

Primary jurisdiction doctrine The principle followed by most courts that they will refuse to hear a controversy between an agency and a citizen until the agency has first decided the case.

Privatization Government contracts with private firms to perform governmental services.

Privileges and immunities Under the U.S. Constitution, rights every citizen has by virtue of U.S. citizenship.

Probate court A court that distributes the estates of deceased persons.

Progressive income tax A tax on income that

becomes progressively higher as income increases.

Progressive movement A trend in early-twentieth-century politics toward curbing the power of state and local political bosses.

Proportional representation In multiple-member constituencies, the division of seats among parties in proportion to each party's proportion of the total vote cast.

Proposition 13 A famous tax limitation adopted by California voters in 1978.

Prosecuting attorney The public officer within a judicial district whose duty it is to carry on judicial proceedings against persons accused of crimes. Also sometimes known as district attorney.

Psychological distance As used here, a feeling of unfamiliarity between citizen and government.

Public housing Government-owned dwellings rented below cost to the poor.

Public opinion Certain opinions held by a portion of the public that bear on a particular matter.

Public-opinion polling The attempt to determine what a large number of people think by questioning a small number of people.

Public relations Doing or saying that which wins the support of that part of the public that is significant to achieving a goal.

Quasi-judicial power The judicial power of administrative agencies.

Quasi-legislative power The rule-making power of administrative agencies.

Quorum The minimum number of members who must be present at an assembly before it can validly conduct business.

Racial gerrymandering Drawing the boundary lines of voting districts in such a way as to unfairly disadvantage one ethnic group in elections.

Readings First, second, and third readings of bills. Each signifies a separate stage of legislative procedure through which bills pass.

Real-property tax A tax levied annually on the value of real estate.

Reapportionment Periodic redrawing of legislative-district lines to keep districts of the same house roughly equal in population.

Recall Removal of public officers by vote of the electorate.

Recidivism rate The percentage of persons who return to crime after being released from the corrections system.

Reciprocal immunity The freedom of federal and state governments from being taxed by each other.

Record A list of accomplishments that generates a positive or negative reaction among voters.

Referendum A vote by the electorate on a particular issue, such as a constitutional amendment.

Register A list of persons who have passed the exam for a particular kind of competitive-service job.

Regressiveness A characteristic of taxes that burden the poor more than the rich.

Regulation-review committees Committees established by some legislatures to screen new rules made by state agencies and to refer questionable ones to the legislature.

Rent-supplement program Government payment of part of the rent of low-income families living in government-approved quarters.

Republican government Rule by representatives of the people rather than by the people themselves.

Reserved power Power given to the states by the U.S. Constitution.

Residence requirement The period of time a person must live in a political unit before acquiring the right to vote in it (usually no more than 30 days).

Revised code A periodically revised collection of books in which all the effective laws of the state are arranged by subject.

Revisor of statutes An employee of the legislature whose principal task is to publish a state code and keep it up to date.

Rules Laws enacted by administrative agencies elaborating other laws that those agencies have been asked by the legislature to enforce.

Rules committee A committee found in most lower houses that regulates certain aspects of a bill's passage through the legislature.

Rule making The power of agencies of the executive branch of government to make rules having the force of law that affect the rights and duties of private citizens.

Runoff primary A second primary election in which only the two top candidates in the first primary are on the ballot.

Sales tax A tax on retail (or wholesale) sales, levied as a percentage of the sale price.

Secretary of the senate The chief administrator of the senate.

Seniority The period of time one has held a particular job or been employed by a particular employer.

Separate but equal doctrine An interpretation of the U.S. Constitution once held by the U.S. Supreme Court that separation of the races by law is constitutional as long as the separate facilities are physically equal.

Separation of powers The division of governmental power among three separate branches: legislative, executive, and judicial.

Sergeant at arms An employee of a legislative body whose duties in and around the legislative chamber are roughly comparable to those of an ordinary police officer.

Sessions laws A book usually published after each session of the legislature listing the bills in chronological order as they were passed.

Session limitations Laws limiting the frequency and duration of meetings of the state legislature.

Single-member district An election district from which only one representative can be elected at any specific election to a specific legislative body.

Small-claims court A court where disputes over small amounts of money can be settled without the need for lawyers, juries, or complex court procedure.

Speaker Presiding officer of the lower house of legislatures.

Special district A one-function government, such as a park district, transportation district, or school district.

Specialized courts A court (or division of a court) that hears only one kind of case, such as probate, divorce, or juvenile cases.

Special legislation Legislation aimed at named parties, such as individuals or corporations.

Special session In states, a meeting of the legislature convened usually by the governor.

Spending power Power of a government (here the federal government) to spend money.

Spoils system A system in which civil-service jobs are filled with persons appointed as a political favor.

Standing committee A permanently established committee of one house of a legislative body.

Stare decisis Let the decision stand. Deciding today's case the same way similar cases were decided in the past.

State auditor A state official charged with checking the legality of all state expenditures that have been made.

State board of education A board that, with the help of a department of education, carries out the state's relationship with elementary and secondary schools.

State superintendent of schools The official who heads the state department of education.

Statute A formal enactment of a legislative body that has become law.

Statutory law The enactments of legislative bodies, rules made by administrative agencies, and constitutions.

Strong mayor A mayor in a mayor-council form of government who has the power to appoint major department heads of the city.

Subdivision regulations Ordinances enacted usually by cities and counties requiring firms engaged in building new neighborhoods to do a variety of things as a condition for receiving a permit to construct a subdivision.

Suburbs Residential districts near the borders of a city, some or all of which may be separately incorporated.

Suicide mechanism The phenomenon by which third parties, after popularizing their main idea, die when that idea is adopted by a major party.

Sunset laws Laws that require termination of certain agencies after a given length of time unless they get a new lease on life from the legislature.

Supremacy clause Article VI of the U.S. Constitution, which says federal law is the supreme law of the land and takes priority over state law.

Surveyor One who determines the length and direction of boundary lines, computes areas, and maps contours.

Tax limits Laws that prohibit governments from levying property taxes in excess of a certain rate.

Team system A system in which the governor and lieutenant governor run as a team and are voted upon as a team.

Tenth Amendment The amendment to the U.S. Constitution that summarizes the division of power between federal and state governments.

Term limitation In some states, a law that limits an elected official, such as the governor, to a certain number of successive terms in office.

Theory of representation Speculation about the various ways members of legislative bodies can or can't, do or don't, and should or should not reflect the wishes of their constituents.

Third party In two-party systems, any party that rarely or never wins elections.

Tort liability act A law by which a state allows itself to be sued for certain wrongs it may commit.

Township In some states, a division of a county, organized much like a county, and possessing functions similar to those of a county.

Treasurer An officer who keeps public money.

Trial courts Courts of general original jurisdiction over serious criminal and civil cases.

Turnover The departure and replacement of employees.

Two-party system A political system in which only two major parties regularly win elections.

Unassembled test A merit-system test for appointment to professional jobs that involves supplying a dossier with information about schooling, experience, and so on.

Unemployment compensation An employer-financed program under which an involuntarily unemployed worker may draw payments for a certain number of weeks.

Uniform state law A proposed law whose sponsors hope will be adopted in identical form in all states.

Unilateral annexation The process of adding territory to a city without an affirmative vote of the inhabitants of the territory being annexed.

Union shop An agency (or company) that requires all its employees to join a particular labor union within a certain period of time after being hired.

Upper house The senate in two-house legislatures.

Urban homesteading A program under which one can buy a structurally sound but deteriorated piece of property from the government for a nominal fee on condition one improve the property.

Veto In state government, the power of a governor to forbid a bill passed by the legislature to become law, unless it is passed over his objection by an extraordinary legislative majority.

Viva voce **vote** A vote taken by voice.

Voir dire To speak the truth. An examination of prospective jurors by the court to determine their competency to serve.

Voter registration A procedure by which prospective voters appear before election officials who certify them as eligible voters.

Voting age Age 18 in all federal, state, and local elections. See the Twenty-sixth Amendment.

Weak mayor A mayor in a mayor-council form of government who has little power over administration of the city.

Welfare clause A clause allowing the federal government to spend money for anything contributing to the general welfare of the people.

Whips Members of a legislative body who help the leader of their house of the legislature.

White primary A device once used in certain one-party states to prevent blacks from voting in party primary elections.

Winner-take-all system An election system that gives all the legislative seats within an election district to the party that gets the most votes in that district. (Unavoidable in single-member districts.)

Workmen's-compensation laws Laws that make employers liable for all industrial injuries and require them to insure themselves against such liability.

Zero-based budgeting The process of beginning the budget-making process by asking each agency to explain and justify why it should get the money at all (that is, more than zero dollars).

Zoning Division of territory into areas (zones) designated by ordinance for specific land uses.

Index

Adjutant general, 370
Administrative procedure act, 342
Administrative tribunals, 341–43
  appeals from, 187
  hearings, 186
Admission to Union, 35
  admitted states, 35
  original states, 35
Admitted states, 35
  legal equality, 36
AFDC, 358
AFSCME, 330
Agency shop, 334
Agriculture
  colleges, 361
  department of, 362
  generally, 361
  political power of, 362
  technology, 362
Air, quality of, 365
Air transportation, 355
Alexander, Herbert E., 72, 106
Annexation, 275–77, 278
Appeals, 207
  of administrative decisions, 342
  of fact questions, 342
  of law questions, 342
Apportionment, 157–60

Appropriations, 291, 296
  supplemental, 297
Arbitration, binding, 351
Aronson, Albert H., 327
Arraignment, 205
Arrest, 204
Articles of Confederation, 23, 35
Assessment, 226, 229–30, 309–11
Assessment appeals, board of, 226
At-large elections, 267
Attorney, district, 231
Auditing, 297–300
  auditor, 298
  controller, 297
  legislative audit committee, 299
  performance, 163, 300
  postauditing, 298
  preauditing, 298
  treasurer, 298
Auditor, county, 229

Back, Kenneth, 310n
Baer, Jon A., 315n
Bahl, Roy, 317
Bail, 205
Baker v. Carr, 148n, 159n, 190n, 362n
Ballots, 62–67
  Australian, 62

Ballots (*cont.*)
  nonpartisan, 67
  office block, 63, 65
  paper, 62
  party column, 63, 64
  voting machines, 63
Banfield, Edward C., 288
Baum, Bernard H., 345
Beckman, Norman, 324n
Bender, Lewis G., 271
Bentham, Jeremy, 147
Benton, J. Edwin, 311n
Beyle, Thad L., 10, 109n, 110n, 113n, 137n, 139
Bibby, John, 106
Bicameralism, 147–50
  federal, 147
  unicameralism, 267
Billingsley, Alan G., 220n, 249
Bill of Rights, 13, 24
Black, Henry C., 198, 251n
Blanton, Ray, 4
Block grant, 30
Board, county, 224
Board of assessment appeals, 226
Bollens, John C., 249, 288
Borough, 222
Boston, 375
Boss rule, 143
Botner, Stanley B., 317
Bowman, Ann O., 10
Bowman, John H., 310n
Break, George, 42
Bribery, 101–104
Brinton, Milward H., 345
Brough, Regina K., 132
Browne, Cynthia E., 20
Brownstone, Meyer, 288
Brown v. *Board of Education,* 188n, 199
Bryan, Frank, 271
Bryan, William Jennings, 143
Brydges, Earl W., 145, 145n
Budget 165, 290–96
  clarity of, 295
  Colorado, 292
  and cost-benefit analysis, 294
  defined, 290
  earmarking, 131, 146
  executive, 292n
  governor's, 130–31, 135, 291
  incremental, 131, 292
  and legislatures, 291
  making by mayor, 263
  politics of, 292
  PPBS, 294
  rationality of, 292, 293
  zero-based, 293

Building codes, 238
Bureaucracy, 262, 264
  agriculture, 361
  college, 353
  corrections, 366–67
  environmental protection, 363
  fire protection, 369
  health, 355
  highway patrol, 369
  labor, 370
  libraries, 354
  licensing boards, 349
  militia, 369
  organization of, 7, 348–51
  police, 367, 367–69
  reorganization of, 350–51
  schools, public, 351–52
  transportation, 354
  welfare, 356–61
Burger, Warren E., 213
Burke, Beverly G., 359n
Burns, James M., 10

Cabinet, 111
  department heads, 324
Calvert, Jerry, 153n
Campaigns
  computers, use of, 88
  cost, 88–90
  finance, 88–92
  management firms, 86–88
  media science, 87
  old-style politics, 88
  organizations, 85
  public opinion polling, 87
  staff, 110
Cannon, Bradley C., 215
Caraley, Demetrios, 288
Carruthers, Garrey, 271
Carter, Jimmy, 99
Categorical aid, 30
Caucus, 58
  precinct, 82
CFR, 201
Chadwick, William, 324n
Chamelin, Neil C., 215
Charity, 361
Charters, 252–55
  classified, 253
  general law, 253
  home rule, 254
  optional, 253
Checks and balances, 12
Chicago, 85
Chicago Transit Authority, 244
Chi, Keon S., 336

Circuit courts, 181n
Cities, small, 271–75
Citizenship, 48
City
  budget, 263
  bureaucracy, 262, 264
  charters, 253–55
  civil service, 262, 264, 325
  commission form, 255
  compared with county, 252
  council, 264–67
  council-manager form, 257–59
  distinguished from county, 222
  elections, 267–71
  forms of government, 255–59
  general law, 253
  home rule, 254
  manager, 257
  mayor, 259–64
  mayor-council form, 259
  mergers with county, 278, 283–86
  mergers with state, 278
  merit system, 262
  municipal corporation, 251
  size, 252
City council, small town, 271–75
Civil case, 195, 201, 208
Civil law, 201
Civil law world, 200
Civil Rights Act, 52
Civil servants, 8, 143, 262, 318–45
  and city council, 264
  civil service commissions, 323, 328
  classification of jobs, 322
  consultants, 328
  department heads, 324
  dismissals, 318, 330
  fitness system, 321
  governor's office, 324
  Hatch Acts, 322
  illegal patronage, 327–30
  job descriptions, 328
  judicial power, 341–43
  legislative power, 337–41
  local governments, 325
  merit systems, 321, 333
  noncompetitive jobs, 324
  Pendleton Act of 1883, 325
  rulemaking by, 337–41
  rural, 273
  spoils system, 321, 327–30
  staff of legislature, 324
  strikes, 332, 351
  temporary appointments, 327
  tests, 323, 328
  unions, 330–35

Clark, Cal, 271
Clark, Janet, 271
Classification of jobs, 322
Clean Air Act, 33
Clerk, county, 227
Clerk, court, 228
Clerk of the house, 164, 172
Closed shop, 334
Code, building, 238
Code, housing, 238
Cohen, Morris, 215
Collective bargaining by teachers, 351
Colleges, 353, 361
Comer, John C., 72, 210
Commerce clause, 27
Commission system, 255
Committees of legislature
  audit, 163
  chairpersons, 167
  conference, 175
  demand procedure, 174
  importance, 165
  interim, 168
  joint, 166
  membership, 167
  number, 166
  power, 166
  rules, 174
  staff of, 161
  standing, 165–68, 172–75
  of the whole, 174
Common law, 197–200
Commonwealth court, 181n
Community development, 30
Compensation,
  of city council, 265
  commission, 164
  of legislature, 154
Confederacy, 23
Confederate States of America, 23
Conference committee, 175
Conservation, energy, 365
Constable, town, 239
Constitution, U.S.
  amendment procedure, 38
  commerce clause, 27
  elections, 46–47
  extradition, 39
  Fifteenth Amendment, 53
  Fourteenth Amendment, 47, 54
  implied powers, 26–27
  judicial interpretation of, 188, 198
  and local governments, 220
  necessary and proper clause, 24, 26
  privileges and immunities, 41
  republican form of government, 36

Constitution, U.S. (*cont.*)
  Seventeenth Amendment, 38
  spending power, 26
  style of, 26
  suits between states, 40
  Tenth Amendment, 23, 24
  territorial integrity, 37
  Twenty-fourth Amendment, 46–54
  Twenty-sixth Amendment, 47
  welfare clause, 26
Constitutional amendment
  difficulty, 14
  frequency, 15–16
  initiation, 13, 38
  process, 13–16
  ratification, 14, 38
Constitutional commissions, 17
Constitutional Convention of 1787, 24, 148
Constitutional conventions, 17
Constitutional law, 26
Constitution, model state, 19, 20
Constitutions, 12–20
  basic principles, 12–13
  defined, 12
  executive interpretation, 18
  interpretation, 18
  judicial interpretation, 18
  legislative interpretation, 18
  length, 16
  new, 18
  revision of, 17–20
  similarities among, 12–13
  writing of, 19
Consultants, 328
Consumer protection, 349
Contracting for service, 282
Controller, 297
Conventions
  constitutional, 17, 38
  nominating, 58, 84
Cook, Rhodes, 72
Cooperative federalism, 28–33
Cornwell, Elmer E., Jr., 20
Coroner, 232
Corrections, 366–67
Corrupt Practice Act, 90
Cost-benefit analysis, 294
Council, city
  attitudes toward their work, 266
  and bureaucrats, 264
  New York, 267, 267n
  offices, 266
  part-time members, 265
  pay, 265
  relations with mayor, 266

  staff, 266
  unicameral, 267
Council-manager system, 257–59
Councils of governments, 281
Counsel, right to, 205
County, 221–39
  assessor, 226, 309–11
  attorney, 231
  auditor, 229
  boards, 224–27
  boroughs, 222
  building codes, 238
  civil service, 325
  clerk, 227
  coroner, 232
  defined, 221
  Denver, 283–85
  distinguished from city, 222
  finance, 239
  health service, 234
  home rule, 233
  managers, 234
  organization, 224
  parish, 222
  parks and recreation, 235
  planning, 235–39
  population, 223
  recorder, 228
  reform of, 232
  rural, 271–75
  services, 234–39
  sheriff, 230
  size, 223
  subdivision regulation, 237
  superintendent of schools, 232
  surveyor, 232
  treasurer, 228
  welfare service, 235
  zoning, 237
Court, clerk, 228
Courts, 178–215
  administrative, 186, 341–43
  appeals, 181
  circuit, 181n
  civil cases, 201
  civil procedure, 208
  of common pleas, 181n
  commonwealth, 181n
  criminal cases, 201
  criminal procedure, 204–8
  district, 181n
  domestic relations, 185
  equity, 203
  of error, 181
  family, 184

federal and state, 187–89
general jurisdiction, 181
judges, 189–93
juries, 193–97
justice of the peace, 180
juvenile, 184
and law, 197–202
local, 179
municipal, 180
organization, 179
of original jurisdiction, 181
probate, 185
reform, 209
small claims, 183
specialized, 183
superior, 181n
supreme, 181n, 189
trial, 181
unified systems, 19
Crane, Wilder, Jr., 177
Crime rate, 367
Criminal case, 201, 204–8
Criminal law, 201
Cronin, Thomas E., 10
Culture, political, 6
Curley, James Michael, 259

Dade County, 279
Dahl, Robert, 95n
Daley, Richard J., 85
Daniels, Bruce C., 249
Death penalty, 194
Debt limits, 143, 313–15
    evading, 314
    local, 313
    New York City's, 315
    state, 146, 313
Delegated powers, 23
Demand procedure, 174
Democracy, 56, 153
    direct, 240
Democratic Party, 76, 79
    in Chicago, 85
Denver, City and County of, 100, 283–85
Denver, James W., 283
Department heads, 111, 114, 120, 324
Dillon's rule, 221
Dillon, John F., 221n, 253n
Direct democracy, 240
    in New England towns, 240
Direct legislation, 68–69
    initiative, 68
    referendum, 68
District attorney, 231
District courts, 181n

Divorce, 39
Domestic relations courts, 185
Dometrius, Nelson C., 133n, 137n, 139
Downing, Rondal G., 215
Drafting office, 162
Dresang, Dennis L., 345
Dual sovereignty, 22–23, 28, 312
Duncombe, Herbert S., 249
Dye, Thomas R., 10, 106, 133n

Earmarking, 131, 146
Eastman, Clyde, 271
Eckstein, O., 317
Education, 4, 8, 30
    cost of, 352
    higher, 353
    of police, 368
    public schools, 351–52
Eisenstein, James, 215
Elazar, Daniel J., 20, 33n
Elections, 44–73, 267–71
    apathy, 269
    at-large, 267
    ballots, 62–67
    blacks, 51–54, 268, 279
    city, 267–71
    district, 267
    election judges, 67
    of federal officials, 37
    federal power over, 46–49, 270
    fraud, 104
    general, 62–68
    initiative, 68
    local control of, 46
    and minorities, 268, 270
    nominations, 58–62
    nonpartisan, 67
    nonvoting, 55
    primary, 58–62
    recall, 70
    referendum, 68
    registration, 49–51
    state power over, 46
    time, place and manner, 47
    voting, 46–56
Elites, 93–98
    antidemocratic, 94
    divided, 94
    economic, 96–98
    iron law of oligarchy, 93
    leaders, 94
Energy, conservation, 365
Environmental protection, 363
    air, 365
    federal role in, 364

Environmental protection (*cont.*)
  pollution defined, 364
  water, 365
Environmental Protection Agency, 33, 365
Epstein, Leon B., 177
Equity, 203
Esseks, J. Dixon, 271
Ethnic politics, 99–100
Exhaustion of remedies doctrine, 342
Expenditures
  growth of, 302
  local, 302
  state, 300–03
Extradition, 39
Extraterritorial jurisdiction, 277

Factions, 92
Family courts, 184
FBI, 103, 367
  entrapment, 103
Federal power, 24
Federal Register, 201
Federal and state courts, 187–89
Federalism, 21–43
  value today, 34–35
Felonies, 181
Fifteenth Amendment, 53
Finance
  campaign, 88–92
  county, 239
  school, 352
Fire protection, 369
Fiscal year, 296
Fitness system, 321
Fitzpatrick, John S., 294n
Fourteenth Amendment, 47, 54
Fox, Douglas M., 350n
Fox, Vernon B., 215
Franklin, Benjamin, 148
Fremont, John C., 77
Frieden, Bernard J., 372
Frohock, Fred M., 472
Full faith and credit, 38

Galvin, John T., 259n
Garaventa, Eugene, 336
Garfield, James A., 325
Garnett, James L., 351n, 372
General assembly, 149
General court, 149
General elections, 62–68
  ballots, 62–68
General law charter, 253
General law city, 253–55

General revenue sharing, 32
Gerrymandering, 157–60
  racial, 53
Gershenfeld, Walter J., 345
Gilbertson, Henry S., 224
Ginsburg, Sigmund G., 327n
Glendening, Parris N., 10, 42
Glick, Henry R., 209, 215
Goldwater, Barry M., 80
Goodall, Leonard E., 372
Goodman, William, 106
Gormley, William T., Jr., 3n
Goulden, Joseph, 215
Governor, 108–39
  advice for, 110–12
  appointments, 111, 114, 119–23, 134
  budgetary power, 130–31, 291
  cabinet, 111
  campaign staff, 110
  guarding time, 111
  incapacitation, 138
  institution of, 109
  isolation, 111
  lack of power, 122
  legislator, 123–26
  lieutenant, 136–38
  manager, 110–13, 135
  maverick, 127
  organizing the bureaucracy, 134
  party leader, 126
  personal staff, 110, 135, 324
  powers, 119–35, 141
  and public opinion, 124–26
  royal, 119
  special sessions, 126
  strength, 133–35
  term, 129
  veto power, 127–29, 175
  who becomes, 113
Graham, Robert W., 317
Graham, Stephen A., 364n
Grants-in-aid, 29–32, 219
Grantsmanship, 31
Graves, W. Brooke, 20
Great Compromise, 148
Gregson, Ronald E., 349n
Grilliot, Harold J., 215
Grofman, Bernard, 195n

Hadley, Arthur T., 55n
Hamilton, Edward K., 270n
Handberg, Roger, 215
Hansen, Kathryn Renner, 271
Hanus, Jerome J., 29n

Hardy, Leroy C., 177
Harrigan, John J., 275n, 288
Hatch Acts, 322
Hawley, Willis D., 106
Health
  county services, 234
  regulation of, 338, 371
  state service, 355
Heard, Alexander, 177
Hearings
  administrative, 186, 341–43
  preliminary, 205
Henry, Nicholas, 10, 372
Henry, Patrick, 24
Hibbeln, Ken, 271
Highway patrols, 370
Highways, 355
Hill, Melvin, Jr., 322n
Home rule, 19, 143, 233, 254
  charter, 254
  city, 143, 254
  county, 233
Horan, James F., 288
House of delegates, 149
Housing, 359
  codes, 238
Howe, Charles B., 177
Howitt, Arnold M., 41
Hrebenar, Ronald J., 106
Hull, Raymond, 135n
Hunter, Floyd, 95n

Immunity, sovereign, 211
Implied powers, 26–27
In re Gault, 185
Income, 4
  tax, 306
Incremental budgeting, 292
Indians, 5
Indictment, 204
Information, 204
Ingster, Bernard, 345
Initiative, 68, 143
  constitutional, 14
Injunction, 203
Insurance, liability, 211
Interest groups, 98–99, 170
  civic associations, 68
  lobbying by, 100
  and occupational licensing, 349
  and political parties, 98–99
  and reorganization, 350–51
  and sunset, 349
Interim committees, 168

Interpretation of constitutions, 18
Interstate relations, 38–41
  extradition, 39
  full faith and credit, 38
  privileges and immunities, 41
  suits between states, 40
Iowa, 21

Jackson, Andrew, 224, 322
Jackson, Byran O., 100
Jacksonian democracy, 141
Jacob, Herbert, 133n, 215
Jaros, Dean, 215
Jeffrey, Terri, 271
Jennings, M. Kent, 373
Jensen, Jens Peter, 308n
Jewell, Malcolm E., 73, 106, 177
Job descriptions, 327
Johnson, William C., 275n, 288
Judge-made law, 197–200
Judges
  administrative law, 341–43
  appointment, 189–92
  election, 67, 190
  hearing officers, 341–43
  Missouri system, 191
  removal, 192
  selection methods, 189–92
Judicial review, 12–13
Junkins, Lowell, 145, 145n
Jury
  challenge for cause, 206
  civil, 195, 208
  function, 193
  instructions to, 207
  mistrial, 207
  peremptory challenges, 206
  selections of, 195, 205
  service on, 195
  size, 195, 205
  stacking, 195
  unanimous verdicts, 194, 207, 212
  voir dire, 206
Justice, barriers to, 212
Justice of the peace, 180
Juvenile courts, 184

Kammerer, Gladys M., 249
Kansas, 374
Kaplan, Marshall, 372
Kayden, Xandra, 106
Kearney, Richard C., 10, 132, 331n
Kent, Calvin A., 311n
Kirkpatrick, Jeane Jordan, 107

Knighton, Lennis M., 317
Koch, Edward I., 100, 259, 288, 333
Krislov, Samuel, 345

Labor, 371
LaFollette, Robert M., 77, 143
Lakewood, 282
Lamm, Richard, 112
Lancaster, Lane W., 249
Land, arable, 6
Lane, Frederick S., 345
Language, 6
Law
  administrative rules, 187, 201
  civil, 201
  common law, 197–200
  criminal, 201
  equity, 203
  judge-made, 197–200
  questions, 181
  separate but equal doctrine, 199
  stare decisis, 197
  statutory, 201
Lee, Robert E., 23
Leftwich, Richard H., 372
Legislation, administrative, 337–41
Legislative council, 162
Legislatures
  apportionment, 157–60
  appropriations, 291, 297
  audit committee, 163, 299
  auditing, 297–300
  bicameralism, 147
  bill drafting, 162, 171
  budget, 165, 291
  clerk, 164, 172
  committees, 165–68, 172–75
  compensation, 143, 154
  confirmation power, 121
  corruption of, 142
  decline, 141
  democratization, 141
  gerrymandering, 157–60
  governor's influence over, 122
  houses of, 149
  interest groups, 170
  legislative council, 162
  limitations on, 146
  organization, 150–53
  oversight, 121
  power, 141
  president pro tem, 168
  procedures, 169–76
  reapportionment, 157–60
  representativeness, 150, 155–60

  revisor of statutes, 162
  secretary of the senate, 164
  sergeant-at-arms, 165
  sessions, 143–46
  size, 150
  speaker of the house, 168
  special sessions, 144
  staff services, 160–65, 324
  terms, 152
  turnover, 152
  veto, 127–29
Lehne, Richard, 372
Lewis, Edward B., 271
Liability
  insurance, 211
  tort, 210–12
Libraries, state, 164, 354
Licensing, 226, 349
Lieutenant governor, 136–38
  duties, 136
  team system, 136
Littlewood, Thomas, 10
Lobbying, 100
  regulation of, 101
Local government, 216–88
  civil servants, 325
  federal involvement with, 219
  legal status, 220
  state aid to, 219
Loewenberg, J. Joseph, 345
Lopach, James J., 249
Lorch, Robert S., 345
Lotteries, 304
Lower house, 149
Luther v. *Borden,* 220n
Lyden, Fremont J., 317
Lynch, Thomas D., 317
Lynn, Arthur D., Jr., 310n
Lyons, W. E., 249

Majority leader, 169
Malapportionment, 158
Maleck, Frederic V., 330n
Maleck Manual, 330n
Manager
  city, 257–59
  county, 234
  town, 240
Mandamus, 204
Mandate, 56, 156
Mandel, Marvin, 3
Marshall, John, 27
Martin, Donald L., 350n
May, Janice C., 20

Mayor
  administrator, 262
  budgeting, 263
  and civil service, 262
  in commission system, 256
  in council-manager system, 257
  Curley, James Michael, 259
  election of, 260
  as innovator, 263
  Koch, Edward I., 100, 259, 288, 333
  in mayor-council system, 259
  small town, 271–75
  and state politics, 259
  strong and weak, 260
  symbol, 262
Mayor-council system, 259
McCallister, Robert B., 271
McCulloch v. Maryland, 27
McGovern, George S., 80
McGraw, Bradley D., 20
McKinsey, Lauren S., 249
McNitt, Andrew D., 45n, 60n
Mecham, Evan, 138
Media
  mass, 3
  newspapers, 2
  science, 87
  television, 3–4
Medicaid, 357
Medicare, 357
Merit system, 143, 262, 321–30, 333
  and governor's staff, 116
  shortcomings of, 121
Metropolitan district, 280
Metropolitan government, 275–86
  annexation, 275–77, 278
  city-county mergers, 278, 283–86
  city-state, 279
  contracting for service, 282
  councils of governments, 281
  Denver, 283–85
  extraterritorial jurisdiction, 277
  Lakewood, 282
  metropolitan district, 280
  New York City, 280, 285–86
  suburbs, 276
  Toronto, 280
  Twin Cities, 282
Miami, 279
Michels, Robert, 93n, 151n
Middleton, Lorenzo, 354n
Miewald, Robert D., 210
Mikesell, John L., 310n
Militia, 369
Mill, 230

Miller, Ernest G., 317
Minority leader, 169
Miranda v. Arizona, 204n
Missouri system, 189, 191
Moakley, Maureen W., 177
Model state constitution, 19, 20
Mollenhoff, Clark R., 10
Moore, Paul, 220n, 249
Moore, Perry, 294n
Morehouse, Sarah McCally, 139
Morgan, David G., 288
Morgan, David R., 331n
Morrill Act of 1862, 29, 362
Muchmore, Lynn, 139
Muckrakers, 142
Multiple-member constituency, 77
Municipal corporation, 251
Municipal courts, 180
Murphy, Russell D., 260n

National Guard, 370
National Labor Relations Act, 335
National obligation to states, 36–37
Necessary and proper clause, 23, 26
Needs test, 357
New England, 375
New England town, 7, 239–41
New York
  City of, 267, 267n, 280, 285–86, 315
  Port of, 244
  State of, 325, 333
Newspapers, 3
Nice, David, 43
Nominations, 58–62
  caucus, 58
  conventions, 58
  primary elections, 58–62
Nonassociation, right of, 334
Noncompetitive jobs, 324
Nonpartisan
  elections, 67, 270
  primary, 62
Nonresidents, 41
Nonvoting, 55
Norris, George, 148

Occupational licensing, 349, 355
O'Donnell, Robert W., 3
Olson, Floyd B., 77n
Ombudsman, 210
One-man-one-vote, 159
One-party states, 92
Opinion polls, 87
Orientals, 6

Original 13 states, 35
O'toole, Laurence J., Jr., 359n

Parish, 7, 222
Parks and recreation, 235
Parsons, Malcolm B., 150
Patterson, Samuel C., 177
Peirce, Neal, 43
Peltason, J. W., 10
Peña, Federico, 100
Pendergast, Tom, 85
Pendleton Act, 325
Performance auditing, 163, 300
Peter, Laurence J., 135n
Petersen, John E., 317
Planning, 235–39
Plessy v. Ferguson, 199
Plunkett, T. J., 288
Plural executive, 119, 134
Pluralism, 34
Police
    education of, 368
    FBI, 367
    highway patrols, 370
    organization, 367
    sheriff, 230
    state, 370
Political action committees, 90
Political corruption, 101–4
Political parties, 74–107
    campaigns, 86–88
    conventions, 58–61, 84
    county, 83
    Democrat, 76
    discipline, 85, 86
    disunity, 126
    finance, 88–92
    functions, 74–76
    governor as leader, 126
    history, 76
    ideology, 79
    membership in, 81
    national, 83
    nominations, 58–62
    organization, 80–86
    precinct, 82
    primary elections, 58–62, 84
    Republican, 77
    state, 83
    third, 78
    two-party system, 76–79
    urban, 85
    ward, 82
Poll
    taxes, 46, 53
    watchers, 67

Pollution, 364
Popular sovereignty, 13
Population, state, 6
Port of New York Authority, 244
PPBS, 294
Precinct, 63, 82
    captain, 82
    caucus, 82
    committeepersons, 82
Preliminary hearing, 205
Prescott, Frank W., 139
President pro tem, 168
Prima facie case, 206
Primary jurisdiction doctrine, 341
Primary elections, 58–62
    blanket, 61
    closed, 61
    nonpartisan, 62
    in one-party states, 92
    open, 61
    presidential, 84
    runoff, 61
Prisons, 366
Privatization, 335–37
Privileges and immunities, 41
Probate
    code, uniform, 186
    court, 185
Proffer, Lanny, 211
Progressive
    income tax, 306
    Movement, 143
Project grant, 30
Property tax
    assessment for, 309–11
    personal, 311
    real, 308–11
    regressiveness of, 308
Proportional representation, 77
Proposition 13, 220n, 315
Prosecuting attorney, 231
Psychological distance, 34
Public opinion, 124–26
Public relations, 116
Public schools, 190n, 220, 232, 244

Quorum, 174

Rabinovitz, Francine F., 73, 270n
Race, 6, 46, 51–54, 68, 81, 99–100, 113, 268, 270
Rae, Douglas, 73
Railroads, 355
Ransone, Coleman B., Jr., 139
Readings of bills, 171
Reagan, Michael D., 43
Reagan, Ronald, 33, 129, 275, 358

Reapportionment, 157–60
Recall, 70, 143
Recorder, 228
Referendum elections, 68
Register, merit system, 328
Registration, voter, 49–51
  good character test, 52
  literacy test, 51
  periodic, 50
  permanent, 50
  understanding test, 52
Regulation, business, 143, 335, 349
Reorganization of bureaucracy, 350–51
Representation, 150
  agent theory, 157
  legislative, 155–60
  mandates, 156
  theories of, 156
Republican form of government, 6, 36, 220
Republican Party, 77, 79
Residence requirement, 48
Revenue
  local, 305
  sharing, 32
  state, 304
  taxation, 304–12
Revised code, 162
Revisor of statutes, 162
Reynolds v. Sims, 148n, 159n
Roman Law, 200
Roosevelt, Theodore, 143
Rosenbloom, David H., 345
Rosenstone, Steven J., 73
Rosenthal, Alan, 177
Ross, Douglas, 43
Royko, Mike, 288
Rulemaking, 201, 337–41
Rules committee, 174
Rural government, 271–75

Sabato, Larry, 107, 113n, 139
Sachs, Barbara Faith, 20
Sales tax, 306
Sandford, Terry, 20
Sanzone, John G., 43
Savas, E. W., 327n, 345
Schechter Case, 343n
Schiller, Bradley R., 373
Schlesinger, Joseph A., 132, 133n
Schmandt, Henry J., 288
Schrag, Philip G., 17
Secretary of the senate, 164
Selectmen, 240
Senators, U.S., direct election of, 143
Sentencing, 207
Separate but equal doctrine, 199

Separation of powers, 12, 141, 337
  negation by lieutenant governors, 137
Seranno v. Priest, 190n
Sergeant-at-arms, 165
Seroka, Jim, 271, 288
Session laws, 163
Sessions, legislative
  frequency, 143
  length, 144
  special, 144
  split, 146
Seventeenth Amendment, 38
Sex, 46, 113
  equality, 19
Sharp, Ansel M., 372
Shumate, Robert V., 177
Simon, Herbert A., 95n
Single-member district, 77
Sloan, R. D., Jr., 271
Small claims court, 183
Smith, Elton C., 359n
Smith, Robert G., 249
Smolka, Richard G., 73
Snavely, Keith, 271
Snelling, Richard A., 32n
Social security, 356
Sokolow, Alvin D., 271
Sovereign immunity, 211
Sovereignty, dual, 22–23, 28
Spanish-surnamed persons, 6
Speaker of the house, 168
Special district, 243–47
  defined, 243
  faults of, 246–47
  need for, 244–46
  number of, 243
  organization, 244
  types, 244
Special legislation, 147
Special sessions, 126, 144
Specialized courts, 183
Speer, Albert, 57
Spending power, 26
Spoils system, 321, 327–30
Stanley, David T., 369
Stare decisis, 197
State police, 370
Statutory law, 201
Steffens, Lincoln, 143, 143n
Stephens, G. Ross, 249
Stillman, Richard J., II, 107
Strikes, 332, 351
Sturm, Albert L., 20
Subdivision regulation, 237
Suburbs, 159, 276
Suicide mechanism, 78

Suits between states, 40
Summons, 208
Sunset, 349
Superintendent of schools, 232
Superior courts, 181n
Supervisors
county, 226
township, 243
Supremacy clause, 28
Supreme Court
in New York, 181n
of the United States, 28, 189
Surveyor, county, 232
Svara, James H., 132
Swindler, William F., 20

Taft-Hartley Act, 90, 203n, 334n
Taney, Roger B., 23
Tax limits, 315
Taxes
cannons of taxation, 306
income, 306
limits on, 315
local, 305
lotteries, 304
personal property, 311
real property, 308–11
reciprocal immunity from, 312
sales, 307
state, 304
Taylor, Thomas G., 288
Television, 3–4
Temporary appointments, 327
Tenth Amendment, 23
Term
governor's, 129, 135
lame ducks, 129
legislative, 152
limitations, 129
Territorial integrity, 37
Test
civil service, 323, 328
needs, 357
Testing
competency, 352
truth in, 352
Third parties, 78
Thomas, Robert D., 43
Thompson, Frank J., 327n, 345
Thorson, John, 33n
Tolchin, Martin, 345
Tolchin, Susan, 345
Toronto, 280
Tort liability
of governments, 210–12
acts, 211

Town, New England, 7, 239–41
Town meetings, 240
Towns, small, 271–75
Townships
political, 241–43
surveyor's, 242
Transportation, 354
Treasurer
county, 228
state, 298
Trial courts, 181
Turnover, legislative, 152
Twin Cities, 282
Twenty-fourth Amendment, 46
Twenty-sixth Amendment, 47, 54
Two-party states, 92

Unemployment
compensation, 361
insurance, 371
Unicameralism, Nebraska, 148
Uniform state law, commission on, 164
Union shop, 334
Unions, public service, 330–35
AFSCME, 330
agency shop, 334
closed shop, 334
growth of, 331
history of, 330
and merit system, 333
national labor law, 335
strikes, 332
teachers, 351
union shop, 334
Universities, 353, 361
Uppal, Jag C., 213
Upper house, 149

Veto, 175
governor's power of, 127–29
item, 128
legislative override, 128
pocket, 129
president's power of, 129
Vines, Kenneth N., 133n, 215
Vote fraud, 104
Voting
age, 46
ballots, 62–67
citizenship, 48
machines, 63
nonvoting, 55
poll taxes, 46
procedure, 63–67
qualifications for, 46–55
race, 46, 51–54

registration, 49–51
residence requirement, 48
sex, 46
Voting Rights Act, 49, 52

Walker, David B., 33n, 43, 275
Wallace, George C., 77
Warren, Robert Penn, 139
Washington, Harold, 100
Water, 41, 365
Watson, Richard A., 215
Watts, Meredith W., Jr., 177
Weinberg, Martha Wagner, 373
Welfare, 356–61
AFDC, 358
clause, 26
county, 235
defined, 356
housing, 359
local charities, 361
medicaid, 357

medicare, 357
needs test, 357
OASDHI, 356
state look-alike programs, 360
Whips, 169
White primary, 53, 81
Wildavsky, Aaron, 317
Wilson, James Q., 288
Wilson, Woodrow, 143
Wolfinger, Raymond E., 73
Woo, Lillian C., 73
Workmen's compensation, 371
Wright, Diel S., 43
Wyner, Alan J., 139

Zeigler, L. Harmon, 373
Zellmer, Steven J., 311n
Zero-based budget, 293
Zimmerman, Joseph F., 73, 139, 267n, 270n
Zolty, Thaddeus C., 271
Zoning, 237